Two Ways to Integrate Technology into Your Course

 **HEINLE** *Learning Center* OR **CourseMate**

 **HEINLE** *Learning Center*

username: Spencerscott allen
password: B28 Craig

iLrn™ Student Features:

- Online Student Activities Manual
- Interactive ebook viewable on an iPad
- Grammar Tutorials
- Access to Audio and Video

- Chapter In-Review Cards
- Auto-Graded Quizzes
- Flashcards
- Diagnostics Study Tool

Students sign in at **ilrn.heinle.com**

ON THE WEB

INTRO SPAN Are you in?

ONLINE RESOURCES

CourseMate Engaging. Trackable. **Affordable.**

CourseMate Student Features:

- Print Student Activities Manual
- Interactive eBook
- Audio and video program
- Auto-Graded Quizzes
- Flashcards

- Student Review Cards
- Web links
- Games: Crossword Puzzles and more

Students sign in at **cengagebrain.com**

D0144583

HEINLE
CENGAGE Learning

EXPLORACIONES
Blitt | Casas

Editor-in-Chief: P.J. Boardman

Publisher: Beth Kramer

Acquisitions Editor: Heather Bradley Cole

Managing Development Editor: Harold Swearingen

Senior Content Project Manager: Esther Marshall

Editorial Assistant: Sara Dyer

Senior Media Editor: Morgen Murphy

Associate Media Editor: Katie Latour

Senior Marketing Manager: Ben Rivera

Marketing Communications Manager:
Glenn McGibbon

Marketing Coordinator: Janine Enos

Executive Marketing Manager, 4 LTR Press:
Robin Lucas

Product Development Manager, 4 LTR Press:
Steven E. Joos

Senior Development Editor Market Strategies:
Elizabeth Kendall

Senior Art Director: Linda Jurras

Senior Print Buyer: Elizabeth Donaghey

Text Designers: Joe Devine and Polo Barrera

Illustrator: Hermann Mejia

Photo Researcher: NesbittGraphics

Permissions Editor: Llanca Letelier

Production Service: NesbittGraphics

Cover Designer: Polo Barrera

Cover Image: ©Walter Bibikow/Photolibrary

Compositor: NesbittGraphics

For product information and technology assistance, contact us at
Cengage Learning Academic Resource Center, 1-800-423-0563
For permission to use material from this text or product,
submit all requests online at **cengage.com/permissions**.
Further permissions questions can be emailed to
permissionrequest@cengage.com.

Library of Congress Control Number: 2010915887

Student Edition (iLrn):
ISBN-13: 978-1-4130-0068-9
ISBN-10: 1-4130-0068-1

Student Edition (CourseMate):
ISBN-13: 978-1-4282-0641-0
ISBN-10: 1-4282-0641-8

Heinle Cengage Learning
20 Channel Center Street
Boston, MA 02210
USA

Cengage Learning is a leading provider of customized learning solutions with office locations around the globe, including Singapore, the United Kingdom, Australia, Mexico, Brazil, and Japan. Locate your local office at **international.cengage.com/region**

Cengage Learning products are represented in Canada by Nelson Education, Ltd.

For your course and learning solutions, visit
www.cengage.com.

Purchase any of our products at your local college store or at our preferred online store **www.ichapters.com**

For your course and learning solutions, visit
academic.cengage.com

Purchase any of our products at your local college store or at our preferred online store **www.ichapters.com**

Printed in the United States of America
3 4 5 14 13 12

DEDICATORIA

To Russ Boersma, who believed in our project from the very beginning and was our eternal support

In memory of Don Swanson, whose enthusiasm for **Exploraciones** was boundless

To my friends and family, and especially my parents, for all their support and understanding
(Mary Ann)

A mi queridísima familia: A Gordon, a mis padres, a mis hermanos Luis, Alfonso y Fernando, a Paty y a mis sobrinos. Gracias por su apoyo y cariño incondicional.

To all my professors and friends at the Foreign Language Department of Colorado State University. Thank you!
(Margarita)

Scope and Sequence

Chapter	Objectives	Vocabulary
CAPÍTULO 1 Hola, ¿qué tal? 	▪ Greet and say good-bye to people in formal and informal situations ▪ Describe your classroom, your friends, and other people ▪ Use numbers up to 100 and exchange telephone numbers ▪ Spell names	**Exploraciones léxicas 1** Greetings, introductions, and good-byes 4 Classroom 4 Alphabet 5 Numbers 0-100 8, 13 **Exploraciones léxicas 2** Descriptive adjectives 18
CAPÍTULO 2 ¿Cómo es tu vida? 	▪ Talk about your classes ▪ Describe your family and tell ages ▪ Talk about what people do routinely ▪ Express ownership	**Exploraciones léxicas 1** Academic subjects 40 **Exploraciones léxicas 2** Family members and pets 54
CAPÍTULO 3 ¿Qué tiempo hace hoy? 	▪ Communicate dates, time, and seasons ▪ Talk about the weather ▪ Discuss clothing ▪ Discuss your likes and dislikes ▪ Use question words to ask for specific information	**Exploraciones léxicas 1** Time 76 **Exploraciones léxicas 2** Clothing 90 Colors 90 Weather 90

Scope and Sequence

Chapter	Objectives	Vocabulary
CAPÍTULO 4 ¿Dónde vives? 	• Describe your town or city • Describe your house • Tell what you and others are going to do in the near future • Request information about the cost of things	**Exploraciones léxicas 1** Places in a city 112 **Exploraciones léxicas 2** Rooms of a house 126 Furniture and appliances 126
CAPÍTULO 5 ¿Estás feliz en el trabajo? 	• Describe your feelings, emotions, and physical states • Talk about ongoing actions • Discuss abilities needed for certain jobs and professions	**Exploraciones léxicas 1** Adjectives of emotion and physical states 148 **Exploraciones léxicas 2** Professions 162
CAPÍTULO 6 ¿Cómo pasas el día? 	• Talk about your daily routine • Discuss your hobbies and pastimes • Talk about sports • Discuss events that occurred in the past	**Exploraciones léxicas 1** Parts of the body 184 **Exploraciones léxicas 2** Sports 198 Sporting equipment 198

Grammar

Reading / Writing

Culture

Scope and Sequence

Chapter	Objectives	Vocabulary
CAPÍTULO 7 ¿Cómo pasaste las vacaciones? 	▪ Request a room in a hotel and any of their services ▪ Use numbers above 100 ▪ Order food in a restaurant	**Exploraciones léxicas 1** Hotel 220 Numbers above 100 220 **Exploraciones léxicas 2** Meals and utensils 234
CAPÍTULO 8 ¿Qué te gustaba de niño? 	▪ Give instructions ▪ Talk about your hobbies and pastimes ▪ Talk about what you used to do in the past	**Exploraciones léxicas 1** Fruit, vegetables, and condiments 256 **Exploraciones léxicas 2** Hobbies and pastimes 270
CAPÍTULO 9 ¿Qué pasó? 	▪ Describe in detail past events ▪ Talk about holidays and celebrations ▪ Give the details of an accident	**Exploraciones léxicas 1** Parties and celebrations 292 **Exploraciones léxicas 2** Navigating the city 306

Grammar	Reading/Writing	Culture

Scope and Sequence

Chapter	Objectives	Vocabulary
CAPÍTULO 10 ¿Estás preparado? 	▪ Discuss daily chores ▪ Give and receive directions ▪ Make travel arrangements ▪ Suggest activities ▪ Make informal and formal requests	**Exploraciones léxicas 1** Taking a trip 328 **Exploraciones léxicas 2** Household chores 342
CAPÍTULO 11 ¿Es la moda arte? 	▪ Express preferences and make comparisons ▪ Describe the state of objects and people	**Exploraciones léxicas 1** Shopping for clothing 364 **Exploraciones léxicas 2** Art 378
CAPÍTULO 12 ¿Qué será del planeta? 	▪ Talk about the future ▪ Talk about what you have done ▪ Discuss the environment ▪ Express your opinions and knowledge about the animal world and the environment ▪ Express doubt and certainty	**Exploraciones léxicas 1** Geography and environment 400 **Exploraciones léxicas 2** Animals 414

Scope and Sequence

Chapter	Objectives	Vocabulary
CAPÍTULO 13 ¿Es tu vida una telenovela? 	• Talk about relationships • Express desires and give recommendations • Talk about popular culture • Discuss emotional reactions to events	**Exploraciones léxicas 1** Personal relations 436 **Exploraciones léxicas 2** Popular culture 450
CAPÍTULO 14 ¿Vivimos en un mundo sin fronteras? 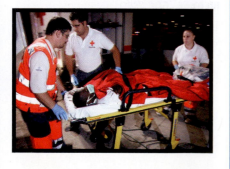	• Discuss health issues with a doctor • Discuss hypothetical situations • Express opinions regarding world issues • Tell what had happened prior to other events in the past	**Exploraciones léxicas 1** Health and medical emergencies 472 **Exploraciones léxicas 2** Political concepts and nationalities 486

Most people who study another language would like to be able to speak it. **Exploraciones** will help you do just that. You'll learn to talk about yourself, your community and the world around you. You'll start out asking and answering questions, then you'll narrate events and make comparisons, and eventually you'll be able to express your opinions. At the same time, you'll read real world samples of the language such as flyers, magazine articles and menus and you'll write letters and e-mails in Spanish.

In order to become a good language learner, it's important to learn to analyze the language and figure out the rules for yourself. In the grammar sections of **Exploraciones,** you'll be guided through a process of observing the language in use and deducing the rules. Eventually, you'll sharpen this skill, and be able to use it beyond this textbook, as you become a successful language learner.

You can't learn a language without studying the cultures of the people who speak it. In every chapter you'll learn about the practices of Spanish-speakers from around the world and the countries they live in. This will enable you to make cultural comparisons, finding both similarities and differences between their cultures and your own. We hope that you'll find the study of the Spanish language exciting and fun, and that it opens many doors in your future explorations.

Organization of Exploraciones

Exploraciones has fourteen chapters, each consisting of two independent parts that are identical in organization. Each chapter starts with the chapter outline and provides a learning strategy. The remainder of each of the chapters is set up in the following manner:

Exploraciones léxicas

You will be introduced to vocabulary through illustrations and lists. Then, in the **Práctica** section, you will work through a series of activities that will require you to speak minimally at first and then progress to more open-ended communicative activities.

En vivo

You will improve your reading skills while continuing to practice vocabulary through authentic readings from a variety of sources such as magazines and websites.

Exploraciones gramaticales

You will be guided through the discovery of the rules for Spanish grammar through a dialogue or paragraph in the **A analizar** section. This section is followed by **A comprobar,** in which you can compare your conclusions with the explanation of the rules. Then in the **A practicar** section, you will practice the grammar concept in a variety of activities.

Conexiones culturales

This section has short cultural information pieces and tasks that encourage you to go beyond the reading and research various aspects of the Spanish-speaking world.

Lectura

This section allows you to learn more about the culture of Spanish-speaking countries while improving your reading skills. Each section starts with a strategy to help you improve your reading in Spanish.

Redacción

At the end of each chapter, you will develop your writing skills through a process-writing, in which you are guided to brainstorm, write a draft and revise.

Exploraciones profesionales

These short career-focused vignettes allow you to observe the Spanish language within a professional context. The **Vocabulario** section provides useful vocabulary and expressions that you would use in a field in which you currently work or in which you may intend to work, while the **Datos importantes** feature gives important information about the career such as education, salary and work environment.

Exploraciones de repaso

At the end of each chapter, there are two pages of review activities. The **Exploraciones de repaso: estructuras** provides a structured review of the grammar concepts from the chapter while the **Exploraciones de repaso: comunicación** lets you practice the vocabulary and grammar through communicative partner activities.

Exploraciones literarias

After every second chapter, there is a literary selection that will introduce you to different writers from throughout the Spanish-speaking world and a sample of their work. You will also learn the basics of literary analysis through the **Investiguemos la literatura** box accompanying each selection.

Study Suggestions

1. Study every day. For most students, it is more effective to study for 15-20 minutes 3 times a day, than to spend one full hour on the subject.

2. Listen to the audio recordings. When studying the vocabulary, take time to listen to the pronunciation of the words. It will help your pronunciation, as well as help you learn to spell them properly.

3. Get help when you need it. Learning a foreign language is like learning math; you will continue to use what you have already learned and to build upon that knowledge. So, if you find you don't understand something, be sure to see your instructor or a tutor right away.

4. Participate actively in class. In order to learn the language, you have to speak it and to learn from your mistakes.

5. Make intelligent guesses. When you are reading, listening to your instructor, or watching a video make intelligent guesses as to the meaning of words you do not know. Use the context, cognates (words that look or sound like English words), intonation, and if possible visual clues such as body language, gestures, facial expressions and images, to help you figure out the meaning of the word.

6. Study with a friend or form a study group. Not only might you benefit when your friend understands a concept that you have difficulty with, but you will have more opportunities to practice speaking as well as listening.

7. Find what works for you. Use a variety of techniques to memorize vocabulary and verbs until you find the ones that are best for you. Try writing the words, listening to recordings of the words, and using flash cards.

8. Review material from previous lessons. Because learning a language is cumulative, it is important to refresh your knowledge of vocabulary, verbs and structures learned in earlier lessons.

9. Avoid making grammar comparisons. While it is helpful to understand some basic grammar concepts of the English language, such as pronouns and direct objects, it is important not to constantly make comparisons and to learn the new structures.

10. Speak Spanish. Try to use Spanish for all your classroom interactions, not just when called on by the instructor or answering a classmate's question in a group activity. Don't worry that your sentence may not be structurally correct; the important thing is to begin to feel comfortable expressing yourself in the language.

Acknowledgments

We would like to express our most sincere gratitude and appreciation to everybody who has played a role in the making of **Exploraciones,** and to those who have supported us. In particular, we are grateful to the instructors and students who used **Exploraciones** in its previous edition, and helped us to improve it. The following faculty has made **Exploraciones** a better book thanks to all their comments and valuable insights:

Metropolitan Community College-Maple Woods: Emily Armstrong, Ruth Heath, Fenton Gardner, Carol Kuznacic, Chad Montuori, Jennifer Rogers, Don Swanson, Jefferson Bingham, Sherri Clayton, James Clutter, Linda Cobb, Jeffrey Finnie, Eugenio González, Jan Good-Bollinger, Nancy Hake, Gary Metzger, Elizabeth Norwat, Sue Willams, ErinWoste-Littlejohn, Chris Yannitelli

Linn-Benton Community College: Brian Keady, Wendy Pilkerton, Claudia Bolais, David Lane, Monica Olvera, Michelle Barnes, and the tutors Diva Rodriguez and Miranda Prince

Butler County Community College: Calisa Marlar, Marsha Mawhirter, Kerry Locke

Kansas State University: Mary Copple, Katherine Brinkman, Angelique Courbou, Adam Miller, Sarah Murdoch

University of Arkansas at Little Rock: David McAlpine and Joy Saunders

There were numerous people who played a role in the production and promotion of the custom version of **Exploraciones,** which allowed us to class test it with over 8,000 students. We would like to thank Bob Tessman, Nathan Anderson, Kalina Ingham Hintz, Kim Fry, Cydney Capell, Cecilia Lause, Kirk Scott, Keith Tudor, Markosa Studios, Lauren Aspenlieder, Tony Sosa, Jacqueline Chávez, Diana Pérez, Bogart Sauza, Ingrid Fernández, and José Vásquez.

We wish to express a giant thank you to the wonderful people who have worked so hard at Cengage to make this project become a reality. We would like to give a very special thank you to Harold Swearingen, our developmental editor; we are most grateful for his thoughtful revisions and the insight that he brought to **Exploraciones**. His patience, humor and enthusiasm were invaluable to us. We would also like to thank Heather Bradley, our acquisitions editor who believed in **Exploraciones** and brought it to fruition. A huge thank you goes to Esther Marshall—we do not know how the project would have been completed without her. Our thanks also go to Ben Rivera, Linda Jurras, and Sara Dyer; Hermann Mejia for the great illustrations, Alice Bowman and Harry Druding from Nesbitt Graphics for their dedicated work and professional contribution, and the other freelancers who worked on this project: Poyee Oster, Luz Galante, Margaret Hines, Grisel Lozano-Garcini.

A very, very special thank you goes to Russ Boersma whom we can credit with the seed of the project. Thank you for supporting us all the way through!

Reviewers and Contributors

Special thanks go to the following professors who have written the outstanding supplements to accompany the book: Mary Copple, Angelique Corbou, Yasmin Diaz, all of Kansas State University, wrote the extensive Testing program; Jennifer Rogers, of Metropolitan Community College—Blue River, prepared the grammar and vocabulary worksheets; Lisa Barboun, of Coastal Carolina University, wrote the Web quizzes; Maria Fidalgo-Eick, of Grand Valley State University, created the cultural Web activities to enhance the culture sections.

We are thankful to the following members of the **Exploraciones** Reviewer Panel who provided thoughtful commentary on the manuscript through detailed reviews during its development:

Luz-Maria Acosta-Knutson, Morton College
Ana Afzali, Citrus College
Tim Altanero, Austin Community College
Lisa Barboun, Coastal Carolina University
Cristian Batalla Candas, University of North
 Carolina—Charlotte
Cathy Briggs, North Lake College
Steve Budge, Mesa Community College
Mary Copple, Kansas State University
Kristy Cross, Orange Coast College
Alicia del Campo, California State University at
 Long Beach
Kent Dickson, California State University at
 Pomona
Ronna Feit, Nassau Community College
Maria Fidalgo-Eick, Grand Valley State
 University
Leah Fonder-Solano, University of Southern
 Mississippi
Jose M. Garcia-Paine, Georgia Perimeter College
Ana Giron, Hill College
Ruth Heath, Metropolitan Community College
 —Penn Valley

Joshua Hoekstra, Bluegrass Community and
 Technical College
Todd Lakin, City Colleges of Chicago—Richard
 J. Daly College
Monica Malamud, San Mateo County
 Community College District
Eric Mayer, Central Washington University
Bryan McBride, Eastern Arizona College
Stephanie Panichelli-Batalla, Wingate University
Graciela Perez-Boruskzo, Pepperdine University
Robert H. Rineer, Lehigh Carbon Community
 College
Jennifer Rogers, Metropolitan Community
 College-Blue River
Laura Ruiz-Scott, Scottsdale Community
 College
Joy Saunders, University of Arkansas, Little
 Rock
Carter E. Smith, University of Wisconsin
 —Eau Claire
Hilde Votaw, University of Oklahoma
Renee Wooten, Vernon College

We are also grateful for the valuable feedback and suggestions offered by the following professors through their participation in live and virtual focus groups, one-on-one interviews, and chapter reviews:

Thomas Acker, Mesa State College
Maria Akrabova, Wichita State University
Sylvia Albanese, Nassau Community College
Luz Maria Alvarez, Johnson County
 Community College
Aleta Anderson, Grand Rapids Community
 College
Margarita Andrade-Robledo, Southwestern
 College
Debra D. Andrist, Sam Houston State University
Emily Armstrong, Metropolitan Community
 College-Longview
Robert Baum, Arkansas State University
Kevin Beard, Richland College
Anne Becher, University of Colorado—Boulder
Flavia Belpoliti, University of Houston
Maria Alejandra Bonifacino, Wichita State
 University

Greg Briscoe, Utah Valley University
Sara Burns, Gainesville State College
Julia Bussade, University of Mississippi-Oxford
Mónica Cabrera, Loyola Marymount University
Gabriela Cambiasso, City Colleges of Chicago
 —Harold Washington College
Kelly Campbell, Saint Michaels College
Doug Canfield, University of Tennessee
Beth Cardon, Georgia Perimeter College
Carmen Carracelas-Juncal, University of
 Southern Mississippi
Lissette Castro, Mount San Jacinto College
Alicia Cipria, University of Alabama
Dennis Cokely, Northeastern University
Sandra Contreras, Kansas State University
Fatima Cornwall, Boise State College
Jose Cortes-Caballero, Georgia Perimeter College
Dulce de Castro, Collin College

Lorena Delgadillo, University of North Carolina—Charlotte

Luis Delgado, City Colleges of Chicago - Olive Harvey College

David Detwiler, Mira Costa Community College

Yasmin Diaz, Kansas State University

Wendy Dodge, University of Central Arkansas

Margaret Eomurian, Houston Community College

Luz Marina Escobar, Tarrant County College, Southeast

Addison Everett, Dixie State College

Dina Fabery, University of Central Florida

Irene Fernandez, North Shore Community College

Alejandro Garza, Tarrant County College, Northwest

Edmund Gert, Rose State College

Scott Gibby, Austin Community College

Patsy Gilbert, Trinity Valley Community College

Juana Goergen, DePaul University

J. T. Golden, Austin Community College

Sandra Contreras Gomez, Kansas State University

Yolanda Gonzalez, Valencia Community College

Vanessa Gutierrez, Palomar College

John Haan, Grand Valley State University

Eduardo Hernandez, Elgin Community College

Jennifer Horvath, Johnston Community College

Antonio Iacopino, William Rainey Harper College

Francisco Javier Iñiguez Becerra, Cabrillo College

Becky Jaimes, Austin Community College

Valerie Job, South Plains College

Lauri Hutt Kahn, Suffolk Community College

Anne Kelly-Glascoe, South Puget Sound Community College

Deborah Kessler, Bradley University

Julie Kleinhans-Urrutia, Austin Community College

Carol Kuznacic, Metropolitan Community College-Longview

Marta LaCorte, City Colleges of Chicago—Harold Washington

Wayne Langehennig, South Plains College—Reese Center

Stephanie Langston, Georgia Perimeter College

Nicole Lasswell, University of Dallas

Luis Latoja, Columbus State Community College

Mercedes Limon, Chaffey College

Jeff Longwell, New Mexico State University

Iraida Lopez, Ramapo College of New Jersey

Guadalupe López-Cox, Austin Community College

Nuria Lopez-Ortega, University of Cincinnati

Gillian Lord, University of Florida

Matthew Lubeck, University of Miami

Lunden MacDonald, Metropolitan State College of Denver

Juan Manuel Soto, El Centro College

Calisa E. Marlar, Butler Community College

Trina Marmarelli, Reed College

Marsha Mawhirter, Butler Community College

Francisco Mazno-Robledo, Washington State University

David McAlpine, University of Arkansas, Little Rock

Alba-Leonor Melo-Carvajal, Richland College

Ivan Miño, Tarrant County College, Southeast

Teresa Moinette, University of Central Oklahoma

Bill Monds, Trinity Valley Community College

Mónica Montalvo, University of Central Florida

Delia Montesinos, Austin Community College

Chad Montouri, Metropolitan Community College-Maple Woods

Rosa-Maria Moreno, Cincinnati State Technical and Community College

Eric Narvaez, Normandale Community College

Ruth Navarro, Grossmont Community College

Mai Nazif, Santa Rosa Junior College

Jose Ramon Nunez, Long Beach City College

Tina Oestreich, Case Western Reserve University

Carmel O'Kane, Northeastern Illinois University

Elizabeth Olvera, University of Texas at San Antonio

Lois O'Malley, Kansas State University

Mirta Pagnucci, Northern Illinois University

James Palmer, Tarrant County College, Northeast

Florencia Pecile, Kirkwood Community College

Carlos Pedroza, Palomar College

Tammy Perez, San Antonio College

Maria Perez, University of Houston

Todd Phillips, Austin Community College

Mercedes Rahilly, Lansing Community College

Dr. Kay Raymond, Sam Houston State University

John Riley, Greenville Technical College

Maria Rocha, Houston Community College

Theresa Ruiz-Velasco, College of Lake County

Lowell "Bud" Sandefur, Eastern Oklahoma State College

John Sanders, Metropolitan Community College—Penn Valley

Bethany Sanio, University of Nebraska-Lincoln

Jose Sanquintin, Piedmont Technical College

Rosalba Scott, University of North Carolina—Charlotte

Inigo Serna, Washington State University

Gilberto Serrano, Columbus State Community College
Virginia Shen, Chicago State University
Paul Siegrist, Fort Hays State University
Marvin Skinner, Strayer University
Stuart Smith, Austin Community College
Irena Stefanova, Contra Costa College
Mingyu Sun, University of Wisconsin- Milwaukee
Cristina Szterensus, Rock Valley College
Gigi Terminel, Whittier College
Tamara Townsend, Wheaton College
Elvira Ventimiglia, Rock Valley College

Natalia Verjat, Tarrant County College, Northeast
Mary Frances Wadley, Jackson State Community College
Alina Waguespack, Austin Community College
Sue Williams, Metropolitan Community College-Maple Woods
Gloria Yampey-Jorg, Houston Community College – Central
Olivia Yanez, College of Lake County
Chris Yanitelli, Metropolitan Community College-Maple Woods
Melissa Young, Georgia State University

In addition to the instructors listed above, hundreds of additional instructors took the time to respond to surveys which gathered information about preferred supplementary items, product packaging formats and other critical issues. We appreciate their time and advice.

We are especially grateful for the feedback and suggestions we have received from thousands of students during the years when the book was being developed and used in the classroom as a custom edition. The comments and suggestions of students who have used this material have informed every aspect of this program. In addition to students who learned from the custom editions, students from the following schools offered extremely useful suggestions about preferences on content, design and the use of technology during focus groups and surveys:

Austin Community College, Bradley University, Butler University, Central Michigan University, Central Piedmont Community College, Cincinnati State and Technical College Clemson University, College of Charleston, DePaul University, George Washington University, Kansas State University, Minnesota State University, North Lake College, Oklahoma University, Rock Valley College, Saint Louis University, Temple University, Trinity College, University of Maryland—College Park, University of Wisconsin—Milwaukee, University of Dallas, University of Texas—Arlington, Washington State University

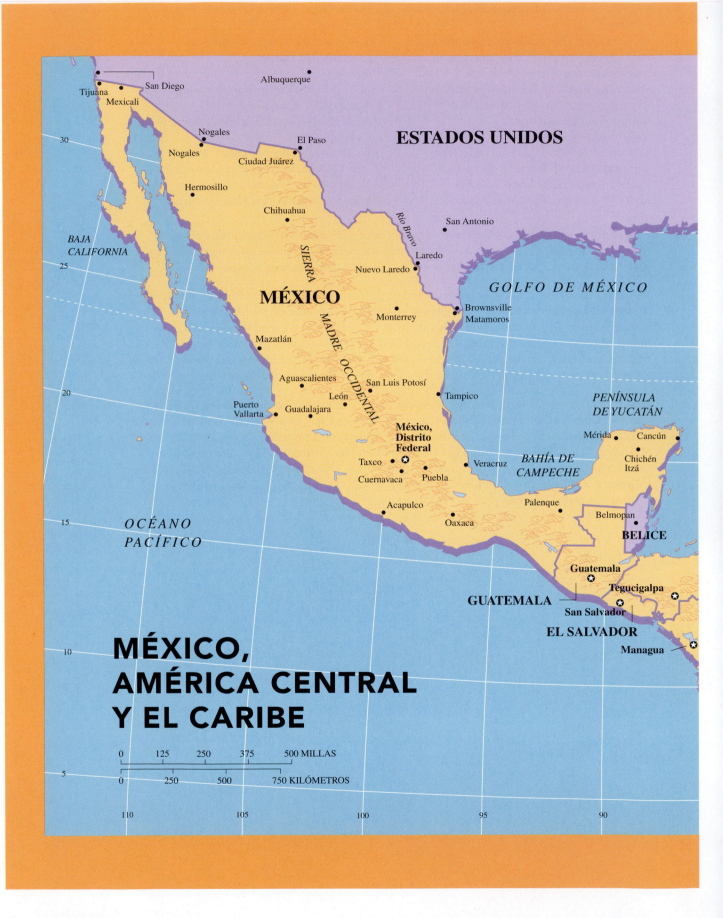

ESTADOS UNIDOS

Albuquerque

San Diego
Tijuana
Mexicali

Nogales
Nogales
El Paso
Ciudad Juárez
Hermosillo

Chihuahua

Río Bravo
San Antonio

BAJA CALIFORNIA

Laredo
Nuevo Laredo

GOLFO DE MÉXICO

MÉXICO

SIERRA

Monterrey

Brownsville
Matamoros

Mazatlán

MADRE OCCIDENTAL

Aguascalientes
San Luis Potosí
León
Tampico

PENÍNSULA DE YUCATÁN

Puerto Vallarta
Guadalajara

Mérida
Cancún

México, Distrito Federal

BAHÍA DE CAMPECHE

Chichén Itzá

Taxco
Cuernavaca
Puebla
Veracruz

Acapulco
Oaxaca
Palenque

Belmopan

OCÉANO PACÍFICO

BELICE

GUATEMALA
Guatemala

Tegucigalpa
San Salvador

EL SALVADOR

Managua

MÉXICO, AMÉRICA CENTRAL Y EL CARIBE

| 0 | 125 | 250 | 375 | 500 MILLAS |
| 0 | 250 | 500 | 750 KILÓMETROS |

30
25
20
15
10
5

110 105 100 95 90

75   70   65   60   55

30

OCÉANO
ATLÁNTICO

25

Miami

Nassau

BAHAMAS

La Habana

20

CUBA

REPÚBLICA
DOMINICANA

San Juan

MAR CARIBE

Santiago
de Cuba   **Puerto Príncipe**

Santo
Domingo

PUERTO
RICO

GUADALUPE —

Kingston

HAITÍ

JAMAICA

HONDURAS

MARTINICA —

15

NICARAGUA

Lago de
Managua

10

Caracas

San José

CANAL DE
PANAMÁ   Colón

Panamá

PANAMÁ

COSTA
RICA

GOLFO
DE
PANAMÁ

VENEZUELA

85   80

COLOMBIA

Bogotá

ESPAÑA

FRANCIA

ANDORRA

200 MILLAS
300 KILÓMETROS
150
200
100
100
50
100
0
0

OCÉANO
ATLÁNTICO

MAR CANTÁBRICO

MENORCA

MALLORCA

Palma

ISLAS
BALEARES

IBIZA

MAR MEDITERRÁNEO

Gerona

Barcelona

Costa
Brava

CATALUÑA

Lérida

NAVARRA
PIRINEOS

Pamplona

Bilbao

Santander

PAÍS VASCO

CANTABRIA

CORDILLERA CANTÁBRICA

PRINCIPADO
DE ASTURIAS

GALICIA

Santiago

Zaragoza

Río Ebro

LA RIOJA

ARAGÓN

Valencia

COMUNIDAD
VALENCIANA

Alicante

Cartagena

SIERRA DE
GUADARRAMA

MADRID

Madrid

Valladolid

Segovia

CASTILLA
Y LEÓN

Salamanca

Toledo

CASTILLA-LA MANCHA

Ciudad Real

MURCIA

Murcia

SIERRA NEVADA

Granada

ANDALUCÍA

Córdoba

Río Guadalquivir

Sevilla

EXTREMADURA

Río Tajo

PORTUGAL

Lisboa

Costa del Sol

Málaga

Cádiz

Estrecho
de Gibraltar

GIBRALTAR (Br.)

CEUTA (Sp.)

MELILLA (Sp.)

Tanger

MARRUECOS

ÁFRICA

ISLAS CANARIAS

LANZAROTE

FUERTEVENTURA

GRAN
CANARIA

Las
Palmas

TENERIFE

GOMERA

LA
PALMA

HIERRO

MILLAS
100
150
0
KILÓMETROS
100
150
0

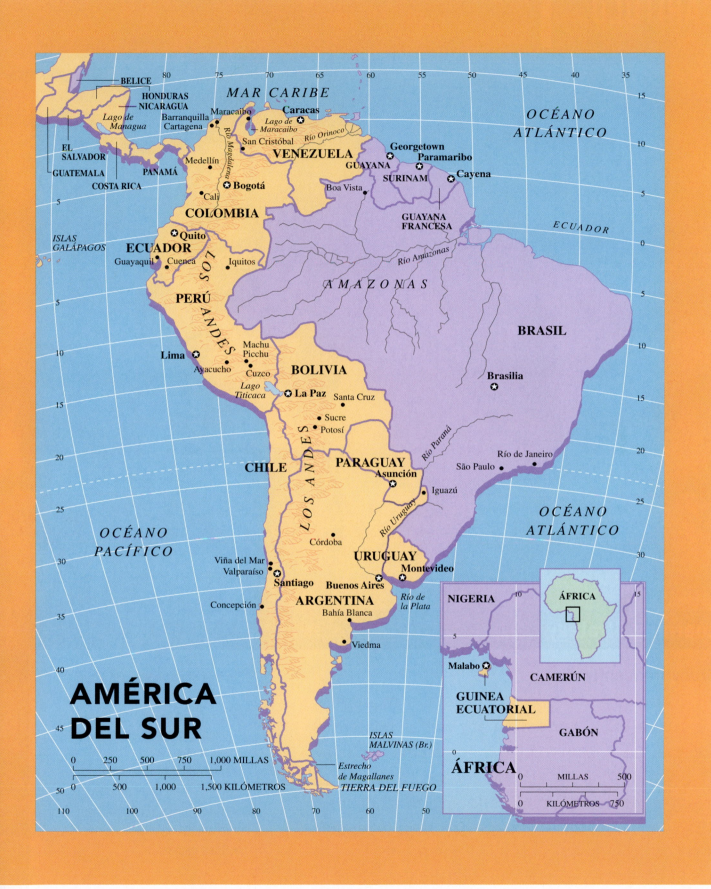

AMÉRICA DEL SUR

BELICE
HONDURAS
NICARAGUA
EL SALVADOR
GUATEMALA
COSTA RICA
PANAMÁ

Lago de Managua
Maracaibo
Barranquilla
Cartagena
San Cristóbal
Medellín
Cali
Bogotá

MAR CARIBE
Caracas
Lago de Maracaibo
Río Orinoco
VENEZUELA
GUAYANA
Georgetown
Paramaribo
SURINAM
Cayena
Boa Vista
GUAYANA FRANCESA

OCÉANO ATLÁNTICO

COLOMBIA

ISLAS GALÁPAGOS
Quito
ECUADOR
Guayaquil
Cuenca
Iquitos

ECUADOR

Río Amazonas
A M A Z O N A S

PERÚ
L O S   A N D E S

Lima
Ayacucho
Machu Picchu
Cuzco

BRASIL

Brasilia

BOLIVIA
Lago Titicaca
La Paz
Santa Cruz
Sucre
Potosí

Río Paraná

Río de Janeiro
São Paulo

CHILE

L O S   A N D E S

PARAGUAY
Asunción
Iguazú

Río Uruguay

OCÉANO ATLÁNTICO

Córdoba

URUGUAY
Viña del Mar
Valparaíso
Santiago
Buenos Aires
Montevideo
Concepción
ARGENTINA
Bahía Blanca
Río de la Plata

OCÉANO PACÍFICO

Viedma

ISLAS MALVINAS (Br.)

Estrecho de Magallanes
TIERRA DEL FUEGO

0   250   500   750   1,000 MILLAS
0   500   1,000   1,500 KILÓMETROS

NIGERIA

ÁFRICA

Malabo
CAMERÚN
GUINEA ECUATORIAL
GABÓN

ÁFRICA

0   MILLAS   500
0   KILÓMETROS   750

Learning Strategy

Study frequently

When learning a foreign language it is important to study every day. Aside from any written homework you may have, plan to spend some time each day learning the current vocabulary and verbs. For most students, it is more effective to study for 15–20 minutes three times a day, than to spend one full hour on the subject. It might also be a lot easier for you to find time to study if you break it into smaller periods.

In this chapter you will learn how to:

- Greet and say good-bye to people in formal and informal situations
- Describe your classroom, your friends, and other people
- Use numbers up to 100 and exchange telephone numbers
- Spell names

Hola, ¿qué tal?

© Blend Images/Jupiter Images

Este es el salón de clases de Mariana. ¿Qué hay en la clase?

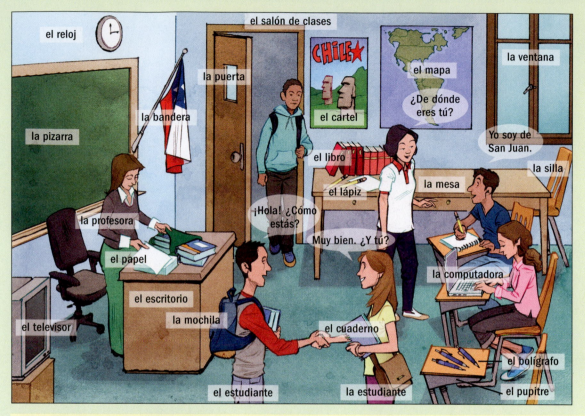

el reloj · el salón de clases · la ventana · la puerta · la bandera · el mapa · la pizarra · el cartel · ¿De dónde eres tú? · el libro · Yo soy de San Juan. · la silla · el lápiz · la mesa · ¡Hola! ¿Cómo estás? · la profesora · Muy bien. ¿Y tú? · el papel · la computadora · el escritorio · la mochila · el cuaderno · el televisor · el bolígrafo · el estudiante · la estudiante · el pupitre

Saludos formales	**Respuestas**	**Despedidas**			
Buenos días.	Buenos días.	Adiós.	*Good-bye.*	Me llamo…	*My name is . . .*
Buenas tardes.	Buenas tardes.	Chao.	*Good-bye.*	Le presento a…	*I'd like to*
Buenas noches.	Buenas noches.		*(informal)*		*introduce you to*
¿Cómo está	Bien, gracias./	Hasta luego.	*See you later.*		*. . . (formal)*
(usted)?	Mal./Regular,	Hasta pronto.	*See you soon.*	Te presento a…	*I'd like to*
	gracias. ¿Y	Hasta mañana.	*See you*		*introduce you to*
	usted?		*tomorrow.*		*. . . (informal)*
		¡Nos vemos!	*See you later!*	Encantado(a).	*Nice to meet you.*
Saludos informales	**Respuestas**	¡Qué tengas un	*Have a nice day!*	Mucho gusto.	*Nice to meet you.*
¡Hola!	¡Hola!	buen día!	*(informal)*	¿Cómo se	*How do you*
¿Cómo estás	Bien, gracias./			escribe…?	*spell . . . ?*
(tú)?	Mal/Regular,	**Presentaciones**			
¿Qué tal?	gracias. ¿Y tú?	¿Cómo te llamas?	*What is your*		
¿Qué hay de	Nada.		*name?*		
nuevo?			*(informal)*		
¿Qué pasa?	Nada.				

INVESTIGUEMOS EL VOCABULARIO
A male would use the form **encantado**, and a female would use the form **encantada**.

Práctica

1.1 **Escucha y responde** Listen to the following list of common classroom items. If the item is in your classroom, give a thumbs-up; if it is not, give a thumbs-down.

CD1-2

.2 En la mochila Indicate which of the following items could go into a student's backpack.

1. la pizarra   3. el papel   5. el bolígrafo   7. la puerta

2. el cuaderno   4. la silla   6. el escritorio   8. los lápices

INVESTIGUEMOS EL VOCABULARIO
Vocabulary often varies from one Spanish-speaking country to another. For example, the word for *pen*:

el bolígrafo (Spain)
la pluma (Mexico)
el lapicero (Peru)

1.3 Un poco de lógica Match each question or statement on the left with a logical response on the right.

1. ¿Cómo te llamas?   **a.** Soy de California.

2. ¿De dónde eres?   **b.** Me llamo Marcos.

3. ¿Cómo estás?   **c.** Nada.

4. ¿Qué hay de nuevo?   **d.** Mucho gusto.

5. Te presento a Jairo.   **e.** Bien, gracias. ¿Y tú?

.4 Mucho gusto First, read the dialogue aloud with a partner. Then, read it again, substituting all the parts in italics with your own information or preferred greetings/farewells.

Estudiante 1: *¡Hola!*
Estudiante 2: *¡Hola!*
Estudiante 1: Me llamo *Rafael.* ¿Y tú? ¿Cómo te llamas?
Estudiante 2: Me llamo *Carlos.*

Estudiante 1: Mucho gusto, *Carlos.* ¿De dónde eres?
Estudiante 2: Soy de *México.* ¿Y tú?
Estudiante 1: Yo soy de *Argentina.*
Estudiante 2: *¡Qué bien!*
Estudiante 1: Bueno... *¡adiós!*
Estudiante 2: *¡Chao!*

🔊 El alfabeto
CD1-3

Letra	Pronunciación de la letra	Letra	Pronunciación de la letra	Letra	Pronunciación de la letra	Letra	Pronunciación de la letra
A	a	H	hache	Ñ	eñe	U	u
B	be	I	i	O	o	V	ve
C	ce	J	jota	P	pe	W	doble ve
D	de	K	ka	Q	cu	X	equis
E	e	L	ele	R	ere	Y	i griega
F	efe	M	eme	S	ese	Z	zeta
G	ge	N	ene	T	te		

1.5 ¿Cómo se escribe...? Read through the following dialogues. Then, using the same format, find out the names of three of your classmates and how to spell them.

1. —¿Cómo te llamas?
—Me llamo Jorge.
—¿Cómo se escribe Jorge?
—J-O-R-G-E

2. —¿Cómo te llamas?
—Me llamo Raquel.
—¿Cómo se escribe Raquel?
—R-A-Q-U-E-L

3. —¿Cómo te llamas?
—Me llamo Xochitl.
—¿Cómo se escribe Xochitl?
—X-O-C-H-I-T-L

INVESTIGUEMOS EL VOCABULARIO
Since 1994 **ch** and **ll** are not considered independent letters. According to the Real Academia, **rr** is not an independent letter either, so it has not been included in this list. Also, you might hear the letter **w** pronounced as "doble u" and the letter **y** as "ye."

What school supplies would you expect to buy for a student entering fifth grade? Make a list. The following is a list of recommended school supplies for students in fifth grade in Mexico. Compare your list of school supplies to the one in the article. Which required supplies were not on your list?

Keith Dannemiller/Corbis

La SEP difunde lista de útiles escolares

Ciudad de México–
La Secretaría de Educación Pública (SEP) dio a conocer la lista oficial de útiles escolares para el próximo ciclo escolar.

Quinto grado

- Cuatro cuadernos, tres de cuadrícula chica y uno de hojas blancas, tamaño carta, de 100 hojas

- Un cuaderno de rayas, de 100 hojas

- Un lápiz del número dos, un bicolor y un bolígrafo

- Una caja de 12 lápices de colores de madera y una goma para borrar

- Un pegamento líquido o un lápiz adhesivo, ambos no tóxicos

- Un juego de geometría con regla graduada de 30 cm., un sacapuntas y unas tijeras de punta roma

- Un compás de precisión

- Un bloc de hojas blancas, tamaño carta, o un paquete de 100 hojas blancas

- Un diccionario escolar

- Una calculadora con las cuatro operaciones básicas (suma, resta, multiplicación y división)

Más allá

What supplies do you use for your classes?

Exploraciones gramaticales

A analizar

Read the following paragraph in which a teacher describes his classroom. Which vocabulary words are singular? Which ones are plural?

> Hay muchas sillas. También hay un escritorio, pero no hay una computadora. No hay carteles, pero hay un mapa. Hay una pizarra. Cuando hay estudiantes también hay muchos libros, cuadernos, lápices y mochilas.

1. How are nouns made plural in Spanish?
2. What is the plural of **lápiz**?

INVESTIGUEMOS LA GRAMÁTICA

Throughout the book, you will be given examples of structures in Spanish and asked to come up with the rules based on those examples. The process of figuring out the rules on your own not only helps you to remember the rules but will also help you to develop important skills such as inference and pattern recognition, which will make you a better language learner.

A comprobar

Gender and number of nouns

1. A noun (**sustantivo**) is a person, place, or thing. In order to make a noun plural:

   - add an **-s** to words ending in a vowel — libro → libros; silla → sillas
   - add an **-es** to words ending in a consonant — profesor → profesores; papel → papeles
   - change a final **-z** to **-c** and add an **-es** — lápiz → lápices

2. You will notice that some nouns lose an accent mark or gain an accent mark when they become plural. You will learn more about accent marks in **Capítulo 2**.

   televisión → televisiones
   examen → exámenes

3. In Spanish, nouns have a gender. In other words, they can be masculine or feminine.

   The endings of nouns not referring to people often indicate a word's gender.

   Masculine nouns:
   - often end in **-o,** such as **el libro** and **el cuaderno**
   - can refer to a man, such as **el profesor** and **el estudiante**

   Feminine nouns:
   - often end in **-a,** such as **la silla** and **la pizarra**
   - can refer to a woman, such as **la profesora** and **la estudiante**

   There are some exceptions such as:

Masculine	Feminine
el día	**la** mano
el mapa	**la** foto
el problema	**la** moto

4. Here are the numbers from 0 to 20.

Los números							
0	cero	7	siete	14	catorce
1	uno	8	ocho	15	quince
2	dos	9	nueve	16	dieciséis
3	tres	10	diez	17	diecisiete
4	cuatro	11	once	18	dieciocho
5	cinco	12	doce	19	diecinueve
6	seis	13	trece	20	veinte

A practicar

1.6 Género Using the rules that you have learned, decide whether the following words are masculine (**M**) or feminine (**F**).

	M	F
1. saludo	_____	_____
2. actriz	_____	_____
3. cafetería	_____	_____
4. rosa	_____	_____
5. doctor	_____	_____
6. teatro	_____	_____
7. mano	_____	_____
8. supervisora	_____	_____
9. mapa	_____	_____
10. autor	_____	_____

1.7 De singular a plural Change the following vocabulary words from singular to plural.

Modelo cuaderno → *cuadernos*

1. mochila
2. lápiz
3. papel
4. pupitre
5. reloj
6. bandera
7. libro
8. cartel

© MARCELODLT/Shutterstock

1.8 **En la clase** Listen to Carolina describe how many of the following items are in her classroom. As you listen, write the number next to each item. Then decide whether each statement is **cierto** or **falso** according to your own classroom.

CD1-4

> **Modelo** You will hear: *Hay once escritorios.*
> You will write: _____11_____ escritorios

1. _____ estudiantes
2. _____ pizarras
3. _____ sillas
4. _____ ventanas
5. _____ mapas
6. _____ computadoras

1.9 **Los útiles** Look at the picture below and identify the school supplies, telling how many there are. Then work with a partner and take turns identifying the school supplies you each have. ¡**OJO!** Pay attention to singular and plural forms of the vocabulary words.

© Mike Flippo/Shutterstock

1.10 **La clase de matemáticas** Work with a partner and take turns saying the following mathematical equations in Spanish and giving their solutions. You will need the following words: **más (+), menos (–)** and **son (=)**.

> **Modelo** 6 + 10 =
> *Seis más diez son dieciséis.*

1. 4 + 5 =
2. 16 – 6 =
3. 20 – 2 =
4. 7 + 9 =
5. 3 + 12 =
6. 11 – 4 =
7. 13 + 1 =
8. 14 + 5 =

Conexiones... a la geografía

Look at the map and write the names of all Spanish-speaking countries that you can locate. Then indicate in what region each country is located: North America (**América del Norte**), Central America (**América Central**), South America (**América del Sur**), the Caribbean (**el Caribe**), Europe (**Europa**), or Africa (**África**). When you finish your list, match each of the countries with its capital city from the box below. **¡OJO!** One of the countries has two capital cities.

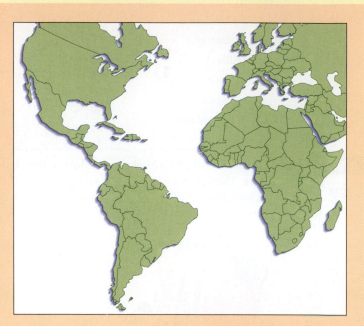

Montevideo	Tegucigalpa	San Juan
Buenos Aires	Lima	San Salvador
La Habana	Asunción	Bogotá
La Paz	Managua	Santiago
Sucre	Madrid	Ciudad de Panamá
Quito	Ciudad de Guatemala	Caracas
Santo Domingo	Ciudad de México	Malabo
San José		

iTunes
Listen to the song "Latino" by Adolescent's Orquesta. What Latin American countries are named?

Comparaciones

How different is the Spanish used in Spain from the Spanish spoken in Latin American countries? It is important to understand that it is the same language and both will be understood in every country where Spanish is spoken. However, there are regional differences in vocabulary as well as accents, just as there are between the English spoken in England and the English used in the United States. Come up with a list of five or six regional vocabulary variations in English and compare your list with a partner's. Do your words fit into specific categories?

What factors do you think influence differences in vocabulary within the same language? Write five words that you would expect to vary in Spanish-speaking countries.

© Jose AS Reyes/Shutterstock

Cultura

Cultural practices and products of Spanish-speaking countries vary from country to country. Putting aside preconceived ideas will help you gain a better understanding of these cultures. Work in groups of three or four to determine if the statements below are true or false. Then, search the Internet to correct the false statements.

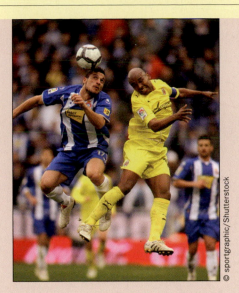

1. All Latin Americans speak Spanish.

2. Flamenco is a popular dance throughout South America.

3. The majority of the population in Spanish-speaking countries is Catholic.

4. **Tortillas** are a typical dish in Spain.

5. Some indigenous people in Mexico and Guatemala still wear traditional clothing.

6. Chiles are a cooking staple in Paraguay, Uruguay, and Argentina.

7. Soccer is the most popular sport in South America.

8. In many Spanish-speaking countries, children can attend school in the morning or the afternoon.

9. Bullfighting is a popular sport in Cuba.

10. In most Spanish-speaking countries, the main meal is between 5:00 and 7:00 P.M.

> Investiga en Internet los deportes más populares en España y Latinoamérica.

Comunidad

If there are any international students or ESL students in your school that are native Spanish speakers, introduce yourself to one of them and find out where he or she is from. You may want to become conversation partners.

A analizar

Read the following paragraph and answer the questions below.

> En el salón de clase hay unas mesas para los estudiantes y un escritorio para la profesora. En el escritorio hay unos libros y una computadora.

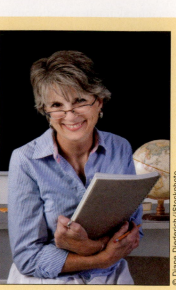

© Diane Diederich/iStockphoto

1. Write the word that comes before each of the following nouns. Do these words change according to the nouns that follow? Explain.

   _____ salón de clase

   _____ mesas

   _____ estudiantes

   _____ escritorio

   _____ profesora

   _____ libros

   _____ computadora

2. What do you think **hay** means?

A comprobar

Definite and indefinite articles and **hay**

1. The definite article *the* is used with a specific noun or a noun that has previously been mentioned. In Spanish, the definite article indicates whether a noun is masculine or feminine as well as whether it is singular or plural. It can be expressed in four different ways.

los artículos definidos

	masculino	femenino
singular	**el**	**la**
plural	**los**	**las**

¿De dónde es **el** profesor?
*Where is **the** professor from?*

2. The indefinite articles *a/an* or *some* are used when referring to a noun that is not specific or that has not previously been mentioned. They also indicate gender (masculine/feminine) and number (singular/plural), and can be expressed in four different ways in Spanish.

los artículos indefinidos

	masculino	femenino
singular	**un**	**una**
plural	**unos**	**unas**

¿Hay **una** ventana en el salón de clases?
*Is there **a** window in the classroom?*

3. **Hay** means *there is* or *there are*. It is used with the indefinite article to talk about singular nouns and to indicate *some* with plural nouns. The indefinite article is often omitted after **hay** in plural expressions.

Hay un escritorio.   No hay lápices.
There is a desk.   *There are no pencils.*

Hay (unas) ventanas.   No hay una pizarra.
There are (some)   *There isn't a board.*
windows.

4. When using **hay** with numbers, do not use an article.

No hay tres libros.   Hay cinco libros.
There aren't three books.   *There are five books.*

21	veintiuno	28	veintiocho	70	setenta
22	veintidós	29	veintinueve	80	ochenta
23	veintitrés	30	treinta	90	noventa
24	veinticuatro	31	treinta y uno	100	cien
25	veinticinco	40	cuarenta	101	ciento uno
26	veintiséis	50	cincuenta		
27	veintisiete	60	sesenta		

INVESTIGUEMOS LA ORTOGRAFÍA

Notice that numbers below 30 are only one word, whereas numbers above 30 take the word **y** *(and)*, for example, **treinta y uno.** Note that with the numbers 21, 31, etc., **uno** changes to **un** when followed by a masculine noun: **Hay treinta y un libros** and **una** when followed by a feminine noun: **Hay treinta y una sillas.**

A practicar

1.11 **¿Lógico o no?** Read the statements and decide if they are logical or not.

1. Hay un cuaderno en la mochila.
2. No hay una puerta en la clase.
3. Hay una estudiante en la clase.
4. Hay cinco libros en el escritorio.
5. Hay unos papeles en la mesa.
6. Hay una pizarra en la silla.

© baranq/Shutterstock

1.12 **Los artículos** Look at the sentences and decide if you need the definite article or the indefinite article. Circle the correct answer.

David es (**1.** un / el) estudiante en (**2.** una / la) universidad de los Estados Unidos. En su salón de clases hay (**3.** unos / los) carteles y (**4.** una / la) ventana. (**5.** Una / La) ventana es muy grande. En (**6.** una / la) mochila de David hay (**7.** unos / los) libros para (**8.** una / la) clase de español de David.

© Monkey Business Images/Shutterstock

1.13 **¿Cuántos hay?** Look at the picture below and take turns answering the following questions.

INVESTIGUEMOS EL VOCABULARIO

Here are some question words you will start to recognize:

¿Dónde?	**¿Qué?**
Where?	*What?*
¿Cuándo?	**¿Quién?**
When?	*Who?*
¿Cuántos(as)?	**¿Por qué?**
How many?	*Why?*

1. ¿Cuántos mapas hay?

2. ¿Cuántas sillas hay?

3. ¿Cuántos libros hay?

4. ¿Cuántos lápices hay?

5. ¿Cuántas banderas hay?

6. ¿Qué más hay? (*What else is there?*)

1.14 **¿Qué hay?** With a partner, take turns asking and answering the questions about the items in your classroom. If you have them in your classroom, tell how many there are. Remember, if there is only one item, you must use **un** or **una.**

Modelo ¿Hay una mesa?
Estudiante 1: *¿Hay una mesa?*
Estudiante 2: *Sí, hay una mesa./No, hay dos mesas./*
No, no hay una mesa.

1. ¿Hay un reloj?

2. ¿Hay una pizarra?

3. ¿Hay una bandera?

4. ¿Hay un mapa?

5. ¿Hay una ventana?

6. ¿Hay un cartel?

7. ¿Hay una computadora?

8. ¿Hay una silla?

© Christopher Futcher/Shutterstock

1.15 **El número, por favor** Look at the page from a tourist guide for Madrid, Spain. What number would you need to call for the following services?

1. atención médica
2. servicio de autobús
3. servicio de taxi
4. medicina
5. información sobre los restaurantes y museos

Números importantes

Madrid

Oficinas de turismo
Aeropuerto Internacional Barajas....................................913 05 86 56
Plaza Mayor..915 88 16 36

Transporte
Estación de autobús (Continental Auto)........................ 917 45 63 00
Tele-Taxi.. 913 71 21 31

Farmacias
Farmacia de la Paloma c/Toledo, 46..............................913 65 39 18
Farmacia del Globo c/Goya...915 75 33 16

Urgencias
Hospital Doce de Octubre Avenida Andalucía, s/n........... 913 90 80 00
Hospital La Paz Paseo Castellana, 241............................917 27 73 39

Puerta de Alcalá

INVESTIGUEMOS EL VOCABULARIO

Phone numbers in most Spanish-speaking countries are often given in pairs. If a number is not even, only the first number is given separately, for example, 5-93-34-76.

1.16 **En la librería** It is the end of the year, and the employees are taking inventory at the bookstore. Tell how many items they have using the verb **hay**.

1. 50 cuadernos
2. 85 diccionarios
3. 100 bolígrafos
4. 78 lápices
5. 94 paquetes de papel
6. 31 libros de español
7. 62 mapas
8. 49 mochilas

© Monkey Business Images/Shutterstock

Lectura

Antes de leer

Look at the advertisement for a school. Using the cognates to help you, answer the questions.

LINGUAMAX

Establecido en 1980, **Linguamax** ofrece clases de inglés y francés para adolescentes y adultos.

- Profesores nativos con mucha experiencia
- Clases con un máximo de 5 estudiantes
- Precios razonables

Los cursos comienzan el 1° de junio

Para más información llame al 1-23-45-67 o visite **Linguamax** en la Avenida Bolívar, 203

¡Cursos de lenguas con garantía de calidad!

Obtenga un descuento del 10% al mencionar esta publicidad

a. When was the school established?

b. What classes are offered at the school?

c. Who can take classes?

d. What are three benefits of taking classes at this school?

e. When do classes begin?

f. How can you get more information?

g. How can you receive a discount?

Now look at the reading on the next page. The red, bold words are cognates. What do they mean?

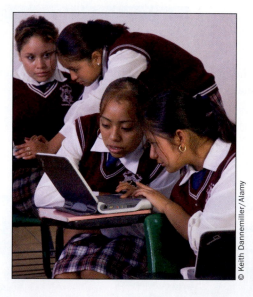

© Keith Dannemiller/Alamy

A leer

countries/right

3 year pre-university course
shifts/attend

free
must buy/supplies

La escuela es para todos

En los **países** latinoamericanos y en España, **la educación** es un **derecho** de los niños. En unos países la escuela **primaria** y la **secundaria** son **obligatorias**. En otros países la **preparatoria** es obligatoria. Para satisfacer la **demanda**, muchas escuelas tienen dos **turnos**: unos niños **asisten** a la escuela por la mañana, y otros por la tarde.

[la educación es un derecho de los niños]

Por lo **general**, los libros de texto son **gratuitos**, pero las familias **deben comprar** otros **útiles** escolares. También en muchos **casos** las **familias** necesitan comprar **uniformes** para los niños porque es **común** usarlos.

Estudiantes en la Plaza de Armas, Lima, Perú

© Author's photo

Comprensión

Decide whether the following statements are true or false.

1. En Latinoamérica la escuela primaria es obligatoria.
2. Todos *(All)* los niños están en la escuela por la mañana.
3. Es necesario comprar *(to buy)* los libros para la escuela.
4. Muchos niños usan uniformes.

Después de leer

Even though school is free, there are many expenses associated with it, such as purchasing uniforms, lab coats, fees for special equipment, etc. What expenses are associated with K-12 in the United States? Can you think of other hidden expenses?

Estas personas van a un concierto. ¿Cómo son?

labels: moreno(a), calvo(a), rubio(a), pelirrojo(a), viejo(a), bajo(a), grande, gordo(a), guapo(a), alto(a), delgado(a), joven, pequeño(a)

Las descripciones de la personalidad

bueno(a) / malo(a)	**Más adjetivos:**		largo(a)	long	**Más cognados:**
cruel / cariñoso(a)	antipático	*unfriendly*	nuevo(a)	new	agresivo(a)
generoso(a) / egoísta	amable	*kind*	perezoso	*lazy*	atlético(a)
idealista / realista	bonito(a)	*pretty*	pobre	*poor*	famoso(a)
inteligente / tonto(a)	corto(a)	*short (length)*	rebelde	*rebel*	honesto(a)
interesante / aburrido(a)	difícil	*difficult*	rico(a)	*rich*	
optimista / pesimista	fácil	*easy*	simpático(a)	*nice*	**Palabras adicionales**
liberal / conservador(a)	feo(a)	*ugly*	trabajador(a)	*hardworking*	el hombre — *man*
paciente / impaciente					el niño — *boy*
serio(a) / cómico(a)					la niña — *girl*
tímido(a) / sociable					la mujer — *woman*

Práctica

1.17 **Escucha y responde** Look at the picture and listen to the different adjectives. Write the letter **D** on one piece of paper and the letter **S** on another. If the adjective you hear describes Don Quijote, hold up the **D**. If it describes Sancho Panza, hold up the **S**.

CD1-5

1.18 **Identificaciones** Look around the classroom and identify someone that fits the following descriptions.

1. pelirrojo	**3.** joven	**5.** moreno	**7.** bajo
2. alto	**4.** atractivo	**6.** rubio	**8.** delgado

1.19 **Sinónimos** Identify a word from the vocabulary list that has a similar meaning.

1. afectuoso	**3.** sincero	**5.** complicado	**7.** simple
2. introvertido	**4.** tolerante	**6.** atractivo	**8.** positivo

1.20 **La personalidad y las profesiones** Make a list of the ideal personality traits for the following jobs.

Modelo profesor
paciente, interesante, inteligente

1. policía	**3.** actor	**5.** político
2. estudiante	**4.** espía *(spy)*	**6.** doctor

1.21 **¡Adivina!** Cristóbal attended an all-boys' school. Look at the photos of his classmates and take turns describing one person at a time without telling which one you are describing. Use as many adjectives as necessary until your partner can guess who you are describing. You might even imagine what their personalities are like.

© Jason Stitt/Shutterstock
© Jerome Tisne/Getty Images
© Tad Denson/Shutterstock
© Michael Jang/Getty Images

1.22 **Veinte preguntas** Follow the steps below to play "twenty questions."

Paso 1 In groups of three, write a list of the names of famous men who are familiar to everybody in the group.

Paso 2 One person in the group chooses a name from the list but doesn't say which name it is. The other two members of the group guess the name by asking yes/no questions.

Modelo *¿Es* (Is he) *joven?*
¿Es rubio?
¿Es alto?

Many people change their hair color. Why do you think this is? The following appeared in the magazine *People en español*. Read the captions. Why did each of these actresses change their hair color?

¿Las prefieres rubias o pelinegras?

ANGÉLICA RIVERA

Ahora que es la novia del gobernador del Estado de México, Enrique Peña Nieto, la actriz ha optado por un color de cabello[1] más conservador, un castaño claro. En una época Rivera llevaba el cabello completamente rubio.

© Notimex/FOTO/Cortesia/COR/ACE/Newscom

WireImage/Getty Images

CAMERON DÍAZ

La actriz de ascendencia cubana casi siempre anda rubia, pero cuando se le antoja[2] meterse un poquito más en la onda latina se obscurece[3] el cabello. ¿O será que los cambios dependen del novio[4] de turno?

[1] hair   [2] she feels like   [3] darkens   [4] boyfriend

Más allá

¿Eres rubio, moreno o pelirrojo? ¿Qué color de pelo prefieres tú?

A analizar

Read the following paragraph in which Mercedes introduces herself and her friends.

> Yo **soy** Mercedes y **soy** de España. Ellos **son** mis amigos, Vilma y David. Vilma **es** de La República Dominicana. Ella **es** un poco tímida. David **es** de Honduras. Él no **es** tímido; **es** muy sociable. Nosotros **somos** estudiantes en Miami. ¿Y tú? ¿De dónde **eres** tú?

1. Does **ellos** refer to one person or more than one person? In the paragraph, who does **él** refer to? And **ella**?

2. The verb **ser** *(to be)* is used throughout the paragraph. Its forms are in bold. Write the appropriate form that is used with each of the following pronouns.

   yo _____   ella   _____

   tú _____   nosotros _____

   él _____   ellos   _____

3. Look at the following conversations, paying attention to the use of **tú** and **usted**. Both mean *you* in English. What do you think the difference is?

A comprobar

Subject pronouns and the verb ser

singular		plural	
yo	I	nosotros/nosotras	we
tú	you (familiar)	vosotros/vosotras	you (familiar in Spain)
usted	you (formal)	ustedes	you (formal)
él	he	ellos	they (group of males or a mixed group)
ella	she	ellas	they (group of females)

INVESTIGUEMOS LA GRAMÁTICA

In Spanish **ser** and **estar** both mean *to be*. You will learn more about **estar** in **Capítulo 4.**

1. When addressing one person, Spanish speakers use either **tú** or **usted** (sometimes abbreviated Ud.). **Tú** is informal. It is used with family, friends, classmates, and children. It denotes familiarity. **Usted** is formal. It is used with people in a position of authority, older people, strangers, and people in a professional setting. It denotes respect and more distance.

2. When referring to groups of females, use **nosotras** and **ellas,** and when referring to groups of males, use **nosotros** and **ellos.** When the groups are mixed, use the masculine forms **nosotros** and **ellos,** as they have a generic meaning that implies the presence of both genders.

3. In Spain, **vosotros** and **vosotras** are used to address a group of people and denote familiarity, and follow the same rules as **nosotros** and **nosotras** with regard to gender; **ustedes** is used to address a group of people and denotes respect. In Latin America, **ustedes** (sometimes abbreviated Uds.) is used to address any group of people, regardless of the relationship.

4. The verb **ser** means *to be*. Just as there are different forms of the verb *to be* in English (*I am, you are, he is*, etc.), there are also different forms of the verb **ser** in Spanish. Changing a verb into its different forms to indicate who is doing the activity is called *conjugating*.

ser

yo	soy	I am	nosotros/nosotras	somos	we are
tú	eres	you are	vosotros/vosotras	sois	you all are
usted	es	you are	ustedes	son	you all are
él/ella	es	he/she is	ellos/ellas	son	they are

5. Use **ser**
   - to describe what someone is like.

     Él **es** alto, pero ellos **son** bajos.
     He is tall, but they are short.
   - to say where someone is from.

     Yo **soy** de Lima, Perú.
     I am from Lima, Peru.

INVESTIGUEMOS LA GRAMÁTICA

Use **de dónde** to ask where someone is from.

¿De dónde **eres** tú?
Where are you from?

A practicar

1.23 **¿Tú o usted?** Which pronoun would you use **to address** each of the following people?

Modelo un niño → *tú*

1. un policía
2. un profesor
3. mamá
4. un amigo
5. el presidente
6. un estudiante en la clase de español

1.24 Sustituciones Which pronoun would you use **to talk about** the following people?

Modelo Rebeca → *ella*

1. Felipe
2. Silvia y Alicia
3. tu amigo y Ricardo
4. Regina

5. la señora Marcos
6. Javier y yo
7. Lola, Ana, Sara y Luis
8. Miguelito

1.25 Parejas Match the subject with the remainder of the sentence.

1. Yo
2. Rafael y Carlos
3. La profesora
4. Tú
5. Maite y yo

a. es joven.
b. somos trabajadores.
c. soy optimista.
d. eres inteligente.
e. son guapos.

1.26 El verbo *ser* Complete the paragraph with the correct form of the verb **ser**.

¡Hola! Yo (1) _____ Antonio y (2) _____ de Santiago, Chile. Mis amigos

(3) _____ Laura y Víctor. Nosotros (4) _____ estudiantes en la Universidad de

Santiago. Laura (5) _____ estudiante de biología y Víctor y yo (6) _____

estudiantes de ciencias políticas. Y tú, ¿también (7) _____ estudiante?

1.27 ¿De dónde son? In groups of three, look at the map and complete the following
sentences telling where the different people are from. Then, find out from the other
members of your group where they are from. Be sure to use the correct forms of the verb **ser.**

Modelo Carolina...
         Carolina es de Chile.

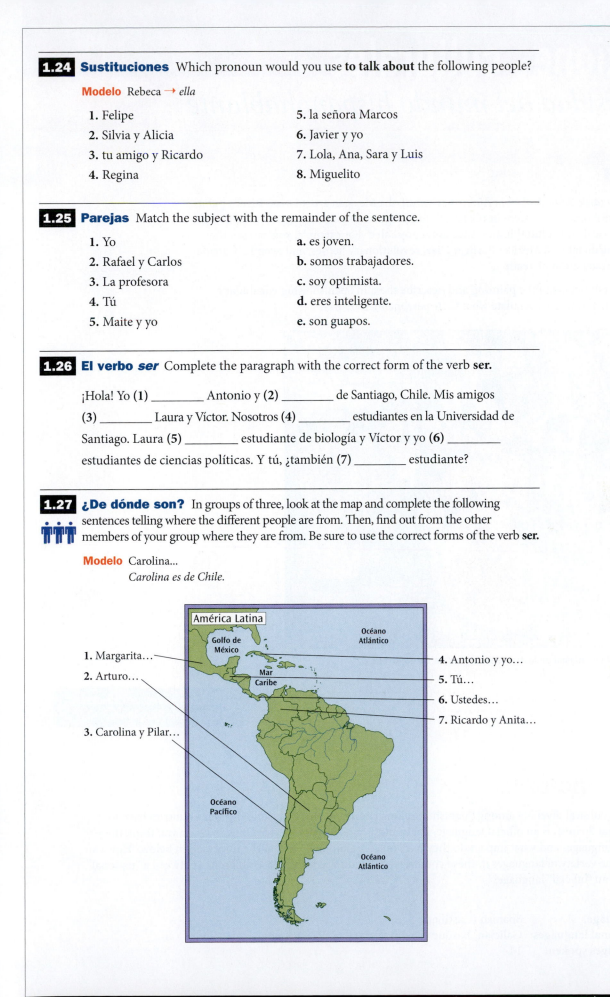

1. Margarita…
2. Arturo…
3. Carolina y Pilar…

4. Antonio y yo…
5. Tú…
6. Ustedes…
7. Ricardo y Anita…

Cultura

In *Sueño de una tarde dominical en la Alameda Central,* the Mexican artist Diego Rivera paints himself along with others who were important to him. Figures of personal significance as well as those of historical and cultural importance are represented. For example, you can see the former president/dictator of Mexico, Porfirio Díaz, revolutionary heroes, and even La Catrina, the cultural representation of death.

Pick three different people in the painting and describe them in Spanish using vocabulary from the chapter. You might speculate what their personalities are like.

Sueño de una tarde dominical en la Alameda Central de Diego Rivera

Investiga en Internet los murales políticos de Diego Rivera.

Comparaciones

There is great cultural diversity among Spanish-speaking countries. One thing all Hispanic countries have in common is that Spanish is an official language, but in most cases it is not the only one. Why do you think there are "official" languages and what impact do they have on communities? Look at the information below. How can you explain the variety of languages in these countries? What do you think is the difference between a "national" language and an "official" language?

SPAIN
Official language: Spanish (Castilian)
Official regional languages: Galician, Basque (Euskara), Catalan, Valenciano
Other languages spoken: 14

MEXICO

National language:	Spanish
Other languages spoken:	298 (náhuatl is the only one spoken by over one million speakers)

GUATEMALA

Official language:	Spanish
Other languages spoken:	55

BOLIVIA

Official languages:	Spanish, Quechua, Aymara
Other languages spoken:	45

UNITED STATES

National languages:	English (official in some states)
Regional languages:	Hawaiian, Spanish (in New Mexico)
Other languages spoken:	178

Source: The Ethnologue Report, Almanaque Mundial 2010

Conexiones... a la geografía

The people in the photos are all from Latin America. In Spanish, tell what country each person is from and describe him or her. If possible, locate the countries using Google Earth. Why do you think there is such great ethnic diversity in Latin America?

Rigoberta Menchú, Guatemala, activista política

Luis Miguel, México, cantante

Evo Morales, Bolivia, presidente

Celia Cruz, Cuba, cantante (RIP)

Lupita Ferrer, Venezuela, actriz

Comunidad

Find out if there are any businesses in your community that have a Spanish-speaking office assistant. Set up a time to meet with the person. When you meet, introduce yourself and tell him or her that you are a Spanish student (**un estudiante de español**). Then find out how he or she uses Spanish in the office.

A analizar

Read the following paragraph in which Cristina introduces herself and her friend, Mario. Then underline the adjectives.

¡Hola! Me llamo Cristina. Yo soy una chica muy extrovertida. Mi mejor amigo, Mario, no es extrovertido. Él es muy tímido. Mario es inteligente, muy simpático e idealista. Yo también soy inteligente y simpática, pero no soy idealista. Soy realista, trabajadora y también soy liberal. Además, Mario es alto, rubio y atlético, y yo soy baja y morena. Mario y yo somos muy diferentes, pero lo importante es que somos buenos amigos.

Using the underlined adjectives as well as what you learned about **encantado** and **encantada,** complete the following chart.

masculine singular	masculine plural	feminine singular	feminine plural
bajo	_____	_____	_____
_____	inteligentes	_____	_____
_____	_____	idealista	_____
liberal	_____	_____	_____
trabajador	_____	_____	_____

A comprobar

Adjective agreement

Adjectives describe a person, place, or thing. In Spanish, adjectives must agree with the person or the object they describe both in gender (masculine/feminine) and in number (singular/plural).

Singular masculine adjectives...		singular	plural
ending in **-o**	masculine	simpático	simpáticos
	feminine	simpática	simpáticas
ending in **-a**	masculine	idealista	idealistas
	feminine	idealista	idealistas
ending in **-e**	masculine	sociable	sociables
	feminine	sociable	sociables
ending in a consonant*	masculine	ideal	ideales
	feminine	ideal	ideales
*exception: ending in **-or**	masculine	trabajador	trabajadores
	feminine	trabajadora	trabajadoras

> **INVESTIGUEMOS LA PRONUNCIACIÓN**
> For pronunciation purposes, **y** *(and)* becomes **e** when followed by a word beginning with the letter(s) **i** or **hi.**

Mi amigo es simpático, sociable e idealista.

Mi amiga también es simpática, sociable e idealista.

Mis amigos son simpáticos, sociables e idealistas.

A practicar

1.28 **¿Quién es?** Listen to the eight descriptive statements and decide which person is being described. In some cases, the description may apply to both. Place a check mark in the appropriate blanks. **¡OJO!** Pay attention to the adjective endings!

CD1-6

1. _____ Jennifer López   _____ Ricky Martin
2. _____ Lorena Ochoa   _____ Sammy Sosa
3. _____ Daisy Fuentes   _____ George López
4. _____ Isabel Allende   _____ Gabriel García Márquez
5. _____ Shakira   _____ Gael García Bernal
6. _____ Penélope Cruz   _____ Paul Rodríguez

1.29 **La atracción de los opuestos** Complete each sentence with an adjective that has the opposite meaning of the underlined word. **¡OJO!** Be sure the adjectives agree with the subject they are describing.

1. Susana es <u>generosa</u> y su esposo es _____.
2. Fernando es <u>tímido</u> y su esposa es _____.
3. Mis amigas son <u>delgadas</u> y sus esposos son _____.
4. Marcos es <u>trabajador</u> y su esposa es _____.
5. Mis amigos son <u>cómicos</u> y sus esposas son _____.
6. Mi amigo es _____ y su esposa es _____.
   (Choose adjectives not used in the sentences above.)

1.30 **En el café** Work with a partner and take turns giving true/false statements about the people in the drawing. You should correct any false statements. **¡OJO!** Be sure the adjectives agree with the subject they are describing.

Modelo Estudiante 1: *Vicente es calvo.*
             Estudiante 2: *Falso, él es rubio.*

1.31 **Los ideales** Complete the following statements expressing your own opinion regarding the ideal characteristics of each subject. Then compare your list with a partner's and come to an agreement on two characteristics for each.

1. La profesora ideal es… No es…
2. El estudiante ideal es… No es…
3. Los amigos ideales son… No son…
4. La madre *(mother)* ideal es… No es…
5. Los políticos ideales son… No son…
6. Las mascotas *(pet)* ideales son… No son…

INVESTIGUEMOS EL VOCABULARIO
Use the words **muy** (*very*) and **un poco** (*a little*) to discuss degrees.

1.32 **El horóscopo** Find your astrological sign below and read the descriptions. Choose two characteristics that describe you. You may use those listed for your sign or choose others that are more accurate. Then, talk to three classmates and find out their signs and the characteristics that describe them.

Modelo Estudiante 1: *¿Cuál es tu signo?*
Estudiante 2: *Yo soy Aries.*
Estudiante 1: *¿Cómo eres tú?*
Estudiante 2: *Yo soy extrovertido(a) y emocional.*

Signo Fechas
Características

 **Aries**

21 de marzo – 20 de abril
extrovertido, obstinado

 **Leo**

24 de julio – 23 de agosto
creativo, vanidoso

 **Sagitario**

23 de noviembre –
21 de diciembre
idealista, indiscreto

 **Tauro**

21 de abril – 21 de mayo
paciente, perezoso

 **Virgo**

24 de agosto –
23 de septiembre
organizado, perfeccionista

 **Capricornio**

22 de diciembre –
20 de enero
práctico, calculador

 **Géminis**

22 de mayo – 21 de junio
intelectual, impaciente

 **Libra**

24 de septiembre –
23 de octubre
activo, indeciso

 **Acuario**

21 de enero –
19 de febrero
independiente, rebelde

 **Cáncer**

22 de junio – 23 de julio
trabajador, emocional

 **Escorpión**

24 de octubre –
22 de noviembre
introvertido, posesivo

 **Piscis**

20 de febrero –
20 de marzo
generoso, dependiente

Redacción

Write a paragraph in which you describe yourself and your best friend.

Paso 1 Create a Venn diagram such as the one below. In the middle section where the circles overlap, write any adjectives that are common to both yourself and your best friend. Write any adjectives that are unique to yourself in the circle on the left and adjectives that are unique to your best friend in the circle on the right.

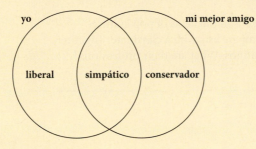

yo   mi mejor amigo

liberal   simpático   conservador

Paso 2 Write a sentence in which you introduce your reader to yourself and to your best friend.

Paso 3 Write two or three sentences in which you describe the qualities that you and your friend have in common.

Paso 4 Write two or three more sentences that describe the qualities that are unique to you and unique to your best friend.

Paso 5 Write a conclusion sentence that wraps up the paragraph.

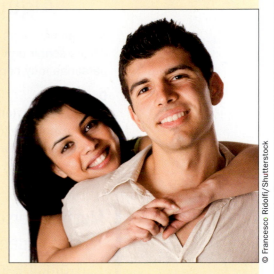

© Francesco Ridolfi/Shutterstock

Paso 6 Edit your paragraph:

1. Do the adjectives agree with the person they describe?
2. Check your spelling, including accent marks.
3. Are there any sentences that could be joined with either y *(and)* or pero *(but)*?
4. Can you vary some of the sentences by using expressions like también *(also)* and los/las dos *(both of us)*?

Lectura

Antes de leer

Write a list of names of famous contemporary U.S. citizens in the fields of pop culture, politics, movies, and sports. Why are they famous? Compare lists with a classmate. Together, try to come up with names of contemporary famous Latinos. What are their professions?

A leer

Algunos famosos de Latinoamérica

Muchas personas de países hispanos se distinguen en todas las áreas y es difícil escribir una lista corta. A continuación hay descripciones de algunas personas muy populares en el mundo contemporáneo.

Deportes

Manu Ginóbili (**julio** 1977), deportista **argentino,** es un excelente jugador de **básquetbol** de la NBA de los Estados Unidos. Habla fluidamente español, inglés e italiano y tiene su propia página en el Internet.

© Bob Pearson/epa/Corbis

> [Muchas personas de países hispanos se distinguen en todas las áreas y es difícil escribir una lista corta.]

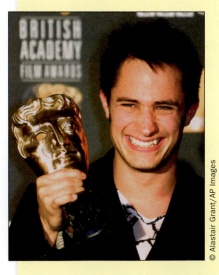
© Alastair Grant/AP Images

teach reading

Cine

Gael García Bernal (noviembre 1978) es actualmente uno de los actores latinoamericanos más **famosos,** gracias a su **participación** en **filmes** como *Los diarios de motocicleta* (2004), *El crimen del Padre Amaro* (2002) y *Babel* (2006). Un dato interesante es que Gael participó en campañas para **enseñar a leer** a los **indígenas** huicholes en el norte de México.

© Matt Sayles/AP Images

Música

Olga Tañón (**abril** 1967) es una cantante y actriz de Puerto Rico. Es famosa en Latinoamérica por su música **rítmica,** y ahora planea grabar **música** en inglés. Tañón participó en la **controversial** versión en español del himno estadounidense en 2006.

Política

Felipe Calderón Hinojosa (agosto 1962) es el **presidente** de México desde diciembre del 2006. Calderón ganó las **elecciones** más controversiales en la historia de México... tan controversiales que muchas personas en México no **reconocen** a Calderón como el presidente. Felipe Calderón es licenciado en **derecho,** con una maestría de la Universidad de Harvard.

law

© Eduardo Verdugo/AP Images

Comprensión

To which of the people mentioned in the reading does the statement refer?

1. Es famosa por su música.
2. Estudió en los Estados Unidos.
3. Es un actor popular.
4. Es atlético.
5. Es puertorriqueña.
6. Juega al básquetbol.

Después de leer

What other famous people do you know from Spanish-speaking countries? Work with a partner to come up with a list of names, then choose one of the people on your list and write a short description of him/her. Read your description to the class and have them guess whom you are describing.

iTunes
Listen to the Mocedades song, "Eres tú". Write down as many cognates as you can as well as words you recognize. What do you think the theme of the song is?

© Yuri Arcurs/Shutterstock

Vocabulario

Sustantivos

buena presencia	*good appearance*
la cita	*appointment*
el formulario	*form*
la oficina	*office*
la reunión	*meeting*

Verbos

contestar el teléfono	*to pick up the phone*
inscribir	*to register*
interpretar	*to interpret*
preparar informes	*to prepare reports*

Frases útiles

¿En qué puedo servirle?
How can I help you?

Un momento, por favor.
One moment, please.

Está ocupado. ¿Desea hacer una cita?
He is busy right now. Would you like to make an appointment?

¿Cuál es su número de teléfono?
What is your phone number?

Más despacio, por favor.
Slower, please.

Disculpe.
Excuse me. I'm sorry.

Necesita hablar con...
You need to speak to . . .

¿Con quién quiere hablar?
Whom do you want to speak to?

Tiene que ver a...
You have to see. . . .

DATOS IMPORTANTES

Educación: Escuela secundaria con entrenamiento especial en tecnología o *community college*; algunos puestos *(some positions)* requieren una licenciatura *(bachelor's degree)*

Salario: Entre $23 000 y $36 000

Dónde se trabaja: Variedad de organizaciones; aproximadamente 90% de los asistentes trabajan en la industria de servicio, como *(like)* la educación, el gobierno *(government)*, la salud *(health)* y ventas *(retail)*

María Bravo es secretaria ejecutiva y trabaja en una escuela privada. Allí hay muchos estudiantes de otros países *(countries)*. Ella necesita comunicarse en inglés y en español continuamente. María se encarga *(is in charge of)* de los trabajos administrativos de la escuela y ayuda *(helps)* a los padres *(parents)* y estudiantes que necesitan información. En el video, María habla con el padre de un estudiante que no habla inglés.

Antes de ver

Administrative assistants and executive secretaries are the connections between a company and their clients. What questions do you think a parent would ask a secretary at a private school? How important do you think it is to have bilingual administrative personnel in a school? Why?

Comprensión

Answer the following questions according to the video.

© Heinle/Cengage Learning

1. ¿Qué tiene que hacer el señor Molina? *(What does Mr. Molina have to do?)*

2. ¿De dónde son el Sr. Molina y su familia? *(Where are Mr. Molina and his family from?)*

3. ¿Cuántos años tiene el hijo del Sr. Molina? *(How old is Mr. Molina's son?)*

4. Según la Sra. Bravo, ¿a qué grado entra el hijo del Sr. Molina? *(According to Mrs. Bravo, what grade will Mr. Molina's son go into?)*

5. ¿Cuántos maestros bilingües hay? *(How many bilingual teachers are there?)*

Después de ver

With a partner, play the roles of the parent of a Latin American student who has just arrived in the United States and the secretary of a school. Greet and introduce yourself to the secretary. The secretary should ask how he/she can help you. Explain what you need.

Here are some useful phrases:

Quiero inscribir a mi hijo.	*I want to register my son.*
¿Cuántos años tiene?	*How old is he?*
Él tiene _____ años.	*He is . . . years old.*

1.33 **¿Qué hay?** A student is in her room studying. Mention five items that are in the room, and then mention one thing that is not.

Modelo *Hay unos libros.*

© Sofos Design/Shutterstock

1.34 **Los famosos** Tell where the following famous people are from. Search the Internet for information on those you don't know.

1. Enrique y Julio Iglesias
2. Marc Anthony
3. Salma Hayek
4. Daisy Fuentes y Gloria Estefan
5. Hugo Chávez
6. Shakira y Juanes

1.35 **Mi amiga Mónica** Complete the paragraph with the appropriate forms of the verb **ser** and the adjectives, as indicated by the words in parentheses.

¡Buenos días! Yo (**1.** ser) _____ Jacobo, y ella (**2.** ser) _____

Mónica. Nosotros (**3.** ser) _____ estudiantes en la Universidad Central

de Venezuela. Mónica (**4.** ser) _____ estudiante de literatura, y es muy

(**5.** inteligente) _____ y (**6.** trabajador) _____ . Las clases (**7.** ser)

_____ muy (**8.** difícil) _____ , pero los profesores son (**9.** bueno)

_____ y (**10.** simpático) _____ .

1.36 **Comunicación** Work with a partner. Using the adjectives below, find three things you have in common. **¡OJO!** Pay attention to the adjective endings.

generoso realista inteligente optimista conservador
cómico tímido atlético trabajador cariñoso

Modelo Estudiante 1: *Yo soy paciente. ¿Eres tú paciente?*
Estudiante 2: *Sí, soy paciente. Yo soy idealista. ¿Eres tú idealista?*
Estudiante 1: *No, no soy idealista.*

1.37 **Diferencias** Working with a partner, one of you will look at the picture on this page, and the other will look at the picture in the Appendix A. Take turns describing the pictures using the expression **hay,** numbers, and the classroom vocabulary. Find the eight differences.

Modelo Estudiante 1: *En A hay una computadora.*
Estudiante 2: *Sí. En B, hay una silla.*
Estudiante 1: *No, en A no hay una silla.*

A.

Vocabulario 1

CD1-7

Saludos

bien	*fine*
buenas noches	*good night*
buenas tardes	*good afternoon*
buenos días	*good morning*
¿Cómo estás?	*How are you? (informal)*
¿Cómo está usted?	*How are you? (formal)*
hola	*hello*
mal	*bad*
nada	*nothing*
¿Qué hay de nuevo?	*What's new?*
¿Qué pasa?	*What's going on?*
¿Qué tal?	*How's it going?*
regular	*so, so*
¿y tú?	*and you? (informal)*
¿y usted?	*and you? (formal)*

Presentaciones

Encantado(a).	*Nice to meet you.*
Me llamo...	*My name is . . .*
Mucho gusto.	*Nice to meet you.*
Le presento a...	*I'd like to introduce you to . . . (formal)*
Te presento a...	*I'd like to introduce you to . . . (informal)*

Despedidas

adiós	*good-bye*
chao	*bye*
Hasta luego.	*See you later.*
Hasta mañana.	*See you tomorrow.*
Hasta pronto.	*See you soon.*
Nos vemos.	*See you later.*
¡Qué tengas un buen día!	*Have a nice day!*

El salón de clases

la bandera	*flag*
el bolígrafo	*pen*
el cartel	*poster*
la computadora	*computer*
el cuaderno	*notebook*
el diccionario	*dictionary*
el escritorio	*teacher's desk*
el (la) estudiante	*student*
el lápiz	*pencil*
el libro	*book*
el mapa	*map*
la mesa	*table*
la mochila	*backpack*
el papel	*paper*
la pizarra	*chalkboard*
el (la) profesor(a)	*professor*
la puerta	*door*
el pupitre	*student desk*
el reloj	*clock*
el salón de clases	*classroom*
la silla	*chair*
el televisor	*television set*
la ventana	*window*

Los números

See pages 8, 13

Palabras adicionales

hay	*there is/there are*
¿De dónde eres tú?	*Where are you from?*
Yo soy de...	*I am from . . .*

Diccionario personal

_____

_____

_____

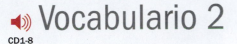

◀))) Vocabulario 2

CD1-8

Adjetivos para describir la personalidad

aburrido(a)	*boring*	interesante	*interesting*
agresivo(a)	*aggressive*	liberal	*liberal*
amable	*kind*	malo(a)	*bad*
antipático(a)	*unfriendly*	optimista	*optimist*
atlético(a)	*athletic*	paciente	*patient*
bueno(a)	*good*	perezoso(a)	*lazy*
cariñoso(a)	*loving*	pesimista	*pessimist*
cómico(a)	*funny*	pobre	*poor*
conservador(a)	*conservative*	realista	*realist*
cruel	*cruel*	rebelde	*rebel*
egoísta	*selfish*	rico(a)	*rich*
famoso(a)	*famous*	serio(a)	*serious*
generoso(a)	*generous*	simpático(a)	*nice*
honesto(a)	*honest*	sociable	*sociable*
idealista	*idealist*	tímido(a)	*timid, shy*
impaciente	*impatient*	tonto(a)	*dumb*
inteligente	*intelligent*	trabajador(a)	*hardworking*

Adjetivos para describir el aspecto físico

alto(a)	*tall*	guapo(a)	*handsome*
bajo(a)	*short*	joven	*young*
bonito(a)	*pretty*	moreno(a)	*dark-skinned/*
calvo(a)	*bald*		*dark-haired*
delgado(a)	*thin*	pelirrojo(a)	*red-haired*
feo(a)	*ugly*	pequeño(a)	*small*
gordo(a)	*fat*	rubio(a)	*blond(e)*
grande	*big*	viejo(a)	*old*

Otros adjetivos

corto(a)	*short (length)*	fácil	*easy*
difícil	*difficult*	largo(a)	*long*

Verbos

ser	*to be*

Palabras adicionales

el hombre	*man*	el (la) niño(a)	*child*
la mujer	*woman*	un poco	*a little*
muy	*very*		

Diccionario personal

_____

_____

Learning Strategy

Listen and repeat vocabulary

When studying the vocabulary, take time to listen to and repeat the pronunciation of the words included on the audio recordings. It will help your pronunciation, which in turn will help you learn to spell them properly. You may want to download the audio onto your MP3 player or cell phone so it will be more accessible.

In this chapter you will learn how to:

- Talk about your classes
- Describe your family and tell ages
- Talk about what people do routinely
- Express ownership

¿Cómo es tu vida?

© Ariel Skelley/Corbis

Exploraciones **léxicas**

En la librería de la universidad hay muchos libros para las clases. ¿Para qué clases son los libros?

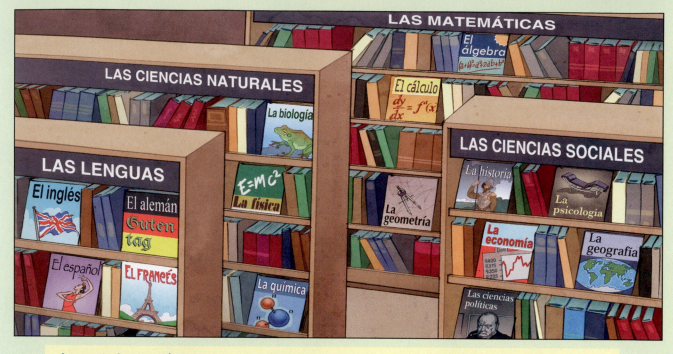

Las materias académicas		Cognados	Palabras adicionales	
la criminología	*criminology*	el arte	el/la compañero(a)	
la expresión oral	*speech*	la filosofía	de clase	*classmate*
la informática	*computer science*	la literatura	la nota	*grade*
la ingeniería	*engineering*	la música	la tarea	*homework*
los negocios	*business*	el teatro		
el periodismo	*journalism*			
la redacción	*writing, composition*			

Práctica

2.1 **Escucha y responde** Listen to the following list of classes. When you hear a humanities class mentioned, raise your left hand; if a science class is mentioned, raise your right hand.

CD1-9

2.2 **Relaciones** Match each course from the first column with a related topic from the second column.

1. _____ periodismo
2. _____ ciencias políticas
3. _____ química
4. _____ alemán
5. _____ veterinaria
6. _____ geometría
7. _____ informática
8. _____ teatro

a. los animales
b. la computadora
c. los eventos internacionales
d. el triángulo
e. los elementos
f. el actor
g. los verbos
h. los presidentes

2.3 **Especialidades** Look at the list of famous people. What classes do you associate with each person?

1. Salvador Dalí
2. Sigmund Freud
3. Cameron Díaz
4. Hugo Chávez
5. Sandra Cisneros
6. Plácido Domingo
7. Sócrates
8. Albert Einstein

2.4 **¿Qué opinas?** Read the statements and decide which ones you agree with and which ones you don't. Then, walk around the classroom and ask your classmates what they think.

Modelo Las clases de informática son difíciles.
    Estudiante 1: *¿Las clases de informática son difíciles?*
    Estudiante 2: *Sí, las clases de informática son difíciles.*
            No, las clases de informática son fáciles.

1. Las clases de historia son buenas.
2. La clase de español es fácil.
3. Las clases de literatura son aburridas.
4. Las clases de ciencias son difíciles.
5. Las clases de matemáticas son mis favoritas.
6. Las clases de arte son interesantes.

> **INVESTIGUEMOS LA GRAMÁTICA**
>
> In order to talk about a specific class or a specific instructor, you can use the expressions **La clase de...** or **El profesor de... El profesor de historia es inteligente.** *The history instructor is intelligent.*

2.5 **Opiniones** With a classmate, take turns completing the sentences with a word from the vocabulary list and finishing the sentences logically.

1. Me gusta (*I like*) la clase de _____ porque (*because*) es...
2. No me gusta mucho la clase de _____ porque es...
3. El profesor/La profesora de la clase de _____ es...
4. Los exámenes en la clase de _____ son...
5. El libro para la clase de _____ es...
6. La tarea de la clase de _____ es...

Me gusta la clase de historia.

© Monkey Business Images/Shutterstock

How many classes does a full-time student in the United States usually take? Look at the plan of study from the Universidad Iberoamericana in Mexico City and answer the questions: ¿Qué carrera (*major*) es? ¿Cuántas clases hay en el primer semestre? ¿y en el segundo? ¿Te gusta (*Do you like*) el plan de estudios? ¿Piensas (*Do you think*) que es fácil o difícil?

© Photos To Go

Una estudiante de la Universidad Iberoamericana en la Ciudad de México

Plan de estudios

Semestre I	Cálculo I y Taller	Algoritmos y Diseño de Programación	Física Universitaria I y Taller	Laboratorio de Física Universitaria I
	Gráficos y Dibujo por Computadora	Introducción a la Ingeniería	Química General	Laboratorio de Química General
Semestre 2	Cálculo II y Taller	Física Universitaria II y Taller	Laboratorio de Física Universitaria II	Álgebra Lineal
	Estructuras Isostáticas	Taller de Geometría	Prácticas de Geometría	

Más allá

Choose another major and list classes you think would be appropriate for the first two semesters of study.

Exploraciones gramaticales

A analizar

Read the following paragraph, paying particular attention to the forms of the verb **tener** in bold. Then answer the questions below.

> Yo **tengo** una clase de psicología este semestre y es muy difícil. **Tengo** miedo de recibir una mala nota. Nosotros **tenemos** mucha tarea y los exámenes **tienen** muchas preguntas (*questions*). Afortunadamente, el profesor **tiene** mucha experiencia y es muy simpático. ¿**Tienes** tú una clase difícil este semestre?

1. What does the verb **tener** mean?
2. Using the examples in the paragraph, complete the chart with the forms of the verb **tener.**

yo _____   nosotros, nosotras _____

tú _____   vosotros, vosotras tenéis

él, ella, usted _____   ellos, ellas, ustedes _____

3. Using context clues to help you, what does the expression **tener miedo** mean?

   a. to have to   **b.** to need   **c.** to be afraid

A comprobar

The verb **tener**

tener (*to have*)			
yo	**tengo**	nosotros(as)	**tenemos**
tú	**tienes**	vosotros(as)	**tenéis**
él, ella, usted	**tiene**	ellos, ellas, ustedes	**tienen**

*Notice that the original vowel **e** changes to **ie** in some of the forms. This is what is known as a stem-changing verb. You will learn more about stem-changing verbs in **Capítulo 3.**

1. There are a number of expressions in which the verb **tener** is used where *to be* would be used in English. The following are noun expressions with the verb **tener:**

tener… años	*to be . . . years old*
tener (mucho) calor	*to be (very) hot*
tener (mucho) cuidado	*to be (very) careful*
tener (mucho) éxito	*to be (very) successful*
tener (mucho) frío	*to be (very) cold*

tener (mucha) hambre	*to be (very) hungry*
tener (mucho) miedo	*to be (very) afraid*
tener (mucha) prisa	*to be in a (big) hurry*
tener (mucha) razón	*to be right*
tener (mucho) sed	*to be (very) thirsty*
tener (mucho) sueño	*to be (very) sleepy*
tener (mucha) suerte	*to be (very) lucky*

2. Unlike adjectives, noun expressions do not change in gender and number.

   Mis hermanos tienen frío.
   My brothers are cold.

   Mi hermana tiene frío.
   My sister is cold.

© Özgür Donmaz/iStockphotos

A practicar

2.6 **¿Qué tienen?** Match the sentences to the appropriate picture.

a.

b.

c.

d.

e.

f.

1. Tenemos hambre. _____
2. Tienen miedo. _____
3. Tengo 5 años. _____
4. Tiene sed. _____
5. ¿Tienes sueño? _____
6. Tiene prisa. _____

2.7 **¿Cuántos años tienes?** Complete the paragraph with the correct forms of the verb **tener.**

Yo soy estudiante en la Universidad de Salamanca y (**1.**) _____ 20 años. Mis amigos Sara y Fernando (**2.**) _____ 19 años. Sara y yo (**3.**) _____ nuestro cumpleaños *(birthday)* en noviembre. Fernando (**4.**) _____ su cumpleaños en diciembre. ¿Y tú? ¿Cuántos años (**5.**) _____?

iTunes
Kumbia Kings is a group from Texas whose music combines cumbia, hip-hop, and R&B. Listen to their song "No tengo dinero." What do you think is the message of the song? What did you like about it? What did you not like about it?

¿Cuántos años tiene? Ask your partner how old the following people are. If you are not sure, guess and use the expression **probablemente.**

Modelo tu profesor de inglés
Estudiante 1: *¿Cuántos años tiene tu* (your) *profesor de inglés?*
Estudiante 2: *Mi* (My) *profesor (probablemente) tiene 35 años.*

1. tú
2. tu mejor amigo (*best friend*)
3. tu profesor de la clase de español
4. el presidente de los Estados Unidos
5. tu actor favorito (¿Cómo se llama?)
6. tu actriz favorita (¿Cómo se llama?)

2.9 **¿Qué tienen?** Describe the scenes using expressions with **tener.**

Modelo Ronaldo
Ronaldo tiene razón.

1. Lola y yo   2. Marcia   3. yo

4. Isabel y Mar   5. tú

2.10 **Entrevista** Interview a classmate using the questions below.

1. ¿Cuántos años tienes?
2. ¿En qué clase tienes mucho sueño?
3. ¿Tienes hambre en la noche?
4. ¿Tienes miedo de un profesor? ¿Cómo se llama?"
5. ¿En qué clase tienes éxito en los exámenes?
6. ¿Tienes frío ahora (*now*)?

Conexiones culturales
La educación

Cultura

One of the largest universities in the world is the **Universidad Nacional Autónoma de México (UNAM).** The university is so large that the applicants have to take their admission exam in a sports stadium. UNAM is considered one of the best universities in the world and is free.

The Central University City Campus of UNAM is one of three universities in the world that was designated as a World Heritage site by UNESCO in 2007. It was designed by over 60 architects, engineers, and artists, and is an exceptional display of twentieth-century modernism. The campus has numerous impressive works of art, such as murals and mosaics. Is there art in your university? Where? What do you think of it?

Sources: Times Higher Education; UNESCO; www.topuniversities.com

La Biblioteca Central de la UNAM fue diseñada por Juan O'Gorman, un artista mexicano.

Investiga en Internet Universidades hispanoamericanas.

Comunidad

Find an international student from a Spanish-speaking country and ask him or her for additional information about their school system. For example, you can talk about the subjects they learn, the price of textbooks, and the number of hours they spend at school every day. The following are some possible questions for your interview:

¿De dónde eres?

¿Qué clases tienes?

¿Es similar la universidad en ____(country)____?

¿Cuántas horas están en la escuela los estudiantes de primaria/secundaria/preparatoria?

¿De dónde eres?

Comparaciones

While in the United States students are required by law to attend school until they are 16, in Mexico students are legally required to attend school until the completion of **secundaria,** or **preparatoria,** depending on the state. After **preparatoria,** Mexican students can choose to go to a **tecnológico** and learn a trade, or attend university. Students have the option of either going to school in the mornings or in the evenings. How does the education system of the United States compare to the Mexican system? Complete the table with the equivalents in the United States.

	México	Estados Unidos
3–5 años	jardín de niños (kinder)	_____
6–11 años	primaria (6 años)	_____
12–14 años	secundaria (3 años)	_____
15–18 años	preparatoria (3 años)	_____
18+	tecnológico/universidad (2–4 años)	_____
	diplomados	_____
	maestría	_____
	doctorado	_____

Conexiones... a la educación

In Spanish-speaking countries, it is common for elementary and secondary students to wear uniforms to school. What are the advantages and disadvantages of using them? Did you ever wear a uniform to school? Are uniforms popular in the United States? Why?

Niñas cubanas en sus uniformes

© Dmitry Matrosov/Shutterstock

A analizar

You will recall from **Capítulo 1** that adjectives are words that describe nouns. Read the paragraph and identify the adjectives. Then, answer the questions below.

> Historia es una clase interesante pero muy difícil. Hay mucha tarea y exámenes muy largos, pero mi profesora es una mujer simpática e inteligente.

Where are the adjectives placed in relation to the noun they describe? What is the exception?

© photos.com

A comprobar

Adjective placement

1. In Spanish, adjectives are generally placed *after* the nouns they describe.

> El cálculo es una clase **difícil.**
> *Calculus is a **difficult** class.*

> La señora Muñoz es una profesora **interesante.**
> *Mrs. Muñoz is an **interesting** professor.*

2. However, adjectives such as **mucho** (*a lot*), **poco** (*few*), and **varios** (*several*) that indicate quantity or amount are placed in front of the object.

> **Muchos** estudiantes estudian francés.
> ***Many** students study French.*

> Tengo **varios** libros para esta clase.
> *I have **several** books for this class.*

> Hay **pocos** estudiantes en clase hoy.
> *There are **few** students in class today.*

3. When using more than one adjective to describe an object, use commas between adjectives and **y** *(and)* before the last adjective.

> Tengo un cuaderno pequeño **y** rojo.
> *I have a small, red notebook.*

> El profesor es un hombre honesto, serio **e** inteligente.
> *The professor is an honest, serious, and intelligent man.*

A practicar

2.11 **Mi clase de español** Listen to the statements about your Spanish class and decide whether they are true (**cierto**) or false (**falso**).

CD1-10 **Modelo** (you hear) La clase de español tiene estudiantes simpáticos.
> *Cierto*

2.12 **¿Cómo son?** Complete the sentences with a logical adjective from the list on the right. Be sure to make the adjective agree with the noun it describes.

Modelo Eva Longoria es una actriz... talentoso
Eva Longoria es una actriz talentosa.

1. Julio César Chávez Jr. es un hombre...
2. Santana es un grupo...
3. Jessica Alba es una mujer...
4. "Bésame mucho" es una canción (*song*)...
5. *Don Quijote de la Mancha* es un libro...
6. Buenos Aires es una ciudad...
7. Puerto Rico es una isla...
8. Gloria y Emilio Estefan son artistas...

a. grande
b. atlético
c. guapo
d. musical
e. argentino
f. mexicano
g. cubano
h. pequeño

¿TE ACUERDAS?
Remember that adjectives must agree in both number (singular/plural) and gender (masculine and feminine) with the object they describe.

2.13 **Mis clases** With a classmate, complete each of the following sentences with the name of a class and an appropriate adjective.

Modelo En la clase de _____ hay un profesor _____ .
En la clase de historia hay un profesor inteligente.

1. El profesor de _____ es un hombre _____ .
2. La profesora de _____ es una mujer _____ .
3. En la clase de _____ tenemos un libro _____ .
4. En la clase de _____ hay unos estudiantes _____ .
5. En la clase de _____ tenemos exámenes _____ .
6. _____ es una clase _____ .
7. En la clase de _____ tenemos tarea _____ .
8. En la clase de _____ hay un estudiante _____ .

2.14 **En busca de...** Circulate throughout the classroom and find eight different students to whom one of the following statements applies. Be ready to report to the class, so remember to ask for the names of your classmates if you don't know them.

1. Tiene una clase difícil.
2. Tiene mucha tarea este semestre.
3. Tiene un profesor rubio.
4. Tiene una computadora nueva.
5. Tiene pocos libros en la mochila hoy (*today*).
6. Siempre (*Always*) tiene notas excelentes.
7. Tiene un lápiz corto.
8. Tiene un compañero de clase muy inteligente.

2.15 Comparaciones Find the five differences in the drawings, then complete the following statement.

En **A** hay…

y en **B** hay…

2.16 Hablemos de las clases Interview a classmate with the following questions.

1. ¿Tienes muchas clases hoy? ¿Qué clases tienes?
2. ¿Tienes un profesor muy simpático este semestre? ¿Cómo se llama?
3. ¿Tienes una clase con pocos estudiantes? ¿Cuántos estudiantes hay?
4. ¿Tienes una clase favorita? ¿Qué clase es?
5. ¿En qué clase tienes exámenes muy largos?
6. ¿En qué clase tienes tarea difícil?

2.17 ¿Tienes...? Use different adjectives to talk about the following items with a partner.
Possible adjectives: **inteligente, simpático, viejo, nuevo, grande, pequeño, difícil, fácil, interesante, aburrido, largo, corto**

Modelo una computadora
Estudiante 1: *¿Tienes una computadora?*
Estudiante 2: *Sí, tengo una computadora nueva.*
Estudiante 1: *Yo tengo una computadora vieja. / Yo también* (also) *tengo una computadora nueva.*

1. una casa/un apartamento
2. un auto
3. unas clases
4. unos profesores
5. una familia
6. un amigo

2.18 **¿Cierto o falso?** Complete the statement below to form four true/false statements that describe the people and objects in the classroom. Then read your statements to your partner, who will tell you whether they are true or false. **¡OJO!** Pay attention to the position of the adjective.

En la clase hay...

Modelo Estudiante 1: *En la clase hay un estudiante pelirrojo.*
Estudiante 2: *Falso.*

2.19 **¿Estás de acuerdo?** Take turns expressing your opinions about something or someone in the following categories. Your partner will have to agree or disagree with you and explain why.

Possible adjectives: **aburrido, bueno, bonito, cómico, grande, guapo, inteligente, interesante, malo, pequeño, simpático, talentoso**

Modelo un atleta
Estudiante 1: *Albert Pujols es un atleta talentoso.*
Estudiante 2: *Estoy de acuerdo. / No estoy de acuerdo. Él es muy viejo.*

1. un actor/una actriz
2. un hombre/una mujer
3. una ciudad (*city*)
4. un profesor
5. un estudiante
6. un programa de televisión

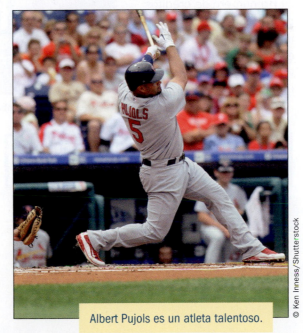

Albert Pujols es un atleta talentoso.

Lectura

Antes de leer

1. The title of this article is **"Otros sistemas universitarios."** Use your knowledge of cognates to deduce what it means, and then mention three ideas that you would expect to find in a text with this title.

2. Work with a partner to ask and answer the following questions.

   a. ¿Cuántas clases tienes este semestre?

   b. ¿Qué clases tienes?

A leer

Otros sistemas universitarios

Las universidades en diferentes partes del *world* **mundo** tienen diferentes sistemas de educación. En muchas universidades de España y Latinoamérica los estudiantes no *need* **necesitan** obtener un cierto número de créditos para graduarse, pero tienen un "plan de estudios", que es una lista de clases que los estudiantes necesitan tener en un semestre.

La Universidad de La Habana en Cuba

© Liset Alvarez/Shutterstock

[en muchas universidades no hay clases de educación general]

En muchas universidades no hay clases de educación general. Un estudiante de literatura tiene diferentes clases de literatura, pero no necesita estudiar matemáticas ni ciencias si no son parte de su plan de estudios. En consecuencia, es necesario especializarse inmediatamente en su área cuando un estudiante inicia la **licenciatura.**

bachelor's degree

En muchas partes del mundo, la educación universitaria es un **derecho** y es prácticamente **gratuita.** Sin embargo, si los estudiantes tienen dinero y lo prefieren, es posible asistir a una universidad privada.

right
free

En muchas partes del mundo, la educación universitaria es un derecho.

Comprensión

Decide whether the statements are true or false. Correct the false statements.

1. En muchas universidades hispanas no existen los créditos.
2. La lista de clases que los estudiantes necesitan tomar se llama "el plan de estudios".
3. Los estudiantes en Latinoamérica y España necesitan tomar clases de educación general.
4. Los estudiantes tienen clases en diferentes facultades.
5. Las universidades privadas también son gratuitas.

Después de leer

Look for a university in a Spanish-speaking country. Then find your major in the index and answer the following questions.

1. ¿Cuántos años de estudios son necesarios para completar la carrera?
2. ¿Qué cursos necesitan tomar?

Esta es la familia de Hernán. ¿Quiénes son las personas en su familia?

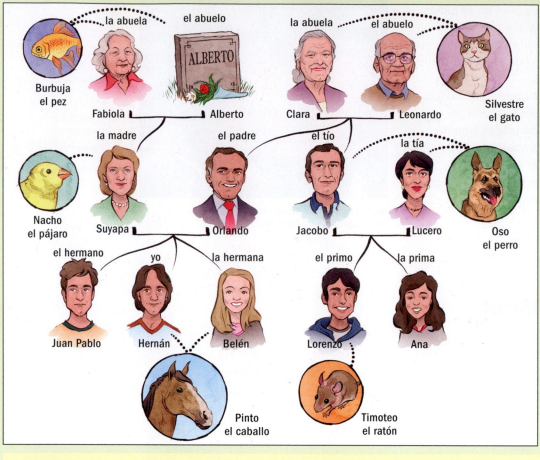

La familia

cuñado(a)	brother-in-law/sister-in-law	padrastro	stepfather
esposo(a)	spouse	los parientes	relatives
hijo(a)	son/daughter	medio(a) hermano(a)	half brother/half sister
nieto(a)	grandson/granddaughter	nuera	daughter-in-law
sobrino(a)	nephew/niece	suegro(a)	father-in-law/mother-in-law
hermanastro(a)	stepbrother/stepsister	yerno	son-in-law
madrastra	stepmother		

Otras relaciones

amigo(a)	friend	la mascota	pet
novio(a)	boyfriend/girlfriend		

Práctica

2.20 **Escucha y responde** Listen to the following statements about Hernán's family. Based on the drawing, give a thumbs up if the statement is true or give a thumbs down if it is false.

CD1-11

2.21 **¿Cómo se llama...?** Give the names of the following people using the information provided in the drawing on p. 54.

1. la madre de Suyapa
2. el padre de Lorenzo
3. los padres de Orlando y Jacobo
4. la hermana de Juan Pablo
5. los tíos de Lorenzo
6. el caballo de Hernán

on p. 54.

2.22 **¿Quién es?** Complete the following sentences about Hernán's family with the appropriate vocabulary word.

1. Suyapa es la _____ de Lorenzo.

2. Fabiola es la _____ de Suyapa.

3. Hernán es el _____ de Orlando.

4. Belén es la _____ de Lorenzo.

5. Jacobo y Orlando son _____.

6. Hernán es el _____ de Jacobo.

7. Clara es la _____ de Leonardo.

8. Fabiola es la _____ de Juan Pablo.

> **INVESTIGUEMOS EL VOCABULARIO**
> Remember that most of the words in the vocabulary can be used to refer to a female by changing the final **o** to an **a**. When talking about a mixed group, the masculine plural form is used:
>
> **hijos** *sons and daughters*
> **hermanos** *brothers and sisters*
> **padres** *parents*
>
> However, note that some words are specific to a gender and cannot change: **nuera** and **yerno**. **La mascota** is used for both male and female pets.

2.23 **Un árbol geneológico** Working with a partner, take turns describing your families. Be sure to include the names, ages, and a brief description of each family member. As you describe your family, your partner will draw your family tree.

> **Modelo** *Mi madre se llama Nora. Ella tiene 52 años. Ella es alta y delgada.*

2.24 **En busca de...** Circulate throughout the classroom and find students to whom the following statements apply. Find a different student for each statement. Take notes and be ready to report to the class.

> **Modelo** Tiene un gato.
> Estudiante 1: *¿Tienes un gato?*
> Estudiante 2: *No, no tengo un gato. / Sí, tengo un gato.*
> Estudiante 1: *(reporting to the class):* ___(name)___ *tiene un gato.*

1. Tiene un hijo.
2. Tiene dos hermanos.
3. Tiene muchos primos.
4. Tiene un caballo.

5. Tiene un padrastro o una madrastra.
6. Tiene una mascota.
7. Tiene esposo.
8. Tiene sobrinos.

> 🎧 **iTunes**
> Pimpinela is an Argentine brother-sister duo whose songs are often conversations between a man and a woman. Listen to their song "Señorita" and write down any family vocabulary words you can hear in the song.

2.25 **¿Cómo son?** Talk to six different classmates and ask each one to describe a member of his or her family or a pet. Be prepared to report your findings to the class.

> **Modelo** Estudiante 1: *¿Cómo es tu abuela?*
> Estudiante 2: *Mi abuela es muy vieja. Ella es baja y gorda.*
> *También es simpática y muy extrovertida.*

To whom do you give greeting cards? On what occasions? Look at the card below. Who is it for?

Gracias por ser mi a**m**iga

Gracias por tu **a**mor

Gracias por la felici**d**ad que traes a nuestra casa

y por el ca**r**iño que tienes para tus hijos

¡Gracias por ser la persona más paci**e**nte del universo!

¡Feliz 10 de mayo!

Más allá

Create a simple greeting card for a family member. You may want to search the Internet for holidays that are observed in Spanish-speaking countries.

Exploraciones **gramaticales**

A analizar

Read the conversation, paying attention to the endings of the words in bold. Then answer the questions.

Paula: ¿**Trabajan** tus padres?

Eva: Sí, mi madre **trabaja** en la universidad. Ella es profesora de historia. Mi padre **trabaja** en una compañía internacional y viaja a México y Estados Unidos con frecuencia.

Paula: ¡Qué interesante! ¿Y tú **trabajas?**

Eva: No, yo no **trabajo.**

1. What does the word **trabajar** mean?

2. You have learned that the verbs **ser** and **tener** have different forms depending upon the subject. The verb **trabajar** also has different forms. Looking at the different forms of the verb **trabajar** in the conversation, complete the following chart.

yo _____	nosotros(as) trabajamos
tú _____	vosotros(as) trabajáis
él, ella, usted _____	ellos, ellas, ustedes _____

A comprobar

Regular -ar verbs

1. An infinitive is a verb in its simplest form. It conveys the idea of an action, but does not indicate who is doing the action. The following are verbs in their infinitive form. You will notice that their English translations are all *to* _____.

ayudar	*to help*	**esquiar**	*to ski*	**necesitar**	*to need*
bailar	*to dance*	**estudiar**	*to study*	**practicar**	*to practice (to*
buscar	*to look for*	**hablar**	*to talk (on the*	**(deportes)**	*play sports)*
cantar	*to sing*	**(por teléfono)**	*phone)*	**preguntar**	*to ask*
caminar	*to walk*	**limpiar**	*to clean*	**regresar**	*to return (home)*
cocinar	*to cook*	**llamar**	*to call*	**(a casa)**	
comprar	*to buy*	**llegar**	*to arrive*	**tomar (café)**	*to take, to*
desear	*to want, to desire*	**mirar (la tele)**	*to look, to*		*drink (coffee)*
enseñar	*to teach*		*watch (TV)*	**trabajar**	*to work*
escuchar	*to listen*	**nadar**	*to swim*	**viajar**	*to travel*

2. You learned that the verbs **ser** and **tener** must be conjugated in agreement with the subject. In other words, they have different forms that indicate who the subject is. The verbs in the list on page 57 all end in -**ar** and are all conjugated in the same way. To form a present tense verb, the -**ar** is dropped from the infinitive and an ending is added that reflects the subject (the person doing the action).

INVESTIGUEMOS LA GRAMÁTICA
When telling where someone travels to, you will need to use the preposition **a** with the verb **viajar**.
Mi familia **viaja a** Puerto Rico.
*My family **travels to** Puerto Rico.*

llegar					
yo	-o	lleg**o**	nosotros(as)	**-amos**	lleg**amos**
tú	-as	lleg**as**	vosotros(as)	-áis	lleg**áis**
él, ella, usted	-a	lleg**a**	ellos, ellas, ustedes	-an	lleg**an**

3. When using two verbs together that are dependent upon each other, the second verb remains in the infinitive.

> Él **necesita viajar** mucho.
> *He needs to travel a lot.*

> Ellas **desean estudiar** inglés.
> *They want to study English.*

However, notice that both verbs are conjugated in the following sentences because they are not dependent on each other.

> Yo **estudio** en la universidad y **trabajo** en un restaurante.
> *I **study** in the university and **work** in a restaurant.*

> Édgar **nada, esquia** y **practica** el tenis.
> *Édgar **swims, skis,** and **plays** tennis.*

4. When creating a negative statement, place the word **no** in front of the verb.

> Ella **no** baila bien.
> *She **doesn't** dance well.*

> No, yo **no** trabajo.
> *No, I **don't** work.*

5. In order to create a simple yes/no question, it is not necessary to use helping words. Simply place the subject after the verb and change the intonation, raising your voice at the end.

> ¿Estudias tú mucho?
> *Do you study a lot?*

> ¿Habla usted español?
> *Do you speak Spanish?*

INVESTIGUEMOS LA GRAMÁTICA
When the recipient of the action (direct object) is a person or a pet, an **a** is used in front of the object. This is known as the **a personal.** It is not translated into English and is not used with the verb **tener.** You will learn more about this concept in **Capítulo 7.**
Los estudiantes buscan **a** la profesora.
Los niños llaman **a** los perros.

A practicar

2.26 **Mi familia y mis amigos** Decide which of the two phrases best completes the sentences. **¡OJO!** You must decide which verb ending agrees with the subject.

1. Mi padre...
   a. mira la tele mucho   **b.** miran la tele mucho

2. Mis padres...
   a. viaja mucho   **b.** viajan mucho

3. Mi esposo...
   a. baila bien   **b.** bailan bien

4. Mi hermana...
   a. toma mucho café   **b.** toman mucho café

5. Mis amigos...
   a. estudia mucho   **b.** estudian mucho

6. Mi profesor de español...
   a. trabaja en la oficina   **b.** trabajan en la oficina

2.27 **Un día ocupado** Fedra and Bruno are very busy. Look at the drawings and describe what they do on a typical day.

Modelo *Fedra y Bruno toman un café.*

1.

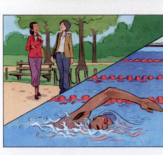

2.

3.

4.

5.

2.28 **¡Yo también!** Place a check mark next to four of the following activities that you do. Then, find four different classmates, each of whom also does one of those activities. When you are finished, report to the class something that you and another classmate both do using the **nosotros** form.

_____ buscar un trabajo

_____ viajar con frecuencia (*frequently*)

_____ mirar la tele mucho

_____ trabajar en un restaurante

_____ cantar bien

_____ cocinar

_____ hablar mucho por teléfono

_____ llamar a un amigo con frecuencia

_____ escuchar la radio

_____ usar la computadora

_____ nadar

_____ comprar muchos regalos (*gifts*)

_____ esquiar

_____ ¿?

2.29 **La familia de Gabriela** Complete the paragraph with the correct form of the verb in parentheses.

Yo (**1.**) _____ (ser) Gabriela, y mi esposo Nicolás (**2.**) _____ (trabajar) en un hospital. Él (**3.**) _____ (pasar – *to spend*) mucho tiempo en el trabajo. Nuestros dos hijos Dora y Ernesto (**4.**) _____ (estudiar) en la universidad. Mi esposo necesita (**5.**) _____ (trabajar) mucho, pero nosotros siempre (**6.**) _____ (tener) vacaciones en julio. La familia (**7.**) _____ (viajar) a Bariloche, Argentina, y nosotros (**8.**) _____ (esquiar). Yo no (**9.**) _____ (esquiar) muy bien, pero es muy divertido.

Cultura

What determines whether a group is considered a family? The painting entitled *La familia presidencial* (1965) was created by Colombian artist Fernando Botero. With this painting, the artist consolidated his now famous style of fat figures. Look at the painting. Do you think that they are a blood family, or are they related in a different way? Can you think of any other groups of people who are considered to be like families?

La familia presidencial de Fernando Botero.

🌐 Investiga en Internet el artista colombiano, Fernando Botero.

Comunidad

Families play a huge role within the different Hispanic cultures. What about in your community? Are there organizations within your community that support families? Make a list of those organizations, and contact them to find out what services are available for Spanish-speaking people.

Mi familia y yo pasamos mucho tiempo juntos.

Comparaciones

What are some of the important events that bring families together in the United States? In Spain and Latin American countries there are numerous events that allow families to get together. Some are religious celebrations such as Christmas (**Navidad**) and **las Posadas,** the nine days of celebration before Christmas re-enacting Mary and Joseph's search for shelter; others are non-religious celebrations such as Mother's Day, Father's Day, Children's Day, and any birthday or anniversary within a family. The **quinceañera,** the 15th birthday of a girl, is a particularly important celebration.

Although the celebrations may seem very similar, there might be important differences. For example, in Mexico Mother's Day is always on May 10th, so it could be any day of the week. Many companies organize activities to honor mothers, and oftentimes allow employees to leave early so they can take their mothers out to eat. If it falls on a weekend, many people will hire a mariachi group and serenade their mothers.

Children's Day takes place on April 30th. It is usually celebrated with big parties at schools, city parades with clowns, and other types of entertainments. Many organizations will give away toys or other items for children on this day. This photo and the one on the previous page are of family events in Latin America. How are these photos similar to ones you might take during your own family events? How are they different?

La Quinceañera es una celebración importante.

Conexiones... a la sociología

In Spanish-speaking countries, the family is very important. It is common for the children to live with their parents until they marry. How can this impact other areas of the society (for example, housing, jobs, eating habits, etc.)? Does it have any impact on the life of college students? What do you think are advantages and disadvantages of living with your family until getting married?

Es común vivir con la familia hasta casarse.

A analizar

Read the paragraph in which Gabino describes his family, and note the words in bold. Then answer the questions below.

> **Mi** familia no es muy grande. **Mis** padres se llaman Enrique y Angélica, y **mi** hermana se llama Chantal. Tenemos dos mascotas; **nuestra** perra se llama Bibi y **nuestro** gato se llama Félix.

The words in bold are used to show possession.

1. What are the two ways of expressing *my* in Spanish? What is the difference between the two forms? Why do you think they are different?

2. What are the two forms of **nuestro** in the paragraph? What is the difference between the two forms? Why do you think they are different?

A comprobar

Possessive adjectives

mi(s)	*my*	**mi** hermano, **mis** hermanos
tu(s)	*your*	**tu** primo, **tus** primos
su(s)	*his, her, its, your*	**su** mascota, **sus** mascotas
nuestro(s), nuestra(s)	*our*	**nuestro** primo, **nuestros** primos, **nuestra** prima, **nuestras** primas
vuestro(s), vuestra(s)	*your*	**vuestro** tío, **vuestros** tíos, **vuestra** tía, **vuestras** tías
su(s)	*their, your*	**su** abuelo, **sus** abuelos

INVESTIGUEMOS LA GRAMÁTICA

When using possessive adjectives in Spanish, keep in mind that the subject pronouns **tú**, **usted, vosotros**, and **ustedes** all mean *you*. Each of the possessive adjectives that indicate *your* corresponds to a different subject pronoun.

tú → tu(s)
usted → su(s)
vosotros/vosotras → vuestro(s)/vuestra(s)
ustedes → su(s)

1. Similar to other adjectives, possessive adjectives agree in number (singular/plural) with the object they modify (that is, the object that is owned or possessed).

> **Mi familia** es muy grande.
> *My family is very large.*

> **Sus padres** hablan italiano.
> *His parents speak italian.*

2. **Nuestro** and **vuestro** agree in gender (masculine/feminine) as well as in number.

> **Nuestra gata** se llama Lili.
> *Our cat is named Lili.*

> ¿Cómo se llaman **vuestras hijas**?
> *What are your daughters' names?*

3. In Spanish, the *'s* does not exist. Instead, if you want to be more specific about who possesses or owns something, it is necessary to use **de.**

> Es la casa **de mi hermano.**
> *It is **my brother's** house.*

> Es **su** casa.
> *It is **his** house.*

> Ella es la hija **de Patricia.**
> *She is **Patricia's** daughter.*

> Ella es **su** hija.
> *She is **her** daughter.*

4. Just as there are contractions in English (can't, don't), there are also contractions in Spanish. However, these contractions are not optional. When using **de** in front of the masculine article **el,** it forms the contraction **del (de + el = del). De** does not contract with the other articles.

> Macarena es la esposa **del** profesor.
> *Macarena is the professor's wife.*

> Max es el perro **de la** familia Pérez.
> *Max is the Pérez family's dog.*

A practicar

2.30 **¿De quién es?** Match the objects with the instructor they belong to and form a sentence.

> **Modelo** el libro de Nietzche/el profesor de filosofía
> *El libro de Nietzsche es del profesor de filosofía.*

1. el libro de Don Quijote	**a.** la profesora de francés
2. los mapas	**b.** el profesor de arte
3. el cartel de París	**c.** la profesora de matemáticas
4. los exámenes de álgebra	**d.** la profesora de español
5. la computadora	**e.** el profesor de geografía
6. los lápices de color	**f.** el profesor de informática

2.31 **Mi familia** Indicate whether each of the sentences requires **mi** or **mis.**

1. (Mi/Mis) madre es bonita. **4.** (Mi/Mis) perro es pequeño.

2. (Mi/Mis) padre es alto. **5.** (Mi/Mis) abuelos son simpáticos.

3. (Mi/Mis) hermanas son cómicas. **6.** (Mi/Mis) amigos son inteligentes.

2.32 **Su familia** Complete the following paragraph with the correct form of **su** or **sus.**

Alberto, David y Óscar son hermanos y tienen un apartamento en Lima. (**1.**) _____ apartamento es pequeño, pero cómodo. Alberto y David comparten (*share*) un cuarto (*bedroom*) y hay muchos carteles en (**2.**) _____ cuarto. (**3.**) _____ hermano, Óscar, tiene un cuarto pequeño. Él tiene dos gatos y un perro. (**4.**) _____ animales molestan (*bother*) mucho a (**5.**) _____ hermanos porque (**6.**) _____ perro siempre está en el sofá y (**7.**) _____ gatos siempre están en la mesa.

El perro de mi hermano siempre está en el sofá.

2.33 **¿De quién es?** Andrés' mother is cleaning the living room where her children have left their things. She is unsure about what belongs to him and what belongs to his sister, Ana. With a partner, take turns playing Andrés and his mother. Look at the picture to decide how Andrés answers her questions. Be sure to use the correct possessive adjective in the proper form.

Modelo

Estudiante 1 (madre): *¿De quién (Whose) es el cuaderno?*
Estudiante 2 (Andrés): *Es su cuaderno.*
Estudiante 2 (madre): *¿De quién son los papeles?*
Estudiante 1 (Andrés): *Son mis papeles.*

1. ¿De quién es la mochila?
2. ¿De quién son los libros?
3. ¿De quién es el diccionario?
4. ¿De quién es el cartel?

5. ¿De quién son los bolígrafos?
6. ¿De quién es la soda?
7. ¿De quién es la pizza?
8. ¿De quién son los CDs?

2.34 **Las cosas *(things)* de nuestros parientes** Describe the following items that your family owns and ask your partner about the items his/her family owns.

Modelo el televisor

Estudiante 1: *Nuestro televisor es nuevo. ¿Cómo es su televisor?*
Estudiante 2: *Nuestro televisor es pequeño.*

1. la casa/el apartamento
2. el auto/los autos
3. la mascota (el perro, el gato, los peces, etc.)
4. la computadora
5. los primos
6. la familia

Redacción

Write a letter to a pen pal and tell him or her about your family and your classes.

Paso 1 Jot down a list of the members of your family.

Paso 2 Beside each person, write down his or her age and two adjectives that describe the person. Be sure to use different adjectives for each person so your paragraph will not be repetitive.

Paso 3 Jot down a list of the classes you are taking.

Paso 4 Choose one of the classes in the list and give an adjective to describe it (**fácil, difícil, aburrido, interesante,** etc). Then jot down a series of phrases about it including the following: how many students are in the class and what they are like, and who the teacher is and what he or she is like.

Paso 5 Start your letter with **Hola** or **¿Qué tal?** (*greetings*) and introduce yourself to your pen pal. Tell your pen pal something about yourself, such as where you are from, your age, or what you are like.

Paso 6 Tell your pen pal whether you have a large or small family. Then tell who each of the members of your family are and give your pen pal some information about each one using the ideas you generated in **Paso 2.**

Paso 7 Begin a second paragraph telling your pen pal that you are a student and where you are studying.

Paso 8 Tell your pen pal what classes you have this semester. Then introduce the class you brainstormed ideas for in **Paso 4,** giving your opinion of the class.

Paso 9 Using the information you generated in **Paso 4,** describe the class.

Paso 10 Finish the letter with **Hasta pronto** or **Tu amigo(a).**

Paso 11 Edit your letter:

1. Are there any sentences that are irrelevant to the topic? If so, get rid of them.
2. Are there any spelling errors?
3. Do your adjectives agree with the person/object they describe?
4. Do your verbs agree with the person doing the action?
5. Are there any sentences you can join using **y** or **pero**?

Lectura

Antes de leer

What does the modern American family look like? What do you think the modern Latin American family looks like?

A leer

La familia típica latinoamericana

change

Es difícil hablar de una familia típica latinoamericana, especialmente porque en todas las sociedades las familias **cambian** para adaptarse a los tiempos modernos. La familia típica latinoamericana urbana tiene pocos hijos, y el hombre y la mujer trabajan. Las familias extendidas son muy importantes, pero en la mayoría de las casas no **viven** muchos familiares: en México, en **promedio** viven 4.2 personas en una casa. En el 74% de las casas viven solamente los padres y los hijos, y solo en el 26% de las casas viven otros

live
average

En México, en promedio viven 4.2 personas en una casa.

© Andy Dean Photography/Shutterstock

such as

[las familias extendidas son muy importantes]

miembros de la familia **como** abuelos, nietos, u otros familiares. Evidentemente, para los mexicanos es muy importante ayudar a los miembros de la familia, pero solo en una de cuatro casas vive un miembro de la familia extendida.

Otro cambio importante es el del **papel** de la mujer. La mayoría de las familias está **encabezada por** hombres, pero el número de familias encabezadas por mujeres **está aumentando** rápidamente.

role
headed by
is increasing

Algunos datos de las familias mexicanas son un buen ejemplo de la tendencia general en Latinoamérica:

- El 75% de las familias nucleares mexicanas tienen hijos.
- El 21% de las familias son parejas que viven en unión libre y no tienen hijos.
- En México hay solamente 7 divorcios por cada 100 matrimonios.
- En la Ciudad de México, las uniones civiles entre miembros del mismo sexo son legales.

Source: DIF (Sistema Nacional para el Desarrollo Integral de la Familia).

Comprensión

Decide whether the following statements are true or false. Correct any false statements.

1. Las mujeres latinoamericanas no trabajan.
2. La familia extendida es muy importante.
3. Ahora hay más (*more*) familias encabezadas por mujeres que antes.
4. En la mayoría de las casas viven tres generaciones (los abuelos, los padres y los hijos).
5. Pocos matrimonios terminan en divorcio.
6. ¿Cómo se comparan estas estadísticas a las de los Estados Unidos?

El número de familias encabezadas por mujeres está aumentando.

© Monkey Business Images/Shutterstock

Después de leer

With three or four other classmates, discuss the following questions:

¿Es importante la familia para ti?
¿Qué personas consideras tú como parte de tu familia?
¿Qué actividades haces (*do you do*) con tu familia?

La educación ▶

La educación ▶

Vocabulario

Sustantivos

el aprendizaje	*learning*
el departamento	*department*
el/la director(a)	*principal*
las horas de clase	*class hours*
la prueba	*quiz*

Adjetivos

aplicado	*studious*
estricto	*strict*
estudioso	*studious*
flexible	*flexible*
organizado	*organized*

Verbos

atrasarse	*to get behind*
calificar	*to grade*
copiarse	*to cheat*
entregar	*to deliver; to hand over*
faltar	*to be absent*
pasar al frente	*to speak in front of the class*
repasar	*to review*

Frases útiles

Su hijo(a) tiene dificultades en....
Your son or daughter has trouble in . . .

¿Entendieron?
Did you understand?

¿Tienen preguntas?
Do you have any questions?

Los trabajos deben estar hechos en computadora.
The papers should be typed.

Por favor, vaya a la oficina del (de la) director(a).
Please go to the principal's office.

La semana que viene hay examen.
You will have an exam next week.

Hoy vamos a estudiar los adjetivos posesivos.

© GoGo Images/JupiterImages

DATOS IMPORTANTES

Educación: Licenciatura o Maestría en Educación o materia específica, como español, historia, matemáticas, etcétera. Algunas escuelas aceptan licenciaturas. Muchos estados requieren una certificación estatal adicional.

Salario: Entre $40 000 y $100 000, dependiendo de la escuela, los títulos y las horas de clases.

Dónde se trabaja: Escuelas públicas y privadas, facultades comunitarias y centros de educación para adultos.

Alejandro Blanco es un maestro con mucha experiencia. Enseña historia en una escuela secundaria pública. En el video hay una entrevista entre Alejandro y la directora de una escuela privada de Miami, donde desea trabajar.

Antes de ver

Interviews are one of the most important steps toward getting a job. In the case of a teacher who wants to work in a private school, what questions do you think he or she will be asked? How do you think speaking Spanish might help someone get a teaching job? What would be a good strategy when interviewing for a job in teaching?

Comprensión

Answer the following questions according to the video.

© Heinle/Cengage Learning

1. ¿Qué enseña el Sr. Blanco?
2. ¿Cuántos años de experiencia tiene como maestro en Boston?
3. ¿Tiene experiencia en Florida? ¿Dónde?
4. ¿Con quién habla español el Sr. Blanco?
5. ¿Qué tipo de maestro es el Sr. Blanco?
6. ¿La directora le ofrece el puesto (position) al Sr. Blanco?

Después de ver

In groups of three, play the role of a teacher and two students. The teacher will tell the students what to expect from their class (quizzes, tests, projects, etc.). The students will ask the teacher questions to be sure they know what they need to do to succeed in the class.

2.35 **La Universidad de Puerto Rico** Complete the paragraph with the appropriate form of the verb or the possessive in parentheses.

(**1.**) _____ (mi) hermana Victoria y yo (**2.**) _____ (estudiar) en la Universidad de Puerto Rico. (**3.**) _____ (nuestro) clases son difíciles y nosotras (**4.**) _____ (tener) mucha tarea. Los profesores son muy amables y (**5.**) _____ (ayudar) mucho. Yo (**6.**) _____ (tener) tres clases: cálculo, biología e inglés. La clase de inglés es muy interesante, y yo (**7.**) _____ (hablar) bien. Victoria (**8.**) _____ (tener) cuatro clases. Ella (**9.**) _____ (tomar) historia, filosofía, literatura y francés. (**10.**) _____ (su) clases favoritas son las de historia y de literatura.

2.36 **Así es mi familia** Add the adjectives in parentheses to the sentences. Be sure to put them in the proper place and in the proper form (masculine, feminine, singular, plural).

1. Tengo una familia. (interesante)
2. Tengo dos hermanas. (pequeño)
3. No tenemos mascotas. (mucho)
4. Tenemos un perro. (cariñoso)
5. Tenemos una gata. (perezoso)
6. Tengo familiares en la ciudad (*city*) donde vivo. (vario)

2.37 **¿Cómo son?** Using the descriptive adjectives in parentheses and the possessive adjectives (**mi, tu, su,** etc.), tell what the family members and pets of the people below are like. **¡OJO!** Be sure to use the correct form of the possessive and descriptive adjectives.

Modelo Natalia tiene perros. (agresivo)   *Sus perros son agresivos.*
Mi hermano tiene una esposa. (rubio)   *Su esposa es rubia.*

1. Geraldo tiene una hermana. (simpático)
2. Mis abuelos tienen gatos. (cariñoso)
3. Nosotros tenemos un caballo. (viejo)
4. Tú tienes primos. (cómico)
5. Yo tengo una sobrina. (bonito)
6. Rufina tiene hijos. (grande)

Tenemos un caballo.

Exploraciones de repaso: comunicación

2.38 **En familia** In groups of three or four, each student chooses a different photo to describe to the rest of the group. Tell the following about the people in the photo: their names, what their relationship is, how old they are, what they are like, and what they are doing.

2.39 **Datos personales** Working with a partner, one of you will look at the chart below and the other will look at the chart in the Appendix A. Take turns asking questions in order to fill in the missing information.

Modelo ¿Cuántos años tiene Diego?   Diego tiene veinte años.
        ¿Qué parientes hay en la familia de Diego?   Diego tiene dos hermanos.
        ¿Qué clase tiene Diego?   Diego tiene informática.
        ¿Diego estudia ahora (now)?   No, Diego limpia la casa.

Nombre	Edad	Familia	Clase	Actividad
Diego	20	dos hermanos	informática	limpia la casa
Alonso	18		química	
Magdalena	22	padrastro		baila salsa
Cristina			historia	
Pablo		dos hijos	arte	
Gabriel		una hermana		mira la tele
Rufina	41			toma un café

Vocabulario 1

CD1-12

Las materias académicas

el alemán	German	la física	Physics
el álgebra	Algebra	el francés	French
el arte	Art	la geografía	Geography
la biología	Biology	la geometría	Geometry
el cálculo	Calculus	la historia	History
las ciencias naturales	Natural Science	la informática	Computer Science
las ciencias políticas	Political Science	la ingeniería	Engineering
		el inglés	English
las ciencias sociales	Social Science	la literatura	Literature
		las matemáticas	Mathematics
la criminología	Criminology	la música	Music
la economía	Economy	los negocios	Business
la educación física	Physical Education	el periodismo	Journalism
		la psicología	Psychology
la expresión oral	Speech	la química	Chemistry
		la redacción	Writing
la filosofía	Philosophy	el teatro	Theater
		la veterinaria	Veterinary Medicine

Expresiones con *tener*

tener... años	to be . . . years old	tener (mucho) miedo	to be (very) afraid
tener (mucho) calor	to be (very) hot	tener (mucha) prisa	to be in a (big) hurry
tener (mucho) cuidado	to be (very) careful	tener (mucha) razón	to be right
tener (mucho) éxito	to be (very) successful	tener (mucha) sed	to be (very) thirsty
tener (mucho) frío	to be (very) cold	tener (mucho) sueño	to be (very) sleepy
tener (mucha) hambre	to be (very) hungry	tener (mucha) suerte	to be (very) lucky

Palabras adicionales

el (la) compañero(a) de clase	classmate	mucho	a lot
el curso	term	la nota	grade
el examen	exam	poco	a little, few
las lenguas	languages	la tarea	homework
		varios	several

Diccionario personal

_____

_____

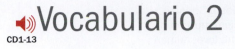

◀)) Vocabulario 2
CD1-13

La familia

el (la) abuelo(a)	*grandfather/ grandmother*	el (la) nieto(a)	*grandson/ granddaughter*
el (la) amigo(a)	*friend*	el (la) novio(a)	*boyfriend/ girlfriend*
el (la) cuñado(a)	*brother-in-law/ sister-in-law*	el padrastro	*stepfather*
el (la) esposo(a)	*spouse*	el padre (papá)	*father*
el (la) hermanastro(a)	*stepbrother/ stepsister*	la pareja	*couple; partner*
		el pariente	*relative*
el (la) hermano(a)	*brother/sister*	el (la) primo(a)	*cousin*
el (la) hijo(a)	*son/daughter*	el (la) sobrino(a)	*nephew/niece*
la madrastra	*stepmother*	el (la) suegro(a)	*father-in-law/ mother-in-law*
la madre (mamá)	*mother*		
el (la) medio(a) hermano(a)	*half brother/ half sister*	el (la) tío(a)	*uncle/aunt*

Las mascotas

el caballo	*horse*	el (la) perro(a)	*dog*
el (la) gato(a)	*cat*	el pez	*fish*
el pájaro	*bird*	el ratón	*mouse*

Los verbos

ayudar	*to help*	limpiar	*to clean*
bailar	*to dance*	llamar	*to call*
buscar	*to look for*	llegar	*to arrive*
caminar	*to walk*	mirar (la tele)	*to look, to watch (TV)*
cantar	*to sing*	nadar	*to swim*
cocinar	*to cook*	necesitar	*to need*
comprar	*to buy*	practicar	*to practice*
desear	*to wish*	(deportes)	*(to play sports)*
enseñar	*to teach*	preguntar	*to ask*
escuchar	*to listen*	regresar (a casa)	*to return (home)*
esquiar	*to ski*	tomar (café)	*to take, to drink (coffee)*
estudiar	*to study*		
hablar (por teléfono)	*to talk (on the phone)*	trabajar	*to work*
		viajar	*to travel*

Diccionario personal

_____

_____

Gustavo Adolfo Bécquer
Biografía
Gustavo Adolfo Bécquer (1836–1870) was a Spanish writer associated with the post-romanticism movement. Some of his recurrent topics are the night, love, human fragility, and death. His best known book was *Rimas y leyendas*, a collection of poems and tales that has become an essential reading for anyone studying Spanish literature.

© Felipe Rodríguez / age fotostock

Antes de leer

1. In your opinion, what is poetry?
2. Have you ever written a poem?
3. Based on the title, what do you think this poem is going to be about?

¿Qué es poesía?

while you pierce

¿Qué es poesía?, dices **mientras clavas**
En mi pupila tu pupila azul.
¡Qué es poesía! ¿Y tú me lo preguntas?
Poesía eres tú.

© OlgaLis/Shutterstock

Rimas, Rima XXI.

Después de leer

A. Comprensión

1. To whom is the poetic voice talking?
2. In your opinion, what is meant by the last line, "Poesía eres tú"?

B. Conversemos

1. Why do people write poetry?

Investiguemos la literatura: La voz poética

The poetic voice is the person that speaks in the poem. It would be incorrect to say that the poet is actually speaking. He or she usually takes on the persona of someone in a particular situation. As you read through a poem, it is important to ask yourself who is speaking.

© Paco Torrente/AFP/Newscom

Gloria Fuertes
Biografía
Gloria Fuertes (1917–1998) was a Spanish writer born in Madrid. She wrote her first poem at the age of fourteen and published her first poems in 1935. She continued writing during the Spanish Civil War (1936–1939) while working as an accountant and a secretary. The civil war had a profound effect on her as she struggled to understand how modern civilizations could go to war over things of little importance with no concern for the children destroyed by it. As a result, a large percentage of her works were written for children.

Antes de leer

1. What do you know about Somalia?
2. What would you expect a poet to write about children in Somalia?

Niños de Somalia

© Kvini/Shutterstock

eat

Yo **como**

Tú comes

Él come

Nosotros comemos

Vosotros coméis

¡Ellos no!

Authorized by Luz María Jimenez, heiress of Gloria Fuertes.

Después de leer

A. Comprensión

1. According to the poem, who eats? Who does not?
2. What do you think is the message of the poem?

B. Conversemos

1. Both Becquer's poem and Fuertes' poem are simple, but they are very different in style. Which poem do you prefer? Why?
2. Do you enjoy reading poetry? Why?

Investiguemos la literatura: Interpretación

It is important to realize that there are often multiple interpretations of a literary piece. Each reader brings his or her own experiences to the reading, and these experiences influence his or her interpretation. So don't be afraid to express your ideas. Look for ways to support them with a part or parts of the text.

Learning Strategy

Understand before moving on

Learning a foreign language is like learning math: you will continue to use what you have already learned and to build upon that knowledge. Therefore, if you find you don't understand something, make an appointment to see your instructor or a tutor right away in order to get some extra help.

In this chapter you will learn how to:

- Communicate dates, time, and seasons
- Talk about the weather
- Discuss clothing
- Discuss your likes and dislikes
- Use question words to ask for specific information

¿Qué tiempo hace hoy?

© Christopher Pillitz/Getty Images

Exploraciones gramaticales

Me gusta/te gusta/le gusta

Regular **-er** and **-ir** verbs

Interrogatives

Stem-changing verbs (e → ie; e → i)

En vivo

La cartelera

La Paz ya tiene su Miss Cholita

Conexiones culturales

Las celebraciones

El clima y la ropa

Lectura

La Navidad en algunos países hispanos

Los trajes tradicionales

▶ Exploraciones profesionales

El turismo

¿Cuál es la fecha? ¿Qué día es hoy?

Días de la semana	Meses		Palabras adicionales	
lunes	enero	julio	el cumpleaños	*birthday*
martes	febrero	agosto	la fecha	*date*
miércoles	marzo	septiembre	hoy	*today*
jueves	abril	octubre	mañana	*tomorrow*
viernes	mayo	noviembre	todos los días	*every day*
sábado	junio	diciembre		
domingo				

1. To tell time, the verb **ser** is used. Use **es la** with **una** and **son las** with all other hours.
   ¿Qué hora es? *What time is it?*
   Son las tres. *It's three o'clock.*   **Es** la una. *It's one.*

2. To tell time from the hour to the half hour (1–30 minutes), use **y** between the hour and the minutes. To tell time after the half hour (31–59 minutes), use **menos** and the minutes until the next hour.

   Son las siete **y** cinco.   Son las tres **menos** veinte.

3. Use **cuarto** to express a quarter before or after the hour, and use **media** to express half past the hour.

   Son las diez y **cuarto.**   Son las once menos **cuarto.**   Son las ocho y **media.**

4. It is also common to express time as read on a digital clock.
   Es la una y cincuenta. *It's one fifty.*   **Son las seis y quince.** *It's six fifteen.*

5. To ask or tell at what time something is done, use the preposition **a.**
   ¿A qué hora trabajas?   *At what time do you work?*
   Trabajo **a** las cuatro de la tarde. *I work at 4:00 in the afternoon.*

6. To express *A.M.* or *P.M.*, use the following expressions: **de la mañana** (*in the morning*), **de la tarde** (*in the afternoon*), and **de la noche** (*in the evening*). To express *noon* use **mediodía** and to express *midnight* use **medianoche.**

INVESTIGUEMOS EL VOCABULARIO
When talking about days and dates:
- to give the date, use the phrase:
  Es el (number) **de** (month).
  Es el once **de** julio.
  It is the eleventh of July.

- to talk about the first of the month use **primero.**
  Es el **primero** de julio.
  It is the first of July.

- the names of the months and days of the week are not capitalized in Spanish.
- use the definite article (**el** or **los**) to talk about something that happens on a particular day or days.
  El examen es **el** miércoles.
  The test is on Wednesday.

  Trabajo **los** viernes y sábados.
  I work on Fridays and Saturdays.

- other than **sábado** and **domingo,** the plural form for other days of the week is the same as the singular form.

  el sábado   los sábados
  el lunes   los lunes

In Spanish calendars, the first day of the week is Monday (**lunes**).

Práctica

3.1 **Escucha y responde** Write the word **mes** on one piece of paper and **día** on another. Listen to a list of months and days of the week. If you hear a month hold up **mes**; if you hear a day of the week, hold up **día**.

CD1-14

3.2 **En orden** Complete the following sequences with the missing word.

1. enero, febrero, marzo, _____
2. viernes, sábado, _____
3. lunes, miércoles, _____
4. septiembre, octubre, _____
5. lunes, martes, _____
6. junio, julio, _____
7. jueves, sábado, _____
8. mayo, agosto, noviembre, _____

3.3 **¿Qué hora es?** Look at the clocks and tell what time it is.

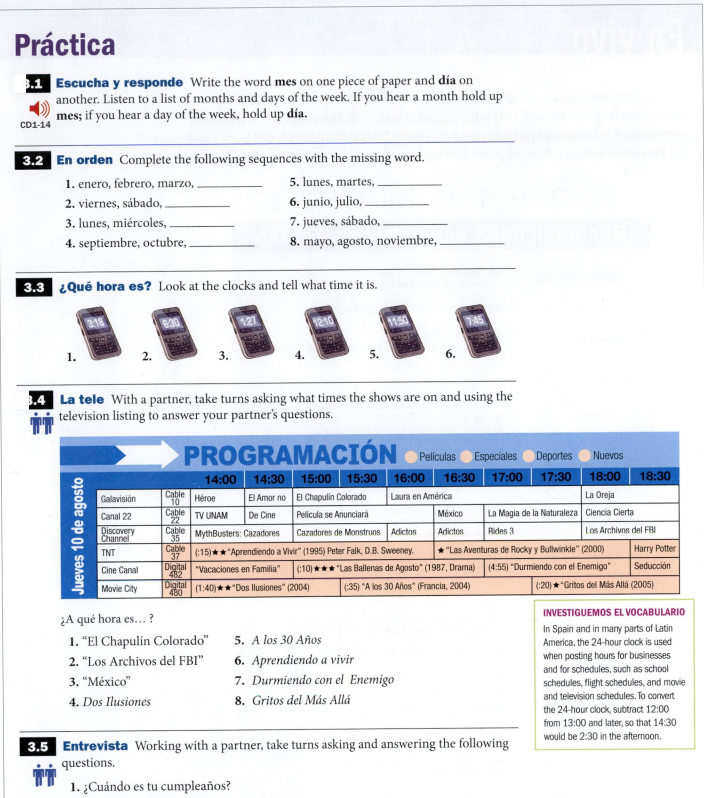

1. 3:18   2. 6:30   3. 1:27   4. 12:10   5. 11:50   6. 7:45

3.4 **La tele** With a partner, take turns asking what times the shows are on and using the television listing to answer your partner's questions.

PROGRAMACIÓN ● Películas ● Especiales ● Deportes ● Nuevos

Jueves 10 de agosto

		14:00	14:30	15:00	15:30	16:00	16:30	17:00	17:30	18:00	18:30
Galavisión	Cable 10	Héroe	El Amor no	El Chapulín Colorado		Laura en América				La Oreja	
Canal 22	Cable 22	TV UNAM	De Cine	Película se Anunciará			México	La Magia de la Naturaleza		Ciencia Cierta	
Discovery Channel	Cable 35	MythBusters: Cazadores		Cazadores de Monstruos		Adictos	Adictos	Rides 3		Los Archivos del FBI	
TNT	Cable 37	(:15)★★ "Aprendiendo a Vivir" (1995) Peter Falk, D.B. Sweeney.				★ "Las Aventuras de Rocky y Bullwinkle" (2000)					Harry Potter
Cine Canal	Digital 482	"Vacaciones en Familia"		(:10)★★★ "Las Ballenas de Agosto" (1987, Drama)				(4:55) "Durmiendo con el Enemigo"			Seducción
Movie City	Digital 480	(1:40)★★ "Dos Ilusiones" (2004)			(:35) "A los 30 Años" (Francia, 2004)				(:20) ★ "Gritos del Más Allá" (2005)		

¿A qué hora es… ?

1. "El Chapulín Colorado"
2. "Los Archivos del FBI"
3. "México"
4. *Dos Ilusiones*
5. *A los 30 Años*
6. *Aprendiendo a vivir*
7. *Durmiendo con el Enemigo*
8. *Gritos del Más Allá*

INVESTIGUEMOS EL VOCABULARIO

In Spain and in many parts of Latin America, the 24-hour clock is used when posting hours for businesses and for schedules, such as school schedules, flight schedules, and movie and television schedules. To convert the 24-hour clock, subtract 12:00 from 13:00 and later, so that 14:30 would be 2:30 in the afternoon.

3.5 **Entrevista** Working with a partner, take turns asking and answering the following questions.

1. ¿Cuándo es tu cumpleaños?
2. ¿Cuándo es el cumpleaños de tu mejor (*best*) amigo?
3. ¿Cuál es tu día feriado (*holiday*) favorito? ¿Cuándo es?
4. ¿Qué mes del año es tu favorito?
5. ¿Qué días tienes clases? ¿A qué hora es tu primera clase de la semana?
6. ¿Trabajas? ¿Qué días trabajas? ¿Normalmente a qué hora trabajas?

INVESTIGUEMOS LA CULTURA

Here are some holidays that are commonly celebrated in most Spanish-speaking countries: **el Día de la Raza** (*Columbus Day*), **el Día de los Muertos** (*Day of the Dead*), **el Día de los Reyes Magos** (*Three Kings Day*), **la Pascua** (*Easter, Passover*), **la Navidad** (*Christmas*), **la Nochebuena** (*Christmas Eve*), **la Semana Santa** (*Holy Week*).

What information does a theater listing generally have? Check the theater listing from a tourist guide to see if that information is included. Then answer the following questions: ¿Qué obras (*plays*) presentan el sábado 7 de noviembre? ¿A qué hora y qué día presentan *Julieta y Romeo*? ¿Qué días hay una obra a la una de la tarde?

NOVIEMBRE

Resumen del 8 encuentro de Teatro

Miércoles 4
La Prohibida 18:00 hrs.
Soplador de Estrellas 20:00 hrs.

Jueves 5
Roma al Final de la Vía 20:00 hrs.

Viernes 6
Anatol 20:00 hrs.
Javiera en el Acuario de los Peces Rotos 20:00 hrs.

Sábado 7
La Inútil Precaución 13:00 hrs.
¡Ay Carmela! 20:00 hrs.

Domingo 8
El Gran Teatro del Mundo 13:00 hrs.
Voces en el Umbral 20:00 hrs.
El Circo: Maroma y Teatro 19:00 hrs.

Lunes 9
Opción Múltiple 18:00 hrs.
Barrionetas 20:00 hrs.

Martes 10
Pedro y el Capitán 18:00 hrs.

Miércoles 11
Sazón de Mujer 20:00 hrs.
Los Invisibles 20:00 hrs.
Clavos de Plata 20:00 hrs.

Jueves 12
El Cepillo de Dientes o Naufragos en el Parque de Atracciones 20:00 hrs.

Viernes 13
Sólo para Machos 18:00 hrs.
Julieta y Romeo 20:00 hrs.

Sábado 14
Las Preciosas Ridículas 13:00 hrs.
Historias de Vivos y Muertos 18:00 hrs.

Domingo 15
Salvemos el Bosque 13:00 hrs.
El Libertino 18:00 hrs.
Mentir está Barato 20:00 hrs.

Lunes 16
La Maestra 18:00 hrs.
La Revolución 20:00 hrs.

Martes 17
Ni Esclavo ni Amo, Simplemente Cucurumbé 18:00 hrs.
Para ti... Sor Juana 20:00 hrs.

Miércoles 18
Un pañuelo el mundo es 18:00 hrs.
Los enemigos 20:00 hrs.

Más allá

Find a local theater listing or one from a city near where you live and choose one of the plays. Then answer the following questions in Spanish.

1. ¿Cómo se llama la obra?
2. ¿Qué días presentan la obra?
3. ¿A qué hora?
4. ¿Cuánto cuesta la entrada? (*How much does the ticket cost?*)

A analizar

Read the paragraph, paying particular attention to the verb **gustar.** Then answer the questions.

> Yo soy Alonso y soy un estudiante colombiano. **Me gusta** el mes de diciembre porque **me gusta** mucho la Navidad. **Me gustan** las decoraciones y la comida especial. ¡Y **me gustan** mucho las fiestas con amigos! También **me gusta** escribir y recibir tarjetas (*cards*), pero no **me gusta** el frío, y aquí hace frío en diciembre.

1. The verb **gustar** is used to express likes and dislikes. What do you think **me gusta** means?

2. When is **gusta** used? And **gustan**?

A comprobar

Me gusta/te gusta/le gusta

1. The Spanish equivalent of *I like* is **me gusta,** which literally means *it pleases me.* The expressions **me gusta** (*I like*), **te gusta** (*you like*), and **le gusta** (*he/she likes*) are followed by singular nouns.

   Me gusta el chocolate.
   *I like chocolate. (Chocolate **pleases me.**)*

   ¿Te gusta la pizza?
   *Do **you like** pizza? (Does pizza **please you**?)*

   Le gusta la comida mexicana.
   *He/She likes Mexican food. (Mexican food **pleases him/her.**)*

2. The expressions **me gustan, te gustan,** and **le gustan** are followed by plural nouns.

   Me gustan los animales.
   *I like animals. (Animals **please me.**)*

   ¿Te gustan tus clases?
   *Do **you like** your classes? (Do your classes **please you?**)*

   Le gustan el béisbol y el fútbol.
   *He/She likes baseball and football. (Baseball and soccer **please him/her.**)*

3. When followed by a verb or a series of verbs, the singular form of **gusta** is always used.

   Me **gusta** correr y nadar.
   I like to run and swim.

Le **gusta** leer novelas de ciencia ficción.
He/She likes to read science fiction novels.

4. Contrary to English, when using **gustar** with a noun, you must use the definite article as well.

   Me gustan **las ciencias.**
   I like science.

   ¿Te gusta **el café?**
   Do you like coffee?

5. To clarify who *he* or *she* is, it is necessary to use an **a** in front of the name.

   A Mario le gustan los perros.
   Mario likes dogs.

   A Alba le gusta cocinar.
   Alba likes cooking.

6. To express different degrees, use the terms **mucho** (*a lot*), **un poco** (*a little*), and **para nada** (*not at all*).

   Me gustan **mucho** los fines de semana.
   I like the weekends a lot.

   Me gusta **un poco** la clase.
   I like the class a little.

   ¡No me gustan los exámenes **para nada!**
   I don't like exams at all!

> **INVESTIGUEMOS EL VOCABULARIO**
>
> When using **gusta** with people, it has a romantic implication. In **Capítulo 8** you will learn the expression **caer bien,** which is used to say that you like a person.
>
> **Me gusta Julio.**
> *I like Julio (as a romantic interest).*

© Patrick Sheandell O'Carroll/PhotoAlto/Getty Images

A practicar

3.6 **Combinaciones lógicas** Decide which phrases in the second column best complete the sentences in the first column.

1. En el restaurante me gustan...
2. En el restaurante no me gusta...
3. En la universidad me gusta...
4. En la universidad no me gustan...
5. En casa me gusta...
6. En casa no me gustan...

a. la clase de inglés.
b. los menús variados.
c. ayudar a mis hijos con su tarea.
d. el servicio malo.
e. los exámenes difíciles.
f. las tareas domésticas (*chores*).

3.7 **¿Qué te gusta?** Complete the following mini-dialogues with **me** or **te** and **gusta** or **gustan.**

1. Elena: Sonia, ¿ _____ _____ mirar la tele?

   Sonia: Sí, _____ _____ mirar la tele mucho.

   Elena: ¿ _____ _____ los programas cómicos?

   Sonia: No, _____ _____ más los programas dramáticos.

2. Hugo: ¿ _____ _____ practicar deportes, Raúl?

   Raúl: Sí, _____ _____ los deportes mucho.

   Hugo: ¿ _____ _____ el básquetbol?

   Raúl: ¡No _____ _____ para nada! _____ _____ el fútbol y el tenis.

3. Marcela: ¿ _____ _____ escuchar música?

   Enrique: _____ _____ escuchar y bailar música rock. ¿Y a ti?

   Marcela: _____ _____ mucho la música. También _____ _____ cantar.

3.8 **Me gusta** Ask your partner if he/she likes the things in the list below. When answering the questions, be sure to tell your partner why. **¡OJO!** You will need to decide whether to use **gusta** or **gustan.**

Modelo sábados
   Estudiante 1: *¿Te gustan los sábados?*
   Estudiante 2: *No, no me gustan los sábados porque trabajo.*
      Sí, me gustan los sábados porque no hay clases.

1. la clase de español
2. las clases
3. el mes de diciembre
4. viajar a otros países (*countries*)
5. las vacaciones
6. los animales

3.9 **Los gustos de Octavio** Look at the pictures below and, using the expression **le gusta(n)**, tell what Octavio likes and doesn't like.

Modelo
No le gusta estudiar.

3.10 **¿Te gusta...?** Circulate throughout the classroom and talk with 10 different students about their likes and dislikes. Be sure to use some of the following expressions: **mucho, un poco,** and **para nada.**

Modelo bailar
  Estudiante 1: *¿Te gusta bailar?*
  Estudiante 2: *Sí, me gusta (mucho) bailar.*
    No, no me gusta bailar (para nada).

1. el café
2. las clases de ciencias
3. practicar deportes
4. la música rock
5. los caballos
6. comprar y escuchar música
7. los chocolates
8. las novelas románticas
9. la Navidad
10. ¿?

3.11 **En común** Choose four of the following items that you like. Then circulate throughout the classroom and interview your classmates to find out if they like the same things. For each of the items you chose, find at least one other classmate who shares your opinion.

_____ los perros
_____ cocinar
_____ la música clásica
_____ los programas cómicos
_____ mirar los deportes

_____ la pizza
_____ los autos rápidos
_____ el fútbol y el béisbol
_____ la universidad
_____ ¿?

Cultura

Guadalupe Posada was a Mexican artist who produced numerous engravings depicting skeletons in everyday scenes, usually having fun. Although Posada's intention originally was satirical, as his work dealt with political and social issues, his art has been consistently used by Mexicans to decorate and celebrate **el Día de los Muertos.** Research and report to the class when and where **el Día de los Muertos** is celebrated and what other activities are typical of **el Día de los Muertos.**

© Giraudon/Art Resource, NY

iTunes

"La Llorona" is a well-known Mexican legend associated with the Day of the Dead. Listen to the song "La Llorona" sung by Lila Downs, a Mexican-American artist whose music is influenced by the music of Mixtec, Zapotec, Maya, and Nahuatl cultures. What is the tone of the song? What words can you understand?

Investiga en Internet otras obras de arte de Guadalupe Posada.

Comparaciones

The following are celebrations in Spain or Latin American countries. Are there similar celebrations in the United States? If so, when are they celebrated? Can you think of holidays that are unique to the United States?

San Fermín	el 7 de julio	Los españoles corren (run) con los toros.
El Día de los Muertos	el 1 y 2 de noviembre	Los mexicanos celebran la muerte (death).
El Día de los Inocentes	el 28 de diciembre	Los latinos hacen bromas (jokes).
El Carnaval	la semana antes del Miércoles de Cenizas	Los latinos cantan y bailan en las calles.
San Juan	el 24 de junio	Los paraguayos juegan (play) con fuego (fire).
El Año Nuevo	el 1º de enero	Los latinos celebran la llegada del nuevo año.
La Tomatina	el último (last) miércoles de agosto	Los españoles pelean (fight) con tomates.
El Día del Estudiante	el 21 de septiembre	Los estudiantes argentinos tienen fiestas en el parque y juegan al fútbol.

Conexiones... a la religión

Another Catholic tradition widely spread in the Spanish-speaking world is the celebration of **el santo.** Each day of the year is attributed to a particular saint, and it is a common practice to give a baby the name of the saint of the day when he or she was born. When babies aren't given the name of the patron saint of their birthday, their **santo** is celebrated like a second birthday. For example, suppose a baby born on October 5 receives the name of Fernando. Fernando will celebrate his birthday on October 5, and then his **santo** on May 30th, **día de San Fernando.** Look at the calendar and determine when these people would celebrate their **santo.**

Óscar de la Renta
Rómulo Gallegos
Gilberto Santa Rosa
Alejandro Fernández
Rufino Tamayo

Febrero

1 San Cecilio	11 Nuestra Sra. de Lourdes	20 San Eugenio
2 San Cornelio	12 San Damián	21 San Pedro Damián
3 San Óscar	13 Santa Maura	22 Santa Leonor
4 San Gilberto	14 San Valentín	23 Santa Marta de Astorga
5 Santa Felicia	15 San Faustino	24 San Sergio
6 Santa Dorotea	16 San Elías	25 San Valerio
7 Santa Juliana	17 San Rómulo	26 San Alejandro
8 San Lucio	18 San Eladio	27 San Basilio
9 San Abelardo	19 San Gabino	28 San Rufino
10 San Jacinto		29 Santa Emma

If you and or your family members have a Christian name, find out when you would celebrate your **santo.**

Comunidad

On the Internet, research the importance of **el Cinco de Mayo** in Mexican history. Then find out how it is celebrated in your community. Why do you think it has become a holiday celebrated more in the United States than in Mexico?

A analizar

Read the paragraph paying particular attention to the forms of the verbs in bold.

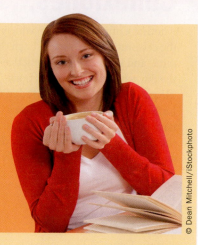

El miércoles es un día muy ocupado. Primero **asisto** a la clase de francés. Es difícil y no **comprendo** mucho. Luego Mariana y yo **asistimos** a la clase de historia donde **aprendemos** sobre la Revolución Cubana. Después Mariana **asiste** a la clase de literatura, y yo **bebo** un café y estudio francés. Después de su clase, Mariana y yo **comemos** con su familia. Ellos **viven** muy cerca (*near*) de la universidad y llegamos rápido. Por la tarde yo **leo** el libro de historia y ella **escribe** una composición.

The verbs in the paragraph (**asistir, comprender, aprender, beber, comer, vivir, leer,** and **escribir**) are **-er** and **-ir** verbs. Using the examples in the paragraph and what you have learned about **-ar** verbs, complete the following charts for the verbs **comprender** and **asistir.**

comprender

yo _____   nosotros(as) _____

tú _____   vosotros(as) _____

él, ella, usted _____   ellos, ellas, ustedes _____

asistir

yo _____   nosotros(as) _____

tú _____   vosotros(as) _____

él, ella, usted _____   ellos, ellas, ustedes _____

A comprobar

Regular -er and -ir verbs

1. In **Capítulo 1** we learned the forms of verbs whose infinitives end in **-ar.** The following are regular **-er** and **-ir** verbs:

Los verbos -er			
aprender (a + infinitive)	*to learn (to do something)*	creer	*to believe*
beber	*to drink*	deber	*should*
comer	*to eat*	leer	*to read*
comprender	*to understand*	vender	*to sell*
correr	*to run*		

Los verbos -ir

abrir	*to open*	recibir	*to receive*
asistir a	*to attend*	vivir	*to live*
escribir (un mensaje)	*to write (a message)*		

2. Regular **-er** and **-ir** verbs follow a pattern very similar to regular **-ar** verbs.

beber

yo	**-o**	beb**o**	nosotros(as)	**-emos**	beb**emos**
tú	**-es**	beb**es**	vosotros(as)	**-éis**	beb**éis**
él, ella, usted	**-e**	beb**e**	ellos, ellas, ustedes	**-en**	beb**en**

escribir

yo	**-o**	escrib**o**	nosotros(as)	**-imos**	escrib**imos**
tú	**-es**	escrib**es**	vosotros(as)	**-ís**	escrib**ís**
él, ella, usted	**-e**	escrib**e**	ellos, ellas, ustedes	**-en**	escrib**en**

Remember the following rules:

To form negative sentences, the word **no** is placed in front of the conjugated verb.

> Los niños no comprenden inglés.

When using two dependent verbs together, the second verb stays in the infinitive.

> Debemos estudiar el lunes.

> Los estudiantes aprenden a hablar español.

To form simple questions, place the subject after the conjugated verb and add the question marks at the beginning and end of the question.

> ¿Vive Alfredo en Bogotá?

A practicar

3.12 **¿Qué tienen?** Choose the most logical verb to complete the sentence.

1. Cuando tengo hambre, yo _____ un sándwich.

    a. como   **b.** creo   **c.** corro

2. Vanesa y Nelson tienen prisa y _____ a clase.

    a. comprenden   **b.** escriben   **c.** corren

3. Cuando tienen calor, mis padres _____ las ventanas.

    a. beben   **b.** asisten a   **c.** abren

4. Belinda y yo tenemos éxito en la clase de cálculo y _____ buenas notas.

    a. vendemos   **b.** recibimos   **c.** aprendemos

5. Cuando Leopoldo tiene sed, _____ agua.

    a. debe   **b.** come   **c.** bebe

3.13 **Mis amigos y yo** Complete the sentences with the correct forms of the verbs indicated.

(leer) Mi amigo Gustavo y yo (1.) _____ muchos libros. Yo (2.) _____
novelas de ciencia ficción y él (3.) _____ novelas de suspenso.

(comer) Durante la semana, la familia (1.) _____ a la una. Por la noche, los niños
(2.) _____ a las ocho, y mi esposa y yo (3.) _____ a las nueve.

(vivir) Mi familia es de Guadalajara, pero yo (1.) _____ en Oaxaca y mi hermana
(2.) _____ en Xalapa. Mis padres todavía (3.) _____ en Guadalajara.

(escribir) Mis amigos y yo siempre (1.) _____ mensajes. Ellos (2.) _____
mensajes todos los días y ahora yo debo (3.) _____ un mensaje para ellos.

3.14 **Un día en la vida de Antonio** With a partner, take turns describing Antonio's
activities; be sure to include the time. Use the -**er** and -**ir** verbs from this lesson as well
as other verbs you know.

3.15 **En busca de...** Circulate throughout the classroom and find classmates who do the
following activities. Be sure to list a different person for each activity.

1. leer novelas románticas
2. recibir buenas notas
3. correr en la mañana
4. beber mucho café

5. vivir en un apartamento
6. escribir muchos mensajes
7. asistir a conciertos
8. comer en McDonalds

3.16 **Entrevista** Take turns asking and answering the following questions.

1. ¿Asistes a clases todos los días?
2. ¿Comprendes al profesor de español?
3. ¿Lees mucho? ¿Lees novelas o revistas (*magazines*)?
4. ¿Dónde vives? ¿Vives con otra persona?
5. ¿A qué hora comes los domingos?
6. ¿Recibes muchos mensajes? ¿De quién?
7. ¿Debes escribir muchas composiciones para (*for*) tus clases? ¿Para qué clases?
8. ¿Crees que (*that*) aprender español es fácil o difícil? ¿Por qué?

3.17 **¿Qué debe hacer?** With a partner, come up with recommendations for what the following people should do. Use the verb **deber** and one of the following verbs.

aprender	asistir	buscar	comer	correr	estudiar
hablar	practicar	ser	trabajar	vender	

> **Modelo** Carla tiene problemas con su novio.
> *Ella debe hablar con su novio.*

1. Julio y Claudia tienen malas notas en sus clases.
2. Mónica no habla español muy bien.
3. Yo necesito dinero.
4. El señor Ortiz desea perder peso (*to lose weight*).
5. Pablo y yo no tenemos muchos amigos.
6. La señorita García desea ser doctora.

3.18 **¿Qué hacen?** Tell your partner about the things you and others do. Choose a subject from the first column and combine it with a verb from the second column. Be sure to add a phrase from the parentheses to complete your sentence. **¡OJO!** Pay attention to the form of the verb.

yo	deber (estudiar, escribir la tarea, leer el libro)
mis compañeros de clase	recibir (buenas notas, muchos mensajes, cartas de su familia)
mis amigos y yo	asistir a (clase de español, muchos conciertos, muchas fiestas)
mi mejor amigo	vivir en (una casa, un apartamento, el campus)
mi profesor de español	comprender (el español, las matemáticas, el inglés)
mi familia	comer (en restaurantes, en la cafetería, mucha pizza)

3.19 **Yo también** Using the verb indicated, tell your partner what you do. Your partner will tell you if he or she does the same activities or not.

> **Modelo** correr
> Estudiante 1: *Yo corro en la mañana.*
> Estudiante 2: *¡Yo también!/Yo corro en la noche.*

1. beber
2. comer
3. leer
4. escribir
5. asistir a
6. deber
7. vivir
8. comprender

© ArtmannWitte/Shutterstock

Lectura

Reading Strategy: Skimming

Skim through the text before reading it thoroughly. You will notice certain key ideas. Without looking up any words, try to identify three main ideas.

Antes de leer

In many countries there are important celebrations and holidays that are unique to the country. Make a list of the holidays that are important in the United States. Which ones do you celebrate and why? Look back at the celebrations mentioned in **Conexiones culturales.** Do you know other celebrations from a Spanish-speaking country? The following reading is about Christmas, a particularly important celebration because the majority of the population in Spain and Latin America is Catholic.

A leer

La Navidad en algunos países hispanos

Muchas de las tradiciones en Latinoamérica son religiosas y tienen sus orígenes en tradiciones españolas. Una de estas tradiciones es la de la Navidad. Para muchos, la celebración de la Navidad se inicia **antes** del 25 de diciembre. Desde noviembre es posible escuchar **villancicos** en los comerciales de televisión y de la radio. En varios países las fiestas se inician el 16 de diciembre y continúan todas las noches hasta el 24 de diciembre. Estas fiestas se llaman *las posadas*. En las posadas muchas personas visitan otras casas en la comunidad.

before

Christmas carols

> [...les gusta cantar villancicos, comer comida tradicional y romper piñatas.]

food

Les gusta cantar villancicos, comer **comida** tradicional y romper piñatas. A los niños les gusta mucho romper piñatas. A veces, también hay *pastorelas,* que son similares a pequeñas obras de teatro con lecciones religiosas o morales.

© Mary Ann Blitt

church

gifts

the Three Kings
ring-shaped bread

En muchos países, el 24 de diciembre (Nochebuena) las personas van a la **iglesia,** comen en familia, y a la medianoche abren los **regalos** de Navidad. El final de las celebraciones de Navidad es el 6 de enero, el Día de los Reyes Magos. En unos países los niños reciben regalos de los **Tres Reyes Magos,** y todos comen la famosa **rosca** de reyes.

© PILAR OLIVARES/Reuters /Landov

Comprensión

Decide whether the following statements are true or false. Correct any false statements.

1. En toda Latinoamérica las celebraciones de Navidad se inician el 25 de diciembre.
2. Las Pastorelas son fiestas en las que las personas cantan villancicos.
3. Es tradicional ir a la iglesia en Nochebuena.
4. El Día de los Reyes Magos, los niños reciben regalos.
5. La rosca de Reyes es una comida tradicional.

Después de leer

With a partner, come up with a list of activities you do to celebrate Christmas (**Navidad**), Hanukkah, Kwanzaa, another winter solstice celebration, or the New Year (**Año Nuevo**).

Modelo *En Navidad cantamos villancicos.*

© Noam Armonn/Shutterstock

En Janucá comemos postres deliciosos.

¿Qué estación es? ¿Qué ropa debes llevar?

El tiempo		La ropa		Los colores	
Hace (muy) buen tiempo.	*The weather is (very) nice.*	**los calcetines**	*socks*	**amarillo**	*yellow*
Hace (muy) mal tiempo.	*The weather is (very) bad.*	**el cinturón**	*belt*	**anaranjado**	*orange*
		la corbata	*tie*	**azul**	*blue*
Hace (mucho) calor.	*It's (very) hot.*	**el impermeable**	*raincoat*	**blanco**	*white*
Hace fresco.	*It is cool.*	**los lentes**	*glasses*	**café**	*brown*
Hace (mucho) frío.	*It's (very) cold.*	**las medias**	*panty hose*	**gris**	*gray*
Hace sol.	*It's sunny.*	**los pantalones**	*pants*	**morado**	*purple*
Hace (mucho) viento.	*It's (very) windy.*	**la pijama**	*pajamas*	**negro**	*black*
Está nublado.	*It is cloudy.*	**el traje**	*suit*	**rojo**	*red*
Está despejado.	*It is clear.*	**el vestido**	*dress*	**rosado**	*pink*
Llueve.	*It's raining./It rains.*	**llevar**	*to wear, to be wearing/ to take/to carry*	**verde**	*green*
Nieva.	*It's snowing./It snows.*				

Práctica

3.20 **Escucha y responde** Vas a escuchar una lista de varios artículos de ropa. Si llevas la ropa cuando hace calor, señala con el pulgar hacia arriba. Si no, señala con el pulgar hacia abajo. (*You are going to hear a list of different articles of clothing. If you wear the clothing when it is hot, give a thumbs up. If not, give a thumbs down.*)

CD1-15

3.21 **¿Qué tiempo hace?** ¿Con qué estación del año relacionas cada descripción del tiempo? (*What season do you associate with each of the weather conditions?*)

1. Hace viento.
2. Nieva.
3. Hace mucho calor.
4. Está despejado.

5. Hace fresco.
6. Llueve.
7. Hace mucho sol.
8. Hace mucho frío.

3.22 **Identificaciones** Encuentra (*Find*) a un compañero de clase que lleva una de las prendas de ropa de la lista. Para el número 10, escoge otro artículo de ropa. (*Find a classmate that is wearing one of the articles of clothing in the list. For number 10, choose another item of clothing.*)

1. unos calcetines blancos
2. una chaqueta
3. un suéter
4. unas botas
5. una camiseta

6. una falda
7. unos pantalones negros
8. un vestido
9. unos tenis
10. ¿?

INVESTIGUEMOS EL VOCABULARIO

Many Latin Americans use the word **el clima** to refer to the weather. Additionally, it is possible to say either **llevar** or use the expression **llevar puesto** to say what you wear.

The following are lexical variations for clothing items:

jacket	**la chamarra** (Mexico)
tennis shoes	**los campeones** (Paraguay)
glasses	**las gafas** (Spain)
socks	**las medias** (Central and South America)
panty hose	**la pantimedia** (Central and South America)
skirt	**la pollera** (Panama and South America)
jeans	**pantalones de mezclilla** (Mexico)
	los mahones (Puerto Rico)
	los vaqueros (Spain)

3.23 **De vacaciones** Con un compañero, túrnense para preguntar sobre el tiempo en los diferentes destinos, y la ropa que necesitan. (*With a partner, take turns asking about the weather in the following destinations, and the clothing that you need.*)

Modelo Cancún / julio
Estudiante 1: *¿Qué tiempo hace en Cancún en julio?*
Estudiante 2: *Hace mucho calor y está despejado.*
Estudiante 1: *¿Qué ropa necesitas?*
Estudiante 2: *Necesito pantalones cortos, sandalias y un traje de baño.*

1. Buenos Aires / diciembre
2. Anchorage / abril
3. Miami / agosto

4. Londres / junio
5. La Habana / septiembre
6. Chicago / marzo

3.24 **¿Cómo son y qué ropa llevan?** Con un compañero, túrnense para describir la ropa que llevan las personas en la pintura *La calle* del pintor colombiano Fernando Botero. (*With a partner, take turns describing what people are wearing in Colombian painter Fernando Botero's painting,* La calle.)

Modelo *Un niño lleva una camiseta roja y pantalones negros.*

🎵 **iTunes**
El Grupo Niche is a Colombian salsa band. Listen to their song "Gotas de lluvia" and write down any vocabulary words you hear.

En vivo

¿Qué es importante para una concursante (*contestant*) en un concurso de belleza? ¿Crees que también esto (*this*) es importante para las concursantes en un concurso de belleza de cholitas (*mujeres indígenas bolivianas*)? Según el artículo, ¿qué ropa usan las cholitas en el concurso? ¿Por qué? ¿Qué es lo más importante para ganar (*to win*) el concurso? En tu opinión ¿por qué es diferente a otros tipos de concursos de belleza? ¿Qué son las *transformers*? ¿Piensas que la palabra tiene una connotación positiva o negativa? ¿Por qué?

La Paz ya tiene su Miss Cholita

Ruxandra Guidi, Bolivia

Las mujeres indígenas de La Paz no tienen que identificarse con certámenes de belleza[1] como Miss Universo o Miss Mundo.

Jose Luis Quintana/Reuters/Landov

Requisitos[2] del concurso
Todas las catorce concursantes entraron con sus faldas a capas[3], o polleras, sus grandes aretes de oro[4], sus caras al natural y trenzas[5] largas.

Estas son las características de las mujeres indígenas de Bolivia, también conocidas[6] aquí como "cholitas".

Las mujeres desfilaron por la pasarela[7] con ropas tradicionales —nada de bikinis aquí— para ser juzgadas por sus personalidades, sus mantas[8] de colores, y sus habilidades de hablar en el idioma[9] aymara.

Mariela Mollinedo dijo unas cuantas palabras con dificultad en aymara, pero su linda cara y su gran sonrisa conquistó a los jueces[10] del evento. Sin embargo, Mollinedo no reinaría como Miss Cholita por mucho tiempo.

Después de pocos minutos, uno de los del jurado[11] vio que las trenzas de Mollinedo eran extensiones falsas, algo que es absolutamente inaceptable entre cholitas.

Las trenzas son la clave
"Las trenzas son algo vital, son como el labio pintado[12] de una señorita", dijo David Mendoza, uno de los jueces del evento.

"Aquí ocurre muchas veces una transformación, muchas personas de origen chola, por el tema de la segregación y del racismo, asumen otro rol de ser señoritas, de tener pantalón y de negar[13] un poco su origen cultural."

Las cholitas que abandonan su peinado[14] o vestimenta tradicional son conocidas aquí como *transformers*.

© Jose Luis Quintana/Reuters/Landov

[1]beauty contests [2]requirements [3]layered [4]gold earrings [5]braids [6]known [7]paraded up and down the catwalk [8]shawls [9]language [10]judges [11]judges panel [12]lips with lipstick [13]deny [14]hairstyle

Más allá
Investiga si hay concursos de belleza étnicos en los Estados Unidos.

Exploraciones gramaticales

A analizar

Lee la conversación entre dos nuevos amigos y observa las preguntas. Después contesta las preguntas que siguen. (*Read the conversation between two new friends and pay attention to the questions. Then answer the questions below.*)

Gustavo: ¿De dónde eres tú?

Rafael: Soy de Paraguay.

Gustavo: ¿Y cómo es Paraguay?

Rafael: Es un país pequeño con mucha historia.

Gustavo: ¿Qué tiempo hace en Paraguay ahora?

Rafael: Paraguay está en el hemisferio sur, entonces es invierno ahora. Hace frío.

Gustavo: ¡Qué interesante! ¿Cuál es tu estación favorita?

Rafael: Me gusta el otoño porque es muy bonito y hace buen tiempo.

© Gawrav Sinha/iStockphoto

1. In Spanish, punctuation for questions is different from that in English. What is the difference?
2. Using the conversation above and what you have learned in previous chapters, identify the interrogatives (question words). What do all of the question words have in common?

A comprobar

Interrogatives

¿cómo?	how?	¿adónde?	to where?	¿quién(es)?	who?	¿cuántos(as)?	how many?
¿cuándo?	when?	¿de dónde?	from where?	¿qué?	what?	¿cuánto(a)?	how much?
¿dónde?	where?	¿por qué?	why?	¿cuál(es)?	which?		

*Notice that all question words have an accent.

1. In most questions:
   - the subject is placed after the verb.
   - the question word is often the first word of the question.
   - it is not necessary to have a helping word such as *do* or *does*.
   - it is necessary to have an inverted question mark at the beginning of the questions and another question mark at the end.

interrogative + verb + subject		
¿Cuándo	es	la fiesta?
¿Dónde	vives	tú?

2. Prepositions (**a, con, de, en, por, para,** etc.) cannot be placed at the end of the question. They *must* be in front of the question word.

   ¿**Para** quién compras ese gorro?
   For whom are you buying that cap?

3. **Quién** and **cuál** must agree in number with the noun that follows, and **cuánto** and **cuántos** must agree in gender.

   ¿**Quiénes** son tus profesores?
   Who are your teachers?
   ¿**Cuántas** blusas tienes?
   How many blouses do you have?

4. There are two ways to express *What?* or *Which?*

¿Cuál? often implies choice. It can be used in front of a verb or the preposition **de,** but is generally not used in front of a noun.

¿**Cuáles** son tus clases favoritas?
What (Which) are your favorite classes?

¿**Cuál** de estos suéteres te gusta?
Which of these sweaters do you like?

¿Qué? is used to ask for a definition or an explanation when it is used in front of a verb. When it is used in front of a noun, it implies choice.

¿**Qué** es?
What is it?

¿**Qué** necesitas llevar?
What do you need to wear?

¿**Qué** ropa te gusta?
What clothing do you like?

A practicar

3.25 **La respuesta lógica** Una chica habla por celular con una amiga en una fiesta. Lee las preguntas y decide cuáles son las respuestas más lógicas. (*A girl talks to a friend at a party on her cell phone. Read the questions and decide which answer is most logical.*)

1. _____ ¿Dónde está la casa de Martín?   **a.** Veinte o treinta.

2. _____ ¿Por qué tienen una fiesta?   **b.** Bluyíns y un suéter.

3. _____ ¿Cuántas personas hay?   **c.** Es el cumpleaños de Osvaldo.

4. _____ ¿Quién está en la fiesta?   **d.** ¡Muy divertida!

5. _____ ¿Cómo es la fiesta?   **e.** En la Avenida Quintanilla.

6. _____ ¿Qué llevas?   **f.** Todos nuestros amigos.

3.26 **¿Qué o cuál?** Decide si debes usar **Qué** o **Cuál(es)** para completar las preguntas. (*Decide whether you should use **Qué** or **Cuál(es)** to complete the questions.*)

1. ¿ _____ estación del año te gusta más?

2. ¿De _____ color es tu chaqueta?

3. ¿ _____ te gusta, el abrigo gris o el negro?

4. ¿ _____ ropa llevas en invierno?

5. ¿ _____ son los guantes de Eugenio?

6. ¿ _____ vestido te gusta llevar a la fiesta?

7. ¿ _____ de las faldas es más larga?

8. ¿Con _____ camisa llevas el pantalón?

En el invierno llevo guantes y una bufanda.

© Tanya Ien/Shutterstock

3.27 **Una conversación por teléfono** Estás en una tienda de ropa con tu amiga Patricia cuando llama por teléfono una amiga de Patricia. Completa la conversación telefónica con las preguntas lógicas de ella. Inventa la última pregunta y la respuesta. (*You are in a clothing store with a friend when her friend Patricia calls. Complete the telephone conversation with Patricia's logical questions. Invent the last question and answer.*)

Amiga: Hola, Patricia.

Patricia: ¿..**1**.. _____?

Amiga: Estoy bien, gracias. De compras (*shopping*) con una amiga.

Patricia: ¿..**2**.. _____?

Amiga: Busco un vestido.

Patricia: ¿..**3**.. _____
_____?

Amiga: Necesito un vestido nuevo porque hay una fiesta este fin de semana.

Patricia: ¿..**4**.. _____?

Amiga: La fiesta es el sábado por la noche.

Patricia: ¿..**5**.. _____
_____?

Amiga: Adriana y Olivia organizan la fiesta.

Patricia: ¿..**6**..?

Amiga: _____ . Bueno, hablamos más tarde. Adiós.

3.28 **De compras** Inventa cinco preguntas relacionadas con la foto. Luego, trabaja con un compañero para que responda tus preguntas. (*Invent five questions related to the photo to ask a classmate. Then, work with a partner and have him/her answer your questions.*)

Modelo *¿Qué compran?*

© Dmitriy Shironosov/Shutterstock

3.29 **Información, por favor** Trabajas en una tienda de ropa y necesitas completar el formulario para una tarjeta de crédito para un cliente. Trabaja con un compañero para que te responda tus preguntas. (*You work in a clothing store and you need to complete the form for a credit card for a customer. Work with a partner and have him/her answer your questions.*)

Modelo Nombre
Estudiante A: *¿Cómo se llama Ud.?*
Estudiante B: *Me llamo…*

**Formulario Para
Una Tarjeta de Crédito**

Nombre

Edad (Age)

Dirección (Address)

Origen

Nombre de esposo(a)

Número de hijos

Trabajo

Conexiones culturales
El clima y la ropa

Cultura

Escribe una lista de asociaciones con la primavera. Luego lee la primera estrofa de una canción popular muy conocida en casi todos los países hispanohablantes. Hay también muchas traducciones al inglés. Después contesta las preguntas. (*Write a list of associations with spring. Then read the first verse of a popular song that is known in most Spanish-speaking countries. There are also many English translations. Afterwards, answer the questions.*)

De colores, de colores se visten los **campos**[1] en la primavera
De colores, de colores son los pajaritos que vienen de afuera
De colores, de colores es el **arco iris**[2] que vemos **lucir**[3]

Y por eso los grandes amores de muchos colores me gustan a mí
Y por eso los grandes amores de muchos colores me gustan a mí.

🌐 Investiga en Internet las otras estrofas de la canción *De colores*.

[1]*fields*   [2]*rainbow*   [3]*to shine*

En tu opinión ¿cuáles de las siguientes palabras describen la canción? ¿Por qué?

triste (*sad*)   alegre (*happy*)   nostálgica   rítmica   rápida   lenta (*slow*)

Comunidad

Investiga las alternativas que hay en tu comunidad para comprar ropa tradicional de países hispanohablantes. ¿Qué ropa hay disponible? ¿De dónde es? ¿Cuánto cuesta?
(*Investigate the alternatives in your community for buying traditional clothing from Spanish-speaking countries. What clothing is available? Where is it from? How much does it cost?*)

Un mercado de Los Ángeles

Comparaciones

La ropa que usan las personas en los países hispanohablantes depende de muchas variables. Por ejemplo, depende de cuántos años tienen, de su posición económica, y de si viven en una ciudad grande o un lugar pequeño. ¿Crees que los jóvenes universitarios se visten de manera similar en todos los países? Observa las fotografías y responde las preguntas.

1. ¿Qué ropa llevan los estudiantes de las fotos? ¿Es similar a la ropa que llevan los estudiantes en tu universidad? Explica las similitudes (*similarities*) y diferencias.

2. ¿Piensas que los españoles y los latinoamericanos se visten (*dress*) como tú?

© Courtesy of Fernando Casas, ITESO

© Dmitriy Shironosov/Shutterstock

Conexiones... a la redacción

Con un compañero, escojan (*choose*) una estación y escriban una lista de adjetivos, actividades y expresiones que asocien con esa estación. Luego, escriban un poema dedicado a esa estación. Recuerden que los poemas normalmente no tienen oraciones completas y que no es necesario tener rima. (*With a partner, choose a season and write a list of adjectives, activities, and expressions that you associate with it. Then, write a poem dedicated to that season. Remember that poems normally don't have complete sentences and that it isn't necessary to have a rhyme.*)

© LianeM/iStockphoto

A analizar

Lee la conversación y observa las formas del verbo **preferir.** (*Read the conversation, paying particular attention to the forms of the verb* **preferir.**)

> **Enrique:** Yo **prefiero** el verano. Hace buen tiempo y me gusta mucho jugar al tenis y al golf. ¿Qué estación **prefieres** tú?
>
> **Anita:** Yo **prefiero** el verano también. No hay clases y me gusta viajar. Nosotros **preferimos** el verano, pero mi hermano **prefiere** el invierno. Le gusta mucho esquiar.

1. Using the examples from the conversation and your knowledge of conjugating verbs, complete the table with the verb **preferir.**

   preferir

   yo _____   nosotros(as) _____

   tú _____   vosotros(as) preferís

   él, ella, usted _____   ellos, ellas, ustedes _____

2. How do the **nosotros** and **vosotros** forms of the verb differ from the other forms?

A comprobar

Stem-changing verbs e → ie and e → i

1. There are a number of verbs that have changes in the root or stem. They are called stem-changing verbs. These verb forms change in all forms except **nosotros** and **vosotros.** Notice that in the verbs below the **e** changes to **ie;** however, the endings are the same as other **-ar, -er,** and **-ir** verbs.

querer (*to want*)

yo	quiero	nosotros(as)	queremos
tu	quieres	vosotros(as)	queréis
él, ella, usted	quiere	ellos, ellas, ustedes	quieren

cerrar (*to close*)

yo	cierro	nosotros(as)	cerramos
tú	cierras	vosotros(as)	cerráis
él, ella, usted	cierra	ellos, ellas, ustedes	cierran

mentir (*to lie*)

yo	miento	nosotros(as)	mentimos
tú	mientes	vosotros(as)	mentís
él, ella, usted	miente	ellos, ellas, ustedes	mienten

© ImageryMajestic/Shutterstock

The verbs listed below are also **e → ie** stem-changing verbs.

comenzar	*to begin*	nevar	*to snow*
empezar	*to begin*	pensar	*to think*
encender	*to turn on*	perder	*to lose*
entender	*to understand*	preferir	*to prefer*

2. The verbs **comenzar** and **empezar** are followed by the preposition **a** when used with an infinitive.

> Él **empieza a** trabajar a las ocho.
> *He begins to (starts) work at 8:00.*

> Ellos **comienzan a** estudiar español.
> *They are beginning to study Spanish.*

3. There are some **-ir** verbs in which the **e** in the stem changes to **i.** As with the **e → ie** stem-changing verbs, these verbs also change in all forms except **nosotros** and **vosotros,** and the endings are the same as regular **-ir** verbs.

repetir (*to repeat*)

yo	rep**i**to	nosotros(as)	repetimos
tú	rep**i**tes	vosotros(as)	repetís
él, ella, usted	rep**i**te	ellos, ellas, ustedes	rep**i**ten

The verbs listed below are **e → i** stem-changing verbs like **repetir.**

competir	*to compete*	servir	*to serve*
pedir	*to ask for*	sonreír	*to smile*
reír	*to laugh*		

4. Notice that the verb **reír** requires an accent mark on the **i** when it is conjugated. The same rule applies for **sonreír.**

reír (*to laugh*)

yo	**río**	nosotros	**reímos**
tú	**ríes**	vosotros	**reís**
él, ella, usted	**ríe**	ellos, ellas, ustedes	**ríen**

5. **Pedir** means *to ask for* (*something*) and **preguntar** means *to ask* (*a question*). The preposition *for* is part of the verb **pedir,** so you should not use **por** or **para** with it.

> Los niños **piden** permiso de sus padres.
> *Children ask permission from their parents.*

> Él **pregunta** si va a nevar.
> *He is asking if it is going to snow.*

A practicar

3.30 **La conclusión lógica** Decide qué conclusión completa cada oración mejor. (*Decide which conclusion best completes each of the sentences.*)

1. Pedro es muy cómico y sus amigos...
2. Nosotros trabajamos en un restaurante donde...
3. Fernando tiene dieciséis años y...
4. Lola es atleta y ella...
5. No me gusta la clase de álgebra porque...
6. Hoy nieva, y mis amigos y yo...

a. compite en las olimpiadas.
b. ríen mucho.
c. queremos esquiar.
d. pide permiso para viajar con sus amigos.
e. no entiendo las matemáticas.
f. servimos comida italiana.

3.31 ¿Qué piensan hacer más tarde? Usando el verbo **pensar,** explica qué piensan hacer las personas y cuándo. (*Using the verb **pensar,** explain what the people plan to do and when.*)

Modelo Raúl

10:00

Raúl piensa correr con el perro a las diez.

1. Silvia y Gisela

4:30

2. Tomás

12:00

3. Lupe y yo

7:45

4. el señor y la señora Márquez

1:30

5. Olga

6:15

6. Y tú ¿qué piensas hacer más tarde?

3.32 Somos iguales Marca cuatro de las siguientes oraciones que sean ciertas para ti. Después, busca cuatro diferentes compañeros para quienes las oraciones también sean ciertas. (*Place a check mark by four of the following sentences that apply to you. Then, find four different classmates to whom one of the sentences also applies.*)

_____ Compito en un deporte.

_____ Quiero viajar a otro país.

_____ Sonrío en las fotos.

_____ No miento.

_____ Enciendo la radio cuando estudio.

_____ Normalmente empiezo a estudiar después de (*after*) las ocho de la noche.

_____ A veces (*Sometimes*) pierdo la tarea.

_____ Pienso comer en un restaurante hoy.

_____ Entiendo al profesor de español.

_____ Pido ayuda con la tarea de español.

Queremos viajar a otro país.

© Herjua/Shutterstock

3.33 Entrevista Entrevista a tu compañero con las siguientes preguntas. (*Interview your classmate with the following questions.*)

1. ¿Quién sirve la comida (*food*) en tu casa/apartamento?

2. ¿Trabajas? Normalmente, ¿a qué hora empiezas a trabajar?

3. ¿Qué tienes que hacer (*to do*) mañana?

4. ¿Qué tienes ganas de hacer durante el fin de semana?

5. ¿Quieres viajar en el verano? ¿Adónde?

6. ¿Pierdes las cosas (*things*) con frecuencia? ¿Qué cosas pierdes con frecuencia?

7. ¿Qué piensas hacer esta noche?

8. ¿Entiendes otra lengua? ¿Cuál?

Redacción

An international student from a Spanish-speaking country is going to attend your university. Write a letter to the student explaining what the climate in your area is like, what people often do during holidays, and advise him/her as to what clothing he or she will need.

Paso 1 Write down the current season. Then write a list of the types of weather you experience in your area during that time.

Paso 2 Jot down things people do in your area as well as any special holidays, celebrations, or events that take place during that time.

Paso 3 Decide whether you are writing to a male or a female student. Then write down a list of clothing items that people wear in your area. Think about what they would wear to school, to go out, and to do any of the activities you wrote down in **Paso 2.**

© Chris Schmidt/iStockphoto

Paso 4 Start your letter by writing the date in Spanish and greeting the student using the expression **Querido(a)** *(Dear)*. Remember to use **Querido** if it is a male student and **Querida** if it is a female student.

Paso 5 Begin your first paragraph by introducing yourself to the international student and telling him or her where you study. Then using the information you generated in **Pasos 1** and **3,** tell him or her what season it is, what the weather is like in your area, and what particular clothing items he/she needs for that climate.

Paso 6 Using the information you generated in **Pasos 2** and **3,** begin a second paragraph and tell him or her what students usually wear to the university. Then explain what kinds of activities people do in their free time and any particular clothing items he or she would need. Be sure to include any special events or holidays and when they are.

Paso 7 Conclude your letter with **Hasta pronto** or **Tu nuevo(a) amigo(a).**

Paso 8 Edit your essay:

1. Are there any sentences that are irrelevant to the topic? If so, get rid of them.
2. Are your paragraphs logically organized or do you skip from one idea to the next?
3. Are there any short sentences you can combine by using **y** or **pero**?
4. Are there any spelling errors?
5. Do your adjectives agree with the object they describe?
6. Do your verbs agree with the subject?

Lectura

Antes de leer

Las personas en las fotos llevan ropa tradicional. Con un compañero relacionen las fotos con el país de donde creen que son. (**Argentina, Cuba o Perú**). Luego contesten las preguntas que siguen. (*The people in the photos are wearing traditional clothing. With a classmate match the photos with the country where you think they are from.* [**Argentina, Cuba, Perú**]. *Then answer the questions below.*)

© Don Tremain/JupiterImages   © Kobby Dagan/Shutterstock   © Laurent Grandadam/AGE Fotostock

1. ¿Qué factores consideran para relacionar las fotografías con los países?
2. ¿Hay ropa tradicional en el estado/la región donde viven? ¿Cómo es?
3. ¿Cuándo usan las personas la ropa tradicional? ¿Por qué?

A leer

Los trajes tradicionales

Muchas regiones del mundo hispano tienen una gran variedad de trajes regionales que indican su cultura y sus tradiciones, y también reflejan su historia y su clima.

En muchas culturas es posible determinar de dónde es una persona solamente por el traje y los colores que lleva, como es el caso de Guatemala. **Sin embargo,** no todas las personas llevan sus trajes tradicionales todo el tiempo. En las **ciudades** las personas prefieren usar ropa moderna, como trajes, vestidos y bluyíns.

> En muchas culturas es posible determinar de dónde es una persona solamente por el traje

Nevertheless

cities

En las ciudades grandes, pocas personas tienen trajes regionales, y los usan solamente en ocasiones especiales como en fiestas nacionales y regionales, en **bodas** y en interpretaciones de bailes folklóricos. En particular, los trajes tradicionales para las danzas y bailes ayudan a narrar historias.

weddings

© Joel Shawn/Shutterstock

Sin embargo, muchos de los indígenas en la región andina de Perú, Bolivia y el Ecuador llevan siempre su ropa tradicional, especialmente los que viven en las comunidades pequeñas. Más al norte, en Guatemala y varias regiones del sur de México, cada comunidad produce ropa con combinaciones de colores y diseños que son únicos. Por esta razón, es posible en muchos casos determinar de dónde es una persona por la ropa que lleva. La ropa indígena refleja las creencias de una comunidad, y muchas veces el estado civil o social de una persona. Para muchos indígenas, la ropa tradicional es una parte vital de su identidad, y un nexo con sus **antepasados.**

ancestors

Comprensión

1. ¿Qué indican los trajes regionales?

2. ¿Qué ropa prefieren llevar las personas en las ciudades?

3. ¿Cuándo usan trajes tradicionales las personas de las ciudades?

4. ¿Qué es posible determinar de una persona de Guatemala y del sur de México mediante su traje tradicional?

Después de leer

Con un compañero, describan un traje tradicional que refleje el clima, la cultura y la historia de una región de su país. ¿Qué llevan los hombres? ¿Y las mujeres? ¿Qué colores se usan? ¿Qué representan los colores? (*With a partner, describe a traditional outfit that reflects the climate, culture, and history of a region of your country. What would the men wear? And the women? What colors are the outfits? What do the colors represent?*)

En Chile no hace frío en diciembre. No necesita abrigo.

© Andresr / Shutterstock

Vocabulario

Sustantivos

el clima	*climate*
el descuento	*discount*
la devolución	*return*
el ecosistema	*ecosystem*
el ecoturismo	*ecotourism*
el medio ambiente	*environment*
la naturaleza	*nature*
el pago	*payment*
la reserva	*reservation*
el seguro	*insurance*
la temporada	*season*

Adjetivos

caluroso	*hot*
diligente	*diligent*
educado	*polite*
húmedo	*humid*
lluvioso	*rainy*
responsable	*responsible*
seco	*dry*

Verbos

averiguar	*to find out*
cobrar	*to charge*
confirmar	*to confirm*
devolver	*to return*
llevar	*to take*
pagar	*to pay*
recorrer	*to go through*

Frases útiles

Tenemos un paquete muy bueno.
We have a great package.

Tenemos descuento para grupos familiares.
We have family plans.

Es temporada alta/baja.
This is high/low season.

¿Me da su número de tarjeta de crédito?
May I have your credit card number?

Este es su número de confirmación.
This is your confirmation number.

DATOS IMPORTANTES

Educación: Estudios secundarios. Certificación de agente de turismo por escuelas privadas o universidades. Algunas universidades ofrecen licenciatura en viajes y turismo. Se requieren conocimientos de computación y se prefieren estudios complementarios en negocios.

Salario: Promedio de $50 000, comisiones de hasta 25% y bonos.

Dónde se trabaja: Agencias de viaje, corporaciones, hoteles y oficinas nacionales de turismo.

Marcela Díaz trabaja en una importante agencia de turismo. Vende paquetes de ecoturismo a distintos lugares de Latinoamérica. En el video vas a ver a Marcela preparando un viaje por teléfono para un nuevo cliente.

Antes de ver

Muchos vendedores trabajan por comisión y reciben dinero extra por cada venta que hacen. Para ellos, los clientes son muy importantes. Necesitan ser educados y diligentes con ellos. ¿Qué esperas de un agente de viajes? ¿Lees la información en Internet antes de llamar a un agente o prefieres hacerle muchas preguntas? ¿Qué tipo de preguntas específicas haces?

Comprensión

1. ¿Qué mira Carlos en la televisión normalmente?
2. ¿Qué país le recomienda Marcela?
3. ¿Qué animal especial vive en El Yunque?
4. ¿Cómo es el clima en Puerto Rico en esa temporada?
5. ¿Qué hacen en Luquillo?
6. ¿Adónde van el último día?

© Heinle/Cengage Learning

Después de ver

En parejas, representen a un agente de viajes y a un cliente que quiere hacer ecoturismo por un país de Latinoamérica. El agente recomienda un lugar de acuerdo con los gustos del cliente. Consideren el clima y hagan recomendaciones de ropa para llevar.

3.34 **Un día en el centro** Escoge el verbo apropiado y completa los párrafos con la forma correcta. (*Choose the appropriate verb and complete the paragraphs with the correct form.*)

A las once, Carmen llama a su amiga Teresa y (**1.**) _____ (pedir/preguntar) si quiere salir a comprar ropa con ella. A Teresa le (**2.**) _____ (gusta/gustan) mucho comprar ropa, y (**3.**) _____ (tener/ser) que buscar un vestido. Ella (**4.**) _____ (abrir/deber) asistir a un evento importante el viernes. Las dos chicas llegan a la tienda (*store*) y (**5.**) _____ (perder/empezar) a buscar ropa. A Teresa le (**6.**) _____ (gusta/gustan) los zapatos, y al final, compra unos zapatos y un vestido elegante.

Después de las compras, Carmen y Teresa (**7.**) _____ (tener/ser) hambre y (**8.**) _____ (entender/querer) comer en el restaurante Río Grande. Carmen (**9.**) _____ (pedir/preguntar) unos tacos, pero Teresa (**10.**) _____ (preferir/cerrar) las enchiladas. Las dos quieren (**11.**) _____ (beber/creer) agua. El mesero (*waiter*) (**12.**) _____ (mentir/servir) la comida y las chicas (**13.**) _____ (comer/correr).

3.35 **Comprensión de lectura** Imagínate que eres profesor y tienes que escribir cinco preguntas de comprensión para los estudiantes sobre este párrafo. **¡OJO!** Las respuestas a las preguntas deben estar en el párrafo. (*Imagine that you are an instructor and need to write five comprehension questions for your students about this paragraph. Attention! The answers to your questions must be in the paragraph.*)

Soy Rómulo y vivo en Montevideo, Uruguay. Hoy es 21 de diciembre, el primer día del verano. El verano es mi estación favorita porque hace buen tiempo. Ahora tengo vacaciones, y mañana mi familia y yo viajamos a Mar del Plata, Argentina. Mis tíos y mis primos viven en Mar del Plata.

3.36 **Explicaciones** Lee las oraciones y usa **gustar** para explicar por qué estas personas no hacen las siguientes actividades. (*Read the sentences and then using the verb **gustar**, explain why the people don't do certain activities.*)

Modelo Frank no estudia. → *No le gustan sus clases.*
Miguel no duerme mucho. → *Le gusta leer por la noche.*

1. Yo no como chocolates.
2. Tú no comes en restaurantes.
3. Laura no limpia su casa.
4. Tomasa no lleva pantalones cortos.
5. Felipe no recibe muchos mensajes electrónicos.
6. Yo no miro televisión.

Exploraciones de repaso: comunicación

3.37 **Descripción de fotos** Escoge una de las fotos y contesta las siguientes preguntas. (*Choose one of the photos and answer the following questions.*)

1. ¿Qué estación es?
2. ¿Qué tiempo hace?
3. ¿Cuál es la relación entre estas (*these*) personas?
4. ¿Qué ropa llevan estas personas?
5. ¿Qué hacen? (*What are they doing?*)

© Photo To Go
© Photo To Go
© Jim Lopes/Shutterstock

3.38 **Mi agenda** Tu compañero y tú deben encontrar una hora para estudiar español. Uno mira la agenda aquí y el otro mira la agenda en el apéndice A. Túrnense para preguntar sobre las horas libres que tienen. (*You and your partner should find a time to study Spanish. One of you look at the agenda on this page, and the other look at the agenda in the appendix, and take turns asking about the times you have available.*)

Modelo Estudiante 1: *¿Quieres estudiar a las nueve?*
Estudiante 2: *No, nado con Armando a las diez.*

miércoles, 20 de octubre	
8:30	
9:15	tomar un café con Alex
10:00	
11:30	estudiar historia
12:00	comer con Natalia
1:15	
2:45	
3:30	asistir a Club de español
4:15	practicar fútbol
5:00	

3.39 **Conversación** Usa las siguientes preguntas para charlar con un compañero. Añade información adicional para que la conversación sea más interesante. (*Use the following questions to chat with a partner. Add additional information to make the conversation more interesting.*)

1. ¿Qué tiempo hace en marzo donde vives? ¿Y en noviembre?
2. ¿Qué ropa llevas durante la primavera?
3. ¿Qué actividades prefieres hacer durante el verano? ¿y en el invierno?
4. ¿Qué te gusta hacer cuando hace sol? ¿y cuando llueve?
5. ¿Prefieres el frío o el calor? ¿Por qué?

Vocabulario 1

CD1-16

Los días de la semana

el lunes	*Monday*		el viernes	*Friday*
el martes	*Tuesday*		el sábado	*Saturday*
el miércoles	*Wednesday*		el domingo	*Sunday*
el jueves	*Thursday*			

Los meses

enero	*January*		julio	*July*
febrero	*February*		agosto	*August*
marzo	*March*		septiembre	*September*
abril	*April*		octubre	*October*
mayo	*May*		noviembre	*November*
junio	*June*		diciembre	*December*

Los verbos

abrir	*to open*		creer	*to believe*
aprender (a + infinitive)	*to learn (to do something)*		deber	*should, ought to*
asistir (a)	*to attend*		escribir (un mensaje)	*to write (a message)*
beber	*to drink*		leer	*to read*
comer	*to eat*		recibir	*to receive*
comprender	*to understand*		vender	*to sell*
correr	*to run*		vivir	*to live*

Palabras adicionales

el cumpleaños	*birthday*		mañana	*tomorrow*
el día	*day*		la medianoche	*midnight*
la fecha	*date*		el mediodía	*noon*
el fin de semana	*weekend*		la semana	*week*
hoy	*today*		todos los días	*every day*

Expresiones importantes

me gusta	*I like*		le gusta	*he/she likes*
te gusta	*you like*			

Diccionario personal

_____

_____

_____

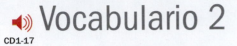 Vocabulario 2

CD1-17

La ropa y los accesorios

el abrigo	*coat*		los lentes	*glasses*
la blusa	*blouse*		las medias	*panty hose*
los bluyíns	*blue jeans*		los pantalones	*pants*
las botas	*boots*		los pantalones cortos	*shorts*
la bufanda	*scarf*			
los calcetines	*socks*		el paraguas	*umbrella*
la camisa	*shirt*		la pijama	*pajamas*
la camiseta	*T-shirt*		las sandalias	*sandals*
el chaleco	*vest*		el sombrero	*hat*
la chaqueta	*jacket*		el suéter	*sweater*
el cinturón	*belt*		los tenis	*tennis shoes*
la corbata	*tie*		el traje	*suit*
la falda	*skirt*		el traje de baño	*swimming suit*
el gorro	*cap*		el vestido	*dress*
los guantes	*gloves*		los zapatos	*shoes*
el impermeable	*raincoat*			

El tiempo

Está despejado.	*It is clear.*		Hace mal tiempo.	*The weather is bad.*
Está nublado.	*It is cloudy.*		Hace sol.	*It's sunny.*
Hace buen tiempo.	*The weather is nice.*		Hace viento.	*It is windy.*
Hace calor.	*It's hot.*		Llueve.	*It rains./It is raining.*
Hace fresco.	*It is cool.*		Nieva.	*It snows./It is snowing.*
Hace frío.	*It's cold.*			

Las estaciones

el invierno	*winter*		la primavera	*spring*
el otoño	*fall*		el verano	*summer*

Los verbos

cerrar (ie)	*to close*		pensar (ie)	*to think*
comenzar (ie)	*to begin*		perder	*to lose*
competir (i)	*to compete*		preferir (ie)	*to prefer*
empezar (ie)	*to begin*		reír (i)	*to laugh*
entender (ie)	*to understand*		repetir (i)	*to repeat*
llevar	*to wear*		querer (ie)	*to want*
mentir (ie)	*to lie*		servir (i)	*to serve*
nevar (ie)	*to snow*		sonreír (ie)	*to smile*
pedir (i)	*to ask for*			

Los colores

see p. 90

Palabras interrogativas

see pp. 93–94

Learning Strategy

Participate

Participate in class. You can't learn another language by simply observing. You have to be willing to actively use it, and to learn from the mistakes you make.

In this chapter you will learn how to:

- Describe your town or city
- Describe your house
- Tell what you and others are going to do in the near future
- Request information about the cost of things

¿Dónde vives?

© PhotoLink/JupiterImages

Exploraciones gramaticales

The verb **estar** with prepositions

The verb **ir** and **ir** + **a** + infinitive

Stem-changing verbs (**o → ue**)

Adjective placement

En vivo

Un directorio para turistas

Casas en venta

Conexiones culturales

Ciudades fuera de lo común

Casas únicas

Lectura

Algunas ciudades únicas de Latinoamérica

Soluciones para la vivienda en Cuba

▶ Exploraciones profesionales

La arquitectura

El señor Ramírez tiene media hora para ir al banco y hacer otras diligencias. ¿Qué más necesita hacer en el centro de la ciudad?

Otros lugares

el bar	bar	el mercado	market
el club	club	la oficina	office
la discoteca	nightclub	el teatro	theater
el edificio	building	el templo	temple
la librería	bookstore	el zoológico	zoo

Los verbos

depositar (dinero)	to deposit (money)
ir	to go
mandar (una carta)	to send (a letter)
mirar una película	to watch a movie
rezar	to pray

Práctica

4.1 **Escucha y responde** Vas a escuchar algunos lugares. Indica con el pulgar hacia arriba si es posible hacer ejercicio en el lugar. Si no, indica con el pulgar hacia abajo.

CD1-18

INVESTIGUEMOS EL VOCABULARIO
The suffix **-ería** is often used to indicate stores where certain products are sold. What is sold in the following stores?
chocolatería
frutería
papelería
tortillería

4.2 **¿Cierto o falso?** Decide si las oraciones son ciertas o falsas. Corrige las oraciones falsas.

1. C F En la biblioteca compramos libros.
2. C F En la discoteca miramos animales.
3. C F Nadamos en la piscina.
4. C F Miramos películas en el cine.
5. C F En el parque compramos medicinas.
6. C F Estudiamos y aprendemos en la tienda.
7. C F En la plaza caminamos y miramos a las otras personas.
8. C F Mandamos cartas en el banco.

4.3 **¡Adivina dónde estoy!** Vas a jugar en un grupo de tres estudiantes. Imagínate que estás en un lugar dentro de la ciudad. Los otros dos tienen que hacer diez preguntas para adivinar (*to guess*) dónde estás, pero sólo puedes responder **sí** o **no.** Túrnense.

Modelo Estudiante 1: *¡Adivina dónde estoy!*
Estudiante 2: *¿Comes en este lugar* (place)*?*
Estudiante 1: *No.*
Estudiante 3: *¿Hay libros y mesas?*
Estudiante 1: *Sí.*

4.4 **Conversemos** Entrevista a tu compañero con las siguientes preguntas.

1. ¿Con qué frecuencia visitas un parque?
2. ¿Cuál es tu supermercado preferido? ¿Por qué?
3. ¿Hay un banco cerca de tu casa? ¿Cómo se llama?
4. ¿Te gusta ir al cine? ¿Qué películas prefieres? (cómicas, de horror, de acción)
5. ¿Cuál es tu restaurante favorito?
6. ¿En qué tienda prefieres comprar tu ropa?
7. ¿Adónde prefieres ir con tus amigos?
8. ¿Te gusta ir a museos? ¿Qué tipo de museo es tu favorito? (de historia, arte, etcétera)

4.5 **¿Con qué frecuencia...?** Para cada actividad, habla con un compañero diferente y pregúntale con qué frecuencia la hace.

Modelo visitar al doctor en el hospital
Estudiante 1: *¿Con qué frecuencia visitas al doctor en el hospital?*
Estudiante 2: *Visito al doctor en el hospital una vez al año.*

1. comprar comida en el mercado
2. rezar en el templo (la iglesia/la sinagoga/la mezquita)
3. leer en la biblioteca
4. mirar películas en el cine
5. visitar el parque
6. depositar cheques en el banco
7. visitar un zoológico
8. bailar en la discoteca

> **INVESTIGUEMOS EL VOCABULARIO**
>
> When saying how many times you do something, use the word **vez.**
>
> **una vez a la semana**
> *once a week*
>
> **dos veces al mes**
> *two times a month*
>
> To say you never do something, use the word **nunca** in front of the conjugated verb.
>
> Yo **nunca** voy al museo.
> *I **never** go to the museum.*

¿Qué anuncios para servicios y lugares crees que puedes encontrar en un directorio para turistas? Lee el siguiente directorio. ¿Qué tipo de lugares hay en el directorio? ¿Cómo se llama el museo de arte en la Avenida Morelos? ¿Qué es "La mano mágica"? ¿Cuántas galerías hay y dónde están?

Source: Galleries and Museums from Tourist Brochure, Oaxaca, Mexico

Más allá

Trabaja con un compañero para inventar otro anuncio para el directorio. Deben pensar en lo siguiente:

¿Qué tipo de lugar es? ¿Cómo se llama? ¿Dónde está?
Si es posible, incluyan ilustraciones o fotos.

Exploraciones gramaticales

A analizar

Las siguientes oraciones describen la ciudad en la página 112. Lee las oraciones y contesta las preguntas que siguen.

El hotel **está** en la calle Santiago.

El hotel **está** enfrente de la iglesia.

El parque **está** detrás de la biblioteca y la sinagoga.

El hotel **está** a la izquierda del restaurante.

El gimnasio **está** a la derecha del cine.

El correo y el banco **están** entre la iglesia y el museo.

El parque **está** lejos de la iglesia.

1. You learned some of the forms of the verb **estar** in **Capítulo 1.** The boldfaced verbs are also forms of the verb **estar.** From what you have already learned and looking at the examples above, fill in the following chart.

   estar

   yo _____   nosotros(as) _____

   tú _____   vosotros (as) _____

   él, ella, usted _____   ellos, ellas, ustedes _____

2. In **Capítulo 1** you used **estar** to tell how someone is doing. How is **estar** used here?

A comprobar

The verb **estar** with prepositions of place

Las preposiciones de posición

a la derecha de	*to the right of*	**en**	*in, on, at*
a la izquierda de	*to the left of*	**encima de**	*on top of*
al lado de	*beside, next to*	**enfrente de**	*in front of, facing*
cerca de	*near*	**entre**	*between*
debajo de	*below*	**fuera de**	*outside*
dentro de	*inside*	**lejos de**	*far from*
detrás de	*behind*		

1. Notice that most of the prepositions include the word **de** (*of*).

   You will remember from **Capítulo 2** that the **de** in front of a masculine noun combines with **el** to become **del** (**de** + **el** = **del**), and that it does not contract with the other articles.

Mi casa está al lado **del** café.
My house is next to the café.

El cine está a la derecha **de** la tienda.
The movie theater is to the right of the store.

2. The verb **estar** is used to express position; therefore, it is used with all prepositions of place.

estar (*to be*)			
yo	**estoy**	nosotros(as)	**estamos**
tú	**estás**	vosotros(as)	**estáis**
él, ella, usted	**está**	ellos, ellas, ustedes	**están**

A practicar

4.6 **¿Qué hacen?** Lee las oraciones y menciona las actividades que las personas hacen en el lugar donde están.

1. Yo estoy en la plaza.

2. Mis hijos están en la escuela.

3. Tú estás en la librería.

4. Mi esposa está en la oficina.

5. Mis amigos están en el café.

6. Mi hermano está en el correo.

7. Mi madre y yo estamos en el parque.

8. Tú estás en el banco.

4.7 **¿Dónde están?** Lee las descripciones y completa las oraciones con la forma apropiada del verbo **estar** y un lugar del vocabulario. Hay varias posibilidades.

Modelo Hay muchos niños. Ellos... *están en la escuela./están en el parque./están en la plaza./ están en el zoológico.*

1. Hay música. Tú...

2. Hay comida (*food*). Yo...

3. Hay muchos libros. Los estudiantes...

4. Hay medicinas. El doctor...

5. Hay escritorios. Nosotros...

6. Hay muchas personas que rezan. La familia...

4.8 **En la capital** Completa las oraciones con la forma correcta del verbo **estar.** Luego, usa los mapas al principio del libro para identificar los países donde están las ciudades.

Modelo Mario ___está___ en Santiago. *Está en Chile.*

1. Yo _____ en Lima.

2. Usted _____ en San José.

3. Gloria y yo _____ en La Habana.

4. Joaquín y Héctor_____ en San Juan.

5. Hugo _____ en Caracas.

6. Tú _____ en Tegucigalpa.

7. Cristina _____ en Quito.

8. Los Gardel _____ en Buenos Aires.

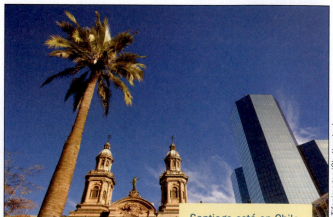

Santiago está en Chile.

4.9 **En la ciudad** Mira el plano, escucha la descripción de la ciudad y decide si cada oración es cierta o falsa. Corrige las oraciones falsas.

CD1-19

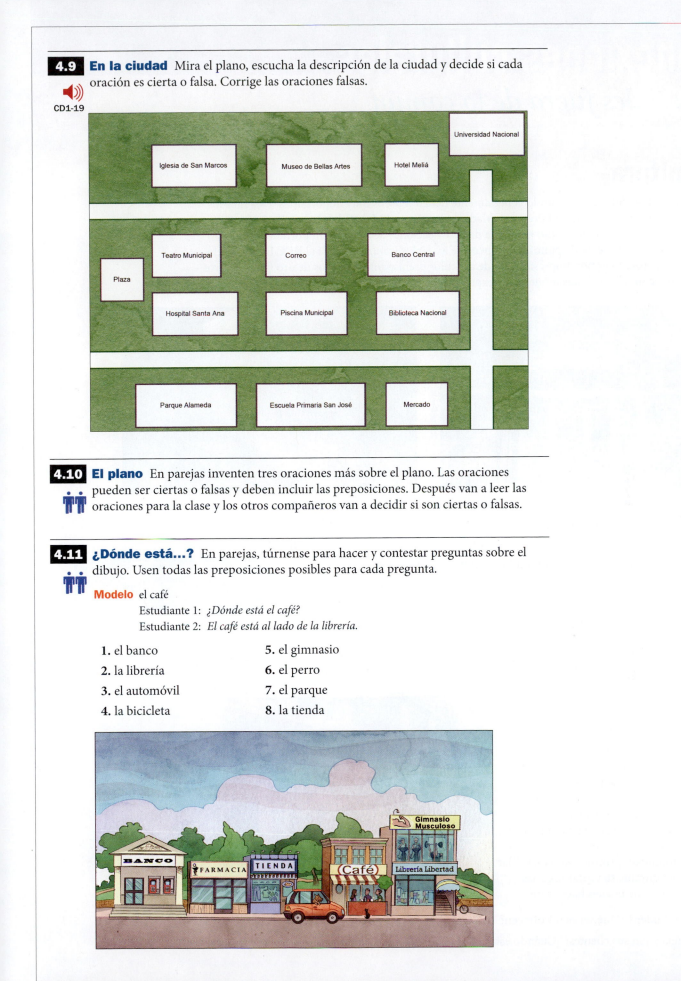

Iglesia de San Marcos

Museo de Bellas Artes

Hotel Meliá

Universidad Nacional

Plaza

Teatro Municipal

Correo

Banco Central

Hospital Santa Ana

Piscina Municipal

Biblioteca Nacional

Parque Alameda

Escuela Primaria San José

Mercado

4.10 **El plano** En parejas inventen tres oraciones más sobre el plano. Las oraciones pueden ser ciertas o falsas y deben incluir las preposiciones. Después van a leer las oraciones para la clase y los otros compañeros van a decidir si son ciertas o falsas.

4.11 **¿Dónde está...?** En parejas, túrnense para hacer y contestar preguntas sobre el dibujo. Usen todas las preposiciones posibles para cada pregunta.

Modelo el café

    Estudiante 1: *¿Dónde está el café?*
    Estudiante 2: *El café está al lado de la librería.*

1. el banco
2. la librería
3. el automóvil
4. la bicicleta

5. el gimnasio
6. el perro
7. el parque
8. la tienda

BANCO   FARMACIA   TIENDA   Café   Gimnasio Musculoso   Librería Libertad

Conexiones culturales
Ciudades fuera de lo común

Cultura

Las grandes ciudades del mundo generalmente tienen museos muy importantes. Dos museos de fama internacional son El Prado en Madrid, España, y el Museo del Oro en Bogotá, Colombia. El Museo del Prado tiene una de las colecciones de arte más importantes del mundo, especialmente de pintores europeos de los siglos (*centuries*) XVI al XIX. El Museo del Oro tiene una colección impresionante de artículos prehispánicos hechos de oro (*gold*) y otros metales, con instalaciones modernas y exposiciones con multimedia.

El Museo del Prado en Madrid

El Museo del Oro en Bogotá

¿De qué artistas crees que hay cuadros en El Prado?

¿Qué civilizaciones prehispánicas crees que están representadas en el Museo del Oro?

¿Qué otros museos de todo el mundo son muy famosos y por qué?

¿Tienes un museo favorito? ¿Cuál? ¿Por qué?

> Investiga en Internet los sitios web oficiales del Museo del Prado y del Museo del Oro.

Comunidad

En las grandes ciudades casi siempre hay áreas con negocios (*businesses*) de comida y productos étnicos. ¿Hay negocios en tu comunidad que sirvan a hispanos, por ejemplo una tienda, un restaurante o una iglesia? Visita uno de estos lugares. Luego, repórtale a la clase sobre tu experiencia. Comenta sobre las semejanzas y las diferencias entre ese negocio y otros negocios de tu comunidad. ¡Aprovecha para hablar español durante tu visita! Algunas preguntas que puedes hacer son:

El barrio chino en Lima, Perú

¿Qué venden? ¿Qué servicios ofrecen?

¿Quiénes son sus clientes? ¿Cuándo está abierta la tienda/el restaurante?

Comparaciones

Las ciudades prehispánicas tenían mucho en común con las ciudades modernas. En la actualidad se conservan muchas ciudades de culturas prehispánicas, como Teotihuacán en México, Tikal en Guatemala y Machu Picchu en Perú. ¿Qué tipo de edificios crees que había en estas ciudades prehispánicas? Por ejemplo, ¿piensas que había supermercados?

Observa el mapa de la Ciudad de Machu Picchu, una ciudad inca en las montañas de los Andes. ¿Hay algún edificio que no haya en tu ciudad? Busca información de los pueblos hopi en Arizona en Internet. ¿Es semejante (*similar*) a Machu Picchu?

Source: http://www.enjoyperu.com/guiadedestinos/machupicchu/mapas

Conexiones... a las relaciones internacionales

Muchas ciudades del mundo participan en un programa de ciudades hermanas. La Asociación Internacional de Ciudades Hermanas es una organización que promueve el respeto mutuo, el entendimiento y la cooperación. Por ejemplo, Miami, Florida, es ciudad hermana de Managua, Nicaragua. El objetivo del programa es conectar a dos ciudades semejantes (*similar*) en superficie, pero en diferentes zonas del mundo, para fomentar el contacto humano. ¿Cuál es la ciudad hermana de la capital de tu estado? ¿Qué actividades y eventos tienen?

A analizar

Lee la conversación y observa las formas del verbo **ir**. Luego, contesta las preguntas que siguen.

> **Rosa:** Los sábados tengo la mañana muy ocupada. Primero, **voy** al banco para depositar un cheque. Del banco, **voy** al correo. Y finalmente, **voy** al mercado para comprar unas frutas.
>
> **Dora:** ¿A qué hora **vas** al banco este sábado? Si quieres, yo te acompaño. Yo también necesito **ir** al correo y al mercado. Y después, **vamos** al Café Rústico en la plaza para tomar algo.
>
> **Rosa:** ¡Qué buena idea! ¡**Vamos!**

© michaeljung/Shutterstock

1. The forms **voy, vas,** and **vamos** in the conversation above are forms of the verb **ir.** Is the verb regular like **vivir** or irregular like **ser**? Explain why.

2. Using the forms presented in the conversation and what you already know about verbs, complete the chart. Why do you think in the phrase **necesito ir,** the verb **ir** is not conjugated?

   ir

yo _____	nosotros _____
tú _____	vosotros _____
él, ella, usted _____	ellos, ellas, ustedes _____

A comprobar

The verb **ir** and **ir** + **a** + infinitive

ir (*to go*)

yo	**voy**	nosotros(as)	**vamos**
tú	**vas**	vosotros(as)	**vais**
él, ella, usted	**va**	ellos, ellas, ustedes	**van**

1. To tell where someone is going, it is necessary to use the preposition **a** (*to*). When asking where someone is going, the preposition **a** is added to the word **dónde** (**adónde**).

   ¿Adónde van ustedes?
   Where are you going?

   Vamos **a** la universidad.
   *We are going **to** the university.*

2. You will recall that just as there are contractions in English (can't, don't), there are also contractions in Spanish, and that in Spanish these contractions are not optional. Similar to the contraction **del**, when using the preposition **a** in front of a masculine noun, it combines with the **el** to form the contraction **al** (**a** + **el** = **al**). The **a** does not contract with the other articles.

   Yo voy **al** cine con mis amigos.
   I am going to the movie theater with my friends.

   Mi familia va **a la** piscina hoy.
   My family is going to the pool today.

3. Similar to English, the verb **ir** can be used to talk about the future. To tell what someone is *going to do,* use the following structure:

ir	+ a +	infinitive
Voy	a	viajar.
Van	a	trabajar.

Vamos a estudiar esta noche.
We are going to study tonight.

Juan **va a ir** al café con Elena.
Juan is going to go to the café with Elena.

A practicar

4.12 **¿Lógico o ilógico?** Lee las siguientes oraciones y decide si son lógicas o no. Si son ilógicas, haz las correcciones.

1. Yo voy a la librería porque necesito estudiar.

2. Mis padres van al teatro porque quieren mirar una película.

3. Mi hermana va a la tienda porque quiere comprar una blusa.

4. Mis amigos y yo vamos al correo para comer.

5. ¿Tú vas a la piscina para nadar?

6. Mis abuelos van a la sinagoga para rezar.

iTunes
Julieta Venegas is a popular Mexican singer, songwriter, and musician. Listen to her song "Me voy". Why do you think she is leaving?

4.13 **Después de las clases** Completa el párrafo con la forma correcta del verbo **ir.**

Después de las clases, mis compañeros **(1)** _____ a casa, y yo **(2)** _____ a la biblioteca con mi amigo Fernando. Nosotros **(3)** _____ al café después para tomar algo. Luego, él **(4)** _____ a su casa, y yo **(5)** _____ al trabajo. ¿Adónde **(6)** _____ tú después de las clases?

4.14 **Las diligencias** Usando el vocabulario y el verbo **ir,** explica adónde van las siguientes personas.

Modelo Tú necesitas comprar un libro. Tú...
        Vas a la librería.

1. Yo necesito depositar un cheque. Yo...

2. Mis hijos tienen clase hoy. Ellos...

3. Mi hermana trabaja como doctora. Ella...

4. Mi esposo y yo estudiamos español. Nosotros...

5. Tú tienes una clase de aeróbic. Tú...

6. Tus amigos y tú quieren ver una película. Ustedes...

7. Mis tíos escriben cartas a sus familiares en Perú. Ellos...

8. A mi sobrino le gustan mucho los animales. Él...

9. Mis padres y yo queremos comer. Nosotros...

10. Tú quieres nadar. Tú...

4.15 **¿Adónde vas y qué vas a hacer?** Usando la forma apropiada del verbo **ir** y el vocabulario, explica adónde van las diferentes personas. Luego, explica qué van a hacer, usando **ir + a + infinitivo.**

Modelo Rosario
Rosario va al zoológico. Va a mirar los animales.

1. yo

2. mis amigos

3. la señora Montero

4. tú

5. Ricardo y yo

6. tu perro y tú

4.16 **¿Qué vas a hacer mañana?** Pregúntale a tu compañero qué va a hacer mañana a las siguientes horas.

Modelo 2:00 P.M.
Estudiante A: *¿Qué vas a hacer (to do) mañana a las dos de la tarde?*
Estudiante B: *Yo voy a correr en el parque.*

1. 8:00 A.M.   **5.** 3:30 P.M.

2. 10:30 A.M.   **6.** 6:45 P.M.

3. 12:00 P.M.   **7.** 8:15 P.M.

4. 1:15 P.M.   **8.** 10:00 P.M.

El reloj del Arco de Santa Catalina, Antigua, Guatemala

© Vulkanette/Shutterstock

4.17 **De vacaciones** Imagínense que van a viajar a Panamá por un fin de semana. Miren el anuncio y decidan qué van a hacer. Pueden usar las siguientes palabras para planear sus actividades. Mencionen por lo menos tres cosas que van a hacer.

la playa (*beach*)   **bucear** (*to scuba dive*)

jugar al golf (*to play golf*)   **hacer piragüismo** (*to go whitewater rafting*)

tomar un crucero (*to take a cruise*) **tomar el sol** (*to sunbathe*)

Modelo Estudiante 1: *¿Adónde vamos a ir el sábado por la mañana?*
Estudiante 2: *Vamos a ir a la playa.*
Estudiante 1: *¿Qué vamos a hacer en la playa?*
Estudiante 2: *Vamos a nadar y a tomar el sol. Yo voy a tomar fotos.*

Panamá es un destino de renombre para negocios y convenciones, quédate unos días más y conviértelo en una experiencia inolvidable.

Panama
se queda en ti

http://www.atp.gob.pa/

4.18 **Tiempo libre** Con un compañero, túrnense para preguntar adónde van en las siguientes situaciones y qué van a hacer.

Modelo Es domingo y no tienes mucha tarea.
Estudiante 1: *Es domingo y no tienes mucha tarea. ¿Adónde vas?*
Estudiante 2: *Voy al templo.*
Estudiante 1: *¿Qué vas a hacer?*
Estudiante 2: *Voy a rezar.*

1. Mañana no hay clase y no necesitas trabajar.

2. La clase de español termina (*ends*) a las diez, y tu siguiente clase comienza a las doce.

3. Son las vacaciones de primavera y vas a recibir un cheque de $800 de los impuestos (*taxes*).

4. Es sábado y hace buen tiempo.

5. Tú recibes un cheque de $50 dólares por tu cumpleaños.

6. Es viernes por la noche.

Lectura

Antes de leer

¿Qué cosas hay en todas las grandes ciudades? ¿Cómo piensas que son las capitales de España y los países latinoamericanos?

A leer

Algunas ciudades únicas de Latinoamérica

they were

La mayoría de las grandes ciudades latinoamericanas combina lo moderno con lo histórico. Algunas de las ciudades **fueron** fundadas mucho antes de la llegada de los españoles, como es el caso de la Ciudad de México (Tenochtitlán), y de Cuzco, capital del imperio Inca en Perú. Hoy día en las dos ciudades se pueden ver ruinas de civilizaciones indígenas al lado de edificios coloniales de unos 400 años de antigüedad.

[Un elegante ejemplo de modernidad se encuentra en Buenos Aires...]

skyscrapers

bridges

Por supuesto, las ciudades más grandes en Latinoamérica tienen **rascacielos** y otras maravillas de la ingeniería, como **puentes** y avenidas de circulación rápida.

Un elegante ejemplo de modernidad se encuentra en Buenos Aires, la capital de Argentina y su ciudad más importante, con más de doce millones de habitantes. "Baires",

as

como la llaman los argentinos, fue fundada en 1536, con el nombre original de "Puerto de Nuestra Señora Santa María del Buen Aire". Los barrios de la ciudad reflejan su pasado de inmigrantes. Es una ciudad cosmopolita y llena de cultura. Es famosa por sus monumentos, como el obelisco, y por tener la

widest

avenida **más ancha** del mundo: la Avenida 9 de julio.

La Boca, Buenos Aires

© Margarita Casas

beautiful

Otra ciudad moderna y de **hermosa** arquitectura es Bogotá. La ciudad de Bogotá es la capital de Colombia y en 2006 fue declarada "capital del libro del mundo" por la UNESCO, gracias a las increíbles bibliotecas de la ciudad.

Cada una de estas ciudades es especial por su arquitectura, sus monumentos, parques, restaurantes, cafés, tiendas y boutiques. Sin duda, como muchas otras ciudades latinoamericanas, son muy atractivas para el turismo.

Bogotá, Colombia

Comprensión

Contesta las preguntas.

1. ¿Qué combinan muchas de las ciudades de Latinoamérica?
2. ¿Cómo se llamaba la capital del imperio Inca en Perú?
3. ¿Cómo llaman los argentinos a su capital?
4. ¿Por qué es famosa Buenos Aires?
5. ¿Por qué fue declarada "la capital del libro del mundo" Bogotá?

Después de leer

Busca una página en Internet con información para turistas en una ciudad de España o Latinoamérica. Después, contesta las preguntas.

1. ¿Qué actividades puedes hacer?
2. ¿Te gustaría visitar la ciudad? ¿Por qué?

Turistas en Caracas

Esta es la casa de Lola. ¿Qué hay en su casa?

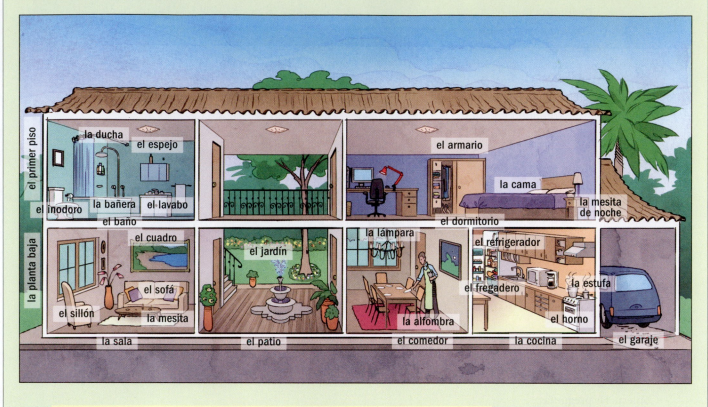

alquilar	*to rent*	**el horno de**	*microwave oven*
el apartamento	*apartment*	**microondas**	
la cafetera	*coffee maker*	**la lavadora**	*washer*
las cortinas	*curtains*	**el lavaplatos**	*dishwasher*
el electrodoméstico	*appliance*	**los muebles**	*furniture*
las flores	*flowers*	**las plantas**	*plants*
la habitación	*room*	**la secadora**	*dryer*

Práctica

4.19 **Escucha y responde** Vas a escuchar algunas oraciones. Indica con el pulgar hacia arriba si la oración es lógica. Si no, indica con el pulgar hacia abajo.

🔊 CD1-20

4.20 **¿Dónde están?** ¿En qué habitación de la casa están los siguientes muebles o aparatos?

1. el horno
2. el sillón
3. el lavabo
4. el lavaplatos
5. el armario
6. la cafetera
7. la mesita de noche
8. la cama

INVESTIGUEMOS EL VOCABULARIO

Notice that **el primer piso** refers to what people in the United States would call the second floor. In many Spanish-speaking countries the first floor is referred to as the ground floor, or **la planta baja.**

INVESTIGUEMOS EL VOCABULARIO

While **el dormitorio** is a very standard word, there are many other words that refer to a bedroom:

el cuarto (Mexico)

la habitación (Mexico, Spain)

la pieza (Mexico)

la alcoba (South America)

la recámara (Latin America)

4.21 **¡Qué desastre!** La casa es un desastre y no puedes encontrar nada. Con un compañero, túrnense para preguntar dónde están los objetos perdidos.

Modelo la corbata
Estudiante 1: *¿Dónde está la corbata?*
Estudiante 2: *Está en la cama.*

1. el teléfono
2. el libro
3. la bota
4. el suéter

5. el paraguas
6. el cuaderno
7. los peces
8. el gato

4.22 **Adivinanza** Mira el dibujo al inicio de la lección. Vas a elegir y a describir tres objetos en dos o tres oraciones. No debes mencionar el objeto en tu descripción. Usa **es para** para describir la función del aparato. Con un compañero túrnense para adivinar el objeto que el otro describe.

Modelo Estudiante 1: *Está en la cocina. Está debajo de la estufa. Es para cocinar.*
Estudiante 2: *¡Es el horno!*

4.23 **Comparemos** Mira una de las casas mientras tu compañero mira la otra. Túrnense para describir las casas y busquen seis diferencias.

Modelo Estudiante 1: *En el baño de Alberto hay un espejo.*
Estudiante 2: *En el baño de Laura no hay espejos.*

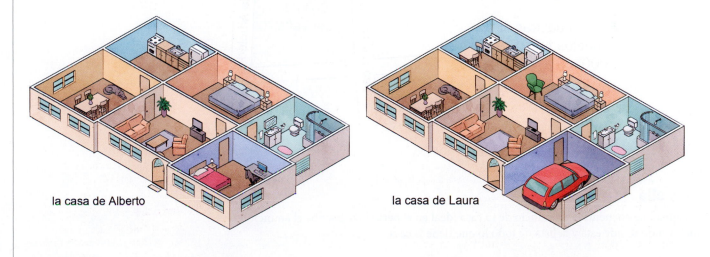

la casa de Alberto

la casa de Laura

¿Qué información hay en la sección de anuncios para apartamentos y casas en el periódico (*newspaper*)? Estos son anuncios para unas casas en venta en Ponce, Puerto Rico. La casa en el modelo Bugambilia tiene dos baños y medio. ¿Qué crees que es un medio baño? ¿Qué piensas que significa "estacionamiento cubierto"? ¿Cuál de las dos casas prefieres? ¿Por qué?

URBANIZACIÓN COLINAS DEL VALLE

CASAS EN VENTA

En una de las mejores zonas de Ponce, cerca de parques y un centro comercial

Modelo Bugambilia
- 3 habitaciones
- 2 baños y medio
- cocina integral
- sala-comedor amplia
- acabados de lujo
- estacionamiento cubierto para un auto

Modelo Rosal
- 4 habitaciones
- 2 baños
- cocina con desayunador
- sala
- comedor
- acabados de lujo
- terraza
- estacionamiento para un auto

Todo lo que necesita para vivir cómodamente.

Visite nuestras casas modelos todos los días de 9:00 am a 9:00 pm.

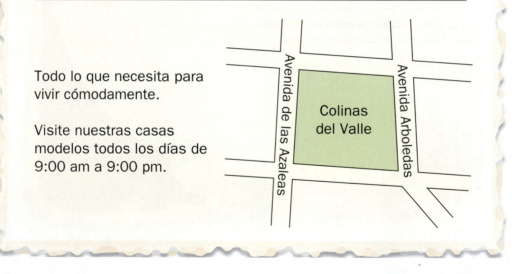

Más allá

Imagina que encuentras el anuncio de tu casa ideal en el periódico. Escribe el anuncio incluyendo dónde está y la lista de todo lo que tiene la casa.

Exploraciones gramaticales

A analizar

Lee la conversación y observa las formas del verbo **poder**.

El estudiante:	¿Cuándo **puedo** ver el apartamento?
La señora:	¿**Puede** venir usted a las tres y media?
El estudiante:	Tengo clase hasta las cuatro. ¿**Podemos** encontrarnos a las cuatro y media?
La señora:	Está bien. Nos vemos a las cuatro y media.
El estudiante:	Perfecto. Hasta luego.

Using your knowledge of stem-changing verbs and the forms in the conversation, complete the chart with the correct forms of the verb **poder**.

poder

yo _____	nosotros(as) _____
tú _____	vosotros (as) _____
él, ella, usted _____	ellos, ellas, ustedes _____

A comprobar

Stem-changing verbs (o → ue)

1. In **Capítulo 3,** you learned about stem-changing verbs. Notice in the verbs below, that the **o** changes to **ue** in all forms except the **nosotros** and **vosotros** forms. Again, the endings are the same as other **-ar, -er,** and **-ir** verbs.

dormir (*to sleep*)

yo	d**ue**rmo	nosotros(as)	dormimos
tú	d**ue**rmes	vosotros(as)	dormís
él, ella, usted	d**ue**rme	ellos, ellas, ustedes	d**ue**rmen

almorzar (*to eat lunch*)

yo	alm**ue**rzo	nosotros(as)	almorzamos
tú	alm**ue**rzas	vosotros(as)	almorzáis
él, ella, usted	alm**ue**rza	ellos, ellas, ustedes	alm**ue**rzan

The verbs listed below are also **o → ue** stem-changing verbs.

costar	*to cost*
devolver	*to return* (*something*)
encontrar	*to find*
llover	*to rain*
morir	*to die*
poder	*to be able to*
recordar	*to remember*
soñar (con)	*to dream* (*about*)

volver (*to return*)

yo	v**ue**lvo	nosotros(as)	volvemos
tú	v**ue**lves	vosotros(as)	volvéis
él, ella, usted	v**ue**lve	ellos, ellas, ustedes	v**ue**lven

© kristian sekulic/Shutterstock

Los niños **duermen** en este dormitorio.
*The children **sleep** in this bedroom.*

Gloria y yo **almorzamos** en la cafetería.
*Gloria and I **eat lunch** in the cafeteria.*

2. The verb **jugar** is conjugated similarly to the **o → ue**
stem-changing verbs, changing the **u** of its stem to **ue**.

jugar *(to play)*			
yo	**ju**ego	nosotros(as)	jugamos
tú	**ju**egas	vosotros(as)	jugáis
él, ella, usted	**ju**ega	ellos, ellas, ustedes	**ju**egan

A practicar

4.24 **Un poco de lógica** ¿Qué verbo completa mejor la oración?

1. Matilde siempre _____ a la casa después de trabajar.
   a. llueve   **b.** vuelve   **c.** almuerza

2. Los niños _____ con el gato en la sala.
   a. juegan   **b.** sueñan   **c.** encuentran

3. Nosotros _____ en la cocina.
   a. dormimos   **b.** volvemos   **c.** almorzamos

4. Rolando no _____ sus libros en el dormitorio.
   a. sueña   **b.** encuentra   **c.** vuelve

5. Mis amigos _____ mirar la tele en la sala.
   a. juegan   **b.** cuestan   **c.** pueden

6. Mi esposo y yo _____ en una cama matrimonial.
   a. dormimos   **b.** podemos   **c.** encontramos

7. Yo _____ el espejo al dormitorio de mi hermana.
   a. encuentro   **b.** vuelvo   **c.** devuelvo

8. Mi habitación es un desastre y no _____ dónde está mi tarea.
   a. recuerdo   **b.** puedo   **c.** duermo

¿Dónde está mi tarea?

© Photos To Go

4.25 **Nuestros sueños** Completa el siguiente párrafo con las formas necesarias del verbo **soñar.**

Todos tienen sueños (*dreams*) para el año nuevo. Yo **(1)** _____ con un trabajo,

y mi esposo **(2)** _____ con comprar un coche nuevo. Nosotros también

(3) _____ con comprar una casa nueva. Mis hermanos **(4)** _____ con unas

vacaciones en la playa. Y tú ¿con qué **(5)** _____?

¿Sueñas con comprar un coche?

© Monkey Business Images/Shutterstock

4.26 ¿Cuánto cuesta? Estás en una tienda en España. Con un compañero, túrnense para preguntar cuánto cuestan los objetos.

> **Modelo** Estudiante 1: *¿Cuánto cuesta el cuadro grande?*
> Estudiante 2: *Cuesta treinta y cinco euros.*

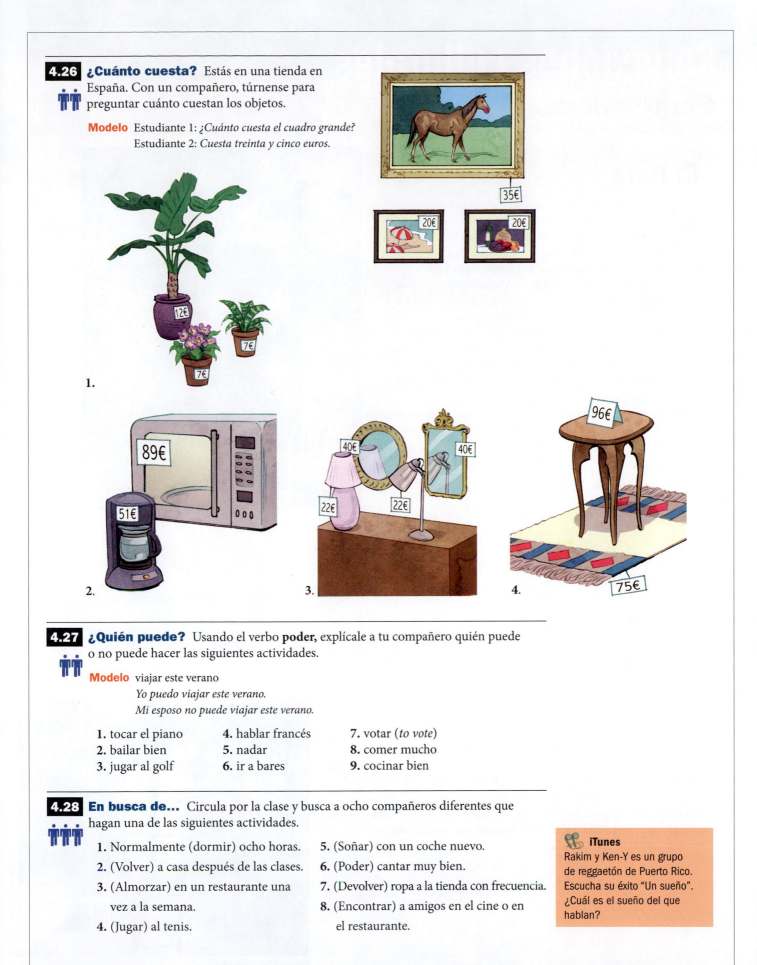

1.

2.

3.

4.

4.27 ¿Quién puede? Usando el verbo **poder,** explícale a tu compañero quién puede o no puede hacer las siguientes actividades.

> **Modelo** viajar este verano
> *Yo puedo viajar este verano.*
> *Mi esposo no puede viajar este verano.*

1. tocar el piano
2. bailar bien
3. jugar al golf
4. hablar francés
5. nadar
6. ir a bares
7. votar (*to vote*)
8. comer mucho
9. cocinar bien

4.28 En busca de... Circula por la clase y busca a ocho compañeros diferentes que hagan una de las siguientes actividades.

1. Normalmente (dormir) ocho horas.
2. (Volver) a casa después de las clases.
3. (Almorzar) en un restaurante una vez a la semana.
4. (Jugar) al tenis.
5. (Soñar) con un coche nuevo.
6. (Poder) cantar muy bien.
7. (Devolver) ropa a la tienda con frecuencia.
8. (Encontrar) a amigos en el cine o en el restaurante.

iTunes
Rakim y Ken-Y es un grupo de reggaetón de Puerto Rico. Escucha su éxito "Un sueño". ¿Cuál es el sueño del que hablan?

Cultura

Es común que las casas de personas famosas se conviertan en (*are converted to*) museos. Por ejemplo, Hernán Cortés, el conquistador español que derrotó (*defeated*) a los aztecas en México, tuvo casas en muchas ciudades de México, y también en España. Probablemente una de las más conocidas es la Primera Casa de Hernán Cortés, en Veracruz, México. Este edificio, que se considera un monumento histórico, está en restauración y es un sitio turístico muy popular.

Ernesto "Ché" Guevara, famoso revolucionario que participó en la Revolución Cubana, también vivió en varias casas que ahora lo homenajean (*pay tribute to him*). Una de las más populares es el Museo Casa del Ché en Alta Gracia, Argentina donde vivió de niño.

Otras casas de personas muy famosas son las siguientes. Busca en Internet para decir quiénes fueron (*were*) estas personas y dónde están sus casas.

La Casa-Museo de Federico García Lorca

La Casa de Pablo Neruda

La Casa-Museo Quinta de Simón Bolívar

© John Mitchell/Alamy

Primera Casa de Hernán Cortés

🌐 Investiga en Internet acerca de otras casas famosas en España y Latinoamérica.

Comunidad

¿Hay casas famosas en tu comunidad? ¿Por qué son famosas?

Visita una casa famosa en tu pueblo o en tu ciudad, o una que esté cerca de ti. Luego, prepara un folleto (*brochure*) con la dirección del museo, las horas y los días que está abierto, recomendaciones de qué ver en el museo, servicios, etcétera. Después, comparte la información con los administradores de la casa famosa, para usarla con los visitantes que hablen español.

© Juan José Pascual/Age Fotostock

Museo Casa del Ché

Comparaciones

Una expresión común en la cultura mexicana es "Mi casa es su casa". Otro ejemplo es "Candil (*lamp*) de la calle, obscuridad de su casa", que se usa para hablar de una persona que es muy amable con las personas fuera de su casa, pero no con las de su familia. Los siguientes son otros refranes (*proverbs*) que se refieren a la casa. ¿Cuál de las fotos asocias con cada refrán? ¿Por qué? ¿Qué valores reflejan? ¿Estás de acuerdo con ellos? ¿Hay equivalentes en inglés?

Casa sin hijos, higuera (*fig tree*) sin higos (*figs*).
Cuando de casa estamos lejanos, más la recordamos.
En la casa en que hay un viejo, no faltará (*lack*) un buen consejo (*advice*).
La ropa sucia (*dirty*) se lava en casa.

¿Cuáles son algunos refranes en inglés que hablan de la casa? ¿Qué valores reflejan? ¿Reflejan valores semejantes o diferentes a los refranes en español?

Conexiones... a la arquitectura

Algunos de los arquitectos más famosos del mundo son Antonio Gaudí (Barcelona, España, 1852–1926) y Luis Barragán (Cd. de México, México, 1902–1988). Antonio Gaudí era un hombre muy religioso. Su obra maestra (*masterpiece*) es la Catedral de la Sagrada Familia, en Barcelona, que todavía está en construcción. Su arquitectura es considerada modernista, pero su estilo es único en el mundo. En contraste, la arquitectura del mexicano Luis Barragán se caracteriza por líneas muy simples y por el uso del color. ¿Qué estilo prefieres? ¿Tienes un arquitecto o un estilo arquitectónico favorito? ¿Quién o cuál?

Casa Milà en Barcelona, una obra de Gaudí

Una fuente diseñada por el arquitecto Luis Barragán

A analizar

Lee el anuncio e identifica los adjetivos. Después contesta las preguntas que siguen.

> Apartamento grande en buena zona, en el primer piso, dos habitaciones amplias y un baño, a buen precio.

1. Where are the adjectives in relation to the nouns they describe? Why do you think the position of the adjectives varies?

2. Which ones have different forms?

A comprobar

Adjective placement

1. As you remember from **Capítulo 2,** other than adjectives of quantity, adjectives are generally placed behind the noun they modify. However, there are some other exceptions. **Bueno** and **malo** are often used in front of the noun they modify, and they drop the **o** when used in front of a masculine singular noun.

> Hace **mal** tiempo.
> *The weather is bad.*
>
> Ella es una **mala** estudiante.
> *She is a bad student.*
>
> Hace **buen** tiempo.
> *The weather is nice.*
>
> Ella es una **buena** estudiante.
> *She is a good student.*

2. Ordinal numbers are numbers that designate position in a sequence (first, second, third, etc.). As with other numbers, ordinal numbers go before the noun they modify. However, they must agree in gender and number. Similar to **bueno** and **malo, primero** and **tercero** drop the **o** when they are used in front of a masculine singular noun.

> El baño está en el **primer** piso.
> *The bathroom is on the first floor.*

Es la **primera** habitación a la derecha.
It's the first bedroom on the right.

Vivo en el **tercer** piso.
I live on the third floor.

Es la **tercera** casa en la calle Rosas.
It's the third house on Rosas Street.

Los números ordinales	
1° primero	6° sexto
2° segundo	7° séptimo
3° tercero	8° octavo
4° cuarto	9° noveno
5° quinto	10° décimo

3. **Grande** can be used in front of a noun; however, its meaning normally changes from *big* to *great*. **Grande** becomes **gran** when used in front of singular nouns.

> Tengo una casa **grande.**
> *I have a **big** house.*
>
> El presidente es un **gran** hombre.
> *The president is a **great** man.*

A practicar

4.29 **Casa Bonita** La tienda Casa Bonita vende muebles, electrodomésticos y otras cosas para la casa. Lee las oraciones y decide si son lógicas o no. Corrige las oraciones ilógicas.

5º dormitorio
4º baño
3º cocina
2º sala
1º jardín

1. Hay refrigeradores en el tercer piso.
2. Hay sofás en el quinto piso.
3. Hay camas en el segundo piso.
4. Hay bañeras en el cuarto piso.
5. Hay hornos en el segundo piso.
6. Hay plantas y flores en el primer piso.

4.30 **El edificio de apartamentos** Con un compañero, túrnense para preguntar e identificar en qué piso viven las diferentes familias en el edificio de apartamentos.

Modelo Estudiante 1: *¿Dónde vive la familia García?*
Estudiante 2: *La familia García vive en la planta baja.*

10º Castillo
9º Cisneros
8º Pérez
7º Casas
6º Gutiérrez
5º Fuentes
4º Álvarez
3º Duarte
2º Rodríguez
1º Gómez
PB García

INVESTIGUEMOS EL VOCABULARIO
In English, to write ordinal numbers using numerals you use 1st, 2nd, 3rd, 4th, etc. In Spanish, when the ordinal number is masculine and ends in **o (primero, segundo, tercero)**, it is written as 1º, 2º, 3º. If it is feminine and ends in an **a (primera, segunda, tercera)**, it is written 1ª, 2ª, 3ª.

4.31 **Unas descripciones** Completa las oraciones, usando el adjetivo entre paréntesis. Piensa en la posición del adjetivo y en la forma correcta.

> **Modelo** Compro un refrigerador. (nuevo)
> *Compro un refrigerador nuevo.*
> Es la habitación a la derecha. (primero)
> *Es la primera habitación a la derecha.*

1. Carmen busca un apartamento. (grande – *big*)
2. Quiero un sofá. (negro)
3. No tengo cuadros. (mucho)
4. Tenemos una planta. (pequeño)
5. Hay rebajas (*sales*) en el departamento de electrodomésticos hoy. (grande – *great*)
6. Es una lavadora. (bueno)
7. Ella va a comprar una alfombra. (nuevo)
8. Esa tienda vende armarios. (bonito)
9. El gato está en el piso. (tercero)

4.32 **En la universidad** En parejas, contesten las siguientes preguntas. Respondan usando los adjetivos de la lista. ¡**OJO** con la concordancia y la posición de los adjetivos!

bueno   malo   interesante   aburrido   viejo   simpático   moderno

antipático   grande   pequeño   primero   tercero   segundo

> **Modelo** Estudiante 1: *¿Cómo es tu libro de matemáticas?*
> Estudiante 2: *Es un buen libro./Es un mal libro.*

1. ¿Cómo es tu universidad?
2. ¿Cómo son los profesores en la universidad?
3. ¿Cómo son los estudiantes en la universidad?
4. ¿Cuál es tu primera clase del día?
5. ¿Cómo es tu clase de español?
6. ¿Qué tipo de estudiante eres?
7. ¿Qué tipo de notas recibes?
8. ¿En qué piso del edificio está tu clase de español?

4.33 **Opiniones** Con un compañero, túrnense para expresar sus opiniones sobre las siguientes personas y cosas. Deben usar los dos elementos indicados y un adjetivo.

> **Modelo** Antonio Banderas / actor
> *Antonio Banderas es un buen actor. / Antonio Banderas es un actor guapo.*

1. el profesor de español / profesor
2. el presidente / hombre
3. el Parque Central / parque
4. Jessica Alba / mujer
5. El Prado / museo
6. *Don Quijote de la Mancha* / libro
7. la clase de español / clase
8. La Casa Blanca / edificio
9. yo / (persona, estudiante, ¿?)

Antonio Banderas es un buen actor.

© cinemafestival/Shutterstock

Redacción

You are going to write a letter to a pen pal in which you tell him or her about where you live. One approach to descriptive writing is to begin with a general idea and to then become more specific. That is what you will do in this letter. In the first paragraph, you will discuss the town or city where you live; in the second paragraph you will describe your house in general, and in the last paragraph you will discuss your favorite room in the house.

Paso 1 Jot down as many adjectives as you can think of that you would use to describe the town or city where you live. Write a list of the things your town or city has to offer: businesses, museums, etc.

Paso 2 Jot down as many phrases as you can about your home in general. Think about the following questions: Do you live in an apartment or a house? Whom do you live with? How would you describe your house (color, big, old, comfortable, etc.)? What rooms are in your house?

Paso 3 Decide which room you like best in your house. Jot down as many phrases as you can about that room. Think about the following questions: Why is it your favorite room? What items do you like in that room? How much time do you spend there? What do you do there?

Paso 4 After your greeting, begin your first paragraph by telling where you live. Then develop the paragraph in which you describe your city or town using the ideas you generated in **Paso 1**.

Paso 5 Write a transition sentence in which you tell where your house is located, such as the street you live on or what you live near. Then, develop the rest of the paragraph in which you describe your house using the information you generated in **Paso 2**.

Paso 6 Begin your third paragraph with a transition sentence that connects the second paragraph with the new idea to be discussed (your favorite room).

> **Modelo** *Hay muchas habitaciones en mi casa, pero mi habitación favorita es la sala.*

Paso 7 Develop the rest of the paragraph using the ideas you generated in **Paso 3**. Be sure to have a concluding statement at the end of the third paragraph. At the end of your letter, ask your pen pal two or three questions about where he/she lives.

Paso 8 Edit your essay:

1. In each paragraph, do all of your sentences support the topic sentence?
2. Are your paragraphs logically organized or do you skip from one idea to the next?
3. Are there any short sentences you can combine by using **y** or **pero**?
4. Are there any spelling errors?
5. Do your adjectives agree with the objects they describe?
6. Do your verbs agree with their subjects?

Lectura

Antes de leer

En general, ¿cómo son las casas en la ciudad donde vives? ¿Es fácil comprar o alquilar una casa? ¿Por qué? ¿Cuál es una ventaja (*advantage*) de este sistema? ¿y una desventaja (*disadvantage*)?

A leer

Soluciones para la vivienda en Cuba

right

Tener una vivienda es una necesidad básica para todos. En Cuba, la vivienda es considerada un **derecho.** Para las personas en Cuba, el costo de la vivienda no es un problema grande. El valor de una casa vendida por el Estado es de aproximadamente US$300, que se deben pagar a 30 años por crédito bancario. El costo al mes es aproximadamente de US$0.60. Se calcula que el 85% de los cubanos son **propietarios** de sus casas. Además los cubanos también pueden alquilar hasta dos habitaciones de su casa para suplementar su economía.

> [En Cuba, la vivienda es considerada un derecho.]

owners

Nevertheless

Sin embargo, el problema de la vivienda es un gran **reto** para este país: hay un déficit de más de 600 000 casas.

challenge

Unas viviendas en La Habana

© Joel Blit/Shutterstock

have damaged

to move
exchange

Además, en los últimos años, varios huracanes **han dañado** muchas otras viviendas que ahora necesitan reparaciones. Obtener una casa en Cuba es muy difícil debido al limitado número de viviendas, pero una vez que se tiene una casa, si una familia quiere **mudarse** a otro lugar, puede **intercambiar** su casa por la de otra familia. Este sistema puede causar problemas cuando una pareja decide tener hijos o quiere divorciarse.

En Cuba las familias pueden intercambiar sus casas.

En años recientes, debido a la dificultad que el gobierno tiene para construir viviendas, está invitando a los ciudadanos a construir sus propias casas, pero no hay una solución fácil ni rápida para proveer viviendas a todos los cubanos que las necesitan.

Comprensión

1. ¿Cuánto cuestan las casas que vende el gobierno en Cuba?
2. ¿Qué pueden hacer los cubanos en sus casas para ganar dinero extra?
3. ¿Por qué es muy difícil encontrar donde vivir en Cuba?
4. ¿Qué tiene que hacer una persona en Cuba para mudarse a otra casa?

Después de leer

Para los turistas que desean visitar Cuba hay varias posibilidades además de los hoteles: pueden alquilar apartamentos o casas que existen específicamente para el turismo.

Imagínate que vas a visitar Cuba con un compañero de clase y van a quedarse en un apartamento para turistas. Escriban una lista de las cosas que quieren tener en el apartamento. Luego, busquen en Internet un apartamento para turistas en Cuba y contesten las preguntas.

1. ¿Tiene todo lo que desean?
2. ¿Por qué te gusta ese apartamento?

Aquí vamos a hacer la entrada del garaje.

© Junial Enterprises/Shutterstock

Vocabulario

Sustantivos

la calefacción central	*central heat*
los cimientos	*foundation*
el (la) dueño(a)	*owner*
la entrada	*entrance*
la fecha de inicio	*starting date*
la finalización	*completion*
el frente	*façade*
la grúa	*crane*
el ladrillo	*brick*
la maqueta	*scale model*
el plano	*plan*

Adjetivos

apurado(a)	*in a hurry*
construido(a)	*built*
creativo(a)	*creative*
preparado(a)	*ready, prepared*
retrasado(a)	*late*

Verbos

cavar	*to dig*
conectar	*to connect*
demoler	*to demolish*
diseñar	*to design*
instalar	*to install*
construir	*to built*

Frases útiles

Con vista a...
With view to . . .

Les presento el nuevo proyecto.
I'm pleased to introduce the new project.

¿Cuántos pisos tiene el edificio?
How many stories are in the building?

El edificio tiene cien unidades.
The building has one hundred units.

Estas son las dimensiones.
These are the dimensions.

Usamos materiales de primera calidad.
We use top-quality materials.

¡Manos a la obra!
Let's get to work!

DATOS IMPORTANTES

Educación: Estudios universitarios completos en arquitectura. Experiencia en compañías constructoras. Capacidad de trabajo en equipo.

Salario: Entre $100 000 y $200 000, dependiendo de la responsabilidad del proyecto de construcción.

Dónde se trabaja: Compañías constructoras, Departamento de Obras Públicas del gobierno, contratistas, consultorías.

Briana Vásquez es arquitecta y trabaja para una importante compañía constructora. Su función es estar a cargo de (*in charge of*) la obra de construcción de edificios de apartamentos. También debe comunicarse con los dueños del edificio. En el video vas a ver a la arquitecta Vásquez mientras habla con uno de los dueños.

Antes de ver

Los arquitectos desarrollan (*develop*) los proyectos de construcción. Luego supervisan a los trabajadores de la construcción para realizar los planos a la perfección.

1. ¿En qué tipo de proyectos trabaja un arquitecto?
2. Imagínate que quieres construir un edificio. ¿Qué preguntas le haces al arquitecto?

Comprensión

1. ¿Qué tipo de apartamentos quiere ofrecer el Sr. Sierra?
2. ¿Qué vista tienen los apartamentos de tres habitaciones?
3. ¿Cómo son los apartamentos de dos habitaciones?
4. ¿Cuántos pisos va a tener el edificio?
5. ¿Qué va a estar al lado de la entrada principal del edificio?
6. ¿Cuándo es la fecha de finalización de la construcción?

© Heinle/Cengage Learning

Después de ver

En grupos pequeños, representen una reunión entre un arquitecto asociado, un trabajador que es el jefe de construcción y un dueño. El dueño piensa construir un edificio de apartamentos. Hagan un diálogo entre las tres personas. Deben decirle al arquitecto lo que quieren tener en su apartamento. El arquitecto puede hacer preguntas específicas.

4.34 **En casa** Completa el párrafo con la forma apropiada del verbo entre paréntesis.

Toda la familia (**1.**) _____ (estar) en casa hoy. Mi esposa y yo (**2.**) _____ (estar) en la cocina. Nosotros siempre (**3.**) _____ (almorzar) a esta hora, y hoy (**4.**) _____ (ir) a preparar unos sándwiches. Los niños (**5.**) _____ (estar) en casa también. Ellos no (**6.**) _____ (poder) jugar en el jardín porque (**7.**) _____ (llover) hoy. Vicente (**8.**) _____ (dormir) en su habitación, y Marisa (**9.**) _____ (jugar) unos videojuegos en la sala. Después de (*After*) comer, mis hijos (**10.**) _____ (ir) al cine con sus amigos, y mi esposa (**11.**) _____ (ir) al supermercado. Creo que yo (**12.**) _____ (ir) a mirar una película aquí en casa.

4.35 **¿Qué van a hacer?** Menciona qué van a hacer estas personas según el tiempo que hace donde viven. Deben usar el futuro (**ir** + **a** + infinitivo).

1. Yo vivo en Antigua y llueve hoy.
2. Kenia vive en Santo Domingo y hace buen tiempo hoy.
3. Yago y Matilde viven en Granada y nieva hoy.
4. Zoila y yo vivimos en Tegucigalpa y hace calor hoy.
5. Hugo y Marisabel viven en Caracas y hace mal tiempo hoy.
6. Cándido vive en Asunción y hace mucho frío hoy.
7. Yo vivo en Bogotá y hace fresco hoy.
8. Ulises vive en La Paz y hace viento hoy.
9. Renata y yo vivimos en San Juan y hace sol hoy.
10. ¿Dónde vives tú? ¿Qué tiempo hace? ¿Qué vas a hacer hoy?

4.36 **Completa las ideas** Completa las siguientes oraciones con la palabra o frase correcta.

1. Hoy voy a _____ ropa nueva.
   (**compro/comprar**)
2. Mi amiga _____ también.
   (**va a ir/va ir**)
3. Vamos a La Galería, una tienda enfrente _____ correo.
   (**de el/del**)
4. En La Galería la ropa no _____ mucho.
   (**costa/cuesta**)
5. La ropa de mujer está en el _____ piso.
   (**primer/primero**)
6. Quiero encontrar una chaqueta _____.
   (**negro/negra**)
7. Ella busca _____.
   (**zapatos bonitos/bonitos zapatos**).
8. Luego _____ almorzar en un restaurante.
   (**podemos/puedemos**)

4.37 **¿Es cierto?** Observa la ilustración de la casa y escribe seis oraciones ciertas o falsas sobre el dibujo (*drawing*). Después, túrnate con un compañero para leer las oraciones y decidir si son ciertas o falsas, y corregir (*correct*) las falsas.

Modelo Estudiante 1: *Hay tres dormitorios.*
Estudiante 2: *Falso, hay dos dormitorios.*
Estudiante 2: *La cocina está a la derecha del comedor.*
Estudiante 1: *Cierto.*

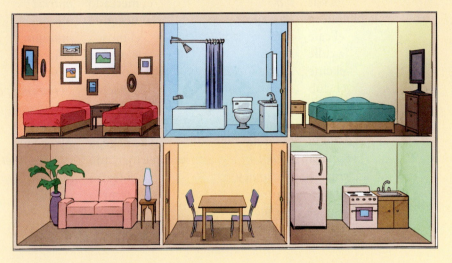

4.38 **Cinco diferencias** Trabaja con un compañero. Uno mira el dibujo aquí y el otro mira el dibujo en el apéndice A. Túrnense para describirlos y buscar cinco diferencias.

🔊 Vocabulario 1
CD1-21

Los lugares

el banco	*bank*		el hotel	*hotel*
el bar	*bar*		el mercado	*market*
la biblioteca	*library*		la mezquita	*mosque*
el café	*cafe*		el museo	*museum*
la calle	*street*		la oficina	*office*
el cine	*movie theater*		el parque	*park*
el club	*club*		la piscina	*swimming pool*
el correo	*post office*		la plaza	*city square*
la discoteca	*nightclub*		el restaurante	*restaurant*
el edificio	*building*		la sinagoga	*synagogue*
la escuela	*school*		el supermercado	*supermarket*
la farmacia	*pharmacy*		el teatro	*theater*
el gimnasio	*gym*		el templo	*temple*
el hospital	*hospital*		la tienda	*store*
la iglesia	*church*		el zoológico	*zoo*
la librería	*bookstore*			

Los verbos

depositar	*to deposit*		mandar	*to send*
ir	*to go*		rezar	*to pray*

Palabras adicionales

la carta	*letter*		la película	*movie*
el dinero	*money*			

Las preposiciones

a la derecha de	*to the right of*		en	*in, on, at*
al lado de	*beside, next to*		encima de	*on top of*
a la izquierda de	*to the left of*		enfrente de	*in front of*
cerca de	*near*		entre	*between*
debajo de	*under*		fuera de	*outside*
dentro de	*inside*		lejos de	*far from*
detrás de	*behind*			

Diccionario personal

_____

_____

_____

_____

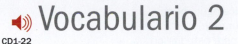

Vocabulario 2

CD1-22

Habitaciones de la casa

el baño	bathroom		el garaje	garage
la cocina	kitchen		el jardín	garden
el comedor	dining room		el patio	patio
el dormitorio	bedroom		la sala	living room

Muebles, utensilios y aparatos electrodomésticos

la alfombra	carpet		el inodoro	toilet
el armario	closet, armoire		la lámpara	lamp
la bañera	bathtub		el lavabo	bathroom sink
la cafetera	coffee maker		la lavadora	washer
la cama	bed		el lavaplatos	dishwasher
las cortinas	curtains		la mesita	coffee table
el cuadro	painting, picture		la planta	plant
la ducha	shower		el refrigerador	refrigerator
el espejo	mirror		la secadora	dryer
la estufa	stove		el sillón	armchair
la flor	flower		el sofá	couch
el fregadero	kitchen sink			
el horno	oven			
el horno de microondas	microwave oven			

Los verbos

almorzar (ue)	to have lunch		jugar (ue)	to play
alquilar	to rent		llover (ue)	to rain
costar (ue)	to cost		morir (ue)	to die
devolver (ue)	to return (something)		poder (ue)	to be able to
			recordar (ue)	to remember
dormir (ue)	to sleep		soñar (ue) (con)	to dream (about)
encontrar (ue)	to find		volver (ue)	to come back

Los números ordinales

See page 134

Palabras adicionales

el apartamento	apartment		el piso	floor
la habitación	room		la planta baja	ground floor
el mueble	furniture			

Diccionario personal

_____

_____

Exploraciones literarias

© Stan Honda/AFP/Newscom

Claribel Alegría
Biografía
Claribel Alegría (1924–) nació en Estelí, Nicaragua, pero cuando era muy joven su familia se mudó (*moved*) a El Salvador. En 1943 viajó a Estados Unidos para estudiar en la Universidad George Washington, donde recibió su título en Filosofía y Letras. Ha publicado varios libros de poesía y narrativa además de testimonios históricos. Una de las grandes influencias en sus obras fue la Guerra Civil en El Salvador (1980–1992). Ahora vive en Managua, Nicaragua.

Antes de leer

1. Mira el título. En tu opinión ¿de qué va a tratar el poema?
2. Examina el poema. ¿Cuáles son las palabras que se usan para expresar el tiempo en el poema?

Instantes

Sólo éste ahora es mío
este momento
el pasado escapó
glimpse the face   y no **vislumbro el rostro** del futuro.

© Piers Cavendish / Impact / HIP / The Image Works

Authorized by the author, Claribel Alegría.

Después de leer

A. Comprensión

1. Según el poema, ¿qué es más relevante: el pasado, el presente o el futuro?
2. ¿Cuál es el mensaje del poema?
3. ¿Cuál es el tono?
4. Por la biografía sabemos que la Guerra Civil en El Salvador influenció la vida y la obra (*life and work*) de Claribel Alegría. ¿Es obvia esta influencia en el poema?

B. Conversemos

¿Qué eventos o experiencias personales pueden influenciar la vida y la obra de una persona?

Investiguemos la literatura: El tono

The tone of a work refers to the attitude that a writer communicates toward a particular subject through the work. It can be playful, formal, angry, loving, etc. You can often identify the tone of a work by paying attention to the author's word choice. Does the author use words or expressions that are positive, negative, or neutral?

Antes de leer

1. Lee el título del poema. ¿De qué piensas que va a hablar?
2. Ahora lee el poema rápidamente, sin usar el diccionario. ¿Qué palabras entiendes? ¿Cambió (*changed*) tu respuesta a la primera pregunta?

No pienses en mañana

No pienses en mañana
ni me hagas promesas
the same   ni tú serás **el mismo**
ni yo estaré presente.
peak   Vivamos **juntos la cima** de este amor
deceit   sin **engaños**
sin miedo
transparentes.

Authorized by the author, Claribel Alegría.

Después de leer

A. Comprensión

1. ¿Cuál es el tono del poema?
2. ¿Cuáles son algunas palabras clave (*key*)?
3. ¿Con quién está hablando la voz poética?
4. ¿Cuál es el mensaje (*message*) del poema? ¿Estás de acuerdo? ¿Por qué?
5. ¿Por qué dice (*says*) que no debe pensar en mañana?
6. ¿Piensas que hay relación entre el poema "No pienses en mañana" y el primer poema "Instantes"? ¿Por qué?

B. Conversemos

1. ¿Te gustan estas* [*these*] poesías? ¿Por qué?
2. En tu opinión, ¿es más importante el pasado, el presente o el futuro? ¿Por qué?

Learning Strategy

Guess intelligently

When you are listening to audio recordings or your instructor, or are watching a video, make intelligent guesses as to the meaning of words you do not know. Use the context, intonation, and if possible, visual clues such as body language, gestures, facial expressions, and images to help you figure out the meaning of words.

In this chapter you will learn how to:

- Describe your feelings, emotions, and physical states
- Talk about ongoing actions
- Discuss abilities needed for certain jobs and professions

¿Estás feliz en el trabajo?

© Aaron Mccoy/Getty Images

Exploraciones gramaticales

Estar with adjectives and present progressive

Ser and **estar**

Verbs with changes in the first person

Saber and **conocer**

En vivo

¿Qué sabes de ti?

Las solicitudes de empleo

Conexiones culturales

Las emociones y el bienestar

Las profesiones y la economía

Lectura

¿Quiénes son más felices?

Profesiones poco comunes

▶ **Exploraciones profesionales**

El trabajo social

Laura trabaja en el Café Simón. Es un lugar muy popular en el centro histórico de la ciudad. ¿Cómo están las personas en el café?

está cansado

está triste

está sorprendida

está feliz

está enamorado

está aburrida

está borracho

está enojada

está avergonzado

está preocupada

Los estados de ánimo

estar alegre	to be happy	**estar divertido(a)**	to be entertained, to be in a good mood	**estar frustrado(a)**	to be frustrated
estar celoso(a)	to be jealous			**estar interesado(a)**	to be interested
estar contento(a)	to be happy, to be content	**estar enfermo(a)**	to be sick	**estar ocupado(a)**	to be busy
estar deprimido(a)	to be depressed	**estar equivocado(a)**	to be wrong	**estar sano(a)**	to be healthy
		estar feliz	to be happy	**estar seguro(a)**	to be sure

Práctica

5.1 **Escucha y responde** Escucha los adjetivos de emoción. Indica con el pulgar hacia arriba (*thumbs up*) si es una emoción positiva o con el pulgar hacia abajo (*thumbs down*) si es una emoción negativa.

CD1-23

5.2 **¿Lógica o ilógica?** Indica si las siguientes oraciones son lógicas o ilógicas.

1. Vamos a tener un examen difícil y estamos felices.
2. Tus amigos te preparan una fiesta sorpresa y estás celoso.
3. Nuestro hijo está muy enfermo. Estamos preocupados.
4. Corriste (*You ran*) 15 kilómetros. Estás cansado.
5. Estás sano porque tienes una F en matemáticas.

5.3 **¿Cómo estás?** Con un compañero, túrnense para expresar sus reacciones ante estas situaciones.

Modelo Tienes tres exámenes y recibes una A en todos.
Estudiante 1: *¡Estoy contento! ¿Y tú?*
Estudiante 2: *¡Yo estoy sorprendido!*

1. Vas de vacaciones a las islas Canarias y pierdes tu pasaporte.
2. Tú y tu novio se casan (*get married*) hoy.
3. Recibes una caja (*box*) de chocolates y los comes todos en un día.
4. Necesitas trabajar pero no puedes encontrar un trabajo.
5. Llegas tarde al aeropuerto y pierdes (*miss*) tu vuelo (*flight*).
6. Encuentras a una persona que no conoces (*that you don't know*) en la sala de tu casa.

Estamos contentos.

5.4 **Asociaciones** Habla con un compañero y explícale qué emoción asocias con lo siguiente (*the following*) y por qué.

Modelo la clase de matemáticas
Estoy frustrado porque no comprendo los problemas de matemáticas. /
Estoy feliz porque me gustan las matemáticas.

1. el lunes
2. el verano
3. la clase de historia
4. el examen final
5. el Día de San Valentín
6. el chocolate
7. el templo (la iglesia, la sinagoga, la mezquita)
8. la universidad

5.5 **Entrevista** Con un compañero, túrnense para hacer y contestar las preguntas.

1. ¿Qué te gusta hacer (*to do*) cuando estás cansado?
2. ¿Qué haces para (*in order to*) no estar nervioso antes de un examen?
3. ¿Cómo estás ahora? ¿Por qué?
4. ¿Qué haces para estar sano?
5. ¿Qué hacen las personas cuando están celosas?
6. ¿Qué día de la semana estás muy ocupado? ¿Por qué?

5.6 **Situaciones** Con un compañero, identifiquen la emoción o el estado de ánimo que tiene la persona en el dibujo y expliquen por qué.

Modelo *Está contento porque es su cumpleaños.*

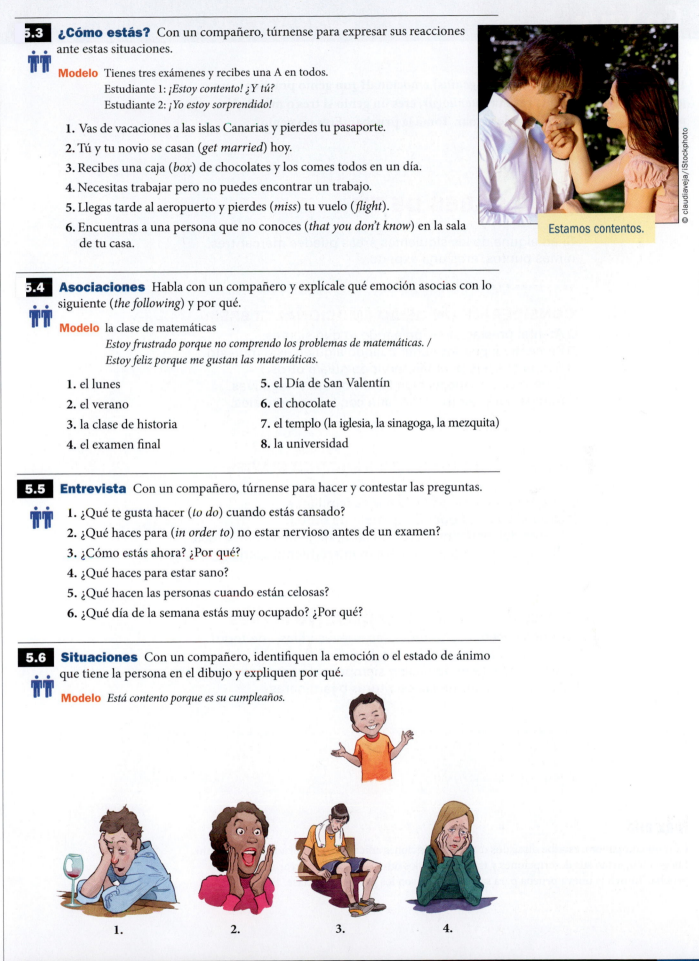

1.   2.   3.   4.

¿Qué tipo de persona es un genio (*genius*) emocional? ¿un genio práctico? ¿un genio creativo? Según la revista *Buenhogar*, eres un genio si tres o más de las acciones describen tu forma de actuar. Toma la prueba. ¿Eres un genio?

¿QUÉ SABES DE TI?

Si en alguna de las siguientes áreas puedes marcar tres o más puntos, eres una experta.

CONSIDÉRATE UN GENIO EMOCIONAL SI ERES:

- ☐ Atenta: prestas atención a todo lo que sientes.
- ☐ Perceptiva: puedes sentir cuando alguien está molesto.
- ☐ Buena consejera: amas servir de guía a otros.
- ☐ Controlada: manejas bien las emociones negativas.
- ☐ Rápida para reír (o llorar): aun con los comerciales.

CONSIDÉRATE UN GENIO PRÁCTICO SI ERES:

- ☐ Una profesional con mapas o direcciones.
- ☐ Coordinadora de las actividades familiares.
- ☐ Organizada: tu hogar es ejemplo de orden.
- ☐ Dueña del estilo: prefieres un corte de pelo simple y fácil de cuidar a uno que requiera mantenimiento diario.

CONSIDÉRATE UN GENIO CREATIVO SI ERES:

- ☐ Curiosa acerca del mundo, las nuevas ideas, ¡de todo!
- ☐ Atenta a lo último (películas, libros, noticias...)
- ☐ Arriesgada: tu imaginación siempre está ocupada.
- ☐ Artista: la mejor de las escritoras o jardineras.

Más allá

Con un compañero, escribe otras dos o tres descripciones adicionales para cada tipo de genio. Luego compartan sus descripciones y trabajen con los otros grupos para crear una nueva prueba. Tomen la nueva prueba para saber quiénes son los genios de la clase.

A analizar

Lee el párrafo y observa los verbos en negritas. Luego, contesta las preguntas que siguen.

Todos están muy ocupados esta tarde. Mi esposo **está trabajando** en la oficina, y mi hijo Bernardo **está corriendo** en el parque. Mi hija Amalia **está escribiendo** una composición en su cuarto. Ella siempre está preocupada por sus notas. Yo **estoy limpiando** la casa.

© claudiaveja/iStockphoto

1. How are the verbs in bold formed?
2. In **Capítulo 4,** you learned to use the verb **estar** to indicate location. Looking at the paragraph again, in what other way is the verb **estar** used?

A comprobar

Estar with adjectives and present progressive

1. Remember that **estar** is an irregular verb:

estar			
yo	**estoy**	nosotros	**estamos**
tú	**estás**	vosotros	**estáis**
él, ella, usted	**está**	ellos, ellas ustedes	**están**

2. Apart from indicating location as you learned in **Capítulo 4,** the verb **estar** is also used to express an emotional, mental, or physical condition.

> Mis padres están felices.
> *My parents **are** happy.*

> Yo estoy cansado hoy.
> *I **am** tired today.*

> Nosotros estamos muy ocupados.
> *We **are** very busy.*

3. The verb **estar** is also used with present participles to form the present progressive. The present progressive is used to describe actions in progress. To form the present participle, add **-ando** (**-ar** verbs) or **-iendo** (**-er** and **-ir** verbs) to the stem of the verb.

> hablar → habl**ando**
> comer → com**iendo**
> vivir → viv**iendo**

> El profesor **está hablando** con Tito ahora.
> *The professor **is talking** to Tito now.*

4. The present participle of the verb **ir** is **yendo.** However, it is much more common to use the present tense of the verb when the action is in progress.

> **Voy** a la iglesia./**Estoy yendo** a la iglesia.
> *I'm going to church.*

5. When the stem of an **-er** or an **-ir** verb ends in a vowel, **-yendo** is used instead of **-iendo.**

> leer – le**yendo**   destruir – destru**yendo**   traer - tra**yendo**

6. Stem changing **-ir** verbs have an irregular present participle. An **e** in the stem becomes an **i**, and an **o** in the stem becomes a **u**.

mentir – m**i**ntiendo	pedir – p**i**diendo
repetir – rep**i**tiendo	servir – s**i**rviendo
dormir – d**u**rmiendo	morir – m**u**riendo

7. In the present progressive, the verb **estar** must agree with the subject; however, you will notice that the present participle does NOT agree in gender (masculine/feminine) or number (singular/plural) with the subject.

Mis hijos están estudiando inglés.
My children are studying English.

Sandra está leyendo su libro de química.
Sandra is reading her chemistry book.

A practicar

5.7 **¿Cierto o falso?** Escucha las oraciones sobre el dibujo y decide si cada oración es cierta o falsa.

CD1-24

5.8 **La fiesta** Estás en una fiesta en la casa de Dalia. Un amigo llama y pregunta qué está pasando en la fiesta. Usa los verbos entre paréntesis en la forma del presente progresivo para explicar qué están haciendo todos.

Modelo yo (hablar por teléfono)
Estoy hablando por teléfono.

1. Dalia (servir la comida)
2. Luis y Alfonso (comer pizza)
3. María Esther (beber una cerveza)
4. Felicia, Marciano y Mateo (jugar a las cartas)
5. Sergio (bailar con su novia)
6. los padres de Dalia (dormir)
7. la hermana de Dalia (leer una novela)
8. el hermano de Dalia (¿?)

5.9 **¿Qué están haciendo?** Con un compañero de clase, decidan dos actividades que estas personas están haciendo.

Modelo Los estudiantes están en la biblioteca.
Están estudiando.
Están buscando libros.

1. El chef Pepín está en la cocina.
2. El presidente está en Camp David.
3. Juanes y Shakira están en el estudio.
4. El profesor de español está en la oficina.
5. David Ortiz está en el parque.
6. Tú estás en la clase de biología.
7. Gabriel García Márquez está en su oficina.
8. Sonia Sotomayor está en Washington, D.C.

El jugador de béisbol, David Ortiz

© Dennis Ku/Shutterstock

5.10 **En la oficina** Usando el presente progresivo, describe lo que están haciendo en la oficina.

Jorge — Eva — Hugo — Delia — Omar — Alma — Paco

5.11 **Un amigo preguntón** Cuando hablas con tu amigo, él siempre empieza la conversación con la pregunta **¿Qué estás haciendo?** Imagínate que tu amigo llama a las siguientes horas. Trabaja con un compañero y contesta su pregunta con diferentes actividades. Túrnense para ser el amigo preguntón.

1. 9:00 de la mañana
2. mediodía
3. 2:00 de la tarde
4. 5:00 de la tarde
5. 8:00 de la noche
6. medianoche

¿Qué estás haciendo?

© Jason Stitt/Shutterstock

Conexiones culturales

Las emociones y el bienestar

Cultura

Algunos grandes artistas produjeron (*produced*) obras de arte en períodos de tristeza y depresión. La pintora mexicana Frida Kahlo (1907–1954) es famosa por sus autorretratos (*self-portraits*), los que muestran su sufrimiento (*suffering*). Cuando tenía 17 años, tuvo un accidente en un tranvía (*streetcar*) y se fracturó la espina dorsal y varios huesos (*bones*). Como resultado, pasó mucho tiempo en el hospital, nunca pudo tener hijos y sufrió de dolor (*pain*) por el resto de su vida (*life*).

Como muchos de los pintores de ese tiempo, el pintor español Francisco de Goya y Lucientes (1746–1828) era pintor de la corte (*court*), y su trabajo era pintar a la familia real (*royal*) y a otros miembros de la aristocracia.

Dos viejos comiendo sopa de Francisco de Goya

© Scala/Art Resource, NY

Private Collection/ © Photo: Jorge Contreras Chacel/ The Bridgeman Art Library

Pensando en la muerte de Frida Kahlo

Después de la invasión de Napoleón y las Guerras Napoleónicas, Goya entró en una gran depresión con una percepción muy negativa de la humanidad. Durante este período, conocido como el Período Negro, pintó una serie de 14 pinturas con temas oscuros (*dark*) y figuras grotescas.

Observa los cuadros de Goya y de Frida Kahlo. ¿Qué emociones producen? ¿Por qué? ¿Qué colores usan los autores?

Investiga en Internet otras obras de Frida Kahlo y Francisco de Goya.

Comunidad

Visita un museo local o uno en el Internet y elige (*choose*) una pintura. ¿Qué hay en la pintura? ¿Qué emociones produce? ¿Cuál es el mensaje de la pintura?

© Shiningcolors/Dreamstime.com

Comparaciones

Con un compañero, discutan en español cinco supersticiones populares en la cultura de ustedes. Después lean la lista de supersticiones del mundo hispano. ¿Hay supersticiones similares a las que discutieron?

1. Pasar por debajo de una escalera (*ladder*) trae mala suerte.
2. Abrir un paraguas dentro de una casa trae mala suerte.
3. Romper un espejo trae siete años de mala suerte.
4. Cruzarse con un gato negro trae mala suerte.
5. Sentir comezón (*itch*) en la mano es señal de que se va a recibir dinero.
6. Para tener un buen año con el dinero, uno debe usar calzoncillos (*underpants*) amarillos para recibir el año nuevo.

Si encontraste (*If you found*) supersticiones parecidas (*similar*), ¿cómo puedes explicar la similitud?

Conexiones... a la literatura

Generalmente, ¿qué emociones puede provocar la poesía? Piensa en un poema que conoces. ¿Qué emociones te provoca?

Salvador Díaz Mirón (1853–1928) fue un periodista (*journalist*), político y poeta de Veracruz, México. Fue uno de los precursores del movimiento modernista. Sus poemas iniciales mostraban fuertes (*strong*) emociones. Desafortunadamente, no se conserva mucho de su obra.

El siguiente es un fragmento de uno de sus poemas. ¿Qué emoción produce? Da ejemplos concretos de las palabras que producen la emoción.

> **iTunes**
> Listen to the song "La Negra Tomasa" by Los Caifanes. What emotions are mentioned in the song?

Rimas

El día con su **manto**	*blanket*
de vívidos colores	
inspira cosas **dulces**:	*sweet*
la risa y la ilusión.	
Entonces la mirada	
se inclina hacia las flores...	
¡Las flores son los versos	
que el **prado** canta al sol!	*meadow*
La noche con su **sombra**,	*shadow*
que deja **ardientes rastros**,	*burning remains*
inspira cosas graves:	
la angustia y la **oración**.	*prayer*
Entonces la mirada	
se eleva hacia los astros...	
¡Los astros son los versos que el cielo canta a Dios!	

A analizar

Lee el párrafo y observa los usos de los verbos **ser** y **estar.** Luego, contesta las preguntas que siguen.

Soy Regina y **soy** de Nueva York. **Estoy** estudiando español en la Universidad Central de Venezuela. **Es** una buena universidad y mis clases **son** interesantes. Ahora **son** las siete de la mañana y **estoy** en la casa de mi familia venezolana. La señora **está** preparando el desayuno en la cocina, y el señor todavía **está** en el hospital. Los dos **son** doctores. ¡Ellos siempre **están** ocupados! Graciela **es** mi hermana venezolana y **es** estudiante en la universidad también. **Es** muy simpática. ¡**Estoy** feliz aquí!

1. What are the uses of **estar** you have learned so far? Find examples in the paragraph.
2. Look at the verb **ser** in the paragraph. What are the different ways in which it is used?

© David Davis/Shutterstock

A comprobar

Ser and estar

1. The verb **ser** is used in the following ways:
   a. to describe characteristics of people, places, or things

   La profesora **es** inteligente.
   *The professor **is** intelligent.*

   Mi coche **es** muy viejo.
   *My car **is** very old.*

   b. to identify a relationship, occupation, or nationality

   Esta **es** mi novia; **es** peruana.
   *This **is** my girlfriend; she **is** Peruvian.*

   Ellos **son** mecánicos.
   *They **are** mechanics.*

   c. to express origin

   Yo **soy** de Cuba.
   *I **am** from Cuba.*

   d. to express possession

   Este libro **es** de Álvaro.
   *This book **belongs** to Álvaro.*

   e. to tell time and give dates

   Es el tres de marzo y **son** las dos.
   *It **is** the third of March, and it **is** two o'clock.*

2. The verb **estar** is used in the following ways:
   a. to indicate location

   El perro **está** enfrente de la casa.
   *The dog **is** in front of the house.*

   b. to express an emotional, mental, or physical condition

   Mi madre **está** enferma hoy.
   *My mother **is** sick today.*

   Las secretarias **están** ocupadas.
   *The secretaries **are** busy.*

   c. in the present progressive

   Estoy estudiando.
   *I **am** studying.*

INVESTIGUEMOS LA GRAMÁTICA

While **estar** is generally used to indicate location, if you want to say where an event takes place, use **ser**.

La fiesta **es** en la casa de Alejandro.
The party is at Alejandro's house.

---

3. It is important to realize that the use of **ser** and **estar** with some adjectives can change the meaning of the adjectives. The use of **ser** indicates a characteristic or a trait, while the use of **estar** indicates a condition. Some common adjectives that change meaning are:

estar aburrido(a)	*to be bored*
ser aburrido(a)	*to be boring*
estar alegre (feliz)	*to be happy* (*emotion*)
ser alegre(feliz)	*to be a happy person*
estar bueno(a)/estar malo(a)	*to be (taste) good/bad (condition)*
ser bueno(a)/ser malo(a)	*to be good/bad (general quality)*
estar guapo(a)	*to look handsome/pretty (condition)*
ser guapo(a)	*to be handsome/pretty (characteristic)*
estar listo(a)	*to be ready*
ser listo(a)	*to be clever*
estar rico(a)	*to be delicious*
ser rico(a)	*to be rich*

Carlos **es** alegre.
Carlos is happy. (a happy person) (personality)
Graciela **está** alegre.
Graciela is happy. (emotion)
La fruta **es** buena.
Fruit is good. (general quality)
Los tomates **están** buenos.
The tomatoes are (taste) good. (present condition)

A practicar

5.12 **¿Es posible?** Mira la foto y lee las oraciones. Decide si es posible o no.

1. Son amigos.
2. Están enojados.
3. Están en la universidad.
4. Son muy viejos.
5. Están hablando.
6. Son de Puerto Rico.

© Alberto L. Pomares G./iStockphoto

5.13 ¿Cómo son o cómo están? Decide cuáles son las formas correctas para terminar las siguientes oraciones. Hay más de una posibilidad para cada oración.

1. Yo estoy…
   a. cansada   b. en clase ahora   c. estudiante   d. enamorado

2. Javier y Marta son…
   a. mis amigos   b. enfermos   c. colombianos   d. enfrente de la clase

3. Madrid es…
   a. en Europa   b. cosmopolita   c. muy bonita   d. la capital de España

4. El profesor de español está…
   a. en la oficina   b. interesante   c. rubio   d. ocupado

5. Nosotros somos…
   a. inteligentes   b. de Chile   c. hermanos   d. preocupados

6. Mis primos son...
   a. profesores   b. cerca de la casa   c. guapos   d. estudiando

7. Tú estás...
   a. mi amigo   b. contenta   c. inteligente   d. detrás del hotel

8. Mi hermano está...
   a. hablando   b. listo   c. peruano   d. viejo

5.14 Una foto En parejas, contesten las preguntas sobre la foto. Inventen la información que no es evidente. **¡OJO!** Atención al uso de los verbos **ser** y **estar**.

© Photos To Go

1. ¿Quiénes son las personas en la foto?
2. ¿Cómo están hoy?
3. ¿Cómo son?
4. ¿De dónde son?
5. ¿Dónde están?
6. ¿Qué están haciendo?

5.15 **¿Ser o estar?** Completa el párrafo con la forma correcta del presente del indicativo de **ser** o **estar**.

Hoy **(1)** _____ el primero de septiembre, el primer día de clases. **(2)** _____ las once y media, y yo **(3)** _____ en la clase de inglés. Yo **(4)** _____ un poco nervioso porque es mi primera clase de inglés. Laura **(5)** _____ mi amiga y ella **(6)** _____ en la clase también. Nosotros **(7)** _____ muy interesados en aprender inglés. El profesor de la clase **(8)** _____ el señor Berg. Él **(9)** _____ alto y delgado y tiene el pelo negro. Es evidente que él **(10)** _____ simpático. Creo que va a **(11)** _____ un buen semestre.

5.16 **¿Cómo eres y cómo estás?** Primero, decide cuáles de los siguientes adjetivos te describen a ti. Luego, pregúntale a tu compañero si esos adjetivos también lo describen a él. Atención al uso de **ser** y **estar** y a las formas de los adjetivos.

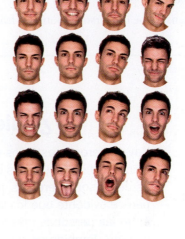
© ZoneCreative/iStockphoto

Modelo contento   Estudiante 1: *¿Estás contento?*
               Estudiante 2: *Sí, estoy contento. /*
               No, no estoy contento.
       rico   Estudiante 1: *¿Eres rica?*
               Estudiante 2: *Sí, soy rica. / No, no soy rica.*

1. enamorado   6. romántico
2. triste   7. enfermo
3. inteligente   8. atlético
4. tímido   9. preocupado
5. cansado   10. optimista

5.17 **Una historia interesante** Con un compañero de clase, escojan uno de los dibujos y describan la escena. Contesten las siguientes preguntas usando los verbos **ser** y **estar.** ¿Quiénes son las personas? ¿Cuál es su relación? ¿Dónde están? ¿Cómo están? ¿Qué está pasando? ¡Sean creativos!

Modelo *El hombre es Tomás y la mujer es Graciela. Son buenos amigos.*
         Están en el hospital porque la madre de Graciela está enferma.
         Ellos están muy preocupados...

Lectura

Reading Strategy: Guessing verb tenses

A useful strategy for understanding a text is to not worry about the exact meaning of a word and to make an educated guess instead. In the case of verbs, if you know the meaning of the verb, you will be able to guess from the context if it refers to the past or to the future. Look at the second paragraph. The verb **publicar** is translated for you. From the context of the paragraph, is the verb used to refer to the past or the future?

Antes de leer

Contesta las preguntas.

1. En general ¿qué necesitas para ser feliz?
2. ¿En qué países piensas que las personas son más felices? ¿Por qué?

A leer

¿Quiénes son más felices?

Hay numerosos estudios sobre la felicidad. Los resultados de estos estudios son diferentes, pero en todos parece evidente que los latinos están entre las personas más felices del planeta. También es evidente que la felicidad no depende del dinero, **sino** de la calidad de las relaciones entre las personas.

but rather

En el 2004, el Worldwatch Institute **publicó** un estudio donde **concluye** que la gente es más rica y más gorda ahora, pero no más feliz. En los Estados Unidos sólo el 39% de las personas piensa que es feliz.

publicar: *to publish*
it concludes

© Monkey Business Images/Shutterstock

El estrés de las personas está relacionado con la necesidad de trabajar muchas horas para poder comprar todo lo que desean. Los estadounidenses trabajan **en promedio** 350 horas más al año que el promedio de los europeos. Es obvio que los estadounidenses están muy ocupados y estresados. **A pesar de** que el estrés puede disminuir la felicidad de la gente, hay

on average

Despite

[**los latinos están entre las personas más felices del planeta**]

que considerar el caso de los mexicanos. En México la gente trabaja más horas en promedio que en los Estados Unidos, pero estudios recientes muestran que los mexicanos están entre las personas más felices del mundo.

Una investigación reciente concluye que los países más felices del planeta son Nigeria y México, seguidos por Venezuela, El Salvador y Puerto Rico. En un estudio un poco posterior siete países latinoamericanos están entre los diez países más felices del mundo: Colombia, Costa Rica, Panamá, Cuba, Honduras, Guatemala y El Salvador. En otro estudio del 2006, Puerto Rico recibió el título de tener a la gente más feliz del planeta. En contraste, muchas de las naciones más industrializadas están en posiciones inferiores en la lista de 178 países: Alemania está en el puesto 81, Japón en el 95, y Estados Unidos en el puesto 150.

© Jacob Wackerhausen/iStockphoto

Aun en los Estados Unidos, los hispanos son el segmento más feliz de la población, a pesar de ganar (como grupo) mucho menos dinero que otros segmentos de la población, y de tener más problemas. Camilo Cruz, experto en el éxito para la comunidad latina residente en los Estados Unidos, explica este fenómeno diciendo que "la felicidad es una decisión personal".

Sources: Redtercermundo.org; Hispanicprwire.com; BBC News

Comprensión

1. En una oración ¿cuál es el tema del artículo?
2. Según el WorldWatch, ¿cuántas personas en los Estados Unidos son felices?
3. Dentro de los Estados Unidos, ¿qué grupo de personas es más feliz en general?
4. ¿Qué países latinoamericanos están en la lista de los más felices?
5. En tu opinión, ¿cómo se puede explicar la generalizada felicidad de los latinos?

Después de leer

Con un compañero, escriban una lista de cuatro o cinco cosas que pueden hacer para ser más felices.

Varios años después de la graduación, Luisa es fotógrafa. Asiste a la reunión para ver a sus compañeros. ¿Qué profesiones tienen ellos?

REUNIÓN DE LA GENERACIÓN DEL 98

la enfermera · el músico · el médico · la mesera · el mecánico · la fotógrafa · el pintor · el actor · la cocinera · el asistente de vuelo · el piloto · el policía · el científico · el deportista

Las profesiones

el (la) abogado(a)	*lawyer*
la actriz	*actress*
el (la) agente de viajes	*travel agent*
el ama de casa	*homemaker*
el (la) arquitecto(a)	*architect*
el bailarín/la bailarina	*dancer*
el (la) cantante	*singer*
el (la) contador(a)	*accountant*
el (la) consejero(a)	*counselor*
el (la) dependiente	*store clerk*
el (la) diseñador(a)	*designer*
el (la) escritor(a)	*writer*
el (la) ingeniero(a)	*engineer*
el jefe/la jefa	*boss*

el (la) maestro(a)	*teacher*
el (la) periodista	*reporter*
el (la) político(a)	*politician*
el (la) psicólogo(a)	*psychologist*
el (la) secretario(a)	*secretary*
el (la) trabajador(a) social	*social worker*
el (la) vendedor(a)	*salesperson*
el (la) veterinario(a)	*veterinarian*

Palabras adicionales

ganar	*to earn; to win*
la entrevista	*interview*
la solicitud	*application; want ad*
el sueldo	*salary*

Práctica

5.18 **Escucha y responde** Vas a escuchar una lista de profesiones. Levanta la mano si una persona que tiene la profesión mencionada lleva uniforme.

CD1-25

5.19 **¿Dónde trabajan?** Relaciona a la persona con su lugar de trabajo.

1. _____ un dependiente
2. _____ un cocinero
3. _____ un pintor
4. _____ un actor
5. _____ un médico

a. un hospital
b. un teatro
c. un restaurante
d. una tienda
e. un estudio

5.20 **¿Qué hacen?** Con un compañero, escriban una actividad que hacen las siguientes personas en su trabajo.

Modelo mesero
Un mesero trae café.

1. maestro
2. secretario
3. enfermero

4. policía
5. ama de casa
6. deportista

5.21 **¿Cuál es su profesión?** ¿Puedes identificar las profesiones de las siguientes personas? Identifica las que sabes (*the ones you know*) y después pregunta a tus compañeros para completar la información. Incluye toda la información adicional posible.

Modelo Jennifer López
Estudiante 1: *¿Cuál es la profesión de Jennifer López?*
Estudiante 2: *Es cantante. También es actriz en* Selena, Gigli *y* El cantante.
Ella es de Puerto Rico.

1. Albert Pujols
2. Carolina Herrera
3. Isabel Allende
4. Antonio Banderas

5. Franklin Chang-Díaz
6. Frida Kahlo
7. Carlos Santana
8. Felipe Calderón

▶ **YouTube**
En tres minutos: Look for Carolina Herrera, Frida Kahlo, or Carlos Santana.

5.22 **Consejero** Imagina que eres consejero y debes recomendarles una profesión a algunos estudiantes, según sus clases favoritas. Túrnate con un compañero.

Modelo las matemáticas y la química
Estudiante 1: *Me gustan las matemáticas y la química. ¿Qué profesión debo estudiar?*
Estudiante 2: *Debes ser científico o ingeniero.*

1. los deportes y la clase de español
2. las clases de historia y de arte
3. la música y bailar
4. la historia y escribir

5. la biología y los animales
6. las lenguas extranjeras y viajar
7. las fiestas y cocinar
8. las leyes (*law*) y la política

5.23 **Veinte preguntas** En grupos de tres, van a turnarse para elegir (*choose*) una profesión sin decir cuál. Tus compañeros van a hacer veinte preguntas para adivinar la profesión. Solamente puedes contestar **sí** o **no.**

Modelo *¿Trabaja en una escuela/oficina/teatro/aeropuerto/ tienda, etcétera?*
¿Trabaja con niños/animales/números, etcétera?
¿Necesita estudiar en la universidad para tener este trabajo?

🎵 **iTunes**
Listen to the Spanish classic "Cuando seas grande" by Argentinian rocker Miguel Mateos. What does the teenager in the song want to be when he grows up?

Cuando buscas un trabajo y lees solicitudes, ¿qué tipo de requisitos (*requirements*) esperas encontrar? Aquí hay unas solicitudes de empleo de un periódico de México. ¿Qué tipo de trabajos ofrecen las solicitudes de empleo? ¿Qué tipo de requisitos tienen? ¿Qué diferencias hay entre estos anuncios y los de los Estados Unidos?

EMPLEO

ARQUITECTO. Empresa solicita Arquitecto o Diseñador. Hombres o mujeres, 25 a 35 años, casado, experiencia programas 3d autocad, etc. Excelente presentación, disponibilidad de horario y para viajar. Interesados comunicarse al 3636-1111 (de 10:00 a 18:00 hrs.).

DEPENDIENTE. Mujer honesta y responsable para trabajar en una óptica en Plaza Fancy, turno completo, sin experiencia y preparatoria terminada. Interesadas enviar curriculum vitae a: plazafancy@empleos.com. Sueldo base $4,000 + Comisión.

CAJERO. Administrador de pizzería, hombre, edad máxima 30 años, zona Ciudad Bugambilias. Contratación Inmediata. Comunicarse al: 3693-9393.

CHOFER particular, buena presentación, experiencia mínima de un año. Llamar al Tel 547-89-4240. Ofrecemos buen sueldo y vacaciones pagadas.

SE Solicita Ama de Casa. Para atender señor solo. Tardes libres. Informes al 345-0900- 2636.

CHOFER. Hotel en Puerto Vallarta solicita chofer de camioneta. Requisitos: Inglés indispensable, disponibilidad de horario para rotar turnos, actitud de servicio. Interesados presentar solicitud en Avenida Hidalgo 7002, en horario de oficina.

CHOFER. Repartidor/Motociclista. Requisitos: 30–40 años, casado, excelente conocimiento de la ciudad, licencia de chofer y motociclista vigentes. Informes al 901-3600-3164.

DENTISTA o pasante para trabajo en clínica dental de Ortodoncia. Turno completo, sexo femenino. Informes al 987- 5567-8133 a mandar curriculum o: ortodoncia@jalisco.com.

EJECUTIVO(A) de ventas con experiencia, auto compacto y disponibilidad para viajar, 25–35 años. Ofrecemos producto de primera necesidad para la industria hotelera, sueldo base más comisión, y prestaciones de ley. Interesados enviar c.v con foto a: gerencia@hotelería.com.

ENFERMERA(O). General/técnica, indispensable cédula profesional. Edad: 25–45 años, estado civil indistinto, experiencia comprobable de tres años. Sueldo según aptitudes. Enviar curriculum a: recursoshumanos@hospital SanJosé.com.

MESEROS y cantineros. Ambos sexos. Requisitos: experiencia mínima de 3 años, excelente presentación, disponibilidad de horario. Presentarse con curriculum o solicitud elaborada en Restaurante Bar Arcoiris, centro histórico, teléfono 987-6543-4571.

RECEPCIONISTA. Requisitos: responsable y con iniciativa, disponibilidad de horario, trato amable, buena presentación, preferentemente soltera, sexo femenino, edad 23 a 35 años, manejo de PC, paquete Office. Citas al Tel: 541-5959-6283, extensión 345 (Recursos humanos).

SE solicita Maestro de Yoga. Experiencia mínima de un año, de 20 a 35 años, interesados llamar al cel: 044-33 3403-3466.

Source: Want ads from Mexican newspaper.

Más allá

Con un compañero escribe una solicitud para un trabajo en otra profesión. Luego compartan su solicitud con otros grupos. ¿Qué profesiones de las otras solicitudes te interesan a ti?

Exploraciones **gramaticales**

A analizar

Lee el párrafo y observa las formas de los verbos.

Yo soy fotógrafo y trabajo para una revista. ¡Me gusta mucho mi trabajo! Siempre vengo a la oficina a las ocho y pongo todo en orden. Durante el día conduzco a diferentes lugares y veo a personas interesantes. Además tengo suerte porque salgo de viaje con frecuencia.

Look at the paragraph again and find the first person (**yo**) form of the following verbs.

venir   **poner**   **ver**   **conducir**   **salir**

A comprobar

Verbs with changes in the first person

1. Some verbs in the present tense are irregular only in the first person (**yo**) form. You have already seen the verb **hacer.**

hacer (*to do, to make*)	
hago	hacemos
haces	hacéis
hace	hacen

The verb **hacer** is used in the following expressions:

hacer la cama *to make the bed*	**hacer** ejercicio *to exercise*
hacer una pregunta *to ask a question*	**hacer** diligencias *to run errands*
hacer un viaje *to take a trip*	

2. The following verbs also have irregular first person forms:

poner (*to put, to set*)	**pongo,** pones, pone, ponemos, ponéis, ponen
salir (*to go out, to leave*)	**salgo,** sales, sale, salimos, salís, salen
traer (*to bring*)	**traigo,** traes, trae, traemos, traéis, traen
conducir (*to drive*)	**conduzco,** conduces, conduce, conducimos, conducís, conducen
dar (*to give*)	**doy,** das, da, damos, dais, dan
ver (*to see*)	**veo,** ves, ve, vemos, veis, ven

3. The following verbs are not only irregular in the first person form, but also have other changes:

decir (*to say, to tell*)	
digo	decimos
dices	decís
dice	dicen

venir (*to come*)	
vengo	venimos
vienes	venís
viene	vienen

seguir (*to follow, to continue*)	
sigo	seguimos
sigues	seguís
sigue	siguen

oír (*to hear*)	
oigo	oímos
oyes	oís
oye	oyen

A practicar

5.24 **¿Quién soy?** Decide quién hace las siguientes actividades.

> **Modelo** Les doy inyecciones a las mascotas.
> *el veterinario*

1. Hago las reservaciones cuando tú quieres viajar.
2. Conduzco un coche con luces rojas y azules. No quieres conducir muy rápido cuando yo estoy cerca.
3. Les traigo la comida a los clientes en el restaurante.
4. Veo a muchas personas enfermas.
5. Escribo artículos, entrevisto a personas famosas y digo la verdad.
6. Oigo los problemas de muchas personas.
7. Muchas personas vienen a mi estudio y yo tomo fotos de ellas.
8. Pongo todo en orden en casa y salgo para comprar comida.

5.25 **Un día ocupado** Completa el párrafo usando los verbos de la lista en la primera persona singular del presente.

conducir	hacer	poner	salir	tener	venir

Soy ama de casa y **(1)** _____ que hacer mucho trabajo todos los días. Primero **(2)** _____ el almuerzo para mis hijos. A las 7:45 ellos suben al (*get into*) auto y **(3)** _____ a la escuela. Después, voy al supermercado, **(4)** _____ a casa y **(5)** _____ la comida en el refrigerador. Más tarde **(6)** _____ otra vez a la escuela para recoger a mis hijos.

Soy ama de casa.

© Trudy Simmons/Shutterstock

5.26 **¿Qué hace Rocío?** Rocío es agente de viajes. Con un compañero, describan lo que hace Rocío. Incluyan todos los detalles posibles y usen los verbos siguientes: **poner, oír, hacer, decir, salir, conducir.**

5.27 **¿Con qué frecuencia...?** Habla con ocho diferentes compañeros de clase y pregúntale a cada uno con qué frecuencia hace una de las siguientes actividades.

todos los días (*every day*)   **a veces** (*sometimes*)   **casi nunca** (*almost never*)
nunca (*never*)

> **Modelo** hacer la cama
> Estudiante 1: *¿Con qué frecuencia haces la cama?*
> Estudiante 2: *Todos los días (A veces/Casi nunca/Nunca) hago la cama.*

1. seguir las recomendaciones de tus amigos
2. salir con amigos
3. ver la televisión
4. decir mentiras (*lies*)
5. conducir el coche a la universidad
6. venir a la clase tarde
7. dar respuestas correctas en clase
8. traer el libro a la clase

5.28 **Preguntas personales** Entrevista a un compañero de clase.

1. ¿Adónde sales los fines de semana? ¿Con quién sales?
2. ¿A qué hora vienes a la universidad? ¿A qué hora regresas a casa?
3. ¿Te gusta ver películas? ¿Qué tipo de películas ves?
4. ¿Siempre haces la tarea? ¿Cuándo haces la tarea?
5. ¿Pones música cuando estudias? ¿Qué tipo de música escuchas?
6. ¿Te gusta conducir? ¿Qué coche conduces?

¿Qué tipo de música escuchas?

Cultura

A mediados del siglo pasado, en México se sintió una necesidad de crear una identidad y de restaurar el orgullo (*pride*) nacional. Comenzó entonces un movimiento artístico para glorificar lo mexicano. En edificios públicos como hospitales, escuelas y edificios del gobierno (*government*) se pintaron murales que representaban momentos y figuras importantes en la historia de México. Se destacan (*stand out*) tres muralistas: Diego Rivera, David Siqueiros y José Clemente Orozco.

Un tema muy importante del arte de este período fue el trabajador mexicano. Mira la pintura de José Clemente Orozco. ¿Cómo presenta Orozco a la clase trabajadora en esta pintura?

La clase trabajadora de José Clemente Orozco (1883–1949)

© Schalkwijk/Art Resource, NY. © 2010 Artists Rights Society (ARS). New York/ SOMAAP Mexico City.

> Investiga en Internet sobre otros murales de José Clemente Orozco.

Comunidad

Lee la sección de solicitudes de trabajo de tu comunidad. ¿Qué empleos hay? ¿Cuántos trabajos puedes encontrar en donde busquen una persona que pueda hablar español? ¿Para qué profesiones son estos trabajos? Repórtaselo a la clase.

© Xavier Subias/AGE Fotostock

Comparaciones

¿Piensas que en los Estados Unidos la gente trabaja mucho? ¿Crees que trabajan más en otros países? Mira la información en el cuadro y contesta las preguntas.

Horas promedio¹ de trabajo por persona (2007)

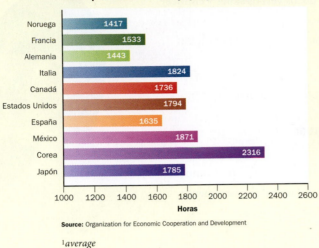

País	Horas
Noruega	1417
Francia	1533
Alemania	1443
Italia	1824
Canadá	1736
Estados Unidos	1794
España	1635
México	1871
Corea	2316
Japón	1785

Horas

Source: Organization for Economic Cooperation and Development

¹*average*

En promedio, ¿cuántas horas trabajan al año en México? ¿Quiénes trabajan más: los españoles o los estadounidenses? ¿Cuántas horas trabajan en Corea? ¿Cómo puedes explicar las diferencias?

Conexiones... a la economía y el comercio

Hay muchas compañías de los Estados Unidos que tienen fábricas (*factories*) en países en vías de desarrollo (*developing*). Estas industrias se llaman **maquiladoras,** y hacen todo tipo de productos, como ropa, zapatos, muebles, productos químicos y electrónicos.

Habla con un compañero sobre las siguientes preguntas. Luego investiga qué compañías de los Estados Unidos tienen maquiladoras en otros países y repórtaselo a la clase.

1. ¿Cuáles son las ventajas (*advantages*) y las desventajas para la compañía? ¿Y para los empleados?
2. ¿Qué efectos tienen las maquiladoras en la economía de los Estados Unidos? ¿y en la economía de los países donde se establecen?

© Ragne Kabanova/Shutterstock

A analizar

Lee las siguientes oraciones y observa el uso de los verbos **saber** y **conocer**.

> Yo soy cocinera. **Conozco** bien a mis clientes y **sé** qué comidas prefieren.
>
> Yo soy policía. **Conozco** muy bien la ciudad y **sé** conducir bien.
>
> Yo soy maestro. **Conozco** a mis estudiantes y **sé** quiénes son sus padres.
>
> Yo soy actor. **Conozco** el teatro y **sé** actuar.

1. What is the first person form of the verb **saber**? And the verb **conocer**?
2. The verbs **saber** and **conocer** mean *to know*. Look at the statements above and explain the difference in their uses.

© photos.com

A comprobar

Saber and conocer

1. As with the other verbs in this chapter, **saber** and **conocer** are irregular in the first person form.

saber	**sé,** sabes, sabe, sabemos, sabéis, saben
conocer	**conozco,** conoces, conoce, conocemos, conocéis, conocen

2. While the verbs **saber** and **conocer** both mean *to know*, they are used in different contexts. **Saber** is used to express knowledge of facts or information as well as skills. **Conocer** is used to express acquaintance or familiarity with a person, place, or thing.

Notice the difference in meaning in the following sentences:

Ana **conoce** Chile. (*familiarity*)
Ana **sabe** dónde está Chile. (*fact*)

Paco **conoce** a Diego. (*acquainted with*)
Paco **sabe** dónde vive Diego. (*information*)

Conozco la poesía de Neruda. (*familiarity*)
Sé que Neruda es un poeta famoso. (*fact*)

3. When using **saber** to mean *to know how to do something,* it is followed by the infinitive.

El ingeniero **sabe diseñar** edificios.
*The engineer **knows how to design** buildings.*

El cantante **sabe cantar.**
*The singer **knows how to sing.***

4. You may recall from **Capítulo 2** that it is necessary to use a personal **a** when the direct object of the verb is a person or a pet. Remember to use the personal **a** with **conocer.**

La profesora **conoce a** los estudiantes.
*The professor **knows** her students.*

El jefe **conoce a** sus empleados.
*The boss **knows** his employees.*

A practicar

5.29 **¿Lógica o ilógica?** Decide si las siguientes descripciones de profesiones son lógicas. Corrige las oraciones ilógicas.

1. La bailarina sabe jugar al fútbol.
2. El periodista conoce a muchas personas famosas.
3. El médico sabe dónde está la farmacia.
4. El contador sabe cantar bien.
5. El veterinario conoce a unos criminales.
6. La secretaria sabe usar la computadora.
7. El psicólogo conoce bien la cocina del restaurante.
8. El escritor conoce las obras (*works*) más importantes de la literatura.

5.30 **Oraciones incompletas** Decide qué opciones pueden completar las siguientes oraciones. Hay más de una posibilidad para cada oración.

1. El médico conoce...
   - **a.** a sus pacientes.
   - **b.** la medicina.
   - **c.** dar inyecciones.
   - **d.** el hospital.

2. El arquitecto sabe...
   - **a.** al ingeniero.
   - b. diseñar casas.
   - **c.** dónde está la casa.
   - d. la ciudad.

3. El científico conoce...
   - **a.** las ciencias.
   - **b.** cómo hacer el experimento.
   - **c.** el laboratorio.
   - **d.** que su trabajo es importante.

4. El consejero sabe...
   - **a.** los problemas de sus clientes.
   - **b.** escuchar bien.
   - **c.** a sus clientes.
   - **d.** a qué hora vienen los clientes.

5.31 **¿Saber o conocer?** Primero completen individualmente las siguientes oraciones con las formas necesarias de los verbos **saber** y **conocer**. Después, túrnense para leer las definiciones y decir cuál es una profesión lógica.

Modelo Estudiante 1: *Yo _____ tocar el piano.*
Estudiante 2: *Un músico.*

1. Yo _____ bien la ley (*law*).
2. Julio _____ pintar bien.
3. Matilde y Simón _____ a muchos médicos.
4. Fabio _____ al presidente.
5. Daniela y yo _____ tomar buenas fotos.
6. Yo _____ dónde están los buenos hoteles.
7. Mario y Luisa _____ los animales.
8. Tú _____ cocinar muy bien.
9. Yo _____ bailar tango.
10. El señor Montero _____ a sus estudiantes.

Bailamos tango.

© Sandra Gligorijevic/Shutterstock

5.32 **Puerto Rico** Con un compañero, túrnense para preguntar si saben o conocen las siguientes cosas.

Modelo Puerto Rico

Estudiante 1: *¿Conoces Puerto Rico?*

Estudiante 2: *Sí, conozco Puerto Rico. / No, no conozco Puerto Rico.*

hablar español bien

Estudiante 1: *¿Sabes hablar español bien?*

Estudiante 2: *Sí, sé hablar español bien. / No, no sé hablar español bien.*

1. dónde está Puerto Rico
2. un puertorriqueño
3. la comida puertorriqueña
4. quién es el gobernador de Puerto Rico
5. San Juan
6. la historia de Puerto Rico
7. cuándo es el día de la Independencia de Puerto Rico
8. bailar salsa

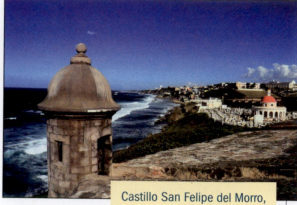

Castillo San Felipe del Morro, San Juan, Puerto Rico

© Colin D. Young/Shutterstock

5.33 **¿Qué saben? ¿Qué conocen?** Con un compañero, túrnense para completar las siguientes oraciones. ¡**OJO** al verbo!

1. **a.** Nosotros conocemos…

   b. Nosotros sabemos…

2. **a.** Los periodistas conocen…

   b. Los periodistas saben…

3. **a.** Un jefe conoce…

   b. Un jefe sabe…

4. **a.** El presidente conoce…

   b. El presidente sabe…

5.34 **En busca de…** Primero, decide qué verbo necesitas usar en cada oración. Luego, busca a ocho compañeros diferentes que respondan positivamente a una de las siguientes preguntas. Después de responder, deben contestar la pregunta adicional.

1. ¿(saber/conocer) a una persona famosa? (¿Quién?)
2. ¿(saber/conocer) un buen restaurante? (¿Cuál?)
3. ¿(saber/conocer) tocar un instrumento musical? (¿Cuál?)
4. ¿(saber/conocer) a una persona de otro país (*country*)? (¿Qué país?)
5. ¿(saber/conocer) el nombre del presidente de Argentina? (¿Cómo se llama?)
6. ¿(saber/conocer) cocinar? (¿Cuál es tu especialidad?)
7. ¿(saber/conocer) muy bien la ciudad donde vives? (¿Cuál es tu lugar favorito?)
8. ¿(saber/conocer) cuál es la capital de Venezuela? (¿Cuál es?)

Redacción

Write a letter to a friend telling him/her about a new job.

Paso 1 Brainstorm a list of jobs that you think are fun or exciting.

Paso 2 Pick one of the jobs from your list of interesting jobs. Jot down as many things as you can about that job: Why do you find it interesting? Where do professionals in that field work? What do they do? What do they have to know? Who do they work with? How much do they work?

Paso 3 Write a list of emotions that you might feel if you were to have a job like the one you described in **Paso 2.**

Paso 4 Imagine that you have the job you described in **Paso 2.** Begin the letter to your friend and ask how he/she is doing. Then say how you are feeling.

Paso 5 Continue your letter telling your friend that you have a new job. Then write a paragraph in which you discuss various aspects of the job using the information you generated in **Paso 2.** Also describe how you are feeling about the job using the list you created in **Paso 3.**

Paso 6 Conclude your letter.

Paso 7 Edit your letter:

1. Is your letter logically organized with smooth sentence transitions?
2. Are there any short sentences you can combine by using **y** or **pero**?
3. Do your verbs agree with the subjects?
4. Do your adjectives agree with the nouns they describe?
5. Did you use **ser** and **estar** properly?
6. Are there any spelling errors?

Lectura

Reading Strategy: Paying attention to parts of speech

You've learned some concrete strategies as to how to make educated guesses about verbs. To guess the meaning of other words, pay attention to the context and the part of speech of the unknown word (verb, noun, etc.). For example, in the sentence *He walked bumptiously*, we might not know the meaning of *bumptiously*, but we know it is an adverb and it refers to the way in which the person walked. Look at the last paragraph on page 175. What part of speech do you think the word **potable** is? What do you think it means?

Antes de leer

Menciona dos profesiones que te parecen poco comunes. ¿Por qué piensas que son poco comunes? ¿Conoces a alguien con una profesión poco común?

A leer

Profesiones poco comunes

cambiar: to change

En un mundo que está **cambiando** muy rápidamente, los trabajos de la gente también cambian a gran velocidad y muchos trabajos ya casi no existen. Los siguientes son trabajos poco comunes y muy modestos que encontramos en algunos pueblos de Latinoamérica.

typewriter

El escribano: Generalmente trabaja en el centro de un pueblo o de una ciudad, donde espera a clientes en la calle, con su **máquina de escribir.** El escribano les ayuda a las personas que no saben leer o escribir, o que no tienen ni una máquina de escribir ni una computadora. Por un poco de dinero, este trabajador escribe a máquina cartas de amor, cartas para la familia o completa solicitudes de trabajo.

> [los trabajos de las personas también cambian a gran velocidad]

while

El ropavejero: Camina por las calles **mientras** va anunciando que compra ropa vieja, periódicos y objetos viejos. Luego, vende los objetos usados.

La lavandera: Para las personas que no están contentas con su lavadora de ropa, o no tienen una, la lavandera es una gran ayuda. Va a la casa de una persona para lavar a mano toda la ropa *dirty* **sucia.**

El organillero: Si tienes suerte, puedes encontrar al organillero en un parque de la ciudad, tocando música con su organillo. Si tienes más suerte, un chimpancé va a estar bailando a la música del organillero, y pidiéndole

© Courtesy of Mary Ann Blitt

Un organillero

cage

dinero a la gente en la calle. Desafortunadamente, esta profesión originada en Europa ya es casi algo del pasado.

El adivinador: Va por el parque con un pajarito en una **jaula.** Cuando el cliente le paga al adivinador, el pájaro selecciona un papel que dice su suerte, igual que un horóscopo.

© Courtesy of Margarita Casas

Una adivinadora le lee la fortuna a un turista.

© Courtesy of Mary Ann Blitt

Un repartidor de agua

Repartidores: Van por toda la ciudad y llevan artículos de gran importancia a las casas de la gente. Hay muchos tipos de repartidores, pero los más importantes son los repartidores de agua **potable,** y los que reparten el gas para cocinar. Otros repartidores van con refrescos o periódicos si una persona se los pide.

Comprensión

Decide si las siguientes afirmaciones son ciertas o falsas. Haz los cambios necesarios para hacer verdaderas las afirmaciones falsas.

1. El adivinador le vende pájaros a la gente que quiere una mascota.
2. La lavandera compra ropa vieja.
3. Algunos repartidores llevan agua a las casas de los clientes.
4. Un escribano tiene una máquina de escribir para enseñarles a sus clientes a leer y a escribir.
5. Los organilleros son muy difíciles de encontrar hoy en día.
6. Los repartidores de gas llevan gasolina para los autos de sus clientes.

Después de leer

En grupos de tres, hablen sobre los trabajos que tienen o los trabajos que consideren interesantes. Incluyan lo siguiente: las habilidades (*skills*) necesarias, la preparación necesaria, el sueldo, lo que les gusta del trabajo y lo que no les gusta del trabajo.

© Rob Marmion/Shutterstock

Vocabulario

Sustantivos

el abuso	*abuse*
el alcohol	*alcohol*
el autoestima	*self-esteem*
la custodia	*custody*
la droga	*drug*
la rehabilitación	*rehabilitation*
la violencia	*violence*

Adjetivos

agresivo(a)	*agressive*
obsesionado(a)	*obsessed*
violento(a)	*violent*

Verbos

dejar de + *infinitive*	*to stop doing something*

Frases útiles

¿En qué puedo ayudarle?
How can I help you?

¿Tiene problemas de salud?
Do you have any health problems?

¿Cuál es su número de seguridad social?
What is your social security number?

¿Cómo se llama la persona encargada de su caso?
What is the name of your case worker?

Voy a referirlo a...
I am going to refer you to . . .

Necesitamos hacer una cita con...
We need to make an appointment with . . .

DATOS IMPORTANTES

Educación: Licenciatura en trabajo social o carrera relacionada, aunque muchos puestos requieren una maestría

Salario: Entre $30 000 y $50 000

Dónde se trabaja: Escuelas primarias y secundarias, hospitales, asilos para ancianos, centros para el tratamiento de abuso, agencias para individuos y familias, el gobierno local o estatal

Ana Correa es trabajadora social y ayuda a personas con diferentes problemas, como la falta de (*lack of*) trabajo, las drogas y la violencia doméstica. En el video vas a ver una entrevista entre Ana y una persona que necesita ayuda.

Antes de ver

1. ¿Cuáles son los problemas sociales más comunes en los Estados Unidos? ¿Hay esos problemas en tu comunidad?
2. ¿Qué tipo de ayuda crees que puede ofrecer un trabajador social para los problemas mencionados en la pregunta #1?
3. ¿Hay lugares en tu comunidad donde puedes ir a ver a un trabajador social?

Comprensión

1. ¿Cómo se llama el hombre que habla con Ana Correa y qué problema tiene?
2. ¿Cómo está el hombre en el momento de la entrevista?
3. ¿Qué datos le pide la trabajadora social?
4. ¿Con quién vive el Sr. Gómez?
5. ¿Con qué compara el alcohol la Sra. Correa?
6. ¿Es el Sr. Correa agresivo?
7. ¿Qué debe hacer el Sr. Gómez?

© Heinle/Cengage Learning

Después de ver

En grupos de tres, representen a una pareja o dos amigos que van a ver a un trabajador social por primera vez. Hablen del problema que uno o los dos tienen, como alcoholismo, drogas, falta de trabajo, etcétera, y cómo el problema afecta su vida familiar o su amistad. El trabajador social debe hacer preguntas y dar consejos.

El consejero debe preguntar sobre:

Nombre de la persona

Dirección y teléfono

Trabajo

Cuál es el problema

Recomendar a un especialista para resolver el problema

La persona debe responder las preguntas del consejero y dar un problema.

Preguntas posibles para el consejero:

¿En qué les puedo ayudar?

¿Cómo estás ahora?

5.35 **Un día en la vida** Completa el siguiente párrafo con la forma necesaria de la palabra entre paréntesis. A veces debes escoger entre dos palabras. **¡OJO!** Algunos de los verbos requieren el uso del presente progresivo.

Me llamo Romina. **(1)** _____ (ser/estar) de Cuzco, Perú, pero **(2)** _____ (ser/estar) en Nueva York. **(3)** _____ (ser/estar) cocinera ¡y me encanta mi trabajo! Ahora estoy **(4)** _____ (trabajar) en un restaurante con un cocinero francés. Estoy **(5)** _____ (aprender) mucho con él.

Yo **(6)** _____ (saber/conocer) a mis clientes muy bien. Ellos **(7)** _____ (venir) al restaurante con frecuencia y **(8)** _____ (decir) que mi comida es la mejor en Nueva York. Algún día quiero **(9)** _____ (ser/estar) dueña (*owner*) de un restaurante andino. Yo **(10)** _____ (saber/conocer) cocinar muy bien... ¡yo **(11)** _____ (hacer) unos platos deliciosos! **(12)** _____ (ser/estar) segura que puedo tener éxito.

5.36 **Descripción personal** Conjuga el verbo en la primera persona **(yo)**, y completa la oración de una forma original para escribir una descripción personal.

1. (Ser)...

2. Hoy (estar)...

3. (Venir) a la clase de...

4. Los fines de semana (salir)...

5. Yo no (saber)...

6. (Conocer) a...

7. No (hacer)...

8. (Conducir)...

5.37 **Texteando** Estás visitando la ciudad de Barcelona, en España, y escribes varios mensajes en tu teléfono celular para decirles a tus amigos lo que estás haciendo en ese momento. Usa el presente progresivo para hablar de tus actividades.

1. 10:30 A.M. – caminar por el parque Güell

2. 1:00 P.M. – comprar recuerdos en las Ramblas

3. 2:00 P.M. – almorzar en el Café 4Gats

4. 4:00 P.M. – visitar el mercado

5. 6:00 P.M. – ver cuadros en el Museo de Picasso

6. 8:00 P.M. – beber y comer en un restaurante de tapas

5.38 **En el trabajo** Usando el presente progresivo, explica qué están haciendo estas personas en el trabajo. Deben usar ocho verbos diferentes.

Modelo Isabel es veterinaria.
  Está ayudando al perro.

1. Leticia es mesera.

2. Ernesto es secretario.

3. Esmeralda es mujer policía.

4. Mario es deportista.

5. Alicia es ama de casa.

6. Marcelo es maestro.

5.39 **Descripción de fotos** Con un compañero describan las siguientes fotos. Deben determinar quiénes son las personas en las fotos, qué relación tienen, cuáles son sus profesiones, qué están haciendo y qué emociones se muestran en las fotos. ¡**OJO** con los verbos **ser** y **estar**!

Modelo *Marta no está contenta. Es escritora y está hablando por teléfono con el editor.*
Él necesita el libro en dos semanas.

5.40 **Información, por favor** Trabaja con un compañero. Uno debe mirar el gráfico en esta página y el otro debe mirar el gráfico en el apéndice A. Túrnense para preguntarse y completar el gráfico con la información necesaria. Necesitan identificar sus profesiones, sus orígenes, dónde están ahora y cómo están. Atención al uso de **ser** y **estar**.

Nombre	Profesión	Origen	Localización	Emoción
Carlota		Madrid	la casa	
Éric				frustrado
César	periodista	San Juan		cansado
Paloma	abogada		el correo	
Samuel		Managua	la oficina	
Camila	diseñadora			divertida

Vocabulario 1

CD1-26

Los estados de ánimo y otras expresiones con el verbo *estar*

aburrido(a)	*bored*		enfermo(a)	*sick*
alegre	*happy*		enojado(a)	*angry*
asustado(a)	*scared*		equivocado(a)	*wrong*
avergonzado(a)	*embarrassed*		feliz	*happy*
borracho(a)	*drunk*		frustrado(a)	*frustrated*
cansado(a)	*tired*		interesado(a)	*interested*
celoso(a)	*jealous*		loco(a)	*crazy*
confundido(a)	*confused*		nervioso(a)	*nervous*
contento(a)	*happy*		ocupado(a)	*busy*
deprimido(a)	*depressed*		preocupado(a)	*worried*
divertido(a)	*to be entertained, to be in a good mood*		sano(a)	*healthy*
			seguro(a)	*sure*
			sorprendido(a)	*surprised*
enamorado(a) (de)	*in love (with)*		triste	*sad*

Palabras adicionales

la salud — *health*

Los verbos

comer	to eat		morir	*to die*
destruir	to destroy		pedir	*to ask for*
dormir	to sleep		repetir	*to repeat*
estar	to be		servir	*to serve*
hablar	to speak		traer	*to bring*
leer	to read		vivir	*to live*
mentir	to lie			

Diccionario personal

_____

_____

_____

_____

_____

_____

_____

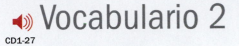

Vocabulario 2

CD1-27

Las profesiones

el (la) abogado(a)	*lawyer*
el actor	*actor*
la actriz	*actress*
el (la) agente de viajes	*travel agent*
el ama de casa	*homemaker*
el (la) arquitecto(a)	*architect*
el (la) asistente de vuelo	*flight attendant*
el bailarín/ la bailarina	*dancer*
el (la) cantante	*singer*
el (la) científico(a)	*scientist*
el (la) cocinero(a)	*cook*
el (la) consejero(a)	*adviser*
el (la) contador(a)	*accountant*
el (la) dependiente	*clerk*
el (la) deportista	*athlete*
el (la) diseñador(a)	*designer*
el (la) enfermero(a)	*nurse*
el (la) escritor(a)	*writer*
el (la) fotógrafo(a)	*photographer*

el (la) ingeniero(a)	*engineer*
el jefe/la jefa	*boss*
el (la) maestro(a)	*elementary/ high school teacher*
el (la) mecánico(a)	*mechanic*
el (la) médico(a)	*doctor*
el (la) mesero(a)	*waiter*
el (la) modelo	*model*
el (la) músico(a)	*musician*
el (la) periodista	*journalist*
el (la) piloto(a)	*pilot*
el (la) pintor(a)	*painter*
el policía/la mujer policía	*police officer*
el (la) político(a)	*politician*
el (la) psicólogo(a)	*psychologist*
el (la) secretario(a)	*secretary*
el (la) trabajador(a) social	*social worker*
el (la) vendedor(a)	*salesperson*
el (la) veterinario(a)	*veterinary*

Palabras adicionales

la entrevista	*interview*
la solicitud	*application; want ad*

el sueldo	*salary*

Los verbos

conducir	*to drive*
conocer	*to know, to be acquainted with*
dar	*to give*
decir	*to say, to tell*
ganar	*to earn*
hacer	*to do, to make*
oír	*to hear*

poner	*to put, to set*
saber	*to know (facts, how to do something)*
salir	*to go out, to leave*
seguir	*to follow*
traer	*to bring*
venir	*to come*
ver	*to see*

Diccionario personal

_____

_____

Learning Strategy

Study with someone else

Study with a friend or form a study group. Not only will you benefit when someone in your group understands a concept that you have difficulty with, but you can also increase your own understanding by teaching others who need extra help. Group study will provide you with more opportunities to speak and listen to Spanish as well.

In this chapter you will learn how to:

- Talk about your daily routine
- Discuss your hobbies and pastimes
- Talk about sports
- Discuss events that occurred in the past

¿Cómo pasas el día?

© Caroline Webber/Photolibrary

Exploraciones gramaticales

Reflexive verbs

Indefinite and negative words

The preterite

Stem-changing verbs in the preterite

En vivo

La higiene

La biografía de Ana Guevara

Conexiones culturales

La vida diaria

Los deportes en España y Latinoamérica

Lectura

La siesta

Deportistas famosos

▶ Exploraciones profesionales

La educación física

Es temprano por la mañana y la familia Cervantes comienza su día.

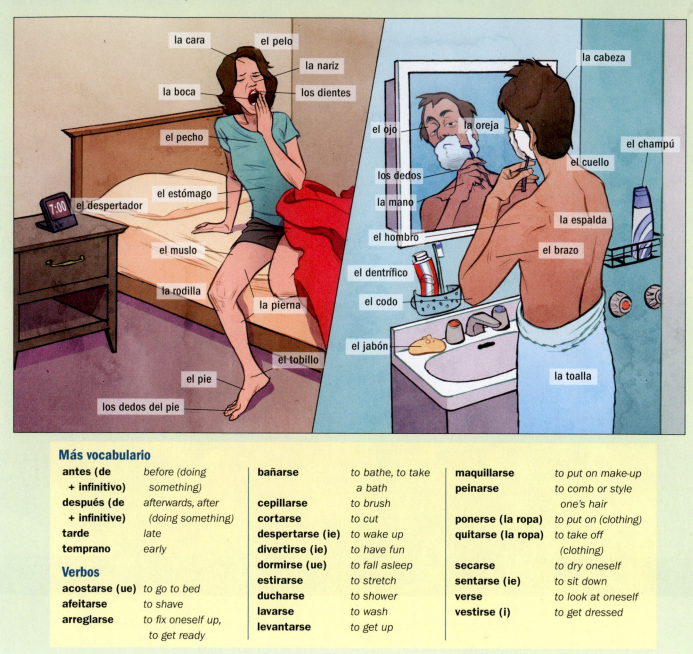

Más vocabulario

antes (de + infinitivo)	*before (doing something)*	**bañarse**	*to bathe, to take a bath*	**maquillarse**	*to put on make-up*
después (de + infinitive)	*afterwards, after (doing something)*	**cepillarse**	*to brush*	**peinarse**	*to comb or style one's hair*
tarde	*late*	**cortarse**	*to cut*	**ponerse (la ropa)**	*to put on (clothing)*
temprano	*early*	**despertarse (ie)**	*to wake up*	**quitarse (la ropa)**	*to take off (clothing)*
		divertirse (ie)	*to have fun*		
Verbos		**dormirse (ue)**	*to fall asleep*	**secarse**	*to dry oneself*
acostarse (ue)	*to go to bed*	**estirarse**	*to stretch*	**sentarse (ie)**	*to sit down*
afeitarse	*to shave*	**ducharse**	*to shower*	**verse**	*to look at oneself*
arreglarse	*to fix oneself up, to get ready*	**lavarse**	*to wash*	**vestirse (i)**	*to get dressed*
		levantarse	*to get up*		

Práctica

6.1 Escucha y responde Vas a escuchar varias partes del cuerpo. Señala la parte del cuerpo que escuches.

CD1-28

6.2 Asociaciones ¿Qué ropa asocias con las siguientes partes del cuerpo?

1. los pies
2. las piernas
3. la cabeza
4. las manos
5. el cuello
6. la espalda y el pecho

6.3 **¿Qué parte del cuerpo es?** Completa las descripciones.

1. _____ está entre la cabeza y los hombros y sirve para mover la cabeza.

2. Tenemos dos _____, y cada uno tiene cinco dedos. Sirven para caminar y bailar.

3. Usamos _____ para hablar y para comer.

4. Tenemos dos _____ en la cara para ver.

5. _____ está en el brazo, entre la mano y el hombro.

6. En la cabeza tenemos dos _____ para escuchar.

7. Yo tengo _____ largo, rubio y rizado.

8. _____ es una parte que conecta la pierna con el pie.

6.4 **No corresponde** Trabaja con un compañero. Observen los grupos de palabras y túrnense para decidir cuál es diferente. Expliquen por qué.

1. los pies	las manos	el cuello
2. los dedos	la boca	la nariz
3. el pelo	el codo	la rodilla
4. el estómago	el diente	la espalda
5. el muslo	la oreja	el tobillo
6. el despertador	el dentrífico	el jabón

6.5 **¿Cuándo?** Con un compañero, túrnense para explicar en qué situaciones una persona tiene que hacer las siguientes actividades.

Modelo ducharse con agua fría
>Estudiante 1: *¿Por qué una persona tiene que ducharse con agua fría?*
>Estudiante 2: *La persona tiene mucho calor.*

1. sentarse al frente de la clase
2. acostarse muy tarde
3. vestirse con ropa muy vieja
4. estirarse
5. levantarse muy temprano
6. afeitarse las piernas
7. cortarse el pelo
8. cepillarse los dientes

INVESTIGUEMOS LA GRAMÁTICA

To say what someone does before or after another activity, use the expressions **antes de** + *infinitive* and **después de** + *infinitive*.

Antes de acostarse, mi hijo lee un libro.
Before going to bed, my son reads a book.

Después de comer, los niños necesitan cepillarse los dientes.
After eating, the children need to brush their teeth.

To say *afterwards*, use **después** followed by the conjugated verb. **Normalmente tomo un café y después voy a la universidad.**
Normally I have coffee and afterwards I go to the university.

6.6 **¿Para qué es?** Usando los nuevos verbos, túrnense para explicar para qué son los objetos.

Modelo el champú → *El champú es para lavarse el pelo.*

1. el despertador	**5.** la cama
2. la toalla	**6.** el dentrífico
3. el jabón	**7.** el cepillo
4. la silla	**8.** la bañera

INVESTIGUEMOS EL VOCABULARIO

In some Latin American countries, **la pasta de dientes** is used rather than **el dentrífico** to say *toothpaste*.

In Mexico **rasurarse** is used to say *to shave* rather than **afeitarse**.

¿Qué le puedes decir a un niño que te pregunta por qué debemos lavarnos las manos? Las siguientes son las recomendaciones de un anuncio público. ¿Cuándo recomiendan lavarse las manos?

LAVAR LAS MANOS

¿No te lavas las manos? ¿Y ahora?

Los gérmenes y las bacterias van a hacer una fiesta en ti y te puedes enfermar, ¡y despídete de divertirte con tus amiguitos! No dejes de lavar tus manos después de usar el baño, después de manipular basura, después de un estornudo, después de jugar con tu animalito preferido. Si tocas dinero no lo dejes para después, ¡los billetes pueden tener bacterias fecales! ¿Te lo imaginas?

haid3r/Shutterstock

Más allá

Ahora escoge una de las siguientes opciones y escribe una explicación para niños.

1. por qué deben lavarse los dientes
2. por qué deben lavarse el pelo y peinarse

© jo unruh/iStockphoto

A analizar

Lee el siguiente párrafo y observa las estructuras de los verbos.

Todas las noches, yo baño a mi hijo a las siete. Acuesto al niño, y después yo **me baño.** Prefiero **bañarme** en la noche porque no tengo mucho tiempo en la mañana. Veo la tele un poco, y **me acuesto. Me despierto** a las seis, **me peino** rápidamente y **me pongo** un pantalón y una camisa. Despierto a mi hijo y preparo su cereal. Mi mamá siempre llega a las siete y media, y yo salgo para la oficina.

1. What is the subject of the verbs in bold in the examples above?
2. What do you notice about the verbs in bold in the paragraph above?
3. Notice the different structures of the verbs **acostar** and **bañar** in the following sentences taken from the paragraph above. How are they different? Why do you think the structures are different?

   Todas las noches, yo **baño** a mi hijo a las siete.
   Acuesto al niño, y después yo **me baño.**
   Veo la tele un poco, y **me acuesto.**

A comprobar

Reflexive verbs

1. Many verbs used to discuss our daily routine (**bañarse, despertarse, vestirse,** etc.) are known as reflexive verbs. Reflexive verbs are used to indicate that the subject performing the action also receives the action of the verb. In other words, these verbs are used to describe actions we do to ourselves.

   Ella **se pone** un vestido azul.
   *She **puts on** (herself) a blue dress.*

   Yo **me levanto** temprano.
   *I **get** (myself) **up** early.*

2. Reflexive verbs are conjugated in the same manner as other verbs; however, they must have a reflexive pronoun. The reflexive pronoun agrees with the subject of the verb.

The following verbs from the section **Vocabulario** are reflexive verbs:

acostarse* (ue)	divertirse* (ie)	ponerse
afeitarse	dormirse* (ue)	quitarse
arreglarse	ducharse	secarse
bañarse	estirarse	sentarse* (ie)
cepillarse	lavarse	verse
despertarse* (ie)	levantarse	vestirse* (i)
*stem-changing verbs		

3. The reflexive pronoun is placed in front of a conjugated verb.

   Nosotros **nos** acostamos tarde.
   We go to bed late.

   Yo **me** estoy durmiendo.
   I am falling asleep.

lavarse

yo	**me** lavo	nosotros	**nos** lavamos
tú	**te** lavas	vosotros	**os** laváis
él, ella, usted	**se** lava	ellos, ellas, ustedes	**se** lavan

4. When using an infinitive, attach the reflexive pronoun to the end. Note that even in the infinitive form, the pronoun agrees with the subject. The pronoun can also be attached to the present participle, but you must add an accent to maintain the original stress.

> ¿Vas a bañar**te** ahora?
> *Are you going to bathe now?*
>
> Estoy lavándo**me** la cara.
> *I am washing my face.*

5. Many verbs can be used reflexively or nonreflexively, depending on who (or what) receives the action.

> Gerardo **se lava** las manos.
> *Gerardo **washes** his (own) hands.*
>
> Felipe **lava** el coche.
> *Felipe **washes** the car.*
>
> (Felipe does not receive the action; the car does.)

> Rebeca **se mira** en el espejo.
> *Rebeca **looks at herself** in the mirror.*
>
> Los niños **miran** a la maestra.
> *The children **look at** the teacher.*
>
> (The children do not receive the action; the teacher does.)

6. When using reflexive verbs, do not use possessive adjectives.

> Silvia se lava **el** pelo.
> *Silvia washes **her** hair.*

7. Some verbs have a slightly different meaning when used with a reflexive pronoun, such as **irse** (*to go away, to leave*) and **dormirse** (*to fall asleep*).

> Liz **se duerme** a las diez todas las noches.
> *Liz **falls asleep** at ten o'clock every night.*
>
> Liz **duerme** ocho horas cada noche.
> *Liz **sleeps** eight hours each night.*

A practicar

6.7 **Conclusiones lógicas** Empareja las columnas para hacer oraciones lógicas.

1. El despertador suena a las ocho y tú...
2. No hay agua caliente, y por eso yo...
3. Empieza la clase de aeróbic, y la profesora...
4. Son las once de la noche, y nosotros...
5. Tengo que ir a una fiesta formal, y yo...
6. Después de comer, ellos...

    a. me pongo un vestido elegante.
    b. se estira.
    c. se cepillan los dientes.
    d. te levantas y te vistes.
    e. nos acostamos.
    f. prefiero no ducharme.

6.8 **Mis hábitos** Habla con un compañero sobre tus hábitos. Conjuga el verbo en la forma apropiada y completa las oraciones.

Modelo Yo (lavarse) el pelo...
    Estudiante 1: *Yo me lavo el pelo con Champú Reina, ¿y tú?*
    Estudiante 2: *Yo me lavo el pelo con Champú Brillo.*

1. Los fines de semana yo (acostarse)...
2. Yo (estirarse) cuando...
3. A veces yo (dormirse) cuando...
4. Yo nunca (ponerse)...
5. En clase de español prefiero (sentarse)...
6. Yo (divertirse) cuando...

6.9 **Entrevista** Entrevista a un compañero con estas preguntas.

1. ¿A qué hora te despiertas de lunes a viernes? ¿y los sábados?
2. Generalmente, ¿cuánto tiempo necesitas para arreglarte?
3. ¿En qué ocasiones te pones ropa elegante?
4. ¿A veces te duermes en clase? ¿En qué clase?
5. ¿Qué haces para divertirte?
6. ¿Prefieres bañarte o ducharte?

6.10 **En el baño** ¿Qué están haciendo estas personas?

1. 2. 3.

4. 5.

6.11 **Una mañana muy apurada** Completa el siguiente párrafo con la forma necesaria del verbo apropiado. ¡**OJO!** Unos verbos son reflexivos y otros no. Después, compara tus respuestas con las de un compañero.

Carmen (**1.**) _____ (despertar/despertarse) y (**2.**) _____ (mirar/mirarse) el reloj. ¡Las siete de la mañana! Los niños deben estar en la escuela a las ocho. Rápidamente va al cuarto de sus hijos y (**3.**) _____ (despertar/despertarse) a Carlos y Víctor. Ellos (**4.**) _____ (levantar/levantarse) y van al baño. Mientras los niños (**5.**) _____ (bañar/bañarse), Carmen (**6.**) _____ (preparar/prepararse) el desayuno (*breakfast*) para ellos. Cuando Carlos y Víctor entran en la cocina para desayunar, Carmen corre al baño y empieza a (**7.**) _____ (arreglar/arreglarse). Ella (**8.**) _____ (maquillar/maquillarse) y (**9.**) _____ (vestir/vestirse). Después, Carmen (**10.**) _____ (llamar/llamarse) a sus hijos. Carlos y Víctor van al baño y (**11.**) _____ (cepillar/cepillarse) los dientes. Carmen (**12.**) _____ (peinar/peinarse) a los chicos y todos salen de la casa a las ocho menos diez.

6.12 **En busca de...** Busca a compañeros que hagan las siguientes actividades. Habla con una persona diferente para cada actividad de la lista. ¡**OJO!** Tienes que decidir si debes usar la forma reflexiva del verbo o no. Luego, comparte la información con la clase.

Modelo (duchar/ducharse) en la noche
Estudiante 1: ¿*Te duchas en la noche?*
Estudiante 2: *Sí, me ducho en la noche.*

1. (levantar/levantarse) temprano los fines de semana
2. preferir (vestir/vestirse) con ropa cómoda
3. (lavar/lavarse) la ropa una vez a la semana
4. normalmente (dormir/dormirse) siete horas
5. preferir (sentar/sentarse) al frente de la clase
6. (poner/ponerse) la mesa antes de comer
7. (afeitar/afeitarse) todos los días
8. (cepillar/cepillarse) a una mascota

Conexiones culturales

La vida diaria

Cultura

Antonio López García (1936–) es un famoso artista español. Comenzó a pintar influenciado por su tío, que era pintor. López García escribió: "Una obra nunca se acaba (*is finished*), sino que se llega al límite de las propias (*own*) posibilidades". Con esta idea describe su propio proceso como pintor, ya que a veces toma muchos años para terminar un cuadro. Muchas de sus obras reflejan momentos de la vida diaria. Algunos críticos definen su estilo como hiperrealista porque sus cuadros parecen casi fotografías. Observa su cuadro *Lavabo y espejo*. ¿Qué objetos reconoces?

> Investiga en Internet otras obras de Antonio López García.

Lavabo y espejo de Antonio López García

© Museum of Fine Arts, Boston. Melvin Blake and Frank Purnell Collection, 2003.4. Photograph © Museum of Fine Arts, Boston. © 2010 Artists Rights Society (ARS). New York/VEGAP Madrid

Comparaciones

Cada país tiene frases y refranes que reflejan la cultura popular. Las siguientes frases populares se relacionan con las partes del cuerpo. Por ejemplo, la frase "no tener dos dedos de frente (*forehead*)" significa que una persona no es inteligente. Dos dedos indican una medida (*measure*) de aproximadamente unos 3 centímetros. Si una persona tiene menos de 3 cms de frente, obviamente no tiene un cerebro (*brain*) muy grande. ¿Puedes adivinar el significado de los refranes después de leer los ejemplos? ¿Conoces alguna frase que signifique lo mismo en inglés?

1. **ser codo**
   ¡Mi novio es muy codo! Nunca me invita a cenar.

2. **hacérsele (a uno) agua la boca**
   Mi mamá hace un flan delicioso. ¡Se me hace agua la boca!

3. **tomar el pelo**
   ¿No hay exámenes en la clase de matemáticas? ¿Me estás tomando el pelo?

4. **no tener pies ni cabeza**
   No entiendo la explicación. No tiene ni pies ni cabeza.

5. **no tener pelos en la lengua**
   Mi hermana no tiene pelos en la lengua y siempre dice lo que piensa.

6. **costar un ojo de la cara**
   ¡Hoy en día (*nowadays*) la gasolina cuesta un ojo de la cara!

> Listen to "Mis Ojos" by the Mexican rock group Maná. Write all the parts of the body mentioned in the song. Listen a second time. What is the tone of the song? Why?

Conexiones... a la música

La siguiente es una canción infantil muy popular para enseñarles a los niños higiene personal. ¿Conoces alguna canción en inglés con el mismo propósito (*goal*)?

Pimpón es un muñeco con manos de cartón.

Pimpón es un muñeco
con manos de cartón
Se lava la carita
con agua y con jabón.
Pimpón es un muñeco
con manos de cartón
Se lava las manitas
con agua y con jabón.

Y cuando las estrellas
comienzan a salir,
Pimpón se va a la cama,
Pimpón se va a dormir.

Comunidad

Como la canción de Pimpón, existen muchos libros para niños que enseñan a tener buenos hábitos de higiene. Pregunta en la librería de tu comunidad si tienen un programa para leerles en español a los niños. Si tu librería no tiene un programa, puedes ser voluntario en un programa bilingüe en un jardín de niños o en escuela primaria. ¡Leer es una magnífica manera de practicar español!

Una mujer le lee a una niña.

A analizar

Lee el siguiente párrafo y observa las expresiones negativas. Luego contesta las preguntas que siguen.

A Lorenzo **no** le gustan las mañanas, por eso siempre se levanta tarde. Cuando se levanta, **no** quiere hablar con **nadie.** Va directamente al baño. **No** se lava la cara **ni** se afeita; simplemente se peina y se cepilla los dientes. **Nunca** toma mucho tiempo para decidir qué ropa ponerse. Después de vestirse, se va corriendo de la casa. **No** tiene **nunca** tiempo para comer **nada.**

© Vincent Ricardel/Getty Images

1. How many negative words are there in each sentence?
2. Where are the negative words placed in relation to the verbs in each sentence?

A comprobar
Indefinite and negative words

1. The following are the most commonly used negative and indefinite words.

Palabras negativas		Palabras indefinidas	
nadie	*no one, nobody*	**alguien**	*someone, somebody*
nada	*nothing*	**algo**	*something*
nunca	*never*	**siempre**	*always*
jamás	*never*	**también**	*also*
tampoco	*neither, either*	**algún (alguno), alguna**	*some*
ningún (ninguno), ninguna	*none, any*	**o… o**	*either . . . or*
ni… ni	*neither . . . nor*		

2. In Spanish, it is possible to use multiple negative words in one sentence. When a negative word follows the verb, it is necessary to place **no** or another negative word in front of the verb, making it a double negative.

    No corro **nunca** en ese parque.
    I **never** run in that park.

    No hay **ni** jabón **ni** dentrífico aquí.
    *There is **neither** soap **nor** toothpaste here.*

    Nunca le das **nada** a **nadie.**
    *You **never** give anything to anyone.*

3. The negative words **nadie, jamás, nunca,** and **tampoco** can also be placed directly before the verb. **Nada** can only be placed before the verb if it is used as the subject.

    Nadie está en el baño ahora.
    No one is in the bathroom right now.

    Tampoco me levanto temprano.
    *I don't get up early **either.***

    Nada es imposible.
    Nothing is impossible.

4. When using the indefinite words **algún, alguno(s), alguna(s),** or the negative words **ningún, ninguno(s), ninguna(s),** they must agree in number and gender with the noun they are describing. When using the negative, the singular form is generally used.

> ¿Tienes **algunos*** animales?
> No, no tengo **ningún** animal.
> (No, no tengo **ninguno.**)
> ¿Tienes **algunas*** plantas?
> No, no tengo **ninguna** planta.
> (No, no tengo **ninguna.**)

*While it is correct to use **algunos(as),** it is more common to use **unos(as).**

A practicar

6.13 **¿Cierto o falso?** Mira el dibujo y decide si estas oraciones son ciertas o falsas.

1. No hay ninguna toalla.
2. No hay ni jabón ni dentrífico.
3. Tampoco hay champú.
4. Ninguna mascota está en el baño.
5. No hay nada encima del lavabo.
6. Nadie se mira en el espejo.
7. El gato no bebe nada.
8. Hay algo al lado del lavabo.

6.14 **Un hotel poco hospitalario** Alguien va a quedarse en un hotel por la noche y tiene varias preguntas para el recepcionista. Contesta las preguntas de forma negativa.

1. ¿Siempre está lleno (*full*) el hotel?
2. ¿Hay algunas toallas en el baño?
3. ¿Tiene champú o jabón?
4. No tengo computadora. ¿El hotel tiene computadoras?
5. ¿Hay algo para comer en el restaurante ahora?
6. ¿Alguien va a limpiar mi cuarto mañana?

Nunca somos simpáticos en este hotel.

6.15 Preguntas personales Entrevista a un compañero con las siguientes preguntas. Si es posible, continúa la conversación con la pregunta entre paréntesis.

1. ¿Vives con alguien? (¿Con quién?)

2. ¿Tienes algunas mascotas? (¿Qué son?)

3. ¿Con qué frecuencia te levantas temprano los sábados: nunca, casi nunca, a veces, siempre? (¿Por qué?)

4. ¿Tienes que hacer algo hoy que no quieres hacer? (¿Qué es?)

5. ¿Te gusta hacer algún deporte? (¿Cuál?)

6. ¿Pasas tu tiempo libre con alguien? (¿Con quién)

6.16 Un sondeo En grupos de cuatro o cinco, túrnense haciendo las preguntas para averiguar (*find out*) quién hace las siguientes actividades. Luego reporten a la clase.

Modelo no tiene ningún hermano
> Estudiante 1: *¿Quién no tiene ningún hermano?*
> Estudiante 2: *Yo no tengo ningún hermano.*

1. no tiene ninguna otra clase

2. no estudia con nadie

3. nunca trabaja los domingos

4. siempre hace la tarea para la clase de español

5. no come nada por la mañana

6. no tiene que compartir (*to share*) el baño con nadie

6.17 En casa Primero, mira el dibujo y decide si las oraciones son ciertas o falsas. Si son falsas, corrígelas. Después, usando las expresiones negativas e indefinidas, inventa tres oraciones más que pueden ser ciertas o falsas. Luego, léele las oraciones a un compañero, quien va a decidir si son ciertas o falsas.

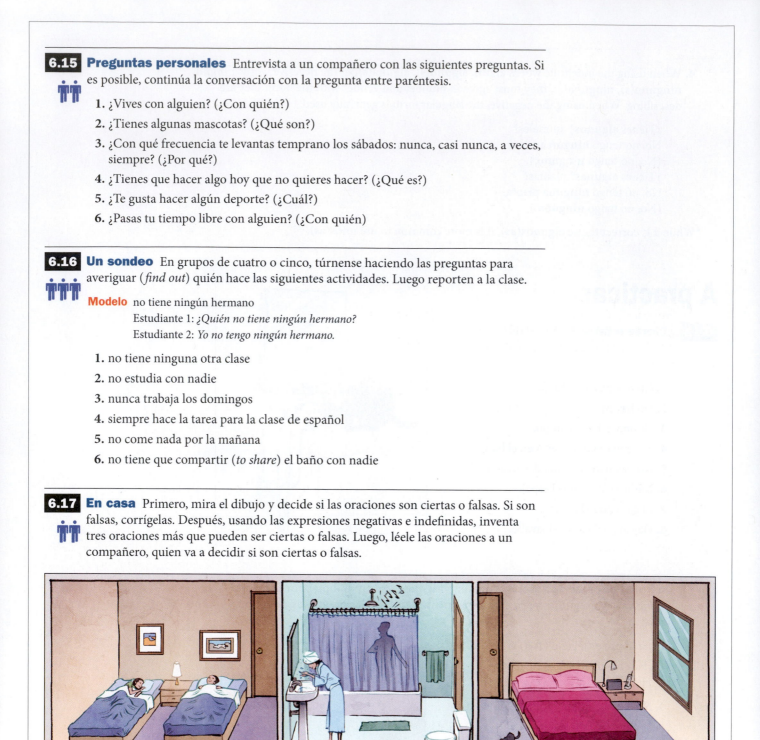

1. Hay algo en la mesita al lado de la cama.

2. No hay ningún niño en la casa.

3. Alguien se arregla en el dormitorio grande.

4. Algunas personas están en el baño.

5. No hay ni gatos ni perros en la casa.

6.18 **La niñera** Una niñera cuida a Jorge, un niño que está de muy mal humor. Completa la conversación con algunas de estas palabras negativas e indefinidas. **¡OJO! Algún** y **ningún** tienen varias formas.

algo	alguien	algún	siempre	o
nada	nadie	ningún	nunca	ni ... ni

Niñera: Jorge, ¿quieres leer _____ cuentos?

Jorge: No, no quiero leer _____ cuento. Es aburrido.

Niñera: ¿Tienes hambre? ¿Quieres comer _____?

Jorge: No, no quiero comer _____.

Niñera: ¿Te gustaría jugar a las cartas _____ al dominó?

Jorge: No me gusta jugar _____ a las cartas _____ al dominó.

Niñera: ¿Quieres invitar a _____ a jugar contigo?

Jorge: No, no quiero invitar a _____. Quiero estar solo.

Niñera: ¿Quieres ir a _____ lugar (*place*)?

Jorge: ¡Sí! Quiero ir a _____ playa para jugar voleibol en la arena con _____ de mis amigos.

Niñera: ¡Por fin! ¡_____ eres tan negativo, Jorge!

6.19 **Los opuestos** Trabaja con un compañero y túrnense para hablar sobre su rutina. El primer estudiante debe decir una idea positiva o negativa, y el segundo estudiante debe decir lo opuesto, aun (*even*) si no es la verdad.

Modelo Estudiante 1: *Yo siempre me ducho por la noche.*
Estudiante 2: *Yo no me ducho por las noches nunca.*
Estudiante 2: *Yo leo algunos libros antes de dormirme.*
Estudiante 1: *Yo no leo ningún libro antes de dormirme.*

Leemos algunos libros antes de dormirnos.

6.20 **¿Qué debo hacer?** Con un compañero túrnense para pedir consejos para conseguir sus metas (*goals*). Cuando das los consejos, menciona lo que debe o no debe hacer tu compañero usando una palabra afirmativa o negativa.

Modelo ayudar a otros
Estudiante 1: *Quiero ayudar a otros.*
Estudiante 2: *Debes buscar algunas oportunidades para trabajar como voluntario.*

1. ahorrar (*save*) dinero
2. conocer a más personas
3. tener buenas notas
4. un nuevo trabajo
5. estar más sano
6. divertirme más

Lectura

Antes de leer

1. ¿Tomas una siesta de vez en cuando? ¿Por qué?

2. ¿Qué personas crees que toman siestas más frecuentemente y por qué?

3. ¿Cuáles son algunas ventajas y desventajas de tomar siestas?

4. ¿En qué países piensas que se toman siestas y por qué?

A leer

La siesta

La costumbre de dormir durante el día por una media hora se originó en Roma, donde se usaba la expresión "hora sexta" para hablar del tiempo dedicado a dormir y descansar después de cinco horas de mucho trabajo. En España "la hora sexta" **se convirtió en** *la siesta.* En el horario tradicional, exportado después a los países latinoamericanos, la gente come con su familia al mediodía y después descansa un poco antes de volver a trabajar.

became

Este tiempo es importante porque la comida al mediodía es la comida principal en muchos de estos países, y es saludable tomar

[recomiendan la siesta
como algo positivo]

tiempo para digerir. Además, en los meses cuando hace mucho calor, nadie quiere salir a la calle durante estas horas—**las más calurosas** del día. Muchos estudios científicos recomiendan la siesta como algo positivo para la salud **ya que** previene problemas cardiacos, ayuda a la digestión y disminuye el estrés.

the warmest

as

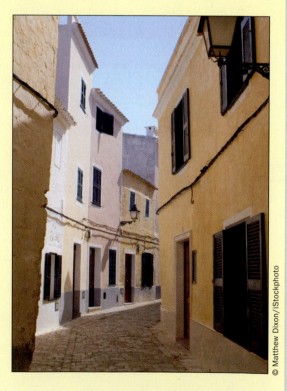

© Matthew Dixon/iStockphoto

Aún más, aunque las personas no siempre usan este tiempo para dormir, la interrupción de las labores permite a las familias reunirse y pasar más tiempo juntas.

En algunos países hay empresas que entienden el valor de la siesta, y dan a sus trabajadores un espacio donde pueden descansar por algunos minutos, para incrementar su productividad, pero desafortunadamente, la hora dedicada a la siesta es una costumbre que está desapareciendo en muchos países. La gente ya casi nunca tiene tiempo para descansar debido principalmente a la presión de la vida en las ciudades, en donde el tiempo es poco, el tráfico y las distancias son grandes, y los negocios prefieren no cerrar para tener algunos clientes más.

© Kravchenko Marina/Shutterstock

Comprensión

1. ¿Cuál es el origen de la palabra *siesta*?
2. ¿Qué hacen las personas durante la hora de la siesta?
3. ¿Cuáles son los beneficios de tomar una siesta?
4. ¿Por qué está desapareciendo esta costumbre?
5. En tu opinión personal ¿crees que la costumbre de la siesta va a desaparecer por completo?

Después de leer

Habla con un compañero para responder a las preguntas.

1. ¿Tú duermes una siesta a veces (*sometimes*)? ¿Por qué?
2. ¿Piensas que es una buena idea dormir siestas?
3. ¿Cuáles son las ventajas y las desventajas de dormir la siesta?

© Photos To Go

Tomar una siesta es una costumbre saludable.

¡Es el verano! Hace buen tiempo y algunas personas de la ciudad salen a disfrutar del buen tiempo.

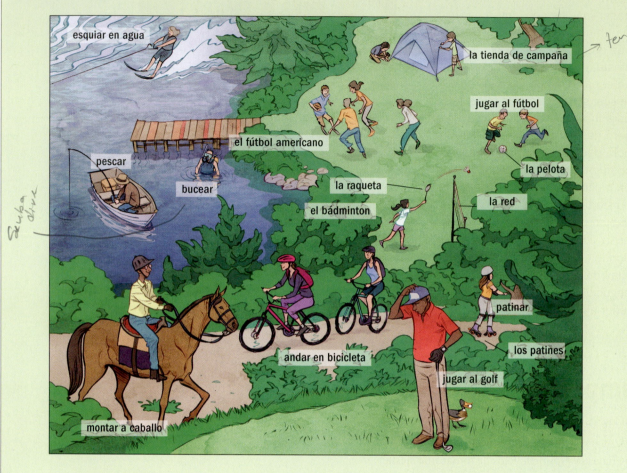

esquiar en agua

la tienda de campaña → tent

jugar al fútbol

el fútbol americano

la pelota

pescar

bucear

la raqueta

la red

el bádminton

patinar

andar en bicicleta

los patines

jugar al golf

montar a caballo

scuba dive

Más vocabulario

el aficionado	fan (of a sport)
el campo	field
la cancha	court
el equipo	team; equipment
la entrada	ticket
el partido	game, match
el saco de dormir	sleeping bag

Cognados

el básquetbol	el tenis
el béisbol	el voleibol
el ping-pong	

Los pasatiempos

acampar	to camp
esquiar en tabla	to snowboard
hacer alpinismo	to go mountain climbing
ir de excursión	to go hiking
levantar pesas	to lift weights
patinar en hielo	to ice skate

INVESTIGUEMOS EL VOCABULARIO

The following are lexical variations:

| el baloncesto | basketball |
| el fanático | fan |

Práctica

6.21 **Escucha y responde** Vas a escuchar algunas actividades. En un papel escribe **deporte** y en otro **equipo.** Si escuchas el nombre de un deporte, levanta el papel que dice **deporte,** y si es equipo para jugar, levanta el papel que dice **equipo.**

CD1-29

6.22 Relaciones ¿Qué actividades o cosas puedes relacionar con los siguientes verbos? Escribe todos los que puedas (*as many as you can*).

1. acampar
2. practicar
3. jugar
4. ir
5. andar
6. patinar
7. hacer

[handwritten notes:]
1. la tienda de campaña
   el saco dormir
   ir de excursión
   hacer alpinismo

2. Jugar al fútbol
   el badminton
   el golf
   Patinar
   montar caballo

3. fútbol, el badminton, golf

4. Ir de excursión, hacer alpinismo

5. andar en bicycleta

6.23 ¿Qué actividad es? Identifica el nombre del deporte que se necesita para completar las oraciones.

1. Es necesario tener dos equipos de seis personas, una pelota y una red para jugar _el voleibol_.
☆ 2. Jugamos _ping pong_ con raquetas, una mesa, una red y pelotas pequeñas.
3. Cuando vamos a acampar dormimos en _el saco de dormir_.
☆ 4. Para jugar al fútbol necesitamos dos _equipos_ de once personas.
5. Es necesario tener una _raqueta_ para jugar tenis.
6. Podemos _pescar_ en el lago (*lake*).
7. El deporte más popular en Europa y Latinoamérica es _fútbol_.
8. A mi hermana le gusta hacer _alpinismo_ en las montañas.

6.24 ¿Qué palabra no corresponde al grupo? Primero, encuentra la palabra que no corresponda (*belong*), y después, compara tus respuestas con las de un compañero. Expliquen por qué no corresponde.

1. pescar	nadar	acampar	bucear
2. la raqueta	la tienda de campaña	la pelota	la red
3. la cancha	el voleibol	el básquetbol	el fútbol
4. patinar en hielo	jugar al golf	esquiar	esquiar en tabla
5. el fútbol	ir de excursión	el voleibol	el básquetbol
6. el aficionado	el saco de dormir	el partido	la cancha

6.25 ¡Adivina! Con un compañero, túrnense para describir artículos (*items*) o actividades asociados con deportes. Deben adivinar lo que el otro describe.

Modelo Estudiante A: *Es un deporte. Para jugar necesitamos dos equipos de cinco personas y una pelota...*
Estudiante B: *Es el básquetbol.*

6.26 En busca de... Circula por la clase y pregúntales a unos compañeros si hacen las siguientes actividades en su tiempo libre. Habla con un compañero diferente para cada actividad. Tu compañero debe dar información adicional. Después repórtenle la información a la clase.

Modelo jugar al ping-pong
Estudiante 1: *¿Juegas al ping-pong?*
Estudiante 2: *Sí, juego al ping-pong en casa de mis amigos.*

1. jugar al fútbol
2. levantar pesas
3. acampar en el verano
4. ver golf en televisión
5. jugar bien al básquetbol
6. estar en un equipo (*team*) deportivo
7. patinar en hielo
8. gustar ver fútbol americano

¿Cuáles son algunos deportistas que admiras? Ana Guevara es una de las grandes deportistas mexicanas de la actualidad. Lee su biografía. ¿En qué deporte compite Ana Guevara? ¿Por qué es una atleta extraordinaria?

Ricardo Mazalan/AP Images

Nombre: Ana Gabriela Guevara Espinoza
País: México
Fecha de nacimiento: 4 de marzo de 1977
Lugar de nacimiento: Nogales, Sonora

En poco tiempo, Ana Gabriela Guevara se ha convertido en la máxima figura del deporte mexicano, logrando ser la mujer más rápida en los 400 metros planos a nivel mundial.

Desde muy joven, Ana mostró su gusto por los deportes y se unió al equipo de básquetbol de su escuela en la secundaria y la preparatoria. Al ver su buen desempeño, fue elegida para la selección de Nogales, donde obtuvo el campeonato estatal.

Debido a su edad, la joven de Sonora no pudo continuar en el equipo, por lo que decidió continuar con otro deporte, y se decidió por el atletismo. En 1996 y 1997, Ana obtuvo sus primeras medallas de oro en la pista, al salir campeona en los 400 y 800 metros en la Olimpiada Juvenil.

Bajo las órdenes del cubano Raúl Barreda, Ana fue invitada por la Federación Mexicana de Atletismo para ser parte de la selección nacional. En 1999, Ana participó en el Mundial bajo techo de Japón y terminó en el cuarto sitio.

Gracias a sus buenas actuaciones durante el año, se decidió que la sonorense fuera la abanderada de la delegación mexicana en los Juegos Panamericanos de Winnipeg. Sin muchos problemas, Ana conquistó la medalla de oro para México en los 400 metros.

El 2002 marcó la mejor época de la mexicana, ya que conquistó la Golden League y el Grand Prix, además de dos medallas de oro en la Copa del Mundo en Madrid. El 3 de mayo de 2003, Ana logró la mejor marca en la historia de los 300 metros ante el público mexicano, que llenó el estadio de Ciudad Universitaria para ver a la nueva estrella del deporte mexicano.

En el Campeonato Mundial de París, Ana Guevara se convirtió en la nueva reina de los 400 metros del atletismo mundial, al cronometrar 48 segundos con 89 centésimas, la mejor marca del año. El 14 de septiembre, la mexicana Ana Guevara estrenó su corona mundial, al ganar por tercer año consecutivo la Gala Atlética de la IAAF en Mónaco.

© Editorial Televisa

Más allá

¿Admiras a algún deportista? ¿Quién? ¿Por qué?

A analizar

Lee el siguiente párrafo y observa las formas de los verbos.

Mis amigos y yo **salimos** para la playa el viernes pasado por la mañana y **volvimos** ayer. El viernes, yo **pasé** todo el día en la playa con Daniel y Óscar. **Tomé** el sol y **nadé** en el mar. Por la noche **paseamos** por el centro y **cenamos** en un restaurante muy bueno. Yo **comí** enchiladas, Daniel **comió** tacos y Óscar **pidió** un chile relleno. Yo **bebí** una soda, y Óscar y Daniel **bebieron** cervezas. ¡Nos **gustó** mucho la comida! El sábado, **nos levantamos** temprano para ir a la playa otra vez. Después de comer, **decidimos** ir de compras. Yo **compré** una camiseta para mi hermano. Óscar **compró** un reloj para su novia, pero Daniel no **compró** nada. El domingo, yo **salí** en un barco y **aprendí** a practicar esquí acuático. Óscar y Daniel **se quedaron** en la playa. Ellos **jugaron** al voleibol con unas chicas que **conocieron.** A las cinco, **subimos** al coche para regresar a casa.

© Tatiana Morozova/Shutterstock

1. Have these events already happened or are they going to happen in the future?
2. All the boldfaced verbs are in the preterite tense. Using the verbs in the paragraph as a model, complete the tables below.

-ar

yo	_____	nosotros(as)	_____
tú	**-aste**	vosotros(as)	**-asteis**
él, ella, usted	_____	ellos, ellas, ustedes	_____

-er/-ir

yo	_____	nosotros(as)	_____
tú	**-iste**	vosotros(as)	**-isteis**
él, ella, usted	_____	ellos, ellas, ustedes	_____

A comprobar

The preterite

1. The preterite is used to discuss actions completed in the past.

   ¿Jugaste al tenis ayer?
   *Did you **play** tennis yesterday?*

   No, **nadé** en la piscina.
   *No, I **swam** in the pool.*

2. To form the preterite of regular **-ar, -er,** and **-ir** verbs, add these endings to the stem of the verb.

INVESTIGUEMOS LA GRAMÁTICA
Notice that the endings for regular **-er** and **-ir** verbs are identical in the preterite.

comer

yo	com**í**	nosotros(as)	com**imos**
tú	com**iste**	vosotros(as)	com**isteis**
él, ella, usted	com**ió**	ellos, ellas, ustedes	com**ieron**

escribir

yo	escrib**í**	nosotros(as)	escrib**imos**
tú	escrib**iste**	vosotros(as)	escrib**isteis**
él, ella, usted	escrib**ió**	ellos, ellas, ustedes	escrib**ieron**

hablar

yo	habl**é**	nosotros(as)	habl**amos**
tú	habl**aste**	vosotros(as)	habl**asteis**
él, ella, usted	habl**ó**	ellos, ellas, ustedes	habl**aron**

3. -ar and **-er** verbs that have stem changes in the present tense do not have a stem change in the preterite. You will learn about **-ir** stem-changing verbs later in this chapter.

cerrar

yo	cerré	nosotros(as)	cerramos
tú	cerraste	vosotros(as)	cerrasteis
él, ella, usted	cerró	ellos, ellas, ustedes	cerraron

volver

yo	volví	nosotros(as)	volvimos
tú	volviste	vosotros(as)	volvisteis
él, ella, usted	volvió	ellos, ellas, ustedes	volvieron

4. Verbs ending in **-car, -gar,** and **-zar** have spelling changes in the first person singular (**yo**) in the preterite. Notice that the spelling changes preserve the original sound of the infinitive for **-car** and **-gar** verbs.

-car	c → qué
tocar	yo **toqué,** tú tocaste, él tocó,…
-gar	g → gué
jugar	yo **jugué,** tú jugaste, él jugó, …
-zar	z → cé
empezar	yo **empecé,** tú empezaste, él empezó, …

5. The third person singular and plural of **leer** and **oír** also have spelling changes. An unaccented **i** always changes to **y** when it appears between two vowels. Notice the use of accent marks on all forms except the third person plural.

leer

yo	leí	nosotros(as)	leímos
tú	leíste	vosotros(as)	leísteis
él, ella, usted	**leyó**	ellos, ellas, ustedes	**leyeron**

oír

yo	oí	nosotros(as)	oímos
tú	oíste	vosotros(as)	oísteis
él, ella, usted	**oyó**	ellos, ellas, ustedes	**oyeron**

A practicar

6.27 **El orden lógico** Héctor y Gustavo pasaron un muy buen fin de semana. Lee las oraciones sobre sus actividades y ponlas en un orden lógico.

_____ Héctor invitó a Gustavo a ir a la playa por el fin de semana.

_____ Los dos salieron para la playa.

_____ Héctor llamó a su mejor amigo, Gustavo.

_____ Gustavo llegó a la casa de Héctor a las siete.

_____ El viernes Héctor volvió a casa después de trabajar.

_____ Gustavo aceptó la invitación con mucho entusiasmo.

_____ Al llegar a la playa, buscaron un hotel.

6.28 **El sábado pasado** En parejas, usen la información de los dibujos para describir lo que Beatriz hizo (*did*) el sábado pasado con su novio Arturo.

INVESTIGUEMOS LOS VERBOS
You will learn irregular preterite verbs in **Capítulo 7;** however you may want to use the verb **ir** in this lesson. It is conjugated in the following manner:

yo	**fui**	nosotros(as)	**fuimos**
tú	**fuiste**	vosotros(as)	**fuisteis**
él, ella,	**fue**	ellos, ellas,	**fueron**
usted		ustedes	

6.29 **¿Qué hiciste?** Con un compañero, completen las siguientes oraciones para hablar de su fin de semana, usando el pretérito. Pueden usar los siguientes verbos u otros verbos.

> **Modelo** Estudiante 1: *Anoche yo comí en un restaurante, ¿y tú?*
> Estudiante 2: *Anoche yo cociné para mi familia.*

| levantarse | trabajar | salir | estudiar | pasar bien/mal |
| limpiar | jugar | mirar | escribir | hablar por teléfono |

1. El fin de semana pasado yo…
2. El viernes por la noche yo…
3. El sábado yo…
4. El sábado por la noche yo…
5. El domingo yo…
6. El domingo por la noche yo…

6.30 **Una entrevista** Con un compañero, túrnense para preguntar y contestar las preguntas.

1. ¿Qué clases tomaste el semestre pasado?
2. ¿Qué cenaste anoche?
3. ¿Jugaste algún deporte el fin de semana pasado? ¿Cuál? ¿Con quién?
4. ¿A qué hora te levantaste esta mañana? ¿A qué hora llegaste a la universidad?
5. ¿Qué hiciste (*did you do*) ayer por la mañana? ¿Y por la tarde?
6. ¿Con quién hablaste por teléfono la semana pasada?

INVESTIGUEMOS EL VOCABULARIO
You might find the following expressions helpful when talking about the past:

anoche	*last night*
ayer	*yesterday*
la semana pasada	*last week*

6.31 **Las vacaciones** Escribe tres actividades que hiciste (*you did*) durante tus últimas (*last*) vacaciones. Luego, busca a tres compañeros diferentes que hicieron una de esas tres actividades también. **¡OJO!** Usa el pretérito.

Conexiones culturales

Los deportes en España y Latinoamérica

Cultura

Los deportes tienen la capacidad de unir al mundo... o de dividirlo. Uno de los eventos deportivos más importantes son los juegos Olímpicos, que comenzaron su historia en Grecia en el año 776 a.C. Aunque se suspendieron por muchos años, en 1896 se retomó la idea, y así nacieron los juegos Olímpicos como los conocemos hoy, un evento que se realiza cada cuatro años. Posteriormente, en 1924, se crearon los juegos Olímpicos de Invierno.

Aunque hasta ahora, de los países hispanos, solamente México y España **han sido sede** (*have hosted*) de los juegos Olímpicos, todos participan en ellos con orgullo (*pride*) y con esperanzas cada cuatro años. Entre los países con más medallas aparecen Cuba (en el lugar 15),

¿Sabes qué significa el logotipo de los juegos Olímpicos?

España (en el lugar 28), Argentina (34) y México (37). El primer y segundo lugar en el total de medallas los tienen Estados Unidos y Rusia.

En parejas, respondan a las siguientes preguntas relacionadas con los juegos Olímpicos y repórtenle las respuestas a la clase.

1. ¿En qué deportes tienen más medallas los países latino-americanos? ¿Por qué crees que tienen más éxito en estos deportes?

2. ¿Qué países hispanohablantes crees que compiten más en los juegos Olímpicos de Invierno? ¿Por qué piensas que algunos compiten más que otros?

3. ¿Por qué piensas que entre los países con más medallas (*medals*) está Cuba?

Yoanka González Pérez

iTunes

Similar to the Olympic Games, the Soccer World Cup is played every four years. The song "La copa de la vida" by Puerto Rican singer Ricky Martin was the theme song for the 1998 World Cup Tournament in France. Listen to the song and then determine what the message is.

Investiga en Internet los atletas de países hispanohablantes que ganaron medallas en los juegos Olímpicos.

Comunidad

Muchos deportistas en los Estados Unidos vienen de países hispanohablantes. Investiga si hay jugadores de países hispanohablantes en tu universidad y escribe una entrevista para ese deportista. Las siguientes son algunas ideas para la entrevista:

¿Por qué le gusta jugar?

¿Con qué frecuencia practica?

¿Quiere ser profesional? ¿Por qué?

¿Cuándo empezó a jugar?

¿Jugaba en un equipo de la escuela secundaria?

¿El deporte le ayudó a llegar a la universidad?

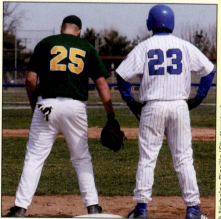

¿Hay deportistas de países hispanohablantes en tu universidad?

Comparaciones

En muchos países de habla hispana se practican deportes en las universidades, pero juegan un papel diferente a los deportes en los Estados Unidos, donde los estudiantes obtienen créditos por practicar deportes. En Latinoamérica los deportes son considerados un entretenimiento y nadie mencionaría sus actividades deportivas en su curriculum vitae (*resumé*), excepto los deportistas. Sin embargo, la mayoría de las universidades tienen equipos deportivos que representan a su alma mater con orgullo.

¿Son importantes las actividades deportivas en tu universidad?

¿Hay becas (*scholarships*) para deportistas en tu universidad?

¿Son importantes las actividades deportivas en tu vida en general?

¿Cuántas horas a la semana practicas deportes?

Busca una universidad en España o en Latinoamérica en el Internet y compara las actividades deportivas que se ofrecen, con las actividades de una universidad en los Estados Unidos.

Practican deportes en la universidad.

© Shelby Ross/Getty Images

Conexiones... a la antropología

Muchas civilizaciones antiguas jugaban juegos de pelota, pero el objetivo no era solamente el entretenimiento, ya que el juego tenía significados religiosos. En el juego de pelota azteca (Tlachtli) la cancha representaba el mundo, y la pelota el sol o la luna. En este juego, la pelota debía atravesar el aro hecho de piedra (*stone*). El juego de pelota azteca tenía una gran semejanza con el juego Pok-a-tok de los mayas, juego en el que los jugadores debían tocar la pelota solamente con los codos, las rodillas o las caderas (*hips*).

¿Conoces el origen de otros deportes o juegos?

Ruinas de un juego de pelota maya en México

© Arvind Balaraman/Shutterstock

A analizar

Lee el siguiente párrafo y observa las formas de los verbos. Luego, contesta la pregunta que sigue.

Fernando **consiguió** unas entradas para un partido de fútbol el sábado pasado. Nos invitó a mí y a Vicente. Fernando y Vicente son grandes aficionados de los Tigres y **se vistieron** de rojo, pero yo **me vestí** de negro porque soy aficionado de los Jaguares. Después de llegar al estadio y sentarnos, **pedimos** algo de comer. Ellos **pidieron** tamales, pero yo **pedí** una quesadilla. Cuando comenzó el partido nos levantamos y gritamos por nuestros equipos. Todos **nos divertimos,** pero creo que ellos **se divirtieron** más porque al final ganó su equipo.

Conseguir, vestirse, pedir, and **divertirse** all have stem changes in the present as well as in the preterite. How are the stem changes different in the preterite?

A comprobar

Stem-changing verbs in the preterite

-Ir verbs that have stem changes in the present tense also have stem changes in the preterite. The third person singular and plural (**él, ella, usted, ellos, ellas,** and **ustedes**) change **e → i** and **o → u.**

pedir

yo	pedí	nosotros(as)	pedimos
tú	pediste	vosotros(as)	pedisteis
él, ella, usted	p**i**dió	ellos, ellas, ustedes	p**i**dieron

Yo **pedí** una quesadilla durante el partido.
Mis amigos **pidieron** tacos.

dormir

yo	dormí	nosotros(as)	dormimos
tú	dormiste	vosotros(as)	dormisteis
él, ella, usted	d**u**rmió	ellos, ellas, ustedes	d**u**rmieron

Other common stem-changing verbs:

conseguir (i)	repetir (i)
divertirse (i)	seguir (i)
morir (u)	servir (i)
preferir (i)	vestirse (i)

¿Se **divirtieron** ustedes?
Sí, nos **divertimos** mucho.

Todos **dormimos** en la tienda de campaña.
Mi hermano **durmió** en una hamaca.

A practicar

6.32 **Un día de esquí** Completa las oraciones de la primera columna para contar la historia de un grupo de amigos que esquiaron un fin de semana.

1. Mis amigos...
2. El viernes yo...
3. El sábado, mis amigos y yo...
4. Al mediodía Sergio tenía hambre y en el café...
5. Al final todos...
6. Después de tanto ejercicio, yo...

a. pidió un bistec.
b. nos vestimos para esquiar.
c. prefirieron ir a esquiar el sábado.
d. dormí muy bien.
e. conseguí el coche de mis papás para ir a las montañas.
f. se divirtieron.

6.33 **En la playa** Completa el siguiente párrafo con la forma correcta del pretérito del verbo indicado. **¡OJO!** No todos los verbos tienen cambio en el radical.

El fin de semana pasado Tomás viajó a Puerto Viejo con su esposa Irma. Antes de salir, Tomás llamó al Hotel Bahía y **(1.)** _____ (pedir) una habitación para dos personas con balcón. **(2.)** _____ (conseguir) una habitación doble. Cuando ellos llegaron, estaban muy cansados. **(3.)** _____ (pedir) servicio a la habitación y **(4.)** _____ (acostarse). Los dos **(5.)** _____ (dormir) bien y **(6.)** _____ (despertarse) temprano. Pasaron el día en la playa y **(7.)** _____ (divertirse) nadando y jugando al sol. **(8.)** _____ (volver) tarde al hotel; se bañaron y **(9.)** _____ (vestirse) para salir a comer. Cuando regresaron al hotel, Tomás decidió quedarse en la habitación leyendo, pero Irma **(10.)** _____ (preferir) relajarse en el sauna antes de acostarse. Al día siguiente, pasaron la mañana paseando por la ciudad. Luego, **(11.)** _____ (almorzar) en el restaurante del hotel y **(12.)** _____ (empezar) el viaje de regreso a casa.

6.34 **Un día de fútbol** Isabel y Mónica son aficionadas al fútbol. En parejas, describan el día que fueron a un partido. Incluyan los siguientes verbos: **acostarse, divertirse, dormirse, preferir, sentarse, vestirse** y **volver.**

6.35 **En el pasado** Con un compañero, túrnense para conjugar el verbo en el pretérito y completar las oraciones de una forma original. Luego, reporten la información a la clase.

Modelo Ayer yo (jugar)...
Estudiante 1: *Ayer jugué al voleibol con mis amigas, ¿y tú?*
Estudiante 2: *Yo no jugué nada, pero mi hermano jugó al básquetbol.*

1. Anoche yo (dormir)...
2. La última vez (*last time*) que fui a mi restaurante favorito, yo (pedir)...
3. El fin de semana pasado yo (almorzar)...
4. Una vez que cociné, yo (servir)...
5. Esta mañana yo (preferir)...
6. El semestre pasado, yo (conseguir)...
7. Este semestre yo (comenzar)...
8. Una vez yo (perder)...

Nos divertimos en el café.

6.36 **Entrevista** Entrevista a un compañero sobre la última vez que asistió a un evento (un partido, una obra de teatro, etcétera).

1. ¿A qué evento asististe?
2. ¿Con quién asististe al evento?
3. ¿Quién consiguió las entradas?
4. ¿Cómo se vistieron para el evento?
5. ¿Sirvieron comida? ¿Qué comida?
6. ¿Se divirtieron en el evento?

6.37 **En busca de...** Circula por la clase y pregúntales a unos compañeros si hicieron las siguientes actividades. Habla con un compañero diferente para cada actividad. Tu compañero debe dar información adicional. Después reporten la información a la clase.

Modelo reír mucho el fin de semana (¿Por qué?)
Estudiante 1: *¿Reíste mucho el fin de semana?*
Estudiante 2: *Sí, reí mucho el fin de semana.*
Estudiante 1: *¿Por qué?*
Estudiante 2: *Porque miré una película cómica.*

1. divertirse durante el fin de semana (¿Dónde?)
2. vestirse elegante recientemente (¿Por qué?)
3. dormir bien anoche (¿Cuántas horas?)
4. pedir ayuda en una clase este semestre (¿Qué clase?)
5. conseguir un trabajo nuevo durante el último año (¿Dónde?)
6. servir la cena esta semana (¿Cuándo?)

Redacción

Write a letter to a friend telling him or her about a sporting event.

© Andresr/Shutterstock

Paso 1 Think of a sporting event you participated in, attended, or watched on TV. Then jot down a list of things you did. Think about the following questions: What was the event? When was it? Did you have to get tickets or make arrangements? Did you have to get up early or stay up late? What did you do before the event? What happened during the event? Did your team win or lose? What did you do after the event?

Paso 2 Begin your letter with a greeting and ask how your friend is. Then, write a topic sentence using an expression of time to tell your friend when you participated in, attended, or watched the sporting event.

> *El 30 de julio yo...*
>
> *La semana pasada yo...*

Paso 3 Using the information you generated in **Paso 1,** recount the events of the day. In order to connect your ideas, use some of the following expressions: **primero, luego, después, entonces** (*then*), and **por último** (*finally*).

Paso 4 Write a concluding statement in which you tell how you felt at the end of the day. Then close your letter.

Paso 5 Edit your letter:

1. Do all of your sentences in each paragraph support the topic sentence?

2. Is the paragraph logically organized with smooth transitions between sentences?

3. Are there any short sentences you can combine with **y** or **pero**?

4. Do your verbs agree with the subject? Are they conjugated properly?

5. Are there any spelling errors? Do the preterite verbs that need accents have them?

Lectura

Reading Strategy: Making notes

In the first **Lectura** of this chapter you learned to make notes as you go. Practice this strategy by writing a brief note next to each paragraph of the following reading. Try to use Spanish for your notes.

¿Qué deportes piensas que son muy populares en España y Latinoamérica? ¿Sabes el nombre de un deportista famoso de estos países?

A leer

Deportistas famosos

pride

A veces un deportista es mucho más que un deportista; a veces los atletas se vuelven símbolos de **orgullo** nacional. Tal es el caso de uno de los jugadores más famosos de fútbol de la historia —el argentino Diego Maradona— quien se convirtió en héroe en la Argentina por su valiosa participación en cuatro Copas del Mundial de Fútbol.

successful

Desafortunadamente, después de una carrera muy **exitosa,** Maradona tuvo problemas de salud debido a su sobrepeso y al uso de drogas. Después de un período de rehabilitación en Cuba, ahora Maradona conduce un exitoso programa de televisión llamado

> [a veces los atletas se vuelven símbolos de orgullo nacional]

El futbolista Diego Maradona de Argentina

"La Noche del Diez", con invitados de todo el mundo. Con su programa, Maradona continúa influenciando la opinión pública en diversas esferas de la vida argentina, inclusive en la política. Recientemente Maradona tuvo la oportunidad de regresar al fútbol como el director técnico de la selección argentina de fútbol en la Copa del Mundo 2010 en Sudáfrica.

Otro atleta distinguido es el español Miguel Induráin, uno de los mejores ciclistas de todos los tiempos, y ganador de cinco Tours de Francia consecutivos entre 1991 y 1995; hay solamente otras cuatro personas en el mundo que pueden decir lo mismo. Además ganó dos Giro-Tour de Italia consecutivos. Induráin creó la Fundación Miguel Induráin, que **apoya** a los deportistas de Navarra, la provincia en España de donde él es originario.

El ciclista español, Miguel Induráin

supports

just

novice
became

Finalmente hay que mencionar a una deportista que realmente **apenas** está comenzando su carrera, la golfista mexicana Lorena Ochoa. A los 25 años consiguió el título de la jugadora del año del Circuito Femenino de Golf Profesional (LPGA, por sus siglas en inglés), sólo tres años después de tener el título de la **novata** del año. En el año 2007 Lorena Ochoa **llegó a ser** la mejor golfista del mundo. La habilidad de Ochoa para jugar al golf también está atrayendo en México a muchos nuevos aficionados de este deporte. Sin duda, Lorena Ochoa estará en las noticias deportivas por muchos años.

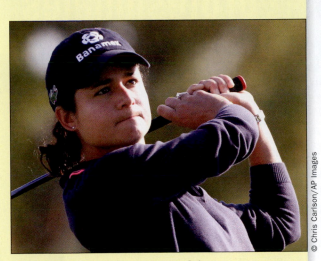
© Chris Carlson/AP Images

La jugadora de golf mexicana, Lorena Ochoa

Comprensión

1. ¿Quiénes son los tres deportistas de los que habla la lectura? ¿De dónde son?
2. ¿Qué problemas tuvo Diego Armando Maradona? ¿Qué hace ahora?
3. ¿Cuántos deportistas ganaron el Tour de Francia cinco veces consecutivas?
4. ¿Qué hace la fundación Miguel Induráin?
5. ¿Qué deporte juega Lorena Ochoa?
6. ¿Qué efecto tiene en México el desempeño (*performance*) de Ochoa como deportista?

Después de leer

Con un compañero de clase, escriban una lista de atletas hispanos que conocen y los deportes que juegan. Luego, escojan uno de la lista y busquen cinco detalles interesantes sobre esa persona para compartirlos con la clase.

El jugador de tenis español, Rafael Nadal

© Neale Cousland/Shutterstock

Vocabulario

Sustantivos

el (la) adolescente	*teenager*
los aparatos	*exercise machines*
la autoestima	*self-esteem*
el calambre	*cramp*
el calentamiento	*warm-up*
la dieta	*diet*
los ejercicios aeróbicos	*aerobics*
el (la) entrenador(a)	*trainer*
el masaje	*massage*
el músculo	*muscle*
la serie	*series/sets*
el sobrepeso	*overweight*

Adjetivos

agotado(a)	*exhausted*
disciplinado(a)	*disciplined*
extenuante	*exhausting*

Verbos

entrenar(se)	*to train oneself*
respirar	*to breathe*
sudar	*to sweat*

Expresiones útiles

estar en buena forma
to be in good shape

¿Qué parte del cuerpo quiere fortalecer?
What part of your body would you like to strengthen?

Descanse.
Take a break.

Haga abdominales.
Do sit-ups.

Haga flexiones.
Do push-ups.

Haga tres series de...
Do three series of . . .

Tome agua.
Drink some water.

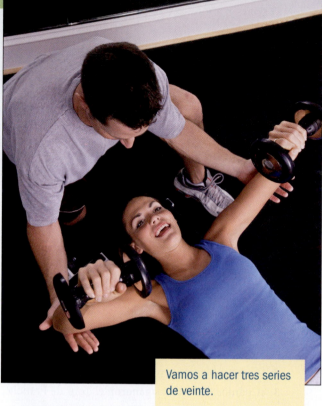

Vamos a hacer tres series de veinte.

© iofoto/Shutterstock

DATOS IMPORTANTES

Educación: Certificación de entrenador personal. Se prefieren profesores de educación física. Otros requisitos adicionales importantes: estudios terciarios y universitarios relacionados con medicina; por ejemplo, asistencia médica, técnica en primeros auxilios, enfermería, etcétera.

Salario: Entre $20 000 y $100 000

Dónde se trabaja: Gimnasios, clubes privados, clubes comunitarios, clubes deportivos profesionales (fútbol, béisbol, boxeo, etcétera)

Ricardo Melo es entrenador personal. Trabaja en un club privado y entrena a personas que quieren bajar de peso o estar en buena forma. En el video vas a ver una entrevista entre Ricardo y la madre de una joven que necesita ir al gimnasio.

Antes de ver

Los entrenadores personales ayudan a personas con diferentes necesidades. ¿Qué tipo de necesidades crees que puede tener una persona que va a un gimnasio? ¿Qué preguntas iniciales le hacen al entrenador? ¿Consideras que el entrenamiento individual es mejor que el entrenamiento en grupo? Explica.

Comprensión

1. ¿Por qué la hija de la Sra. Matos necesita ir al gimnasio?

2. ¿Cuántos años tiene la hija?

3. ¿Dónde hace gimnasia la hija de la Sra. Matos?

4. ¿Qué tipo de ejercicios recomienda el entrenador para empezar a trabajar las piernas?

5. ¿Qué otros ejercicios recomienda el entrenador?

6. Según el entrenador, ¿con qué debe combinar el programa de ejercicio?

© Heinle/Cengage Learning

Después de ver

En parejas, representen a un entrenador personal y a una persona que necesita su ayuda. Expliquen por qué la persona busca al entrenador. ¿Quiere estar en buena forma? ¿Desea fortalecer una parte del cuerpo? ¿Tiene algún problema físico? ¿El médico le recomendó hacer ejercicio? ¿Hay algo que no puede hacer? El entrenador le explica un plan para esa situación.

6.38 **¿Con qué frecuencia?** Mira las actividades en la lista y menciona con qué frecuencia las haces.

> **Modelo** ducharse por la noche
> *Me ducho por la noche una vez a la semana./*
> *Nunca me ducho por la noche.*

1. afeitarse
2. cepillarse los dientes
3. levantarse temprano
4. bañarse en la bañera
5. acostarse tarde
6. dormirse con la tele encendida (*turned on*)
7. ponerse ropa elegante
8. lavarse la cara

¿Con qué frecuencia te afeitas?

© Junial Enterprises/Shutterstock

6.39 **El pesimista** Diego es el entrenador de un equipo de fútbol muy malo. Un reportero le hace una entrevista. Imagina que eres Diego y contesta las preguntas, usando expresiones negativas.

1. ¿Siempre ganan los partidos?
2. ¿Hay alguien famoso en el equipo?
3. ¿Hay algunos buenos jugadores en el equipo?
4. ¿Compite el equipo en torneos nacionales o internacionales?
5. ¿Hay alguna posibilidad de ganar el próximo partido?
6. ¿Quiere usted decir algo más?

6.40 **De pesca** Completa los párrafos con la forma apropiada del pretérito del verbo entre paréntesis.

Esta mañana yo **(1.)** _____ (despertarse) temprano para ir de pesca con mis amigos Alfredo y César. **(2.)** _____ (vestirse), **(3.)** _____ (comer) un poco de fruta, **(4.)** _____ (tomar) un café, y **(5.)** _____ (salir) de casa. En media hora **(6.)** _____ (llegar) al lago (*lake*) y mis amigos **(7.)** _____ (llegar) un poco después.

Nosotros **(8.)** _____ (pasar) toda la mañana en el agua. Alfredo y yo **(9.)** _____ (pescar) unos peces bonitos. ¡Pobre César! Él no **(10.)** _____ (conseguir) nada, pero **(11.)** _____ (divertirse) mucho. A las dos nosotros **(12.)** _____ (decidir) ir a comer. **(13.)** _____ (comer) en un restaurante cerca del lago; luego mis amigos **(14.)** _____ (volver) a sus casas y yo a la mía (*mine*).

6.41 **Un pasado interesante** Trabaja con un compañero. Túrnense para hacer y contestar las preguntas sobre las fotos. Deben usar el pretérito en todas las respuestas.

1.

© Vladimir Mucibabic/Shutterstock

a. ¿Qué hizo (*What did he do*) anoche?
b. ¿Por qué durmió en el coche?
c. ¿Qué pasó cuando se despertó?

2.

© Jaimie Duplass/Shutterstock

a. ¿Quién llamó?
b. ¿Qué pasó?
c. ¿Qué hizo la mujer después?

3.

© Losevsky Pavel/Shutterstock

a. ¿Adónde viajaron?
b. ¿Qué hicieron allí (*What did they do there*)?
c. ¿Qué pasó cuando regresaron?

4.

© Photos To Go

a. ¿Adónde corrió?
b. ¿Por qué llegó tarde?
c. ¿Qué pasó cuando llegó?

6.42 **Unos monstruos** Trabaja con un compañero. Uno mira el dibujo aquí, y el otro mira el dibujo en el apéndice A. Túrnense para describir los monstruos. Deben encontrar las cinco diferencias.

🔊 Vocabulario 1

Los verbos reflexivos

acostarse (ue)	to lie down, to go to bed	estirarse	to stretch
afeitarse	to shave	irse	to leave, to go away
arreglarse	to get ready	lavarse	to wash
bañarse	to bathe, to shower (Mex.)	levantarse	to get up
		maquillarse	to put on make-up
cepillarse	to brush	peinarse	to comb or style one's hair
cortarse	to cut	ponerse (la ropa)	to put on (clothing)
despertarse (ie)	to wake up	quitarse (la ropa)	to take off (clothing)
divertirse (ie)	to have fun	secarse	to dry oneself
dormirse (ue)	to fall asleep	sentarse (ie)	to sit down
ducharse	to shower	verse	to see oneself
		vestirse (i)	to get dressed

Las partes del cuerpo

la boca	mouth	la mano	hand
el brazo	arm	el muslo	thigh
la cabeza	head	la nariz	nose
la cara	face	el ojo	eye
el codo	elbow	la oreja	ear
el cuello	neck	el pecho	chest
el dedo	finger	el pelo	hair
el dedo (del pie)	toe	el pie	foot
el diente	tooth	la pierna	leg
la espalda	back	la rodilla	knee
el estómago	stomach	el tobillo	ankle
el hombro	shoulder		

Palabras adicionales

antes de + infinitive	before (doing something)	después de + infinitive	after (doing something)
el champú	shampoo	el jabón	soap
el dentrífico	toothpaste	tarde	late
el despertador	alarm clock	temprano	early
		la toalla	towel

Expresiones indefinidas y negativas

algo	something	ni… ni	neither . . . nor
alguien	someone, somebody	ningún (ninguno), ninguna	none, any
algún (alguno), alguna	some	nunca	never
jamás	never	o… o	either . . . or
nada	nothing	siempre	always
nadie	no one, nobody	también	also
		tampoco	neither, either

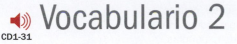

Vocabulario 2

CD1-31

Los deportes

el alpinismo	*mountain climbing*
el bádminton	*badminton*
el básquetbol	*basketball*
el béisbol	*baseball*
el fútbol	*soccer*
el fútbol americano	*American football*

el golf	*golf*
el ping-pong	*ping-pong, table tennis*
el tenis	*tennis*
el voleibol	*volleyball*

El equipo

el campo	*field*
la cancha	*court*
el equipo	*equipment, team*
el patín	*skate*
la pelota	*ball*

la raqueta	*racquet*
la red	*net*
el saco de dormir	*sleeping bag*
la tienda de campaña	*camping tent*

Los verbos

acampar	*to go camping*
andar (en bicicleta)	*to walk (to ride a bike)*
bucear	*to scuba dive*
esquiar en el agua	*to water-ski*
esquiar en tabla	*to snowboard*
hacer alpinismo	*to climb mountains*

ir de excursión	*to hike*
ir de pesca	*to go fishing*
levantar pesas	*to lift weights*
montar a	*to ride (an animal)*
patinar	*to skate*
patinar en hielo	*to ice skate*
pescar	*to fish*

Palabras adicionales

el (la) aficionado(a)	*fan (of a sport)*
la entrada	*ticket*
el partido	*game*

anoche	*last night*
ayer	*yesterday*
la semana pasada	*last week*

Diccionario personal

_____

_____

_____

_____

_____

_____

© Used by permission of Donato Ndongo

Donato Ndongo
Biografía
Donato Ndongo-Bidyogo (1950–) es un escritor, político y periodista de Guinea Ecuatorial. Su trabajo profesional ha incluido varios puestos en universidades españolas, y más de diez años trabajando para la agencia de noticias (*news*) EFE en África central. También trabajó como director adjunto del Centro Cultural Hispano-Guineano en Malabo. Dentro de su labor política, destaca como fundador del Partido del Progreso de Guinea Ecuatorial en 1984.

Como escritor, Ndongo es autor de libros de ficción, ensayos y poesía. Algunas de sus obras más destacadas incluyen *Historia y Tragedia de Guinea Ecuatorial* (1977), y la antología de literatura ecuatoguineana titulada *Las tinieblas de tu memoria negra*.

Ndongo ha vivido en el exilio desde 1994, cuando se marchó a España debido a su oposición al gobierno de Teodoro Obiang. Entre 2005 y 2009, Ndongo trabajó como profesor visitante de la Universidad de Missouri en Columbia. Después de su estancia en los Estados Unidos, regresó a España.

Antes de leer

1. El título del poema que vas a leer es Cántico. ¿Qué piensas que significa esta palabra?
2. El poema habla de lo que un poeta debe hacer. En tu opinión ¿cuáles son los deberes ú objetivos de un poeta?

Cántico

Yo no quiero ser poeta para cantar a
África.
Yo no quiero ser poeta para glosar
lo negro.
5 Yo no quiero ser poeta así.
El poeta no es cantor de
bellezas.   *beauties*
El poeta no luce la brillante
piel negra.

10 El poeta, este poeta no tiene voz
para **andares ondulantes** de   *undulating gait*
hermosas damas
de pelos **rizados** y **caderas**   *curly / hips*
redondas.

15 El poeta llora su **tierra**   *land*
inmensa y pequeña
dura y frágil
luminosa y oscura
rica y pobre.

20 Este poeta tiene su mano
atada   *tied*
a las **cadenas** que atan a su   *chains*
gente.
Este poeta no siente nostalgia
25 de glorias pasadas.

Yo no canto al sexo exultante
que huele a jardín de rosas.
lips Yo no adoro **labios** gruesos
que saben a mango fresco.
30 Yo no pienso en la mujer encorvada
basket/wood bajo su **cesto** cargado de **leña**
empty con un niño chupando la teta **vacía.**
Yo describo la triste historia
de un mundo poblado de blancos
35 negros
rojos y
amarillos
pool que saltan de **charca** en charca
sin hablarse ni mirarse.

40 El poeta llora a los muertos
que matan manos negras
en nombre de la Negritud.
Yo canto con mi pueblo

una vida pasada bajo el cacaotero
45 para que ellos **merienden** cho-co-la-te. *snack*
Si su pueblo está triste,
el poeta está triste.
Yo no soy poeta por **voluntad** divina. *will*
El poeta es poeta por voluntad humana.

50 Yo no quiero la poesía
que solo deleita los oídos de los poetas.
Yo no quiero la poesía
que se lee en noches de vino tinto
y mujeres **embelesadas**. *spellbound*

55 Poesía, sí.
Poetas, sí.
Pero que sepan lo que es el hombre
y por qué sufre el hombre
y por qué **gime** el hombre. *groan*

Courtesy of the author, Donato Ndongo.

Después de leer

A. Comprensión

1. Según la voz narrativa, ¿qué es importante decir en las poesías?
2. ¿Cuál es el mensaje del poema?
3. ¿Cuál es el tono? ¿Por qué?
4. ¿Cuál es el tema?
5. Encuentra dos descripciones que hablan de la vida en Guinea Ecuatorial. ¿Qué emoción te producen?

Investiguemos la literatura: El tema

The theme of a literary text refers to the underlying ideas, what the piece is really about. To find it, look for patterns and ideas that are restated in different parts of the work. It is not the subject of the work, but more of a view of the human experience and attitude. Oftentimes the theme can be identified by asking questions such as: Are the characters in control of their lives? Does fate control them? How should people treat each other? How can we tell the false from the genuine? Is it right to resist or oppose authority?

B. Conversemos

1. En tu opinión ¿se debe mezclar (*to mix*) la poesía con la política y los problemas sociales? ¿Por qué?
2. ¿Conoces otros autores que piensan que la poesía debe tener un elemento social? ¿Quién?
3. Escribe una lista de temas políticos o sociales que piensas que son buen tema para una poesía.

Learning Strategy

Try a variety of memorization techniques

Use a variety of techniques to memorize vocabulary and verbs until you find the ones that work best for you. Some students learn better when they write the words, others learn better if they listen to recordings of the words while looking over the list, and still others need to use flashcards.

In this chapter you will learn how to:

- Request a room in a hotel and any of their services
- Use numbers above 100
- Order food in a restaurant

¿Cómo pasaste las vacaciones?

HOTEL ROMA REIAL
RESTAURANT - BAR

HOTEL ROMA
RESTAURANT

HOTEL RO
RESTAUR

© Kevin Foy / Alamy

Kevin Foy / Alamy

Exploraciones gramaticales

Irregular verbs in the preterite

Por and **para** and prepositional pronouns

Direct object pronouns I

Direct object pronouns II

En vivo

Un folleto de un hotel

Un menú para un restaurante

Conexiones culturales

Lugares excepcionales

¡Tanta comida!

Lectura

¿Dónde quedarse: hoteles, moteles, pensiones o albergues?

La comida rápida en Latinoamérica

▶ Exploraciones profesionales

La hotelería

El señor y la señora Buendía acaban de llegar a su hotel en Bogotá. Se van a quedar cuatro días y esperan tener unas vacaciones fabulosas.

Verbos

el alojamiento	*lodging*	**alojarse**	*to lodge, to stay*	**trescientos**	*300*
la clase turista	*economy class*		*(in a hotel)*	**cuatrocientos**	*400*
la habitación	*single/double/*	**bajar**	*to go down*	**quinientos**	*500*
sencilla/	*triple room*	**quedarse**	*to stay*	**seiscientos**	*600*
doble/triple		**subir**	*to go up*	**setecientos**	*700*
el (la) turista	*tourist*			**ochocientos**	*800*
el viaje todo	*all-inclusive trip*	### Los números		**novecientos**	*900*
pagado (VTP)		**cien**	*100*	**mil**	*1000*
de lujo	*luxurious*	**ciento uno**	*101*	**dos mil**	*2000*
		doscientos	*200*	**un millón**	*1 000 000*

Práctica

7.1 **Escucha y responde** Vas a escuchar una serie de ocho números. Si el número es mayor (*greater*) que el número que tú ves en la lista, señala con el pulgar hacia arriba. Si es menor (*lesser*), señala con el pulgar hacia abajo.

CD1-32

a. 150	**b.** 340	**c.** 570	**d.** 768
e. 990	**f.** 1619	**g.** 20 308	**h.** 215 365

INVESTIGUEMOS EL VOCABULARIO

In Latin America, **la camarera** is a maid; however, in Spain **la camarera** is a waitress.

In Spain, **sauna** is feminine; however, it is masculine in the majority of Latin America.

7.2 **En el hotel** Completa las ideas con las palabras del vocabulario que aparecen abajo. No necesitas usarlas todas.

maletas	huéspedes	toallas	ascensor	sauna
recepción	recepcionista	botones	habitación	camarera

1. Para entrar en nuestra ___habitacion___ necesitamos una llave.
2. Cuando llegamos a un hotel, hablamos con el ___receptionista___.
3. El ___botones___ es la persona que lleva nuestras maletas a la habitación.
4. Los ___huespedes___ de la habitación 415 desean pedir un taxi.
5. Nuestra habitación está en el décimo piso. ¿Hay ___ascensor___? Preferimos no usar las escaleras porque tenemos muchas ___maletas___.
6. ¡Qué habitación tan limpia! Debemos recordar darle una buena propina (*tip*) a la ___camarera___.

.3 **Relaciona las palabras** Empareja una palabra de la primera columna con una de la segunda. Después trabaja con un compañero, turnándose para comparar sus respuestas y explicar la relación entre las dos palabras. Es posible relacionar con más de una palabra.

Modelo la toalla
   la camarera
   La camarera trae las toallas a la habitación.

1. la habitación	**a.** el recepcionista
2. el botones	**b.** la puerta
3. el ascensor	**c.** el sauna
4. la recepción	**d.** las maletas
5. el baño	**e.** las escaleras
6. la llave	**f.** sencilla
7. el huésped	**g.** la camarera

.4 **¿Cuánto cuesta?** Un compañero y tú están en un hotel en Nicaragua y desean ir de excursión. Túrnense para preguntar cuánto cuestan las siguientes excursiones.

Modelo Paseo en bote por el lago Nicaragua (c 600)
   Estudiante 1: *¿Cuánto cuesta el paseo en bote por el lago Nicaragua?*
   Estudiante 2: *Cuesta seiscientos córdobas.*

1. Excursión de un día en Managua (c 550)
2. Cena con baile folklórico (c 320)
3. Excusión de 2 días a Puerto Cabezas (c 1239)
4. Paseo de un día a la Ciudad de León (c 653)
5. Paseo para visitar todos los museos de Managua (c 257)
6. Excursión de 3 días a Ocotal y Baká (c 3 985)

7.5 **Entrevista** Trabaja con un compañero para conversar sobre las siguientes preguntas.

1. ¿Cuándo fue la última vez que te alojaste en un hotel? ¿Por qué te quedaste en el hotel? ¿Recuerdas cuánto pagaste por la habitación?
2. De los hoteles que conoces ¿qué hotel te gusta más y por qué?
3. En tu opinión ¿quién tiene el trabajo más difícil en un hotel (el/la recepcionista, el botones o la camarera)? ¿Por qué?
4. En tu opinión ¿qué servicios o artículos es muy importante tener en una habitación?

Cuando te quedas en un hotel, ¿qué servicios te gusta tener? Este es un folleto (*brochure*) de un hotel en México. Mira el folleto y contesta las siguientes preguntas: ¿Cuánto cuesta el paquete con una habitación sencilla en el Hotel Las Olas? ¿en el Hotel Las Playas? ¿y en el Hotel Amanecer? ¿Cuánto cuesta el paquete con una habitación doble en el Hotel Las Olas? ¿en el Hotel Las Playas? ¿y en el Hotel Amanecer? ¿Cuánto cuesta el paquete con una habitación triple en el Hotel Las Olas? ¿en el Hotel Las Playas? ¿y en el Hotel Amanecer?

Puerto Vallarta

¡Ahora usted puede conocer Puerto Vallarta, con nuestros paquetes desde $3,820*!

¡Con nuestros VTP (Viaje Todo Pagado), no hay excusa para no tomar unas vacaciones!

	Habitación sencilla	Habitación doble	Habitación triple
Hotel Las Olas	$4,950	$4,200	$3,820
Hotel Las Playas	$5,100	$4,420	$3,999
Hotel Amanecer	$6,560	$4,660	$4,250

Todos nuestros hoteles ofrecen:
T.V. a color con cable en todas
  las habitaciones
Alberca
Internet inalámbrico
Restaurante y bar
Lavandería y tintorería
Estacionamiento
Caja de seguridad

Photos: © Evok20/Shutterstock

* Los precios son por persona y están en pesos mexicanos.

Más allá

Con un compañero escojan uno de los hoteles en el folleto y preparen un diálogo entre un recepcionista y un cliente que desea una habitación de hotel. Deben incluir en su conversación: los saludos, las fechas de la reservación, el tipo de habitación, el nombre del cliente, la reservación con tarjeta de crédito y las despedidas. Después, presenten su diálogo a la clase.

A analizar

Lee el siguiente párrafo y observa las formas de los verbos en negritas.

El fin de semana pasado **fui** a Viña de Mar con mi familia, y nos quedamos en el Hotel del Mar. El sábado por la mañana todos **fuimos** a la playa. Por la tarde mi padre y mi hermano **fueron** a un museo, y mi madre, mis hermanas y yo **fuimos** de compras. Más tarde toda la familia **fue** al Restaurante El Barco para cenar. ¡La comida estuvo deliciosa, y los meseros **fueron** excelentes! El domingo **fui** al Jardín Botánico con mi familia, y luego regresamos a la playa antes de volver a casa. ¡**Fue** un viaje corto pero muy divertido!

1. The verbs **ser** and **ir** are irregular in the preterite; however they are both conjugated the same. Look at the paragraph above and decide which of the verbs is **ser** and which is **ir.**

2. Using the forms in the paragraph above and what you learned about the preterite in **Capítulo 6,** complete the chart below with the appropriate forms of **ser/ir** in the preterite.

yo _____	nosotros _____
tú _____	vosotros ___fuisteis___
él, ella, usted _____	ellos, ellas, ustedes _____

A comprobar

Irregular verbs in the preterite

1. There are a number of verbs that are irregular in the preterite. The verbs **ser** and **ir** are identical in this tense.

ser/ir

yo	**fui**	nosotros(as)	**fuimos**
tú	**fuiste**	vosotros(as)	**fuisteis**
él, ella, usted	**fue**	ellos, ellas, ustedes	**fueron**

2. The verbs **dar** and **ver** are conjugated similarly.

dar

yo	**di**	nosotros(as)	**dimos**
tú	**diste**	vosotros(as)	**disteis**
él, ella, usted	**dio**	ellos, ellas, ustedes	**dieron**

ver

yo	**vi**	nosotros(as)	**vimos**
tú	**viste**	vosotros(as)	**visteis**
él, ella, usted	**vio**	ellos, ellas, ustedes	**vieron**

3. Other irregular verbs can be divided into three groups. Notice that there are no accents on these verbs and that they all take the same endings (with the exception of the 3rd person plural of the verbs with **j** in the stem).

Verbs with *u* in the stem: poner		
yo	puse	nosotros(as) pus**imos**
tú	pus**iste**	vosotros(as) pus**isteis**
él, ella, usted	pus**o**	ellos, ellas, ustedes pus**ieron**

Other verbs with the same pattern		
andar	**anduv-**	saber **sup-**
estar	**estuv-**	tener **tuv-**
poder	**pud-**	

Verbs with *i* in the stem: hacer		
yo	hice	nosotros(as) hic**imos**
tú	hic**iste**	vosotros(as) hic**isteis**
él, ella, usted	hiz**o**	ellos, ellas, ustedes hic**ieron**

Other verbs with the same pattern	
querer	**quis-**
venir	**vin-**

Verbs with *j* in the stem: decir		
yo	dije	nosotros(as) dij**imos**
tú	dij**iste**	vosotros(as) dij**isteis**
él, ella, usted	dij**o**	ellos, ellas, ustedes dij**eron**

Other verbs with the same pattern		
conducir	**conduj-**	traducir **traduj-**
producir	**produj-**	traer **traj-**

4. The preterite of **hay** is **hubo** (*there was, there were*).

Hubo un accidente en la habitación.	***There was*** an accident in the room.
Hubo problemas en ese hotel.	***There were*** problems in that hotel.

> **INVESTIGUEMOS LA GRAMÁTICA**
>
> As with the present tense of **haber** (**hay**), there is only one form in the preterite (**hubo**) regardless of whether it is used with a plural or singular noun.

A practicar

7.6 **Un día ocupado** Lee las oraciones sobre lo que hicieron todos en el hotel ayer. Los verbos subrayados (*underlined*) están en el pretérito. Decide cuál es el infinitivo del verbo.

1. Los huéspedes <u>fueron</u> al sauna del hotel para relajarse.
2. El turista <u>vino</u> al hotel por dos noches.
3. La camarera <u>puso</u> las toallas en el baño.
4. Los botones <u>trajeron</u> las maletas al cuarto.
5. El recepcionista le <u>dio</u> la llave al huésped.

7.7 **Unas fechas importantes** Con un compañero, decidan en qué año ocurrieron los siguientes acontecimientos históricos, y después túrnense para hacer oraciones completas con la información.

Modelo Manuel de Falla (componer–*to compose*) *El amor brujo*   1915
Manuel de Falla compuso *El amor brujo* en *1915.*

1. Hernán Cortés (estar) en México.   **a.** 1492
2. (Haber) una revolución en Cuba.   **b.** 1808
3. Napoleón (querer) conquistar España.   **c.** 1959
4. Cristóbal Colón (hacer) su primer viaje a las Américas.   **d.** 1519
5. Miguel Hidalgo (dar) el grito (*shout*) de independencia en México.   **e.** 1810

7.8 **La semana pasada** Primero, conjuga el verbo en el pretérito y luego completa la oración de una manera lógica. Después, compara tu semana con la de un compañero de clase.

Modelo yo (hacer)…
Estudiante 1: *La semana pasada hice una fiesta. ¿Qué hiciste tú?*
Estudiante 2: *La semana pasada yo hice la cena para mi familia.*

La semana pasada…

1. yo (conducir)…
2. mi amigo (estar)…
3. mis amigos y yo (ir)…
4. yo (tener) que…
5. uno de mis profesores (decir)…
6. mis compañeros y yo (poder)…
7. yo (ver)…
8. mis compañeros de clase (traer)…

7.9 **¿Qué pasó?** Con un compañero, túrnense para describir qué pasó en el hotel. Deben usar los siguientes verbos en el pretérito.

decir **hacer** **ir** **poner** **ponerse** **querer** **traer**

7.10 **En busca de…** Busca a ocho compañeros diferentes que hicieron las siguientes actividades. Cuando encuentres a alguien que responda positivamente, debes pedirle más información.

1. conducir a la universidad hoy (¿A qué hora?)
2. estar en una fiesta durante el fin de semana (¿Dónde?)
3. ir de compras recientemente (¿Qué compró?)
4. traer su almuerzo de la casa hoy (¿Qué comida preparó?)
5. tener un examen la semana pasada (¿En qué clase?)
6. poder hacer la tarea anoche (¿Para qué clase?)
7. ver una buena película recientemente (¿Cuál?)
8. hacer un viaje el año pasado (¿Adónde?)

iTunes
Listen to the song "La fuerza del destino" by the Spanish pop group Mecano. What preterite verbs do you recognize? What is the theme of the story told in the song?

Cultura

En España, existen hoteles muy originales que se llaman paradores. Los paradores son hoteles ubicados (*located*) en castillos, monasterios, fortalezas u otros edificios históricos. De esta manera, los españoles conservan sus monumentos nacionales y artísticos. Los paradores son económicamente razonables y tienen un estándar de servicio muy alto. Un parador muy famoso es el Parador San Francisco, en Granada, España. El edificio data del siglo (*century*) XIV, y sirvió como convento en el siglo XV. Este parador es uno de muy pocos en España que recibe la clasificación de Parador Museo.

En el Internet o en una guía turística, busca información sobre otro parador en España para saber:

¿Qué tipo de edificio histórico es?

¿Qué servicios ofrece?

¿Cuánto cuesta?

🌐 Investiga en Internet sobre otros paradores de España.

El Parador San Francisco, un convento del siglo XV en Granada, España

Comparaciones

Los hoteles no siempre son una opción cuando se quiere visitar lugares diferentes. Por ejemplo, para pasar la noche en las islas artificiales de los Uros, en el lago Titikaka en Perú, se debe pasar la noche con una familia en una casa hecha en su totalidad de una planta llamada totora (con la que también están hechas las islas).

Para otra visita excepcional, es posible visitar las cuevas (*caves*) Pedro Antonio de Alarcón, en Granada, España, donde los moros se refugiaron durante su expulsión de Granada hace cientos de años. Hoy en día, cada cueva es un apartamento con una cocina, un dormitorio y un baño. Algunas cuevas tienen incluso un lujoso jacuzzi o chimenea.

En las islas de los Uros se debe pasar la noche en una casa hecha de totora.

Otro hotel poco usual es el Hotel de Sal en el Salar de Uyuni en Bolivia. Este hotel está hecho completamente de sal.

¿Sabes de hoteles poco convencionales en Estados Unidos? ¿Por qué son diferentes y en dónde están?

Conexiones... a la economía

En muchos países donde se habla español el turismo es un motor importante de la economía. Por ejemplo, España es el tercer país más visitado del mundo. España recibe cada año más turistas que su población total. México está en el décimo lugar en esta lista, pero muchos otros países hispanos son importantes destinos turísticos, como Costa Rica, país que promueve el ecoturismo, o Cuba, famosa en Europa por sus hermosas playas.

Por estas razones, en muchos otros países de habla española los turistas encuentran servicios adicionales, como cambiar dinero en la recepción del hotel. A veces se aceptan pagos en moneda extranjera (*foreign currency*).

¿Qué impacto crees que el turismo puede tener en la economía de una región, y en su cultura?

© RAFAEL PEREZ/Reuters /Landov

Es posible cambiar dinero en la recepción del hotel.

Comunidad

Visita un hotel en tu comunidad que tenga información para sus clientes en español y consigue un folleto (*brochure*). ¿Hay expresiones que no conoces en el folleto? ¿Cuáles son y qué piensas que significan?

Encuentra un empleado hispano y haz preguntas sobre el hotel. Por ejemplo, puedes preguntar: ¿Hay muchos empleados que hablan español? ¿En qué áreas trabajan? ¿Los empleados del hotel hablan otros idiomas? ¿Reciben muchos huéspedes hispanos? ¿De qué países vienen?

© erwinova/Shutterstock

¿Hay muchos empleados que hablan español?

A analizar

Lee el párrafo y observa los usos de **por** y **para**.

> ¡**Por** fin tengo vacaciones! Mi esposa y yo salimos **para** Santo Domingo mañana. Encontramos un hotel con muchos servicios **para** los huéspedes. Hay una piscina **para** nadar y un sauna **para** relajarse, y está a un buen precio. Tenemos una habitación doble **por** una semana **por** DOP $14 000.*
>
> *pesos dominicanos

In what ways is **por** used? And **para**?

© Yuri Arcurs/Shutterstock

A comprobar

Por and para and prepositional pronouns

1. Por is used to indicate:

a. cause, reason, or motive (*because of, on behalf of*)

Por la lluvia, no vamos a la piscina hoy.
Because of the rain, we are not going to the pool today.

Hicieron sacrificios **por** sus hijos.
They made sacrifices on behalf of their children.

b. duration, period of time (*during, for*)

Van a estar en el hotel **por** dos noches.
They will be in the hotel for two nights.

c. exchange (*for*)

Él compró los libros **por** 200 dólares.
He bought the books for $200.

Gracias **por** el regalo de cumpleaños.
Thank you for the birthday gift.

d. general movement through space (*through, around, along, by*)

Pedro caminó **por** el parque.
Pedro walked through (by) the park.

Para llegar a la piscina, tienes que pasar **por** el gimnasio.
To get to the pool, you have to pass by the gym.

e. expressions

por ejemplo	*for example*	**por** supuesto	*of course*
por eso	*that's why*	**por** fin	*finally*
por favor	*please*		

2. Para is used to indicate:

a. goal, purpose (*in order to, used for*)

Vamos al lago **para** pescar.
We are going to the lake (in order) to fish.

El sauna es **para** relajarse.
The sauna is for relaxing.

b. recipient (*for*)

Ella compró un regalo **para** su amiga.
She bought a gift for her friend.

c. destination (*to*)

Salen **para** las montañas el sábado.
They are going to the mountains Saturday.

d. deadline (*for, due*)

La tarea es **para** mañana.
The homework is for (due) tomorrow.

e. contrast to what is expected (*for*)

Para una habitación doble, no es muy grande.
For a double room, it isn't very big.

f. expressions

para siempre	*forever*	**para** variar	*for a change*
para colmo	*to top it all off*	**para** nada	*not at all*

3. In **Capítulo 1,** you learned to use subject pronouns (**yo, tú, él,** etc.). Except for **yo** and **tú,** these same pronouns are used after prepositions.

mí	nosotros(as)
ti	vosotros(as)
él	ellos
ella	ellas
usted	ustedes

El regalo es para **ti.**
A **mí** me gusta pescar. (emphasis)

4. Instead of using **mí** and **ti** with **con, conmigo** and **contigo** are used.

Vamos al parque **contigo.**
*We'll go to the park **with you.***

A practicar

INVESTIGUEMOS LA GRAMÁTICA
You learned negative expressions in **Capítulo 6.** The negative of **con** is **sin** (*without*), and it takes the same personal pronouns as the other prepositions.

No quiero viajar sin **ti.**

7.11 **Unas preguntas** Lee las preguntas de un recepcionista de hotel y decide cuál es la respuesta más lógica.

1. ¿Para cuándo necesita usted la habitación?
2. ¿Para cuántas personas es la habitación?
3. ¿Por cuánto tiempo van a quedarse?
4. ¿Cuándo llegan al hotel?
5. ¿Cómo prefiere pagar por la habitación?
6. ¿Por qué viajan a Sevilla?

a. dos
b. para ver la Feria de Abril
c. con tarjeta de crédito
d. cuatro días
e. el 15 de abril
f. por la tarde

7.12 **La Semana Santa** Completa el siguiente párrafo con **por** y **para.**

Voy (**1.**) _____ Antigua (**2.**) _____ ver la celebración de la Semana Santa. Ayer
(**3.**) _____ la tarde llamé al hotel (**4.**) _____ conseguir una reservación (**5.**) _____
cuatro noches. Como mi amigo Julián va conmigo, quería una habitación doble
(**6.**) _____ nosotros. La recepcionista dijo que en ese
momento había una promoción (**7.**) _____ esa fecha: al
quedarnos (**8.**) _____ tres noches, recibimos la cuarta noche
(**9.**) _____ solo diez dólares por persona. ¡(**10.**) _____
supuesto que a mí me gustó mucho la promoción! Le di las
gracias a la recepcionista (**11.**) _____ la información
e hice una reservación.

La celebración de la Semana Santa en Antigua, Guatemala

© Jenkedco/Shutterstock

7.13 **Planes para el día** Fernando llama a su amiga Verónica. Completa la conversación con **por** o **para** o el pronombre preposicional apropiado. **¡OJO!** También es posible usar **conmigo** o **contigo**.

Fernando: Hola, Verónica. Voy a ir a la playa. ¿Quieres ir (**1.**) _____ hoy?

Verónica: ¡A (**2.**) _____ me gusta mucho la playa! ¡(**3.**) _____ (Por/Para) supuesto que voy (**4.**) _____!

Fernando: Vamos a salir temprano (**5.**) _____ (por/para) la mañana (**6.**) _____ (por/para) tener todo el día en la playa. También van a ir José, Pablo y Catarina con (**7.**) _____.

Verónica: ¡Qué bueno! ¿Qué quieres que lleve (*take*)?

Fernando: Si quieres, puedes llevar algo (**8.**) _____ (por/para) tomar.

Verónica: ¿A (**9.**) _____ te gusta la limonada?

Fernando: Sí, me gusta.

Verónica: No tengo coche hoy. ¿Te molesta venir (**10.**) _____ (por/para) (**11.**) _____?

Fernando: (**12.**) _____ (Por/Para) nada. Paso (**13.**) _____ (por/para) (**14.**) _____ a las ocho.

Verónica: Bueno, voy a estar lista. ¡Hasta entonces!

Fernando: ¡Chao!

Pasamos todo el día en la playa.

7.14 **Necesito información** Imagínense que están en un hotel y uno de ustedes es el recepcionista y el otro es el huésped. Respóndanse las preguntas que aparecen a continuación.

Estudiante 1 (el recepcionista):

    1. ¿Para qué fecha necesita una habitación?

    2. ¿Por cuántas noches se va a quedar?

    3. ¿Para cuántas personas es la habitación?

Estudiante 2 (el huésped):

    1. ¿Cómo puedo pagar por la habitación?

    2. ¿Hay un ascensor para subir a la habitación?

    3. ¿Por qué necesita el número de mi tarjeta de crédito?

Su número de tarjeta de crédito, por favor.

7.15 **Oraciones incompletas** Con un compañero, completen las oraciones. Deben pensar en los usos diferentes de **por** y **para.**

    1. a. Voy al hotel por…

      b. Voy al hotel para…

    2. a. Los huéspedes suben a la habitación por…

      b. Los huéspedes suben a la habitación para…

    3. a. Por ser un buen empleado del hotel,…

      b. Para ser un buen empleado del hotel,…

    4. a. Vamos a viajar por…

      b. Vamos a viajar para…

    5. a. El huésped llamó a la recepción por…

      b. El huésped llamó a la recepción para…

    6. a. Encontramos una habitación doble por…

      b. Encontramos una habitación doble para…

7.16 **En la recepción** Con un compañero, túrnense para explicar lo que hicieron Manuel y las otras personas según (*according to*) los dibujos. **¡OJO!** Deben usar el pretérito y **por** o **para.**

 iTunes
Carlos Ponce is a Puerto Rican singer and actor. One of his hits is a song called "Rezo." What do you think the song will be about? Listen to the song and compare your answers. What phrases do you hear with **por**? And with **para**?

7.17 **Una foto** Con un compañero, escojan una de las fotos e inventen una historia basada en la foto. Deben incluir varios usos de **por** y **para** en su historia.

© Photos To Go

© Losevsky Pavel/ Shutterstock

Lectura

Antes de leer

Aparte de los hoteles ¿qué diferentes tipos de alojamiento (*lodging*) conoces? ¿Por qué unos tipos de alojamiento son más caros que otros?

A leer

¿Dónde quedarse: hoteles, moteles, pensiones o albergues?

Cuando vamos de viaje, a la hora de elegir un hotel probablemente lo primero en que pensamos es en el dinero, pero hay otras decisiones importantes, como la privacidad y la comodidad. Para seleccionar mejor nuestro alojamiento es importante entender la clasificación internacional.

Hoteles: Un hotel es un edificio entero con habitaciones para los turistas. El precio depende del lujo y de los servicios que se ofrecen. Casi todos los países clasifican los hoteles con un sistema de cinco **estrellas;** mientras más estrellas tiene un hotel, es mejor. Los hoteles de cuatro y cinco estrellas siempre tienen aire acondicionado y **calefacción** en las habitaciones, y además tienen tiendas, buenos restaurantes y otras

stars

heat

Un hotel muy lujoso en El Salvador

© Andre Nantel/Shutterstock

high quality facilities

[**mientras más estrellas tiene un hotel, es mejor**]

instalaciones de calidad. Un hotel de cinco estrellas tiene habitaciones muy grandes, pero un hotel de una estrella tiene habitaciones muy pequeñas. Aunque la mayoría de los países usan el sistema de estrellas para catalogar los hoteles, hay diferencias en la clasificación de un país a otro. Por ejemplo, un hotel de tres estrellas en España puede ser muy diferente a un hotel de tres estrellas en Costa Rica. Algunos países usan categorías adicionales, como "Gran Turismo", "Diamante" o "Turismo Mundial" para distinguir los hoteles más lujosos y exclusivos.

Moteles: Los moteles están situados fuera de los núcleos urbanos y cada habitación tiene una entrada independiente. Las áreas comunes (salones, comedores, etcétera) son más pequeñas que las de los hoteles.

Hostales y pensiones: Los hostales y pensiones no cumplen con requisitos de los hoteles como tener habitaciones grandes y un restaurante.

Nevertheless

Sin embargo, siempre tienen agua caliente, recepción y un salón social con televisión, y al menos un baño para cada cinco habitaciones.

Albergues juveniles: Uno de los alojamientos más económicos que existe son los albergues juveniles.

Despite

Pese a su nombre, no son solamente para jóvenes; personas de todas las edades pueden hacerse miembros y quedarse allí por la noche. Generalmente ofrecen **literas** en

bunk beds

cuartos para varias personas, y a veces uno debe traer sus propias

sheets

sábanas. También hay generalmente una cocina y, sobre todo, muchas oportunidades para conocer a personas de otros países. Los albergues casi siempre tienen también un salón de TV, biblioteca, sala de estar y cuarto de lavandería.

Un hostal en España

© J.D. Dallet/AGE Fotostock

Comprensión

¿Cierto o falso? Corrige las afirmaciones falsas.

1. Los hoteles de tres estrellas siempre tienen aire acondicionado.
2. Los mejores hoteles que hay en todo el mundo son los de cinco estrellas.
3. Los hostales y pensiones ofrecen baños privados en cada habitación.
4. Los moteles son iguales a los hoteles, pero más baratos.
5. Los albergues juveniles no tienen baños privados.
6. Los albergues juveniles no son solamente para jóvenes.

Después de leer

Imagina que tú y tu compañero van a viajar a un país hispanohablante. En Internet o en una guía turística, busquen un ejemplo de cada uno de los siguientes alojamientos: un hotel, un motel, un hostal o una pensión y un albergue juvenil. Lean los detalles de cada alojamiento y escriban una lista de los beneficios de cada uno. Luego, decidan en cuál prefieren quedarse y expliquen por qué.

El señor Buenrostro está de visita en Michoacán para asistir a una conferencia.
Después de instalarse en su habitación, baja al restaurante de su hotel para comer.

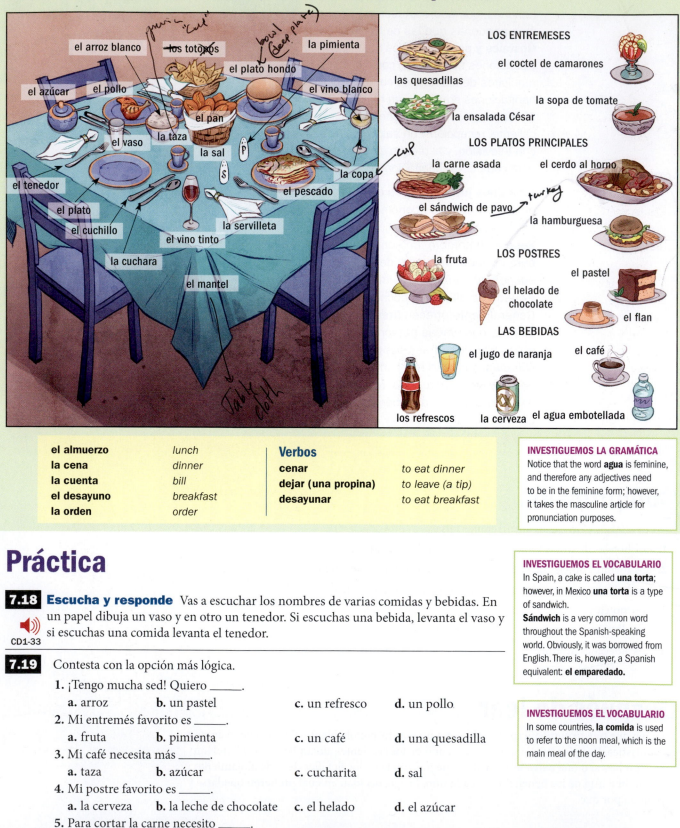

el almuerzo	lunch
la cena	dinner
la cuenta	bill
el desayuno	breakfast
la orden	order

Verbos

cenar	to eat dinner
dejar (una propina)	to leave (a tip)
desayunar	to eat breakfast

INVESTIGUEMOS LA GRAMÁTICA

Notice that the word **agua** is feminine, and therefore any adjectives need to be in the feminine form; however, it takes the masculine article for pronunciation purposes.

Práctica

7.18 **Escucha y responde** Vas a escuchar los nombres de varias comidas y bebidas. En un papel dibuja un vaso y en otro un tenedor. Si escuchas una bebida, levanta el vaso y si escuchas una comida levanta el tenedor.

CD1-33

7.19 Contesta con la opción más lógica.

1. ¡Tengo mucha sed! Quiero _____.
   a. arroz b. un pastel c. un refresco d. un pollo
2. Mi entremés favorito es _____.
   a. fruta b. pimienta c. un café d. una quesadilla
3. Mi café necesita más _____.
   a. taza b. azúcar c. cucharita d. sal
4. Mi postre favorito es _____.
   a. la cerveza b. la leche de chocolate c. el helado d. el azúcar
5. Para cortar la carne necesito _____.
   a. un cuchillo b. una cuchara c. una servilleta d. la sal

INVESTIGUEMOS EL VOCABULARIO

In Spain, a cake is called **una torta**; however, in Mexico **una torta** is a type of sandwich.
Sándwich is a very common word throughout the Spanish-speaking world. Obviously, it was borrowed from English. There is, howeyer, a Spanish equivalent: **el emparedado.**

INVESTIGUEMOS EL VOCABULARIO

In some countries, **la comida** is used to refer to the noon meal, which is the main meal of the day.

7.20 **Relaciona las columnas** Relaciona las palabras de la primera columna con las de la segunda que tengan alguna relación. Después, con un compañero túrnense para decir qué relación hay entre ellas.

Modelo café... bebida → *El café es una bebida.*

1. _____ el cerdo		**a.** la sal
2. _____ el pastel		**b.** el vaso
3. _____ vino		**c.** un postre
4. _____ sopa		**d.** la carne
5. _____ jugo		**e.** el plato principal
6. _____ pimienta		**f.** taza
7. _____ las enchiladas		**g.** una copa
8. _____ té		**h.** la cuchara

7.21 **Encuesta** Encuentra a seis personas que hacen las siguientes actividades. Contesten con oraciones completas y después reporten a la clase.

Modelo desayunar cereal todos los días
Estudiante 1: *¿Desayunas cereal todos los días?*
Estudiante 2: *Sí, siempre desayuno cereal todos los días.*

1. pedir postre siempre cuando come en un restaurante
2. su comida favorita es el desayuno
3. saber hacer flan
4. comer carne más de tres veces a la semana
5. no tomar cerveza nunca
6. cenar frente al televisor

7.22 **En un restaurante** En parejas, túrnense para hacer el papel (*play the role*) de mesero y de cliente (*customer*).

Mesero: Buenas tardes, (señor/señorita/señora). ¿Prefiere la sección de fumar o de no fumar?

Cliente: _____

Mesero: ¿Desea una bebida?

Cliente: _____

Mesero: ¿Qué prefiere como plato principal?

Cliente: _____

Mesero: ¿Y le gustaría (*would you like*) un postre?

Cliente: _____

Mesero: ¿Necesita algo más (*something else*)?

Cliente: _____

Mesero: ¡Buen provecho! (*Enjoy!*)

© Photos To Go

Generalmente ¿qué comidas hay en el menú de un restaurante de comida mexicana? El siguiente es el menú de un restaurante de México. ¿Están las comidas que mencionaste? ¿Has probado (*Have you tasted*) todas las comidas y bebidas que aparecen en el menú? De las que conoces ¿cuáles son tus favoritas? ¿Qué piensas que significan estas palabras en el menú: albóndigas, atún, rebanada? ¿Por qué crees que el café americano especifica que incluye dos tazas?

EL GATO AZUL MENÚ

*Nota: Todos los precios están en pesos mexicanos.

Entremeses
Coctel de camarones......................$79.00
Orden de quesadillas......................$40.00

Pastas
Espagueti con albóndigas................$55.00
Coditos con atún...........................$55.00

Sopas
Arroz a la mexicana........................$35.00
Sopa de tortilla..............................$40.00
Sopa de verduras..........................$42.00

Ensaladas
Ensalada verde.............................$30.00
Ensalada del Chef..........................$55.00
Ensalada de pollo/atún...................$60.00

Platos principales
Enchiladas de pollo/carne/queso......$65.00
Carne asada.................................$75.00
Chiles rellenos..............................$70.00
Pollo al horno...............................$55.00
Chuletas de cerdo con chipotle.........$68.00

Hamburguesa con queso.................$65.00
Sándwich de pavo...........................$55.00

Postres
Flan..$35.00
Fruta (papaya, mango o melón)..........$35.00
Helado (vainilla, chocolate o fresa).....$28.00
Pastel de chocolate (rebanada).........$35.00
Pastel Tres leches..........................$35.00
Pay de manzana............................$35.00

Bebidas
Refrescos (coca-cola, sidral mundet)....$10.00
Jugos naturales
(naranja, tomate, piña, toronja)...........$19.50
Cervezas nacionales........................$19.00
Vino (blanco, rosado, tinto) copa.......$30.00
Té negro.......................................$20.00
Café americano (dos tazas)..............$22.50
Café capuchino..............................$35.00
Café frappé...................................$38.00
Café expreso.................................$30.00
Café con licor de café.....................$40.00
Leche...$20.00
Agua embotellada (natural/con gas).....$22.00

INVESTIGUEMOS LA CULTURA
En muchos países latinoamericanos salir a tomar café con los amigos es una tradición social muy importante. El café se relaciona con la idea de pasar tiempo hablando con los amigos, y no es común ver a personas conduciendo y bebiendo café.

INVESTIGUEMOS LA GRAMÁTICA
When using a noun to describe another noun, you must use the preposition **de** between them.
Pastel **de** chocolate
Helado **de** vainilla

Más allá

Imagínate que quieres abrir un restaurante con la mejor comida de Latinoamérica. Investiga en Internet la comida de varios países hispanohablantes. Luego escribe un menú con al menos tres platos para cada categoría (entremeses, ensaladas, sopas o pastas, plato principal, postres y bebidas). Debes incorporar platos de por lo menos cinco países diferentes.

Exploraciones gramaticales

A analizar

Lee el siguiente diálogo y observa los pronombres de objeto directo en negritas.
Luego, contesta las preguntas que siguen.

Mesero: Buenas tardes. ¿Están listos?

Laura: Sí. ¿La ensalada de camarones tiene chile?

Mesero: No, no **lo** tiene.

Laura: Bien, **la** voy a pedir entonces.

Emilio: Y yo quiero los tacos de pescado, por favor.

Mesero: Lo siento, no **los** tenemos ahora. No hay más pescado.

Emilio: Bueno, en ese caso quiero las enchiladas supremas.
¿De qué son?

Mesero: Son de pollo.

Emilio: Bueno, **las** voy a pedir.

1. What do **lo** and **la** mean in the dialogue above? And **los** and **las**?

2. Pronouns take the place of a noun. In the above dialogue, the words in bold are direct object pronouns. Identify what each of the pronouns in the dialogue replaces.

3. Where are the pronouns in bold placed?

4. What pronoun would you use to replace **el arroz**? And **las cervezas**?

A comprobar

Direct object pronouns I

1. A direct object is a person or a thing that receives the action of the verb. It tells who or what is being [*verb*].

   Juan pide **pollo.**
   Juan is ordering chicken. (The chicken is what is being ordered.)

   Elena invita a **Natalia** a comer.
   Elena is inviting Natalia to eat. (Natalia is who is being invited.)

2. In order to avoid repetition, the direct object can be replaced with a pronoun. In Spanish, the pronoun must agree in gender and number with the direct object it replaces.

   ¿Tienes **las tazas**?
   *Do you have **the cups**?*

   Sí, **las** tengo.
   *Yes, I have **them**.*

In answering the question, it is not necessary to repeat the direct object, **las tazas**; therefore, it is replaced with the pronoun **las.**

3. The following are the third person direct object pronouns:

	singular		plural	
masculino	**lo**	*it, him, you (formal)*	**los**	*them, you*
femenino	**la**	*it, her, you (formal)*	**las**	*them, you*

4. The direct object pronoun is placed in front of the conjugated verb.

   ¿Comes carne?
   Do you eat meat?

   No, no **la** como.
   No, I don't eat it.

5. When using a verb phrase that has an infinitive or a present participle (**-ando, -iendo**), the pronoun can be placed in front of the conjugated verb, or it can be attached to the infinitive or the present participle. Notice that an accent is necessary when adding the pronoun to the end of the present participle.

La voy a invitar. / Voy a invitar**la**.
*I am going to invite **her**.*

¿**Lo** quieres comer? / ¿Quieres comer**lo**?
*Do you want to eat **it**?*

Él **lo** está sirviendo. / Él está sirviéndo**lo**.
*He is serving **it**.*

A practicar

7.23 **En el restaurante** Lee la siguiente conversación e identifica el objeto o persona que el pronombre reemplaza (*replaces*).

Sr. Ortega: ¿Quieres el menú?

Sra. Ortega: No, no <u>lo</u>¹ necesito. Ya sé qué quiero.

Sr. Ortega: ¿Sí? ¿Vas a pedir el pollo como siempre?

Sra. Ortega: No, no <u>lo</u>² quiero comer hoy. Voy a pedir la carne asada.

Sr. Ortega: Yo voy a pedir<u>la</u>³ también. ¿Pedimos una botella de vino?

Sra. Ortega: Sí, <u>la</u>⁴ podemos pedir.

Sr. Ortega: Bueno, estamos listos. ¿Dónde está el mesero? No <u>lo</u>⁵ veo.

Sra. Ortega: Allí está. ¿Por qué no <u>lo</u>⁶ llamas?

Sr. Ortega: ¡Señor!

7.24 **La redundancia** Lee el siguiente párrafo y escríbelo de nuevo usando los pronombres para evitar (*avoid*) repeticiones.

El mesero llega con los menús y pone los menús en la mesa. Jimena y Tomás miran los menús. A Jimena le gusta el pollo asado y decide pedir pollo asado. Pero Tomás prefiere el pescado y pide pescado. Las ensaladas parecen (*seem*) deliciosas y los dos quieren ensaladas. Tomás ve al mesero y llama al mesero. El mesero

¡Tenemos muchos platos para lavar!

© zolwiks/Shutterstock

recomienda el vino blanco, pero ellos no quieren vino blanco; prefieren pedir vino tinto. En poco tiempo, la comida llega y ellos disfrutan (*enjoy*) la comida. Pero al final no tienen suficiente dinero para pagar la cuenta cuando el mesero trae la cuenta. El mesero les dice que tienen muchos platos para lavar; los dos van a la cocina y lavan platos.

7.25 **¿Quién lo hace?** Mira los dibujos. Con un compañero, túrnense haciendo preguntas con las palabras y contestándolas. Cuando contesten, deben usar pronombres de objeto directo.

Modelo (Look at drawing #1.) comer/ensalada
Estudiante 1: *¿Quién come la ensalada?*
Estudiante 2: *Eva **la** come.*

1.

a. tomar/sopa   **b.** comer/pan

2.

a. servir/tacos   **b.** servir/hamburguesas

3.

a. necesitar/tenedor   **b.** necesitar/cuchara

4.

a. tomar/cerveza   **b.** tomar/refresco

7.26 **¿Para qué es?** Con un compañero túrnense para explicar lo que hacemos con las siguientes cosas. Deben usar los pronombres de objeto directo en las respuestas y dar explicaciones completas.

Modelo el arroz
Estudiante 1: *¿Qué hacemos con el arroz?*
Estudiante 2: *Lo servimos con los frijoles./Lo ponemos en la paella./Lo cocinamos en agua.*

1. el refresco   **3.** la ensalada   **5.** el azúcar   **7.** la sopa
2. el helado   **4.** las enchiladas   **6.** los camarones   **8.** los tomates

---

7.27 **Entrevista** Túrnense para hacer y contestar todas las siguientes preguntas. **¡OJO!** Necesitan usar pronombres de objeto directo para reemplazar (*replace*) las palabras subrayadas (*underlined*) cuando contesten para evitar la repetición.

1. ¿Desayunaste esta mañana? ¿Tomaste <u>café</u>?

2. ¿Trajiste <u>el almuerzo</u> a la universidad? ¿Qué comiste?

3. ¿A qué hora cenaste anoche? ¿Quién preparó <u>la cena</u>?

4. ¿Cocinaste esta semana? ¿Preparaste <u>verduras</u>?

5. ¿Comiste <u>postre</u> después de la cena anoche? ¿Qué comiste?

6. ¿Tomaste <u>refrescos</u> con el almuerzo? ¿Qué tomaste?

7. ¿Quién limpió <u>la cocina</u> en tu casa después de la cena anoche? ¿Lavó <u>los platos</u> a mano?

Cultura

A veces un lugar para comer se vuelve casi tan importante como un monumento para una ciudad debido tanto a la comida como a la historia del lugar. Por ejemplo 4Gats, en Barcelona, fue un lugar de reunión para muchos artistas famosos, como Pablo Picasso. Las guías para turistas (*tourist guides*) incluyen estos lugares, y los llaman "el mejor lugar para comer comida típica", o títulos similares.

Otros ejemplos famosos incluyen La Casa de los Azulejos, un edificio histórico construido en 1731 en la Ciudad de México. El edificio obtuvo su nombre debido a los mosaicos (*tiles*) con que está decorado. Este edificio se usa como restaurante (Sanborn's) y tiene una importante colección de arte, incluido un mural de José Clemente Orozco. La Casa de los Azulejos es un lugar de reunión donde los residentes de la ciudad acostumbran reunirse a la hora del café.

También en la Ciudad de México se encuentra el Tenampa, una famosa cantina en el corazón de Plaza Garibaldi, la que se considera el corazón de la música de mariachis.

En Madrid, La Casa del Sobrino de Botín es bien conocida. Hemingway la hizo famosa a nivel internacional al mencionarla en su novela *The Sun Also Rises*.

Otro ejemplo muy conocido es La Cabaña, en Buenos Aires. La Cabaña es el restaurante especializado en carnes más viejo de la capital argentina. Su libro de visitas tiene la firma de visitantes muy famosos, entre ellos Charles de Gaulle, Henry Kissinger, Richard Nixon, el Rey Juan Carlos, Joan Crawford y Walt Disney, para mencionar solo a algunos.

Piensa en una ciudad de un país hispano que te interesa conocer, y busca información sobre algún restaurante o café famoso.

La Casa de los Azulejos en la Ciudad de México.

© Halogenure

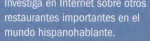
Investiga en Internet sobre otros restaurantes importantes en el mundo hispanohablante.

Comunidad

Visita un supermercado de tu comunidad y busca la sección de comida de otras partes del mundo. Luego prepara un reporte, usando las siguientes preguntas para guiarte.

¿Hay comida latinoamericana o española?

¿Qué productos encuentras?

Mira las etiquetas (*labels*). ¿Dónde están hechos?

¿Te sorprende la cantidad de productos de otros países? ¿Por qué?

¿Hay otras tiendas con comida de otros países? ¿Las conoces y las visitas?

© Monkey Business Images/Shutterstock

¿Qué productos latinoamericanos hay?

Conexiones... a la salud

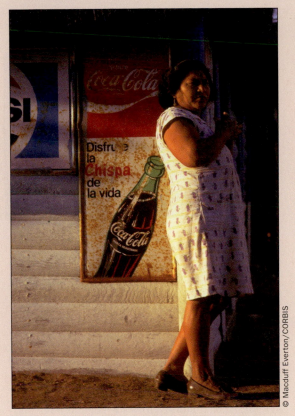

En México consumen muchos refrescos.

Muchas personas piensan que somos lo que comemos (*we are what we eat*). En estos tiempos modernos, mucha gente no tiene tiempo para preparar comida, y esto puede afectar negativamente los hábitos alimenticios. Una consecuencia de estos cambios es la gran cantidad de personas obesas que hay en algunas sociedades. Los países con más gente obesa en el mundo son Estados Unidos, México y el Reino Unido. El caso de México puede explicarse, en parte, por el dramático consumo de refrescos. Los mexicanos consumen en promedio 149 litros de refrescos por año.

Escribe una lista de productos que piensas que tienen un gran impacto en el peso (*weight*) de las personas. Después, entrevista a tres compañeros de la clase para saber si también piensan que estos productos son malos para la salud. Reporta la información a la clase.

Comparaciones

¿Dónde compras la comida? ¿Vas a tiendas especializadas? En España y Latinoamérica, siempre ha sido (*it has been*) muy común comprar la comida en diferentes tiendas pequeñas en vez del supermercado. La siguiente es una lista de diferentes tipos de tiendas. ¿Qué productos crees que venden en los siguientes lugares?

1. una tortillería

2. una heladería

3. una panadería

4. una frutería

5. una lechería

6. una carnicería

7. una chocolatería

¿Cuáles son las ventajas (*advantages*) de ir a las tiendas especializadas? ¿Y las desventajas? ¿Dónde compras tú esos (*those*) productos? ¿Puedes encontrar estas tiendas especializadas donde vives?

En esta tienda venden quesadillas.

A analizar

Lee las siguientes oraciones y observa los pronombres de objeto directo en negritas.

> ¿**Me** comprendes?
>
> Sí, **te** comprendo.

© Photos To Go

1. What do the pronouns **me** and **te** refer to?

2. How would you translate the sentences?

A comprobar

Direct object pronouns II

In the last **Exploraciones gramaticales** section, you learned about third person direct object pronouns. The following are all of the direct object pronouns.

	singular		plural	
first person	**me**	*me*	**nos**	*us*
second person	**te**	*you*	**os**	*you (plural)*
third person	**lo, la**	*it, him, her, you (formal)*	**los, las**	*they, you*

1. As with the third person direct object pronouns, these pronouns are placed in front of the conjugated verb. They can also be attached to an infinitive or a present participle. Remember that an accent is necessary when adding the pronoun to the present participle.

El mesero **nos** ve.
*The waiter sees **us**.*

Te quiero invitar a cenar./Quiero invitar**te** a cenar.
*I want to invite **you** to dinner.*

Ana **me** está llamando./Ana está llamándo**me**.
*Ana is calling **me**.*

2. The following are some of the verbs that are frequently used with these direct object pronouns:

ayudar	escuchar	querer
buscar	felicitar *(to congratulate)*	saludar *(to greet)*
conocer	invitar	ver
creer	llamar	visitar
encontrar	llevar	

A practicar

7.28 **¿Qué significa?** Decide cuál traducción es correcta.

1. No te entiendo.

    a. I don't understand you.   **b.** You don't understand me.

2. Mi madre me llama todos los días.

    a. My mother calls me every day.   **b.** I call my mother every day.

3. ¿Te esperan tus amigos?

    a. Are you waiting for your friends?   **b.** Are your friends waiting for you?

4. No nos ven.

    a. They don't see us.   **b.** We don't see them.

7.29 **Algunas preguntas** Decide cuál es la respuesta correcta.

1. ¿Quién me llama?

   a. Héctor te llama.   **b.** Héctor me llama.

2. ¿Te comprenden tus padres?

   a. Sí, te comprenden.   **b.** Sí, me comprenden.

3. ¿Me ayudas con la tarea?

   a. Sí, te ayudo.   **b.** Sí, me ayudas.

4. ¿Cuándo te invitan a comer?

   a. Te invitan a comer hoy.   **b.** Me invitan a comer hoy.

5. ¿Vas a visitarnos mañana?

   a. Sí, voy a visitarnos.   **b.** Sí, voy a visitarlos.

6. ¿El profesor los vio a ustedes?

   a. Sí, nos vio.   **b.** Sí, los vio.

7.30 **En clase** Contesta las preguntas referentes a los hábitos del profesor de español. Debes usar el pronombre **nos** en las respuestas.

Modelo ¿El profesor de español los invita a ustedes a fiestas?
   Sí, nos invita a fiestas. / No, no nos invita a fiestas.

¿El profesor de español…

1. los comprende a ustedes?
2. los conoce bien?
3. los ayuda a ustedes con la tarea?
4. los escucha cuando ustedes tienen problemas?
5. los llama a casa?
6. los lleva a comer en un restaurante mexicano?
7. los saluda en los pasillos (*hallways*)?
8. los ve fuera de la clase?
9. los invita a ser sus amigos en su página de Facebook?
10. los felicita cuando hacen un buen trabajo?

7.31 **¡Ayuda!** Completa la siguiente conversación con el pronombre **me, te** o **nos.**

Susana: Simón, ¡yo (**1.**) _____ necesito! ¡No entiendo francés!

Simón: ¿El profesor siempre habla con ustedes en francés?

Susana: Sí, solo nos habla en francés, pero no lo comprendemos a él, ni él (**2.**) _____ comprende a nosotros. ¿(**3.**) _____ ayudas con mi tarea?

Simón: Por supuesto. Yo (**4.**) _____ puedo ayudar esta tarde si quieres.

Susana: ¡Sí! Entonces ¿(**5.**) _____ vas a llamar luego?

Simón: Sí, yo (**6.**) _____ llamo después de trabajar.

Susana: ¡Qué bueno! ¡(**7.**) _____ quiero, Simón!

Necesito ayuda con mi tarea de francés.

© Andresr/Shutterstock

7.32 Una noche en el restaurante Con un compañero, túrnense para describir lo que pasó anoche en el restaurante. Deben completar lo que dijeron las diferentes personas en cada escena, usando los pronombres de objeto directo **me, te** y **nos**.

7.33 La telenovela Imagínate que eres un actor de telenovelas (*soap operas*). Con un compañero, túrnense para leer las preguntas y las exclamaciones, y para responder de una manera original y dramática. Usen pronombres de objeto directo en las respuestas. ¡Sean creativos!

Modelo ¿Quieres a tu esposa?
Estudiante 1: *¿Quieres a tu esposa?*
Estudiante 2: *No, no la quiero, pero ella es muy rica.*

1. ¿Me quieres?
2. ¿Me vas a querer siempre?
3. ¿Quién te besa (*kiss*) cada noche?
4. ¡¿No nos vas a llevar contigo?!
5. ¡No me comprendes!
6. ¿Me estás engañando (*cheating on*)?
7. ¿Nos vas a abandonar?
8. ¡Nunca me escuchas!

¿Me quieres?

7.34 Preguntas personales Entrevista a un compañero de clase con las siguientes preguntas.

Modelo Estudiante 1: *¿Quién te cree siempre?*
Estudiante 2: *Mi esposo (mi madre, mi mejor amigo, etc.) me cree siempre.*

1. ¿Quién te comprende?
2. ¿Quién te quiere mucho?
3. ¿Quién te invita a comer con frecuencia?
4. ¿Quién te llama por teléfono y habla y habla y habla…?
5. ¿Quién te ayuda con la tarea de español?
6. ¿Quién te visita con frecuencia?
7. ¿Quién te escucha cuando tienes problemas?
8. ¿Quién te busca cuando necesita dinero?
9. ¿Quién los visita a ti y a tu familia con frecuencia?
10. ¿Quién los saluda a ti y a tus compañeros de clase todos los días?

Redacción

Write a letter to a friend telling him or her about a trip you took.

Paso 1 Think about a time that you took a trip and stayed in a hotel. Jot down some things about your stay: Where did you go? Whom did you go with? When did you arrive at the hotel? What kind of a room did you have? How many nights did you stay? Did you do anything in the hotel, such as go to the pool, the gym or the restaurant? What time did you leave? If you have not traveled and stayed in a hotel, invent the information.

Paso 2 Think about a restaurant you visited during your trip. Jot down as many things as you can about your visit to the restaurant. Think about the following questions: When did you go? What did you order? If there was someone else with you, what did he/she order? What did you particularly like about what you ate?

Paso 3 After greeting your friend, write a sentence or two in which you tell when you took a trip and where you went.

Paso 4 Write the rest of your paragraph telling him/her about your hotel stay using the information you generated in **Paso 1.** Be sure to organize your information logically.

Paso 5 Begin a second paragraph telling your friend what restaurant you went to and when you went there.

Paso 6 Write the rest of the paragraph about the visit to the restaurant using the information you generated in **Paso 2.**

Paso 7 Write a concluding sentence for your letter in which you sum up your trip. Your concluding statement should let your reader know that you have finished.

> **Modelo** *Realmente, fue un muy buen viaje.*

Paso 8 Edit your letter:

1. Can you add some more details?
2. Are the paragraphs logically organized?
3. Are there any spelling errors?
4. Did you use the correct forms of the preterite in your letter?

Lectura

Antes de leer

¿Qué comidas se consideran "comida rápida" en los Estados Unidos? ¿Existe una diferencia entre comida rápida y comida chatarra (*junk food*)? ¿Cuál?

A leer

La comida rápida en Latinoamérica

has changed / century

Todos sabemos que la vida **ha cambiado** mucho en el último **siglo,** especialmente en las grandes ciudades, donde hoy en día hay poco tiempo para hacer todo lo que debemos hacer. ¿Cómo afecta esta **falta de tiempo** nuestros hábitos alimenticios?

lack of time

Preparar comida consume mucho tiempo, así que mucha gente busca soluciones para **ahorrar** ese tiempo. Las soluciones para este problema

save

[. . . no tiene sentido que una persona coma mientras maneja. . .]

son diferentes según el país. Por ejemplo, en muchos países latinos, donde pasar tiempo con la familia es muy importante, no **tiene sentido** que una persona coma mientras maneja su automóvil. Para la hora de la comida, muchas amas de casa ocupadísimas se detienen en locales de comida rápida (o "comida corrida") para comprar platillos **caseros** para su familia. De esta manera, no tienen que llegar a casa a preparar comida, solamente deben servirla. Los platillos que se compran en estos locales tienen la ventaja de ser variados y de cambiar todos los días. ¿Qué venden? ¡De todo! Diferentes variedades de sopa, carnes guisadas, verduras y hasta postres. Como el negocio no necesita mucho espacio y hay pocos empleados, pueden proveer comida muy semejante a la que se elabora en casa a un precio razonable.

make sense

homemade

Otra comida rápida popular es el pollo asado. Hay grandes compañías que lo venden muy **barato, a semejanza** de las grandes compañías en Estados Unidos que venden hamburguesas.

cheap / like

Una pupusería en El Salvador

© rj lerich/Shutterstock

Un pincho de puerco

Sin embargo, el negocio de la comida rápida no se limita a la comida para toda la familia: también hay un gran mercado para la comida chatarra. ¿Quién no tiene hambre a mediodía o a media tarde? Para satisfacer esos **antojos,** en cualquier pueblo o ciudad de Latinoamérica se encontrarán puestos en la calle o pequeños locales donde se puede comprar comida barata de acuerdo al gusto local. Por ejemplo, en los

However

cravings

países andinos (Perú, Ecuador y Bolivia especialmente) se compran papas en la calle, preparadas de mil maneras diferentes. En El Salvador se venden pupusas, en Puerto Rico los pinchos, y en el Paraguay el chipá. Aunque los ingredientes de la comida chatarra no son necesariamente los mismos que los de la comida que se compra en los Estados Unidos, los resultados son igual de **apetecibles.**

El chipá paraguayo

appetizers

Comprensión

Decide si las siguientes afirmaciones son ciertas o falsas, según la lectura. Corrige las ideas falsas.

1. En Latinoamérica, la gente (*people*) tiene mucho tiempo para cocinar.
2. Los locales de comida rápida venden comida como hamburguesas, pizza y pollo asado.
3. La gente generalmente no come mientras conduce su automóvil en los países latinos.
4. Las papas pueden ser un tipo de comida rápida en algunos países como Perú y Bolivia.
5. El pollo asado es una comida popular.

Después de leer

Con un compañero, túrnense para hacer y contestar las preguntas.

¿Comes comida rápida/chatarra con frecuencia? ¿Por qué?
¿Qué comidas rápidas prefieres?
¿Hay otras cosas que haces para ahorrar el tiempo con la comida?

Vocabulario

Sustantivos

el aire acondicionado	*air conditioning*
la cancelación	*cancellation*
el cibercafé	*cybercafé*
la conexión a Internet	*Internet connection*
la estancia	*stay*
la reserva	*reservation*
el servicio de habitación	*room service*
el servicio de lavandería	*laundry service*

Adjetivos

cómodo	*comfortable*
dispuesto	*willing*
silencioso	*quiet*

Verbos

relajarse	*to relax*

Expresiones útiles

Estoy aquí para servirle.
I'm here to help you.

¿Cuántos días va a quedarse?
How long will you stay?

¿Necesita una habitación doble o sencilla?
Do you need a double or a single room?

¿Cuántas llaves quiere?
How many keys do you want?

¿Quiere que lo despertemos?
Would you like to be called in the morning?

El desayuno se sirve a las...
Breakfast is served at . . .

Debe dejar la habitación a las...
You should leave the room by . . .

Por la mañana servimos desayuno continental.

© Image Source/JupiterImages

DATOS IMPORTANTES

Educación: Título universitario en negocios o relaciones públicas. Se prefiere personal bilingüe y técnicos en turismo.

Salario: Entre $40 000 y $120 000, dependiendo de la experiencia y la categoría del hotel.

Dónde se trabaja: Hoteles internacionales, administración de villas, condominios de lujo.

Lorena Libreros es la gerente de un hotel internacional. Ella recibe a turistas de todo el mundo y les ofrece las mejores habitaciones, según las necesidades de cada persona. En el video vas a ver a la Sra. Librero cuando habla con un turista que quiere quedarse en el hotel.

Antes de ver

Los gerentes de hotel siempre están dispuestos a ayudar a sus clientes. Los días que una persona pasa en un hotel deben ser agradables (*pleasant*) y con todas las comodidades posibles. ¿Qué personalidad debe tener un gerente de hotel? ¿Cuántos idiomas cree que tiene que hablar un gerente de hotel? ¿Qué preguntas haces cuando quieres quedarte en un hotel?

Comprensión

1. ¿Por qué el Sr. Santos no puede encontrar habitaciones libres en ningún hotel?

2. ¿Cuántas noches se va a quedar el Sr. Santos?

3. ¿Por qué consigue una habitación en el Hotel Reina?

4. ¿Qué tipo de habitación pide?

5. ¿Qué problema tuvo la semana pasada en otro hotel?

6. ¿En qué partes del Hotel Reina se puede usar computadora?

7. ¿Cuántas comidas se sirven en el Hotel Reina?

© Heinle/Cengage Learning

Después de ver

En parejas, representen a un gerente de hotel y un turista que quiere hospedarse allí. El hotel puede ser lujoso o sencillo. Dependiendo de las necesidades del turista, el gerente debe dar las respuestas apropiadas.

7.35 **Una reservación** Para evitar (*avoid*) repeticiones, reemplaza las palabras en cursiva con el pronombre de objeto directo. ¡**OJO** con la posición del pronombre!

Recepcionista: Buenas tardes. Hotel Miramar. ¿En qué le puedo servir?

Cliente: Necesito una habitación doble.

Recepcionista: ¿Para cuándo necesita *la habitación doble*?

Cliente: Para el 8 de agosto. ¿Tienen una habitación con balcón?

Recepcionista: Sí, todas las habitaciones tienen *balcón*.

Cliente: ¿Tiene ascensor el hotel?

Recepcionista: No, no tenemos *ascensor*.

Cliente: ¿Hay un botones para llevar las maletas a la habitación?

Recepcionista: Sí, el botones puede subir *las maletas* a la habitación.

Cliente: Muy bien, quiero hacer una reservación.

Todas las habitaciones tienen balcón.

7.36 **Ayer y hoy** Completa las siguientes oraciones con el pretérito del verbo en cursiva. ¡**OJO** con el sujeto!

1. Hoy no *conducimos* porque ayer _____ mucho para llegar al hotel.

2. Prefiero *andar* al parque porque ayer no _____.

3. Mi esposa quiere *ver* la ciudad porque ayer no la _____.

4. Nuestros hijos *van* a la piscina hoy porque ayer llegamos tarde y no _____.

5. Hoy *podemos* disfrutar (*enjoy*) el día, pero ayer no _____ hacer nada.

6. ¿Y tú? ¿Qué vas a *hacer* hoy que no _____ ayer?

7.37 **¿Por o para?** Lee las siguientes oraciones y substituye las palabras en cursiva con **por** o **para**.

1. Ayer Renato decidió ir a un restaurante *a* cenar.

2. A las ocho salió de su casa *al* restaurante.

3. *A causa de* no tener una reservación, no pudo sentarse inmediatamente.

4. Esperó *durante* media hora.

5. *Al* fin, un señor lo llevó a una mesa.

6. Tenían un especial: una pizza de queso *a* 50 pesos y decidió pedirla.

7. Luego pidió un helado *de* postre.

7.38 **Sondeo** En grupos de tres o cuatro contesten las siguientes preguntas. Luego compartan las respuestas con la clase.

1. ¿Prefieres comer en un restaurante o en casa? ¿Por qué?
2. ¿Cuántas veces a la semana almuerzas en un restaurante?
3. ¿Cuántas veces al mes cenas en un restaurante?
4. ¿Cuál es tu restaurante favorito? ¿Qué pides allí?
5. ¿Cuándo fue la última vez (*last time*) que fuiste a un restaurante? ¿Cuál fue?

7.39 **Comparemos** Trabaja con un compañero. Uno va a mirar el dibujo en esta página y el otro va a mirar el dibujo en el apéndice A. Túrnense para describir los dibujos y encontrar cinco diferencias.

7.40 **¿Y en tu casa?** Habla con un compañero sobre quién hizo las siguientes actividades en tu casa la semana pasada. Deben usar los pronombres de objeto directo y el pretérito cuando contesten las preguntas.

Modelo servir la comida
Estudiante 1: *¿Quién sirvió la comida en tu casa?*
Estudiante 2: *Mi madre la sirvió. ¿Y en tu casa?*
Estudiante 1: *Mi esposo la sirvió.*

1. poner la mesa
2. comprar la comida
3. preparar el desayuno
4. lavar los platos
5. cocinar la cena
6. limpiar la cocina

En mi casa, mi madre sirvió la comida.

Vocabulario 1

CD1-34

El hotel

el alojamiento	*lodging*
el ascensor	*elevator*
el (la) botones	*bellhop*
el (la) camarero(a)	*maid*
las escaleras	*stairs*
la habitación	*room*
el (la) huésped	*guest*
la llave	*key*
la maleta	*suitcase*
la recepción	*reception*
el (la) recepcionista	*receptionist*
el sauna	*sauna*
el transporte	*transportation*
el (la) turista	*tourist*

Verbos

alojarse	*to lodge, to stay (in a hotel)*
bajar	*to go down*
quedarse	*to lodge, to stay*
subir	*to go up*

Palabras adicionales

la clase turista	*economy class*
disponible	*available*
doble	*double*
lujo	*luxury*
sencillo	*single*
triple	*triple*
el viaje todo pagado (VTP)	*all-inclusive trip*

Los números

cien	*100*	setecientos	*700*
ciento uno	*101*	ochocientos	*800*
doscientos	*200*	novecientos	*900*
trescientos	*300*	mil	*1000*
cuatrocientos	*400*	dos mil	*2000*
quinientos	*500*	un millón	*1 000 000*
seiscientos	*600*		

Diccionario personal

_____
_____
_____
_____
_____
_____
_____
_____

CAPÍTULO 7

252

🔊 Vocabulario 2

CD1-35

Los utensilios

la copa	*wine glass*	la servilleta	*napkin*
la cuchara	*spoon*	la taza	*cup*
el cuchillo	*knife*	el tazón	*serving bowl*
el mantel	*tablecloth*	el tenedor	*fork*
el plato	*plate*	el vaso	*glass*
el plato hondo	*bowl*		

La comida

el arroz	*rice*	la naranja	*orange*
el azúcar	*sugar*	el pan	*bread*
la bebida	*drink*	el pastel	*cake*
el café	*coffee*	el pavo	*turkey*
el camarón	*shrimp*	el pescado	*fish*
la carne	*meat*	la pimienta	*pepper*
el cerdo	*pork*	el pollo	*chicken*
la cerveza	*beer*	el postre	*dessert*
el coctel	*cocktail*	el refresco	*soda*
la ensalada	*salad*	la sal	*salt*
el entremés	*appetizer*	el sándwich	*sandwich*
el flan	*flan*	la sopa	*soup*
la fruta	*fruit*	el tomate	*tomato*
la hamburguesa	*hamburger*	los totopos	*tortilla chips*
el helado	*ice cream*	el vino blanco	*white wine*
el jugo	*juice*	el vino tinto	*red wine*

Verbos

cenar	*to eat dinner*	desayunar	*to eat breakfast*
dejar (una propina)	*to leave (a tip)*		

Palabras adicionales

al horno	*baked*	la cuenta	*bill*
el almuerzo	*lunch*	el desayuno	*breakfast*
asado(a)	*grilled*	frito(a)	*fried*
la cena	*dinner*	la orden	*order*
la comida	*food, lunch*	el plato principal	*main dish*

Diccionario personal

_____

_____

Learning Strategy

Review material from previous chapters

Because you continue to use vocabulary, verbs, and grammar you learned in past chapters, it is important to review the information you learned earlier. It's helpful to make flashcards for each chapter and review them often, to go back to the **Exploraciones de repaso** section in earlier chapters to be sure you can still do the activities, and to complete the **Hora de reciclar** activities in your Student Activities Manual.

In this chapter, you will learn how to:

- Give instructions
- Talk about your hobbies and pastimes
- Talk about what you used to do in the past

¿Qué te gustaba de niño?

© Ariel Skelley/Getty Images

La señora Montero escoge frutas y verduras frescas y baratas en el mercado.

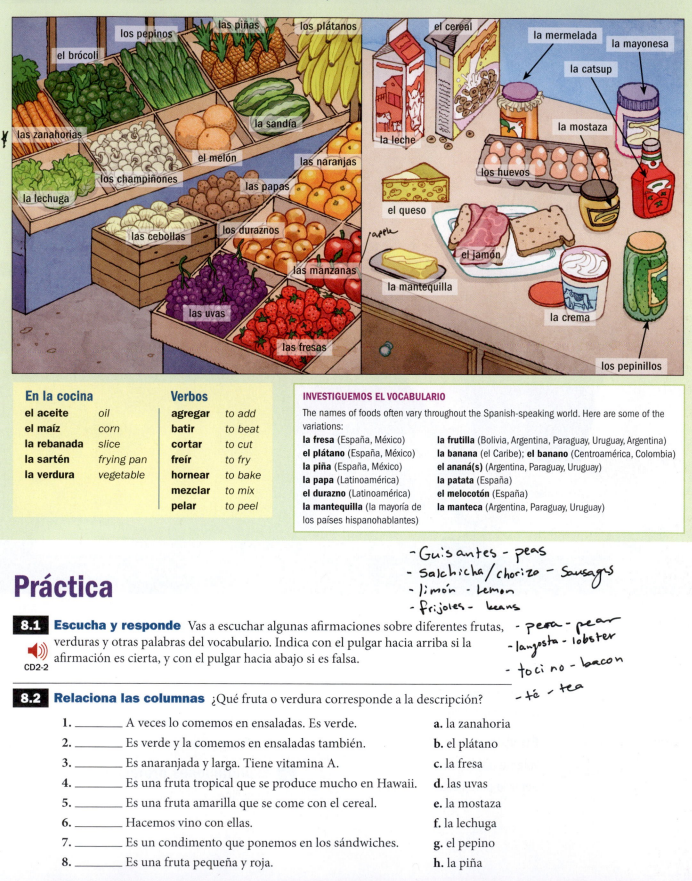

En la cocina

el aceite	*oil*
el maíz	*corn*
la rebanada	*slice*
la sartén	*frying pan*
la verdura	*vegetable*

Verbos

agregar	*to add*
batir	*to beat*
cortar	*to cut*
freír	*to fry*
hornear	*to bake*
mezclar	*to mix*
pelar	*to peel*

INVESTIGUEMOS EL VOCABULARIO

The names of foods often vary throughout the Spanish-speaking world. Here are some of the variations:

la fresa (España, México)	**la frutilla** (Bolivia, Argentina, Paraguay, Uruguay, Argentina)
el plátano (España, México)	**la banana** (el Caribe); **el banano** (Centroamérica, Colombia)
la piña (España, México)	**el ananá(s)** (Argentina, Paraguay, Uruguay)
la papa (Latinoamérica)	**la patata** (España)
el durazno (Latinoamérica)	**el melocotón** (España)
la mantequilla (la mayoría de los países hispanohablantes)	**la manteca** (Argentina, Paraguay, Uruguay)

Práctica

- Guisantes - peas
- Salchicha/chorizo - Sausages
- limón - Lemon
- frijoles - beans
- pera - pear
- langosta - lobster
- tocino - bacon
- té - tea

8.1 **Escucha y responde** Vas a escuchar algunas afirmaciones sobre diferentes frutas, verduras y otras palabras del vocabulario. Indica con el pulgar hacia arriba si la afirmación es cierta, y con el pulgar hacia abajo si es falsa.

CD2-2

8.2 **Relaciona las columnas** ¿Qué fruta o verdura corresponde a la descripción?

1. _____ A veces lo comemos en ensaladas. Es verde.   **a.** la zanahoria
2. _____ Es verde y la comemos en ensaladas también.   **b.** el plátano
3. _____ Es anaranjada y larga. Tiene vitamina A.   **c.** la fresa
4. _____ Es una fruta tropical que se produce mucho en Hawaii.   **d.** las uvas
5. _____ Es una fruta amarilla que se come con el cereal.   **e.** la mostaza
6. _____ Hacemos vino con ellas.   **f.** la lechuga
7. _____ Es un condimento que ponemos en los sándwiches.   **g.** el pepino
8. _____ Es una fruta pequeña y roja.   **h.** la piña

8.3 **Los ingredientes** Trabaja con un compañero para decidir qué ingredientes se necesitan para preparar estas comidas. Ustedes deciden la comida para el número seis.

Modelo un sándwich
Para preparar un sándwich necesitamos pan, mayonesa, mostaza, queso y jamón.

1. una ensalada verde
2. una sopa de verduras
3. una hamburguesa

4. un omelet
5. unos nachos
6. ¿?

8.4 **Descripciones** Trabaja con un compañero. Túrnense para escoger una fruta, un vegetal o un ingrediente de una de las fotos y para describírselo a su compañero sin decir el nombre.

Modelo Estudiante 1: *No es ni fruta ni vegetal. Lo usamos para hacer sándwiches.*
Estudiante 2: *El pan.*

© Photos To Go

© Photos To Go

8.5 **En busca de...** Circula por la clase y busca a ocho compañeros diferentes que hagan las siguientes actividades. Después deben reportar a la clase.

Modelo beber leche todos los días
Estudiante 1: *¿Bebes leche todos los días?*
Estudiante 2: *Sí, bebo leche todos los días con el desayuno.*

1. desayunar huevos
2. almorzar en la cafetería de la escuela
3. poner catsup en mucha de su comida
4. ser vegetariano
5. comer papas fritas frecuentemente
6. saber cocinar un omelet
7. preferir la mermelada de fresa
8. su verdura favorita es el brócoli

8.6 **La lista del supermercado** Primero, escribe una lista de diez productos que compras regularmente en el supermercado. Después, trabaja con un compañero para hablar sobre sus listas.

Modelo Estudiante 1: *Yo compro tomates todas las semanas.*
Estudiante 2: *¿Por qué? (¿Cuántos? / ¿Cuánto cuestan? / ¿Cómo los usas?)*
Estudiante 1: *Los compro porque le gustan a mi familia. ¿Tú qué compras?*

¿Qué comida compras con frecuencia en el supermercado? Mira el anuncio de un supermercado de España para ver si hay algunos de esos productos. ¿Reconoces todos los artículos? ¿Son parecidos (*similar*) los precios a los que encuentras tú en el supermercado?

MERCADONA

SUPERMERCADOS DE CONFIANZA

1/4 kilo de queso manchego orgánico a solo **3.45 €**

Leche entera de vaca a solo **.92 €** el litro

Jugo de naranja marca Valencia a solo **1.98 €** en envase de un litro

Espárragos importados en envase de 300 gr. a solo **.95 €**

Mayonesa marca Hidalgo de 500 ml. a solo **1.39 €**

Kilo de Fresas importadas a solo **1.20 €**

Duraznos en almíbar en envase de un kilo a solo **1.10 €**

Ofertas válidas del 7 al 14 de febrero.

Más allá

Diseña un anuncio parecido para un supermercado local.

A analizar

Lee la conversación de un programa de televisión. Presta atención a las palabras en negritas y luego contesta las preguntas que siguen.

Laura: Pues, aquí estamos con el chef Julián. ¿Qué **nos** vas a preparar hoy, Julián?

Julián: **Les** voy a preparar un sándwich cubano. Es muy fácil de preparar.

Laura: ¿Qué es el sándwich cubano?

Julián: Es un sándwich caliente muy popular en Cuba. ¿**Te** gustan el jamón y el queso?

Laura: ¡**Me** encantan!

Julián: Entonces, **te** va a gustar este sándwich.

© Photos To Go

1. You've learned that a direct object is the thing or person acted upon, for example, **Corté las papas.** or **Vi al cocinero.** What is an indirect object?

2. Why is the verb **encantan** conjugated in the third person plural form?

A comprobar

Indirect object pronouns

1. An indirect object is not affected directly by the action of the verb. It is usually a person and tells **to whom** or **for whom** something is done.

> Él siempre **le** dice la verdad **a su novia**.
> *He always tells the truth **to his girlfriend**.*
> (**to whom** the truth is told)

> **Le** compro un regalo **a mi amigo**.
> *I am buying a gift **for my friend**.*
> (**for whom** the gift is bought)

2. When using the indirect object pronoun, it is possible to add **a** + prepositional pronoun or **a** + noun to either clarify or emphasize. Although it may seem repetitive, it is common to include the indirect object pronoun, even if the indirect object is clearly identified.

> El mesero **le** llevó la comida **a la señora**.
> *The waiter took the food **to the lady**.*

> Jorge **me** escribió **a mí**.
> *Jorge wrote **to me**. (not to someone else)*

3. Indirect object pronouns

yo	**me**	nosotros(as)	**nos**
tú	**te**	vosotros(as)	**os**
él, ella, usted	**le**	ellos, ellas, ustedes	**les**

4. As with the direct object pronoun, the indirect object pronoun is placed in front of a conjugated verb or can be attached to an infinitive or a present participle.

> **Le** pregunté cuánto cuesta.
> *I asked **him/her** how much it costs.*

> Quiero prepara**rte** un sandwich.
> *I want to make **you** a sandwich.*

> El mesero está sirviéndo**le** al cliente.
> *The waiter is serving the customer.*

5. The following are some of the verbs that are frequently used with these indirect object pronouns:

contar (ue)	*to tell*	pedir	
dar		prestar	*to lend*
decir		preguntar	
devolver (ue)		servir	
mostrar (ue)	*to show*		

6. In **Capítulo 3** you learned the verb **gustar**. **Gustar** always takes the indirect object pronoun and is conjugated according to the subject that follows it.

> A él **le gusta** el melón.
> *He likes melon. (Melon is **pleasing to him**.)*
>
> A los niños no **les gusta** el brócoli.
> *The children don't **like** broccoli.*

The following are verbs similar to **gustar**. They also take an indirect object pronoun and are conjugated according to the subject that follows them.

caer (bien/mal)	*to like/dislike a person*
encantar	*to really like, to enjoy immensely*
fascinar	*to fascinate*
importar	*to be important*
interesar	*to interest*
molestar	*to bother*

> **Me encanta** la fruta fresca.
> *I **love** fresh fruit. (Fresh fruit **delights me**.)*
>
> ¿**Te molesta** ir al supermercado?
> *Does it **bother you** to go to the supermarket?*

A practicar

8.7 **¿Qué les gusta?** Completa las oraciones lógicamente.

1. A mí me gusta comprar la comida en el supermercado _____.
2. A mis amigos no les gusta comer en _____.
3. A mi amigo le encantan las frutas, especialmente _____.
4. A mi mejor amigo y a mí nos fascina la comida _____.
5. A mi esposo/novio le caen mal los meseros que _____.

8.8 **Sondeo** En grupos de cuatro o cinco, hablen sobre sus hábitos gastronómicos usando los verbos y las expresiones indicados. Cada estudiante debe escribir el número de estudiantes que contestan **sí** y el número que contestan **no**. Después, repórtenle la información a la clase.

Modelo gustarle las frutas
> Estudiante 1: *¿A quién le gustan las frutas?*
> Estudiante 2: *Me gustan mucho.*
> Estudiante 3: *No me gustan (para nada).*

	sí	no
molestarle ir al supermercado	_____	_____
fascinarle las comidas exóticas	_____	_____
encantarle cocinar	_____	_____
interesarle la nutrición	_____	_____
importarle comer saludablemente	_____	_____
gustarle las verduras	_____	_____

8.9 **Oraciones incompletas** Selecciona la conclusión más lógica para las siguientes oraciones. Luego, explica a quién se refiere el pronombre indicado.

1. Hoy es el cumpleaños de Rosa...
2. El niño tiene mucha hambre...
3. Los abuelos de Paulino fueron al mercado...
4. Unos amigos vienen a cenar...
5. Mis padres fueron a un restaurante...
6. Cecilia tiene sed...

a. y sus padres **le** van a dar una manzana.
b. y **le** traigo un jugo de piña.
c. y el mesero **les** sirvió la comida.
d. y su mamá **le** está preparando un pastel.
e. y **le** compraron frutas.
f. y **les** voy a servir una sopa de verduras.

8.10 **Tú y tu mejor amigo** Entrevista a un compañero sobre su mejor amigo.

1. ¿Le cuentas tus secretos a tu mejor amigo?
2. ¿Le prestas dinero a tu mejor amigo?
3. ¿Siempre le dices la verdad a tu mejor amigo?
4. ¿Le das regalos a tu mejor amigo?
5. ¿Le pides consejos (*advice*) a tu mejor amigo?
6. ¿Le escribes mensajes de texto a tu mejor amigo?

8.11 **La cena** Completa la conversación entre la mesera y el cliente con los pronombres de objeto indirecto. Luego explica qué pasó, usando el pretérito de los verbos indicados.

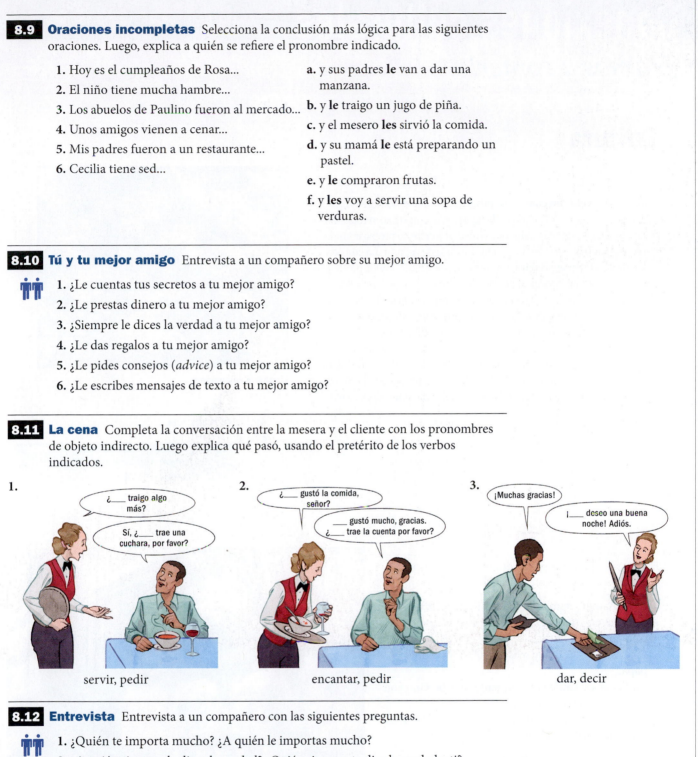

1.
¿____ traigo algo más?
Sí, ¿____ trae una cuchara, por favor?

servir, pedir

2.
¿____ gustó la comida, señor?
____ gustó mucho, gracias. ¿____ trae la cuenta por favor?

encantar, pedir

3.
¡Muchas gracias!
¡____ deseo una buena noche! Adiós.

dar, decir

8.12 **Entrevista** Entrevista a un compañero con las siguientes preguntas.

1. ¿Quién te importa mucho? ¿A quién le importas mucho?
2. ¿A quién siempre le dices la verdad? ¿Quién siempre te dice la verdad a ti?
3. ¿A quién le pides ayuda con la tarea de español? ¿Quién te pide ayuda a ti?
4. ¿A quién le escribes cartas o mensajes electrónicos? ¿Quién te escribe a ti? ¿Alguien te escribe cartas de amor?
5. ¿A quién le pides consejos (*advice*)? Normalmente ¿te dan buenos consejos? ¿Alguien te pide consejos a ti?
6. ¿Quién te da regalos para tu cumpleaños? ¿A quién le das regalos de cumpleaños?
7. ¿Qué les prestas a tus amigos? ¿Siempre te devuelven tus cosas? ¿Qué te prestan tus amigos a ti?
8. ¿Quién te cae bien a ti? ¿A quién le caes muy bien?

Conexiones culturales

¡Vamos a comer!

Cultura

Comida como cultura

"**La comida es cultura cuando se produce,** porque el hombre no utiliza solo lo que se encuentra en la naturaleza (como hacen todas las demás especies animales), sino que ambiciona crear su propia comida, superponiendo la actividad de producción a la de captura. **La comida es cultura cuando se prepara,** porque una vez adquiridos los productos básicos de su alimentación, el hombre los transforma mediante el uso del fuego y una elaborada tecnología que se expresa en la práctica de la cocina. **La comida es cultura cuando se consume,** porque el hombre aun pudiendo comer de todo, elige su propia comida con criterios ligados ya sea a la dimensión económica y nutritiva del gesto, ya sea a valores simbólicos de la misma comida. De este modo, la comida se configura como un elemento decisivo de la identidad humana como uno de los instrumentos más eficaces para comunicarla." (Massimo Montanari)

La paella valenciana

1. ¿Estás de acuerdo con la opinión expresada por Massimo Montanari? Explica tu respuesta.

2. ¿Cuáles son ejemplos de comidas que se identifican con culturas específicas?

3. ¿Qué comidas representan a tu cultura y por qué?

> Investiga en Internet comida que simboliza otras partes del mundo hispano.

Comparaciones

En la mayoría de los países donde se habla español la dieta es muy diferente. Por ejemplo:

- En Sudamérica no se comen chile ni tortillas.
- En Uruguay se come más carne que en cualquier otro país del mundo.
- En Bolivia y Perú hay más de 2000 variedades de papa.
- En España y Chile generalmente se bebe vino con la comida a mediodía.
- En México, en promedio, cada persona bebe 150 litros de refrescos al año.

¿Cómo se comparan tus hábitos alimenticios con los de las personas de los países que se mencionan arriba?

En México los refrescos son muy populares.

Conexiones... a la gastronomía

La comida es una parte muy importante de las tradiciones y cultura de cada país. Los siguientes son algunos ejemplos.

En Argentina, Paraguay y Uruguay se bebe un té que se hace con una yerba llamada mate. Hay varias formas de prepararlo y beberlo, pero en la más tradicional se hace con hojas secas de mate y agua caliente. Se prepara y se bebe en un recipiente hecho con el fruto de la calabaza (*gourd*), y se bebe con una bombilla (*straw*). El té se pasa de persona a persona, así que beber mate es una actividad social.

Un platillo tradicional de Costa Rica es el Gallo Pinto. Este plato se prepara con arroz, pollo, frijoles y otros ingredientes que le dan un sabor especial, como cebolla y cilantro. Hay muchas variaciones de este platillo. De hecho, el arroz y los frijoles son la base para platillos importantes de otros países, como Moros y Cristianos, de Cuba.

Abajo hay una lista de otros platillos. Escoge cuatro de ellos e investiga qué son y qué ingredientes se necesitan para prepararlos.

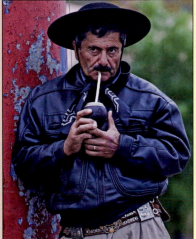
Un gaucho uruguayo bebiendo mate

Bolivia: chicha
Chile: empanadas
Colombia: buñuelos
Ecuador: ceviche
España: gazpacho
Honduras: baleada
Panamá: chocao panameño
Paraguay: sopa paraguaya
La República Dominicana: tostones
Venezuela: hallacas

En el Almanaque al final del libro puedes encontrar más platillos tradicionales de cada uno de los países donde se habla español.

Gallo pinto

Comunidad

¿Hay restaurantes latinoamericanos en tu comunidad? Puedes explorar uno nuevo para ti, y probar platillos nuevos y deliciosos. Usa las expresiones que aprendiste en el **Capítulo 7** para pedir tu comida en español. Luego, comparte tu experiencia con la clase.

Si no hay ningún restaurante cerca, encuentra uno en Internet y busca un platillo nuevo para ti. Puedes escribir un mensaje para preguntar qué ingredientes se usan para preparar el platillo.

¿Hay un restaurante latinamericano en tu comunidad?

A analizar

Lee la explicación para preparar el sándwich cubano y observa los verbos. Luego, contesta las preguntas que siguen.

© REDAV/Shutterstock

Primero, **se necesita** un pedazo de pan francés. **Se corta** el pan a lo largo y **se pone** mostaza en las dos partes. **Se ponen** unas rebanadas delgadas de puerco asado y jamón en una de las rebanadas de pan. Luego **se pone** queso suizo encima del jamón. **Se ponen** unos pepinillos y **se coloca** encima la otra rebanada de pan. El sándwich **se cocina** en una sartén hasta que esté tostado y el queso esté derretido.

1. In what forms (person) are the verbs conjugated?

2. What pronoun is used in all of the highlighted verbs? Does it have a reflexive meaning like we saw with the verbs **sentarse** and **lavarse**?

3. How do you determine whether to use the singular or the plural form?

A comprobar

Constructions with **se**

1. The pronoun **se** is used when the person or thing performing an action is either unknown or unimportant. The verb is then conjugated in the third person form. The singular form is used with singular nouns and the plural form with plural nouns. Notice that the subject can either precede or follow the verb.

> **Se cocina** la carne en una sartén.
> *The meat **is cooked** in a frying pan.*

> La receta **se prepara** fácilmente.
> *The recipe **is easily prepared.***

> **Se cortan** los tomates.
> *The tomatoes **are cut.***

> Las papas **se pelan** primero.
> *The potatoes **are peeled** first.*

2. When followed by an infinitive, the verb is often conjugated in the singular form.

> **Se recomienda** tomar agua y dormir ocho horas.
> *It is recommended that one drink water and sleep eight hours.*

3. When the verb is not used with a noun, it is conjugated in the third person singular. The pronoun **se** translates to *one, you,* or *they* in English.

> En Paraguay **se come** a las dos de la tarde.
> *In Paraguay **they eat** at two in the afternoon.*

> **Se dice** que las zanahorias son buenas para los ojos.
> *They say that carrots are good for your eyes.*

> **Se vive** bien en España.
> *One lives well in Spain.*

A practicar

8.13 **Un poco de lógica** Mira las siguientes instrucciones para preparar una ensalada y decide cuál es un orden lógico.

    a. _____ Se sirve la ensalada.

    b. _____ Las verduras se ponen en un tazón.

    c. _____ Se mezcla todo.

    d. _____ Se sacan la lechuga, los tomates y el pepino del refrigerador.

    e. _____ Se mezcla el aceite de oliva con el vinagre.

    f. _____ Se cortan las verduras.

    g. _____ Se pone el aderezo (*dressing*) encima de las verduras.

8.14 **El mercado** Mira las fotos e identifica la comida que se vende en los mercados.

Un mercado en Ecuador © XuRa/Shutterstock

Un mercado en Perú © David Petit/Shutterstock

8.15 **Costumbres** Cambia el verbo para usar una construcción con **se** en las siguientes oraciones.

    1. En Argentina normalmente _____ (desayunar) un pan tostado con café.

    2. En Ecuador _____ (tomar) muchos diferentes jugos de fruta.

    3. En Latinoamérica _____ (ir) al mercado para comprar comida fresca todos los días.

    4. En Guatemala los frijoles negros _____ (comer) con frecuencia.

    5. En Latinoamérica _____ (preparar) la comida más fuerte al mediodía.

    6. En México las salsas picantes _____ (servir) al lado de la comida.

    7. En Paraguay _____ (consumir) mucha carne.

    8. En Latinoamérica no _____ (comprar) muchas verduras congeladas (*frozen*).

    9. En Cuba _____ (cenar) entre las nueve y las diez de la noche.

    10. En España _____ (salir) a menudo (*often*) a comer tapas por la noche.

8.16 **Unos niños mal educados** Mira el dibujo.
Con un compañero, túrnense para explicarles a
estos niños lo que se hace o no se hace a la mesa.
Deben usar una construcción con **se**.

Modelo *No se habla con comida en la boca.*
Se come y después se habla.

8.17 **Buenos modales** Lee el siguiente artículo sobre los buenos modales, y luego comenta
lo que se debe hacer a la mesa y lo que no se debe hacer, usando una construcción con **se**.

La etiqueta
a la mesa

La etiqueta es una muestra
de civilización y de consideración
para los otros. Nosotros tenemos
que ser buenos ejemplos, y para
que nuestros hijos tengan
buenos hábitos, es necesario
que practiquen en casa y no solo
cuando están de visita en otra
casa o en un restaurante.

Tenemos que enseñarles a:

· Masticarᵃ con la boca
  cerrada.
· Mantener las dos manos
  encima de la mesa, pero no
  poner los codos en la mesa.
· Comer la fruta con un
  tenedor.
· Dejar la servilleta en la
  mesa, y no ponerla al cuello.
· No limpiarse la nariz a la
  mesa.
· No eruptar a la mesa.

Chew

© Monkey Business Images/Shutterstock

¿Es la etiqueta de Latinoamérica diferente a la de los Estados Unidos? ¿Cómo?

8.18 **¿Qué se hace?** Con un compañero, túrnense para explicar qué se hace con las siguientes cosas. Usen una construcción con **se.**

1. el cuchillo
2. el vaso
3. el azúcar
4. los jugos

5. las frutas
6. la mantequilla
7. los huevos
8. el helado

8.19 **La tortilla española** Con un compañero, miren los siguientes dibujos y expliquen cómo se prepara una tortilla española.

Vocabulario útil: pelar (*to peel*), **batir** (*to beat*), **voltear** (*to flip*)

Tortilla española

© Mihai Petre/Shutterstock

8.20 **¿Cómo se hace?** Con un compañero, escojan una de las siguientes metas (*goals*), o inventen su propio tema, y escriban un mínimo de 5 cosas que se pueden hacer para lograrlo (*achieve it*). Deben usar una construcción con **se.**

Modelo perder peso
Se va al gimnasio todos los días. Se camina en el parque. Se comen muchas frutas y verduras. Se toman menos refrescos. Se pide comida saludable en los restaurantes.

1. hacerse millonario
2. conquistar a un hombre/una mujer
3. conseguir una A en la clase de español
4. hacer una cena romántica perfecta
5. conseguir un buen trabajo
6. tener una fiesta sorpresa para alguien
7. terminar los estudios universitarios en tres años
8. comprar un coche nuevo

iTunes
Laura Pausini, an Italian singer, has recorded numerous songs in Spanish. Listen to her song, "Cuando se ama" and write down the **se** constructions that you hear.

Lectura

Antes de leer

Escribe una lista de comidas que se consumen durante el Día de Acción de Gracias. ¿Qué ingredientes se necesitan para prepararlas? ¿Conoces una comida típica de algún país latinoamericano? ¿Qué comida? ¿Qué ingredientes se necesitan?

A leer

Los alimentos del Nuevo Mundo

where they used to live

Es obvio que en épocas anteriores, los hombres y las mujeres comían los alimentos que estaban disponibles en la zona **donde habitaban.** Debido a las diferencias climáticas y geográficas, los animales y plantas del Nuevo Mundo (el continente americano) eran muy diferentes a los que existían en Europa.

Hoy en día, gracias al avance en las comunicaciones del mundo, y a las nuevas técnicas de transporte y preservación de los alimentos, es posible comer productos que

were harvested

se **cosecharon** o produjeron a miles de kilómetros de distancia. Nuestro mundo

used to be

era muy diferente antes de la llegada de los Europeos al Nuevo Mundo.

[puedes imaginar el resto del mundo sin chocolate...]

¿Puedes imaginar tu dieta sin leche, sin queso, sin carne de res o sin naranjas ni plátanos? Estos son solo algunos de

were not available

los productos que **no había** en el Nuevo Mundo. Por otra parte, ¿puedes imaginar el resto del mundo sin chocolate, vainilla, tomates, maíz, papas, chiles o pavos? La lista de productos americanos es larga,

goes well beyond

y su importancia **va mucho más allá** del gusto por estos productos. Un buen ejemplo es el de las papas, las cuales le salvaron la vida a millones de europeos durante el período de escasez que siguió a la Segunda Guerra Mundial en Europa.

Si se piensa en la economía de varios países ¿puedes imaginar a Suiza o a Bélgica sin chocolates? ¿Puedes imaginar las típicas pizzas italianas sin tomate? ¿o

spicy

la **picante** comida de la India sin chile?

Hay más de 3800 variedades de papas en los Andes.

Tanto el tomate como el maíz, la vainilla y el cacao se originaron en Mesoamérica, el territorio que hoy es parte de México y de Centroamérica. De hecho, las palabras *tomate* y *chocolate* vienen de las palabras del náhuatl *tomatl* y *xocolatl*. *Ahuacatl* y *chilli* son palabras náhuatl para *aguacate* y *chile*, más plantas nativas de las Américas.

Un poco más al sur se originan la papa y la quinoa —un cereal que aunque no es muy conocido en los Estados Unidos, se considera que puede ser la solución al problema del hambre en el mundo, debido a su gran valor nutritivo.

peanuts

flavors

¿Y qué sería de la dieta de los países asiáticos sin chiles o sin **cacahuates**? Los helados europeos no serían tan populares sin los **sabores** de chocolate y vainilla, y las papas a la francesa no existirían. Estos productos son solo una pequeña parte de las aportaciones del Nuevo Mundo para el resto del planeta.

El maíz se originó en Mesoamérica.

© rj lerich/Shutterstock

Comprensión

1. ¿Cuáles son cuatro productos originarios de las Américas que son importantes en las celebraciones culturales de Estados Unidos? ¿Por qué?

2. ¿Qué frutos tomaron su nombre del idioma náhuatl, el idioma de los aztecas?

3. ¿Qué es la quinoa y por qué es importante?

4. En tu opinión ¿cuáles tres productos de América tienen mucha importancia en la economía mundial? ¿Por qué?

5. ¿Qué productos muy importantes en tu dieta personal no había en América antes de la llegada de los europeos?

Después de leer

Cada región o país tiene su comida típica. ¿Qué factores externos ayudan a determinar la comida típica de una región? ¿Qué comida es típica donde vives? ¿Por qué? Con un compañero, explíquenle al resto de la clase cómo preparar una comida típica de su estado o tu región.

Los tiempos cambian, así como también cambian las actividades favoritas de los niños.

Juegos		Verbos		Palabras adicionales	
el ajedrez	chess	chatear	to chat on the Internet	el juguete	toy
las cartas	playing cards	contar (ue) (cuentos,	to tell (short stories,	el permiso	permission
las damas	checkers	historias, chistes)	stories, jokes)	el recreo	recess
el dominó	dominos	cuidar (a niños)	to care for (children)		
las escondidas	hide and seek	hacer travesuras	to do mischievous things		
		ir de paseo	to go for a walk		
		pelear	to fight, to argue		
		portarse (bien/mal)	to behave well/badly		
		tejer	to knit		

Práctica

8.21 **Escucha y responde** Vas a escuchar una serie de actividades populares entre los niños. Si es un juego, indica con tu pulgar hacia arriba. Si es otro tipo de actividad, indica con el pulgar hacia abajo.

CD2-3

8.22 **¿Cierto o falso?** Mira el dibujo de **Exploraciones léxicas** y decide si las siguientes oraciones son ciertas o falsas. Corrige las oraciones falsas.

1. La niñera está muy feliz.
2. Dos niñas dibujan en la pared.
3. Una niña salta la cuerda en el jardín.
4. Un niño lee un libro.
5. Un niño trepa un árbol.
6. Un gato mira a unos niños que hablan por teléfono en su celular.

8.23 **¿Qué dicen estos niños del tercer año?** Completa las ideas con una palabra de la lista de vocabulario (no las necesitas todas). Si es un verbo, debes conjugarlo.

cuento	pelear	muñecas	recreo	travesuras	saltar
permiso	videojuegos	cometa	juguete	contar	

Juanito: Mi mamá dice que soy malo porque hago muchas _____.

Anita: En la escuela podemos comer y jugar a la hora del _____.

Luisito: Mis hermanos y yo _____ chistes.

Mónica: Yo nunca _____ con mi hermana porque soy una buena niña.

Sofía: Yo tengo muchas _____, pero mi favorita es una *Barbie*.

Pepito: Mi padre siempre me cuenta un _____ por la noche. Mi favorito es el de "Cenicienta" (*Cinderella*).

Roberto: Cuando hay viento, me gusta ir al parque y volar una _____.

Sarita: Si quiero salir con mis amigas, tengo que pedir _____ a mi mamá o mi papá.

Emilia: Yo prefiero jugar _____ con mis amigos en la computadora.

8.24 **Asociaciones** Con un compañero, decidan qué palabra no pertenece al grupo. Luego expliquen por qué.

1. el dominó	las canicas	el permiso	las damas
2. jugar	coleccionar	el recreo	volar
3. la cometa	el carrito	el cuento	la muñeca
4. la niñera	las cartas	el ajedrez	las escondidas
5. andar en patineta	tejer	saltar la cuerda	trepar árboles

8.25 **Explicaciones** Con un compañero, túrnense para describir las siguientes palabras sin decir cuál es. Tu compañero debe adivinar qué palabra describes.

los carritos	el cuento	los videojuegos	el recreo	tejer	coleccionar
las canicas	las damas	la muñeca	las tiras cómicas	el dominó	
la cometa	las escondidas	la niñera	chatear	la patineta	

8.26 **Los niños de hoy** Habla con un compañero para expresar sus opiniones.

1. ¿Tienes hijos, nietos, sobrinos o hermanos menores? ¿Cuántos? ¿Cómo se llaman? ¿Qué les gusta hacer?
2. ¿Cuáles son las actividades que los niños de hoy hacen?
3. ¿Conoces alguna canción para niños? ¿Cuál? ¿Sabes si los niños todavía cantan esa canción?
4. Si tienes hijos o cuidas a niños con frecuencia, ¿qué hacen que tú nunca hiciste?

Piensa en una fiesta infantil que diste (o a la que fuiste) de niño. ¿Qué juegos había? Lee el siguiente anuncio de servicios para fiestas infantiles. ¿Qué piensas que significa "payasos"? ¿y "magos"? ¿Cómo sabes? ¿Había estas actividades en la fiesta de cumpleaños en la que pensaste?

¡En PEQUES tenemos todo para sus Fiestas infantiles!

- payasos
- magos
- maquillaje
- piñatas con los personajes de moda de las películas y de la televisión
- carritos de hot dogs, hamburguesas y algodones de azúcar
- organizamos actividades y juegos

PEQUES le ofrece paquetes para todos los presupuestos. Garantizamos una fiesta inolvidable para sus pequeñines.

Más allá

Imagina que estás planeando una fiesta de cumpleaños para tus hijos o tus sobrinos. Diseña las invitaciones e incluye una lista de las actividades que va a haber para los niños.

A analizar

Lee el siguiente párrafo y presta atención a los verbos en negritas. Luego contesta las preguntas que siguen.

Cuando **era** niña **tenía** una amiga que se **llamaba** Julia. **Vivía** cerca y siempre **iba** a su casa para jugar a la mamá. Yo **tenía** una muñeca rubia, muy bonita. También me **gustaba** jugar con mi hermano, pero a veces él me **molestaba** mientras **jugaba** con mis amigas. Él **era** más grande y me **hacía** daño cuando **patinábamos** o **trepábamos** los árboles. Por la noche mi madre siempre me **leía** cuentos. Me **fascinaban** los cuentos de hadas. Pero cuando mi mamá **apagaba** la luz, siempre **veía** cosas raras. **Pensaba** que **había** un monstruo en mi cuarto. Entonces ella **ponía** la música de Cri-Cri, así no **tenía** miedo y me **dormía.**

The verbs in bold are in the imperfect tense.

1. What are the endings of the -**ar** verbs? And the -**er**/-**ir** verbs?

2. What are the forms of the verb **ser**? And **ver**? And **ir**?

3. Does the imperfect describe actions in the past, present, or future?

A comprobar

The imperfect

1. To form the imperfect of regular verbs, add the following endings to the stem:

-ar verbs cantar	
cantaba	cantábamos
cantabas	cantabais
cantaba	cantaban

-er/-ir verbs leer	
leía	leíamos
leías	leíais
leía	leían

ir			
yo	iba	nosotros(as)	íbamos
tú	ibas	vosotros(as)	ibais
él, ella, usted	iba	ellos, ellas, ustedes	iban

2. The verbs **ser, ir,** and **ver** are the only irregular verbs in the imperfect.

ser			
yo	era	nosotros(as)	éramos
tú	eras	vosotros(as)	erais
él, ella, usted	era	ellos, ellas, ustedes	eran

ver			
yo	veía	nosotros(as)	veíamos
tú	veías	vosotros(as)	veíais
él, ella, usted	veía	ellos, ellas, ustedes	veían

3. There are no stem-changing verbs in the imperfect. All verbs that have changes in the stem in the present or the preterite are regular.

> Mis hijos **juegan** un juego de mesa.
> Yo **jugaba** con mi muñeca.

> Ayer mis hijos **se divirtieron** en el Parque del Retiro.
> Ellos siempre **se divertían** en el parque.

4. One of the uses of the imperfect is to describe past habits or routines. In English, we frequently use the expression *used to*. It is often used with expressions such as **siempre, todos los días, todos los años, con frecuencia, a menudo** (*often*), **normalmente, generalmente, a veces,** etc.

> De niño, siempre **andaba** en bicicleta.
> *As a child, I always **used to ride** my bike.*

> Todos los veranos, **íbamos** a la playa.
> *Every summer we **went** to the beach.*

5. Another use of the imperfect is to describe an action in progress at a particular moment in the past where there is no emphasis on when the action began or ended.

> ¿Qué **hacías** a las tres?
> *What **were you doing** at three o'clock?*

> Yo **paseaba** en el parque.
> *I **was walking** in the park.*

> **INVESTIGUEMOS LA GRAMÁTICA**
> You will recall that the present progressive describes actions in progress in the present. It is also possible to use the imperfect of **estar** with the present participle.
>
> Los niños **estaban jugando** un juego de mesa.
> *The children **were playing** a board game.*

A practicar

8.27 Cuando era adolescente Lee las siguientes oraciones e indica si son ciertas o falsas según tu experiencia.

1. Yo veía muchas películas.
2. Yo salía con mis amigos todos los días.
3. Yo iba a la escuela en autobús.
4. Yo tenía buenas notas en la escuela.
5. Yo practicaba muchos deportes.
6. Yo leía las tiras cómicas.
7. Yo hablaba mucho por mi teléfono celular.
8. Yo tocaba un instrumento.

8.28 Mi niñez Cambia el verbo a la forma necesaria del imperfecto y completa las siguientes ideas.

Modelo mi niñera me (contar)...
Cuando era niña, mi niñera me contaba cuentos.

Cuando era niño(a),...

1. mis hermanos y yo (comer) mucho...
2. mi familia (ir) con frecuencia a...
3. mis amigos (jugar)...
4. me (encantar)...
5. no me (gustar)...
6. mi mejor amigo (tener)...
7. mis padres me (castigar - *to punish*) cuando...
8. yo (leer)...

8.29 **¿Qué hacían?** Con un compañero, túrnense para identificar las actividades que hacían las personas en el parque cuando el fotógrafo sacó esta foto.

8.30 **Busco un compañero** Vas a preguntarles a ocho compañeros diferentes si ellos hacían las siguientes actividades cuando eran niños. Tus compañeros deben dar un poco de información adicional. Si tu compañero responde negativamente, hazle otra pregunta.

Modelo montar a caballo
Estudiante 1: *¿Montabas a caballo cuando eras niña?*
Estudiante 2: *Sí; tenía un caballo que se llamaba Pegaso.*

1. tocar el piano
2. hacer travesuras
3. comer muchos dulces
4. navegar en Internet
5. ir de vacaciones con la familia
6. pelear con sus hermanos
7. jugar videojuegos
8. hacer fiestas en su cumpleaños

8.31 **Entrevista** Entrevista a un compañero sobre sus actividades mientras estaba en la escuela secundaria. Da mucha información al contestar las preguntas.

1. ¿Qué te gustaba hacer en las vacaciones cuando estabas en la escuela secundaria?
2. ¿Tienes hermanos? ¿Qué hacían ellos?
3. ¿Quién cocinaba? ¿Qué comida te gustaba más?
4. ¿Trabajaban tus padres? ¿Dónde?
5. ¿Tenías una mascota? ¿Cómo se llamaba?
6. ¿Cómo se llamaba tu mejor amigo? ¿Qué hacías con él?
7. ¿Qué te decían tus maestros en la escuela?
8. ¿Qué hacías después de regresar de la escuela?

Cultura

¿A quién no le gusta la música? La música es un elemento cultural de todas las sociedades. Algunos géneros musicales se originaron en otros lugares del mundo, y luego se popularizaron por todo el planeta. Lo que conocemos como música latina es, en realidad, una mezcla de géneros y culturas. Por ejemplo, el danzón es un género de música bailable que se originó en Cuba a finales del siglo XIX. Otro ejemplo es el tango, que define tanto a la música como al baile. El tango se originó en Argentina y Uruguay, y se caracteriza por el uso del bandoneón (*a type of accordion*). Uno de los más importantes artistas del tango, Enrique Santos Discépolo, lo definió como "un pensamiento triste que se baila".

A continuación aparece una lista de otros géneros musicales que se escuchan en España y Latinoamérica. ¿Cuáles conoces? ¿Conoces grupos o cantantes de Estados Unidos que incorporen estos ritmos en su música?

la salsa (popular en los países del Caribe, especialmente Cuba)
el bolero (especialmente popular en España y México)
el vallenato (originario de Colombia)
los corridos (son originarios de México)
la samba (música brasileña)
los sones (hay tipos diferentes de sones, en particular los cubanos y los mexicanos)
el mambo (baile cubano)
el merengue (popular en países del Caribe, Centroamérica, Colombia y Venezuela)
la cumbia (muy popular en Panamá, Venezuela, Perú y sobre todo en Colombia)

En Argentina se baila el tango.

Investiga en Internet grupos o cantantes que incorporen ritmos latinos en su música.

Comparaciones

La música es una forma muy importante de transmitir mensajes en casi todas las culturas. A continuación aparece un fragmento de una canción de Maná, un grupo de rock mexicano, muy popular en toda Latinoamérica. ¿Cuál piensas que es el tema y el mensaje de la canción? ¿Puedes dar ejemplos de canciones en inglés con mensajes de este tipo? ¿Qué dicen?

iTunes
Listen to Maná's song. Is the style of this song similar to a group or an artist you know? Do you like the song?

Justicia, tierra y libertad

Justicia, tierra y libertad... Justicia, tierra y libertad

Oye tú mi canto, oye, oye

Oye tú mi llanto, oye, oye

Hermanos y hermanas de otras razas...

de otro color y un mismo corazón,

rezas y rezas y nada enderezas

por eso hagamos la revolución, de amor.

Estamos exigiendo todo el respeto

respeto al indio y a su dignidad

ya lo dijo Villa, dijo Zapata.

Reproduced by permission of Hal Leonard Corporation, Milwaukee, WI.

El grupo de rock mexicano, Maná

Por el Mar de las Antillas anda un barco de papel, un libro de poesía donde, como en toda su obra, la influencia afro-cubana es muy importante, tanto en la forma como en los temas.

En algunos países, poesías que originalmente no fueron escritas para niños son muy populares entre los pequeños. Un ejemplo importante es la poesía del nicaragüense Rubén Darío, uno de los poetas latinoamericanos más influyentes, y reconocido como el padre de la corriente literaria del modernismo. Una poesía de Darío que es muy popular entre todas las generaciones es "A Margarita Debayle", un cuento y una bella poesía que los padres les repiten a sus hijos en todos los países de Hispanoamérica.

Fuera del ámbito de la literatura, otra persona que dedicó su vida a los niños fue el mexicano Francisco Gabilondo Soler, "Cri-Cri", quien escribió cientos de cuentos y canciones para niños. En los años 50, fue muy popular, gracias a la radio. Hoy, las canciones de Cri-Cri siguen siendo muy populares entre los niños, particularmente los de México.

Ruben Darío

© Hulton Archive/Getty Images

Comprensión

Decide si las siguientes oraciones son ciertas o falsas. Corrige las afirmaciones falsas.

1. Los niños latinoamericanos conocen solamente cuentos tradicionales de su país.
2. Nicolás Guillén escribió canciones para niños.
3. Rubén Darío fue un autor para niños.
4. "A Margarita Debayle" es un poema.
5. Las canciones de Cri-Cri eran populares en la televisión en los años 50.

Después de leer

Hay muchos cuentos conocidos en todo el mundo, como son los cuentos de Perrault. Dos ejemplos famosos son "Caperucita Roja" (*Little Red Riding Hood*) y "Pulgarcito" (*Tom Thumb*). Busca historias para niños en Internet, y tráelas a la clase para compartir con tus compañeros. Consejo: busca las historias usando palabras en español.

Una chef trabaja en la cocina de un restaurante.

© Photo To Go

Vocabulario

Sustantivos

el berro	*watercress*
el bife de lomo	*sirloin*
la caloría	*calorie*
el (la) camarero(a)	*waiter (waitress)*
el carbón	*charcoal*
la carne (de res)	*beef*
el chimichurri	*Argentine steak sauce*
el choclo	*corn*
el chorizo	*Italian sausage*
el condimento	*spice*
la empanada	*turnover*
la especialidad	*specialty*
el matambre	*flank steak*

Adjetivos

arrollado	*rolled*
hervido	*boiled*
relleno	*stuffed*
tierno	*tender*
vegetariano	*vegetarian*

Verbos

descubrir	*to discover*

Frases útiles

a fuego lento
low heat

a la parrilla
on the grill

Se corta finito.
Cut in small slices.

Se sirve caliente/frío.
Serve hot/cold.

vuelta y vuelta
cooked on both sides

DATOS IMPORTANTES

Educación: Título de chef otorgado por escuelas de cocina internacional o título universitario de licenciatura en artes culinarias y hospedaje. Para trabajar en restaurantes finos se requieren años de experiencia.

Salario: Entre $25 000 y $75 000, dependiendo de la experiencia y la categoría del restaurante.

Dónde se trabaja: Restaurantes, hoteles, clubes privados, compañías de servicios para fiestas y eventos, cruceros.

Miguel Casas es el chef de un restaurante de especialidades argentinas. Trabaja en ese lugar desde hace diez vas a ver y los clientes del restaurante están muy satisfechos con la comida. En el video vas a ver al chef Casas hablar con un cliente.

Antes de ver

Los chefs son los supervisores de cocinas. Deben estar al tanto de todos los platos que se preparan para que los clientes queden contentos. ¿Qué instrucciones crees que les da un chef a sus cocineros? ¿Qué tipo de conversación puede tener un chef con un cliente? ¿Qué piensas de la costumbre de algunos chefs de salir al comedor para hablar con los clientes? Explica.

Al ver

1. ¿En qué tipo de restaurante trabaja el chef Casas?
2. ¿Quién llamó al chef Casas?
3. ¿Cómo cocinan la carne en ese restaurante?
4. ¿Qué tipo de carne comió la señorita?
5. ¿Qué ensalada comió?
6. ¿Qué tipo de vino tomó?
7. ¿Con qué rellenan las empanadas en ese restaurante?

© Heinle/Cengage Learning

Después de ver

En parejas, representen a un chef que le da instrucciones a un cocinero muy joven y sin experiencia que hace muchas preguntas. Otra opción es representar a un chef que sale a hablar con un cliente del restaurante. ¿El cliente se queja o lo felicita? ¿Cómo responde el chef?

8.37 **Repetitivo** Primero indica si las palabras subrayadas son objetos directos o indirectos. Luego reemplaza los objetos directos con pronombres, haciendo los cambios necesarios a los objetos indirectos.

> **Modelo** Un hombre llama a una mujer e invita a <u>la mujer</u> a comer en un restaurante.
> la mujer es objeto directo → *Un hombre llama a una mujer y la invita a comer en un restaurante.*

1. Una mujer saluda a los clientes y lleva a <u>los clientes</u> a la mesa.
2. Los clientes piden los menús y ella <u>les</u> da <u>los menús</u>.
3. Los clientes piden las bebidas y el mesero <u>les</u> lleva <u>las bebidas</u>.
4. El cocinero prepara la comida y el mesero <u>les</u> sirve <u>la comida</u> a <u>los clientes</u>.
5. Los clientes quieren ver los postres y el mesero <u>les</u> muestra <u>los postres</u>.
6. Los clientes quieren dejar una buena propina y dejan <u>la propina</u> en la mesa.

8.38 **La niñera** Usando una construcción con **se** y los verbos indicados, explica qué se hace para ser una buena niñera.

1. (Llegar) a la hora indicada.
2. (Escuchar) las instrucciones de los padres.
3. No (hablar) por teléfono.
4. (Jugar) videojuegos con los niños.
5. No (pelear) con los niños.
6. (Contar) historias antes de acostar a los niños.
7. (Mirar) la tele después de acostar a los niños.
8. (Contestar) el teléfono cuando llaman los padres.

© Jenkedco/Shutterstock

Se lee con los niños.

8.39 **La juventud de los famosos** Decide cuáles eran las actividades de estas personas famosas cuando eran más jóvenes. Si no las reconoces a todas, usa la lógica para adivinar (*guess*). Luego forma oraciones completas, usando el imperfecto de los verbos.

1. Jorge Luis Borges
2. Selena
3. Rafael Nadal
4. Pablo Picasso
5. Ellen Ochoa
6. Alex Rodríguez
7. Jessica Alba
8. Carolina Herrera

a. vivir en la República Dominicana
b. gustarle dibujar y pintar
c. asistir a clases de actuación
d. jugar al tenis y al fútbol
e. ir a muchas fiestas elegantes
f. cantar en un grupo con sus hermanos
g. leer mucho
h. ser excelente en la clase de matemáticas

8.40 Crucigrama Trabaja con un compañero. Uno de ustedes va a usar el crucigrama en esta página, y el otro va a usar el crucigrama en el apéndice A. Ayuda a tu compañero a completar su crucigrama, explicándole las palabras en español. No debes mencionar la palabra que aparece en tu crucigrama.

Modelo #0 horizontal
Se hace de los tomates. Se pone en la hamburguesa.

8.41 Hace 50 años Mucho ha cambiado (*has changed*) en los últimos 50 años. Con un compañero, expliquen las diferencias entre hoy y el pasado. Deben usar el imperfecto.

Modelo el transporte
Estudiante 1: *Hoy muchas familias tienen dos o más coches, pero en el pasado muchas familias sólo tenían un coche.*
Estudiante 2: *Es cierto, y hoy la gasolina cuesta mucho, pero en el pasado era más económica.*

1. la familia
2. el trabajo
3. la comunicación
4. la comida
5. los pasatiempos
6. los restaurantes

8.42 ¿A quién...? Habla con un compañero sobre sus reacciones o las de otras personas a los siguientes temas.

Modelo gustar / las películas de terror
Estudiante 1: *¿A quién le gustan las películas de terror?*
Estudiante 2: *A mí me gustan las películas de terror. / A Stephen King le gustan las películas de terror.*

1. interesar / la política
2. encantar / el invierno
3. molestar / los cigarros
4. fascinar / las ciencias
5. importar / mucho el dinero
6. molestar / las personas que hablan mucho
7. caer bien / los niños
8. importar / tener buenas notas

🔊 Vocabulario 1
CD2-4

Frutas

el durazno	*peach*	la piña	*pineapple*
la fresa	*strawberry*	el plátano	*banana*
el melón	*melon*	la sandía	*watermelon*
la naranja	*orange*	las uvas	*grapes*

Verduras

el brócoli	*broccoli*	la papa	*potato*
la cebolla	*onion*	el pepino	*cucumber*
la lechuga	*lettuce*	la zanahoria	*carrot*
el maíz	*corn*		

Lácteos y otros alimentos

la catsup	*ketchup*	la mantequilla	*butter*
el cereal	*cereal*	la mayonesa	*mayonnaise*
la crema	*cream*	la mermelada	*jam*
el huevo	*egg*	la mostaza	*mustard*
el jamón	*ham*	el pepinillo	*pickle*
la leche	*milk*	el queso	*cheese*

Verbos

agregar	*to add*	mezclar	*to mix*
batir	*to beat*	mostrar (ue)	*to show*
cortar	*to cut*	pelar	*to peel*
freír	*to fry*	prestar	*to lend*
hornear	*to bake*		

Palabras adicionales

la rebanada	*slice*

Diccionario personal

_____

_____

_____

_____

_____

Vocabulario 2

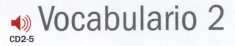

CD2-5

Juegos y juguetes

el ajedrez	*chess*		las damas	*checkers*
las canicas	*marbles*		el dominó	*dominos*
el carrito	*toy car*		las escondidas	*hide and seek*
las cartas	*playing cards*		el juego de mesa	*board game*
el chiste	*joke*		la (el) muñeca(o)	*doll*
la cometa	*kite*		la patineta	*skateboard*
el cuento	*story*		la tira cómica	*comic strip*
la cuerda	*(jumping) rope*		el videojuego	*videogame*

Verbos

chatear	*to chat*		pelear	*to fight; to argue*
contar	*to tell (a story); to count*		portarse (bien/mal)	*to behave (well/badly)*
dibujar	*to draw*		saltar	*to jump*
hacer travesuras	*to do mischievous things*		tejer	*to knit*
ir de paseo	*to go for a walk*		tocar (el piano)	*to play (the piano)*
			trepar (un árbol)	*to climb (a tree)*
			volar	*to fly*

Palabras adicionales

el juguete	*toy*		el recreo	*recess*
la niñera	*baby-sitter*		el teléfono celular	*cell phone*
el permiso	*permission*		la travesura	*mischief*

Diccionario personal

_____

_____

_____

_____

_____

_____

_____

_____

José Martí
Biografía
José Martí (1853–1895) fue un poeta, ensayista y periodista cubano. Publicó sus primeros poemas en el periódico de su escuela. Martí empezó a resentir a los españoles cuando el gobierno de España, que en ese tiempo controlaba Cuba, cerró las escuelas. Poco después el gobierno español lo envió a prisión por seis años acusado de subversión (*treason*). Después de estar exiliado en España, Martí fue a Estados Unidos, en donde formó el Partido Revolucionario Cubano y promovió la independencia de España. En 1895 regresó a Cuba y murió unos meses después en la Batalla de Dos Ríos, antes de que Cuba consiguiera su independencia. Hoy es conocido como el poeta nacional de Cuba y el Padre de la Independencia.

Antes de leer

1. Probablemente, la obra más conocida de José Martí es "Versos sencillos" (*Simple verses*). Estos versos se hicieron muy famosos cuando fueron convertidos en una canción popular llamada "Guantanamera". ¿Sabes dónde está Guantánamo? ¿Qué crees que significa "Guantanamera"?

2. ¿De qué piensas que puede hablar un poema titulado "Versos sencillos"?

Investiguemos la literatura: El verso
Verse refers to a written work with rhyme and sometimes with meter (the basic rhythmic structure of a line). It can refer to one line or to a complete poem. A verse or a stanza is generally called **una estrofa.**

Versos sencillos

Yo soy un hombre sincero
grows De donde **crece** la palma,
Y antes de morirme quiero
to cast/soul **Echar** mis versos del **alma.**

5 Con los pobres de la tierra
Quiero yo mi suerte echar:
creek; mountain range El **arroyo** de la **sierra**
sea Me complace más que el **mar**

	Mi verso es de un verde claro	Yo pienso, cuando me alegro	
bright red	10 Y de un **carmín encendido:**	Como un escolar sencillo,	
injured deer	Mi verso es un **ciervo herido**	En el canario amarillo,–	
mountain / ayuda	Que busca en el **monte amparo.**	¡Que tiene el ojo tan negro!	

Mi verso es de un verde claro
10 Y de un **carmín encendido:**
Mi verso es un **ciervo herido**
Que busca en el **monte amparo.**

bright red
injured deer
mountain / ayuda

Yo quiero salir del mundo
Por la puerta natural:
15 En un carro de **hojas** verdes
A morir me han de llevar.

leaves
They should take me when I die

No me pongan en lo **oscuro**
A morir como un traidor:
¡Yo soy bueno, y como bueno
20 Moriré de cara al sol!

darkness

© Joel Bit/Shutterstock

Yo pienso, cuando me alegro
Como un escolar sencillo,
En el canario amarillo,–
¡Que tiene el ojo tan negro!

25 Yo quiero, cuando me muera,
Sin **patria,** pero sin **amo,**
Tener en mi **losa** un ramo
De flores,– ¡y una bandera!

country; master
grave

Cultivo una rosa blanca,
30 En julio como en enero,
Para el amigo sincero
Que me da su mano franca.

Y para el cruel que **me arranca**
El corazón con que vivo,
35 **Cardo** ni **ortiga** cultivo:
Cultivo la rosa blanca.

tears out
thistle / nettle

Tiene el leopardo un abrigo
En su monte seco y **pardo:**
Yo tengo más que el leopardo,
40 Porque tengo un buen amigo.

dark

Versos sencillos, José Martí.

Después de leer

A. Comprensión

1. En tu opinión, ¿qué es muy importante para la voz poética?
2. ¿Qué palabras usa el poeta para describir a Cuba?

B. Conversemos

1. Mártí menciona ideas importantes para él en este poema. ¿De qué hablarías (*would speak*) tú en un poema sobre lo que es importante?
2. En estos versos, Marti describe a su país. ¿Cuáles son adjetivos que puedes usar en un poema para describir a tu país?

CAPÍTULO 9

Learning Strategy

Remember Spanish and English have different structures

Grammar is an essential part of any language. While it is helpful to understand and compare basic concepts of the English language, such as pronouns and direct objects, it is important to learn the new structures and avoid directly translating from English to Spanish.

In this chapter you will learn how to:

- Describe past events in detail
- Talk about holidays and celebrations
- Give the details of an accident

¿Qué pasó?

© Josu Altzelai/AGE Fotostock

En todas las épocas del año hay celebraciones para divertirse y pasar tiempo con la familia y los amigos.

Celebraciones

el bautizo	*baptism*
la boda	*wedding*
el brindis	*toast*
los desfiles	*parades*
los fuegos artificiales	*fireworks*
los novios	*bride and groom*
las posadas	*a nine-day celebration before Christmas*
la quinceañera	*a girl celebrating her 15th birthday*
los quince años	*a girl's fifteenth birthday*

el santo	*saint's day (similar to a second birthday, based on the name)*
la serenata	*serenade*

Verbos

casarse (con)	*to get married (to)*
celebrar	*to celebrate*
cumplir años	*to be/to turn years old*
romper	*to break*

Práctica

9.1 **Escucha y responde** En un papel dibuja un pastel y en otro, una bandera. Si escuchas una palabra relacionada con un cumpleaños, levanta el pastel. Si es una palabra relacionada con la celebración del Día de Independencia, levanta la bandera. Levanta los dos si la palabra está relacionada con las dos celebraciones.

CD 2-6

> **INVESTIGUEMOS EL VOCABULARIO**
> While in most of Latin America **bocadillos** means *appetizers*, in Spain a **bocadillo** is a sandwich on a baguette.

9.2 **¿Qué es?** Relaciona las palabras en la segunda columna con las oraciones en la primera columna.

1. _____ Los usamos para decorar.
2. _____ Lo comemos después de apagar las velas.
3. _____ La rompemos para obtener muchos dulces.
4. _____ Las enviamos a los amigos cuando vamos a dar una fiesta.
5. _____ Son las dos personas que se van a casar.
6. _____ Los comemos durante las fiestas y las celebraciones.
7. _____ Lo servimos para el brindis del Año Nuevo.
8. _____ Muchas personas caminan por la calle y hay música.

a. la piñata
b. el champán
c. los globos
d. el pastel
e. el desfile
f. los bocadillos
g. las invitaciones
h. los novios

9.3 **¿Qué celebraron las siguientes personas?** Completa las oraciones con una palabra apropiada del vocabulario.

1. Mi hermana se casó con su novio y tuvieron _____ muy grande.

2. Mi mejor amiga cumple quince años hoy, y va a tener una fiesta de _____.

3. En una ceremonia en la iglesia le dimos un nombre a nuestro hijo. Fue su _____.

4. En México las nueve fiestas antes de la Navidad se llaman _____.

5. ¡Terminé mis estudios en la universidad! Celebro mi _____ hoy.

6. Mis padres se casaron hace treinta años. Mañana es su _____.

7. Hoy es el cumpleaños de mi novia y quiero darle _____ con un grupo de mariachis.

8. Para celebrar el Año Nuevo y la Independencia, muchas veces hay _____ por la noche. ¡Son espectaculares!

9.4 **En busca de...** Circula por la clase para buscar personas que hicieron las siguientes actividades. Pide información adicional para reportársela a la clase. Usa el pretérito.

Modelo una serenata alguna vez (¿cuándo?)
        Estudiante A: *¿Participaste en una serenata alguna vez?*
        Estudiante B: *Sí, participé una vez.*
        Estudiante A: *¿Cuándo?*
        Estudiante B: *El 15 de abril, porque fue el cumpleaños de mi novia.*

1. tener una fiesta en su último (*last*) cumpleaños (¿cuándo?)

2. dar un regalo recientemente (¿a quién?)

3. preparar una fiesta para niños recientemente (¿por qué?)

4. cenar en un restaurante para celebrar su cumpleaños (¿cuál?)

5. asistir a una boda recientemente (¿de quiénes?)

6. preparar un pastel de cumpleaños para un amigo (¿qué tipo?)

7. romper una piñata en una fiesta (¿qué fiesta?)

8. tener más de quince invitados en una celebración (¿qué celebración?)

9.5 **Una fiesta** Imagina que un compañero y tú van a dar una fiesta. Discutan todos los detalles y después compartan sus planes con la clase.

1. ¿Qué van a celebrar? (cumpleaños, bautizo, graduación, boda, fin de curso, etcétera)

2. ¿Dónde y cuándo va a ser la celebración?

3. ¿A quién van a invitar?

4. ¿Cómo van a decorar?

5. ¿Qué van a ofrecerles a los invitados para beber y comer?

6. ¿Qué actividades va a haber en la fiesta? (música viva, baile, juegos, etcétera)

7. ¿A qué hora va a terminar su fiesta?

8. ¿Van a hacer algo después de la celebración? ¿Qué?

¿A quién van a invitar a la fiesta?

© bikeriderlondon/Shutterstock

¿Qué eventos se anuncian generalmente en la sección de sociedad de un periódico? En muchos países latinoamericanos se anuncian las fiestas de quince años. ¿Qué tipo de información se incluye en el anuncio?

De plácemes, los Pelayo Carrillo
Gran fiesta por los XV años de Ivonne

Por ERIKA M. ARECHIGA VILLEGAS

Un día muy especial fue el que vivió Ivonne Verónica Pelayo Carrillo, quien compartió su felicidad con sus padres, Roberto Pelayo Gaytán y Esperanza Carrillo de Pelayo, quienes prepararon una gran fiesta para celebrar el décimo quinto aniversario de vida de su hija.

© La familia Pelayo Carrillo

La cita tuvo lugar en punto de las 19:00 hrs., llegando puntualmente la quince-añera, quien lució bonito vestido chanel, confeccionado en raso color coral y el ramo en tonalidades rosadas, armoni-zando con su atuendo.

Junto con sus padres y padrinos, Daniel Jaimes Torres y Laura Arreola de Jaimes, dio inicio la misa de acción de gracias, en la cual el párroco oficiante mencionó bellas palabras para la festejada y la exhortó a continuar siendo una joven feliz.

Al término de la eucaristía se trasladaron al salón de fiestas del Club de Leones, donde se dio la bienvenida a los invitados de la familia anfitriona.

Allí disfrutaron de gran velada y la quinceañera, en compañía de sus chambelanes, bailó el inolvidable vals, propio de estas fiestas.

Entre los invitados captamos a Luis Pelayo Gaytán, Edmundo Galván y Martha de Galván, Oscar Aguirre, Lilia Carrillo, Lilia de Pelayo, Enrique Ojeda, Francisco Gaytán, Celia Treviño, Luis Pelayo Carrillo y Erick Pelayo, entre otros.

Los anfitriones hicieron disfrutar aún más la recepción. Fue servida una deliciosa cena, la cual fue acompañada por vinos nacionales con los que se brindó por la felicidad de la quinceañera.

Courtesy of the Carillo family.

Más allá

Imagina que eres un reportero para la sección de sociedad de un periódico local. Debes escribir la reseña de una gran fiesta de aniversario o de una boda.

A analizar

Mira los siguientes párrafos y observa los diferentes usos del pretérito y el imperfecto.

> Ella se llamaba Fátima y era muy guapa, con el pelo largo y negro. Llevaba un vestido rojo y estaba sentada en el sofá, hablando con una amiga.
>
> Me acerqué a ella. Le pedí bailar conmigo y aceptó. Pasamos el resto de la noche hablando. Al final de la noche, le pedí su número de teléfono y me lo dio.

1. Which of the paragraphs provides background information? What tense is used?
2. Which paragraph has actions that advance the story? What tense is used?

A comprobar

A comparison of the preterite and imperfect

Imperfect

1. As you learned in **Capítulo 8** the imperfect is used to express past actions in progress or habitual actions in the past.

   > Todos **bailaban** en la fiesta.
   > *Everyone **was dancing** at the party.*

   > Siempre **tenía** una piñata en mis fiestas.
   > *I always **used to have** a piñata at my parties.*

2. The imperfect is also used to describe conditions, people, and places in the past. When telling a story, it communicates background information or details. The order in which these sentences occur is often unimportant.

   > **Era** medianoche y **llovía.**
   > *It **was** midnight, and it **was raining**.*

   > Ella **tenía** quince años y **era** alta.
   > *She **was** fifteen and **was** tall.*

   > **Se llamaba** Lourdes.
   > ***Her name was** Lourdes.*

   > La sala **estaba** decorada con globos.
   > *The living room **was** decorated with balloons.*

Preterite

The preterite is used to narrate the main events of a story that have already happened. In other words, they are the past actions that advance the story. Unlike the imperfect, the order of events is important.

> Él **entró** en el café, **pidió** un café con leche, lo **tomó** y le **pagó** al mesero.
> *He **entered** the café, **ordered** a coffee with milk, **drank** it, and **paid** the waiter.*

> Sandra **cortó** el pastel y se lo **sirvió** a los invitados.
> *Sandra **cut** the cake and **served** it to the guests.*

A practicar

9.6 **Los cumpleaños** Sandra celebra su cumpleaños todos los años, pero el año pasado fue una ocasión especial porque celebró sus quince años. Lee las oraciones y decide cuáles se refieren a las celebraciones cuando era niña y cuáles se refieren a su fiesta de quinceaños. ¡OJO! Presta atención a los verbos.

1. Bailó el vals con su novio.
2. Rompía una piñata.
3. Sus padres la despertaban con "Las mañanitas".
4. Su madre le compró un vestido elegante.
5. Había un payaso (*clown*) con globos.
6. Su padre hizo un brindis durante la fiesta.

9.7 **La fiesta sorpresa** Completa las siguientes oraciones con la forma necesaria del pretérito o imperfecto del verbo indicado, según el caso.

Descripciones:

1. _era_ (ser) el ocho de agosto.
2. _era_ (ser) mi cumpleaños.
3. Ya _tenía_ (tener) treinta años. *already*
4. _eran_ (ser) las siete de la tarde.

5. Yo _llevaba_ (llevar) ropa de trabajo.
6. Yo _estaba_ (estar) un poco triste.
7. No _había_ (haber) luces en la casa.

Acciones principales:

1. Yo _abrí_ (abrir) la puerta.
2. Yo _encendí_ (encender) la luz.
3. Mis amigos _gritaron_ (gritar): "¡Sorpresa!"

4. Mi novio me _besó_ (besar).
5. Nosotros _comimos_ (comer) pastel.
6. Todos me _dijeron_ (dar) regalos.

9.8 **¡Qué sorpresa!** Mira el dibujo. En parejas, túrnense para describir lo que pasaba cuando los padres de Claudia llegaron a casa.

9.9 ¿Qué pasó? Este es el comienzo de una historia. Son las descripciones de la escena. Con un compañero, completen el párrafo con cuatro o cinco oraciones que cuenten lo que pasó. **¡OJO!** Deben usar el pretérito porque van a narrar la historia.

Era el 10 de junio, el día de la boda de Alejandra y Rafael. Rafael llevaba un traje negro y estaba frente a la iglesia. Todos los invitados esperaban la llegada de la novia. A las 10:00...

9.10 Una entrevista Piensa en la última fiesta en que estuviste. Luego, hazle las siguientes preguntas a un compañero y contesta sus preguntas. Deben usar pretérito e imperfecto.

Descripciones:

Im.

1. ¿Qué (llevar) puesto tú?
2. ¿Cuántas personas (haber) en la fiesta?
3. ¿Cómo (ser) el lugar de la fiesta?
4. ¿Cómo (estar) tú ese día?

Acciones principales:

P.

1. ¿A qué hora (llegar) tú a la fiesta?
2. ¿Qué (hacer) después de llegar?
3. ¿(Pasar) algo interesante en la fiesta?
4. ¿A qué hora (volver) a tu casa?

9.11 La fiesta Este grupo de jóvenes estaba en una fiesta cuando sacaron la foto que aparece a continuación. Con un compañero inventen los detalles de la fiesta. Primero, usando el imperfecto, describan la fiesta (¿Qué tiempo hacía? ¿Cuántas personas había? ¿Qué ropa llevaban?). Luego, cuenten qué pasó en la fiesta, usando el pretérito y las expresiones **primero, después, luego** y **entonces.**

© Photos To Go

Cultura

La corrida de toros *(bullfight)* forma parte de muchas fiestas en España, México y en algunos otros países de Latinoamérica. Durante la Edad Media en España la aristocracia se divertía toreando *(bullfighting)* a caballo. En el siglo XVIII se abandonó esta tradición, y la gente de la clase trabajadora empezó a torear a pie.

Sin embargo, el toreo en su forma tradicional es una tradición tan controversial que hasta en una región de España ha sido prohibida: en el verano del 2010, la región de Cataluña decidió que a partir del 2012 no se realizarán más corridas de toros en su territorio.

Hoy en día existen diversos eventos de exhibición con toros. Muchos de ellos son exhibiciones acrobáticas de los participantes y no involucran matar al animal o hacerle daño *(harm)* en modo alguno.

Para algunos, torear es un arte.

Hay gente contra el toreo.

Investiga en Internet sobre el movimiento contra las corridas de toros.

Conexiones... a la literatura

Octavio Paz (1914–1998) fue un notable poeta y ensayista mexicano, ganador del Premio Nobel de Literatura (1990). Entre las muchas obras de importancia que escribió se encuentra el libro de ensayos *El laberinto de la soledad*. El libro se compone de nueve ensayos y habla de lo que Octavio Paz consideraba la psicología del mexicano. Aunque fue escrito en 1950 y las condiciones en el país han cambiado significativamente, esta obra continúa siendo lectura obligada para muchos porque analiza el efecto psicológico que tuvo la conquista en el pueblo mexicano. El siguiente es un extracto de ese libro:

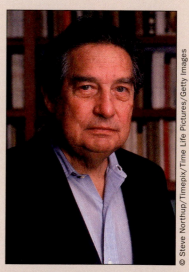

Octavio Paz

El solitario mexicano ama las fiestas y las reuniones públicas. Todo es ocasión para reunirse. Cualquier pretexto es bueno para interrumpir la marcha del tiempo y celebrar con festejos y ceremonias hombres y acontecimientos... Los países ricos tienen pocas [fiestas populares]: no hay tiempo, ni humor.

De acuerdo con tus conocimientos, ¿qué opinas sobre lo que expresa Paz en la cita mencionada arriba? ¿Es cierto también para tu cultura?

Comunidad

¿Qué festejos son importantes en tu comunidad?

En los países hispanohablantes existen numerosas celebraciones y algunas de ellas también se festejan ahora en los Estados Unidos, aunque de manera diferente a como se celebran en el país donde se originaron. Un ejemplo notable es el Cinco de Mayo, una fiesta que es más grande en los Estados Unidos que en México.

¿Puedes pensar en otra celebración con raíces hispanas? ¿Qué se hace? ¿Cómo puedes participar en estos eventos? Investiga si es posible ser voluntario en la planeación, aprovechando tus conocimientos del idioma español. Repórtale a la clase las posibilidades que encuentres.

Un desfile para el Cinco de Mayo en St. Paul, Minnesota

Comparaciones

¿Sabes qué es un Carnaval? ¿Alguna vez fuiste a uno? ¿Qué hacía la gente? En Latinoamérica hay algunos carnavales que tienen fama internacional. Por ejemplo, el Carnaval de Panamá es un evento muy esperado (*anticipated*) en ese país. El carnaval dura cuatro días y cinco noches y en algunas ciudades de Panamá, como en Las Tablas, hay desfiles con carros alegóricos (*floats*). Además, miles de personas se reúnen al aire libre para celebrar los culecos, bailes populares en los que se arroja agua sobre los participantes, quienes terminan empapados (*drenched*). Otro gran ejemplo es el Carnaval de Montevideo en Uruguay. Es el carnaval más largo del mundo y tiene un sabor original, gracias a la influencia africana.

Investiga un poco más sobre los carnavales en Latinoamérica y explica cómo se comparan con el Mardi Gras de Nueva Orleans. ¿En qué aspectos son semejantes? ¿Cómo son diferentes? ¿Cuándo se celebran y por cuánto tiempo?

Carnaval en Montevideo, Uruguay

Una banda musical durante el Carnaval de Montevideo

iTunes

Listen to the song "Abriendo Puertas" by Cuban singer Gloria Estefan. The song talks about the New Year. What is the tone of the song? What are some of the things the New Year will bring?

A analizar

Mira las oraciones y observa los verbos.

Invité a todos nuestros amigos a la fiesta, limpié la casa y después la decoré con globos. Mientras mi esposa hacía el pastel, yo preparaba unos bocadillos. Los primeros invitados llegaron mientras ponía la mesa.

Identify the verb tense in each of the sentences above. Then explain why that particular tense was used.

A comprobar

Uses of the preterite and the imperfect

When telling a story or relating a past event, the action usually can be expressed in one of three ways:

1. Two simultaneous actions:

When there are two actions going on at the same time in the past, they are both in progress, and therefore both verbs will be conjugated in the imperfect. The conjunctions **mientras** (*while*) and **y** are often used in these sentences. This can be visually represented in the following manner:

≈

Él **escuchaba** mientras ella **hablaba.**
*He **listened** while she **spoke.***

Todos **bailaban** y **cantaban.**
*Everyone **was singing** and **dancing.***

2. A series of completed actions:

When there is a series of separate and complete actions in the past, the verbs will all be conjugated in the preterite. This can be visually represented in the following manner:

↓   ↓   ↓   ↓

La señora Cisneros **llevó** el pastel a la mesa. Los niños **cantaron** "Las mañanitas", y después Rosita **apagó** las velas. La señora **cortó** el pastel y se lo **sirvió** a los niños.
*Mrs. Cisneros **took** the cake to the table. The children **sang** "Las mañanitas," and then Rosita **blew out** the candles. Mrs. Cisneros **cut** the cake and **served** the children.*

3. One action in progress when another begins:

In the past, when an action is in progress and a second action begins or is completed, both the preterite and the imperfect are used. The imperfect is used for the action in progress and the preterite is used for the new action that began or interrupted the first action. This can be visually represented in the following manner:

Mientras **terminábamos** las peparaciones, los invitados **empezaron** a llegar.
*While we **were finishing** the preparations, the guests **began** to arrive.*

Todos **se divertían** en la fiesta, cuando **llegó** la policía.
*Everyone **was having fun** at the party, when the police **arrived**.*

A practicar

9.12 **Fotos y descripciones** Decide cuál de las dos oraciones describe mejor cada foto.

1. En 1980 **tuve** un hijo.
2. En 1980 **tenía** dos hijos.

a.    b.

3. Mientras Sara hablaba por teléfono tomaba café.
4. Mientras Susana hablaba por teléfono le sirvieron un café.

a.    b.

5. Gema leía cuando Rocío le hizo una pregunta.
6. Rosendo leía mientras Gilda hacía una llamada.

a.    b.

9.13 **La fiesta de cumpleaños** El sábado pasado Felipe celebró su cumpleaños. Para saber lo que pasó, completa las oraciones con la forma apropiada del verbo entre paréntesis. **¡OJO!** Presta atención al uso del pretérito y el imperfecto.

Dos acciones simultáneas

1. Alicia y Ernesto bailaban mientras el grupo musical (tocar) un vals.
2. Mientras sus padres hablaban, Carlitos (dormir).

Dos acciones consecutivas

3. Jimena se rió cuando Rudy (contarle) un chiste.
4. Hugo se levantó e (hacer) un brindis por el cumpleaños de Felipe.

Una acción en progreso cuando comienza una nueva acción

5. El mesero le sirvió pastel a Jimena mientras ella (hablar) con Rudy.
6. Mientras los invitados disfrutaban (*were enjoying*) de la fiesta, Delia (darle) un regalo a Felipe.

9.14 **¡Acción!** Túrnense para escoger y actuar una de las oraciones de cada par *(pair)* sin decirle a su compañero cuál se está actuando. El otro estudiante debe decidir cuál de las dos oraciones está presentando su compañero. Luego, decidan cómo actuar las otras oraciones.

1. **a.** Se estiró y se levantó.

   b. Se estiraba mientras se levantaba.

2. **a.** Escribía su tarea cuando sonó el teléfono y lo contestó.

   b. Escribía su tarea mientras hablaba por teléfono.

3. **a.** Se sentó y leyó un libro.

   b. Estaba sentado y leía un libro.

4. **a.** Mientras dibujaba una flor dijo: "Me gusta".

   b. Dibujó una flor y dijo: "Me gusta".

5. **a.** Tomó una copa de champán y se durmió.

   b. Se durmió mientras tomaba una copa de champán.

6. **a.** Bailaba mientras comía su pastel de cumpleaños.

   b. Comió su pastel de cumpleaños y bailó.

9.15 **Cuéntame** Con un compañero miren las siguientes fotos. Usando los verbos indicados, escriban dos oraciones para describir lo que pasó. **¡OJO!** Presten atención al uso del pretérito y el imperfecto.

1.

© tonobalaguerf/Shutterstock

a. escribir, escuchar

b. trabajar, sonar *(to ring)* el teléfono

2.

© AVAVA/Shutterstock

a. llevar el pastel, cantar

b. apagar las velas *(blow out the candles)*, cortar

3.

© Karin Hildebrand Lau/Shutterstock

a. pegarle a *(to hit)*, mirar

b. romper, correr

4.
© angelo gilardelli/Shutterstock

a. casarse, salir

b. salir, tirar arroz

9.16 **El quinceaños** Mayra celebró su quinceaños ayer. Completa las oraciones para explicar lo que pasó ese día. **¡OJO!** Presta atención al uso del pretérito y del imperfecto.

1. Eran las tres de la tarde cuando Mayra...
2. Mientras ella se arreglaba, sus padres...
3. Cuando Mayra llegó a la iglesia, sus amigos...
4. Cuando la misa *(mass)* terminó, todos...
5. Los invitados empezaron a llegar a la fiesta, mientras...
6. Mientras el grupo musical tocaba el vals, Mayra...
7. Después de que cortaron el pastel,...
8. Cuando la fiesta terminó,...

9.17 **Unas fiestas** Con un compañero escojan una de las fotos para relatar lo que pasó, usando el pretérito y el imperfecto. Deben incluir ejemplos de lo siguiente: una serie de acciones consecutivas, una acción en progreso cuando comienza una nueva acción y dos acciones simultáneas.

Lectura

Antes de leer

¿Conoces alguna celebración de algún país hispano? ¿Qué celebración? ¿Qué se hace?

A leer

El Día de los Muertos

Latinoamérica tiene una gran reputación por sus numerosas y variadas celebraciones. Muchas de ellas son de origen religioso, y otras son el resultado de la historia y de la mezcla de tradiciones particulares de cada nación. Entre las celebraciones más conocidas está el Día de los Muertos.

El Día de los Muertos se celebra en México y Centroamérica.

Antes de la llegada de los españoles al Nuevo Mundo, los aztecas y otras civilizaciones mesoamericanas creían que había vida después de la muerte, así que enterraban a sus seres queridos con ofrendas como cerámica y **joyas.** También creían que los muertos podían regresar un día al año. Esta celebración ocurría aproximadamente a la mitad del año, en julio o agosto. Sin embargo, cuando los europeos llegaron y quisieron imponer su religión,

jewelry

> [Creían que los muertos podían regresar un día al año]

decidieron permitirles a los indígenas que celebraran a sus muertos en noviembre, el Día de Todos los Santos en la religión católica. Los españoles esperaban que, con los años, los indígenas simplemente comenzaran a observar la celebración católica, y dejaran sus creencias atrás. Esto nunca ocurrió: las creencias europeas se mezclaron con las de los indígenas. Hoy en día, el Día de los Muertos se celebra en todo México y Centroamérica, y cada vez más personas adoptan la celebración.

Según la tradición, se piensa que el Día de los Muertos es cuando los muertos regresan a este mundo. Ellos son bienvenidos y esperados por todos. Sus familias limpian sus tumbas, llevan flores y preparan comidas especiales para este día.

La parte más típica de la celebración es la creación de **ofrendas** con todo lo que le gustaba a la persona cuando vivía: música, comida, flores, y otros elementos tradicionales, como velas y **cempasuchitl.** Un elemento que no puede faltar en ninguna celebración es el pan de muertos, un pan que se prepara solamente para esta ocasión y se come en todas partes. El Día de los Muertos no es un día triste, sino un día para celebrar a los **seres queridos** que han muerto, en compañía de aquellos que todavía están con nosotros.

offerings

marigolds

loved ones

Comprensión

Decide si las afirmaciones son ciertas o falsas, y corrige las falsas.

1. Todas las celebraciones de Latinoamérica se originan en la religión.
2. Los aztecas creían que después de esta vida no había nada.
3. Los españoles crearon la celebración del Día de los Muertos para ayudar a convertir a los aztecas al catolicismo.
4. El Día de los Muertos combina creencias mesoamericanas y europeas.
5. Muchas familias limpian las tumbas de sus familiares en este día.
6. El pan de muertos se come durante todo el año, en honor a los muertos.

Después de leer

En México durante la celebración del Día de los Muertos, se escriben *calaveras*, poemas cómicos que se burlan de (*make fun of*) figuras famosas. Lee la calavera dedicada a Salma Hayek. ¿Cómo se describe a Salma Hayek? Con un compañero escriban una calavera original.

© Calavera: Salma Hayek: authorized by José Hernandez.

SALMA HAYEK

This mexican señorita
que es tan pretty y tan bonita
a todo el world presumía
los gifts de la cirugía

When la Muerte came for ella
que se monta on her burro:
-Don't me lleves -dijo ella.
But la Muerte, en un susurro:
-So you think you're great estrella,
but you filmas puro churro...

En la ciudad hay que tener mucho cuidado y prestar atención al tráfico.

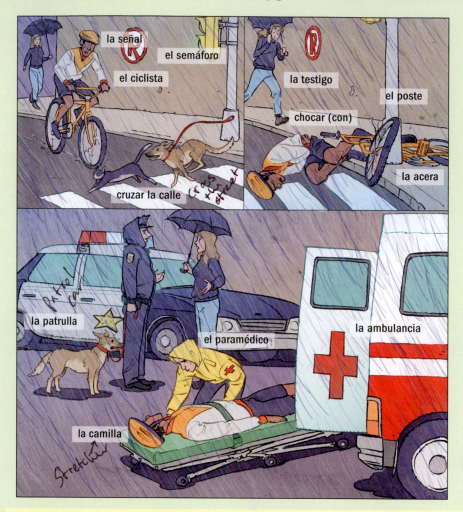

la señal
el semáforo
el ciclista
cruzar la calle (Cross the street)
la testigo
chocar (con)
el poste
la acera
la patrulla (patrol car)
el paramédico
la ambulancia
la camilla (Stretcher)

INVESTIGUEMOS EL VOCABULARIO

While **el parquímetro** is more commonly used, in some countries it is referred to as **el estacionómetro**. Another common term used for *driver* is **el automovilista**.

la carretera	highway	
el (la) conductor(a)	driver	
el cruce	crosswalk	
la esquina	corner	
el límite de velocidad	speed limit	
la multa	fine, ticket	
el parquímetro	parking meter	
el peatón (la peatona)	pedestrian	
(los peatones)		
el puente	bridge	
el servicio de emergencia	emergency service	

Los verbos

atravesar (ie)	to cross
atropellar	to run over
bajar de	to get out of (a vehicle)
caer(se)	to fall
dañar	to damage (el daño = the damage)
distraerse	to get distracted
estacionar	to park
parar	to stop
pasarse un semáforo en rojo	to run a red light

pasarse una señal de PARE	to run a STOP sign
subir a	to get into (a vehicle)
tropezar (ie)	to trip

Expresiones adicionales

de repente	suddenly
estar dañado(a)	to be damaged
estar herido(a)	to be injured (like a wound)

Práctica

roto = broken

romper - to break

9.18 **Escucha y responde** Vas a escuchar algunas ideas sobre el tráfico en la ciudad y los accidentes. Si la idea es lógica, indícalo con el pulgar hacia arriba. Si la idea no es lógica, señala con el pulgar hacia abajo.

CD 2-7

9.19 **¿Qué palabra es más lógica?** Escoge la palabra que completa la oración lógicamente.

1. El policía me dio una (patrulla/multa) por conducir a exceso de velocidad.
2. Cuando el semáforo está en rojo, es necesario (parar/pasarse).
3. El ciclista (atravesó/atropelló) la calle con cuidado.
4. Los peatones deben caminar por la (señal/acera).
5. El automovilista (se cayó/se distrajo) y no vio a los peatones atravesando (la calle/el semáforo).
6. Hay mucho tráfico en la (carretera/esquina) hoy.

9.20 **El testigo** Mira el dibujo del accidente en la página 306. Lombardo se pegó en la cabeza y no está seguro de lo que le pasó. Lee las declaraciones que Lombardo le dio al asistente médico y decide si son ciertas o falsas y corrige las falsas.

1. Cuando iba en mi bicicleta, un perro se atravesó enfrente de mí.
2. Para no chocar, di vuelta a la izquierda y choqué con una señal.
3. Afortunadamente (*Luckily*) había una ambulancia estacionada en la calle.
4. Un testigo llamó por teléfono para informarle a la policía de mi accidente.
5. En la calle no había señales de tráfico.
6. Afortunadamente mi bicicleta no se dañó.

9.21 **Una conversación** Habla con un compañero sobre las preguntas. Después, repórtenle su conversación a la clase.

1. ¿Tienes licencia de conducir? ¿Chocaste el coche de tus padres cuando estabas aprendiendo a conducir?
2. Cuando conduces un auto ¿respetas a los peatones? Cuando caminas por la calle ¿te respetan los automovilistas?
3. ¿Respetas siempre todas las señales de tráfico? ¿el límite de velocidad?
4. ¿Es difícil estacionarse en la ciudad o el pueblo donde vives? ¿Es caro?
5. ¿Siempre atraviesas la calle en los cruces o en las esquinas?
6. ¿Prefieres conducir, andar en bicicleta o usar el transporte público? ¿Por qué?
7. ¿Cuál es el límite de velocidad en tu estado? ¿Te parece bien? ¿Por qué?

9.22 **¿Es verdad?** Observa la escena y túrnate con un compañero para hacer afirmaciones ciertas o falsas sobre ella. El estudiante que escucha deber decidir si es cierto o falso lo que dice su compañero, y corregir las afirmaciones falsas.

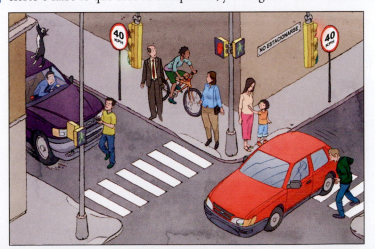

Cuando eres peatón en las calles de la ciudad ¿qué medidas tomas para caminar seguro por la ciudad? ¿y para atravesar una carretera? Lee el siguiente artículo de un periódico español sobre la seguridad peatonal. ¿Cuáles son las recomendaciones del artículo?

Aprenda a caminar seguro por ciudad y por carretera

1 ZONAS PEATONALES. Cuando haya zonas peatonales hay que caminar por ellas y nunca invadir la calzada. Si no hay zona peatonal, se debe caminar lo más cerca posible a los edificios y mejor por la izquierda, para ver venir de frente a los coches. Nunca caminar por los bordillos de las aceras.

© Entienou/iStockPhoto

2 ENTRADAS A LOS PÁRKINGS. Hay que tener especial cuidado con las entradas y salidas de automóviles por las aceras, garajes o talleres.

3 POR DÓNDE CRUZAR. Cruce siempre por los pasos de peatones. No corra pero tampoco se detenga en medio de la calzada. Si no hay pasos de cebra, cruzar siempre por las esquinas. Además, hay que comprobar que no existe peligro y caminar en línea recta.

4 POR CARRETERA. Camine por el arcén izquierdo y lo más alejado posible al borde de la calzada. Evite la ropa oscura.

5 CRUZAR POR CARRETERA. No cruce cerca de curvas, cambios de rasante o en zonas con obstáculos que impidan ver la circulación.

Más allá

Ahora escribe una lista de cinco consejos para andar en bicicleta por la ciudad.

Modelo *Se debe llevar ropa clara porque los conductores pueden vernos mejor.*

3

Exploraciones gramaticales

A analizar

Lee las siguientes oraciones y observa los diferentes usos de los verbos.

© Thomas Eckstadt/iStockPhoto

Me **sentía** feliz caminando en un día muy bonito.

Me **sentí** muy mal cuando vi que la señora en el coche negro estaba herida.

Había un testigo.

Hubo un accidente.

1. Look at the first set of sentences. Which sentence communicates an ongoing emotion? Which communicates a change in emotion? Explain.

2. Based on the second set of sentences, explain how the meaning of **haber** changes with the use of the imperfect or preterite.

A comprobar

Preterite and imperfect with emotions and mental states

You learned in the first part of the chapter that past actions in progress are expressed in the imperfect, and that the preterite is used to relate new or completed actions in the past. The same concept is applied to emotions or mental states.

Era un día bonito y ella **se sentía** feliz.
*It was a beautiful day and she **felt** happy.*
(an ongoing emotion)

Cuando escuché la noticia, **me sentí** mal.
*When I heard the news, I **felt** bad.*
(a change in emotion)

1. The following verbs are often used to express a change in emotion or feeling and are usually used with the preterite:

aburrirse	*to become bored*
alegrarse	*to become happy*
asustarse	*to become frightened*
enojarse	*to become angry*
frustrarse	*to become frustrated*
sorprenderse	*to be surprised*

Me asusté cuando vi el accidente.
I was (became) frightened when I saw the accident.

Los testigos **se alegraron** cuando descubrieron que nadie estaba herido.
*The witnesses **were (became) happy** when they discovered that nobody was hurt.*

2. The verb **sentirse** is a stem-changing verb and is often used to express how one feels.

Hoy **me siento** bien.
*I **feel** fine today.*

Se sintieron tristes cuando se fue.
*They **felt** sad when he left.*

3. It is also common to use the verb **ponerse** (*to become*) to express a change of emotion.

ponerse + adjective (**triste, feliz, furioso, nervioso,** etc.)

Cuando se murió mi perro, **me puse** triste.
*When my dog died, I **became** sad.*

4. The verbs **conocer, saber, haber, poder,** and **querer** are not action verbs but rather they refer to mental or physical states. As with action verbs, using them in the imperfect implies an ongoing condition, whereas using them in the preterite indicates the beginning or completion of the condition.

	imperfect	preterite
conocer	*to know, to be acquainted with*	*to meet*
saber	*to know (about)*	*to find out*
haber	*there was/were (descriptive)*	*there was/there were (occurred)*
poder	*was able to (circumstances)*	*succeeded in*
no poder	*was not able to (circumstances)*	*failed to*
querer	*wanted*	*tried to*
no querer	*didn't want*	*refused to*

Cuando llegué no **conocía** a nadie, pero más tarde **conocí** a Inma.
*When I arrived, I didn't **know** anyone, but later I **met** Inma.*

A practicar

9.23 **Reacciones lógicas** Decide qué verbo completa mejor la oración.

1. Cuando vi el coche pasarse el semáforo en rojo, yo...   **a.** me alegré
2. Cuando chocó con mi coche, yo...   **b.** me asusté
3. Cuando vi el daño a mi coche, yo...   **c.** me sorprendí
4. Cuando la policía le dio una multa, el otro conductor...   **d.** me puse triste
5. Cuando recibí el cheque del seguro *(insurance)*, yo...   **e.** se enojó

9.24 **¿Cómo estaba?** Usando expresiones con **tener** o **estar,** explica cómo estaba Renato ayer, según sus actividades.

Modelo Desayunó cuatro huevos, cereal, dos plátanos y un vaso de leche.
       Tenía hambre.

1. Se puso un suéter, unos guantes y un gorro.   5. Salió con su novia a cenar.
2. Mientras conducía, escuchaba música.   6. Estaba en una fiesta.
3. Tenía un examen de álgebra.   7. Se acostó muy tarde.
4. Visitó a su abuela en el hospital.   8. Tuvo una pesadilla *(nightmare)*.

9.25 **¿Cuándo fue?** Con un compañero túrnense para preguntar sobre la última vez que sintieron las siguientes emociones. Deben explicar las circunstancias de la situación.

Modelo asustarse
       Estudiante 1: *¿Cuándo fue la última vez que te asustaste?*
       Estudiante 2: *Me asusté el lunes porque no podía encontrar mi composición.*

¿Cuándo fue la última vez que...?

1. enojarse   5. preocuparse
2. aburrirse   6. frustrarse
3. ponerse triste   7. ponerse nervioso
4. alegrarse   8. sorprenderse

9.26 **Una entrevista** En parejas, túrnense para responder las siguientes preguntas.

1. ¿Cuándo conociste a tu mejor amigo?
2. ¿Hiciste ayer algo que no querías hacer? ¿Qué?
3. ¿Supiste un secreto recientemente? ¿Qué?
4. ¿Conocías a alguien en la clase de español antes de este curso? ¿A quién?
5. ¿Hubo un buen concierto en tu comunidad recientemente? ¿De qué?
6. ¿Ya podías hablar español cuando llegaste a la universidad? ¿Por qué?

INVESTIGUEMOS EL VOCABULARIO

The word **ya** can mean *already*, *yet*, or *anymore*, depending upon the context. If it is a question, it will usually mean *yet*.

¿**Ya** terminaste la tarea?
Have you finished your homework yet?

Ya terminé la tarea.
I already finished my work

Ya no hacen relojes como este.
They don't make watches like these anymore.

9.27 **Mini-conversaciones** Completa las conversaciones con la forma del pretérito o del imperfecto del verbo indicado, según el caso.

1. —Cuando salí para la universidad esta mañana, _____ (haber) mucho hielo (*ice*) en las calles.
   —Sí, y escuché en la radio que _____ (haber) muchos accidentes.
2. —¿_____ (Saber) tú que Manuel estuvo en el hospital ayer?
   —Sí, lo _____ (saber) cuando llegué a la oficina.
3. —¿_____ (poder) tú conseguir (*get*) el coche de tu hermano?
   —No, él no _____ (querer) prestármelo.
4. —Fui a una fiesta el sábado.
   —¿_____ (Conocer) a alguien?
   —Yo ya _____ (conocer) a muchas de las personas en la fiesta, pero _____ (conocer) a una chica que se llama Dora.
5. —Yo _____ (querer) ir a la playa ayer pero no _____ (poder).
   —¿Por qué?
   —Porque _____ (enfermarse).

9.28 **Cuéntame** Yadira tuvo un accidente el fin de semana pasado y les cuenta a sus amigos lo que pasó. Cuenta lo que pasó cambiando los verbos en negritas al pretérito o al imperfecto, según convenga.

Es[1] sábado por la noche. **Estoy conduciendo**[2] a casa y **estoy**[3] muy nerviosa porque **hay**[4] mucha lluvia y no **puedo**[5] ver bien. De repente un animal **cruza**[6] la calle enfrente de mi coche y yo **me sorprendo**[7]. No **sé**[8] qué tipo de animal **es**[9], pero no **quiero**[10] atropellarlo. **Intento**[11] frenar (*to brake*), pero no **puedo**[12] controlar el coche. El coche **empieza**[13] a salirse de la calle y **me asusto**[14]. Afortunadamente solo **termino**[15] en una zanja (*ditch*) y no **choco**[16] con nada.

9.29 **El accidente de Teo** Describe lo que le pasó a Teo. Usa el pretérito y el imperfecto, y los verbos indicados, según el caso.

Vocabulario útil: **el cigarrillo** *cigarette* **la cima** *top* (*of the mountain*) **la serpiente** *snake*

1. haber, conocer, sentirse **2.** ofrecer, querer **3.** saber, poder, alegrarse

4. ver, asustarse, caerse **5.** estar triste, querer, poder

Conexiones culturales
El tráfico y los accidentes

Cultura

"Yo sufrí dos accidentes graves en mi vida, uno en el que un autobús me tumbó al suelo… el otro accidente es Diego."

La artista mexicana, Frida Kahlo

Aunque parezca increíble, fue gracias a un accidente automovilístico que surgió una de las grandes figuras del arte en México: Frida Kahlo. Frida tenía apenas unos dieciocho años cuando, un día, mientras regresaba de la escuela, el tranvía (*streetcar*) en el que viajaba se accidentó. Frida se fracturó la columna vertebral, la clavícula, la pelvis, una pierna y varias costillas. Pasó mucho tiempo en el hospital, y nunca pudo recuperarse completamente de este accidente. Mientras estaba en reposo (*rest*) absoluto después del accidente, ella empezó a pintar, actividad que marcó el resto de su vida.

Además de ser una gran pintora, Frida se distinguió como una de las intelectuales más distinguidas de la época, y promovió (*promoted*) el amor por su patria (*native homeland*) de muchas maneras, incluyendo la ropa que vestía. Además, tanto Kahlo como Rivera participaron activamente en la política. Por ejemplo, cuando comenzó la Guerra Civil en España, Frida se organizó con otras mujeres para crear un comité de ayuda a los Republicanos españoles. Otro ejemplo conocido es que ambos pintores intercedieron por León Trotsky para que el gobierno mexicano le concediera el exilio político. Tras la llegada de Trotsky a México, se hospedó en la casa de Kahlo y Rivera. La vida de esta artista fue polémica e influyente mucho más allá del arte que creó.

Investiga más sobre la vida de Frida Kahlo después del accidente.

> 🌐 Investiga en Internet sobre el artista Diego Rivera.

Comparaciones

De acuerdo a un artículo publicado por *USA Today*, en los Estados Unidos hay 191 millones de conductores y 204 millones de vehículos. Otras estadísticas muestran que en promedio los estadounidenses hacen cuatro viajes en auto por día. De acuerdo al Ministerio de Tierras, Infraestructura y Transporte del Japón, en los Estados Unidos hay 765 vehículos por cada mil habitantes — más que en cualquier país del mundo. El único país hispano en la lista de los países con más vehículos es España, en el lugar número 15, con 471 automóviles por cada mil habitantes. En Colombia hay menos de 5 millones de autos, para aproximadamente 40 millones de personas.

Elige tres países hispanos y averigua cuántos automóviles hay por persona en esos países. ¿Cómo se compara a los Estados Unidos? ¿Cuáles son algunas consecuencias de tener o no tener muchos automóviles en una ciudad o en un país? ¿Qué piensas que es mejor para la economía? ¿y para el medio ambiente?

Hay mucho tráfico en las carreteras de España.

Conexiones... a la ingeniería

Uno de los grandes proyectos de la ingeniería es la construcción de una carretera que comunique todos los países de América, desde Alaska hasta Chile. Este proyecto, de hecho, está casi completo. Se llama la carretera Panamericana, y es un sistema colectivo de carreteras que recorren más de veinticinco mil kilómetros. Solamente falta un pequeño tramo *(stretch)* para completarla.

La carretera pasa por montañas, selvas *(jungles)* y desiertos, y ofrece vistas increíbles. Como resultado de pasar por diferentes zonas con climas y terrenos variados, la carretera no es uniforme, y en algunas partes del año se cierran porciones porque son peligrosas a causa de la lluvia.

Investiga en el Internet dónde está el tramo que falta y por qué algunas personas se oponen a su construcción. ¿Qué efecto tienen en el medio ambiente y en la economía las grandes carreteras?

La carretera Panamericana

© Melissa Farlow/Getty Images

Comunidad

¿Qué servicios de emergencia hay en tu ciudad? ¿Piensas que son suficientes? ¿Ofrecen servicios en español? Si no hay información escrita, considera traducir un folleto con la información básica, para ayudar a la población que habla español.

© age fotostock/SuperStock

¿Hay servicios de emergencia en español?

A analizar

Lee el diálogo y observa los verbos en el pretérito y el imperfecto.

> **Policía:** Buenas tardes, señora. ¿Usted **fue** testigo del accidente?
>
> **Señora:** Sí, señor...
>
> **Policía:** ¿Qué **hacía** usted cuando **ocurrió** el accidente?
>
> **Señora:** Siempre **caminaba** por la calle Sol con mi perrito en las tardes. **Me gustaba** porque **podía** llegar al parque fácilmente. Pero, la semana pasada **decidí** cambiar mi ruta porque ahora hay mucho tráfico.
>
> **Policía (impaciente):** Sí, señora, pero ¿qué **hacía** en la calle Naranjos hoy?
>
> **Señora:** **Caminaba** con mi perrito Negrito. **Me sentía** muy feliz porque **había** sol. Mientras **caminaba**, **miraba** las flores en los jardines. De repente **oí** un ruido terrible y **vi** que **hubo** un accidente. **Me sentí** muy mal cuando **vi** que la señora en el coche negro **estaba** herida.
>
> **Policía:** ¿Sabe usted qué **pasó**?
>
> **Señora:** No **pude** ver mucho porque no **llevaba** mis gafas, pero me parece que el coche negro **se pasó** el semáforo en rojo.
>
> **Policía:** Bueno, gracias por su ayuda, señora.

Write a list of the circumstances in which you would use preterite and in which you would use imperfect. Can you find any examples of those uses in the dialogue above?

A comprobar

Preterite and imperfect: An overview

You have already learned that the preterite is the narrative past and is used to express an action that is *beginning* or *ending*, while the imperfect is the descriptive past that is used to express an action *in progress* (*middle*). Here is an overview of how the two tenses are used:

Preterite

1. A past action or series of actions that are completed as of the moment of reference

   Vi al ladrón y **llamé** a la policía.

2. An action that is beginning or ending

   Empezó a estudiar a las siete.

   Vivimos en Madrid por tres años.

3. A change of condition or emotion

   Tuve miedo cuando escuché el ruido (*noise*).

Imperfect

1. An action in progress with no emphasis on the beginning or end of the action

   Llovía y **hacía** viento.

2. A habitual action

   Siempre **leía** antes de acostarme.

3. Description of a physical or mental condition

   Era alto y moreno y **tenía** el pelo largo.

   Estaba muy nervioso.

4. Other descriptions, such as time, date, and age

   Eran las tres de la tarde.

   Era el primero de octubre.

   Tenía sesenta años.

A practicar

9.30 **Esquí en Bariloche** Lee el párrafo y observa el uso de los verbos. Después, contesta las preguntas al final.

Cuando Rogelio era niño, iba a esquiar con su familia durante las vacaciones de invierno. Siempre se divertían mucho. El invierno pasado decidió ir a Bariloche para esquiar con sus amigos. La primera mañana hacía sol y estaba muy entusiasmado por salir a esquiar. Se puso los esquíes y subió la montaña. Mientras bajaba la pista (*slope*), disfrutaba la sensación del viento en la cara. De repente, un chico joven cruzó enfrente de él, y Rogelio se asustó y se cayó. No pudo levantarse y bajó la pista resbalando (*sliding*). Por fin paró antes de chocar contra un árbol. Mientras sus amigos corrían hacia (*toward*) él, se levantó y se quitó los esquíes. Estaba mojado y tenía frío, entonces decidió regresar al hotel y tomar un chocolate caliente.

1. ¿Qué hacía Rogelio cuando era niño?
2. ¿Qué hizo el año pasado?
3. ¿Cómo se sentía Rogelio al comenzar el día?
4. ¿Cómo reaccionó Rogelio cuando el joven cruzó enfrente de él?
5. ¿Qué hizo al final? ¿Por qué?

9.31 **Un accidente en bicicleta** Mayda habla sobre un accidente que tuvo con su bicicleta. Completa las oraciones con la frase apropiada para saber lo que pasó.

1. Tenía una bicicleta roja cuando...
   a. era niña.   **b.** fui niña.
2. Cuando salía con mi bicicleta, siempre...
   a. tenía mucho cuidado.   **b.** tuve mucho cuidado.
3. Ese día...
   a. hacía mucho sol.   **b.** hizo mucho sol.
4. Yo iba por la calle cuando...
   a. un coche se pasaba un alto.   **b.** un coche se pasó un alto.
5. Me atropelló porque...
   a. no podía parar.   **b.** no pude parar.
6. Cuando el conductor vio que estaba herida...
   a. se preocupaba.   **b.** se preocupó.
7. Él me hablaba mientras...
   a. esperábamos la ambulancia.   **b.** esperamos la ambulancia.

9.32 **Oraciones incompletas** Un reportero de la radio habló con varias personas sobre sus experiencias en la calle. Con un compañero, completen sus oraciones usando el pretérito y el imperfecto, según sea necesario.

1. Ivonne: Yo caminaba por la acera cuando de repente...
2. Eric: Mi amigo conducía mientras...
3. Esperanza: Mientras mi hija y yo esperábamos en el semáforo...
4. Cristián: Yo siempre iba muy rápido por la calle, pero una vez...
5. Pricila: Mi padre era un buen conductor y siempre...
6. Ima: Cuando vi el accidente...

9.33 Un accidente Completa el siguiente párrafo con la forma necesaria del pretérito o del imperfecto del verbo indicado.

Esta mañana **(1.)** _____ (haber) un accidente a las ocho y media. En ese momento, yo **(2.)** _____ (caminar) por la calle Montalvo con mi amiga Reina. De repente, nosotros **(3.)** _____ (oír) un ruido (*noise*) y **(4.)** _____ (ver) que un coche acababa de chocar contra un árbol. Un hombre mayor **(5.)** _____ (bajar) del coche. Él **(6.)** _____ (estar) muy pálido y **(7.)** _____ (tener) una herida en la cabeza. Nosotros lo **(8.)** _____ (ayudar) a sentarse en la acera. Mientras él **(9.)** _____ (descansar *to rest*), Reina **(10.)** _____ (llamar) a una ambulancia. Nosotros **(11.)** _____ (estar) muy preocupados por él, pero **(12.)** _____ (calmarse) un poco cuando **(13.)** _____ (llegar) la ambulancia. Los paramédicos lo **(14.)** _____ (poner) en la camilla y lo **(15.)** _____ (llevar) al hospital.

9.34 El venado (*The deer*) Con la ayuda de tu compañero describe lo que les pasó a Margarita y a Marián. Usa el pretérito y el imperfecto e incluye muchos detalles.

Redacción

Write an e-mail to a friend telling about a day in your life that was particularly memorable. ¡OJO! You will need to use the preterite and the imperfect.

Paso 1 Think about an event that was particularly memorable. It might be a special day such as a birthday or your wedding, or it might be a day something terrible happened such as an accident.

Paso 2 Jot down a list of phrases that set the scene. Consider how you were feeling as the day began, where and when the event took place, and what the weather was like.

Paso 3 Write a list of chronological events that took place that day.

Paso 4 Greet your friend and begin your e-mail telling him/ her what event you experienced. Then begin your story using the information you generated in **Paso 2** to set the scene.

Paso 5 Write a few paragraphs that tell the story using the information you generated in **Paso 3.**

Paso 6 Be sure to elaborate on the chronological development of the event by adding details such as descriptions and emotions.

Paso 7 Conclude your e-mail telling your friend how the event ended and how you felt at the end.

Paso 8 Edit your e-mail:

1. Is the information clearly organized?
2. Did you include ample details?
3. Is the e-mail logically organized with smooth transitions between sentences?
4. Are there any short sentences you can combine with **y** or **pero**?
5. Do your verbs agree with the subject? Are they conjugated properly?
6. Did you use the preterite and the imperfect accurately?
7. Are there any spelling errors? Do the preterite verbs that need accents have them?

Lectura

Antes de leer

¿Cuál es la diferencia entre una leyenda y un cuento? ¿Qué es una leyenda urbana? ¿Conoces alguna leyenda urbana? ¿Cuál?

A leer

Leyendas urbanas

Una leyenda se puede definir como un relato que no se puede comprobar, pero que se basa en personas, hechos o lugares que realmente existen o existieron. Es decir, es un relato fantástico con un fondo histórico que pretende explicar el presente. Un tipo de leyenda muy común es aquella en donde se explica cómo apareció un lugar, como un volcán o una montaña. Dos ejemplos son las leyendas paraguayas (de origen guaraní) de cómo apareció el pájaro ñandú en la Tierra, y la leyenda que explica cómo apareció el Salto del Guairá.

En cambio, las leyendas urbanas son historias relativamente modernas que no intentan explicar el presente. Se trata simplemente de historias con elementos increíbles que circulan sin ninguna evidencia de que sean verdaderas. Ocasionalmente están basadas en un hecho que realmente llegó a ocurrir.

Son muchas y muy variadas las leyendas urbanas que se escuchan hoy en día. Curiosamente, muchas veces las mismas historias se escuchan en países diferentes. A veces el escenario de la historia es España, a veces México, Paraguay, Puerto Rico o cualquier otro país. A continuación aparece la leyenda de *La muchacha de la curva,* leyenda urbana, de la que existen numerosas versiones.

Un pájaro ñandú

© Alfredo Cerra/Shutterstock

La muchacha de la curva: Era una noche lluviosa. Un automovilista conducía solo por la carretera, cuando vio a una muchacha haciendo autostop. Él se detuvo y la dejó subir a su automóvil. Le preguntó adónde iba. La muchacha le respondió y el automovilista la llevó hasta su casa, y la vio caminar hacia la puerta mientras él arrancaba y se alejaba.

$$\left[\text{ “¡Es ella!”, exclamó. }\right]$$

Al día siguiente, el hombre decidió regresar para buscar a la muchacha, porque era muy bonita. Cuando llegó a la casa en donde la había dejado la noche anterior, tocó a la puerta. Una mujer vieja le abrió. El hombre preguntó por la muchacha y la mujer respondió que allí no vivía ninguna joven. Sin embargo, la mujer invitó al hombre a entrar. En la sala, el hombre vio una fotografía de la muchacha en la pared. “¡Es ella!”, exclamó.

La mujer le dijo al hombre: “Era mi hija. Hace veinte años ella iba conduciendo por la carretera. Estaba muy obscuro y llovía. Entonces llegó a la curva donde usted la recogió. Esa noche llovía tanto que ella no vio las señales. Su auto **resbaló** y mi hija perdió el control y chocó. Murió inmediatamente. Ahora, cada año, el mismo día, en el mismo lugar y a la misma hora en que ocurrió el accidente, mi hija aparece y le pide a algún conductor que la **traiga** a casa, que es adonde ella iba esa noche.”

slid

bring

Llovía tanto que ella no vio las señales.

© Dgrilla/Shutterstock

Comprensión

1. ¿Cuáles son algunas diferencias entre una leyenda y una leyenda urbana?
2. ¿Por qué piensas que las mismas historias se escuchan en diferentes países?
3. En la leyenda de la chica de la curva ¿qué hizo el automovilista cuando vio a una chica haciendo autostop?
4. ¿Qué supo el automovilista al final de la historia?

iTunes

Spanish singer Julio Iglesias' song "Pájaro Choguí" recounts a Paraguayan legend. Listen to the song and tell what the legend is.

Después de leer

Investiga una leyenda urbana y cuéntasela a un compañero, o inventen su propia leyenda, usando las siguientes palabras del vocabulario:

ambulancia	tropezar	automovilista
el cruce	el puente	atravesar
atropellar	caer(se)	distraerse

Vocabulario

Sustantivos

la audiencia	*hearing*
el cinturón de seguridad	*seat belt*
la corte	*court*
los derechos	*rights*
la infracción	*violation*
la licencia de conducir	*driver's license*
la placa	*licence plate*
el registro	*registration*
el vehículo	*vehicle*

Adjetivos

imparcial	*impartial*
justo	*fair*

Verbos

apelar	*appeal*
averiguar	*to find out*
cometer	*to commit*

Frases útiles

licencia de conducir y registro del vehículo
driver's license and registration

Usted cometió una infracción.
You made a violation.

dar una advertencia
to give a warning

exceso de velocidad
speed limit violation

prohibido girar en U
no U turn

Tiene el derecho de apelar.
You have the right to appeal.

Licencia de conducir y registro del vehículo, por favor.

© Hill Street Studios/Getty Images

DATOS IMPORTANTES

Educación: Estudios secundarios completos. Algunos departamentos requieren uno o dos años de cursos universitarios. En ciertos casos se exige título universitario. Se recomiendan cursos complementarios relacionados con educación física.

Salario: Entre $65 000 y $140 000, dependiendo de la agencia, el estado y la experiencia.

Dónde se trabaja: Departamentos de Policía Estatal.

Robert Licata es un policía estatal. Trabaja en las autopistas para que los conductores respeten las reglas de tránsito. En el video vas a ver al Sr. Licata que habla seriamente con un(a) conductor(a).

Antes de ver

Los policías estatales deben ser imparciales cuando hablan con los conductores que cometen infracciones. Simplemente les dicen qué infracción cometieron, qué derechos tienen y qué deben hacer. También deben tener cuidado, porque no saben si las personas que están en los vehículos pueden atacarlos. ¿Cómo te sientes si un policía detiene tu vehículo? ¿Crees que es conveniente hablar mucho con el policía? ¿Como reaccionas si crees que no cometiste ninguna infracción?

Al ver

1. ¿Qué le pide el policía al conductor cuando se acerca al auto?
2. ¿En dónde cometió infracciones el conductor?
3. ¿Qué infracciones cometió?
4. ¿Qué excusa da el conductor por las infracciones cometidas?
5. ¿Por qué cantidad es la multa que le da el policía?
6. ¿Por qué el policía no le dio una advertencia?
7. ¿Qué averiguó el policía con la placa del vehículo?
8. ¿Qué solución posible le da el policía al conductor?

© Heinle/Cengage Learning

Después de ver

En parejas, representen a un policía de cualquier departamento y a una persona que hizo algo incorrecto. Demuestren cómo debe actuar el policía, qué le pide, qué preguntas hace y cómo responde la persona.

9.35 **Una fiesta de quince años** Completa el párrafo con la forma necesaria del pretérito o del imperfecto del verbo entre paréntesis.

El sábado pasado yo (1.) _____ (ir) a una fiesta de quince años.

(2.) _____ (Haber) muchas personas, y yo (3.) _____ (conocer) a

Rosaura. Yo (4.) _____ (hablar) con la quinceañera Zulema cuando la

(5.) _____ (ver) entrar. (6.) _____ (Ser) muy guapa y (7.) _____

(llevar) un vestido azul. Zulema me (8.) _____ (decir) que (9.) _____

(ser) su prima. Yo (10.) _____ (querer) conocerla, y Zulema nos

(11.) _____ (presentar). Yo le (12.) _____ (pedir) bailar, y ella

(13.) _____ (aceptar). Nosotros (14.) _____ (bailar) toda la noche y

(15.) _____ (divertirse) mucho. Ahora Rosaura es mi novia.

9.36 **El periodista** Un periodista habla con un testigo sobre el accidente que vio. Primero, decide si se debe usar el pretérito o el imperfecto en las preguntas. Luego, mira los dibujos y contesta las preguntas.

1. ¿Qué tiempo (hacer)?
2. ¿Quién (conducir) el coche rojo?
3. ¿A qué hora (ocurrir) el accidente?
4. ¿Qué (pasar)?
5. ¿(Haber) testigos?
6. ¿Cuándo (llegar) la ambulancia?

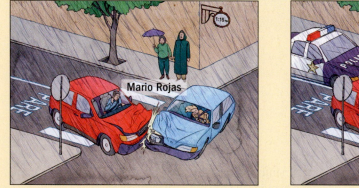

9.37 **El Año Nuevo** Ramiro habla de la fiesta del Año Nuevo. Completa sus oraciones para contar lo que pasó. Deben usar el pretérito y el imperfecto.

1. Cuando era niño siempre...
2. El año pasado decidí hacer una fiesta y...
3. Los invitados empezaron a llegar mientras yo...
4. Me alegré mucho cuando...
5. Algunas personas bailaban mientras otras...
6. Cuando el reloj dio la medianoche, todos...

9.38 **¿Qué es?** En parejas, túrnense para escoger un objeto en uno de los dibujos. Explíquenselo a su compañero sin decir la palabra.

9.39 **Una historia interesante** Con un compañero escojan fotos diferentes y describan lo que pasó usando las preguntas como guia. ¡**OJO** al uso del pretérito y del imperfecto!

1. ¿Dónde estaban? ¿Por qué?
2. ¿Qué hacían?
3. ¿Qué pasó?
4. ¿Cómo se resolvió la situación?

© Photos To Go

© Photos To Go

© michaeljung/Shutterstock

9.40 **Contradicciones** Tu compañero y tú son testigos de un accidente, pero hay diferencias entre las dos versiones. Mira uno de los dibujos y tu compañero va a mirar el otro en el apéndice A. Busquen las cinco diferencias. Después narren lo que ocurrió en el accidente, usando el pretérito y el imperfecto.

◄)) Vocabulario 1

CD 2-8

En la fiesta

los bocadillos	*snacks*
el brindis	*toast*
el champán	*champagne*
las decoraciones	*decorations*
el desfile	*parade*
los dulces	*candies*
los fuegos artificiales	*fireworks*
los globos	*balloons*
el grupo de música	*music group/ band*

la invitación	*invitation*
el invitado	*guest*
los novios	*bride and groom*
el pastel	*cake*
la piñata	*piñata*
la quinceañera	*girl celebrating her fifteenth birthday*
el regalo	*gift*
la serenata	*serenade*
la vela	*candle*

Las celebraciones

el aniversario	*anniversary*
el bautizo	*baptism*
la boda	*wedding*
el cumpleaños	*birthday*
la graduación	*graduation*

las posadas	*nine-day celebration before Christmas*
los quinceaños	*a girl's fifteenth birthday celebration*
el santo	*saint's day*

Verbos

brindar	*to toast*
casarse (con)	*to get married (to)*
celebrar	*to celebrate*

cumplir años	*to be/to turn years old*
romper	*to break*

Diccionario personal

_____

_____

_____

_____

_____

_____

_____

_____

_____

_____

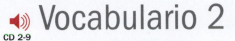

◀)) Vocabulario 2
CD 2-9

En la calle

la acera	*sidewalk*
la ambulancia	*ambulance*
la camilla	*stretcher*
la carretera	*highway*
el (la) ciclista	*cyclist*
el (la) conductor(a)	*driver*
el cruce	*crosswalk*
la esquina	*corner*
el límite de velocidad	*speed limit*
la multa	*fine, ticket*
el (la) paramédico(a)	*paramedic*

el parquímetro	*parking meter*
la patrulla	*police car*
el peatón (la peatona) (los peatones)	*pedestrian*
el poste	*post*
el puente	*bridge*
el semáforo	*traffic light*
la señal	*sign*
el servicio de emergencias	*emergency service*
el (la) testigo(a)	*witness*

Los verbos

aburrirse	*to become bored*
alegrarse	*to become happy*
asustarse	*to become frightened*
atravesar (ie)	*to cross*
atropellar	*to run over*
bajar de	*to get out of (a vehicle)*
caer(se)	*to fall*
chocar (con)	*to crash (into something)*
cruzar	*to cross*
dañar	*to damage*

distraerse	*to get distracted*
enojarse	*to become angry*
estacionar	*to park*
frustrarse	*to become frustrated*
pasarse un semáforo en rojo	*to run a red light*
pasarse una señal de PARE	*to run a STOP sign*
sentirse	*to feel*
sorprenderse	*to be surprised*
subir a	*to get into (a vehicle)*
tropezar (ie)	*to trip*

Expresiones adicionales

de repente	*suddenly*
estar dañado(a)	*to be damaged*
estar herido(a)	*to be injured*

Diccionario personal

_____

_____

_____

_____

_____

Learning Strategy

Use Spanish any time you talk in class

Try to use Spanish for all your classroom interactions, not just when called on by the instructor or answering a classmate's question in a group activity. Don't worry that your sentence may not be structurally correct; the important thing is to begin to feel comfortable expressing yourself in the language. You might even initiate a conversation with your instructor or another classmate before or after class.

In this chapter, you will learn how to:

- Discuss daily chores
- Give and receive directions
- Make travel arrangements
- Suggest activities
- Make informal and formal requests

¿Estás preparado?

© Digital Vision/JupiterImages

Exploraciones gramaticales

Relative pronouns

Formal and **nosotros** commands

Informal commands

Commands with pronouns

En vivo

Tips de viaje

Limpieza en el hogar

Conexiones culturales

La economía del turismo

Los trabajadores

Lectura

¿Adónde ir de vacaciones?

Mexicanos... con escoba y aspiradora

Exploraciones profesionales

La seguridad de aeropuertos

La señora Torres no viaja con frecuencia, pero sabe que es mejor viajar con poco equipaje.

Más vocabulario

la aduana	customs
a tiempo	on time
el asiento	seat
la estación de autobuses	bus station
la llegada	arrival
el reclamo de equipaje	baggage claim
retrasado	delayed
la sala de espera	waiting room
la salida	departure
la visa	visa

Para viajar en avión

abordar	to board
el (la) agente de seguridad	security agent
aterrizar	to land
el cinturón de seguridad	safety (seat) belt
la conexión	connection
despegar	to take off
el equipaje de mano	carry-on luggage
la escala	layover
pasar por seguridad	to pass through security
el pase de abordar	boarding pass
el vuelo	flight

Para viajar por tren

el coche cama	sleeping car
la litera	bunk (on a train)
la parada	stop

INVESTIGUEMOS EL VOCABULARIO

In Latin America a plane or train ticket is **un pasaje** or **un boleto; un boleto** also refers to a ticket for an event. However, in Spain, a train or a plane ticket is **un billete,** and a ticket for an event is **una entrada.**

It is also important to note that while **primera clase** is used for both trains and airplanes, **segunda clase** is used for trains, and for air travel the second class is known as **clase turista.**

A practicar

10.1 **Escucha y responde** Vas a escuchar una serie de ideas sobre viajar por tren o por avión. Indica con el pulgar hacia arriba si son lógicas, y con el pulgar hacia abajo si son ilógicas.

CD 2-10

10.2 **A viajar** Escribe la palabra lógica del vocabulario que mejor complete la oración.

En el aeropuerto:

1. Debemos obtener _____ antes de subirnos al avión.
2. En el mostrador de la aerolínea, un dependiente nos pregunta si preferimos ventanilla o _____.
3. Antes de _____ y de aterrizar, debemos ponernos _____.

En la estación de trenes:

4. Este tren no hace ninguna _____: va directo a su destino.
5. Compramos un boleto en _____ y después caminamos al _____ para abordar el tren.
6. _____ nos pide nuestros boletos en el tren.

10.3 **Asociaciones** Con un compañero, relacionen las palabras de las dos columnas y expliquen la relación entre ellas.

1. _____ retrasado   **a.** el equipaje
2. _____ la taquilla   **b.** el revisor
3. _____ ventanilla   **c.** a tiempo
4. _____ aterrizar   **d.** la salida
5. _____ facturar   **e.** el boleto
6. _____ el asistente de vuelo   **f.** la visa
7. _____ la llegada   **g.** el pasillo
8. _____ el pasaporte   **h.** despegar

10.4 **Situaciones** En parejas, túrnense para hablar sobre las fotografías. Usen las preguntas de la lista para entrevistarse.

¿Quiénes son las personas y dónde están?   ¿Adónde van a viajar?
¿Qué están haciendo y por qué?   ¿Cómo crees que va a ser su viaje?

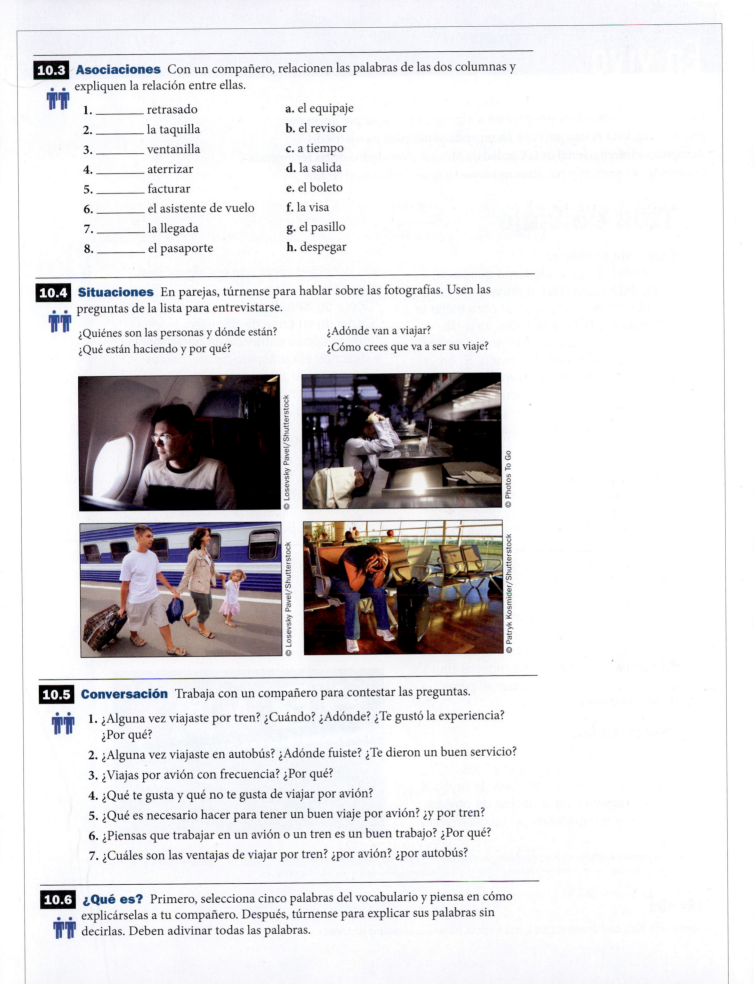

© Losevsky Pavel/Shutterstock

© Photos To Go

© Losevsky Pavel/Shutterstock

© Patryk Kosmider/Shutterstock

10.5 **Conversación** Trabaja con un compañero para contestar las preguntas.

1. ¿Alguna vez viajaste por tren? ¿Cuándo? ¿Adónde? ¿Te gustó la experiencia? ¿Por qué?
2. ¿Alguna vez viajaste en autobús? ¿Adónde fuiste? ¿Te dieron un buen servicio?
3. ¿Viajas por avión con frecuencia? ¿Por qué?
4. ¿Qué te gusta y qué no te gusta de viajar por avión?
5. ¿Qué es necesario hacer para tener un buen viaje por avión? ¿y por tren?
6. ¿Piensas que trabajar en un avión o un tren es un buen trabajo? ¿Por qué?
7. ¿Cuáles son las ventajas de viajar por tren? ¿por avión? ¿por autobús?

10.6 **¿Qué es?** Primero, selecciona cinco palabras del vocabulario y piensa en cómo explicárselas a tu compañero. Después, túrnense para explicar sus palabras sin decirlas. Deben adivinar todas las palabras.

Escribe tres recomendaciones para un amigo que va a viajar por avión por primera vez. Esta es una guía con recomendaciones para pasajeros del Aeropuerto Internacional de la Ciudad de México. ¿Ves alguna de las recomendaciones para tu amigo? ¿Qué otras recomendaciones se dan en el texto?

Tips de viaje

Cómo viajar mejor:

Antes de su vuelo tome suficiente agua, esto le ayudará a prevenir el dolor de cabeza; no coma mucho para evitar la indigestión y la hipertensión; trate de dormir durante el viaje e intente caminar un poco por el pasillo del avión. Si en algún momento se siente mal hable con el personal de vuelo o del aeropuerto para recibir asistencia. Si usted padece de alguna enfermedad, consulte a su médico antes de viajar.

Menores de edad:

*Se consideran menores de edad a las personas entre 5 a 17 años de edad.
*Los menores de 5 años de edad, deben viajar con un familiar o conocido.
*Mayores de 15 años de edad es opcional el pago por concepto de acompañante de la aerolínea.
*En el área de información de la aerolínea, se proporcionan los formatos que deben llenarse para que el menor pueda viajar; es necesario mostrar una identificación oficial y realizar el pago correspondiente.

Objetos perdidos:

En caso de que haya olvidado su equipaje o algún otro objeto en los ambulatorios o en las bandas de rayos X, puede preguntar en la oficina de objetos perdidos y recuperarlos en su caso. Para

ello deberá cumplir con los siguientes requisitos:
*Copia de identificación
*Copia de su pase de abordar
*Indicar dónde extravió sus pertenencias y describir el contenido de su maleta
Es importante aclarar que usted cuenta solamente con 3 meses para recuperar su equipaje o el bien extraviado.

OFICINAS DE OBJETOS PERDIDOS:

Ubicación en T1: Mezzanine oficina 102
Tel. 2482 2289
Horario Lunes a Viernes de 09:00 a 21:00 hrs.
Sábado y Domingo de 09:00 a 14:00 hrs.
Ubicación en T2: Local TLL-01
Tel. 2598 7169
Horario Lunes a Viernes de 09:00 a 21:00 hrs.
Sábado y Domingo de 09:00 a 14:00 hrs.

© Robert Paul van Beets/Shutterstock

Source: http://www.aicm.com.mx/informacionalpasajero/Archivos/GuiaAeropuerto, Internacional de la Ciudad de México.

Más allá

Escribe una lista con recomendaciones lógicas para una estación de trenes.

Exploraciones gramaticales

A analizar

Lee las siguientes definiciones y observa el uso de los pronombres **que** y **quien**. Después contesta las preguntas que siguen.

> La agente es la persona **con quien** debes hablar para conseguir un boleto.
> El revisor es la persona **a quien** tienes que darle el boleto.
> El asistente de vuelo es la persona **que** sirve las bebidas en el avión.
> El pasaporte es el documento **que** necesitas para viajar a otro país.
> El pase de abordar es el papel **que** necesitas para abordar el avión.

© Jack Hollingsworth/JupiterImages

1. How are **que** and **quien** used in the sentences above?

2. How do you determine whether you should use **que** or **quien**?

A comprobar

Relative pronouns

1. The relative pronouns **que** and **quien** are used to combine two sentences with a common noun or pronoun into one sentence.

> Rodrigo tiene un coche.
> *Rodrigo has a car.*

> El coche no consume mucha gasolina.
> *The car doesn't consume a lot of gas.*

> Rodrigo tiene un coche **que** no consume mucha gasolina.
> *Rodrigo has a car **that** doesn't use much gas.*

2. **Que** is the most commonly used relative pronoun. It can be used to refer to people or things.

> Este es el tren **que** va a Córdoba.
> *This is the train **that** goes to Córdoba.*

> El hombre **que** tiene la camisa azul es el conductor.
> *The man **that** has the blue shirt is the driver.*

3. **Quien(es)** refers only to people and is used after a preposition (**a, con, de, para, por, en**).

> Esta es la señora **a quien** le debes dar el boleto.
> *This is the lady **to whom** you should give the ticket.*

> Las personas **con quienes** viajo están en mi clase.
> *The people **with whom** I am traveling are in my class.*

4. **Quien(es)** may replace **que** when the dependent clause is set off by commas.

> Los pasajeros, **quienes/que** viajan en este vuelo, ya abordaron.
> *The passengers, **who** are traveling on this flight, already boarded.*

*Notice that the relative pronouns **que** and **quien(es)** do not have accents.

INVESTIGUEMOS LA GRAMÁTICA

In English, the relative pronoun can sometimes be omitted; however in Spanish it must be used.

Los boletos **que** compraste son para primera clase.
*The tickets **(that)** you bought are for first class.*

A practicar

10.7 **Conclusiones lógicas** Decide qué frase de la segunda columna completa mejor la oración.

1. Hay un vuelo que...
2. No tienen los documentos que...
3. Hay alguien en el mostrador con quien...
4. Siempre revisan el equipaje que...
5. Él es el conductor que...
6. Hay varios pasajeros a quienes...

a. puedes hablar.
b. conduce el autobús.
c. parece (*seems*) sospechoso.
d. no hace escala.
e. no les permitieron abordar el avión.
f. necesitan para entrar en el país.

10.8 Completa el siguiente párrafo con los pronombres relativos **que** y **quien(es)**.

Matilde es la amiga con (**1.**) _____ paso mucho tiempo los fines de semana. El fin de semana pasado decidimos visitar a una amiga (**2.**) _____ vive en Ciudad del Este. Nos encontramos en la estación de autobús (**3.**) _____ está en el centro. Allí compramos los boletos y subimos al autobús (**4.**) _____ estaba estacionado. El autobús estaba lleno y tuve que sentarme al lado de una señora (**5.**) _____ viajaba con su hijo.

Después de unas horas llegamos a Ciudad del Este y vimos a nuestra amiga Pilar, (**6.**) _____ estaba muy contenta de vernos. Cuando llegamos a la casa, Teresa y Daniela, las chicas con (**7.**) _____ vive Pilar, abrieron la puerta. Pasamos horas charlando en la sala; nos contamos historias de nuestras familias, de los chicos con (**8.**) _____ salimos, de las clases (**9.**) _____ tenemos este semestre... de todo. Finalmente, a las doce decidimos (**10.**) _____ era hora de acostarnos.

Matilde es la amiga con quien fui a Ciudad del Este.

10.9 **Oraciones cortas** Con un compañero, usen los pronombres relativos **que** y **quien(es)** para formar una oración, incorporando la segunda oración a la primera.

Modelo Tengo una maleta. La maleta es muy grande.
Tengo una maleta que es muy grande.

1. Tengo el boleto. Compré el boleto en la taquilla.
2. Los pasajeros subieron al autobús. El autobús llegó a la parada.
3. Zacarías es un amigo. Yo voy a viajar con Zacarías.
4. El revisor les pidió los boletos a los pasajeros. Los pasajeros viajaban en tren.
5. El agente miró mi pasaporte. El agente estaba sentado en el mostrador.
6. Ella es la agente. Puedes hablar con ella.
7. Aquí está el asiento. El asiento corresponde a tu boleto.
8. Debes escuchar a la asistente de vuelo. La asistente de vuelo está hablando.

10.10 **Oraciones incompletas** Con un compañero, completen las siguientes oraciones de una forma original. Usen los pronombres relativos **que** o **quien(es)**.

Modelo Tuve una clase...
Estudiante 1: *Tuve una clase que fue muy difícil, ¿y tú?*
Estudiante 2: *Tuve una clase que no me gustó.*

1. Tengo un libro...
2. Conozco a una persona...
3. Tengo un amigo...
4. Mi mejor amigo es la persona...
5. Hay muchas personas...
6. Vi una película...
7. Tuve un profesor...
8. Tengo unos amigos...

10.11 **Definiciones** Con un compañero, túrnense para dar una definición de una de las siguientes palabras. Tu compañero debe decidir cuál es la palabra que estás definiendo. Deben usar pronombres relativos.

Modelo el asistente de vuelo → *Es una persona que sirve refrescos en un avión.*
el pase de abordar → *Es un papel que necesitas para abordar un avión.*

el boleto	el pasaporte	el pasajero
el revisor	el andén	la taquilla
el autobús	el equipaje	la revisión de equipaje

Es la persona que nos sirve refrescos.

© Dmitriy Shironosov/Shutterstock

10.12 **A conocernos** En parejas, túrnense para preguntar y responder. Comiencen sus respuestas con las palabras entre paréntesis y usen pronombres relativos como en el modelo. Deben explicar sus respuestas.

Modelo ¿Qué día de la semana es más ocupado (el día de la semana)
Estudiante 1: *¿Qué día de la semana estás más ocupado*
Estudiante 2: *El día de la semana que estoy más ocupado es el lunes porque tengo cuatro clases.*

1. ¿Qué música te gusta? (la música)
2. ¿Con quién hablas cuando tienes problemas? (la persona)
3. ¿Qué materia es muy difícil para ti? (la materia)
4. ¿Qué día feriado te gusta más? (el día feriado)
5. ¿Para quiénes compras muchos regalos? (las personas)
6. ¿Qué tienda prefieres para comprar ropa? (la tienda)
7. ¿Qué profesión te parece (*seems*) interesante? (la profesión)
8. ¿A quién le dices tus secretos? (la persona)

Conexiones culturales

La industria del turismo

Cultura

Los grandes festivales son una gran oportunidad para ver la cultura de un país y una oportunidad para atraer turistas. Unos ejemplos muy conocidos son el Festival de San Fermín, en Pamplona, España, y el de la Tomatina, en Buñol, España. Hay muchos más festivales y carnavales de gran interés en otros países hispanos, por ejemplo: en Bolivia se celebra el Festival de Oruro, una de las más grandes celebraciones de la cultura andina. El carnaval es un ejemplo de sincretismo, ya que originalmente celebraba a la Pachamama (una diosa inca que representa a la madre naturaleza), pero se mezcló con tradiciones católicas de los europeos cuando los españoles impusieron su religión. La celebración se centra ahora alrededor de la Virgen del Socavón, virgen que apareció en una importante mina de plata (*silver*) en 1789.

El Festival de Oruro en Bolivia
© Gary Yim/Shutterstock

Investiga y escribe una descripción de uno de estos festivales.

El Carnaval de Barranquilla, Colombia
El Carnaval del País (Carnaval de Gualeguaychú), Argentina
El Festival Casals, Puerto Rico
El Festival del Tango de Buenos Aires, Argentina
El Festival Iberoamericano de Teatro, Colombia
El Festival Internacional Cervantino, Guanajuato, México

> 🌐 Investiga en Internet los festivales de San Fermín y el de la Tomatina.

Comparaciones

A veces es necesario obtener una visa para visitar ciertos países. El requisito depende de la nacionalidad del viajero, y del tiempo que va a permanecer de visita en otro país. Los ciudadanos de los Estados Unidos generalmente no necesitan visa para visitar España ni para viajar a la mayoría de los países hispanoamericanos si la visita va a durar menos de tres meses, pero hay excepciones, como Paraguay, que requiere visa. Para conseguirla, se debe completar una solicitud que se puede obtener fácilmente en las páginas del Internet del Consulado de Paraguay. La visa debe enviarse al consulado, junto con el pasaporte, dos fotografías y la cuota (*fee*) debida. En realidad, la obtención de la visa es sencilla comparada con los requisitos de otros países.

¿Qué requisitos piden para visitar los Estados Unidos?
© Gualberto Becerra/Shutterstock

Si tienes amigos latinoamericanos, pregúntales qué requisitos les piden para visitar los Estados Unidos. Si no conoces a ningún latinoamericano, investiga en Internet. Averigua (*Find out*) si los requisitos son los mismos para los ciudadanos de España. Después, repórtale a la clase la información sobre los requisitos.

Conexiones... a la economía

De acuerdo con la UNWTO (*United Nations World Tourism Organization*), más de 50 millones de personas visitan España cada año (la cifra fue de 57 millones en el 2008) y unos 22 millones visitan México anualmente. ¿Qué efecto piensas que tiene el turismo en países como España y México? ¿Y en los Estados Unidos? ¿Cuánto dinero gastas tú cuando vas de vacaciones? ¿Quién crees que trabaja más en carreras relacionadas con el turismo: los hombres o las mujeres? ¿Qué porcentaje de personas en el mundo crees que trabaja en turismo? A continuación puedes leer algunas estadísticas sorprendentes sobre el turismo:

El Aeropuerto Internacional Ezeiza en Buenos Aires, uno de los más importantes en Sudamérica

- En 2008 las llegadas de turistas internacionales en todo el mundo fueron 922 millones, 18 millones más que en 2007, lo que representa un crecimiento del 2%.
- Se espera que continúe un crecimiento sostenido, a pesar de la crisis financiera del 2009 que produjo una caída significativa de la demanda turística.
- Se calcula que entre el 6 y el 7% del total de puestos de trabajo en el mundo están relacionados con el turismo.
- En 2008, más de la mitad de las llegadas de turistas internacionales fue originada por viajes de placer. Aproximadamente el 15% de los turistas internacionales dijo que viajaba por negocios y motivos profesionales, y un 27% por razones personales como visitar a amigos o parientes, o para hacerse tratamientos de salud.
- Más de la mitad de los viajeros llegó a sus destinos mediante transporte aéreo (52%), y el 48% viajó por carretera, por ferrocarril o por barco.

Sources: http://unwto.org/facts/menu.html

Comunidad

Visita un lugar turístico o un hotel de tu comunidad y entrevista a un turista. Si es posible, elige a alguien que hable español. Averigua de dónde es, por qué está en los Estados Unidos, por cuánto tiempo, qué le gusta, qué no le gusta, qué lugares visitó y qué lugares va a visitar. Después, repórtale la información a la clase.

¿De dónde son ustedes?

A analizar

Lee la bienvenida que el capitán de un avión les da a los pasajeros. Después contesta las preguntas que siguen.

En nombre del capitán y la tripulación (*crew*) del vuelo 650 con destino a Asunción, les damos la bienvenida a Aerolíneas Sudamericanas. El tiempo de vuelo es de aproximadamente dos horas y cuarenta minutos. Por favor **pongan** su equipaje de mano debajo de sus asientos, o en los compartimientos en la parte superior de la cabina. **Apaguen** todos los aparatos electrónicos y **ajusten** el cinturón de seguridad. Por favor, **miren** hacia el frente y **escuchen** con atención las instrucciones de su asistente de vuelo sobre lo que deben hacer en caso de una emergencia.

The verbs in bold are commands. What are the infinitives for those verbs? What do you notice about how they are conjugated?

A comprobar

Formal and **nosotros** commands

1. When we tell someone to do something, we use commands, known as **mandatos** in Spanish. Formal commands are used with people you would address with **usted** and **ustedes**; however, these personal pronouns must be left out when using commands. To form these commands, drop the **-o** from the present tense first person (**yo** form) and add the opposite ending (**-e(n)** for **-ar** verbs, and **-a(n)** for **-er** and **-ir** verbs).

present tense first person		formal command
hablo	→	habl**e(n)**
hago	→	hag**a(n)**
sirvo	→	sirv**a(n)**

Muestre su boleto al revisor.
Show your ticket to the controller.

Facturen su equipaje primero.
Check in your bags first.

*Notice that verbs that have a stem change or are irregular in the present follow the same pattern in formal commands.

2. Negative formal commands are formed by placing **no** in front of the verb.

No pierdan los pasaportes.
Don't lose the passports.

3. Infinitives that end in **-car**, **-gar**, and **-ger** have spelling changes in order to maintain the same sound as the infinitive. Infinitives that end in **-zar** also have a spelling change.

-car	buscar → bus**que**(n)
-gar	llegar → lle**gue**(n)
-ger	escoger → esco**ja**(n)
-zar	empezar → empie**ce**(n)

4. The following verbs have irregular command forms.

dar	**dé (den)**
ir	**vaya(n)**
saber	**sepa(n)**
ser	**sea(n)**

5. To make suggestions with *Let's*, use commands in the **nosotros** form. **Nosotros** commands are very similar to formal commands. Add **-emos** for **-ar** verbs, and **-amos** for **-er** and **-ir** verbs.

infinitive	formal command	*nosotros* command
sacar	saque(n)	saqu**emos**
beber	beba(n)	beb**amos**
venir	venga(n)	veng**amos**

Estamos atrasados. **¡Corramos!**
We are late. **Let's run!**

Salgamos por la mañana.
Let's leave *in the morning.*

6. The irregular verbs are also similar in the **nosotros** form.

dar	**demos**
saber	**sepamos**
ser	**seamos**

7. **Ir** has two different forms. While it is possible to use **vayamos,** the present tense **vamos** is often used with affirmative commands and **vayamos** with negative commands.

> **¡Vamos** a Perú!
> *Let's go to Peru!*

> **No vayamos** en tren.
> *Let's not go by train.*

8. **-Ar** and **-er** verbs with stem changes do not change in **nosotros** commands. However, **-ir** verbs do have a stem change.

infinitive	present tense	*nosotros* command
cerrar	cerramos	cerremos
volver	volvemos	volvamos
pedir	pedimos	p**i**damos
dormir	dormimos	d**u**rmamos

A practicar

10.13 **¿Qué hago?** Pablo y Verónica van a hacer su primer viaje internacional y les preguntan a sus amigos qué tienen que hacer. Ordena sus recomendaciones lógicamente.

_____ Pasen por la aduana.

_____ Compren los boletos.

_____ Lleguen al aeropuerto dos horas antes del vuelo.

_____ Consigan sus pasaportes.

_____ Facturen las maletas.

_____ Confirmen el vuelo el día anterior.

10.14 **¿Qué dicen?** En parejas, túrnense para dar un mandato lógico de lo que las siguientes personas dirían (*would say*). Usen los verbos entre paréntesis.

Modelo el agente de la aduana a un turista (abrir)
Abra su maleta.

1. un asistente de vuelo a los pasajeros (poner)

2. un agente de seguridad a un pasajero (venir)

3. un agente de viajes a un cliente (conseguir)

4. un agente en el aeropuerto a un pasajero (ir)

5. un profesor a sus estudiantes (escribir)

6. un policía a un automovilista (conducir)

7. un guía a un grupo de turistas (mirar)

8. un revisor en el tren a un pasajero (comprar)

10.15 **Instrucciones** Eres un huésped en el hotel y pides instrucciones del recepcionista. Mira el plano y lee las instrucciones. Debes indicar dónde estás al final.

Vocabulario útil: seguir derecho *to go straight* **doblar a la derecha/a la izquierda** *to turn right/left* **cruzar** *to cross* **la cuadra** *block*

© Bruce Raynor/Shutterstock

1. Siga derecho por la calle Guevara. Doble a la izquierda en la calle Picasso. Siga derecho hasta la calle República. Está enfrente.

2. Siga derecho en la calle Bolívar hasta la calle República y doble a la derecha. Pase la biblioteca y en la calle Constitución, doble a la derecha otra vez. Está a la izquierda.

3. Siga derecho en la calle Bolívar hasta la calle Córdoba. Doble a la derecha. Cruce la calle Picasso y luego doble a la izquierda en la calle Colón. Pase el parque y está a la derecha.

10.16 **Perdidos** Ustedes son turistas y no conocen la ciudad. Con un compañero, túrnense para preguntarse cómo se llega del hotel a los diferentes lugares y para darse instrucciones. Usen el plano de la **Actividad 10.15.**

Modelo el café
Estudiante 1: *¿Cómo llego al café?*
Estudiante 2: *Salga por la calle Bolívar y vaya hasta la calle Córdoba. Doble a la derecha y camine una cuadra. El café está en la esquina de Córdoba y la calle Picasso.*

1. el museo
2. la playa
3. el banco
4. el restaurante
5. la catedral
6. la biblioteca
7. el correo
8. el Teatro Apolo

10.17 **¿Qué recomiendas?** Con un compañero, denle tres recomendaciones a cada una de las siguientes personas. Usen los mandatos formales.

Modelo El señor Sánchez va a salir de viaje.
Lleve poco equipaje.

1. La señorita Laredo siempre se aburre en los vuelos largos.
2. La señora Ramírez tiene miedo de viajar en avión.
3. Los señores Márquez siempre tienen mucha hambre cuando viajan.
4. El señor Vargas siempre olvida cosas cuando viaja.
5. La señora Castro va a viajar en tren por primera vez.
6. Los señores Gómez van a viajar con sus hijos pequeños en autobús.
7. Está nevando y la aerolínea canceló el vuelo de Miguel.
8. José Ramón está viajando de México a Madrid y el pasajero a su lado ronca (*snores*).

iTunes
Mecano was a Spanish pop group. Listen to their song "No me enseñen la lección." What does the student ask of the teacher? Can you identify with this student's experience?

10.18 **Un viaje** Con un compañero, hagan planes para hacer un viaje. Usen los mandatos en la forma de **nosotros** para expresar sus deseos.

Modelo adónde quieren ir
Estudiante 1: *Vamos a Cancún.*
Estudiante 2: *¡Buena idea! / No, vamos a Puerto Rico.*

1. adónde quieren ir
2. cuándo quieren salir
3. cuánto dinero quieren llevar
4. cómo quieren viajar
5. dónde quieren dormir
6. qué quieren hacer
7. qué recuerdos (*souvenirs*) desean comprar

10.19 **Una escena** Con un compañero, escojan una de las fotos e inventen el diálogo. Usen mandatos en la conversación.

Lectura

Reading Strategy: Visualizing and paraphrasing
While you read, form mental pictures of scenes, characters, and events. It will help you remember the content of the text and the words. In addition to visualizing, stop after each paragraph and think how you would explain ideas from the text with your own words. Take a few moments to jot down your summary of the paragraph. This will help to ensure you understand what you are reading, and will give you notes for reference later.

Antes de leer

1. En tu opinión ¿qué lugares son los que más atraen a los turistas?

2. ¿Qué sitios de Latinoamérica o España piensas que son los más populares entre los turistas? ¿Por qué?

3. ¿Deseas visitar algún país donde se habla español? ¿Cuál y por qué?

A leer

¿Adónde ir de vacaciones?

Todos los países en donde se habla español ofrecen una cantidad impresionante de atractivos turísticos, ya sea por su geografía o por su interés cultural, e incluso por su interés deportivo. El turismo es importante para la economía de muchos países hispanos, por ejemplo, España recibe más de 52 millones de visitantes al año. Esta cifra es más significativa porque la población total de España es de aproximadamente unos 40 millones de habitantes. En México, tan solo en la ciudad de Cancún hay alrededor de 30 000 habitaciones para turistas. Esta ciudad recibe más de dos millones y medio de visitantes cada año. Para Costa Rica, el turismo es la mayor fuente de ingresos. El turismo le da trabajo a más del 13% de la población de este país. Sería imposible resumir en un artículo breve la gran diversidad de lugares de interés, así que en este espacio vamos a describir solamente tres destinos con muchos atractivos que son poco conocidos entre los turistas estadounidenses.

Bariloche, Argentina.
Esta ciudad está en la Patagonia, Argentina, en una zona montañosa. Casi inmediatamente después de su fundación empezaron a llegar los primeros turistas. Sin embargo, fue con la construcción de los medios de transporte que Bariloche se hizo popular. Aunque en 1912 llegó el primer avión a este lugar, cuando se hizo realmente popular fue con la llegada de los **ferrocarriles** en 1934. En esta época se iniciaron en esta zona los deportes invernales como el esquí y el snowboard.

> [El turismo es importante para la economía de muchos países]

railways

Hoy en día, Bariloche es una hermosa ciudad turística, **rodeada de** paisajes increíbles, ideal para practicar deportes invernales y para hacer

surrounded by

Bariloche, Argentina

© Alvaro Pantoja/Shutterstock

innumerables actividades como ir de excursión, visitar museos, montar a caballo y practicar el rafting.

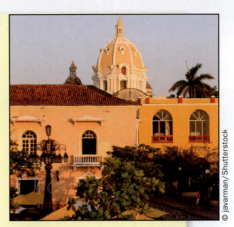
Cartagena, Colombia

Cartagena, Colombia

Cartagena es una ciudad especial por muchas razones. Su centro histórico fue declarado Patrimonio de la Humanidad por la UNESCO en 1985. Debido a su localización y al hecho de ser puerto y **bahía,** en Cartagena se guardaban el oro y otros tesoros antes de embarcarlos a España. En consecuencia, la ciudad prosperó mucho, pero desafortunadamente también atrajo los ataques frecuentes de piratas. Por eso, para finales del siglo XVIII, casi toda la ciudad estaba rodeada por 19 kilómetros de **murallas** que la protegían. Algunos muros llegaron a tener 15 metros de ancho y 12 metros de alto.

bay

walls

Cartagena fue también el principal puerto al que llegaron los esclavos traídos de África, lo que explica el rico legado cultural de ritmos y arte africanos que se encuentra en la región.

Cartagena es actualmente el puerto de exportación más importante de Colombia, y le ofrece al turista una bellísima ciudad histórica, hoteles de primera clase, una gastronomía única, museos de interés, una espectacular vida nocturna y, por supuesto, unas playas a la altura de las más famosas playas del Caribe.

Surfear es un deporte popular en El Salvador.

El Sunzal, El Salvador

Para los amantes de surfear, El Sunzal es un nombre mundialmente reconocido, y que se está haciendo muy popular. La industria del turismo de El Salvador es la que más rápido se está desarrollando en Centroamérica. Además de las bellas playas que este país ofrece, El Salvador también cuenta con volcanes y montañas, parques nacionales y oportunidades para hacer ecoturismo. Tiene además atracciones históricas, como Joya de Cerén, una comunidad que se conoce como "la Pompeya de Centroamérica" debido a que fue **cubierta** por una erupción volcánica en el año 600 antes de Cristo.

covered

Comprensión

1. ¿Dónde está Bariloche y cuándo se hizo popular?
2. ¿Por qué fue importante Cartagena durante la época colonial?
3. ¿Por qué la mayor parte de Cartagena está dentro de murallas?
4. ¿Cuáles son los atractivos de El Salvador para los turistas?

Después de leer

Piensa en una ciudad fascinante que visitaste alguna vez, y escribe una lista de ideas por las que piensas que es una ciudad especial. Después, comparte tus ideas con un compañero, y escucha las suyas.

2

Exploraciones léxicas

Es sábado y la familia Carrillo está limpiando la casa. ¿Qué están haciendo?

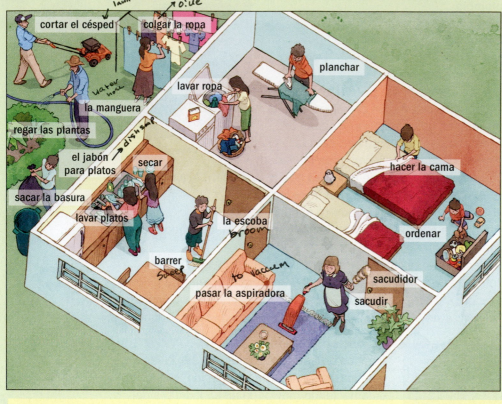

cortar el césped | colgar la ropa | lavar ropa | planchar | la manguera | regar las plantas | el jabón para platos | secar | hacer la cama | sacar la basura | lavar platos | la escoba | ordenar | barrer | la escoba | pasar la aspiradora | sacudidor | sacudir

Los verbos

el bote de basura	trash can	los quehaceres	chores	guardar	to put away
el burro	ironing board	sucio	dirty	poner la mesa	to set the table
el cortacésped	lawn mower	el trapeador	mop	recoger	to pick up
la plancha	iron	el trapo	cleaning cloth, rag	recoger la mesa	to clear the table
				trapear	to mop

Práctica

10.20 **Escucha y responde** Vas a escuchar una serie de quehaceres y de artículos de limpieza. Levanta la mano derecha si el quehacer o producto se relaciona con la cocina, y levanta la mano izquierda si se relaciona con el jardín.

CD2-11

10.21 **¿Qué se necesita?** Relaciona los quehaceres con los objetos que se necesitan para hacerlos.

1. __E__ planchar la ropa   **a.** el sacudidor
2. __h__ lavar los platos   **b.** la escoba
3. __g__ cortar el césped   **c.** la toalla
4. __b__ barrer   **d.** el trapeador
5. __A__ sacudir   **e.** el burro
6. __C__ secar los platos   **f.** la manguera
7. __F__ regar las plantas   **g.** el cortacésped
8. __D__ trapear   **h.** el jabón

10.22 ¿Con qué frecuencia? Con un compañero, túrnense para preguntar con qué frecuencia se hacen los quehaceres. **¡OJO!** Deben usar el **se** pasivo cuando respondan.

Modelo sacudir
   Estudiante 1: *¿Con qué frecuencia se sacude en tu casa?*
   Estudiante 2: *Se sacude una vez a la semana.*

1. lavar la ropa
2. planchar
3. barrer el piso de la cocina
4. pasar la aspiradora

5. cortar el césped
6. hacer las camas
7. limpiar los baños
8. sacar la basura

10.23 Una fiesta Imagina que vives en la casa de los dibujos. Tus amigos y tú van a dar una gran fiesta para toda la clase. Con un compañero, decidan lo que deben hacer antes de la fiesta, y lo que van a tener que hacer después de la fiesta. Sean creativos.

10.24 Busca a alguien Circula por la clase y busca a compañeros que hacen/hicieron las siguientes actividades. Después vas a reportale la información a la clase.

1. Lavó la ropa ayer.
2. Nunca riega las plantas.
3. Hizo su cama esta mañana.
4. Detesta lavar los platos.
5. Cuelga la ropa para secarla.
6. Nunca corta el césped.
7. Vive con alguien que limpia el baño.
8. Planchó algo la semana pasada.

10.25 Una entrevista Trabaja con un compañero para contestar las preguntas y luego repórtale la información a la clase.

1. ¿Qué quehacer te gusta menos? ¿Cuál te gusta más?
2. En tu opinión ¿qué quehacer es el más importante? ¿Cuál es el menos importante?
3. ¿Con qué frecuencia haces los siguientes quehaceres: lavar la ropa, planchar, barrer el piso de la cocina, pasar la aspiradora, sacudir, hacer la cama, limpiar el baño, sacar la basura?
4. ¿Crees que los niños deben ayudar en casa? ¿Qué quehaceres deben hacer?
5. ¿Alguna vez contrataste (*did you hire*) a alguien para limpiar tu casa? ¿Por qué?

En tu opinión, ¿cuáles son las labores domésticas más fastidiosas (*bothersome*)? El siguiente artículo tiene algunas recomendaciones para ayudar con la limpieza de la casa. Después de leerlo decide qué consejos puedes seguir para la limpieza de tu casa, y qué consejos no te sirven. Explica por qué.

Limpieza en el hogar

La limpieza del hogar para muchas mujeres es una tarea fastidiosa. Muchas de nosotras nos esforzamos por ver las cosas perfectas y quizás dedicamos mucho tiempo a la limpieza de cada rincón de nuestro hogar.

© baki/ Shutterstock

Aquí le damos varios consejos para mantener impecable varias cosas que son más difíciles de que queden en perfecto estado con el uso diario.

Muchas veces es fastidioso limpiar hornos, la plancha, electrodomésticos y un sin fin de cosas que usamos a diario, por eso le damos algunos trucos para que los use y nos cuente cómo le resultaron.

- El principal enemigo de un tostador son los residuos de pan. Por eso hay que mantenerlo siempre limpio. Así, durará más tiempo y evitará mayor consumo de electricidad.

- Para que el planchado de las camisas sea más fácil, inmediatamente después de lavarlas cuélguelas en ganchos, acomode los cuellos y estire la tela con las manos. Esto le ayudará a ahorrar tiempo de planchado.

- Aproveche el agua en donde coció papas peladas para limpiar objetos de plata; frótelos con una franela humedecida en esta agua hasta quitar todas las manchas.

- Aproveche las propiedades lubricantes de las cáscaras de plátano

para limpiar las hojas de sus plantas de ornato, frotándolas suavemente con la cara interna para darles brillo.

- Para suavizar la ropa disuelva tres cucharadas de vinagre blanco en una taza con agua, agregue esta mezcla a la lavadora en el ciclo de enjuague; si lava a mano, después de enjuagar su ropa déjela remojando con la mezcla antes de ponerla a secar. Cuando la ropa se seque no conservará ningún olor.

- Para limpiar la regadera y las llaves de baño, basta con pasarles un trapo húmedo con vinagre caliente. Quedarán brillantes.

- Para no gastar en la compra de limpiadores químicos para baño y cocina, emplee una mezcla de carbonato con agua y limón, o agua caliente con vinagre y limón. Estos ingredientes son efectivos en la mayoría de las labores de limpieza.

Más allá

Escribe tu propia lista de cinco consejos para hacer más fáciles algunas labores de la casa.

A analizar

Lee la conversación y observa las formas de los verbos. Luego contesta las preguntas.

> Olivia: ¡**Mira** esta casa! ¡Es un desastre!
>
> Carlos: No te **preocupes.** Yo te ayudo.
>
> Olivia: Gracias. En el baño, **limpia** el inodoro, el lavabo y el espejo.
>   **Trapea** el piso también, por favor.
>
> Carlos: ¿Y los platos en la cocina?
>
> Olivia: No **laves** los platos. Yo los voy a lavar.

In the conversation above, the informal (**tú**) commands are in bold.

1. How are the affirmative commands formed?

2. How are the negative commands formed?

A comprobar

Informal commands

1. Informal commands are used with people you would address with **tú**. To form the affirmative informal commands, use the third person singular (**él/ella**) of the present tense.

infinitive	affirmative *tú* command
lavar	lava
barrer	barre
sacudir	sacude

Limpia tu cuarto.
Clean your room.

¡Riega las plantas!
Water the plants!

*Notice that stem-changing verbs keep their changes in the informal command forms.

2. The following verbs have irregular forms for the affirmative informal commands.

decir	**di**	salir	**sal**
hacer	**haz**	ser	**sé**
ir	**ve**	tener	**ten**
poner	**pon**	venir	**ven**

Hijo, **haz** la cama, por favor.
*Son, **make** your bed, please.*

3. When forming negative informal commands use the formal **usted** commands and add an **-s.**

infinitive	*usted* command	negative *tú* command
ayudar	**ayude**	**no ayudes**
poner	**ponga**	**no pongas**
conducir	**conduzca**	**no conduzcas**
decir	**diga**	**no digas**
ir	**vaya**	**no vayas**

No dejes tus zapatos en el piso.
Don't leave your shoes on the floor.

No cuelgues la ropa sucia.
Don't hang up the dirty clothes.

4. In Spain, the **ustedes** commands are formal. To give commands to two or more friends or family members, they use **vosotros** commands. **Vosotros** affirmative commands are formed by dropping the **-r** from the infinitive and replacing it with a **-d**. Negative commands are formed by using the base of the **usted** commands and adding the **vosotros** ending (**-éis, -áis**).

infinitive	affirmative *vosotros* command	negative *vosotros* command
cerrar	cerr**ad**	**no cerréis**
hacer	hac**ed**	**no hagáis**
ir	**id**	**no vayáis**

A practicar

10.26 **¿Lógico o ilógico?** La señora Martín quiere que su hija limpie su cuarto. Lee los siguientes mandatos y decide si son lógicos o no. Corrige los mandatos ilógicos.

1. Recoge todos los libros.
2. Pon la ropa en la ducha.
3. Guarda las muñecas, por favor.
4. Haz la cama.
5. Barre los muebles.
6. No juegues ahora.
7. Ve a la sala a mirar la tele.
8. No saques la basura.

10.27 **Problemas en casa** Imagina que vives con una persona muy desconsiderada. Forma mandatos informales para decirle qué debe y qué no debe hacer.

1) put into usted commands

1. _Pase_ (Pasar) la aspiradora en la sala.
2. _limpie_ (Limpiar) el baño.
3. _haga_ (Hacer) tu cama.
4. _Ponga_ (Poner) tu ropa en tu cuarto.
5. _saque_ (Sacar) la basura.
6. _Barra_ (Barrer) el piso de la cocina.
7. No _dé_ (dar) fiestas tan tarde.
8. No _ponga_ (poner) la música muy fuerte (*loud*).
9. No _deje_ (dejar) los platos en el fregadero.
10. No te _lleve_ (llevar) mis cosas sin pedírmelas.
11. No _fume_ (fumar) en la casa.
12. No _traiga_ (traer) amigos a casa sin avisarme.

Negative (marginal note bracketing items 7–12)

10.28 **Te lo pido** Habla con ocho compañeros diferentes y pídeles que hagan una de las siguientes actividades, usando los mandatos.

1. saltar como un conejo (*rabbit*)
2. cerrar los ojos
3. escribir su nombre en la pizarra
4. contar hasta veinte en español
5. bailar
6. dibujar una flor
7. subir un pie
8. apagar y encender la luz

10.29 **Un conflicto moral** Cuando tomamos decisiones, a veces hay un conflicto en la conciencia. Con un compañero, túrnense para hacer los papeles (*play the roles*) de la conciencia.

Modelo Estudiante 1 (el diablo): ¡*Toma la cerveza!*
Estudiante 2 (el ángel): ¡*No tomes la cerveza!*

1.

2.

3.

4.

5.

6.

10.30 **Tengo un problema** Con un compañero, mencionen dos mandatos informales lógicos (uno afirmativo y otro negativo) para cada una de las siguientes situaciones.

1. La mascota de tu compañero de casa es un lobo (*wolf*).

2. Una amiga tiene problemas en su matrimonio.

3. A un amigo no le gusta su trabajo.

4. Tu hermano quiere hacer un viaje, pero no sabe adónde ir.

5. Un compañero de clase recibe malas notas en los exámenes de español.

6. Una amiga quiere perder peso (*weight*).

7. Un amigo tiene dolor de cabeza (*headache*).

8. Tu vecino siempre tiene fiestas ruidosas.

🎵 **iTunes**
Listen to Puerto Rican singer Olga Tañon's song "Desilusióname." Make a list of all of the requests that you hear. What would you ask of a person you want to forget?

Conexiones culturales

Los trabajadores

Cultura

Este cuadro del pintor boliviano Melchor Pérez Holguín (1660–1732) muestra a la Virgen María y a su esposo, José, en una pausa durante su viaje a Egipto. La producción de Pérez Holguín se basó en cuadros encargados por órdenes religiosas. En sus obras *(works)*, el artista mezcla elementos de la pintura europea de la época con elementos populares y de su país, Bolivia. Se nota, por ejemplo, que la ropa de la Virgen y la manta en el suelo son tradicionales de la región de la Paz, Oruro y Cochabamba, y la gente las lleva todavía hoy en día. Por otra parte, los querubines son tradicionales en el arte europeo.

¿Qué están haciendo la Virgen y los ángeles en el cuadro? ¿Qué otros quehaceres piensas que tenían que hacer?

> 🌐 Investiga en Internet otras obras de Melchor Pérez Holguín.

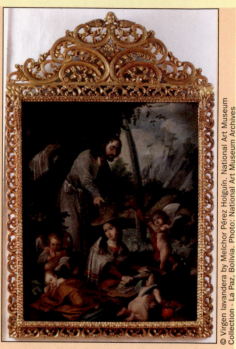

© Virgen lavandera by Melchor Pérez Holguín. National Art Museum Collection - La Paz, Bolivia. Photo: National Art Museum Archives

Virgen lavandera de Melchor Pérez Holguín

Comparaciones

¿Cuánto tiempo pasas haciendo quehaceres? ¿Crees que las mujeres pasan más tiempo limpiando que los hombres? El siguiente es un resumen de las horas que los españoles, los mexicanos y los estadounidenses dedican al trabajo doméstico cada semana. Observa la información. ¿Te sorprende? ¿Por qué?

Horas totales de trabajo doméstico semanal	
mujeres españolas	34,15 horas
hombres españoles	8,05 horas
mujeres mexicanas	36,5 horas
hombres mexicanos	13,82 horas
mujeres estadounidenses	28 horas (casadas y con hijos)
hombres estadounidenses	10 horas (casados y con hijos)

Sources: A study by FUNCAS (Fundación de Cajas de Ahorros) "En torno a la familia española: Análisis y reflexiones desde perspectivas sociológicas y económicas." European Sociological Review, 2008.

"Exactly how much housework does a husband create?" University of Michigan in Ann Arbor, 2008.

¿Cómo se pueden explicar las diferencias entre los hombres y las mujeres de España, México y los Estados Unidos?

© Andersen Ross/Jupiterimages

¿Quién pasa más tiempo haciendo los quehaceres?

Comunidad

En los Estados Unidos viven muchos ancianos (*elderly people*) que no hablan inglés. Busca una organización que ofrezca oportunidades para voluntarios y ofrece ayudar a un anciano que no hable inglés con los quehaceres de su casa.

¿Hay oportunidades para voluntarios en tu comunidad?

Conexiones... a la biología

Un nuevo tipo de productos se hace cada vez más popular en los mercados: los productos de limpieza biológicos. En particular el jabón para lavar ropa hecho con enzimas naturales puede limpiar sin dañar la ropa, el medio ambiente o la salud.

Las enzimas para quitar manchas se obtienen con bacterias modificadas genéticamente. Su uso comenzó en 1913, cuando el químico alemán Otto Rhöm usó una enzima digestiva del páncreas de animales para mejorar el proceso de limpieza. Así se empezó a fabricar y comercializar el primer jabón enzimático. La producción masiva de enzimas provenientes de bacterias y hongos comenzó a mediados del siglo XX.

Más recientemente, un grupo de investigadores de la Universidad de Chile, descubrió que el krill, un minúsculo habitante del mar antártico, produce enzimas capaces de actuar a solo 20°C. Asencio, el líder de este grupo de científicos, le explicó al periódico *El Mercurio* el significado de este descubrimiento para la industria de la limpieza:

"Si en nuestro país se lava ropa un millón de veces al día y, en promedio, cada lavado requiere 20 litros de agua a 50°C, este hallazgo podría reducir a la mitad la energía que se gasta para calentar toda esa agua."

Se puede lavar la ropa con productos naturales.

Según el libro *Biotecnología* (2007) escrito por la doctora en genética María Antonia Muñoz de Malajovich, de nacionalidad argentina, "en la actualidad más del 60% de la producción industrial de enzimas se basa en técnicas de biotecnología moderna". Tan solo en 2009 se calcula que el mercado mundial de enzimas fue de alrededor de 2,4 millones de dólares, y seguirá aumentando, según el pronóstico de Malajovich.

Source: Productos de limpieza biológicos, bt Débora Frid, 08-ene-2010.
http://biotecnologia.suite101.net/article.cfm/la_ciencia_de_quitar_las_manchas

Lee las etiquetas de los productos que tienes en casa para la limpieza de ropa. ¿Cuántos usan enzimas?

A analizar

Lee el siguiente párrafo y observa la posición de los pronombres.

> ¡Hijo! ¡Tu cuarto es un desastre! Recoge tu ropa y cuélgala. Y tus zapatos, no los pongas sobre la cama; ponlos en el armario.

Identify the pronouns in the paragraph above. Where are the pronouns in relation to the verbs?

© Joel Sartore/Getty Images

A comprobar

Commands with pronouns

1. When using affirmative commands, the pronouns are attached to the end of the verb.

> **Ponla** en el armario.
> *Put it in the closet.*

> **Hazlo** ahora mismo.
> *Do it now.*

2. When using negative commands, the pronouns are placed directly before the verb.

> Compra los chocolates, pero **no los comas.**
> *Buy the chocolates, but **don't eat them.***

> Es mi suéter; **no te lo pongas.**
> *It's my sweater; **don't put it on.***

> Guardad vuestros zapatos; **no los dejéis** en la sala.
> *Put away your shoes; **don't leave them** in the living room.*

3. When adding the pronoun(s) creates a word of three or more syllables, an accent is added to the syllable where the stress would normally fall.

lava	lávalos
limpia	límpiala
da	dámelo

> Lava los platos y **sécalos** después.
> *Wash the dishes and **dry them** afterwards.*

> Plancha la ropa y **tráemela.**
> *Iron the clothes and **bring them to me.***

A practicar

10.31 **¿Te ayudo?** Un amigo ofrece ayudarte a limpiar la casa. Mira las preguntas del amigo y escoge la respuesta lógica.

1. _____ ¿Saco la basura?　　　**a.** No, no la laves.

2. _____ ¿Lavo los platos?　　　**b.** Sí, límpialo.

3. _____ ¿Seco los platos?　　　**c.** No, no la limpies.

4. _____ ¿Limpio el lavabo?　　**d.** Sí, lávalos.

5. _____ ¿Lavo la ropa?　　　　**e.** No, no los seques.

6. _____ ¿Limpio la cocina?　　**f.** Sí, sácala.

10.32 **La pareja dispareja** Félix comparte un apartamento con Óscar. Félix es muy ordenado y Óscar es muy desordenado. Félix quiere que Óscar limpie su cuarto. Completa sus ideas con el mandato informal y el pronombre.

¡Óscar! ¡**(1.)** _____ (Levantarse)! Tienes que limpiar este cuarto. Mira toda la ropa en el piso. **(2.)** _____ (Recogerla) y **(3.)** _____ (colgarla). Pero ese pantalón está sucio; no **(4.)** _____ (guardarlo) en el armario. **(5.)** _____ (Ponerlo) en la lavadora. Y tus zapatos, no **(6.)** _____ (dejarlos) aquí. Mira el bote de basura. ¡Está lleno! **(7.)** _____ (Sacarlo). ¡No **(8.)** _____ (mirarme) así! ¡Eres un desastre!

10.33 **Limpia tu cuarto** Tu hija está en casa limpiando su cuarto. De vez en cuando te manda un mensaje con una pregunta. Contesta sus preguntas, usando mandatos informales y los pronombres apropiados.

Modelo ¿Tengo que sacar la basura?
Sí, sácala ahora. / No, no la saques ahora; puedes sacarla más tarde.

1. ¿Puedo mirar un video ahora?

2. ¿Tengo que hacer la cama?

3. ¿Dónde pongo los zapatos?

4. ¿Puedo comer unos chocolates ahora?

5. ¿Qué hago con la ropa arrugada (*wrinkled*)?

6. ¿Dónde pongo mis papeles?

7. ¿Tengo que pasar la aspiradora?

8. ¿Puedo tomar una cerveza ahora?

10.34 **¿Qué dicen?** Usa los verbos indicados en forma de mandato informal y los pronombres apropiados para decir lo que las personas quieren en cada ilustración.

Modelo hacer → *Hazla.*

1. ordenar, limpiar

2. no mirar, apagar

3. no planchar, guardar

4. colgar

5. sacar, lavar

6. regar, cortar

10.35 **Consejos** Con un compañero, túrnense para pedir y dar consejos (*advice*). Contesten las preguntas con mandatos informales y los pronombres necesarios.

Modelo Roberto dejó su CD en mi casa. ¿Le devuelvo (*to return*) el CD?
Estudiante 1: *Roberto dejó su CD en mi casa. ¿Le devuelvo el CD?*
Estudiante 2: *Sí, devuélveselo. / No, no se lo devuelvas.*

1. Encontré el diario de mi novia. ¿Lo leo?
2. Puedo obtener las respuestas para el examen de matemáticas. ¿Las obtengo?
3. El jueves es el cumpleaños de Patricia y hay una gran fiesta. Tengo un examen en la clase de biología el viernes. ¿Estudio biología?
4. Tengo un buen amigo que quiere usar mi coche, pero tiene un mal récord de conducir. ¿Le presto mi coche?
5. Vi al novio de María besando a otra chica. ¿Le digo algo a María?
6. Quiero ir a esquiar con mis amigos pero tengo que trabajar. Puedo decirle a mi jefe que estoy enfermo. ¿Llamo a mi jefe y le miento?
7. Tengo que comprar un regalo para mi abuela, pero quiero comprar una nueva camisa para mí. No tengo dinero para los dos. ¿Me compro la camisa?
8. Rafael quiere copiar mi tarea para la clase de inglés. ¿Le doy mi tarea?

10.36 **¡A limpiar!** Un amigo se va de vacaciones por dos semanas y tú vas a cuidar su casa. Con un compañero, túrnense para preguntar sobre las responsabilidades en la casa y para responder, usando el mandato informal y los pronombres necesarios.

Modelo el gato
Estudiante 1: *¿Le doy de comer al gato?*
Estudiante 2: *Sí, dale de comer.*

1. el césped	3. la basura	5. el correo	7. las ventanas
2. las plantas	4. los perros	6. el periódico	8. las luces

10.37 **En casa** Con un compañero, túrnense para hacer el papel (*role*) del esposo y de la esposa. Deben usar mandatos para decirle al otro qué debe o no hacer.

© Patrick Hermans/Shutterstock

Redacción

Write an e-mail to a student coming from Spain or Latin America to live with your family for a year.

Paso 1 Jot down a list of things that someone coming to live with your family should know about your family. Think about the following: Who lives in the house? What is your house like? Where will the student stay?

Paso 2 Jot down a list of things that the student would need to know about life with your family. Think about the following: daily routine, eating habits, house "rules," and cultural differences.

Paso 3 Jot down a list of questions you would need to ask in order to get the student's arrival information, such as city where the flight will come from, flight number, time of arrival, etc.

Paso 4 Greet the student and write your first paragraph, in which you give the student basic knowledge about your family and house. Use the information you generated in **Paso 1**; however, keep in mind that this paragraph should be more advanced than when you first learned this vocabulary.

Paso 5 Write a transition sentence, with which you will now begin to write a paragraph with advice for the student. Use the ideas you generated in **Paso 2** and the commands you learned in this chapter.

Paso 6 Write your final paragraph asking the student for his/her flight information using the ideas you generated in **Paso 3.** Then conclude your letter.

Paso 7 Edit your e-mail:

a. Do you have smooth transitions between sentences? between the two paragraphs?

b. Do your verbs agree with the subject? Are they conjugated correctly?

c. Do your adjectives agree with the items they describe?

d. Have you used the proper forms for any commands?

Lectura

Antes de leer

1. Según tu experiencia, ¿quién pasa más tiempo limpiando la casa: los hombres o las mujeres? ¿Por qué?

2. ¿Crees que los hombres mexicanos ayudan más en la casa que los hombres estadounidenses? Explica tu respuesta.

A leer

Mexicanos... con escoba y aspiradora

David Cuen, BBC Mundo

El trabajo doméstico suele causar problemas entre parejas. La cantidad y calidad del esfuerzo que cada uno imprime a los quehaceres del hogar —como barrer, trapear, aspirar o lavar la ropa— varía no sólo entre parejas sino también, al parecer, entre países.

Un estudio que será publicado en la European Sociological Review de la Universidad de Oxford, encontró que son los hombres mexicanos los que dedican mayor cantidad de horas a la semana a las labores del hogar.

De acuerdo con la investigación que se llevó a cabo en 34 países, los hombres nacidos en México dedican 13,82 horas a la semana a los quehaceres en la casa.

> [los hombres nacidos en México dedican 13,82 horas a la semana a los quehaceres]

La cifra es aún más relevante si se considera que, por ejemplo, en Japón los hombres sólo pasan 2,52 horas semanales en las labores domésticas.

México, Brasil y Chile bajo la lupa

México aparece en el estudio junto a Chile y Brasil y el profesor Knud Knudsen, de la Universidad de

Los mexicanos dedican más de 13 horas semanales al trabajo doméstico.

© Hans Zeegers/age fotostock

Stavanger, Noruega, uno de los autores del informe habló con BBC Mundo al respecto.

"Es muy interesante lo que descubrimos. Estos tres países sobresalen al menos por dos cosas. Primero, en estos países tanto los hombres como las mujeres están realizando más trabajo doméstico que en otras partes del mundo", reveló.

"Los latinoamericanos parecen pasar más tiempo en casa y con su familia, así que quizá disfrutan más que otros el trabajo doméstico o la vida hogareña", aseguró Knudsen.

Sin embargo, el coautor del estudio también informó que hay diferencias entre estos tres países.

"Por ejemplo, la división del trabajo en casa en Brasil está más o menos en línea con la tendencia global. La mexicana, sin embargo, pareciera ser una sociedad más igualitaria, mientras que la equidad de género en Chile parece menos marcada", dijo Knudsen a BBC Mundo.

© Rob Byron/Shutterstock

Y aunque a los mexicanos se les suele vincular con el estereotipo del machismo, los investigadores concluyeron que eran muy trabajadores en casa basándose en una encuesta de valores sociales que se levantó en 34 países a miembros de matrimonios o parejas en unión libre.

En la mitad de los casos se permitió que contestara el hombre y en la otra mitad la que otorgó la respuesta fue la mujer.

Claves en la casa

Knudsen, quien realizó la investigación junto a Kari Waerness del Instituto de Sociología de Noruega, explicó que uno de los hallazgos más interesantes de esta investigación es el hecho de que los llamados factores macroeconómicos influyen directamente en la vida cotidiana de las personas y las familias.

La cantidad de trabajo que se realiza en casa está vinculado directamente a la equidad de género en el país, y el desarrollo económico de la nación en cuestión.

Así que si confiamos en esta investigación, los mexicanos están trabajando en su casa por factores muy diferentes al de tener siempre la última palabra frente a su mujer. Una última palabra que suele ser: "Sí mi vida" o "lo que tú digas mi amor".

Comprensión

1. De acuerdo al artículo, ¿en cuál de estos tres países trabajan más los hombres en el hogar: México, Chile o Brasil? ¿En cuál trabajan menos?

2. ¿Qué explicación ofrecen los autores de la investigación para explicar sus resultados?

3. ¿Qué tienen en común México, Chile y Brasil, según Knudsen?

4. ¿Cuál es, en tu opinión, la conclusión más importante de la investigación?

Después de leer

Hoy en día son muy numerosos los hogares (*homes*) en donde trabajan el hombre y la mujer. En consecuencia, deben dedicar menos tiempo a los quehaceres de la casa. En los hogares donde se gana más dinero, es común que las familias dediquen parte de sus ingresos a contratar a una persona que ayude con las tareas domésticas. Con un compañero, conversen sobre las siguientes preguntas:

1. Según su experiencia ¿conocen a muchas personas que contraten a alguien para limpiar su casa?

2. ¿Qué tipo de persona contratarían (*you would hire*) para limpiar?

3. ¿Creen que son muchas las personas que trabajan en la limpieza? ¿Piensan que este trabajo es importante para la economía de su país?

Vocabulario

Sustantivos

la Administración de Seguridad en el Transporte	*Transportation Security Administration (TSA)*
la bandeja	*tray*
la cinta transportadora	*conveyor belt*
la computadora portátil	*laptop computer*
el detector de metales	*metal detector*
el envase	*container*
el equipo de rayos X	*X-ray machine*
la requisa	*pat down inspection, body search*
la máquina de Avanzada Tecnología de Imágenes	*Advanced Imaging Technology (AIT) machine*
el proceso de revisión	*screening process*

Verbos

colocar	*to place*
detectar	*to detect*
permanecer inmóvil	*to remain still*

Frases útiles

Coloque su computadora portátil en la bandeja, por favor.
Please place your laptop in the tray.

No se permite llevar envases de líquido o gel en el equipaje de mano.
Carrying containers of liquid or gel in your carry-on luggage is not permitted.

Hay que ponerlos en una bolsa de plástico transparente con capacidad para un cuarto de galón.
You must put them in a quart-size transparent plastic bag.

Entre a la máquina y permanezca inmóvil.
Enter the machine and remain still.

© Gene Chutka/iStockPhoto

Saque su computadora portátil, por favor.

DATOS IMPORTANTES

Educación: Estudios secundarios completos o el equivalente. Algunos trabajos requieren por lo menos un año de experiencia en seguridad o seguridad de aeropuertos. Se recomiendan cursos complementarios relacionados con la seguridad.

Salario: Entre $24 000 y $40 000

Dónde se trabaja: En aeropuertos

Enrique Santiago llega tarde al aeropuerto. Tiene prisa pero antes de abordar el avión, tiene que pasar por seguridad. En el video, el agente que trabaja para la Administración de Seguridad en el Transporte le explica el proceso de revisión.

Antes de ver

Los consejos que da la Administración de Seguridad en el Transporte a los pasajeros son ir al aeropuerto temprano y tener paciencia. El proceso de revisión puede ser largo, pero es necesario. ¿Siempre llegas al aeropuerto temprano? ¿Qué consejos puedes darle a una persona que piensa viajar en avión?

Al ver

1. ¿Con quién habla Enrique por teléfono?
2. ¿Por qué tiene prisa Enrique?
3. ¿Dónde se pone el equipaje de mano?
4. ¿Por qué no puede llevar Enrique la botella de agua a la puerta de salida?
5. ¿Qué tiene que hacer Enrique con los zapatos?
6. ¿Qué le da Enrique al agente en vez del pase de abordar?

© Heinle/Cengage Learning

Después de ver

En parejas, representen a un agente de la Administración de Seguridad en el Transporte y a un pasajero en el aeropuerto. El agente debe explicarle al pasajero el proceso de revisión. El pasajero debe hacerle preguntas: ¿Puedo llevar este envase? ¿Me quito el cinturón? ¿Dónde pongo mi computadora portátil?

10.38 **¿Qué tiene que hacer?** Trabajas en un hotel y hay un nuevo empleado. Dile lo que tiene que hacer usando mandatos formales.

Modelo planchar → *Planche la ropa todos los días.*

1. barrer
2. guardar
3. sacudir
4. colgar
5. hacer
6. lavar
7. poner
8. ordenar

© ronstik/Shutterstock

Planche la ropa todos los días.

10.39 **Sugerencias** Un amigo va a viajar en avión por primera vez. Completa las sugerencias para él usando los mandatos informales. **¡OJO!** Hay mandatos afirmativos y negativos.

1. No _____ (tener) miedo.
2. _____ (Sentarse) al lado de la ventanilla.
3. _____ (Poner) los líquidos en el equipaje que vas a facturar.
4. No _____ (llegar) tarde al aeropuerto.
5. _____ (Ir) a la sala de espera después de conseguir el pase de abordar.
6. No _____ (levantarse) durante el despegue.
7. _____ (Beber) mucha agua durante el vuelo.
8. Si es posible, _____ (dormir) durante el vuelo.
9. No _____ (traer) mucho equipaje de mano.
10. _____ (Llevar) comida si vas a tomar un vuelo largo.

10.40 **Ayuda doméstica** Usa los pronombres relativos **que** y **quien(es)** para formar una oración, incorporando la segunda oración a la primera.

Modelo Hay muchas personas. Esas personas necesitan ayuda doméstica.
Hay muchas personas que necesitan ayuda doméstica.

1. La señora trabaja en una agencia que provee (*provides*) servicios domésticos. Hablé con la señora ayer.
2. Tienen muchos empleados. Los empleados son muy responsables.
3. La muchacha se llama Florinda. Contraté a la muchacha.
4. Florinda tiene mucha experiencia. Consiguió la experiencia cuidando a niños pequeños.
5. A ella le gusta trabajar con familias. Las familias tienen niños.
6. Ella debe planchar los uniformes. Los niños llevan los uniformes a la escuela.
7. También tiene que limpiar el baño de los niños. El baño está en el primer piso.

10.41 **Al viajar** Entrevista a un compañero con las siguientes preguntas.

1. ¿Con qué frecuencia viajas?
2. ¿Prefieres viajar en avión o en coche? ¿Por qué?
3. ¿Alguna vez viajaste en tren? ¿Adónde fuiste?
4. ¿Alguna vez viajaste en primera clase? ¿Vale la pena (*Is it worth it*) pagar más para viajar en primera clase?
5. ¿Qué haces para pasar el tiempo durante el viaje?
6. ¿Te sientes nervioso antes de viajar? ¿Por qué?
7. ¿Prefieres visitar lugares turísticos, o lugares poco conocidos? ¿Por qué?

¿Alguna vez viajaste en tren?

10.42 **Una encuesta** En grupos de tres o cuatro estudiantes, hablen de quién hace los siguientes quehaceres en su casa. Si alguien vive solo, debe contestar desde el punto de vista de su familia de origen. Luego, comparen sus respuestas con las de otro grupo. ¿Hay algunos de los quehaceres que se consideran estereotípicamente de hombres o de mujeres? ¿Por qué crees que existe este estereotipo?

1. comprar la comida
2. cortar el césped
3. lavar la ropa
4. lavar los platos
5. limpiar el baño
6. pasar la aspiradora
7. planchar
8. preparar la comida
9. sacar la basura
10. sacudir

¿Quién prepara la comida en tu casa?

10.43 **En la agencia de viajes** Trabaja con un compañero. Uno de ustedes es el agente de viajes, y mira la información en esta página. El otro es el cliente y mira la información en el apéndice A. El cliente llama al agente de viajes para comprar un boleto. El agente de viajes debe intentar encontrar el mejor boleto para el cliente y conseguir su información (nombre, teléfono, etc.) y su tarjeta de crédito.

el agente de viaje

Los siguientes asientos para Santiago, Chile están disponibles (*available*):
- Vuelo 514–Sale el jueves a la 1:00 de la tarde con una escala en Caracas, y llega a las 11:15 de la noche. Hay un asiento en el pasillo. ($675)
- Vuelo 386–Sale el jueves a las 8:20 de la mañana directo a Santiago, y llega a las 4:05 de la tarde. Hay un asiento en la ventanilla. ($750)
- Vuelo 624–Sale el miércoles a las 2:45 de la tarde directo a Santiago, y llega a las 10:30 de la noche. Hay un asiento en la ventanilla. ($775)

Vocabulario 1

CD 2-12

De viaje

a tiempo	*on time*	el (la) pasajero(a)	*passenger*
la aduana	*customs*	el pasaporte	*passport*
el asiento	*seat*	el pasillo	*aisle*
el boleto	*ticket*	la primera clase	*first class*
la conexión	*connection*	retrasado	*delayed*
el equipaje	*luggage*	la sala de espera	*waiting room*
el equipaje de mano	*hand luggage*	la salida	*departure*
		la segunda clase	*second class*
la llegada	*arrival*	la ventanilla	*window*

En el aeropuerto

el aeropuerto internacional	*international airport*	la puerta (de salida)	*gate*
el (la) agente de seguridad	*security agent*	el reclamo de equipaje	*baggage claim*
el cinturón de seguridad	*safety (seat) belt*	la revisión de equipaje	*luggage screening*
la escala	*layover*	la visa	*visa*
el mostrador	*counter*	el vuelo	*flight*
el pase de abordar	*boarding pass*		

En la estación de tren

el andén	*platform*	el (la) revisor(a)	*controller*
el coche cama	*sleeping car*	la taquilla	*ticket window*
la litera	*bunk*	el vagón	*car, wagon*
la parada	*stop*		

Los verbos

abordar	*to board*	facturar equipaje	*to check luggage*
aterrizar	*to land*	pasar por seguridad	*to go through security*
despegar	*to take off*	seguir derecho	*to go straight*
doblar	*to turn*		

Diccionario personal

_____

_____

_____

_____

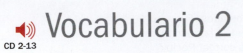

Vocabulario 2

CD 2-13

La limpieza

la basura	*trash, garbage, litter*
el bote de basura	*trash can*
el burro	*ironing board*
el cortacésped	*lawnmower*
la escoba	*broom*
el jabón para platos	*dish soap*
la manguera	*hose*

la plancha	*iron*
el quehacer	*chore*
el sacudidor	*duster*
sucio	*dirty*
el trapeador	*mop*
el trapo	*cleaning cloth, rag*

Verbos

barrer	*to sweep*
colgar (ue)	*to hang*
cortar (el césped)	*to cut, to mow (the lawn)*
guardar	*to put away*
hacer la cama	*to make the bed*
lavar platos	*to do the washing up*
lavar ropa	*to do laundry*
ordenar	*to tidy up, to straighten up*

pasar la aspiradora	*to vacuum clean*
planchar	*to iron*
poner la mesa	*to set the table*
recoger (la mesa)	*to pick up (to clear the table)*
regar (ie)	*to water*
sacar la basura	*to take the trash out*
sacudir	*to dust*
secar	*to dry*
trapear	*to mop*

Diccionario personal

_____

_____

_____

_____

_____

_____

_____

_____

_____

_____

_____

_____

_____

Marco Denevi
Biografía
Marco Denevi (1922–1998) nació en Buenos Aires. Fue un importante novelista, dramaturgo, abogado y periodista que se destacó (*stood out*) por sus cuentos cortos. Recibió el Premio Kraft en 1955 por su primera novela *Rosaura a las diez*. Más tarde ganó el Primer Premio en la revista *Life* en español y el Premio Argentores, los cuales le hicieron ganar prestigio internacional. En 1980 empezó a practicar el periodismo, escribiendo artículos sobre temas políticos y problemas sociales.

© Wikipedia

Antes de leer

1. ¿Qué efecto pueden tener los celos en una relación?
2. ¿Te consideras una persona celosa?

No hay que complicar la felicidad

Un parque. Sentado bajo los árboles, ella y él se besan.

Él: Te amo.

Ella: Te amo.

Vuelven a besarse.

5 **Él:**   Te amo.

Ella: Te amo.

Vuelven a besarse.

Él: Te amo.

Ella: Te amo.

10 *Él se pone violentamente de pie.*

Él: ¡Basta! ¿Siempre lo mismo? ¿Por qué, cuando te digo que te amo, no contestas que amas a otro?

Ella: ¿A qué otro?

feed   **Él:**   A nadie. Pero lo dices para que yo tenga celos. Los celos **alimentan** al
deprived   15   amor. **Despojado** de este estímulo, el amor languidece. Nuestra felicidad es demasiado simple, demasiado monótona. Hay que complicarla un poco. ¿Comprendes?

guessed   **Ella:**   No quería confesártelo porque pensé que sufrirías. Pero lo has **adivinado.**

Él: ¿Qué es lo que adiviné?

20 *Ella se levanta, se aleja unos pasos.*

Ella: Que amo a otro.

Él: Lo dices para complacerme. Porque te lo pedí.

Ella: No. Amo a otro.

© Tudor Voinea/Shutterstock

	Él:	¿A qué otro?
	25 **Ella:**	No lo conoces.
		Un silencio. Él tiene una expresión sombría.
	Él:	Entonces ¿es verdad?
	Ella:	(*Dulcemente*) Sí. Es verdad.
		Él se pasea haciendo ademanes de furor.
pretend	30 **Él:**	Siento celos. **No finjo**, créeme. Siento celos. Me gustaría matar a ese otro.
	Ella:	(*Dulcemente*) Está allí.
	Él:	¿Dónde?
	Ella:	Allí, detrás de aquellos árboles.
	Él:	¿Qué hace?
	35 **Ella:**	Nos espía. También él es celoso.
	Él:	Iré en su busca.
	Ella:	Cuidado. Quiere matarte.
	Él:	No le tengo miedo.
		Él desaparece entre los árboles. Al quedar sola, ella ríe.
	40 **Ella:**	¡Qué niños son los hombres! Para ellos, hasta el amor es un juego.
		Se oye el disparo de un revolver. Ella deja de reír.
	Ella:	Juan.
		Silencio.
	Ella:	(*Más alto*) Juan.
	45	*Silencio.*
	Ella:	(*Grita*) ¡Juan!
		Silencio. Ella corre y desaparece entre los árboles. Al cabo de unos instantes se oye el
bloodcurdling		*grito* **desgarrador** *de ella.*
	Ella:	¡Juan!
curtain		*Silencio. Después desciende* **el telón.**

© Denevi, Marco, *Falsificaciones*, Buenos Aires, Corregidor, 2010.

Investiguemos la literatura: Lector activo

Active reading is a literary technique that does not give the reader all of the information, thus forcing him/her to become actively involved in the reading and to come to his/her own conclusions.

Después de leer

A. Comprensión

1. ¿Por qué se queja (*complains*) él de la relación?

2. ¿Qué recomienda él para mejorar la relación?

3. ¿Por qué tiene celos él?

4. En tu opinión ¿qué pasa al final?

5. ¿Qué significa del título?

B. Conversemos

1. En el drama "él" dice que "Los celos alimentan el amor". ¿Estás de acuerdo? ¿Por qué?

2. ¿Te identificas con el hombre o con la mujer de la historia? ¿Por qué?

CAPÍTULO 11

Learning Strategy

Find ways to use your language in real-life settings

Seek out international students from Spanish-speaking countries, or if possible, visit a local restaurant or shop where there are native speakers, and initiate a conversation. Explore opportunities to travel or to study abroad. Using the language in different social interactions will help to increase your proficiency as well as your confidence.

In this chapter you will learn how to:
- Express preferences and make comparisons
- Describe the state of objects and people

¿Es la moda arte?

© Marcelo Del Pozo/Reuters/Corbis

Esta semana hay buenas rebajas en los centros comerciales y muchos clientes van de compras.

Las telas

el algodón	cotton
la lana	wool
el lino	linen
la mezclilla	denim
la piel	leather
la seda	silk

Adjetivos

apretado	tight

barato	cheap, inexpensive
caro	expensive
cómodo	comfortable
de moda	fashionable
hecho a mano	handmade

Verbos

hacer juego	to match
probarse (ue)	to try on
quedar	to fit

Expresiones útiles

¡Qué pantalones tan elegantes!	What elegant pants!
¡Qué lindos zapatos!	What pretty shoes!
¡Qué bien te queda esa falda!	That skirt really fits you well!
¡Qué color tan bonito!	What a pretty color!
¡Qué caros!	How expensive!

Palabras adicionales

la prenda	garment
la talla	size (clothing)

INVESTIGUEMOS LA GRAMÁTICA

The verb **quedar** can be used with an adjective or an adverb to tell how a piece of clothing fits someone or looks on someone. Like the verb **gustar,** it requires the indirect object pronoun and is conjugated in the third person singular or plural in agreement with the subject.

El vestido **me queda** muy bonito.   *The dress **looks** pretty **on me.***

Los bluyíns **te quedan** bien.   *The blue jeans **fit you** well.*

A practicar

11.1 **Escucha y responde** Vas a escuchar seis ideas relacionadas con las compras. Indica con el pulgar hacia arriba si es lógica, y con el pulgar hacia abajo si es ilógica.

CD2-14

11.2 **La palabra que falta** Lee las siguientes oraciones y completa las ideas con una palabra lógica del vocabulario.

1. Estos zapatos cuestan muy poco dinero; están muy _____.

2. ¡Qué cara! Voy a necesitar mi _____ para pagar la blusa.

3. Los bluyíns generalmente están hechos de _____.

4. La falda me _____ muy bien. ¡Voy a comprarla!

5. No me gustan los estampados a rayas ni a cuadros. Prefiero la ropa _____.

6. Mi sobrino es muy alto. Creo que le voy a comprar la talla _____, pero mi sobrina no es muy pequeña ni muy alta; ella necesita una camiseta de talla _____.

11.3 **Una conversación desordenada** Con un compañero, decidan cuál es el orden correcto de la conversación. Después lean el diálogo, cambiando las palabras en cursivas para hacer una conversación original.

dependiente

1. ¿Desea algo más?
2. Puede pagar en la caja, y gracias por su compra.
3. Tenemos *unos zapatos* muy *elegantes* y están rebajados.
4. Buenas tardes. ¿Puedo ayudarlo?
5. ¿Cuál es su *número*?
6. Sí, claro. ¿Cómo le quedan?

cliente

a. Uso *el número 39 o 39 ½*.
b. No, es todo. ¿Dónde pago?
c. ¿Puedo probármelos?
d. Me quedan *bien*. ¡*Me los llevo*!
e. Sí por favor. Busco *unos zapatos negros, formales*.
f. Muy amable, adiós.

11.4 **Críticos de la moda** Trabaja con un compañero para imaginar que son críticos de la moda. Observen las fotografías y describan la ropa que llevan las personas, utilizando muchos adjetivos. Túrnense para describir la ropa, y el segundo estudiante debe responder con exclamaciones.

Modelo Estudiante 1: *La modelo lleva una camiseta estampada en color azul.*
Estudiante 2: *¡Qué moderna y cómoda es la camiseta!*
Estudiante 1: *También lleva una bufanda a rayas.*

11.5 **Conversemos** Trabaja con un compañero para hablar de sus opiniones sobre las compras de ropa. Piensa en lo siguiente: ¿Te gusta vestir a la moda? ¿Dónde prefieres comprar tu ropa y por qué? ¿Qué estilos y telas prefieres? ¿Cómo prefieres pagar por tus compras? ¿Cuándo fue la última vez que fuiste de compras? ¿Adónde fuiste? ¿Qué compraste?

> **iTunes**
> Estrellas de la Academia is a group of young singers who have participated in a TV show similar to *American Idol*. "Bazar" is a cover of a song by Flans, a Mexican pop group made up of three women. Listen to the song. What items of clothing does the woman look for? What happens afterwards?

¿Conoces algunos casos de moda criticada por ser escandalosa? Un ejemplo reciente ocurrió en México, donde se diseñó un vestido para la Señorita México que fue muy criticado porque representaba la Guerra de los Cristeros, una guerra religiosa que ocurrió en la primera mitad del siglo XX, y en la que murieron muchas personas. Una conocida periodista mexicana, Soledad Loaeza, se refirió al episodio como "una falta de respeto inadmisible para los muertos de esa época y una banalización de un episodio histórico". Observa la foto del vestido. ¿Por qué crees que fue criticado? ¿Qué piensas que simboliza?

AHORCADOS Y FUSILADOS, LOS MOTIVOS

A la izquierda, Rosa María Ojeda, ganadora del concurso Nuestra Belleza, durante la presentación, el pasado 9 de marzo, del traje típico que portará en el concurso *Miss* Universo. A la derecha, un detalle del vestido, en el cual se aprecian ejecuciones de los rebeldes cristeros ■

http://www.jornada.unam.mx/2007/04/14

Más allá

Investiga el traje regional de alguna región del mundo hispanohablante. ¿Cuál es la historia del traje? ¿Tiene algún significado?

A analizar

Lee la conversación y contesta las preguntas que siguen.

Vendedora:	¿Prefiere usted **este** vestido negro, o le gusta más **ese** vestido?
Cliente:	Creo que me gusta más el vestido negro.
Vendedora:	¿Cuál de las blusas prefiere, **esta** blusa a rayas o **esa** de lunares?
Cliente:	Prefiero la blusa de lunares.
Vendedora:	¿Te gustan **esos** zapatos también?
Cliente:	Sí, pero me gustan más **estos.**

1. Using the examples in the conversation above and what you already know about agreement in Spanish, complete these charts.

	masculine	feminine			masculine	feminine
singular	ese	_____		singular	este	_____
plural	_____	_____		plural	_____	_____

2. Demonstrative adjectives and pronouns communicate the location of a person or an object. Which is used with an item that is close to you? Which is used with an item that is farther from you?

A comprobar

Demonstrative adjectives and pronouns

1. Demonstrative adjectives are used to point out specific people, objects, or places. The demonstrative adjective you use depends on how close you are to the object.

este	*this*	close to the speaker
ese	*that*	at a short distance
aquel	*that*	at a long distance

este	sombrero	**esta**	falda
estos	zapatos	**estas**	botas
ese	sombrero	**esa**	falda
esos	zapatos	**esas**	botas
aquel	sombrero	**aquella**	falda
aquellos	zapatos	**aquellas**	botas

2. As with other adjectives, demonstrative adjectives must agree in gender and number with the item they describe.

3. A demonstrative adjective is placed in front of the noun it modifies.

¿Por qué no te pruebas **este** suéter de lana?
*Why don't you try on **this** wool sweater?*

No me gusta **esa** camisa estampada.
*I don't like **that** printed shirt.*

Aquellos zapatos de piel están en rebaja.
Those leather shoes are on sale.

4. Demonstrative pronouns replace the noun and have the same forms as demonstrative adjectives.

> Prefiero esta chaqueta, no **esa.**
> *I prefer this jacket, not **that one.***

> Ese vestido es más caro que **este.**
> *That dress is more expensive than **this one.***

5. The demonstrative forms **esto** and **eso** are neuter and are used to refer to something abstract such as an idea or a situation. They are also used to refer to items not yet identified.

> ¿Qué es **esto?**
> *What is **this?***

> Esta ropa es de muy buena calidad y **eso** es importante.
> *This clothing is of very good quality and **that** is important.*

A practicar

11.6 **Los maniquíes** La vendedora habla con una cliente sobre la ropa que llevan los maniquíes. Escucha lo que dice y decide de cuál de los tres maniquíes habla.

CD2-15

11.7 **Decisiones, decisiones** Dos amigas fueron de compras. Completa su conversación, usando los adjetivos y los pronombres demostrativos.

Gisela: No sé qué comprar. **(1.)** _____ chaqueta que tienes tú es muy bonita, pero **(2.)** _____ aquí es más barata.

Adela: A mí me gusta **(3.)** _____ pantalón que tienes tú.

Gisela: ¿De veras? Yo creo que prefiero **(4.)** _____ pantalón en el estante (*rack*) allá. ¿Y qué piensas de **(5.)** _____ zapatos aquí?

Adela: **(6.)** _____ son bonitos, pero me gustan más **(7.)** _____ aquí.

Gisela: ¡Mira allá! **(8.)** _____ zapatos están en rebaja.

Adela: ¡Vamos!

11.8 **La moda de hoy** Con un compañero túrnense para describir la ropa que llevan los estudiantes de la clase. Usen los adjetivos y los pronombres demostrativos.

Modelo Estudiante 1: *Esta es una camisa a cuadros.*
Estudiante 2: *Esa es una camisa a rayas.*

11.9 **¿De quién es?** Abel y su hermano Aarón comparten (*share*) un cuarto. Su ropa está revuelta (*mixed up*) y Abel quiere organizarla. Con un compañero túrnense para hacer el papel de Abel e identificar de quién es cada artículo. Deben usar los pronombres demostrativos **este** y **ese** en la forma apropiada.

Modelo *Esta es su chaqueta de piel. Ese es mi gorro.*

11.10 **De compras** Vas de compras con un amigo. Uno de ustedes está más cerca de la colección **A** y el otro está cerca de la colección **B**. Túrnense para preguntar sobre las preferencias del otro, usando los adjetivos y pronombres demostrativos. Debes usar **este** para las prendas en la colección más cercana a ti, y **ese** para las prendas en la colección más cercana a tu compañero. **¡OJO!** Pongan atención a la forma de los adjetivos demostrativos.

Modelo Estudiante 1: *¿Prefieres estas gafas de sol o esas?*
Estudiante 2: *Prefiero estas.*

A

© Alexander Kalina/Shutterstck

B

© Andrey Armyagov/Shutterstck

© Alexander Kalina/Shutterstck

© Andrey Armyagov/Shutterstck

Conexiones culturales
La moda

Cultura

En todo el mundo existen grupos étnicos y culturales que son fácilmente reconocibles por vestirse de una forma particular. Uno de estos grupos es el de las llamadas cholas, mujeres indígenas bolivianas. Según parece, la historia de las cholitas comienza en la Colonia, cuando muchas mujeres indígenas inmigraron a las ciudades. Estas campesinas querían adaptarse a la vida de la ciudad, y comenzaron a vestirse elegantemente con el típico y elegante sombrero de bombín que usaban las europeas en esos tiempos, aunque solo las mujeres casadas tenían derecho a usarlo. Otros elementos indispensables de la vestimenta de las cholas eran, y siguen siendo, la pollera (falda), blusa, manta *(poncho)* y botas negras. Mientras que la moda de las mujeres europeas cambió mucho a través de los años, las cholitas continúan apegadas a su elegante moda, aunque ha habido *(there have been)* algunos pequeños cambios.

¿Puedes pensar en otros grupos de personas que sean fácilmente reconocibles por su ropa? ¿Quiénes son? ¿Qué ropa llevan? ¿Hay algún grupo semejante en tu área geográfica?

Cholitas comprando ropa en el mercado

© Margarita Casas

 Investiga en Internet sobre trajes tradicionales de países hispanophablantes.

Comunidad

No todas las personas tienen la ropa que necesitan para su familia. Considera organizarte con otros estudiantes y donar ropa a alguna institución de caridad que se encargue de distribuirla a personas necesitadas. Pueden poner etiquetas en español e inglés en las cajas donde pongan la ropa. O si prefieren, pueden buscar una organización que envíe ropa a zonas pobres de países en desarrollo, como Guatemala y Nicaragua.

¿Hay organizaciones en tu comunidad que distribuyen ropa donada?

© vesilvio/Shutterstock

370 *trescientos setenta* | **Capítulo 11**

Comparaciones

Vestirse apropiadamente es un concepto relativo, ya que depende del lugar donde está una persona, de su género, edad e incluso religión. Una persona puede estar vestida apropiadamente con unos pantalones cortos y una camiseta si está en la playa, pero la misma combinación es probablemente poco deseable en una iglesia, o para trabajar en una oficina.

En el contexto de los estudiantes universitarios, aunque se deben evitar las generalizaciones, puede decirse que los estudiantes en países hispanos prefieren llevar ropa cómoda como bluyíns, pero los combinan con ropa más formal que una simple camiseta. Es posible que los estudiantes en universidades privadas se preocupen más por estar a la moda que los estudiantes en las universidades públicas.

En grupos, contesten las siguientes preguntas sobre su universidad.

1. ¿Creen que es importante la moda en su universidad? ¿Por qué lo creen? Den ejemplos concretos.
2. En promedio ¿cuánto gastan en ropa al mes? ¿Compran ropa de moda o de marcas prestigiosas?
3. ¿Qué ropa es apropiada para estudiar en su universidad?

Después, busquen a estudiantes universitarios de algún país hispanohablante (de su universidad, o en el Internet), y háganles las mismas preguntas. ¿Hay diferencias importantes? ¿Qué diferencias?

Muchos estudiantes de la Universidad Nacional de México se visten informalmente.

Conexiones... al diseño

¿Puedes nombrar a cinco diseñadores famosos? Carolina Herrera es una diseñadora venezolana que nació en la alta sociedad de Venezuela, y vivió siempre entre grupos distinguidos, dentro de los que se dio a notar por su apariencia física y su buen gusto para vestir. No fue sino hasta 1980, cuando ya tenía cuarenta años, que Herrera decidió iniciarse como diseñadora.

La siguiente es una lista de otros diseñadores hispanos. Algunos de ellos son muy populares en los Estados Unidos. ¿Los conoces?

Óscar de la Renta
Paloma Picasso
Roberto Giordano
Angel Sánchez
Thalía Sodi

En el Internet, busca las biografías y algunos de los diseños de uno de estos diseñadores. Después, comparte la información con la clase y, si es posible, muestra algunos modelos. ¿Te gustan los diseños? ¿Alguien en la clase diseña ropa?

Un desfile de moda de los diseños de Carolina Herrera en Nueva York

A analizar

Lee la siguiente conversación y observa las expresiones de comparación.

Lorena: La falda negra es bonita y no es tan cara como la falda azul.

Carolina: Tienes razón, pero creo que prefiero la falda azul porque es un poco más larga que la falda negra. ¿Qué te parece esta blusa roja con la falda?

Lorena: Me gusta, y esa blusa cuesta menos que la blusa de seda.

1. How does the black skirt compare to the blue skirt? What expressions are used to make the comparisons?

2. How does the silk blouse compare to the red blouse? What expression is used to make the comparison?

A comprobar

Comparisons

1. Comparisons of equality

The following construction is used to compare two people or things that have equal qualities:

> **tan** *(as)* + adjective/adverb + **como** *(as)*

La blusa roja es **tan bonita como** la azul.
*The red blouse is **as pretty as** the blue one.*

Yo no canto **tan bien como** mi esposo.
*I don't sing **as well as** my husband.*

The following construction is used to compare two people or things of equal quantity:

> **tanto(s)**
> **tanta(s)** *(as much, many)* + noun + **como** *(as)*

Ella tiene **tantos zapatos como** Esmeralda.
*She has **as many shoes as** Esmeralda.*

Úrsula gastó **tanto dinero como** Eva.
*Ursula spent **as much money as** Eva did.*

The following construction is used to compare equal actions:

> verb + **tanto como**

Él trabaja **tanto como** ella.
*He works **as much as** she does.*

2. Comparisons of inequality

The following constructions are used to compare two people or things that have unequal qualities:

> **más** *(more)*
> **menos** *(less)* + adjective/noun/adverb + **que** *(than)*

La seda es **más cara que** el algodón.
*Silk is **more expensive than** cotton.*

Pilar compró **menos ropa que** su hermana.
*Pilar bought **less clothing than** her sister.*

Pancho conduce **más rápido que** Iván.
*Pancho drives **faster than** Iván.*

The following construction is used to compare unequal actions:

> verb + **más/menos que**

El sombrero cuesta **menos que** los guantes.
*The hat costs **less than** the gloves.*

The following adjectives and adverbs do not use **más** or **menos** in their constructions:

bueno/bien	→ **mejor**	*better*
joven	→ **menor**	*younger*
malo/mal	→ **peor**	*worse*
viejo (age of a person)	→ **mayor**	*older*

Aquí tienen **mejores precios que** allí.
*Here they have **better prices than** there.*

Diana es **menor que** Federico.
*Diana is **younger than** Federico.*

3. Superlatives
Superlatives are used when someone or something is referred to as *the most, the least, the best,* etc. This is expressed through the following construction:

> article (**el, la, los, las**) + noun (optional) + **más/menos** + adjective

Este traje es **el traje más caro** (de esta tienda).
*This suit is **the most expensive suit** (in the store).*

Esta talla es **la más grande**.
*This size is **the biggest**.*

As with the other comparisons, when using **bueno/bien, malo/mal, joven,** and **viejo** (age), you must use the irregular constructions **mejor, peor, menor,** and **mayor**.

Esta tienda tiene **las mejores** rebajas.
*This store has **the best** sales.*

4. The preposition **de** is often used with superlatives to express *in* or *of*.

Este vestido es el más bonito **de** todos.
*This dress is the prettiest **of** all.*

Son las mejores rebajas **del** año.
*They are the best sales **of** the year.*

A practicar

11.11 **¿Qué piensas?** Lee las siguientes oraciones y decide si estás de acuerdo o no. Debes explicarle tus razones a la clase.

1. Una chaqueta de piel cuesta tanto como una chaqueta de lana.
2. Una camisa a cuadros es más bonita que una camisa a rayas.
3. Pagar en efectivo es mejor que pagar con una tarjeta de crédito.
4. La ropa rebajada no es tan buena como la ropa a precio normal.
5. El precio de la ropa es menos importante que la calidad (*quality*).
6. Las mujeres gastan (*spend*) tanto dinero en la ropa como los hombres.
7. La ropa hecha (*made*) en El Salvador es más cara que la ropa hecha en los Estados Unidos.
8. La ropa de marca (*name brand*) es mejor que la ropa sin marca.
9. El algodón es más cómodo que la mezclilla.
10. La moda es menos importante para los hombres que para las mujeres.

¿Quién gasta más en ropa?

© Deklofenak/Shutterstock

11.12 **A comparar** Mira las vitrinas (*display windows*) de una tienda. Con un compañero, túrnense para comparar dos artículos, usando las expresiones **más... que, menos... que** y **tan... como.** Pueden usar estos adjetivos o seleccionar otros: **bonito, feo, barato, caro, largo, corto, grande, pequeño, elegante.**

Modelo *La blusa rosada es más cara que la camisa a rayas.*

11.13 **Opiniones** Con un compañero, expresen sus opiniones sobre los siguientes temas. Escojan dos ideas dentro de cada categoría y compárenlas.

Modelo la ropa - estilos
    Estudiante 1: *La ropa lisa es más bonita que la ropa estampada.*
    Estudiante 2: *En mi opinión las camisas a rayas son tan bonitas como las camisas lisas.*

1. la ropa
    a. telas (*materials*)   **b.** prendas   **c.** tiendas de ropa

2. la educación
    a. universidades   **b.** clases   **c.** profesores

3. el tiempo libre
    a. restaurantes   **b.** cantantes/grupos de música   **c.** deportes

11.14 **Comparaciones de grupo** En grupos de tres o cuatro, contesten las siguientes preguntas sobre los integrantes de su grupo.

1. ¿Quién es el mayor?
2. ¿Quién es el menor?
3. ¿Quién es el más alto?
4. ¿Quién es el más bajo?
5. ¿Quién es el mejor estudiante?
6. ¿Quién es el mejor artista?
7. ¿Quién es el mejor atleta?
8. ¿Quién tiene el pelo más largo?
9. ¿Quién tiene el coche más nuevo?
10. ¿Quién tiene la familia más grande?

¿Quién es más alta?

11.15 **El mundo hispanohablante** Decide cuál de los tres países, ciudades o conceptos en cada (*each*) lista es el más grande, pequeño, antiguo (*old*), etcétera. Debes usar los adjetivos enfrente de la línea para crear cada superlativo.

Modelo grande: Santiago / Buenos Aires / Ciudad de México
   La Ciudad de México es la más grande.

1. grande: México / Argentina / Chile
2. pequeño: El Salvador / la República Dominicana / Puerto Rico
3. antiguo: la civilización maya / la civilización azteca / la civilización inca
4. nuevo: Perú / Panamá / Cuba
5. poblado (*populated*): Argentina / Colombia / Venezuela
6. alto: Cuzco / Quito / Santiago

11.16 **El mejor** Usando las palabras indicadas y los superlativos, expresen sus opiniones.

Modelo interesante / libro
   Estudiante 1: *El libro más interesante es* Don Quijote.
   Estudiante 2: *En mi opinión los libros más interesantes son los libros de Harry Potter.*

1. rápido / coche
2. caro / restaurante
3. bueno / actor o actriz
4. difícil / materia
5. tonta / película
6. malo / programa de televisión
7. talentoso / grupo musical
8. bueno / equipo de fútbol americano

¿Cuál es el libro más interesante?

Lectura

Reading Strategy: Identifying patterns

When you read, look for patterns that are common in all texts, such as opening statements, arguments for or against a point of view, and conclusions. Detect the general purpose of the text and, finally, evaluate: form your own opinion about the subject.

Antes de leer

Con un compañero hablen de las siguientes preguntas.

1. ¿Qué significa **escandalosa**?
2. ¿Por qué razones se puede clasificar alguna ropa como escandalosa?
3. Actualmente (*Currently*), ¿hay ropa que se considera escandalosa? ¿Por qué?
4. Lee el título del artículo. ¿Qué creen que va a decir el artículo?

A leer

Las tapadas: una moda escandalosa

Durante la época de la Colonia en Lima, la capital de Perú, nació una moda que fue producto de la competencia entre las mestizas (de descendencia indígena y europea) y las criollas (descendientes de europeos). Las criollas, por una parte, preferían vestidos europeos que acentuaban su **cintura.** Entonces las mestizas, que eran generalmente de talla más grande, comenzaron a usar sayas, faldas muy amplias que solo dejaban ver los pies.

waist

Estas faldas eran de seda y normalmente de color azul, castaño, negro o verde. Las mujeres que seguían esta moda llevaban una **correa** a la cintura y, lo más importante, usaban un **manto** que les **cubría** la cara, la cabeza y la parte superior del cuerpo, por lo que solamente se les podía ver un ojo a estas mujeres.

belt
cloak
covered

Con esta moda, las mestizas **ocultaban** sus defectos, y era imposible

hid

La moda de las tapadas

[estos vestidos les dieron a las tapadas de Lima una gran libertad en esta época]

distinguir a una mujer de otra. En otras palabras, este traje era completamente anónimo, ya que no era posible distinguir a la persona. Se conocen muchas historias de **tapadas** que "atraparon" a sus propios maridos **coqueteando** con ellas

covered ones
flirting

© Geoffrey Clements/CORBIS

(hay que recordar que sus caras estaban tapadas, así que los hombres no sabían que estaban hablando con sus esposas). El anonimato de estos vestidos les dio a las tapadas de Lima una gran libertad en esa **época**: podían beber alcohol en público, ir a las corridas de toros, y pasear por la ciudad.

at that time

El **comportamiento** de las tapadas fue considerado obsceno, y desde 1561 tanto los **virreyes** del Perú como la Iglesia Católica quisieron prohibir el uso de la vestimenta, imponiendo multas a las mujeres que usaban el manto. Sin embargo, la prohibición solo aumentó su uso. No fue hasta finales del siglo XIX, con la llegada de la moda francesa, que empezaron a desaparecer la saya y el manto.

behavior

viceroys

Durante la existencia de las tapadas en Lima, fueron el tema de muchas obras de arte y también de varias comedias del dramaturgo Manuel Ascencio Segura. Además, participaron en el inicio de la revolución peruana, ayudando a pasar mensajes a los revolucionarios, usando sus trajes para no ser identificadas. Como se puede ver, la moda de las tapadas tuvo singular importancia en la historia del Perú.

Comprensión

Decide si las siguientes afirmaciones son ciertas o falsas, y corrige las falsas.

1. Las criollas y las mestizas de Lima usaban una moda diferente en la época colonial.
2. Las mestizas, en general, eran mujeres más pequeñas que las criollas.
3. Las criollas usaban un manto para cubrir sus defectos.
4. La moda de las tapadas les permitió tener más libertad.
5. La moda de las tapadas desapareció en el siglo XVI.

Después de leer

Habla con un compañero de clase sobre las siguientes preguntas.

1. ¿Te parece escandalosa la moda de las tapadas? ¿Por qué?
2. ¿Hay alguna moda actual que te parezca (*that seems to you*) escandalosa? ¿Por qué?
3. Piensen en ropa que en otra época o en otra cultura se considera (consideraba) escandalosa. ¿Por qué es (era) escandalosa?

A Gabriela le encanta el arte y va a todas las exhibiciones que ofrece el museo de arte de la ciudad donde vive.

los cuadros

el arte abstracto

el paisaje

el retrato

la naturaleza muerta

el autorretrato

el mural

la escultura

el artista

la exhibición de máscaras

Más vocabulario

la galería	gallery
el grabado	engraving; print
el (la) modelo	model
la obra	work (of art, literature, theater, etc.)
el óleo	oil painting
la paleta	palette
el pincel	paintbrush
la tinta	ink

Verbos

apagar	to turn off
apreciar	to appreciate, enjoy
diseñar	to design
esculpir	to sculpt
exhibir	to exhibit
posar	to pose

Adjetivos

complicado	complex
conservador	conservative
cubista	cubist
impresionista	impressionist
realista	realistic
sencillo	simple
surrealista	surrealist
tradicional	traditional
vanguardista	revolutionary; avant-garde

Práctica

11.17 **Escucha y responde** Primero, escribe "A" en un pedazo de papel y "B" en otro. Después vas a escuchar una serie de adjetivos para describir el arte que aparece en Actividad 11.21 en la próxima página. Para cada adjetivo, levanta el papel si la descripción se refiere a la foto A o a la B.

CD2-16

11.18 **¿Cuál es la palabra?** Completa con una palabra lógica del vocabulario.

1. En _____ se exhiben muchas obras de arte.
2. Los estudiantes de pintura copiaron _____ más famosos del museo.
3. Cuando un artista pinta un cuadro de él mismo, el cuadro se llama _____.
4. Una pintura hecha sobre una pared *(wall)* tiene el nombre de _____.
5. Muchas ciudades tienen en sus calles _____ de personas famosas.
6. Un _____ es una persona que posa para un artista.

11.19 **La lógica** Las siguientes ideas son ilógicas. Corrígelas de manera que sean lógicas.

Modelo El artista compró muchas de sus obras en la exhibición.
El artista <u>vendió</u> muchas de sus obras.

1. Muchas galerías asisten a exhibiciones de arte.
2. El escultor posa para una escultura.
3. La naturaleza muerta es un cuadro en el que aparecen animales muertos.
4. Un muralista es una obra que el artista pinta en una pared.
5. El pintor usa la paleta para pintar en el pincel.
6. Un cuadro surrealista es un cuadro en el que un pintor se pinta a sí mismo.

11.20 **¡A adivinar!** En grupos de tres, elijan una palabra del vocabulario de la lista que sigue y explíquensela a sus compañeros sin decirla. Los otros estudiantes pueden hacer preguntas. Túrnense para explicar. El objetivo es adivinar el mayor número de palabras en ocho minutos.

Modelo el mural
Estudiante 1: *Es un tipo de arte que un pintor hace en una pared.*
Estudiante 2: *El mural.*

complicado	realista	la máscara	el paisaje	la escultura
la paleta	vanguardista	la escultura	el óleo	el arte abstracto
posar	el mural	el pincel	la galería	el retrato

11.21 **Un análisis de arte** Trabaja con un compañero para hablar sobre dos pinturas muy diferentes. Usen las siguientes preguntas para ayudar con su análisis.

¿En qué estilo se pintó?   ¿Qué emoción evoca?

¿Qué hay en la pintura?   En tu opinión ¿qué quiere decir el artista?

¿Qué colores usó el artista?

A

© Erich Lessing / Art Resource, NY

Valencianas en la playa de Joaquín Sorolla y Bastida

B

Schalkwijk/Art Resource, NY. © D.R. Rufino Tamayo/Herederos/ México/2010 Fundación Olga y Rufino Tamayo, A.C.

Naturaleza con pie de Rufino Tamayo

🎧 **iTunes**
Listen to the Spanish pop group Mecano's song "'Eungenio' Salvador Dalí". In what ways does the person express admiration for the artist and his work?

Muchas veces los museos organizan actividades y exhibiciones especiales para niños. ¿Qué tipo de actividades crees que son comunes en estos museos? Observa la información sobre el Museo Kaleidoscopio, en Bogotá. ¿Cuáles son cuatro actividades diferentes que este museo ofrece para los niños?

Este verano el Museo Kaleidoscopio ha preparado una serie de actividades para despertar tu sed del conocimiento por las artes y la historia...¡participa y trae a tus padres!

Descubre al artista dentro de ti

Descripción: Curso de verano para niños
Objetivo: Desarrollar la creatividad y aprender sobre el arte
Fechas: Lunes, miércoles y viernes de 10:00 a 2:00 pm
Dirigido a: Niños de 5 a 12 años

En este taller aprenderás sobre algunos de los grandes pintores en la historia mundial, y también tendrás la oportunidad de explorar nuestra colección. Además, habrá oportunidades para pintar.

Descubre las artesanías y la cerámica de Latinoamérica

Descripción: Taller de fin de semana para niños
Objetivo: Aprender sobre las diferentes demostraciones artísticas de varios países latinoamericanos
Fechas: Sábados y domingos de 4:00 a 6:00 pm
Dirigido a: Niños de 6 a 12 años

En este taller aprenderás sobre diferentes tipos de arte de los países latinoamericanos. Podrás crear tus propias molas (típicas de Panamá), pintar en papel amate, hacer esculturas en papel maché, y pintar piezas de cerámica en estilos típicos de los países andinos.

Más allá

Imagina que eres el director de un museo. Decide qué tipo de museo es y diseña una actividad para niños.

A analizar

Lee la conversación y observa las palabras en negritas.

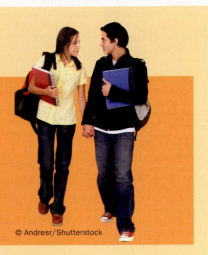

> Rafael: ¿Te interesa ir conmigo a la exposición de las obras de Picasso el sábado?
>
> Teresa: ¡Por supuesto! Estoy muy **interesada** en las obras de Picasso, especialmente en las de su período rosado.
>
> Rafael: Entonces ¿a qué hora vamos?
>
> Teresa: ¡Ay, se me olvidó! El sábado estoy **ocupada.** Tengo planes para visitar a mi tía en Ponce. ¿Está **abierto** el museo el viernes por la tarde?
>
> Rafael: Sí. Vamos el viernes por la tarde.

© Andresr/Shutterstock

1. The words in bold are adjectives. Identify the verb that each of the adjectives is derived from.

A comprobar

Estar with the past participle

1. To form the past participle, place **-ado** on the end of the stem of **-ar** verbs and **-ido** on the stem of **-er** and **-ir** verbs.

hablar	habl**ado**
beber	beb**ido**
vivir	viv**ido**

The following verbs have irregular past participles:

abrir	**abierto**	morir	**muerto**
decir	**dicho**	romper	**roto**
despertar	**despierto**	poner	**puesto**
devolver	**devuelto**	ver	**visto**
escribir	**escrito**	volver	**vuelto**
hacer	**hecho**		

> **INVESTIGUEMOS LA GRAMÁTICA**
>
> Notice that the common irregular participles end in **-to** or **-cho.** Other irregular past participles end in **-so,** such as **imprimir → impreso** (printed) and **confundir → confuso** (confusing).

2. The past participle can be used as an adjective to indicate condition and is often used with the verb **estar.** You have already learned some of them, such as **aburrido, cansado,** and **muerto.** Like other adjectives, they must agree in gender and number with the nouns they describe.

> Los estudiantes **están interesados** en el arte.
> *The students **are interested** in art.*
>
> El museo no **está abierto** los lunes.
> *The museum **is not open** on Mondays.*

3. As is common with most adjectives in Spanish, the past participles can also be placed after the noun they describe.

> Me gustan más sus obras **pintadas.**
> *I like his **painted** works better.*
>
> Salvador Dalí es un pintor **conocido.**
> *Salvador Dalí is a **well-known** painter.*

A practicar

11.22 **Mi salón de clases** Mira alrededor de tu salón de clases y decide si las oraciones son ciertas o falsas.

1. Hay una ventana rota.
2. Las luces están apagadas.
3. Hay algo escrito en la pizarra.
4. La puerta está abierta.
5. Las sillas están hechas de plástico.
6. Todos los estudiantes están despiertos.

11.23 **La casa** Entrevista a un compañero con las siguientes preguntas.

1. ¿Está hecha tu cama? ¿Quién la hizo?
2. ¿Está ordenado tu cuarto? ¿Por qué?
3. ¿Dejaste abiertas las ventanas de tu casa? ¿Por qué?
4. ¿Dejaste encendidas las luces de tu casa? ¿Por qué?
5. ¿Está lavada tu ropa? ¿Quién la lava?
6. ¿Están muertas las plantas en tu casa? ¿Por qué?
7. ¿Tienes algo que está roto? ¿Qué es?
8. ¿Tienes algo hecho en otro país? ¿Qué es y de dónde es?

Mis plantas no están muertas.

© Monkey Business Images/Shutterstock

11.24 **¿Qué ves?** Túrnense con un compañero para preguntar si ven lo siguiente. **¡OJO!** Recuerden que el participio necesita concordar con el objeto que se describe.

Modelo algo abierto
> Estudiante 1: *¿Ves algo abierto?*
> Estudiante 2: *Sí, la puerta está abierta. / No, no hay nada abierto.*

1. algo escrito en inglés
2. algo hecho de metal
3. alguien casado
4. algo colgado en la pared
5. algo roto
6. alguien cansado
7. algo pintado de rojo
8. algo encendido

11.25 **La clase de arte** Lee las siguientes oraciones sobre una clase de arte y explica las condiciones de los sujetos, usando el verbo **estar** y el participio pasado del verbo subrayado (*underlined*).

Modelo La planta del profesor <u>murió</u>.
> *La planta del profesor está muerta.*

1. Cuando el profesor entró en la clase, <u>encendió</u> las luces y <u>cerró</u> la puerta.
2. Él <u>colgó</u> su suéter.
3. Luisa <u>se sentó</u> al lado de Julián.
4. Ella <u>tiene mucho interés</u> en Julián.
5. Pero Julián <u>se ocupa</u> de su pintura.
6. Inés, la chica al lado de Julián, <u>se aburre</u> en la clase.
7. Ella <u>se durmió</u> en la clase.
8. El profesor <u>escribió</u> la tarea en la pizarra.
9. Al escribir la tarea, <u>rompió</u> la tiza (*chalk*).
10. El profesor <u>se frustra</u> y termina la clase temprano.

11.26 **Preocupado** Es medianoche y tu pareja no te deja dormir porque está muy preocupada. Con un compañero, túrnense para preguntar si su pareja hizo lo siguiente. Debe responder con el participio pasado. **¡OJO!** Recuerden que el participio necesita concordar con el objeto que se describe.

Modelo ¿Abriste la ventana?
　　　Estudiante 1: *¿Abriste la ventana?*
　　　Estudiante 2: *Sí, está abierta. / No, no está abierta.*

1. ¿Estás despierto?
2. ¿Apagaste las luces en la sala?
3. ¿Cerraste la puerta?
4. ¿Encendiste la alarma?
5. ¿Colgaste tu ropa?
6. ¿Guardaste los platos limpios?
7. ¿Preparaste el almuerzo para mañana?
8. ¿Escribiste el cheque para el alquiler?

11.27 **El teatro** Con un compañero, túrnense para describir el escenario del teatro, usando los participios como adjetivos. Busquen las cinco diferencias.

Vocabulario útil: **el perchero** *coat rack*

Cultura

El arte no se limita a la pintura y a las esculturas que se exhiben en los grandes museos. La mayoría de las culturas tienen expresiones artísticas muy particulares. En esta sección vamos a explorar las molas y los alebrijes.

En las islas de San Blas, Panamá, existe una tribu indígena conocida como los cunas, quienes son famosos por sus molas, que son una forma de arte textil. Las molas se hacen con fragmentos de tela de colores vivos, y muchas veces tienen diseños abstractos y geométricos. En el pasado las molas se usaban solamente para vestir, pero hoy en día se usan también como artículos decorativos.

Una mola de Panamá

En el estado de Oaxaca, México, algunos artistas especializados se dedican a crear animales fantásticos, hechos de madera. Los artesanos tallan la madera y la decoran en colores brillantes. Los alebrijes casi siempre son una combinación de diferentes partes de animales. Por ejemplo, un alebrije puede tener el cuerpo de una jirafa, las patas (pies de un animal) de un caballo, la cabeza de un pájaro y la cola de un gato. No hay dos iguales.

Investiga otra forma de arte típico de otro país y reporta a la clase.

Un alebrije de Oaxaca, México

🌐 Busca en Internet otros ejemplos de molas y alebrijes.

Comunidad

El arte no solamente está en los museos. ¿Qué se hace en tu comunidad para promoverlo? ¿Y en tu universidad? Con un compañero, piensen en un proyecto para promover el arte en la comunidad, como crear un mural u organizar una competencia de arte. ¿Qué tipo de arte desean promover? ¿Qué necesitan hacer? ¿Dónde? Si es posible, realicen su proyecto.

Mural en una calle en San Francisco

Comparaciones

A pesar de que hay innumerables culturas diferentes dentro de los países donde se habla español, el orgullo por sus artistas es muchas veces internacional. Las grandes obras de arte, inclusive las de literatura, unen a la gente de todos estos países.

Un billete mexicano de 200 pesos

Sería imposible mencionar a todos los grandes artistas, entre los que hay numerosos escritores. Sin embargo, en ninguna lista se puede dejar de mencionar a Pablo Neruda (1904–1973), ganador del Premio Nobel de Literatura y autor de algunos de los poemas más hermosos que se han escrito en español. Neruda, además, estuvo comprometido con ideales políticos y sociales que lo hicieron muy popular entre los latinoamericanos. Aún a treinta años de su muerte, Pablo Neruda es tan querido que para celebrar los cien años de su nacimiento, algunos de los cantantes más populares de España y Latinoamérica le dedicaron un disco lleno de homenajes a Neruda y a su poesía: "Neruda en el Corazón".

Otra autora importante, muy anterior a Neruda, fue la poetisa mexicana Sor Juana Inés de la Cruz (1648–1695), quien decidió hacerse monja *(nun)* para poder seguir estudiando. Sor Juana escribió poesía, teatro y ensayos. Quizás su poema más conocido es uno en el que les reclama a los hombres su doble estándar para juzgar a la mujer y al hombre. El gobierno de México ha honrado la memoria de Sor Juana, poniendo su retrato en uno de los billetes del país.

¿Hay autores en la literatura escrita en inglés que sean reconocidos y admirados por todos los países en donde se habla inglés? ¿Quiénes son y por qué se hicieron tan importantes?

Conexiones... a la filosofía

La siguiente es una colección de citas sobre el arte que dan varios artistas famosos de paíces diferentes. Expliquen con sus propias palabras qué quieren decir, y después digan si están de acuerdo con ellas y por qué.

> El arte es una mentira que nos acerca a la verdad. **Picasso**
> El arte es el mediador de lo inexpresable. **Goethe**
> El arte no reproduce lo visible, sino que hace visible lo que no siempre lo es. **Paul Klee**
> Canto para no morir, porque el arte es la lucha *(struggle)* contra la muerte. **Carlos Cano**
> Los espejos se emplean para verse la cara; el arte para verse el alma *(soul)*. **G. B. Shaw**
> El arte es inútil, pero el hombre es incapaz de prescindir de *(to do without)* lo inútil. **E. Ionesco**
> En Andalucía se vive el arte, en Inglaterra o en los Estados Unidos se cuelga en las paredes. **Lindsay Kemp**
> En los mejores días del arte no existían los críticos del arte. **Oscar Wilde**

Estampilla postal que conmemora la obra de Pablo Picasso

A analizar

Lee el párrafo y observa las estructuras de los verbos.

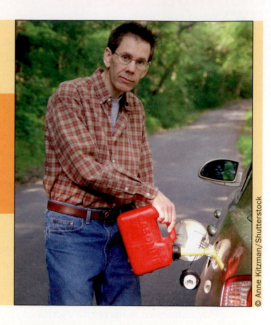

> ¡Qué día! Iba al museo cuando un policía me paró. Me pidió la licencia, pero cuando saqué la billetera no estaba. Le dije al policía: "**¡Se me quedó** en casa!" Luego el coche se paró. Pensé: "**¡Se me acabó** la gasolina!" Cuando por fin llegué al museo, estaba cerrado. Entonces exclamé: "**¡Se me olvidó** que no abren los domingos!"

1. In which person (1st, 2nd, or 3rd) have the verbs been conjugated? Why?
2. What pronouns appear before the verbs?
3. Recalling some of the ways that **se** can be used, what do you think it means here?

A comprobar

Se to indicate accidental occurrences

1. In **Capítulo 8,** you learned to use the pronoun **se** in order to indicate that the subject is either unknown or unimportant. Use the following construction with **se** to indicate unintentional or accidental occurrences:

> **se** + indirect object pronoun + verb

> **Se me** rompió el plato.   *I broke the plate (accidentally).*
> A Diego **se le** perdieron las llaves.   *Diego lost his keys (unintentionally).*

Notice that the verb agrees with subject (**el plato** and **las llaves**) and that the person affected by the event becomes the indirect object (**me** and **A Diego . . . le**).

2. The following are common verbs used with this construction.

acabar	*to finish*	perder	*to lose (an object)*
Se me acabó la gasolina.	*I ran out of gas.*	**Se nos perdió** la tarea.	*We lost our homework.*
apagar	*to turn off*	olvidar	*to forget*
Se les apagó la computadora.	*Their computer went out.*	A ella **se le olvidó** el lápiz.	*She forgot her pencil.*
caer	*to fall*	quedar	*to remain (behind)*
Se les cayeron los libros.	*They dropped their books.*	**Se me quedó** el dinero en casa.	*I left the money at home.*
descomponer	*to break down (a machine)*	romper	*to break*
Se me descompuso el coche.	*My car broke down.*	¿**Se te rompió** el vaso?	*Did you break the glass?*

A practicar

11.28 **El pintor olvidadizo** El pintor no pudo terminar su obra porque le ocurrieron muchos accidentes. Combina los elementos de las dos columnas para formar oraciones lógicas.

1. Al pintor se le olvidó...
2. Al pintor se le apagaron...
3. Al pintor se le acabaron...
4. Al pintor se le rompieron...
5. Al pintor se le perdió...
6. Al pintor se le quedó...

a. las luces
b. los pinceles
c. el número de teléfono del modelo
d. la paleta
e. las pinturas
f. el óleo en casa

11.29 **Un mal día** Completa el párrafo con la forma apropiada del verbo entre paréntesis.

¡Ayer tuve una exposición de mi arte en una galería y todo me salió mal! Primero, **(1.)** _____ (perder) las obras de cerámica que tenía que llevar a la galería. **(2.)** _____ (olvidar) que las puse en un lugar seguro. Por fin las encontré y salí para la galería. A medio camino **(3.)** _____ (acabar) la gasolina. ¡Tuve que caminar un kilómetro a la gasolinera más cercana! Al llegar me di cuenta de que mi billetera *(wallet)* **(4.)** _____ (quedar) en casa. Afortunadamente tenía un poco de dinero en mi pantalón y pude pagar la gasolina. Llegué a la galería tarde. Mientras llevaba las piezas del coche a la sala de exposición, **(5.)** _____ (caer) una y **(6.)** _____ (romper). Por fin comenzó la exposición y vendí unas piezas. Por lo menos la noche terminó bien.

11.30 **¿Qué pasó?** Con un compañero, describan la situación y expliquen lo que les pasó a las personas.

Modelo *El hombre pintaba un mural cuando se le acabó la pintura.*
No tenía dinero para comprar más.

11.31 **No se hizo** Estas personas no pudieron hacer su trabajo por diferentes razones. Explica lo que les pasó usando el verbo indicado con el **se** accidental.

Modelo el piloto / descomponer
Al piloto se le descompuso el avión.

1. la profesora / acabar
2. los estudiantes / olvidar
3. el ama de casa / romper
4. el periodista / descomponer
5. los cocineros / caer
6. el pintor / perder
7. las bailarinas / quedar
8. los actores / apagar

11.32 **En busca de...** Circula por la clase para hacerles las siguientes preguntas a diferentes compañeros. Busca a alguien que responda afirmativamente a la primera pregunta. Después hazle la pregunta entre paréntesis. Usa la expresión **alguna vez** en la pregunta.

Modelo acabar la tinta en medio de un proyecto (¿Qué?)
Estudiante 1: *¿Alguna vez se te acabó la tinta en medio de un proyecto?*
Estudiante 2: *Sí, se me acabó la tinta en medio de un proyecto.*
Estudiante 1: *¿Qué proyecto?*
Estudiante 2: *Una composición para la clase de inglés el semestre pasado.*

1. descomponer el coche a la mitad del camino (*in the middle of the road*) (¿Dónde?)
2. romper algo valioso (*valuable*) (¿Qué?)
3. perder algo importante (¿Qué?)
4. apagar la computadora en medio de una tarea importante (¿Qué tarea fue?)
5. quedar en casa algo importante durante algún viaje (¿Qué?)
6. olvidar el nombre de alguien en el momento de hacer una presentación (*introduction*) (¿De quién?)
7. quemar (*burned*) la comida (¿Qué?)
8. olvidar el cumpleaños de alguien (¿Qué hiciste?)

11.33 **Excusas** Hay muchos problemas en la clase de arte. Con un compañero, túrnense para dar excusas y explicar lo que pasó. Usen los siguientes verbos.

acabar   apagar   caer   descomponer   olvidar   perder   quedar   romper

Modelo ¿Por qué no estuviste en clase?
Se me olvidó poner el despertador.
Se me perdieron las llaves del coche.

1. ¿Por qué no tienes la tarea?
2. ¿Por qué no tienes el libro?
3. ¿Por qué no estudiaste para el examen?
4. ¿Por qué no terminaste la pintura?
5. ¿Por qué no llegó el modelo?
6. ¿Por qué llegó tarde el profesor?

¿Por qué no estudiaste para el examen?

Redacción

Write an e-mail to a friend in which you tell him/her about your shopping habits.

Paso 1 Think about whether or not you like shopping for clothing, and then jot down two or three reasons why.

Paso 2 Write a list of a few of your shopping preferences. Think about the following: Where do you prefer to go? Do you prefer to shop alone or to go with someone else? How long do you usually spend shopping? Is being in fashion important to you? Do you prefer to buy name brands? Are sales important to you?

Paso 3 Think about a time recently when you went shopping for clothing, and jot down some of the details. Think about the following: Where did you go? What were you looking for? Who went with you? How did you feel that day? What did you buy?

© Andresr/Shutterstock

Paso 4 Begin your e-mail with a greeting, and then ask your friend if he/she likes to go shopping for clothing. Then write a topic statement in which you express your thoughts about shopping. (You like or don't like it, it is your favorite pastime, you only shop because you have to, etc.)

Paso 5 Finish your initial paragraph using some of the ideas you generated in **Paso 2.**

Paso 6 Begin your second paragraph with a transition sentence in which you introduce the topic of a particular shopping trip. Then using some of the ideas you generated in **Paso 3,** write a description of that shopping experience.

Paso 7 Conclude your e-mail and sign off.

Paso 8 Edit your e-mail:

a. Do you have smooth transitions between sentences? Between the two paragraphs?

b. Do your verbs agree with the subject? Are they conjugated correctly?

c. Did you use the preterite and the imperfect appropriately in the second paragraph?

d. Do your adjectives agree with the items they describe?

Lectura

Antes de leer

Contesta las preguntas.

1. ¿Quién es tu artista favorito? ¿Por qué?

2. ¿Conoces a algún artista de España o Latinoamérica? ¿Quién? ¿Te gusta su arte?

3. En tu opinión ¿qué se necesita para ser artista?

A leer

Remedios Varo

Una de las grandes artistas del siglo XX fue la pintora española Remedios Varo, nacida en 1908 en Anglés, España. Como muchos artistas, Remedios Varo **desarrolló** desde muy joven un interés por la pintura. Fue **apoyada** por su

developed

supported

© Christie's Images/CORBIS

XX de Remedios Varo

padre, un ingeniero que la enseñó a dibujar y a los quince años la ayudó a ingresar a la Academia de San Fernando en Madrid, a pesar de la oposición de su madre.

Allí conoció a su futuro esposo, Gerardo Lizárraga, con quien se mudó a París cuando ambos finalizaron sus estudios en la Academia. Posteriormente, se trasladaron a Barcelona, donde Remedios trabajó en publicidad.

Poco después Varo se divorció y volvió a casarse con Benjamín Peret. Su segundo esposo, un poeta, la introdujo a un grupo exclusivo de artistas surrealistas encabezado por Andrés Bretón. La pintora fue influenciada enormemente por este movimiento.

> Una de las grandes artistas del siglo XX fue la pintora española Remedios Varo

Más tarde, la Guerra Civil española la hizo emigrar nuevamente a Francia, en donde **permaneció** hasta 1941, año de la invasión nazi. En ese año, Remedios se exilió definitivamente en México,

remained

país que acogió a numerosos exiliados españoles en aquellos años, muchos de ellos artistas. En México, gracias al apoyo de su tercer marido, Walter Gruen, de Austria, Remedios se dedicó por completo a su pintura, la que antes combinaba con trabajos publicitarios. En 1955 hizo su primera exhibición colectiva en la Ciudad de México, y un año más tarde tuvo su primera exhibición individual. Durante este período conoció a otros artistas importantes, como Diego Rivera, Frida Kahlo, Octavio Paz, Gunther Gerzso, y también a su gran amiga Leonora Carrington, otra artista surrealista.

Su obra se caracteriza por figuras estilizadas, realizando acciones simbólicas. En sus cuadros se pueden ver recuerdos de su infancia, así como los horrores de la guerra y la búsqueda del conocimiento a través de la psicología y la filosofía.

Al parecer, Remedios regaló la mayoría de sus cuadros, ya que para ella el valor de la pintura estaba en el proceso de la creación artística. En 1963 Remedios Varo murió de un ataque cardiaco a la edad de 55 años.

© OMAR TORRES/AFP/Getty Images

Foto de la artista Remedios Varo

Sources: Remedios Varo: http://www.analitica.com/va/arte/dossier/1960859.asp
Latin Art Museum: http://www.latinartmuseum.com/remedios_varo.htm

Comprensión

1. ¿Cuándo se interesó por el arte Remedios Varo? ¿Cómo la apoyó su padre?
2. ¿En qué países vivió Varo después de salir de España a consecuencia de la guerra?
3. ¿Cuántas veces se casó?
4. ¿Por qué decidió dedicarse exclusivamente al arte?
5. ¿Qué hizo con la mayoría de sus cuadros?

Después de leer

Escoge uno de los artistas de España o de Latinoamérica que se listaron en la sección **Antes de leer.** Investiga sobre su vida y sus obras y preséntale la información a la clase.

Las ventas ▶

Vocabulario

Sustantivos

la calidad	*quality*
la comisión	*commission*
el descuento	*discount*
la devolución	*return*
la línea	*style*
el proveedor	*wholesaler*
la temporada	*season*

Adjetivos

importado	*imported*

Verbos

descubrir	*to discover*

Expresiones útiles

¿En qué le puedo servir?
How can I help you?

¿Qué talla usa?
What's your size?

Están en oferta.
They are on sale.

Aceptamos tarjeta de crédito.
We take credit cards.

Pase por la caja.
Please go to the cash register.

Aquí está su vuelto.
Here is your change.

Gracias por su compra.
Thanks for shopping.

¿Qué le parecen estos?

© Fuse/JupiterImages

DATOS IMPORTANTES

Educación: Estudios secundarios. Estudiantes universitarios preferiblemente. Se requiere buena presencia y buen servicio de atención al cliente.

Salario: Entre $25 000 y $40 000 + comisiones y bonos.

Dónde se trabaja: En centros comerciales, tiendas particulares, exposiciones de moda.

Luis Collado trabaja en una tienda de ropa. Es el vendedor estrella *(star)* de la tienda y hace diez años que trabaja para que todos los clientes compren ropa apropiada para su estilo y para cada estación. En el video vas a ver a Luis mientras atiende a María Elisa, una señora que quiere comprar ropa para el trabajo.

Antes de ver

Muchos vendedores trabajan por comisión, y reciben dinero extra por la ropa que venden. Algunos vendedores son muy amables, pero a otros realmente no les importa la atención al cliente. ¿Qué espera usted de un vendedor? ¿Qué preguntas le hace?

Al ver

1. ¿Qué tipo de ropa busca la señora?
2. ¿En qué mes están?
3. ¿Qué tipo de ropa le muestra primero el vendedor?
4. ¿Qué se prueba la señora en el probador?
5. ¿Qué talla de pantalones usa la señora?
6. ¿Cómo quiere pagar la señora? ¿Por qué?
7. ¿Qué recibe la señora por ser una nueva clienta?

© Heinle / Cengage Learning

Después de ver

En parejas, representen a un vendedor de ropa y a un cliente potencial que quiere comprar algo pero no sabe qué. El vendedor le ayuda a decidir la ropa ideal según el estilo, el cuerpo y las necesidades del cliente (evento, ropa informal, fiesta, trabajo, etcétera). El cliente toma una decisión y compra o no la ropa.

11.34 **¿Qué piensas?** Usando los elementos indicados, escribe tus opiniones, usando superlativos como el del modelo.

Modelo arte / popular: la pintura, la escultura, la máscara
La pintura es la más popular de las artes.

1. museo / grande: Le Louvre, El Prado, El Museo Metropolitano
2. artista / talentoso: Pablo Picasso, Fernando Botero, Frida Kahlo
3. estilo / interesante: el abstracto, el paisaje, el retrato
4. escultura / conocido: *Venus de Milo, David, El pensador*
5. pintura / famoso: *La Mona Lisa* de Da Vinci, *La noche estrellada* de Van Gogh, *El Grito* de Munch
6. pintor / excéntrico: Salvador Dalí, Remedios Varo, Andy Warhol

11.35 **Descripciones** Completa las oraciones con la forma apropiada del participio pasado de los verbos entre paréntesis.

1. Frida Kahlo y Diego Rivera estaban _____ (casar).
2. Hay muchos libros _____ (escribir) sobre el arte latinoamericano.
3. Francisco Goya está _____ (morir).
4. La artesanía de Latinoamérica está _____ (hacer) a mano.
5. Carmen Lomas Garza es una artista _____ (conocer).
6. Diego Velázquez estaba _____ (interesar) en pintar la vida típica en España.
7. Hay varios cuadros de Pablo Picasso _____ (colgar) en los museos de Nueva York.
8. Mucha de la cerámica de las civilizaciones antiguas está _____ (romper).

11.36 **¡Qué día!** Usando el **se** accidental y el verbo entre paréntesis, explica lo que le pasó a Valentina ayer.

Modelo Se levantó tarde. (olvidar)
Se le olvidó poner el despertador.

1. Todas sus notas para la reunión se mojaron (*got wet*). (caer)
2. Su bolígrafo no escribía y no pudo tomar notas en la reunión. (acabar tinta)
3. Tampoco pudo tomar notas con su lápiz. (romper)
4. No tuvo los reportes para su jefe. (olvidar)
5. A la hora de almorzar no pudo comer nada. (quedar)
6. El coche se paró camino a su casa. (descomponer)
7. No pudo llamar a nadie con su celular. (apagar)
8. Cuando llegó a casa, no pudo entrar. (perder)

11.37 **El mural** En el **Capítulo 5,** aprendiste sobre el movimiento de los muralistas después de la Revolución mexicana. Los siguientes son algunos ejemplos de murales modernos. Con un compañero, túrnense para describirlos lo mejor posible y explicar qué mensaje quiere transmitir el artista. Luego, indiquen si les gusta el mural o no.

Murales de artistas desconocidos

11.38 **Un pedido** Trabaja con un compañero. Uno de ustedes es vendedor, y el otro es el cliente. El cliente necesita ropa para un viaje a la playa. Mira la página del catálogo que aparece a continuación (*below*) y llama para hacer un pedido. Debes comprar tres prendas. El vendedor necesita ver el apéndice A para contestar las preguntas del cliente y conseguir su información (nombre, teléfono, etcétera) y su tarjeta de crédito.

Modelo Estudiante 1: *Buenas tardes.*
Estudiante 2: *Buenas tardes. Necesito una camiseta de algodón azul en talla extra grande.*
Estudiante 1: *Lo siento. No la tenemos en talla extra grande.*
Estudiante 2: *¿Qué colores tienen en talla extra grande?*

C1050 Camiseta de algodón
Colores:
■ azul   ■ negro
■ amarillo   ■ beige
Tallas: P, M, G, XG
Precio: 25 €

C4325 Camisa con estampado hawaiano
Colores:
■ azul   ■ rojo
■ verde
Tallas: P, M, G, XG
Precio: 35 €

B2219 Blusa de lunares
Colores:
▨ blanco/negro   ▨ negro/rosado
▨ rojo/blanco
Tallas: P, M, G, XG
Precio: 42 €

P6750 Pantalones cortos a rayas
Colores:
▨ blanco/azul   ▨ blanco/verde
▨ gris/negro   ▨ café/beige
Tallas: P, M, G, XG
Precio: 55 €

P7382 Pantalones cortos a cuadros
Colores:
▨ azul/verde   ▨ negro/rojo
▨ rosado/gris
Tallas: P, M, G, XG
Precio: 48 €

F9124 Falda con estampado de flores
Colores:
▨ blanco/rosado (P, G, XG)
▨ azul marino/rojo (P, M, XG)
▨ anaranjado/amarillo (P, M, G, XG)
Tallas: P, M, G, XG
Precio: 57 €

Vocabulario 1

CD2-17

En la tienda

la bolsa	*purse*		la prenda	*garment*
la caja	*cash register*		el probador	*dressing room*
el efectivo	*cash*		la talla	*size (clothing)*
el número	*size (shoe)*		la tarjeta de crédito	*credit card*

Telas

el algodón	*cotton*		la mezclilla	*denim*
la lana	*wool*		la piel	*leather*
el lino	*linen*		la seda	*silk*

Estilos

a cuadros	*plaid*		de moda	*fashionable*
a rayas	*striped*		estampado	*patterned*
de lunares	*with polka dots*			

Verbos

hacer juego	*to match*		quedar	*to fit*
probarse (ue)	*to try on*			

Adjetivos

apretado	*tight*		grande	*large*
barato	*cheap, inexpensive*		hecho a mano	*handmade*
			liso	*solid*
caro	*expensive*		mediano	*medium*
chico	*small*		rebajado	*on sale*

Expresiones útiles

¡Qué pantalones tan elegantes!	*What elegant pants!*		¡Qué color tan bonito!	*What a pretty color!*
¡Qué lindos zapatos!	*What pretty shoes!*		¡Qué caros!	*How expensive!*
¡Qué bien te queda esa falda!	*That skirt really fits you well!*			

Comparaciones

mayor	*older (age)*		menor	*younger*
mejor	*better*		peor	*worse*

Demostrativos

aquel	*that (over there)*			
ese	*that*			
este	*this*			

Palabras adicionales

allá	*over there*
allí	*there*
aquí	*here*

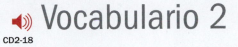
Vocabulario 2

CD2-18

El arte

el arte abstracto	*abstract art*
el autorretrato	*self-portrait*
la escultura	*sculpture*
la exhibición	*exhibit*
la galería	*gallery*
el grabado	*engraving; print*
la máscara	*mask*
el mural	*mural*
la naturaleza muerta	*still life*

la obra	*work (of art, literature, theater, etc.)*
el óleo	*oil painting*
el paisaje	*landscape*
la paleta	*pallet*
el pincel	*paintbrush*
el retrato	*portrait*
la tinta	*ink*

Verbos

acabar	*to finish*
apagar	*to turn off*
apreciar	*to appreciate; to enjoy*
descomponer	*to break down (a machine)*
diseñar	*to design*

esculpir	*to sculpt*
exhibir	*to exhibit*
olvidar	*to forget*
posar	*to pose*
quedar	*to remain (behind)*
romper	*to break*

Adjetivos

complicado	*complex*
conservador	*conservative*
cubista	*cubist*
impresionista	*impressionist*
realista	*realistic*

sencillo	*simple*
surrealista	*surrealist*
tradicional	*traditional*
vanguardista	*revolutionary; avant-garde*

Diccionario personal

_____

_____

_____

_____

_____

_____

_____

CAPÍTULO 12

Learning Strategy

Get a good dictionary

While you should not look up every Spanish word that you don't understand, a bilingual dictionary can be useful. Look for one that has complete entries, including idiomatic expressions. Ask your instructor for some recommendations. When you look up an English word for its Spanish translation, pay attention to the parts of speech. That way you won't select the wrong form, such as a noun when you want an adjective. If the entry has a number of options, look up some of the words in the Spanish-English section to ensure that you choose the correct word.

In this chapter you will learn how to:

- Talk about the future
- Talk about what you have done
- Discuss the environment
- Express your opinions and knowledge about the animal world and the environment
- Express doubt and certainty

¿Qué será del planeta?

© J.D. Dallet/age fotostock

La naturaleza nos ofrece las vistas más bellas del planeta y cada uno de sus componentes es vital para preservar el balance del medio ambiente.

El medio ambiente

la contaminación	contamination, pollution
la deforestación	deforestation
los desechos industriales	industrial waste
la ecología	ecology
el esmog	smog
la naturaleza	nature
el petróleo	oil
el reciclaje	recycling
los recursos naturales	natural resources

Los verbos

destruir	to destroy
preservar	to preserve
proteger	to protect

Otros lugares

la bahía	bay
el desierto	desert
el llano	plains
la pampa	grasslands
la península	peninsula
la selva	jungle
el valle	valley

Palabras adicionales

el árbol	tree
el cactus	cactus
la cascada	cascade, waterfall (small)
la catarata	waterfall (large)

INVESTIGUEMOS LA GRAMÁTICA

The verb **destruir** is conjugated similar to the verb **oír.**

La contaminación **destruye** la naturaleza.

Las compañías **destruyeron** el bosque.

A practicar

12.1 **Escucha y responde** Vas a escuchar una serie de ideas. Indica con el pulgar hacia arriba si la idea es lógica, y con el pulgar hacia abajo si es ilógica.

CD2-19

12.2 Un poco de lógica Decide cuál de las palabras completa la oración lógicamente.

1. Me encanta ir a la (costa / colina) y disfrutar del mar y de la arena.
2. En (el llano / la selva) hay muchos insectos y animales exóticos.
3. El (valle / cielo) está entre muchas montañas.
4. Unas de las (cataratas / pampas) más impresionantes son las del Niágara y las de Iguazú.
5. En un (bosque / desierto) hay muchos árboles.
6. En medio del valle hay (una isla / un lago).
7. El (esmog / petróleo) es un recurso natural no renovable.
8. Una península está rodeada (*surrounded*) por (el mar / las pampas) por tres lados.

12.3 ¿Cuál es diferente? Trabaja con un compañero para decidir qué palabra no corresponde (*belongs*) a la lista. Deben explicar por qué.

1. la montaña   el mar   el río   el lago
2. la costa   la bahía   la pampa   la península
3. el llano   las palmeras   el pasto   el árbol
4. las montañas   las colinas   la selva   el volcán
5. las cataratas   el medio ambiente   la ecología   la naturaleza
6. las olas   el mar   el valle   la arena

12.4 Las descripciones Trabaja con un compañero. Túrnense para describir las fotografías. Den todos los detalles posibles para cada fotografía.

1.

© Galyna Andrushko/Shutterstock

3.

© urosr/Shutterstock

2.

© Chris Howey/Shutterstock

4.

© javarman/Shutterstock

12.5 Opiniones Con un compañero, van a discutir si están de acuerdo o no con las siguientes afirmaciones, o si son verdaderas en el caso de ustedes. ¡OJO! Deben explicar por qué.

1. Me preocupa la ecología y por eso reciclo plásticos, papeles y aluminio.
2. Utilizo el transporte público para usar menos gasolina.
3. La contaminación del aire es un gran problema en mi comunidad.
4. Uso toda el agua que quiero porque se puede procesar y reciclar.
5. En realidad no tiene ningún impacto en la ecología lo que una persona hace.
6. Una persona tiene el derecho de hacer lo que quiera con su propiedad privada.
7. Es importante conservar nuestros recursos naturales.

El futuro del mundo son los niños; por eso es importante que ellos aprendan a cuidar nuestro planeta desde pequeños. En tu opinión, ¿a qué edad podemos empezar a enseñarles a los niños sobre el reciclaje? El siguiente es un artículo acerca de cómo y qué enseñarles a los niños. ¿Qué sugerencias se hacen? ¿Piensas que son buenas ideas?

Consejos de cómo explicar a los niños acerca del reciclaje de residuos

El día 17 de mayo se celebra el día mundial del reciclaje. Más que celebraciones, son necesarias actitudes día tras día. A partir de los 3 años de edad, los niños ya pueden aprender a separar los residuos. Al principio, la enseñanza viene del ejemplo que dan sus padres. Si, desde pequeño, el niño observa el cuidado y el hábito de separar los materiales (cristales, cartones, plástico, etc.), también compartirá del mismo comportamiento después. El cuidado del medio ambiente empieza dentro de nuestras casas.

Cómo explicar el reciclaje a los niños

Lo primero es enseñarles cómo seleccionar la basura y dónde debemos depositarla. Los residuos pueden ser separados en 5 grupos: el de papel, vidrio, plástico, restos de comida, y otros más orientados al aceite, juguetes, pilas, etc. Existen cinco tipos de contenedores donde debemos verter la basura:

1. Contenedor azul: destinado para el papel y cartón
2. Contenedor verde: destinado para el vidrio, cristal
3. Contenedor amarillo: para los envases de plástico y brik[1], aparte del metal
4. Contenedor gris: para los restos de comida, es decir, para la materia orgánica y también para otros tipo de restos como las plantas, los tapones de corcho, las telas, la tierra, cenizas, colillas, etc.
5. Contenedores complementarios: para tirar restos de aceite, juguetes rotos y pilas

© Margarita Casas

Por qué tenemos que reciclar

Es necesario explicar paso a paso el porqué tenemos que reciclar. Los niños necesitan saber el porqué de las cosas para poder hacerlo. Es necesario hacerles entender que el reciclaje existe para evitar la destrucción de nuestro medio ambiente.

Qué podemos hacer

Podemos seguir la regla de las cuatro erres: reducir, reutilizar, reciclar y recuperar. Reducir la cantidad de basura, reutilizar envases y bolsas, reciclar materiales como el plástico, y recuperar materiales para volver a utilizarlos.

Paralelamente a la educación medio ambiental que den a sus hijos, los padres también deben seguir algunas pautas de sugerencias en su día a día:

1. Elegir con cuidado los productos que se compran, considerando las posibilidades de reutilización de los envases
2. Evitar comprar los productos con demasiado envoltorio
3. Siempre que sea posible, reciclar las bolsas de supermercado para envolver la basura o para llevarlas cuando salgas de compras
4. Reciclar los papeles que utilizamos en casa, reutilizando ambas caras
5. Sacar fotocopias de doble faz
6. Hacer que los niños usen más la pizarra que los papeles
7. Comprar bebidas en botellas recuperables

[1]box, such as for juice

Más allá

Los consejos que leíste son para enseñarles a niños pequeños. ¿Qué se debe hacer para informar a más adultos sobre el reciclaje? Escribe cinco ideas.

Exploraciones gramaticales

A analizar

Lee el siguiente párrafo y observa las formas de los verbos. Luego, contesta las preguntas que siguen.

© advent/Shutterstock

> Si seguimos consumiendo recursos a este ritmo, dentro de menos de cien años los bosques **desaparecerán** totalmente y **necesitaremos** dos planetas del tamaño de la Tierra para satisfacer la demanda humana. Los recursos naturales se **harán** más escasos, ecosistemas completos **dejarán** de existir y muchas comunidades **tendrán** problemas relacionados con la agricultura y la salud. Si nosotros no protegemos este planeta, que es el único que tenemos, ¿quién lo **hará**?

1. In what tense are the verbs in bold: past, present, or future?

2. Using the examples in the paragraph above and what you already know about verb conjugation, complete the following verb chart.

yo necesitaré	nosotros _____
tú _____	vosotros _____
él, ella, usted _____	ellos, ellas, ustedes _____

yo haré	nosotros _____
tú _____	vosotros _____
él, ella, usted _____	ellos, ellas, ustedes _____

A comprobar

Future tense

1. You learned in **Capítulo 4** to express the future using the construction **ir** + **a** + infinitive. It is often used in spoken Spanish and generally refers to something that will happen in the near future. It is also common to use the present tense to express near future.

   Voy a pescar en el lago este fin de semana.
   I'm going to fish at the lake this weekend.

   Salgo para las montañas mañana.
   I'm leaving for the mountains tomorrow.

2. Another way to express what will happen is to use the future tense; however, it tends to be a little more formal and is generally used to refer to a more distant future. To form the future tense, add the endings to the infinitive (rather than to the verb stem, as is done with most other verb tenses). Note that **-ar, -er,** and **-ir** verbs take the same endings.

hablar			
yo	hablar**é**	nosotros(as)	hablar**emos**
tú	hablar**ás**	vosotros(as)	hablar**éis**
él, ella, usted	hablar**á**	ellos, ellas, ustedes	hablar**án**

volver			
yo	volver**é**	nosotros(as)	volver**emos**
tú	volver**ás**	vosotros(as)	volver**éis**
él, ella, usted	volver**á**	ellos, ellas, ustedes	volver**án**

ir			
yo	ir**é**	nosotros(as)	ir**emos**
tú	ir**ás**	vosotros(as)	ir**éis**
él, ella, usted	ir**á**	ellos, ellas, ustedes	ir**án**

The following are irregular stems for the future tense:

decir	**dir-**	querer	**querr-**
haber	**habr-**	saber	**sabr-**
hacer	**har-**	salir	**saldr-**
poder	**podr-**	tener	**tendr-**
poner	**pondr-**	venir	**vendr-**

Habrá 20 personas en la excursión.
*There **will be** 20 people on the excursion.*

Los turistas **irán** a la isla primero.
*The tourists **will go** to the island first.*

Allí **verán** el volcán.
*There **they will see** the volcano.*

3. The future tense is also used to express probability or to speculate about present conditions.

Si Octavio no está aquí, **estará** enfermo.
If Octavio is not here, he might be sick.

¿Quién **será**?
Who could it be? (Who might it be?)

Imagino que el presidente **tendrá** unos cincuenta años.
*I imagine the president **must be** about 50 years old.*

A practicar

12.6 **Predicciones para el futuro** Lee las siguientes predicciones para el año 2050 y decide si estás de acuerdo o no. Explica tu respuesta.

1. El cielo será gris a consecuencia de la contaminación.
2. Los políticos crearán más leyes para proteger la naturaleza.
3. No dependeremos tanto del petróleo.
4. No existirán muchos de los animales que existen hoy en día.
5. Habrá menos agua potable en el mundo.
6. La gente tendrá menos aparatos eléctricos.
7. Los edificios se harán con materiales reciclados.
8. Los científicos podrán clonar animales que se extinguieron hace mucho tiempo.

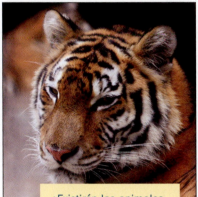

¿Existirán los animales que existen hoy en día?

© Pshenichka/Shutterstock

12.7 **Nace un ecologista** Toño hace una lista de sus resoluciones para el año nuevo. Usa el futuro simple para completar las ideas.

1. Yo _____ (usar) menos electricidad y _____ (apagar) las luces al salir de un cuarto.
2. Yo les _____ (decir) a mis amigos que deben comprar solamente productos ecológicos.
3. En el supermercado mi esposa y yo _____ (pedir) solamente bolsas de papel o _____ (tener) bolsas de tela reusables.
4. Nosotros no _____ (conducir) un coche que consuma mucha gasolina; _____ (comprar) uno más económico.
5. Yo les _____ (explicar) a mis hijos que es importante reciclar y ellos _____ (aprender) a proteger el medio ambiente.
6. No _____ (llevar) a mis hijos a la escuela en coche; nosotros _____ (poder) conversar mientras caminamos juntos a la escuela.

12.8 **En busca de...** Pregúntales a ocho personas diferentes si harán las siguientes actividades después de terminar el curso (semestre, trimestre, etcétera). Después pídeles información adicional para reportársela a la clase. Recuerden que necesitan buscar a alguien que conteste que **sí**.

> **Modelo** seguir estudiando el español (¿Dónde?)
> Estudiante 1: *Seguirás estudiando español?*
> Estudiante 2: *Sí, seguiré estudiando español.*
> Estudiante 1: *¿Dónde?*
> Estudiante 2: *Tendré otra clase en esta universidad.*

1. hacer un viaje (¿Adónde?)
2. buscar un trabajo (¿Qué tipo de trabajo?)
3. obtener un título (*diploma*) (¿En qué carrera [*major*]?)
4. volver a la universidad para el próximo curso (¿Qué clases tomará?)
5. salir con amigos para celebrar (¿Adónde?)
6. casarse (¿Cuándo?)
7. no poder descansar (¿Qué hará?)
8. mudarse (*to move*) (¿Adónde?)

12.9 **En el año 2030** Túrnense para hacer predicciones sobre el año 2030 en las siguientes categorías. Tu compañero te dirá también lo que piensa. Sean originales.

> **Modelo** la salud
> Estudiante 1: *Los científicos encontrarán una medicina para curar el cáncer.*
> Estudiante 2: *Es posible, pero habrá nuevas enfermedades.*

1. la escuela	5. las vacaciones
2. el trabajo	6. los amigos
3. la casa	7. el dinero
4. la familia	8. ¿?

12.10 **¿Qué pasará?** Mira los dibujos. Con un compañero, expresen conjeturas sobre las circunstancias. Piensen en quiénes son, por qué están allí, cuál es la situación, cómo se sienten y qué harán después.

> **Modelo** *Seguramente ellos serán esposos y estarán de vacaciones en una isla. Imagino que será su primer aniversario y estarán muy felices. Creo que cada noche saldrán a comer y a bailar.*

 iTunes
Listen to Mexican pop singer Paulina Rubio's song "Volverás." What will her ex do?

1.

2.

3.

4.

5.

Conexiones culturales
La diversidad geográfica

Cultura

Algunos artistas se dedican a plasmar (*to create*) los paisajes de su tierra. Estos artistas reciben el nombre de paisajistas. Uno de los paisajistas más famosos en la historia de México fue Gerardo Murillo (1875–1964). Murillo es más conocido como "Dr. Atl", que significa "agua" en náhuatl. En su juventud, recibió una beca *(scholarship)* del gobierno mexicano para estudiar en Europa. Murillo recibió un doctorado en Filosofía y Derecho de la Universidad de Roma en 1898. Su estancia en Europa influyó en él por el contacto que tuvo con el arte del renacimiento italiano, y con el movimiento impresionista de ese tiempo. A su regreso comenzó a pintar activamente y a enseñar arte. En 1920 estudió vulcanología. Por su interés en los volcanes, los pintó en numerosos cuadros. A la derecha aparece una reproducción de uno de sus paisajes. ¿Qué hay en el paisaje? ¿Conoces algún paisajista famoso de los Estados Unidos o de algún otro país?

Volcán Iztaccíhuatl

© Volcan Iztaccíhuatl (oil on canvas), Atl, Dr. (Gerardo Murillo) (1875-1964)/Private Collection Photo: Michel Zabe/AZA INBA/The Bridgeman Art Library International

🌐 Investiga en Internet la leyenda relacionada con los volcanes Popocatepl e Iztaccíhuatl.

Conexiones... a la geografía

Algunos parques nacionales que se localizan en países donde se habla español son lugares espectaculares gracias a su localización. Entre los más espectaculares se encuentran los parques al sur de Argentina y Chile. Uno de los más conocidos es el Parque Nacional Los Glaciares, que es el segundo más grande de Argentina. Fue creado en 1937 y declarado Patrimonio de la Humanidad por la UNESCO en 1980. En Chile también hay numerosos parques nacionales, entre los que se distingue el Parque Nacional Torres del Paine, en la región antártica chilena. Aunque fue fundado en 1959, recibió su nombre actual en 1970, y en 1978 la UNESCO lo nombró Reserva Mundial de la Biosfera. En ambos parques pueden admirarse también algunos glaciares impresionantes. Los glaciares son masas de hielo compactado que tardan miles de años en formarse. Son una importante fuente de agua potable, pero la mayoría de los glaciares del mundo está desapareciendo a una velocidad alarmante.

Investiga qué parques nacionales son el orgullo de estos y de otros países hispanos. ¿Qué los hace tan especiales?

Glaciar Perito Moreno en la Patagonia argentina

© Margarita Casas

Comparaciones

Biodiversidad es un término que se usa para referirse a la gran variedad de especies que habitan nuestro planeta. Gracias a la diversidad geográfica de algunos países, estos tienen también una enorme variedad de animales y plantas.

El lago Titikaka

- El 25% de la tierra de Costa Rica está protegido a través de parques nacionales, mientras que solo el 15% de Venezuela está protegido. ¿Qué porcentaje del territorio de los Estados Unidos está protegido?

- Colombia tiene el segundo lugar en especies vegetales, con 49 000 especies diferentes. Solamente Brasil cuenta con más especies, pero tiene un territorio siete veces más grande que el de Colombia. ¿Cuántas especies vegetales hay en los Estados Unidos y cómo se compara al tamaño de Colombia?

- Colombia tiene el 19,4% de todas las aves (birds) del mundo. (África entera el 15%.) Otro país con una biodiversidad impresionante es Costa Rica, que tiene más variedades de aves (850) que los Estados Unidos y Europa juntos. ¿Cuántas especies de aves hay en los Estados Unidos?

- México tiene el 10% de toda la biodiversidad del mundo. ¿Qué porcentaje de biodiversidad tienen los Estados Unidos?

- El volcán más alto del mundo está en la región entre Argentina y Chile: el Nevado Ojos del Salado. Tiene una altura de 6870 metros ¿Cuál es el volcán más alto de Norteamérica y qué altura tiene?

- El lago navegable más alto del mundo es el lago Titikaka, entre Bolivia y Perú. ¿Sabes cuál es el lago más alto de Norteamérica?

- La catarata más alta del mundo es El Salto del Ángel en Venezuela. ¿Cuál es la segunda?

- El desierto de Atacama en Chile es el más seco del mundo. ¿Sabes cuál es el desierto más grande?

Comunidad

Elige un lugar que te parezca muy importante conservar y diseña un cartel en español con los datos más importantes sobre el lugar. Después da razones para protegerlo.

Palabras útiles

apreciar	preservar
educar	el equilibrio
proteger	el cambio
la interdependencia	climático
cuidar	

La selva en Nicaragua

© Monkey Business Images/Shutterstock

A analizar

Lee las siguientes oraciones y contesta las preguntas al final.

Mi esposa y yo **hemos hecho** muchas cosas increíbles. Ella **ha escalado** varias montañas, y yo **he explorado** una selva. Juntos, **hemos nadado** en el mar y **hemos visto** unas cataratas impresionantes. Todavía no **hemos explorado** un volcán, pero nuestro próximo viaje será a El Salvador, en donde escalaremos uno.

1. You will recognize the past participles (**hecho, nadado, visto,** etc.) in the paragraph above. How does their usage differ from those you learned in **Capítulo 11**?

2. Do the verbs express past, present, or future?

A comprobar

Present perfect

1. The present perfect is used to express actions that we have and have not done. It combines the present tense of the verb **haber** with the past participle.

haber			
yo	**he**	nosotros(as)	**hemos**
tú	**has**	vosotros(as)	**habéis**
él, ella, usted	**ha**	ellos, ellas, ustedes	**han**

2. You will remember from **Capítulo 11** that to form the regular past participles, you need to add **-ado** to the end of the stem of **-ar** verbs, and **-ido** to the stem of **-er** and **-ir** verbs.

hablar	habl**ado**
beber	beb**ido**
vivir	viv**ido**

The following verbs have accents in the past participles:

creer	**creído**	oír	**oído**
leer	**leído**	traer	**traído**

3. When using the past participle with **estar,** it must agree in gender and number with the subject because it functions as an adjective. However, when using the participle with **haber,** it is part of the verb, and it does not agree with the subject.

> Ella **ha trabajado** mucho esta semana.
> Ellos **han ido** a la costa.

4. When using direct object, indirect object, or reflexive pronouns, they are placed in front of the conjugated form of **haber.**

> No **se** han despertado todavía.
> Ya lo he visto.

5. In Spanish, the present perfect is generally used as it is in English to talk about something that has happened or something that someone has done. It is usually either unimportant when it happened or it has some relation to the present.

> ¿Alguna vez **has ido** a las montañas?
> *Have you* ever *gone* to the mountains?

> **He perdido** el mapa y no sé dónde estamos.
> *I've lost* the map and don't know where we are.

¿Te acuerdas?

Remember the irregular past participles from **Capítulo 11.** Note the past participle of **despertar** becomes **despertado** when it is used in the present perfect.

abrir	**abierto**	romper	**roto**
decir	**dicho**	poner	**puesto**
escribir	**escrito**	ver	**visto**
hacer	**hecho**	volver	**vuelto**
morir	**muerto**	devolver	**devuelto**

6. The following expressions are often used with the present perfect:

alguna vez	*ever*
no... todavía	*not . . . yet, still . . . not*
nunca	*never*
recientemente	*recently*
ya	*already*

Ya hemos ido a esa playa.
*We have **already** been to that beach.*

No han llegado **todavía**.
*They have **not** arrived **yet**.*

¿**Alguna vez** has escalado una montaña?
*Have you **ever** climbed a mountain?*

> **INVESTIGUEMOS LA GRAMÁTICA**
> In Spain it is much more common to use the present perfect rather than the preterite when referring to anything that happened that same day.
>
> Hemos nadado en el mar esta mañana.
> *We swam in the sea this morning.*

A practicar

12.11 **¿Son ecológicos?** Lee lo que dice Adela sobre sus actividades y las de sus amigos y familiares. Decide si las diferentes actividades son ecológicas o no. Explica tu respuesta.

1. Yo siempre he comprado agua en botellas de plástico.
2. Mis amigos y yo hemos empezado a reciclar papel.
3. Esta semana mis amigos han ido a la universidad en autobús.
4. Mi hermano siempre se ha bañado todos los días por veinte minutos.
5. Este año mis padres han puesto un jardín con verduras al lado de la casa.
6. Mi tío siempre ha preferido tener un coche grande.
7. Mis padres y yo siempre hemos pedido bolsas de plástico en el supermercado.
8. Este verano he abierto las ventanas en vez de encender el aire acondicionado.

12.12 **¿Qué has hecho?** Con un compañero, completen las siguientes oraciones con información sobre sus experiencias personales.

Modelo Yo he ido a...
Yo he ido a Puerto Rico. / Yo he ido a una isla.

1. He estado en...
2. He vivido en...
3. He roto...
4. He escrito...
5. He hecho...
6. He visto...
7. He comido...
8. He comprado...

12.13 **De campamento** Martín y su amigo Gerardo están en un campamento en la tundra argentina. Completa su historia con verbos lógicos de la lista, usando la forma necesaria del presente perfecto.

Este es nuestro quinto día de excursión. Hasta ahora, (**1.**) _____
(caminar) más de 100 kilómetros, pero no (**2.**) _____ (ver) ningún
animal salvaje, excepto un grupo de castores (*beavers*) que (**3.**) _____
(destruir) muchos árboles. Es una lástima ver tantos árboles destruidos. Hace mucho
frío por la noche y por eso yo no (**4.**) _____ (dormir) bien y me siento
muy cansado. Además, yo tampoco (**5.**) _____ (comer) muy bien porque
Gerardo trajo una comida enlatada (*canned*) horrible. Sin embargo, debo admitir
que todos nosotros (**6.**) _____ (divertirse) mucho. A Gerardo le encanta
la fotografía y (**7.**) _____ (tomar) muchas fotos para compartir a nuestro
regreso. ¿Alguna vez (**8.**) _____ (hacer) tú este tipo de excursión?

12.14 ¿Quién lo ha hecho? Con un compañero, túrnense para preguntar y contestar quién ha hecho las siguientes actividades. Si pueden, mencionen otros datos sobre la persona.

Modelo cantar desde (*since*) su niñez
Estudiante 1: *¿Quién ha cantado desde su niñez?*
Estudiante 2: *Christina Aguilera.*

1. escribir más de quince novelas
2. ganar un Grammy
3. hacerse famoso como comediante
4. jugar con los Boston Red Sox
5. no estar de acuerdo con la política de los Estados Unidos
6. vender más de 30 millones de álbumes
7. ser político por más de doce años
8. producir películas

a. Christina Aguilera
b. Julieta Venegas
c. Carlos Santana
d. Hugo Chávez
e. Antonio Banderas
f. Felipe Calderón
g. George López
h. Isabel Allende
i. David Ortiz

12.15 ¿Qué ha pasado? Trabaja con un compañero para describir lo que ha pasado en los dibujos. Usen el presente perfecto y den muchos detalles.

Modelo *Ella ha venido a la playa con un amigo. El amigo ha ido a nadar y ella se ha dormido y se ha quemado.*

12.16 Alguna vez En grupos de tres o cuatro pregúntense si alguna vez han hecho las siguientes actividades. Luego repórtenle la información a la clase.

¿Alguna vez...?

1. nadar en el mar ¿dónde?
2. ver un volcán ¿dónde?
3. ir a una isla ¿cuál?
4. navegar en un río ¿en cuál?
5. escalar una montaña ¿cuál?
6. pescar en un lago ¿qué?
7. perderse en un bosque ¿qué hizo?
8. estar en una selva ¿dónde?

El volcán Cotopaxi en Ecuador

© Steve Herrmann/Shutterstock

12.17 Este año Entrevista a tu compañero sobre lo que ha hecho este año.

Modelo leer un libro (¿Cuál?)

Estudiante 1: *¿Has leído un libro este año?*
Estudiante 2: *Sí, he leído un libro.*
Estudiante 1: *¿Cuál?*
Estudiante 2: *Leí* Cien años de soledad.

1. hacer un viaje (¿Adónde?)
2. escribir una carta (¿A quién?)
3. visitar a unos amigos o parientes (¿Qué hicieron?)
4. mudarse (*to move*) (¿Adónde?)
5. tener una fiesta (¿Cuándo?)
6. comprar un coche (¿Qué coche?)
7. ir a un concierto (¿De quién?)
8. encontrar un nuevo trabajo (¿Dónde?)

12.18 Hechos Con un compañero, túrnense para hablar de lo que han hecho con respecto a los siguientes temas.

Modelo compras

Estudiante 1: *Yo he comprado una casa.*
Estudiante 2: *¿De veras? Yo he comprado un coche nuevo este año.*

1. estudios   5. comida
2. trabajos   6. deportes
3. viajes   7. hazañas (*feats*)
4. relaciones   8. ¿?

12.19 Latinos famosos Identifica a los latinos en las fotos. Luego menciona todo lo que puedas sobre lo que han hecho.

Modelo *Es Rafael Nadal. Ha jugado al tenis desde los cuatro años. Ha ganado una medalla de oro en las Olimpiadas y ha ganado Wimbledon dos veces.*

© lev radin/Shutterstock

1.
© Gustavo Miguel Fernandes/Shutterstock

2.
© Helga Esteb/Shutterstock

3.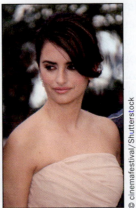
© cinemafestival/Shutterstock

4.
© Debby Wong/Shutterstock

Lectura

Antes de leer

1. ¿Alguna vez has visitado un parque nacional? ¿Cuál?

2. ¿Puedes nombrar algunos parques nacionales famosos en los Estados Unidos? ¿Por qué es importante mantener los parques nacionales?

A leer

Los parques nacionales de Costa Rica y de Ecuador

Costa Rica fue uno de los primeros países en Latinoamérica en reconocer la importancia de la protección de los recursos naturales. Desde 1970, casi el 25% de su territorio ha sido declarado parque nacional o zona de protección.

Costa Rica es un país que se distingue por su respeto a la ecología y a la preservación del medio ambiente. Su sistema de parques nacionales refleja la preocupación por

[es un país que se distingue por su respeto a la ecología y a la preservación del medio ambiente]

Una cascada en La Paz, Costa Rica

conservar la flora y la fauna del país. El éxito de sus parques nacionales es evidente al contemplar los hermosos paisajes de este país: cascadas cristalinas, playas, montañas y ríos para explorar, así como sitios arqueológicos e históricos.

Esto ha sido posible gracias a que los costarricenses consideran el **ambientalismo** una responsabilidad nacional. En este pequeño país existen 205 especies de mamíferos, 845 especies de aves (pájaros), 160 especies de anfibios, 218 especies de reptiles y 1013 especies de peces de agua dulce.

Los parques nacionales de Costa Rica también son de una gran importancia económica ya que se han convertido en importantes centros de atracción para los turistas ecológicos que visitan Costa Rica. El país ha desarrollado una importante infraestructura hotelera para satisfacer la demanda de este turismo sin **dañar** al medio ambiente. Costa Rica es, sin duda, un ejemplo a seguir en materia de ecología.

Ecuador es otro país pequeño que también cuenta con una red importante de reservas ecológicas y parques nacionales públicos y privados. De entre todos sus

environmentalism

harming

parques, no hay duda de que el más conocido es el Parque Nacional Galápagos, establecido en 1959. Se calcula que las islas se formaron hace más de ocho millones de años, pero fueron descubiertas apenas en 1535 por casualidad. Por mucho tiempo las Galápagos fueron utilizadas por piratas ingleses como escondite. Las islas se hicieron famosas originalmente porque Darwin concibió su teoría de la evolución gracias a lo que observó en estas islas.

En la actualidad, el Parque Nacional Galápagos está compuesto por más de 30 islas y tiene una extensión de 693 700 hectáreas. En él abundan especies que no existen en ninguna otra parte del mundo, por lo que tiene mucha importancia. Debido al delicado equilibrio de las islas, existen guías de **comportamiento** muy específicas para los visitantes. Por ejemplo, no es posible visitar las islas sin un guía especializado; no se debe acercar a ningún animal a menos de dos metros, para no alterar su comportamiento; no se debe introducir ningún organismo vivo, y jamás se deben comprar recuerdos que incluyan partes de animales. A pesar de estas rigurosas reglas, las Galápagos están en la lista de Patrimonio Universal en **peligro,** y hay quien piensa que eventualmente se prohibirá el acceso a los visitantes.

behavior

danger

Pelícanos en las islas Galápagos

Comprensión

1. ¿Qué porcentaje del territorio costarricense ocupan los parques nacionales y las zonas de protección?
2. ¿Cómo muestra Costa Rica el respeto por su tierra?
3. ¿Dónde es evidente el éxito de los parques nacionales?
4. ¿Por qué los parques nacionales tienen una gran importancia económica?
5. ¿Desde hace cuántos años existe el Parque Nacional Galápagos?
6. ¿Por qué se hicieron famosas las Galápagos?
7. ¿Cuáles son dos reglas importantes que se deben seguir cuando se visitan las islas?
8. En tu opinión ¿tienen los Estados Unidos una estrategia de conservación similar a la de Costa Rica? Explica las semejanzas y diferencias.

Después de leer

Costa Rica es uno de los países latinoamericanos que más se esfuerza (*makes an effort*) por proteger su ecología. Escoge otro país de hispanohablantes e investiga lo que hacen sus habitantes para conservar la naturaleza. Luego, descríbele a la clase el área y los esfuerzos que se hacen para protegerla.

La vida en una granja no es fácil. Hay muchos animales que cuidar.

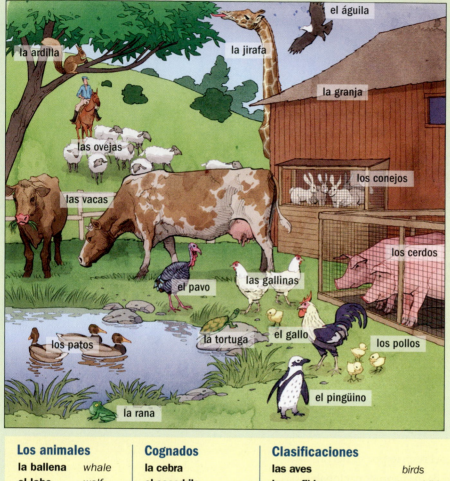

Los animales

la ballena	whale
el lobo	wolf
el mono	monkey
el oso	bear
el tiburón	shark
el toro	bull
el venado	deer
el zorro	fox

Cognados

la cebra
el cocodrilo
el elefante
el gorila
el jaguar
el león
la llama
la serpiente
el tigre

Clasificaciones

las aves	birds
los anfibios	amphibians
los mamíferos	mammals
los reptiles	reptiles

Palabras adicionales

cazar	to hunt
la caza	hunting
la jaula	cage
el peligro (de extinción)	danger (of extinction)

Práctica

12.20 Escucha y responde Escucharás algunas ideas sobre el hábitat de los animales. Si piensas que una idea es cierta, levanta la mano. Si es falsa, no hagas nada.

CD2-20

12.21 **Identificaciones** Decide a qué grupo corresponden los siguientes animales.

| anfibio | ave | mamífero | pez | reptil |

Modelo el gorila *mamífero*

1. el cocodrilo
2. el pingüino
3. el tiburón
4. el águila
5. la serpiente
6. la llama
7. la gallina
8. el delfín
9. la rana

12.22 **La personalidad de los animales** Observa la lista de descripciones y con un compañero decidan qué animales se asocian con cada descripción. Luego decidan si son verdaderos estos estereotipos de los animales o si son mentira. Expliquen por qué.

Modelo tonto
el burro, la vaca

1. inteligente
2. loco
3. chistoso
4. sucio
5. limpio
6. leal (*loyal*)
7. perezoso
8. majestuoso

12.23 **Asociaciones** ¿Qué sabes de estos animales? Con un compañero, túrnense para dar una idea informativa sobre los animales. Deben usar por lo menos una palabra de la siguiente lista.

| selva | bosque | mar | basura | huevos |
| ratones | domesticado | peligroso | desierto | |

Modelo ballenas–océanos
Las ballenas viven en los océanos.

1. osos
2. leones
3. zorros
4. delfines
5. tortugas
6. serpientes
7. lobos
8. vacas

12.24 **Los alebrijes** Los alebrijes son animales fantásticos que se hacen con madera en el estado de Oaxaca en México. Estas artesanías mezclan diferentes partes de animales. Por ejemplo, un alebrije puede tener cabeza de coyote, alas de gallina y patas (*feet*) de cocodrilo.

Debes inventar un alebrije y dibujarlo. Después, trabaja con un compañero y túrnense para describir sus alebrijes. Mientras un estudiante describe su alebrije, el otro estudiante deberá dibujarlo sin ver el dibujo original.

Alebrijes de Oaxaca, México

© Margarita Casas

Vocabulario útil: **ala** *wing* **pata** *leg* **plumas** *feathers*
cola *tail* **lomo** *back*

12.25 **Entrevista** Entrevista a un compañero con las siguientes preguntas.

1. Aparte de tus mascotas, ¿cuál es tu animal favorito? ¿Por qué?
2. ¿Piensas que los derechos de los animales son importantes? ¿Por qué?
3. ¿Con qué frecuencia vas al zoológico? ¿Qué animales prefieres visitar?
4. ¿Te gustaría (*Would you like*) vivir con muchos animales en una granja? ¿Por qué?
5. ¿Te gustaría hacer un safari? ¿Por qué?

¿Cuáles son algunos animales en peligro de extinción? El siguiente artículo habla de algunos animales que están en peligro ahora. ¿Cuáles son? ¿Por qué están en peligro de extinción?

Cuatro especies animales en peligro de extinción en 2010

publicado el viernes 21 mayo 2010 por Me en: Animales Naturaleza EcoComunicados Información Peligro de Extinción

Esta es una de esas listas que nunca es inoportuno recordar: la de **los animales más amenazados, aquellos que están a un paso de extinguirse en la naturaleza y, en el caso de algunos, de desaparecer definitivamente de la faz de este planeta.** Tal es el caso del rinoceronte de Java, el mamífero grande más raro de la Tierra y del que quedan 70 ejemplares en toda la Tierra.

El pingüino de Magallanes, bautizado en honor al explorador Fernando de Magallanes, con quien se encontró en 1520, vive en las costas de Argentina, Chile y las Islas Malvinas. Está amenazado por la pesca comercial y el cambio en las corrientes oceánicas y en la temperatura del mar. El Fondo Mundial para la Naturaleza cree que estas pudieron ser las razones de que, **en 2009, cientos de estos pingüinos aparecieran muy enfermos o muertos en las playas de Río de Janeiro.**

Pingüinos de Magallanes en Argentina

La vaquita marina no es de las especies marinas más conocidas. **De esta marsopa endémica de México no existen, de acuerdo con la organización Vaquita Marina, más de 600 individuos en el mundo.** Habita en el Golfo de California y la principal amenaza que enfrenta son las redes pesqueras, en las que anualmente mueren atrapados entre 40 y 80 ejemplares.

El murciélago de Florida, Eumops floridanus, solo vive en el sur del estado estadounidense de Florida. Es uno de los murciélagos más grandes y raros, y las autoridades de Florida lo han clasificado como amenazado pues, **de acuerdo con Bats Conservation International,** la especie solo ha sido vista pocas veces desde 1960.

Source: Ecología blog

Más allá

Cada región del mundo tiene especies de animales que están en peligro de extinción, o especies que se han convertido en plagas y amenazan a otros animales. Con un compañero, elijan a uno de estos animales y expliquen cuál es su situación y qué se debe hacer para corregir el problema.

A analizar

Lee las siguientes oraciones y observa los verbos en negritas. Luego, contesta las preguntas.

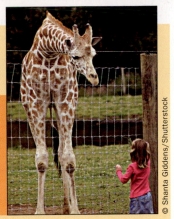

Es buena idea que **visitemos** el zoológico este fin de semana.

Es probable que yo **lleve** a toda la familia.

Es una lástima (*a shame*) que no **vayas** con nosotros.

Es posible que **haya** jirafas sin manchas (*spots*).

Es interesante que los chimpancés **sean** muy sociables.

1. The verbs in bold are subjunctive. What verb form is similar?
2. What expressions precede the verbs?

A comprobar

Subjunctive with impersonal expressions

Until now, all the verb tenses you have studied (present, preterite, imperfect, future, etc.) have been in the indicative. The indicative is an objective mood that is used to state facts and to talk about things that you are certain have occurred or will occur.

> **Las águilas están en peligro.**   *Eagles are endangered.*

In contrast, the subjunctive is a subjective mood that is used to convey uncertainty, anticipated or hypothetical events, or the subject's wishes, fears, doubts, and emotional reactions.

> **Es terrible que las águilas desaparezcan.**   *It is terrible (that) the eagles may disappear.*

The present subjunctive

1. You will notice that the subjunctive verb forms are very similar to formal commands. To form the present subjunctive, drop the -**o** from the first person (**yo**) present tense form and add the opposite ending. Add the -**er** endings for -**ar** verbs, and the -**ar** endings for -**er** and -**ir** verbs.

hablar	
hable	hablemos
hables	habléis
hable	hablen

comer	
coma	comamos
comas	comáis
coma	coman

vivir	
viva	vivamos
vivas	viváis
viva	vivan

2. Verbs that are irregular in the first person present indicative have the same stem in the present subjunctive.

> Es importante que **conduzcas** con cuidado porque hay venados.

3. Stem-changing -**ar** and -**er** verbs follow the same pattern as in the present indicative, changing in all forms except the **nosotros** and **vosotros** forms.

> Es bueno que **podamos** hacer algo, pero es necesario que todos **empiecen** a pensar en el medio ambiente.

4. Stem-changing -**ir** verbs follow the same pattern as in the present indicative, however there is an additional change in the **nosotros** and **vosotros** forms. The additional stem change is similar to that in the third person preterite (**e → i** and **o → u**).

> Es mejor que nosotros **durmamos** en la casa y que los animales **duerman** afuera.

5. You will recall that the formal commands of verbs whose infinitives end in -**car**, -**gar**, and -**zar** have spelling changes. These same spelling changes occur in the subjunctive as well. There is also a spelling change for verbs ending in -**ger**; change the **g** to **j** and add the subjunctive ending.

> Es terrible que no se **proteja** a los animales.

> Es malo que el gallo **empiece** a cantar tan temprano.

6. The subjunctive of the following verbs is irregular: **dar** (**dé**), **haber** (**haya**), **ir** (**vaya**), **saber** (**sepa**), and **ser** (**sea**). You will notice that once again the subjunctive form is similar to the formal command forms.

> Es imposible que **vayas** a la granja mañana.

> Es horrible que **haya** tantos animales en peligro de extinción.

7. Impersonal expressions do not have a specific subject and can include a large number of adjectives: **es bueno, es difícil, es importante, es triste,** etc. They can be negative or affirmative.

The following are impersonal expressions:

es buena/mala idea	es mejor	es ridículo
es horrible	es necesario	es terrible
es imposible	es posible	es una lástima
es increíble	es probable	*(it's a shame)*
es justo	es raro	es urgente
(it's fair)	es recomendable	

8. When using an impersonal expression to convey an opinion or an emotional reaction, it is necessary to use the subjunctive with it. While in English the conjunction *that* is optional, in Spanish, it is necessary to use the **que** between the clauses.

> **Es importante que protejamos** a los animales.
> *It is important that we protect the animals.*

> **Es una lástima que haya** animales en peligro de extinción.
> *It's a shame (that) there are animals in danger of extinction.*

INVESTIGUEMOS LA GRAMÁTICA

When there is no specific subject, the infinitive is generally used after the impersonal expression.

Es imposible ver a todos los animales.
It is impossible to see all the animals.

A practicar

12.26 **Es lógico** Combina las dos columnas para crear ideas lógicas.

1. No es necesario que yo...
2. Es importante que todos nosotros...
3. Es urgente que el gobierno...
4. Es mejor que tú...
5. Es increíble que unos animales...

a. haga leyes (*laws*) para proteger la ecología.
b. se extingan rápidamente.
c. compre ropa o zapatos de piel.
d. pensemos en las otras criaturas que también viven en la tierra.
e. sigas las regulaciones de la caza.

12.27 **¿Es buena idea?** Un amigo vive en un apartamento y va a adoptar una nueva mascota. Lee las siguientes afirmaciones, decide si son buenas ideas o no, y completa las oraciones con la forma necesaria del subjuntivo del verbo entre paréntesis.

(No) Es buena idea que él...

1. _____ (buscar) un animal de un refugio (*shelter*).

2. _____ (decidir) si quiere un perro o un gato.

3. le _____ (pagar) un depósito al propietario del apartamento.

4. _____ (adoptar) un perro grande.

5. _____ (consultar) con su compañero de casa.

6. _____ (tener) prisa al tomar su decisión.

iTunes
Joaquín Sabina is one of the more famous contemporary Spanish composers and musicians. Listen to his song "Es mentira." What are the lies mentioned in the song? Why does the person lie?

12.28 **En un zoológico loco** Con un compañero, miren el dibujo y túrnense para hablar sobre sus reacciones/recomendaciones, usando expresiones impersonales y el subjuntivo.

Modelo *Es raro que no haya hielo en la jaula de los pingüinos.*

12.29 **El safari** Un amigo va a hacer un safari en Guinea Ecuatorial. Hablen sobre sus reacciones/recomendaciones, completando las siguientes oraciones.

1. Es buena idea que...   5. Es mala idea que...
2. Es necesario que...   6. Es probable que...
3. Es importante que...   7. Es imposible que...
4. Es recomendable que...   8. Es increíble que...

12.30 **Consejos para un amigo** Trabaja con un compañero para darle al menos seis consejos a una persona que piensa asistir a tu universidad. Deben usar expresiones impersonales diferentes y el subjuntivo. Luego compartan los consejos con la clase.

Modelo *Es buena idea que viva cerca de la universidad.*

Cultura

En todas las culturas, los animales han sido usados para protagonizar cuentos para niños, fábulas y otras historias. El escritor guatemalteco Augusto Monterroso utilizó animales para escribir fábulas modernas, muchas veces impregnadas de crítica social y de un humor cínico. Monterroso (1921–2003) nació en Honduras, pero su familia era de Guatemala, y allí creció. Debido a cuestiones políticas, tuvo que exiliarse en 1944. Al principio vivió en Chile y Bolivia, y finalmente se mudó a México, en donde vivió la mayor parte de su vida. Es famoso por sus cuentos cortos, y es también el autor del cuento más corto de la historia de la literatura universal: *Y cuando despertó, el dinosaurio todavía estaba allí.*

La siguiente fábula es una de las más conocidas de Monterroso.

La fábula del burro y la flauta

Investiga en Internet otras fábulas hispanohablantes.

El burro y la flauta

Tirada en el campo estaba desde hacía tiempo una Flauta que ya nadie tocaba, hasta que un día un Burro que paseaba por ahí resopló fuerte sobre ella haciéndola producir el sonido más dulce de su vida, es decir, de la vida del Burro y de la Flauta.

Incapaces de comprender lo que había pasado, pues la racionalidad no era su fuerte y ambos creían en la racionalidad, se separaron presurosos, avergonzados de lo mejor que el uno y el otro habían hecho durante su triste existencia.

En tu opinión ¿cuál es la crítica que hace el autor en esta fábula?

Comunidad

En muchas partes del mundo hispanohablante hay organizaciones que necesitan voluntarios para proteger, curar y darles albergue a animales. Aún si no puedes viajar a alguno de estos países, considera dedicar unas horas para trabajar de voluntario en algún albergue de tu comunidad, especialmente si necesitan a una persona que hable español.

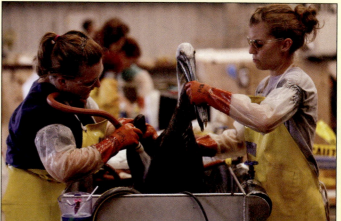

© A.J. Sisco/UPI/Landov

Voluntarias limpian a algunos pelicanos después del desastre petrolero en el Golfo de México.

Comparaciones

Se calcula que existen de 5 a 50 millones de especies diversas en nuestro planeta, aunque hasta la fecha solo se han descrito alrededor de 1.4 millones.

El número total de especies conocidas en cada país es muy diferente. Algunos países son mucho más biodiversos que otros. Por ejemplo, en México hay 64 878 especies aproximadamente. ¿Sabes cuántas especies habitan en los Estados Unidos?

La siguiente tabla muestra cinco países muy ricos por su cantidad de plantas, anfibios, reptiles y mamíferos. Investiga qué lugar ocupan los Estados Unidos en cada una de estas categorías. ¿Te sorprenden los resultados? ¿Por qué? ¿Puedes mencionar algunas especies que vivan solamente en el territorio de los Estados Unidos?

© Vladimir Melnik/Shutterstock

Existen de 5 a 50 millones de especies diversas en nuestro planeta.

**Los países con más biodiversidad en el mundo
(País y número de especies)**

Plantas	Anfibios	Reptiles	Mamíferos
Brasil, 55 000	Brasil, 516	México, 707	Indonesia, 519
Colombia, 45 000	Colombia, 407	Australia, 597	México, 439
China, 30 000	Ecuador, 358	Indonesia, 529	Brasil, 421
México, 26,000	México, 282	Brasil, 462	China, 410
Australia, 25 000	Indonesia, 270	India, 433	Zaire, 409

Source: Instituto Nacional de Ecología, México

Conexiones... a la ecología

De acuerdo a la Unión Internacional para la Conservación de la Naturaleza (IUCN por sus siglas en inglés), un 40% de todos los organismos puede considerarse en peligro de extinción. Según el U.S. Fish and Wildlife Service, hay aproximadamente 1375 animales y plantas en peligro de extinción, tan solo en los Estados Unidos (julio, 2010).

La siguiente lista es de varias especies de animales que están en peligro de extinción. Elige una y averigua: ¿Dónde vive este animal? ¿Por qué está en peligro? ¿Qué se debe hacer para preservarla? ¿Por qué se debe preservar? Repórtale a la clase lo que aprendiste.

© nouseforname/Shutterstock

Una iguana de las islas Galápagos

el axolotl	el murciélago gris
la tortuga gigante	el ocelote
el quetzal	el jaguar
la iguana de las islas Galápagos	el oso grizzly
el perico puertorriqueño	la ballena jorobada
la tortuga verde	el puma

A analizar

Lee parte de la conversación y observa los verbos en negritas. Luego, contesta las preguntas.

© Eric Isselée/Shutterstock

> **Horacio:** Oye, Ivana, ¿sabías que los hipopótamos pueden correr más rápido que el hombre?
>
> **Ivana:** No, no creo que **sea** posible. Creo que **son** demasiado gordos para poder correr tan rápido.
>
> **Horacio:** Es evidente que **es** uno de los animales más pesados (*heavy*), y dudo que **pueda** correr muy rápido por mucho tiempo, pero es cierto que **puede** correr hasta 19 millas por hora. Lo leí en un artículo de una universidad prestigiosa.
>
> **Ivana:** Bueno, no pienso que **tengan** información incorrecta en sus artículos, así que debe ser cierto. ¡Qué interesante!

1. Which of the verbs in bold are in the subjunctive? Which are in the indicative?

2. What expressions precede the verbs in the subjunctive? And in the indicative?

A comprobar

Subjunctive with expressions of doubt

1. When expressing doubt or uncertainty about an action or a condition, you must use the subjunctive. The following are some common expressions of doubt that require the use of the subjunctive:

Dudar que	No estar seguro(a) que
No creer que	No ser cierto/verdad/ obvio/evidente que
No pensar que	
No suponer que	

> **Dudo que** la cebra **corra** más rápido que el león.
> *I doubt that the zebra runs faster than the lion.*
>
> **No pensamos que** los elefantes **duerman.**
> *We don't think that the elephants are sleeping.*

2. When using the expressions below to affirm a belief or express certainty, you must use the indicative.

Creer que	Estar seguro(a) de que
Pensar que	Ser cierto/verdad/ obvio/evidente que
Suponer que	

> **Creo que** la preservación de la ecología **es** importante.
> *I believe that the conservation of the ecology is important.*
>
> **Es obvio que necesitamos** hacer algo.
> *It is obvious that we need to do something.*

> **INVESTIGUEMOS LA GRAMÁTICA**
>
> While the expressions **negar** and **dudar** always require the subjunctive, there is variation in the use of **no negar** and **no dudar.** With these expressions, some speakers will use the subjunctive (*doubt*) or the indicative (*certainty*), depending on the speaker's intention. You might prefer to use an expression of certainty like **estoy seguro(a)** or **es cierto** if you mean that you are completely sure about something.

> **INVESTIGUEMOS LA GRAMÁTICA**
>
> When using the verbs **pensar** and **creer** in a question, it is possible to use the subjunctive in the dependent clause as you are not affirming a belief.
>
> ¿Crees que **haya** suficiente comida para los animales?

A practicar

12.31 **¿Qué animal es?** Lee las oraciones y decide a cuál de los animales se refiere cada una.

el águila	el oso polar	la serpiente
el toro	la tortuga	la vaca

1. Creo que vive en el desierto.
2. Es obvio que produce leche.
3. Dudo que sea muy rápida.
4. No creo que le gusten las temperaturas muy altas.
5. No es cierto que le moleste el color rojo.
6. Pienso que es el símbolo de los Estados Unidos.

12.32 **Oraciones incompletas** Completa las oraciones con la frase apropiada. **¡OJO!** Algunas oraciones necesitan el subjuntivo y otras no.

1. Creo que el caballo...
   - **a.** es un animal fuerte.
   - **b.** sea un animal fuerte.
2. Dudo que la tortuga...
   - **a.** corre rápido.
   - **b.** corra rápido.
3. Supongo que las gallinas...
   - **a.** tienen miedo del zorro.
   - **b.** tengan miedo del zorro.
4. Estoy seguro que el camello...
   - **a.** no necesita agua.
   - **b.** no necesite agua.
5. No pienso que la oveja...
   - **a.** come carne.
   - **b.** coma carne.
6. No es cierto que los pingüinos...
   - **a.** saben volar (*to fly*).
   - **b.** sepan volar.
7. No creo que el elefante...
   - **a.** salta.
   - **b.** salte.
8. Es obvio que el cocodrilo...
   - **a.** no puede sacar la lengua (*tongue*).
   - **b.** no pueda sacar la lengua.

12.33 **En el reino de los animales** En parejas, decidan si son ciertas las siguientes oraciones. Luego usen las expresiones de duda para expresarle sus creencias (*beliefs*) a la clase. **¡OJO!** Usa el subjuntivo solo si tienes duda.

Modelo La cebra es blanca y negra.
Es obvio que la cebra es blanca y negra.
El pez puede vivir fuera del agua.
No creo que el pez pueda vivir fuera del agua.

1. El hipopótamo es carnívoro.
2. Se escucha a un león rugir (*to roar*) a cinco millas.
3. La boa vive en África.
4. Una tortuga puede vivir más de cien años.
5. A los gorilas les gusta tomar una siesta por la tarde.
6. Todos los osos duermen en el invierno.
7. El tigre es el más grande de los felinos.
8. Las rayas de cada cebra son únicas.
9. El gallo canta para despertar a las gallinas.
10. Algunas ardillas pueden medir (*measure*) hasta un metro.

12.34 **En clase** Completa el siguiente párrafo con la forma apropiada del verbo entre paréntesis. **¡OJO!** Algunos verbos requieren el subjuntivo y otros el indicativo.

Miguel: Profesor, ¿es verdad que **(1.)** _____ (haber) muchos animales en peligro de extinción?

Profesor: Sí, es cierto. Es obvio que muchas personas no **(2.)** _____ (pensar) en el medio ambiente y no creen que sus acciones **(3.)** _____ (afectar) el mundo mucho. Yo creo que todos **(4.)** _____ (deber) hacer nuestra parte.

Miguel: Dudo que yo **(5.)** _____ (poder) cambiar las cosas (*make a difference*).

Profesor: No creo que **(6.)** _____ (saber) todo lo que puedes hacer. Es cierto que tú **(7.)** _____ (ser) nada más una persona, pero hay muchas organizaciones que buscan voluntarios.

12.35 **¿Qué piensas?** Usando las expresiones de duda, expresa tus opiniones acerca de las circunstancias en los dibujos.

Modelo *Es obvio que la niña quiere comprar el perro.*
Dudo que la madre le compre el perro.

1.
2.
3.

4.
5.

12.36 **En mi opinión** En grupos de tres, expresen sus opiniones sobre los siguientes temas usando el subjuntivo o el indicativo con las expresiones **(no) creer, (no) dudar, (no) pensar, (no) suponer, (no) estar seguro que** y **(no) ser cierto/evidente/verdad/obvio que.**

Modelo la crueldad con los animales
Creo que el abuso de los animales es un crimen.
Dudo que las personas crueles con los animales sean buenos padres.

1. ser vegetariano
2. la caza
3. la extinción de algunos animales
4. usar pieles de animales

5. la corrida de toros
6. los zoológicos
7. el problema de los gatos y perros callejeros (*stray*)
8. las peleas de gallos o de perros

Redacción

An editorial in a newspaper is an opinion piece. Imagine that you work for a newspaper and have been asked to write an editorial in which you express your opinion on an animal issue or an environmental issue.

Paso 1 Pick one of the following topics about which you have an opinion: water conservation, recycling, vegetarianism, hunting, or zoos. Or you may choose to come up with your own topic.

Paso 2 In order to write a good argument, it is important to think of both sides of the issue. Write down a list of pros and cons related to the issue.

Paso 3 Pick two of the items you wrote in **Paso 2** that support your view on the issue. Then jot down other ideas related to each of the points you have chosen. As you write your support, you may want to keep in mind some of the counterarguments you came up with in **Paso 2.**

> **Modelo** *el zoológico ayuda a educar a la gente*
> *a. la gente puede observar los hábitos de los animales*
> *b. la gente aprende a apreciar los animales*
> *c. el zoológico tiene información sobre los animales*

Paso 5 Write a topic sentence in which you express your opinion on the animal issue you have chosen to write about. Decide which of the points you chose in **Paso 3** you would like to begin your argument with, and then write your first paragraph using the information you generated. You may want to include an opposing argument and refute it in your paragraph.

Paso 6 Write a transition sentence that will introduce your second point. You may think about using expressions such as **además de** (*besides*), **por otra parte** (*moreover*), or **aparte de** (*aside from*).

Paso 7 Using the information you generated on the second point in **Paso 3**, write your second paragraph.

Paso 8 Write a concluding paragraph in which you restate your opinion and summarize your arguments. When restating your opinion, you should not use the same sentence you began your essay with; rather, find another way to express your point of view.

Paso 9 Edit your paragraph:

a. Do all of the sentences in each paragraph support your topic sentence? If not, get rid of them.

b. Do you have smooth transitions between sentences and between paragraphs?

c. Do your verbs agree with the subject? Are they conjugated correctly?

d. Did you use any expressions that require you to use the subjunctive?

Lectura

Reading Strategy: Test your comprehension at the end of a reading

Remember to practice the strategy suggested in the first part of the chapter: test your comprehension at the end by writing a short summary.

Antes de leer

1. ¿Conoces alguna historia sobre animales fantásticos? ¿Cuál?

2. ¿Cuáles son otros animales fantásticos de los que has oído?

3. ¿Por qué crees que hay historias sobre animales fantásticos?

4. ¿Piensas que existen o existieron? Explica por qué.

A leer

Animales fantásticos

Los animales han inspirado la creatividad y la imaginación de los hombres desde tiempos ancestrales, pero muchas veces lo que existe en la realidad parece más increíble que lo que puede hacer la imaginación, como se ve en la variedad y forma de algunos animales que viven en nuestro planeta. Cada año se descubren animales que parecen sacados de libros de ciencia ficción, en especial algunos organismos que viven en las profundidades de los océanos.

Una interpretación artística del Chupacabras

De la misma manera, por mucho tiempo se ha hablado de animales que nadie ha podido comprobar que existan. Algunos ejemplos conocidos son los de un tipo de dinosaurio que vive en Escocia (el monstruo del lago Ness), el Yeti (el abominable hombre de las nieves), el de Sasquash (similar al Yeti, pero que habita supuestamente en el noroeste de los Estados Unidos), y el cada vez más célebre Chupacabras.

La historia del Chupacabras se inicia en los años 90, cuando empiezan a aparecer numerosos animales muertos sin **sangre,** como caballos, ovejas, **cabras,** gallinas y perros. El primer **avistamiento** del Chupacabras se reportó en Puerto Rico, pero en la actualidad hay personas que aseguran haberlo visto en lugares tan alejados como Argentina, Colombia

blood
goats
sighting

[se dice que es una mezcla de coyote o perro sin pelo, de rata, y hasta de canguro]

y Chile. Sin embargo, la mayoría de los reportes siguen siendo de Puerto Rico, la República Dominicana, México y los Estados Unidos.

© Fortean/Sibbick/TopFoto/The Image Works

Según las personas que dicen haberlo visto, el Chupacabras es una mezcla de animales diferentes: se dice que es una mezcla de coyote o perro sin pelo, de rata, y hasta de canguro. Algunos le encuentran parecido con las gárgolas de la mitología europea. En lo que todos están de acuerdo, es en que el Chupacabras tiene forma humanoide y mide aproximadamente un metro de alto. También es un hecho que el interés acerca del Chupacabras ha dado como resultado una gran cantidad de publicidad y de artículos para el mercado: es fácil encontrar camisetas, tazas, libros y sombreros con la imagen del Chupacabras. Su existencia real seguirá siendo un misterio, pero su aparición en el cine, en la televisión, en los cómics, en videojuegos, en las leyendas urbanas y hasta en la música, no es ficticia.

Comprensión

Completa las ideas según la información de la lectura.

1. Algunos animales fantásticos son...
2. En los años 90 empezaron a encontrar...
3. El Chupacabras se vio por primera vez en...
4. Varios testigos reportan que el Chupacabras es una mezcla de...
5. Varios países donde la gente dice haber visto al Chupacabras son...
6. Los países donde más dicen ver al Chupacabras son...
7. Hoy en día, el Chupacabras aparece en....

Después de leer

En parejas, escriban una lista de otros animales que han despertado la imaginación de los humanos, y algunas películas o programas de televisión famosos que se inspiran en animales. Luego, escriban una idea para una película en la que un nuevo animal sea el protagonista de la historia. ¿Qué ocurre en la película? ¿Cómo termina?

© Ruslan Kudrin/Shutterstock

Vocabulario

Sustantivos

la biodiversidad	*biodiversity*
el calentamiento	*warming*
la capa de ozono	*ozone layer*
el combustible	*fuel*
la energía	*energy*
el inversionista	*investor*
el molino de viento	*windmill*
el panel solar	*solar panel*

Adjetivos

contaminante	*pollutant*
destructivo	*destructive*
híbrido	*hybrid*
no renovable	*nonrenewable*
químico	*chemical*
renovable	*renewable*
útil	*useful*

Verbos

ahorrar	*to save*
conservar	*to preserve*
proponer	*to propose*
recuperar	*to recuperate*

Expresiones útiles

Hay que aprovechar los recursos.
We should make use of the resources.

Se debe crear conciencia.
We should make people aware.

evitar el calentamiento
to avoid global warming

invertir hoy para ganar mañana
(lit.) *to invest today to earn tomorrow;*
(fig.) *to act today to receive the benefits later*

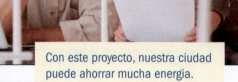

Con este proyecto, nuestra ciudad puede ahorrar mucha energia.

© Jose Luis Pelaez Inc/Blend Images/Getty Images

DATOS IMPORTANTES

Educación: Estudios universitarios. Maestría en ingeniería con especialización en el medio ambiente.

Salario: Entre $60 000 y $150 000, dependiendo de la agencia, la compañía y la experiencia.

Dónde se trabaja: En agencias del gobierno y agencias privadas. En agencias de conservación de recursos naturales. En constructoras comprometidas a proteger el medio ambiente. En agencias de regulaciones legales.

Olga Saldívar es una ingeniera ambiental. Trabaja para una compañía que aprovecha los recursos renovables. En el video verás una presentación de la ingeniera Saldívar sobre un proyecto para ahorrar energía.

Antes de ver

Los trabajos relacionados con el medio ambiente tienen como meta (*goal*) reducir la contaminación. Algunas personas se dedican directamente a la limpieza del medio ambiente y otras, como los ingenieros ambientales, desarrollan (*develop*) máquinas para producir energía sin polución.

¿Qué problemas ambientales observas en la vida diaria? ¿Qué soluciones propones? Piensa en un invento para mejorar el medio ambiente. ¿Cómo se lo explicas a un ingeniero ambiental?

Al ver

1. ¿En qué tipo de ciudad vive la ingeniera Saldívar?

2. ¿Dónde quiere poner paneles solares compactos?

3. ¿Qué recurso renovable usará con esos paneles?

4. ¿Qué ahorrará la gente al usar estos paneles?

5. ¿Qué plan tiene la ingeniera para usar menos combustible?

6. ¿Qué instalará en las fábricas?

7. ¿Qué piensa el inversionista del plan?

8. ¿Qué piensa la ingeniera que ocurrirá si ellos realizan el proyecto?

© Heinle/Cengage Learning

Después de ver

En parejas, representen a un ingeniero ambiental que desarrolló un invento para proteger el medio ambiente. Mientras uno de ustedes explica de qué se trata, cómo funciona y cuáles son los beneficios, el otro hace preguntas correspondientes para saber más sobre ese invento.

12.37 **Hablemos de mascotas** Completa la conversación con el presente perfecto del verbo entre paréntesis.

Viviana: ¿Qué animales **(1.)** _____ (tener) tú de mascota?

Magda: Yo nunca **(2.)** _____ (adoptar) animales. Mi familia siempre

(3.) _____ (vivir) en apartamentos, así que no había espacio para

mascotas, ¿y tú? Viviana: Yo **(4.)** _____ (tener) ratones, pollos, conejos,

gatos, perros y un pájaro, pero desde que mi esposo y yo nos mudamos a esta

ciudad, no **(5.)** _____ (volver) a adoptar mascotas. No tenemos tiempo

para cuidarlas, así que nosotros **(6.)** _____ (decidir) esperar. Yo siempre

(7.) _____ (decir) que no es justo tener una mascota si no tienes tiempo

para ella.

12.38 **En el zoológico** Éric va a ir al zoológico con su esposa y sus dos hijos mañana. Completa las oraciones usando los verbos entre paréntesis en el futuro y da una conclusión lógica.

Modelo Yo (comprar)...
 Compraré comida para los animales.

1. Mi familia y yo (ir)...

2. Mi esposa (hacer)...

3. Los niños (poder)...

4. Mi hija (ver)...

5. Yo (tener)...

6. Todos (estar)...

7. Los animales (dormir)...

8. El zoológico (cerrarse)...

© Muellek Josef/Shutterstock

Me encanta darles de comer a los monos.

12.39 **Viaje a Costa Rica** Fabricio va a hacer un viaje a Costa Rica con su amigo Marcelo. Usa los diferentes elementos para completar sus comentarios. Debes decidir entre el indicativo y el subjuntivo del verbo subrayado (_underlined_). ¡OJO! No olvides usar **que** en las oraciones.

Modelo no creo / Costa Rica / <u>tener</u> / desierto
 No creo que Costa Rica tenga desierto.

1. es buena idea / yo / <u>llevar</u> / un traje de baño / para ir a la costa

2. supongo / <u>haber</u> / volcanes activos

3. es verdad / los costarricenses / <u>cuidar</u> / la naturaleza de su país

4. es posible / nosotros / <u>navegar</u> / en kayak / en el río Sarapiquí

5. no pienso / Marcelo / <u>conocer</u> / el Valle Central

6. creo / Marcelo y yo / <u>viajar</u> / a la selva

7. es probable / yo / <u>ver</u> / muchos animales

8. es cierto / Costa Rica / <u>ofrecer</u> / muchas oportunidades para divertirse

12.40 **En contacto con la naturaleza** Habla con un compañero sobre sus experiencias con la naturaleza.

1. ¿Te gusta pasar tiempo en contacto con la naturaleza? ¿Por qué?

2. ¿Cuándo fue la última vez que estuviste en contacto con la naturaleza? ¿Dónde? ¿Qué hiciste?

3. ¿Alguna vez has visitado un parque nacional? ¿Cuál? ¿Qué viste en el parque?

4. ¿Adónde irás en el futuro para disfrutar de la naturaleza?

5. En tu opinión, ¿es importante que hagamos algo para preservar la naturaleza? ¿Por qué?

6. ¿Crees que el esfuerzo (*effort*) de una persona es suficiente para lograr (*achieve*) un cambio? ¿Por qué?

12.41 **El experto** Con un compañero túrnense para pedirle consejos al experto sobre lo que se puede hacer en cada situación. Deben usar una expresión impersonal **(es... que).** Presten atención al uso del subjuntivo.

Modelo Muchas compañías contaminan el agua.
Estudiante 1: *Muchas compañías contaminan el agua. ¿Qué recomiendas?*
Estudiante 2: *Es buena idea que escribas a los presidentes de las compañías.*

1. Muchos animales no tienen un lugar para vivir.

2. Hay basura en las calles.

3. Hay cientos de miles de botellas de plástico en la basura.

4. Se necesita mucho petróleo para los coches.

5. Los bosques están desapareciendo.

6. Quedan pocas fuentes de agua potable.

7. El agujero de ozono sigue creciendo.

8. El aire de muchas ciudades está muy contaminado.

12.42 **La granja** Mira uno de los dibujos y tu compañero va a mirar el otro en el apéndice A. Túrnense para describir las granjas y encontrar las cinco diferencias.

🔊 Vocabulario 1
CD2-21

El medio ambiente *The environment*

el árbol	*tree*	la ecología	*ecology*
la arena	*sand*	el esmog	*smog*
el cactus	*cactus*	la naturaleza	*nature*
la cascada	*cascade, waterfall (small)*	la nube	*cloud*
		la ola	*wave*
la catarata	*waterfall*	la palmera	*palm tree*
el cielo	*sky*	el pasto	*grass, pasture*
la contaminación	*contamination, pollution*	el petróleo	*oil*
		el reciclaje	*recycling*
la deforestación	*deforestation*	los recursos naturales	*natural resources*
los desechos industriales	*industrial waste*	el volcán	*volcano*

Lugares

la bahía	*bay*	el mar	*sea*
el bosque	*forest*	la montaña	*mountain*
la colina	*hill*	la pampa	*grasslands*
la costa	*coast*	la península	*peninsula*
el desierto	*desert*	el río	*river*
la isla	*island*	la selva	*jungle*
el lago	*lake*	el valle	*valley*
el llano	*plains*		

Verbos

destruir	*to destroy*	proteger	*to protect*
preservar	*to preserve*		

Diccionario personal

_____

_____

_____

_____

_____

_____

_____

_____

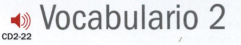
Vocabulario 2

Los animales

el águila (*f.*)	*eagle*	el mono	*monkey*
la ardilla	*squirrel*	el oso	*bear*
la ballena	*whale*	la oveja	*sheep*
la cebra	*zebra*	el pato	*duck*
el cerdo	*pig*	el pavo	*turkey*
el cocodrilo	*crocodile*	el pingüino	*penguin*
el conejo	*rabbit*	el pollo	*chick*
el elefante	*elephant*	la rana	*frog*
la gallina	*hen*	la serpiente	*snake*
el gallo	*rooster*	el tiburón	*shark*
el gorila	*gorilla*	el tigre	*tiger*
el jaguar	*jaguar*	el toro	*bull*
la jirafa	*giraffe*	la tortuga	*turtle*
el león	*lion*	la vaca	*cow*
la llama	*llama*	el venado	*deer*
el lobo	*wolf*	el zorro	*fox*

Clasificaciones

los anfibios	*amphibians*	los mamíferos	*mammals*
las aves	*birds*	los reptiles	*reptiles*

Palabras adicionales

la caza	*hunting*	la jaula	*cage*
cazar	*to hunt*	el macho	*male*
la granja	*farm*	el peligro (de	*danger (of*
la hembra	*female*	extinción)	*extinction)*

Diccionario personal

_____

_____

_____

_____

_____

_____

_____

Mario Benedetti
Biografía

Mario Benedetti (1920–2009) nació en Paso de los Toros, Uruguay. A los cuatro años su familia se mudó a Montevideo, donde asistió al Colegio Alemán de Montevideo y comenzó a escribir poemas y cuentos. A causa de problemas económicos, tuvo que dejar la escuela y trabajar para ayudar a su familia, pero terminó sus estudios por su cuenta (*on his own*). En 1949, publicó su primer libro de cuentos, por el cual recibió el Premio del Ministerio de Instrucción Pública. Así comenzó una larga carrera como escritor. Benedetti publicó más de 80 libros, incluyendo poemas, cuentos, novelas, ensayos y dramas. A causa de un golpe de estado, tuvo que salir de su país y vivió en el exilio por doce años en Argentina, Perú, Cuba y España. En 1983, finalmente pudo regresar al Uruguay, donde continuó escribiendo. Mario Benedetti recibió numerosos premios internacionales por su trabajo. Murió el 19 de mayo del 2009, y este día fue declarado luto nacional en Uruguay.

Antes de leer

1. ¿Crees que es importante aprender otros idiomas? ¿Por qué?
2. ¿Qué es lo más difícil de aprender otros idiomas?

El hombre que aprendió a ladrar

discouragement/ to give up

bark

Lo cierto es que fueron años de arduo y pragmático aprendizaje, con lapsos de **desaliento** en los que estuvo a punto de **desistir**. Pero al fin triunfó la perseverancia y Raimundo aprendió a **ladrar.** No a imitar ladridos, como suelen hacer los chistosos o se creen tales, sino verdaderamente a ladrar. ¿Qué lo había

training

5 impulsado a ese **adiestramiento**? Ante sus amigos se autoflagelaba con humor: "La verdad es que ladro por no llorar". Sin embargo, la razón más valedera era su amor casi franciscano hacia sus hermanos perros. Amor es comunicación.

¿Cómo amar entonces sin comunicarse?

Para Raimundo representó un día

10 de gloria cuando su ladrido fue por fin comprendido por Leo, su hermano perro, y (algo más extraordinario aún) él comprendió el ladrido de Leo. A partir de ese día, Raimundo

lay down

15 y Leo **se tendían** por lo general en los atardeceres, bajo la glorieta, y dialogaban sobre temas generales.

A pesar de su amor por los hermanos perros, Raimundo nunca había imaginado que Leo tuviera una tan sagaz visión de mundo.

20   Por fin, una tarde se animó a preguntarle, en varios sobrios ladridos: Dime Leo, con toda franqueza: ¿qué opinas de mi forma de ladrar? La respuesta de Leo fue **escueta** y sincera: Yo diría que lo haces bastante bien, pero tendrás que mejorar. Cuando ladras, todavía se te nota el acento humano.

simple

Investiguemos la literatura: La metáfora

A metaphor is a figure of speech in which an object or an idea is used in place of another, implying that there is a similarity between the two. For example, *The snake took every last thing I had.* The implication is that the person that took the things is like a snake. An extended metaphor is a metaphor that continues beyond the initial sentence; it can sometimes be an entire work.

Después de leer

A. Comprensión

1. ¿Por qué quiso aprender a ladrar Raimundo?
2. ¿Cuál fue el momento de gloria para Raimundo?
3. Según Leo, ¿por qué todavía tiene que mejorar Raimundo?
4. Este cuento es una metáfora extendida. ¿Cuál es la comparación?

B. Conversemos

1. En el cuento se dice "Amor es comunicación". Explica la importancia de esta cita. ¿Estás de acuerdo? ¿Por qué?
2. ¿Piensas que tener un acento extranjero es malo? ¿Por qué?

Learning Strategy

Find ways to expose yourself to the language outside of the classroom

Download some of the songs in the iTunes suggestions throughout the textbook. Watch a Spanish language film or buy a magazine or newspaper published in Spanish. Not only will this help you to increase your vocabulary, but you will also become more familiar with structures and expressions used by native speakers as well as increase your knowledge about the culture.

In this chapter you will learn how to:
- Talk about relationships
- Express desires and give recommendations
- Talk about popular culture
- Discuss emotional reactions to events

¿Es tu vida una telenovela?

© Alexander Tamargo/Getty Images

Exploraciones gramaticales
Reciprocal verbs
Subjunctive with expressions of desire
Subjunctive with expressions of emotion
Subjunctive with adjective clauses

En vivo
Una boda paso a paso
Las fotonovelas

Conexiones culturales
El cortejo
¡De película!

Lectura
Tradiciones nupciales
Las telenovelas

Exploraciones profesionales
Los medios de comunicación

Las relaciones románticas pueden evolucionar de maneras muy diferentes, algunas más tradicionales que otras.

enamorarse de

la cita

proponer matrimonio

el anillo

el compromiso

la madrina

el padrino

la ceremonia

los recién casados

la luna de miel

dar a luz

estar embarazada

el nacimiento

el divorcio

el noviazgo	engagement, relationship	**comprometerse (con)**	to get engaged (to)	**Palabras adicionales**	
la pareja	couple	**divorciarse (de)**	to divorce	**la adolescencia**	adolescence
el (la) prometido(a)	fiancé(e)	**enamorarse (de)**	to fall in love (with)	**el estado civil**	civil status
la recepción	wedding reception	**llevarse (bien/mal)**	to (not) get along	**la juventud**	youth
el (la) soltero(a)	single person	**nacer**	to be born	**la madurez**	maturity
la unión libre	common-law union	**odiar**	to hate	**la muerte**	death
el (la) viudo(a)	widower (widow)	**querer**	to love	**la niñez**	childhood
		romper (con)	to break up (with)	**la vejez**	old age
Verbos		**separarse (de)**	to separate (from)		
abrazar	to hug				
besar	to kiss				

A practicar

13.1 **Escucha y responde** Vas a escuchar una serie de afirmaciones. Levanta la mano si la afirmación te parece lógica. No hagas nada si la afirmación es ilógica.

CD 2-23

13.2 **Diferencias** Decide qué palabra no corresponde al grupo y explica por qué.

1. enamorarse	divorciarse	comprometerse	llevarse bien
2. la ceremonia	el anillo	el compromiso	proponer matrimonio
3. dar a luz	estar embarazada	extrañar	el nacimiento
4. romper	separarse	divorciarse	besar
5. el padrino	los novios	el soltero	la madrina
6. el viudo	el casado	el prometido	el novio

13.3 **Mis planes** Completa el párrafo con la palabra apropiada del vocabulario.

Ayer le di (1.) _____ a mi novia para comprometernos, porque llevamos cuatro años de noviazgo y estoy seguro de que ella es el amor de mi vida. Planeamos tener (2.) _____ en una iglesia pequeña y tener (3.) _____ muy sencilla, con muy pocos invitados. Mi novia y yo deseamos ir de (4.) _____ en un crucero por Puerto Rico y otras islas del Caribe. Mi novia ahora está (5.) _____ y nuestro primer hijo va a (6.) _____ en julio del próximo año. Ella quiere (7.) _____ en el hospital donde ella nació en Puerto Rico.

13.4 **Un poco de lógica** Con un compañero, relacionen las palabras de las dos columnas y expliquen la relación.

Modelo el anillo – el novio

El novio pone el anillo en la mano de la novia durante la ceremonia.

1. el nacimiento	**a.** la juventud
2. la ceremonia	**b.** estar embarazada
3. separarse	**c.** el anillo de compromiso
4. besar	**d.** la pareja
5. la unión libre	**e.** recién casados
6. la luna de miel	**f.** divorciarse
7. comprometerse	**g.** los novios
8. la adolescencia	**h.** los padrinos

> **INVESTIGUEMOS LA GRAMÁTICA**
>
> In Spanish, there are numerous verbs that consist of a root verb and a prefix, such as **conseguir**, which consists of the root of **seguir**, and **sonreír**, whose root is **reír**. The root of the verb **proponer** is **poner**; therefore, it is conjugated in the same way as **poner: propongo, propuse, he propuesto,** etc. Some other similar verbs are:
>
> | | |
> |---|---|
> | **oponer** | **detener** |
> | **posponer** | **mantener** |
> | **suponer** | **obtener** |

13.5 **Entrevista** Con un compañero, túrnense para responder las preguntas. Den mucha información.

1. ¿Cuál es tu estado civil: casado, soltero, divorciado o viudo?

2. ¿Cuándo fue la última vez que fuiste a una boda? ¿Cómo y dónde fue la boda? ¿Había muchas personas? ¿Te gustó la ceremonia? ¿Hubo una fiesta después? ¿Qué había para comer y beber?

3. ¿Tienes un amigo que esté comprometido? ¿Cuánto tiempo llevan de noviazgo? ¿Cuándo van a casarse?

4. ¿Has ido de luna de miel? ¿Adónde fuiste y por cuánto tiempo? Si no has ido, habla de la luna de miel de algún amigo o pariente, o de la luna de miel que quieres para ti si te casas un día.

Para muchas personas, una boda es uno de los eventos más importantes de su vida, y por eso la celebran con una gran fiesta y numerosos invitados. ¿Qué consejos le darías (*would you give*) a una persona que está planeando una boda? A continuación aparece una guía para planear bodas. ¿Qué se aconseja con respecto a los invitados? ¿Qué se recomienda para planear el presupuesto (*budget*)?

1 Imagínate tu boda perfecta

Antes de anunciarle al mundo que estás comprometida, y que todo el mundo asuma que está invitado a tu boda:

- Habla primero con tu pareja y decidan la fecha, el tamaño, la formalidad y el estilo de la boda que desean, para que esta sea una boda que los identifique como pareja.
- Para inspiración puedes visitar las diferentes galerías de fotos, y ver la última moda en bodas.

© iofoto/Shutterstock

2 Haz una lista de invitados

Esto es algo muy importante que hay que decidir desde el principio.

- Recuerda que muchos de tus invitados van a llevar pareja, y cuentan por dos personas.
- Entre más personas invites, tu presupuesto será más alto.
- Utiliza nuestra herramienta muy conveniente: mi lista de invitados de mi planificador, la cual te ayudará a hacer esto de una forma muy fácil y organizada.
- Una muy buena idea sería hacer una lista A: "Personas que tienen que asisitir", y otra lista B: "Personas que nos gustaría incluir". Al enviar tus invitaciones con tiempo, si los invitados de la lista A no pueden asistir, todavía tienes oportunidad de invitar a algunos de la lista B, y no se van a sentir como que han sido incluidos a última hora.
- Busca *Tips sobre cómo reducir tu lista de invitados.*

3 Haz un presupuesto

La realidad es que todo el glamour y belleza de la boda cuesta dinero, y desarrollar un presupuesto realista ahora, puede evitarte muchos contratiempos más adelante.

© Ingrid Balabanova/Shutterstock

- Toma una calculadora, habla con tus padres y tu pareja, y empieza a hacer tu presupuesto.
- Una vez sepas los elementos sin los cuales no podrías vivir, esto te dará una idea más clara de cómo distribuir el presupuesto.
- Te damos la herramienta de mi presupuesto en mi planificador, para que tengas un estimado de cuánto debes gastar en cada categoría.

Más allá

Imagínate que estás ayudando a planear un evento importante, como un gran cumpleaños, un aniversario o un funeral. Escribe una lista de ideas sobre los preparativos que deben hacerse antes, durante y después del evento.

A analizar

Lee el siguiente párrafo y observa los verbos en negritas. Luego, contesta las preguntas.

Me llamo Florencia y este es mi esposo Camilo. **Nos conocimos** en la escuela primaria. En la escuela secundaria **nos hablamos** más y **nos entendimos** mejor. **Nos besamos** por primera vez la noche de la graduación. Empezamos a salir como pareja, y al terminar la universidad **nos casamos**.

1. Who is the subject for each of the verbs?
2. The word **nos** is an object pronoun. Who does it refer to?

A comprobar

Reciprocal verbs

1. In **Capítulo 6** you learned to use reflexive pronouns when the subject of the sentence does something to himself or herself.

   Ellos **se miran** en el espejo.
   *They **look at themselves** in the mirror.*

2. In English the expressions *each other* and *one another* express reciprocal actions. In order to express a reciprocal action in Spanish, use the plural reflexives.

   Ellos **se miran** con amor.
   *They **look at each other** with love.*

3. Only the plural forms (**nos, os,** and **se**) are used to express reciprocal actions as the action must involve more than one person.

   Los novios **se besaron.**
   *The bride and groom **kissed each other**.*

   Mi amiga y yo **nos escribimos.**
   *My friend and I **write to each other**.*

4. It is usually evident by context whether the verb is reflexive or reciprocal. However, if there is need for clarification, **el uno al otro** can be used. The expression must agree with the subject(s); however, if there are mixed sexes, the masculine form is used for both.

   Se lavaron el pelo **el uno al otro.**
   *They washed **each other's** hair.*

   Nos peinamos **la una a la otra.**
   *We did **each other's** hair.*

   Todos se respetan **los unos a los otros.**
   *They all respect **each other**.*

5. When used in the infinitive form after another verb, the pronoun can be attached to the verb or placed in front of the conjugated verb.

   Nos vamos a amar para siempre.
   We will love each other forever.

   Quieren comprender**se.**
   They want to understand each other.

© hartphotography/Shutterstock

A practicar

13.6 **¿Lógico o ilógico?** Decide si las siguientes oraciones son lógicas o no. Corrige las oraciones ilógicas.

1. Los amigos se escuchan.
2. Los amigos se hablan cuando hay un problema.
3. Los amigos se odian.
4. Los amigos se ayudan con frecuencia.
5. Los amigos normalmente no se entienden.
6. Los amigos se insultan.

13.7 **Pedro y Sara** Describe el proceso de la relación de Pedro y Sara usando los verbos recíprocos.

Modelo Pedro le escribió cartas de amor a Sara. Sara le escribió cartas de amor a Pedro.
Pedro y Sara se escribieron cartas de amor.

1. Pedro conoció a Sara en la fiesta. Sara conoció a Pedro en la fiesta.
2. Pedro le habló a Sara. Sara le habló a Pedro.
3. Pedro entendió bien a Sara. Sara entendió bien a Pedro.
4. Pedro empezó a llamar a Sara por teléfono. Sara empezó a llamar a Pedro por teléfono.
5. Pedro abrazó y besó a Sara. Sara abrazó y besó a Pedro.
6. Pedro se enamoró de Sara. Sara se enamoró de Pedro.
7. Pedro se casó con Sara. Sara se casó con Pedro.

13.8 **En la recepción** En parejas, túrnense para explicar lo que pasa en la recepción. **¡OJO!** Algunos de los verbos están en forma recíproca y otros son reflexivos.

13.9 **Tu mejor amigo y tú** En parejas, túrnense para entrevistarse sobre su relación con su mejor amigo, usando las siguientes preguntas.

1. ¿Dónde y cuándo se conocieron tú y tu mejor amigo?
2. ¿Por qué se hicieron mejores amigos?
3. ¿Con qué frecuencia se hablan por teléfono?
4. ¿Con qué frecuencia se ven? ¿Dónde se encuentran?
5. ¿Se dan regalos? ¿Cuándo?
6. ¿Se ayudan con sus problemas?
7. ¿Se escriben por correo electrónico?
8. ¿Se pelean de vez en cuando?
9. ¿Alguna vez se han dejado de hablar?

13.10 **Una historia de amor** En parejas, elijan una fotografía. Usando algunos de los verbos recíprocos indicados, narren la historia de amor de la pareja: ¿Dónde se conocieron? ¿Qué se dijeron? ¿Por qué se enamoraron? ¿Cómo va a ser su futuro? Luego léanle su cuento a la clase para que sus compañeros decidan a cuál de las fotos corresponde.

| conocerse | besarse | enamorarse | comprometerse |
| casarse | separarse | hablarse | divorciarse |

© Photos To Go

© Lisa F. Young/Shutterstock

© Blaj Gabriel/Shutterstock

© Andy Dean Photography/Shutterstock

Conexiones culturales
El cortejo

Comparaciones

Entre los jóvenes españoles, la palabra "cortejar" prácticamente ha caído en desuso, como la práctica misma de envolver a la persona amada en detalles que, finalmente, la harán caer en nuestros brazos.

No siempre fue así. Los llamados "tunos", jóvenes estudiantes de escasos recursos que aparecieron en el siglo XIII, se ganaban la vida entonando canciones en las tabernas. Por las noches utilizaban sus habilidades musicales para enamorar a sus doncellas. La costumbre estaba tan arraigada, que muy posiblemente fue adoptada siglos después, con algunas variaciones, en las colonias españolas de América Latina.

Actualmente en España solo quedan algunos grupos aislados de tunos. Se trata de jóvenes aficionados a la música y a la tradición y, sobre todo, a la vida nocturna. Ataviados con trajes de época y con una característica capa, y acompañados de guitarras, recorren las calles en busca de mujeres a las que cortejar mientras interpretan canciones populares a puerta cerrada en un bar, o con una serenata a la intemperie.

Pero hoy esta es una excepción. Así como los jóvenes españoles prefieren decir "te quiero" a decir "te amo", ahora en España se habla mucho más de "ligar" que de "cortejar".

En casi todo el mundo, pues, el amor es hoy mucho menos romántico. Pero al mismo tiempo es más directo. Y, por lo tanto, más libre.

¿Cómo ha cambiado el cortejo en tu cultura? ¿Qué prácticas ya no se usan? ¿Qué nuevas prácticas hay?

"El arte de cortejar alrededor de la planeta", Selecciones de Reader's Digest.

Tunos españoles

© Picture Contact / Alamy

> Investiga en Internet sobre los tunos de hoy en día.

Conexiones... a la música

La música es una de las formas favoritas de todas las culturas para hablar del amor. El siguiente es un fragmento de una canción clásica de la música mexicana, escrita por Consuelo Velázquez (1916–2005). ¿Cuál es el tono de la canción (triste, alegre, etcétera)? ¿Por qué? ¿Por qué crees que esta canción se hizo muy famosa?

La canción *Bésame mucho* habla del amor.

© Photos To Go

Bésame mucho
Bésame, bésame mucho
Como si fuera esta noche
La última vez.
Bésame, bésame mucho
Que tengo miedo a perderte
Perderte después.

Quiero tenerte muy cerca
Mirarme en tus ojos
Verte junto a mí.
Piensa que tal vez mañana
Yo ya estaré lejos
Muy lejos de aquí.

Comunidad

Busca anuncios de bodas en un periódico local para la comunidad hispana o en un periódico en línea escrito en español. ¿Cuáles son las diferencias y las similitudes con los anuncios que se ven en periódicos para la comunidad anglohablante (*English speaking*)?

¿Cómo son los anuncios de bodas?

Cultura

Las relaciones personales pueden ser diferentes de país a país, especialmente donde hay una mezcla de culturas. En algunos países latinoamericanos las costumbres del cortejo reflejan la unión de creencias y tradiciones europeas con las indígenas. Un ejemplo de ello son los ritos de noviazgo quechuas en Perú, en donde algunas bodas, en la superficie, parecen ser la tradicional boda católica en la que hay una ceremonia y después se festeja la unión con música, comida y bailes. A consecuencia de la globalización, muchas de las bodas de esta región tienen elementos típicos occidentales, como una novia vestida de blanco y con un velo, o música que no es tradicional de la región, como un grupo de mariachi u otro tipo de música extranjera.

Un joven quechua

Todavía es posible ver bodas más tradicionales en algunas regiones quechuas, pero las diferencias más grandes entre un matrimonio quechua y un matrimonio moderno en Perú o en Ecuador no se encuentran durante la celebración de la boda, sino en lo que ocurrió antes de ella. Muchos pueblos quechuas siguen una tradición inca llamada *sirvinakuy* que en quechua significa "servirse el uno al otro". Según esta tradición, los padres de la pareja hacen una alianza basada en los intereses de los jóvenes. Se dice que una pareja entra en un período de *sirvinakuy*, cuando uno de ellos se va a vivir a la casa de los padres del otro. Durante esta época la pareja vive y duerme junta, ayudando a los padres de él o de ella. La pareja no puede casarse hasta que tengan un hijo, comprobando así que pueden tener familia. Es entonces cuando finalmente se celebra la boda.

¿Cuáles son las ventajas y las desventajas de *sirvinakuy*? ¿Cómo se conocen las parejas dentro tu cultura?

A analizar

Lee el párrafo y observa los verbos en negritas.

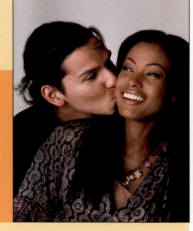

Mi novia y yo queremos casarnos este verano y ¡todos tienen una opinión acerca de la boda! Yo prefiero tener una boda sencilla, pero mi novia quiere que **tengamos** una boda grande y elegante. Nuestros amigos esperan que **haya** una gran fiesta después de la boda, pero yo quiero que **sea** pequeña y que **tengamos** una luna de miel fantástica. Mis padres quieren que **nos casemos** en la iglesia donde ellos se casaron, pero los padres de mi novia piden que **nos casemos** en su jardín. ¡Creo que lo mejor sería escaparnos para casarnos!

1. The verbs in bold are in the subjunctive. What are the expressions in the first clause?
2. In the second sentence, what is the difference between the structure of **prefiero tener** and **quiere que tengamos**?

A comprobar

Subjunctive with expressions of desire

1. When expressing the desire to do something, you use a verb of desire or influence such as **querer** or **preferir** followed by an infinitive.

> **Prefiero ir** a la recepción contigo.
> *I prefer to go to the reception with you.*

> **Él quiere comprar** un anillo para su novia.
> *He wants to buy a ring for his girlfriend.*

2. When expressing the desire for someone else to do something, you use a verb of influence plus **que** followed by the subjunctive.

> **Prefiero que vayas** a la recepción conmigo.
> *I prefer (that) you go to the reception with me.*

> **Ella quiere que su novio le compre** un anillo.
> *She wants her boyfriend to buy a ring for her.*

3. You will notice that when there are two different subjects and the verb in the main clause is in the indicative, the verb in the second clause is in the subjunctive.

Main clause		Dependent clause
(Yo) Prefiero	que	(tú) **vayas** a la recepción conmigo.
Ella quiere	que	su novio le **compre** un anillo.

4. There are other verbs besides **querer** and **preferir** that express desire or influence. These verbs also require the use of the subjunctive when there are different subjects in the two clauses.

desear	*to desire*
esperar	*to hope, to wish*
insistir (en)	*to insist*
mandar	*to order*
necesitar	*to need*
pedir	*to ask for, to request*
recomendar	*to recommend*
sugerir	*to suggest*

> Edwin **espera que vayan** a Puerto Rico para la luna de miel.
> *Edwin **hopes that they will go** to Puerto Rico for the honeymoon.*

> Sus padres **recomiendan que viajen** a México.
> *His parents **recommend (that) they travel** to Mexico.*

5. Ojalá is another way to express hope. This expression does not have a subject and therefore does not change forms. It always requires the use of the subjunctive in the dependent clause; however, the use of **que** is optional.

Ojalá (que) los recién casados sean muy felices.
I hope (that) the newlyweds will be very happy.

A practicar

13.11 **La recepción** Durante la recepción de una boda, los invitados hicieron un brindis con sus deseos para los recién casados. Relaciona las dos columnas para averiguar (*find out*) cuáles fueron los deseos.

1. Ojalá que los novios...
2. Queremos que los padres de los recién casados...
3. Esperamos que el matrimonio de los nuevos esposos...
4. Yo le recomiendo a la novia que...
5. Sugerimos al novio que...
6. Yo insisto en que los invitados...

a. los ayuden durante su matrimonio.
b. hagan otro brindis por los novios.
c. siempre se amen.
d. le diga siempre la verdad a su esposo.
e. sea muy largo y muy feliz.
f. no vea fútbol cada fin de semana.

13.12 **El consejero matrimonial** Juanita y Pablo fueron a un consejero matrimonial y tomaron notas de sus consejos, pero las notas están incompletas. Ayúdalos a completarlas, usando los verbos en paréntesis en el subjuntivo.

Para el esposo:

Sinceramente, deseo que (**1.**) _____ (solucionar) sus problemas con su esposa.

Espero que usted (**2.**) _____ (ayudar) con los quehaceres de la casa.

Insisto en que usted (**3.**) _____ (mantener) una buena comunicación con su esposa.

Para la esposa:

Necesito que usted (**4.**) _____ (venir) a mi oficina dos veces por semana con su suegra.

Le pido que no le (**5.**) _____ (mentir) a su esposo.

Yo recomiendo que (**6.**) _____ (leer) mi libro sobre matrimonios con problemas.

Para los dos:

Les sugiero que (**7.**) _____ (encontrar) tiempo para salir juntos.

Les pido que no me (**8.**) _____ (pagar) con tarjeta de crédito.

Recomiendo que hablen con un consejero matrimonial.

© Junial Enterprises/ Shutterstock

Entre la gente Con un compañero, miren los dibujos y completen las oraciones de una manera lógica.

El hombre espera que…
La mujer quiere que…
Sus amigos desean que…

La chica desea que…
Los padres piden que…
El muchacho espera que…

La mujer insiste en que…
El hombre prefiere que…
El niño necesita que…

Las chicas esperan que…
Los chicos desean que…
Ojalá que…

13.14 **Preferencias** Con un compañero, hablen de lo que quieren que hagan sus amigos y familiares en las situaciones indicadas. **¡OJO!** Deben usar el subjuntivo.

Modelo Vas a casarte.
Estudiante 1: *Quiero que mi novia se arregle muy bonita. ¿Y tú?*
Estudiante 2: *Yo quiero que venga mi hermana de California.*

1. Es tu cumpleaños.

2. Estás enfermo.

3. Te va a proponer matrimonio tu pareja.

4. Acabas de (*just*) tener un bebé.

5. Tu pareja va de viaje por dos semanas.

6. Acabas de mudarte a una casa nueva.

13.15 **Querida Teresa** Teresa trabaja para un periódico dando consejos a las personas que le escriben con sus problemas. Con un compañero, túrnense para hacer el papel (*role*) de Teresa y contesten las cartas con sus recomendaciones. Usen el subjuntivo y los siguientes verbos.

esperar   insistir   mandar   necesitar   pedir   recomendar   sugerir

Querida Teresa: Soy estudiante de inglés, y quiero aprender a hablar bien. La clase es muy difícil y tengo malas notas en la clase. ¿Qué me recomienda? -Perdido

Querida Teresa: Mi esposo y yo hemos estado casados por 15 años, pero recientemente hemos tenido muchos problemas. La semana pasada él mencionó la posibilidad de divorciarnos. Yo lo quiero mucho. ¿Qué debo hacer? -Casada y enamorada

Querida Teresa: Mi novio me propuso matrimonio y vamos a casarnos este verano. El problema es que no tenemos mucho dinero para la boda. ¿Qué podemos hacer? —Pobre y comprometida

Querida Teresa: Me han ofrecido un nuevo trabajo en otro estado. Es un muy buen trabajo y me van a pagar más, pero mi esposa no quiere que nos mudemos (*move*). ¿Qué hago? -Entre la espada y la pared

Querida Teresa: Mi hija tiene 16 años, y ahora está muy rebelde. No quiere ir a clases ni hacer la tarea. Sale con sus amigos y siempre llega muy tarde. Creo que está usando drogas. ¿Qué me sugiere? -Preocupada

13.16 **Expectativas** A veces las personas que nos rodean (*around us*) esperan algo de nosotros. Entrevista a un compañero de clase, usando las siguientes preguntas.

1. ¿Qué te piden tus amigos que hagas?
2. ¿Qué quiere tu mejor amigo que hagas?
3. ¿Qué esperas tú que tus amigos hagan?
4. ¿Qué te recomienda el profesor de español?
5. ¿Qué le sugieres tú al profesor de español?
6. ¿Qué sugiere tu médico que hagas?
7. ¿Qué insiste tu jefe que hagas?
8. ¿Qué quieres tú que hagan tus compañeros de trabajo?

> **iTunes**
> Listen to Colombian singer Juanes' song "A Dios le pido." Make a list of the verbs in the subjunctive. What is it he asks of God?

13.17 **Todos tienen problemas** Con un compañero, van a hacer los papeles (*roles*) del consejero y del cliente. Escojan una de las fotos. El cliente debe explicar su problema y el consejero va a darle recomendaciones usando el subjuntivo y los verbos a continuación. Luego, escojan otra foto y cambien de papel.

esperar   insistir   mandar   necesitar   pedir   recomendar   sugerir

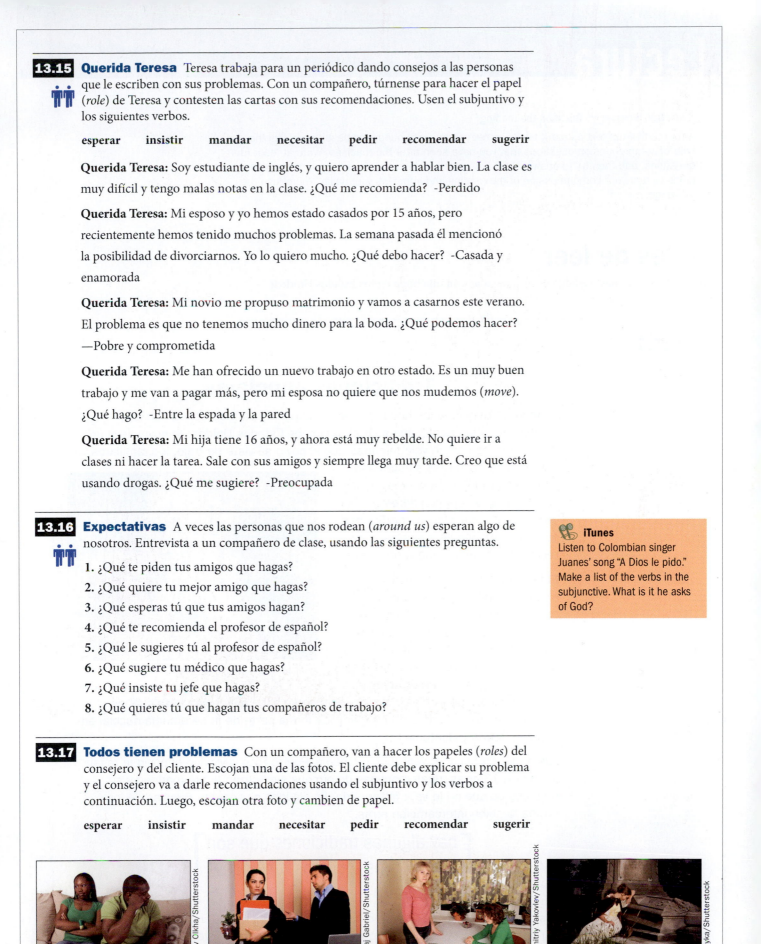

© Lev Olkha/Shutterstock © Blaj Gabriel/Shutterstock © Dmitriy Yakovlev/Shutterstock © Anyka/Shutterstock

Lectura

Antes de leer

¿Cuáles son algunas tradiciones relacionadas con una boda en los Estados Unidos?

A leer

Tradiciones nupciales

En muchos aspectos las bodas típicas en España y Latinoamérica son muy semejantes a las bodas que se realizan en los Estados Unidos: la novia lleva un vestido blanco con un velo mientras que el novio se viste de traje, los familiares y amigos de los novios asisten a la ceremonia y luego a una recepción, y la iglesia se decora con flores y velas. Sin embargo, hay algunas tradiciones que son particulares a ciertas regiones del mundo hispanohablante.

El anillo es un símbolo de amor

© Francois Etienne du Plessis/Shutterstock

rope

El lazo: Durante la ceremonia en México es tradicional que una pareja casada ponga un lazo en figura de ocho sobre la cabeza de los novios, representando la unión entre los dos. Los aztecas tenían una práctica semejante en la que **amarraban** las

tied

puntas de las túnicas de los novios, pero no se sabe a ciencia cierta cuál es el origen de esta costumbre porque también forma parte de la ceremonia nupcial en España, Bolivia y Guatemala.

Las arras: En España, Venezuela, Panamá, Puerto Rico y México el novio le regala a la novia 13 arras, unas **monedas** de oro que simbolizan la prosperidad y su promesa de que no le va a **faltar** nada. En algunos países, las familias de los novios también intercambian arras.

coins
to lack

> [hay algunas tradiciones que son particulares a ciertas regiones del mundo hispanohablante]

Los anillos: El anillo es un símbolo muy importante del amor que se tiene la pareja y representa la fidelidad que se prometen el uno al otro. En España y en la mayor parte de Latinoamérica se intercambian los anillos durante la ceremonia,

Hay semejanzas y diferencias en las tradiciones de bodas.

pero en Argentina y Chile **se entregan** en una fiesta donde se celebra el compromiso de los novios. En Chile se lleva el anillo en la mano derecha hasta el día de la boda, cuando lo cambian a la mano izquierda.

are given

Los padrinos: El padrino es una figura muy importante en la boda, aunque su función varía un poco entre Latinoamérica y España. En España el padrino de la boda, quien lleva a la novia al altar, suele ser su padre, aunque es posible que sea otro familiar. En algunas comunidades él le regala **el ramo** de flores a la novia durante la ceremonia.

bouquet

En México hay entre cinco y ocho padrinos que **se encargan** de diferentes partes de la ceremonia, como los padrinos de lazo, que le ponen el lazo a la pareja durante la ceremonia, o las madrinas de ramo, que se encargan de los ramos de flores: uno para ofrecerle a la Virgen de Guadalupe y el otro que **se lanza** en la recepción. Típicamente los padrinos ayudan con los gastos económicos de la boda, por ejemplo, la madrina del pastel es responsable de comprar el pastel.

are responsible

is tossed

La procesión: En la mayoría de los países latinoamericanos, el padre de la novia la lleva al altar para entregársela a su esposo, pero en algunas partes de El Salvador la ceremonia comienza sin la novia ni su familia. Siete hombres salen de la iglesia para acompañar a la novia y a su familia a la iglesia. En Chile y en Argentina, es común que los padres acompañen a la pareja al altar y que se queden junto a ellos para presenciar la ceremonia.

A pesar de las grandes semejanzas en las tradiciones que rodean las bodas, sobreviven algunas diferencias regionales que reflejan los valores culturales de cada grupo.

Sources: ArtículosInformativos.com.mx, Boston Bridal Shows, Bodas.net

Comprensión

Decide si las ideas son ciertas o falsas y corrige las ideas falsas.

1. En España y Latinoamérica, generalmente la novia viste un vestido blanco.
2. Las arras son un símbolo de amor.
3. La costumbre de poner un lazo en forma del número ocho se originó entre los aztecas.
4. Los padrinos y madrinas de una boda ayudan con los gastos.
5. En Chile y Argentina el anillo se entrega en una fiesta antes de la boda.
6. En toda Latinoamérica, el padre entrega a la novia en el altar.

En la televisión hay una gran variedad de programas para todos los gustos.

La televisión

los anuncios comerciales	TV commercials
la cablevisión	cablevision
el canal	TV channel
la clasificación	TV rating (for adults, for the whole family, etc.)
el patrocinador	sponsor
la programación	programming
la telenovela	soap opera
el televidente	television viewer
la televisión por satélite	satellite television

El Internet

las redes sociales	social networks

El cine

la butaca	seat
el éxito de taquilla	box office hit
las golosinas	candy
las palomitas de maíz	popcorn

Verbos

chatear	to chat online
censurar	to censor
hacer clic (en)	to click (on)

limitar	to limit
transmitir	to broadcast

Práctica

13.18 **Escucha y responde** Escucha las palabras y decide si se relacionan con el cine o con la televisión. Indica con el pulgar hacia arriba si la idea se refiere al cine, y el pulgar hacia abajo si se refiere a la televisión. Si las palabras se refieren a las dos, extiende los cinco dedos.

CD 2-24

13.19 **¿Cierto o falso?** Corrige las ideas que sean falsas.

1. C F Un locutor es una persona que habla en los anuncios de televisión o radio.
2. C F Generalmente las telenovelas son programas infantiles.
3. C F Los conductores de un programa de televisión son los choferes de los actores.
4. C F Los canales de televisión transmiten anuncios comerciales.
5. C F Cuando mandamos un correo electrónico escribimos con el ratón.
6. C F La clasificación de un programa de televisión depende del tipo de audiencia.

13.20 **¿Qué es?** Completa las oraciones con palabras de la lista de vocabulario.

1. Un programa de televisión que está dirigido a los niños es para una audiencia _____. Pero un programa que sólo pueden verlo las personas mayores de 18 años es para _____.
2. Casi todos los canales interrumpen sus programas para transmitir varios _____ que generalmente duran 30 segundos.
3. A veces es necesario modificar las películas y otros programas de televisión para que toda la familia pueda verlos. La acción de cortar ciertas escenas se llama _____.
4. Si contratamos cablevisión podemos ver más _____ de televisión.
5. La persona que oímos en los anuncios en la tele o en la radio es _____.
6. En Latinoamérica, las _____ más populares son Facebook, Hi5 y Sónico.

13.21 **Relaciones** Con un compañero, relacionen las dos columnas para crear ideas lógicas. Expliquen la relación entre las dos palabras.

Modelo transmitir   la cablevisión
    *Algunos programas de televisión **se transmiten** solamente por **cablevisión**.*

1. el ratón
2. el locutor
3. el patrocinador
4. los dibujos animados
5. las revistas
6. las palomitas de maíz

a. los deportes
b. los artículos
c. los anuncios
d. las golosinas
e. los programas infantiles
f. el tablero

13.22 **Opiniones** En grupos de tres, van a dar sus opiniones sobre las siguientes afirmaciones. ¿Están de acuerdo o no? Justifiquen sus respuestas.

1. La televisión es el medio de comunicación más importante.
2. Hay demasiados programas para adultos en horarios para toda la familia.
3. Es importante censurar el contenido de algunos programas de televisión.
4. Las telenovelas no tienen ningún valor social o educativo.
5. La televisión hace que los televidentes no piensen ni sean creativos.
6. Gracias a la televisión estamos mejor informados y más educados que en el pasado.
7. No se debe permitir que algunos patrocinadores se anuncien en televisión.
8. Paso más horas en las redes sociales de Internet que viendo televisión.
9. Prefiero ver las películas en DVD en mi casa en vez de ir al cine.
10. A veces compro revistas o alquilo películas basándome solamente en la portada (*cover*).

iTunes
Listen to Guatemalan singer Ricardo Arjona's song "Frente al televisor." What is he watching? Why is he watching television?

En vivo

Las fotonovelas son un pasatiempo popular que ha sobrevivido a pesar de la competencia de la programación en cablevisión y satélite, de los DVDs, de las computadoras y de los éxitos de taquilla. ¿Cuál piensas que es la definición de una fotonovela? Lee el artículo sobre las fotonovelas para responder a las siguientes preguntas. ¿Cómo se cree que se originaron las fotonovelas? ¿Cuántas copias se llegan a publicar de cada fotonovela? ¿En qué aspectos es diferente la fotonovela mexicoamericana?

Las fotonovelas

Como su nombre lo dice, las fotonovelas son novelas, pero están narradas visualmente a partir de fotografías. En México las fotonovelas tuvieron su origen en las historietas de siglo, que eran versiones ilustradas de obras populares de la literatura europea. Algunas personas piensan que el origen de las fotonovelas está en la mercadotecnia, ya que, al parecer, se incluían pequeños segmentos ilustrados de relatos románticos en los paquetes de cigarrillos. Para saber cómo continuaba la historia, había que seguir comprándolos semana tras semana.

Desde el siglo XIX hasta hoy en día, las fotonovelas se publican en numerosos episodios. Estas historias eventualmente dieron forma a la serie original que se centró en la vida mexicana contemporánea. Popular hasta el día de hoy, la historieta moderna tiene objetivos tan variados como el entretenimiento, la educación y la política. El tiraje de un ejemplar puede ser de hasta 250 mil ejemplares, por lo que llegan a un enorme y variado público de lectores. Debido al tiraje tan elevado, se puede hablar de que circulan en el país alrededor de 30 millones de historietas y fotonovelas cada mes.

Dentro de la comunidad mexico-americana en los Estados Unidos la fotonovela tiene una manifestación distinta, donde proporciona un canal para que la comunidad exprese sus preocupaciones sociales a través de un lenguaje visual innovador. Activistas y grupos religiosos también han recurrido a la fotonovela como una herramienta de organización para la divulgación, la educación y el proselitismo.

Aunque las fotonovelas parecen simples, esta impresión es engañosa. Los argumentos[1] tienden a ser melodramáticos, con temas como el ascenso social a la riqueza, los secretos de familia sobre amores prohibidos entre personas de diferentes clases sociales, etcétera. Más recientemente, los argumentos han tratado de temas sociales, o incluso de elementos sobrenaturales, como fantasmas.

[1]plots

Sources: Public Broadcasting Service and *La Crónica de Hoy: Historietas y revistas, no libros, lecturas favoritas del mexicano.*

Más allá

Imagínate que un compañero y tú están escribiendo una fotonovela original, y tienen que diseñar una página con cuatro escenas. Escriban una descripción de las fotografías y el diálogo de los personajes.

A analizar

Lee las siguientes oraciones y observa los verbos en negritas.

Al director le gusta **llegar** temprano al trabajo y le molesta que los actores **lleguen** tarde.

Muchas personas están contentas de poder **bajar** películas del Internet, pero los cines temen que esto **tenga** un mal efecto en la taquilla.

A los niños les encanta **ver** la tele, pero a sus padres les preocupa que **vean** demasiados programas violentos.

Some of the verbs are in the subjunctive and others are not. Why do you think this is?

A comprobar

Subjunctive with expressions of emotion

1. When expressing an emotion or feeling about something, it is necessary to use the subjunctive if there are two different subjects. Again, the verb in the main clause is in the indicative, and the verb in the dependent clause is in the subjunctive.

Main clause		Dependent clause
Me alegra	que	el programa **se transmita** por la noche.
Él tiene miedo de	que	el gobierno **censure** la programación.

2. Some verbs that express emotion are:

estar contento de	to be glad; to be pleased
estar triste de	to be sad
sentir	to be sorry, to regret
temer/tener miedo de	to fear

Temo que haya demasiados programas violentos.
I am afraid that there are too many violent programs.

Los niños **están contentos de** que su madre les permita ver los dibujos animados.
The children are glad that their mother allows them to watch cartoons.

3. Other verbs that express emotion are:

alegrar	to make happy	**molestar**	to bother
enojar	to make angry	**preocupar**	to worry
encantar	to love	**sorprender**	to surprise
gustar	to like		

You will recall that the verbs **gustar, encantar,** and **molestar** require the use of the indirect object. The other verbs in this list also require the use of the indirect object.

Al director **le** preocupa que los actores no lleguen a tiempo.
The director is worried the actors won't arrive on time.

Me sorprende que haya tantos anuncios comerciales.
It surprises me that there are so many commercials.

4. If there is only one subject, the **que** is not necessary and the infinitive is used with the expression of emotion rather than the subjunctive.

Estoy contento de **ayudar** con el documental.
I am happy to help with the documentary.

Sentimos no **poder** asistir al estreno.
We regret not being able to attend the debut.

A practicar

13.23 **Un poco de lógica** Lee las siguientes oraciones y decide si las reacciones son lógicas o no. Después corrige las oraciones ilógicas.

1. Me alegra que no transmitan mi programa favorito hoy.
2. A los productores les preocupa que el programa no tenga éxito.
3. Los padres temen que sus hijos miren dibujos animados.
4. A los actores les molesta que la compañía haya cancelado su programa.
5. Nos sorprende que el público se ría durante la serie cómica.
6. Elisa siente que el abuelo tenga cáncer.

13.24 **En el foro** Hoy están grabando una telenovela, y hay muchas emociones en el foro *(set)*. Completa las oraciones con la forma apropiada del verbo entre paréntesis. **¡OJO!** Algunos verbos están en el subjuntivo y otros en el infinitivo.

1. Al director le enoja que los actores _____ (hacer) muchos errores y que _____ (tener) que repetir las escenas.
2. A Rosalía le preocupa que Pedro _____ (ir) a olvidar lo que tiene que decir.
3. A Bernardo le alegra _____ (poder) ser parte de la telenovela.
4. A Gustavo no le gusta que su papel *(part)* no _____ (ser) más importante.
5. A Vicente le encanta _____ (besar) a Lupita, pero a ella le molesta que él no _____ (cepillarse) los dientes.
6. A todos les sorprende que el director _____ (frustrarse).

13.25 **Oraciones incompletas** Con un compañero, túrnense para completar las siguientes oraciones. **¡OJO!** Las oraciones deben tener dos sujetos.

1. Al profesor de español le molesta que...
2. Al presidente le preocupa que...
3. El patrocinador está triste de que...
4. Los niños se sienten mal de que...
5. A los estudiantes de español les sorprende que...
6. Mi familia está contenta de que...
7. A los reporteros les gusta que...
8. Los comediantes temen que...

> **INVESTIGUEMOS LA GRAMÁTICA**
>
> You learned in **Capítulo 9** that the reflexive form of the verb **sentir** means to *feel* and is used with an adverb or an adjective. This would also require the subjunctive if there are two subjects.
>
> **Me siento** mal de que no puedas ir al cine con nosotros.
> *I feel badly* that you can't come to the movie theater with us.

13.26 **Hablando de la tele** Trabaja con un compañero para expresar sus opiniones sobre la televisión.

Modelo alegrar
   Estudiante 1: *Me alegra que haya una gran variedad de programas.*
   Estudiante 2: *Me alegra que se pueda bloquear los programas inapropiados para los niños.*

sorprender   **gustar**   **molestar**   **preocupar**   **temer**   **enojar**

> **INVESTIGUEMOS LA GRAMÁTICA**
>
> In **Capítulo 9** you learned that the reflexive verbs **alegrarse, enojarse, preocuparse,** etc., are used to express a change in emotion or feeling. These verbs would also require the subjunctive.
>
> Me alegro de que **vayas** a casarte.
> *I am happy that you are going to get married.*
>
> Sus padres se preocupan de que no **estén** listos.
> *Their parents are worried that they are not ready.*

13.27 **El safari** Con un compañero expliquen lo que pasa en los programas y las reacciones emocionales de los personajes.

Vocabulario útil:

la base base

el extraterrestre extraterrestrial

el príncipe prince

el dragón dragon

el ladrón thief

engañar to cheat on

la princesa princess

Modelo *El jugador corre a primera base. A sus compañeros de equipo les alegra que pueda correr tan rápido. Al otro jugador le preocupa que llegue a la base.*

1.

2.

3.

4.

5. Mi respuesta es.... $1500 $1500

6.

13.28 **Los noticiarios** Imagínate que escuchas las siguientes noticias en un noticiario. Con un compañero, túrnense para expresar una reacción. Deben usar el subjuntivo y una expresión de duda o de emoción o una expresión impersonal.

Modelo Un ciudadano dice que vio un fantasma en el ayuntamiento (*town hall*).
No creo que existan los fantasmas.
Me sorprende que haya fantasmas en el ayuntamiento.
Espero que el fantasma sea bueno.

1. Dos personas están heridas después de un accidente de coche.

2. Van a cancelar el Super Tazón (*Super Bowl*) este año.

3. Los científicos creen que han encontrado una cura para el cáncer.

4. Una niña de 6 años desapareció de su casa.

5. El presidente dice que la economía va a mejorar el próximo año.

6. Han descubierto que hay vida en el planeta Marte.

7. El departamento de salud va a empezar un estudio sobre los hábitos de los ratones.

8. Un prisionero escapó de la prisión estatal.

Conexiones culturales

¡De película!

Cultura

En años recientes, el cine latinoamericano ha producido películas excepcionales, muchas de las cuales han sido muy exitosas en los Estados Unidos. Por ejemplo, *El laberinto del fauno* (traducida al inglés como *Pan's Laberynth*) es un filme dirigido por Guillermo del Toro, un cineasta mexicano que desde el inicio de su carrera ha creado películas con una temática relacionada con la Guerra Civil Española. En *El laberinto del fauno*, Guillermo del Toro y su equipo crearon unos efectos visuales increíbles para narrar la historia de una niña que crea un mundo imaginario ante la horrible realidad de la guerra. Esta película ganó 3 Óscares, además de haber ganado 68 premios internacionales y haber obtenido otras 58 nominaciones.

El director Guillermo del Toro

Elige una de las películas de la lista y mírala. Después escribe una crítica de la película. Usa las preguntas como guía: ¿Cuál es la trama de la película? ¿Cómo es la actuación en la película? ¿Piensas que la película tiene un mensaje social? ¿La recomiendas? ¿Por qué?

*El secreto de sus ojos** (Argentina)   *Amores perros* (México)
Nueve reinas (Argentina)   *Voces inocentes* (México)
El padre de la novia (Argentina)   *La nana* (Chile)
Frida (México)   *María llena de gracia* (Colombia)
El laberinto del fauno (México)   *La misma luna* (México – Estados Unidos)

> 🌐 Investiga en Internet sobre la vida y la filmografía de Guillermo del Toro.

INVESTIGUEMOS EL VOCABULARIO

¡De película! is an expression that means that something is very cool, for example, *¡La fiesta estuvo de película!* The following are some other ways to say that something is cool. They can be used as adjectives with the verb **estar** or in an exclamation with the word **qué**.

¡Qué padre!   *How cool!*
¡Ese coche está chévere!   *That car is cool!*

padre	(Mexico)
guay	(Spain)
chévere	(numerous countries in Latin America)
copado	(Argentina, Uruguay)
sólido	(Panamá)
bacán	(Chile)

*recibió el Óscar para La Mejor Película Extranjera en 2010

Comparaciones

En el mundo actual en donde los sistemas de comunicación son excelentes, es muy común que un programa que fue exitoso en un país se adapte para producirse en otro país.

Los siguientes son programas de la televisión estadounidense originales de la televisión hispana. Por ejemplo, el programa de Betty la Fea era originalmente una telenovela colombiana. Fue tan exitosa que se hicieron nuevas versiones en numerosos países, incluyendo una versión en chino. La adaptación estadounidense se transmitió en un formato más típico del país, con episodios semanales en vez de diarios.

> *Betty la fea (Ugly Betty)*
> *Nada más que la verdad (The Moment of Truth)*

Programas de la televisión hispana que se adaptaron de series originales estadounidenses:

> *100 mexicanos dijeron (Family Feud)*
> *La niñera (The Nanny)*
> *Amas de casa desesperadas (Desperate Housewives)*
> *Trato hecho (Let's Make a Deal)*

¿Creen que los programas tienen diferencias importantes al ser adaptados a otro país? ¿Por qué?

Betty la fea de la telenovela colombiana

Conexiones... a la literatura

Rosario Castellanos (1925–1974) fue una escritora y poeta mexicana muy influyente. Se destacó por sus escritos de orientación feminista aun en una época en la que no se hablaba mucho sobre este tema. Castellanos también trabajó como representante de México en el exterior. Murió accidentalmente mientras era embajadora de México en Israel.

El siguiente es uno de sus poemas, titulado "Telenovela". Antes de leer, escribe un par de ideas que piensas que sean comunes en las telenovelas. Mientras lees, busca esas ideas. Después de leer contesta las preguntas.

Telenovela

El sitio que dejó vacante Homero,
el centro que ocupaba Scherezada
(o antes de la invención del lenguaje, el lugar
en que se congregaba la gente de la tribu
para escuchar al fuego)
ahora está ocupado por la Gran Caja Idiota. [...]

Porque aquí, en la pantalla, una enfermera
se enfrenta con la esposa frívola del doctor
y le dicta una cátedra
en que habla de moral profesional
y las interferencias de la vida privada. [...]

Porque una novia espera al que se fue;
porque una intrigante urde mentiras:
porque se falsifica un testamento;
porque una soltera da un mal paso
y no acierta a ocultar las consecuencias.

Pero también porque la debutante
ahuyenta a todos con su mal aliento.
Porque la lavandera entona una aleluya
en loor del poderoso detergente.

Porque el amor está garantizado
por un desodorante
y una marca especial de cigarrillos
y hay que brindar por él con alguna bebida
que nos hace felices y distintos. [...]

Cuando el programa acaba
la reunión se disuelve.
Cada uno va a su cuarto
mascullando un —apenas— "buenas noches".

Y duerme. Y tiene hermosos sueños prefabricados.

1. ¿Cuál es la idea central de la primera estrofa? ¿y en las siguientes dos estrofas?
2. ¿Cuál es la idea central de la cuarta estrofa? ¿y en la última parte?
3. En tu opinión ¿cuál es el mensaje del poema?

Comunidad

En la mayoría de las ciudades de los Estados Unidos es posible recibir al menos un canal de televisión en español. Elige un segmento de la programación (de unas 2–3 horas) y analízalo. ¿Qué tipo de programas hay? ¿Quiénes son los patrocinadores? ¿A qué audiencia se dirigen? ¿Te gustó alguno de los programas? ¿Por qué? ¿Crees que estos programas ayuden a la población hispana de la comunidad? ¿Por qué?

En los Estados Unidos recibimos canales de televisión en español.

A analizar

Lee la conversación y observa los verbos en negritas.

Germán: ¿Qué quieres mirar, mi amor?

Catalina: Quiero ver un programa que **sea** cómico.

Germán: Hay una película cómica que **parece** divertida. Comienza en una hora.

Catalina: ¿No hay nada que **comience** ahora?

Germán: No, no hay ningún programa que **sea** cómico, pero hay un drama que **tiene** unos actores muy buenos.

Catalina: Bueno, vamos a mirarlo.

You will notice that some of the verbs are in the indicative and others are in the subjunctive. Using what you have already learned about the use of the subjunctive, why do you think this is?

A comprobar

Subjunctive with adjective clauses

1. When using an adjective clause (underlined in the examples below) to describe something that the speaker knows exists the indicative is used.

   Quiero ver la telenovela que **comienza** a las ocho.

   En ese programa hay un conductor que **es** muy cómico.

2. However, when using an adjective clause (underlined in the examples below) to describe something that the speaker does not know exists or believes does not exist the subjunctive is used.

   Quiero ver una telenovela que **sea** intrigante.
   I want to see a soap opera that is intriguing.

   ¿Hay un buen programa que **comience** ahora?
   Is there a good show that starts now?

   No hay ningún canal que **tenga** un documental esta noche.
   There is no channel that has a documentary tonight.

3. Some common verbs used with adjective clauses that can require either the subjunctive or the indicative are: **buscar, necesitar,** and **querer.**

   Busco un televisor que **tenga** una pantalla grande.
   I am looking for a television that has a big screen.

   Busco el televisor que **tiene** una pantalla grande.
   I am looking for a television that has a big screen.

In the first sentence the person does not have a specific television in mind and does not necessarily know if one exists, while in the second sentence he/she is looking for a specific television.

4. When asking about the existence of something, it is also necessary to use the subjunctive, as you do not know whether or not it exists.

   ¿Conoces a alguien que no **mire** la tele?
   Do you know anyone that doesn't watch TV?

   ¿Hay alguna película que **sea** romántica?
   Is there a romantic movie?

5. When using negative words, such as **nadie** or **ninguno,** to express the belief that something does not exist, it is necessary to use the subjunctive in the adjective clause.

   No conozco a nadie que no **mire** la tele.
   I don't know anyone that doesn't watch TV.

   No hay ninguna película que **sea** romántica.
   There is no movie that is romantic.

INVESTIGUEMOS LA GRÁMATICA

When you do not have a specific person in mind or do not know if someone exists, it is not necessary to use the personal **a** in the main clause, except with **alguien** or **nadie.**

La estación de radio **busca un locutor** *que pueda trabajar por la noche.*

¿Conoces a alguien que busque trabajo?

A practicar

13.29 **¿Estás de acuerdo?** Lee las oraciones y decide si estás de acuerdo o no. Explica por qué.

1. Hoy en día no hay nadie que tenga televisor en blanco y negro.
2. La producción de programas de televisión es una profesión que paga bien.
3. Me molestan los anuncios comerciales que hay en la televisión.
4. Prefiero mirar programas que tengan mucha acción.
5. No hay ningún canal local que ofrezca buena programación.
6. Es importante que los niños no vean programas que tengan contenido para adultos.

13.30 **Un nuevo teléfono celular** Hoy en día se puede hacer mucho con los celulares, como mirar la tele, escuchar música y sacar fotos. ¿Qué otros avances puede haber en el futuro? Conjuga los verbos en el subjuntivo para completar las ideas. Después di si estás de acuerdo o no con la afirmación.

Quiero tener un teléfono celular que...

1. (poder) mandar documentos por fax
2. (grabar) las conversaciones
3. (servir) para abrir y cerrar el coche automáticamente
4. (traducir) del inglés al español
5. (tener) una luz para poder usarla como una linterna
6. (ser) tan delgado como una tarjeta de crédito

13.31 **¿Qué buscas?** Usando el subjuntivo, explica lo que buscan las personas en los dibujos.

Modelo *El muchacho busca un programa que sea cómico y que comience a las siete.*

1.

2.

3.

4.

5.

13.32 Un invento increíble Con un compañero diseñen un invento y dibújenlo. Luego completen las siguientes oraciones para explicarle su invento a la clase.

Queremos inventar un(a) _____ que...
Nuestro invento tendrá _____ que...

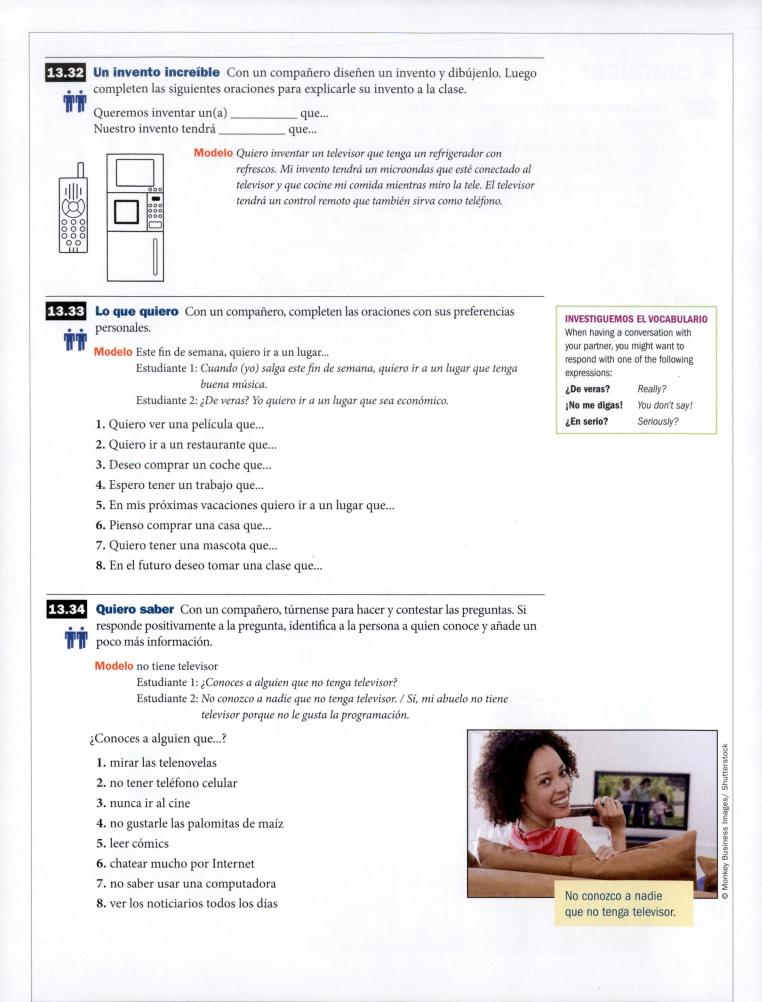

Modelo *Quiero inventar un televisor que tenga un refrigerador con refrescos. Mi invento tendrá un microondas que esté conectado al televisor y que cocine mi comida mientras miro la tele. El televisor tendrá un control remoto que también sirva como teléfono.*

13.33 Lo que quiero Con un compañero, completen las oraciones con sus preferencias personales.

Modelo Este fin de semana, quiero ir a un lugar...
Estudiante 1: *Cuando (yo) salga este fin de semana, quiero ir a un lugar que tenga buena música.*
Estudiante 2: *¿De veras? Yo quiero ir a un lugar que sea económico.*

1. Quiero ver una película que...
2. Quiero ir a un restaurante que...
3. Deseo comprar un coche que...
4. Espero tener un trabajo que...
5. En mis próximas vacaciones quiero ir a un lugar que...
6. Pienso comprar una casa que...
7. Quiero tener una mascota que...
8. En el futuro deseo tomar una clase que...

INVESTIGUEMOS EL VOCABULARIO
When having a conversation with your partner, you might want to respond with one of the following expressions:

¿De veras?	*Really?*
¡No me digas!	*You don't say!*
¿En serio?	*Seriously?*

13.34 Quiero saber Con un compañero, túrnense para hacer y contestar las preguntas. Si responde positivamente a la pregunta, identifica a la persona a quien conoce y añade un poco más información.

Modelo no tiene televisor
Estudiante 1: *¿Conoces a alguien que no tenga televisor?*
Estudiante 2: *No conozco a nadie que no tenga televisor. / Sí, mi abuelo no tiene televisor porque no le gusta la programación.*

¿Conoces a alguien que...?

1. mirar las telenovelas
2. no tener teléfono celular
3. nunca ir al cine
4. no gustarle las palomitas de maíz
5. leer cómics
6. chatear mucho por Internet
7. no saber usar una computadora
8. ver los noticiarios todos los días

No conozco a nadie que no tenga televisor.

© Monkey Business Images/ Shutterstock

Redacción

Write a dramatic scene from a soap opera or a TV drama. It should be written as a script with stage directions in parentheses.

Paso 1 Think of a dramatic problem that would involve two people, such as a marriage proposal or a break-up. Then brainstorm where the scene would take place. Jot down down some ideas such as where the two characters are, what is around them, what they are doing, etc.

Paso 2 Think about what might be said in a conversation of this nature and jot down some key sentences and questions along with some responses to those statements/questions.

© Deborah Cloyed Shutterstock

Paso 3 Write an initial paragraph in which you describe the scene in detail using the information generated in **Paso 1.**

Paso 4 Using the information you generated in **Paso 2,** create a dramatic dialogue between the two characters. Because communication involves more than words, you will need to include gestures, tone, actions, etc., in parentheses.

Paso 5 Edit your script:

  a. Are the stage directions clear?

  b. Read the dialogue out loud. Does it flow? Does it seem "natural"?

  c. Do your adjectives and your verbs agree with the subject?

  d. Do you have a **personal a** where necessary? And indirect object pronouns?

  e. Did you check your spelling, including accents?

Lectura

Antes de leer

1. ¿Cuáles son las características generales de las telenovelas?

2. ¿Cuáles son dos telenovelas muy conocidas en los Estados Unidos?

3. ¿Conoces alguna telenovela latinoamericana? ¿En qué son diferentes a las de los Estados Unidos?

4. ¿Piensas que las telenovelas tengan algún valor?

5. En lo personal ¿te interesan las telenovelas?

A leer

Las telenovelas latinoamericanas: más que un entretenimiento

stations

Las telenovelas latinoamericanas son la columna vertebral de muchas **emisoras** de televisión en Latinoamérica. Se transmiten en todos los horarios, y satisfacen la demanda de todas las audiencias. Quienes creen que las telenovelas son solo para amas de casa, deben echar un **vistazo** a los distintos subgéneros que han nacido en las últimas décadas: telenovelas históricas para los más intelectuales, telenovelas para niños, telenovelas de problemática social, y hasta telenovelas dirigidas a los hombres. Según los productores, este género promueve cambios sociales, ayuda a educar a la gente sobre temas de interés social, como el **SIDA,** la homosexualidad o la inmigración, y hasta ha ayudado a salvar vidas.

glance

AIDS

Las telenovelas latinoamericanas se transmiten alrededor del mundo.

[**este género promueve cambios sociales**]

Las telenovelas latinoamericanas han evolucionado mucho desde su aparición. En un principio casi todas las telenovelas eran la típica historia de **Cenicienta,** en donde una humilde mujer se enamoraba de un amor imposible —generalmente un hombre rico de buena familia. La protagonista debía **luchar** contra innumerables

Cinderella

struggle

desgracias, pero al final se quedaba con el hombre de sus sueños. Aunque todavía hoy en día se producen telenovelas de este tipo, también es cierto que se producen muchas otras con una temática más interesante que atrae a televidentes muy diversos. A veces se convierten en fenómenos sociales, como es el caso del grupo musical Rebelde, creado en una telenovela, pero que ahora hace **giras** por todo el mundo, atrayendo multitudes y llenando estadios. Es común que muchas de estas telenovelas se traduzcan a docenas de otros idiomas, y rompan récords en el número de televidentes en países tan diferentes como Rusia, China y Rumania.

tours

Una gran ventaja del formato de la telenovela latinoamericana es que tiene una duración limitada, generalmente alrededor de seis meses, lo que la hace mucho más versátil que la telenovela estadounidense. Los culebrones latinoamericanos (otro nombre con que se conoce a las telenovelas) son producto de exportación, y se transmiten en más de cien países alrededor del mundo. De hecho, se consideran una gran fuente de empleo que promueve la economía de los países que las producen, y no sería de extrañar que en el futuro cercano este formato empiece a atraer a mayor número de televidentes dentro de los Estados Unidos.

Comprensión

1. ¿Cuáles son dos diferencias importantes entre las telenovelas de los Estados Unidos y las telenovelas latinoamericanas?
2. ¿Qué temas de interés social han tratado algunas telenovelas?
3. Según el texto, ¿qué se creó a partir de la telenovela *Rebelde*?
4. ¿Cómo afectan la economía las telenovelas?
5. En tu opinión, ¿qué hace populares a estas historias en tantos países con culturas tan diferentes?
6. En tu opinión ¿de qué puede tratar una telenovela dirigida a niños?
7. ¿Conoces a alguien que vea telenovelas? Si contestas que sí, ¿sabes por qué le gustan?

Después de leer

Investiga los temas de algunas de las novelas que se transmiten en la actualidad por los canales de televisión en español. ¿Tienen algún mensaje social?

© Music4mix/Shutterstock

"Más sabe El Diablo" se transmite en más de 70 países.

Salimos al aire en un minuto.

© Ricardo Azoury/Corbis

Vocabulario

Sustantivos

la cámara	*camera*
el (la) camarógrafo(a)	*camera person*
el (la) entrevistado(a)	*interviewee*
el foro	*set*
el guión	*script*
el (la) invitado(a)	*guest*
el maquillaje	*makeup*
el micrófono	*microphone*
el vestuario	*dressing room*

Adjetivos

atento	*attentive*
neutro	*neutral*
presentable	*presentable*
puntual	*punctual*
simpático	*appealing*

Verbos

despedirse	*to say good-bye*
guiar	*to guide*
presentarse	*to introduce yourself*

Expresiones útiles

salir al aire
to be on the air

seguir el guión
to follow the script

mirar fijo a la cámara
to look straight into the camera

Vamos a comerciales.
Let's go to commercials.

DATOS IMPORTANTES

Educación: Estudios universitarios o terciarios en comunicación y/o negocios

Salario: Entre $35 000 y $140 000, dependiendo de los años de experiencia, en un rango de 1 a 20 años.

Dónde se trabaja: En canales de televisión locales o nacionales, públicos o privados. En canales de televisión por cablevisión o satélite.

Ruth Oviedo es productora de televisión. Trabaja en un canal privado de cable y está preparándose para un nuevo programa. En el video verás a Ruth dándole instrucciones a una persona.

Antes de ver

Los productores de programas de televisión trabajan detrás de las cámaras. Los televidentes no los ven, pero ellos hacen lo más importante de lo que vemos en TV. Las notas, el entretenimiento y el formato de los programas son idea de los productores. ¿Qué tipo de programas te parece que es más interesante para producir? ¿Qué ideas o qué formato nuevo presentarías? ¿Cuántos actores o presentadores necesitarías? Presenta ideas novedosas.

Al ver

1. ¿A quién le da instrucciones Ruth?
2. ¿Dónde estará Ruth durante el programa?
3. ¿Qué ropa no le gusta a Jorge?
4. ¿Qué es lo primero que debe hacer Jorge al empezar el programa?
5. ¿Quién es el invitado de hoy?
6. ¿Qué tiene que hacer Jorge con la ropa durante el concurso?
7. ¿Quién participará en el concurso?
8. ¿Cuándo salen al aire?

© Heinle/Cengage Learning

Después de ver

En grupos de tres, representen a un productor de televisión dando instrucciones antes de la grabación de un programa. Las otras personas pueden ser actores, presentadores o personal técnico.

13.35 **La tele** Completa el párrafo con la forma apropiada del verbo entre paréntesis. **¡OJO!** Tendrás que usar el subjuntivo, el indicativo o el infinitivo.

Los Marino no quieren que su hijo Édgar **(1.)** _____ (ver) la tele mucho. Prefieren que **(2.)** _____ (pasar) más tiempo jugando afuera y leyendo. A Édgar le molesta que sus padres **(3.)** _____ (apagar) la tele después de una hora y que no le **(4.)** _____ (permitir) verla más. Esta noche él quiere **(5.)** _____ (ver) una película que **(6.)** _____ (empezar) a las ocho. Entonces, Édgar les pide a sus padres que le **(7.)** _____ permiso para verla. Su padre le dice que sí, pero insiste en que **(8.)** _____ (terminar) su tarea primero. A Édgar le alegra **(9.)** _____ (poder) ver la película, y promete terminar su tarea.

13.36 **Relaciones** Mira los dibujos y explica lo que pasa. Debes usar la forma recíproca de los verbos indicados en el presente del indicativo.

1.

amar, extrañar (*to miss*), escribir

2.

pelear, gritar (*to yell*), mirar

3.

conocer, dar la mano, besar

13.37 **Lo que se busca** Completa las oraciones con la forma apropiada del verbo entre paréntesis y con una conclusión lógica.

1. Al buscar una pareja, algunas personas buscan a alguien que (ser)...
2. Al salir en una cita, hay personas que buscan un lugar que (tener)...
3. Al casarse algunas parejas quieren tener una boda que (costar)...
4. Algunos recién casados prefieren vivir en un lugar que les (ofrecer)...
5. A veces después de tener hijos, los padres necesitan un trabajo que les (permitir)...
6. Si la pareja se divorcia, es buena idea conseguir un abogado que (ser)...

13.38 **Una telenovela** Las siguientes fotos son de varias escenas de telenovelas. En parejas, elijan una e inventen los detalles. Piensen en lo siguiente: ¿Quiénes son los protagonistas? ¿Cuál es la trama? ¿Qué pasa en esta escena? ¿Cómo se va a resolver la situación? Deben usar diferentes ejemplos del subjuntivo en la descripción.

© CURAphotography/Shutterstock
© Martin Novak/Shutterstock
© Doreen Salcher/Shutterstock
© Photos To Go

13.39 **¿Cuál es la pregunta?** Trabaja con un compañero. Uno de ustedes debe ver las preguntas en esta página, y el otro debe verlas en el apéndice A. Es una competencia y el ganador (*winner*) es quien tiene más puntos. Obtienes puntos cuando adivinas la pregunta <u>exacta</u> que tiene tu compañero. Para ayudarte, tu compañero te va a decir la respuesta a la pregunta. Tienes tres oportunidades para adivinar cada pregunta.

Modelo ¿Qué es extrañar?
Estudiante 1: *Es cuando no estás con una persona y estás triste. Piensas mucho en la persona.*
Estudiante 2: *¿Qué es extrañar?*

1. 10 puntos: ¿Qué es la luna de miel?
2. 20 puntos: ¿Qué es divorciarse?
3. 30 puntos: ¿Qué es un soltero?
4. 40 puntos: ¿Qué es un nacimiento?
5. 50 puntos: ¿Qué hacemos en la adolescencia?
6. 100 puntos: ¿Qué es enamorarse?

13.40 **¿Qué ves?** Habla con un compañero sobre sus hábitos en cuanto a la tele y al cine.

1. ¿Con qué frecuencia vas al cine? ¿Compras algo de comer o beber? ¿Qué?
2. ¿Te gusta mirar la tele? Aproximadamente, ¿cuántas horas miras la tele en una semana?
3. ¿Qué tipo de programas te gusta? ¿Tienes un programa favorito? ¿Cuál es?
4. ¿Qué tipo de programas no te gusta? ¿Por qué?
5. En tú opinión, ¿cómo nos beneficia (*benefit*) la televisión? ¿Cómo nos perjudica (*harm*)?
6. ¿Crees que deben censurar las películas y los programas de televisión por su contenido violento o sexual? ¿Por qué?

Vocabulario 1

CD 2-25

Relaciones personales

el anillo	*ring*	la pareja	*couple*
la ceremonia	*ceremony*	el (la) prometido(a)	*fiancé(e)*
la cita	*date*		
el compromiso	*engagement*	la recepción	*wedding reception*
la luna de miel	*honeymoon*	el (la) recién casado(a)	*newlywed*
la muerte	*death*		
el nacimiento	*birth*	el (la) soltero(a)	*unmarried person*
el noviazgo	*engagement, relationship*	la unión libre	*common-law union*
		el (la) viudo(a)	*widower (widow)*

Verbos

abrazar	*to hug*	llevarse (bien/mal)	*to (not) get along*
besar	*to kiss*		
comprometerse (con)	*to get engaged (to)*	mandar	*to order*
dar a luz	*to give birth*	nacer	*to be born*
desear	*to desire, to wish*	odiar	*to hate*
divorciarse (de)	*to divorce*	proponer (matrimonio)	*to propose (marriage)*
enamorarse (de)	*to fall in love (with)*	querer	*to love*
esperar	*to hope*	romper (con)	*to break up (with)*
estar embarazada	*to be pregnant*	separarse (de)	*to separate (from)*
extrañar	*to miss*	sugerir	*to suggest*
insistir (en)	*to insist (on)*		

Palabras adicionales

la adolescencia	*adolescence*	la muerte	*death*
el estado civil	*civil status*	la niñez	*childhood*
la juventud	*youth*	la vejez	*old age*
la madurez	*maturity*		

Diccionario personal

_____

_____

_____

_____

_____

◀)) Vocabulario 2

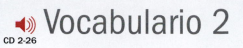

La televisión

el anuncio comercial	*commercial*
la audiencia	*audience*
la cablevisión	*cablevision*
el canal	*TV channel*
la clasificación	*TV rating (for adults, for the whole family, etc.)*
el concurso	*game show*
el conductor	*TV host*
el control remoto	*remote control*
el documental	*documentary*
los dibujos animados	*cartoons*

el (la) locutor(a)	*announcer*
el noticiario	*news*
el patrocinador	*sponsor*
la programación	*programming*
el reproductor de DVDs	*DVD player*
la telenovela	*soap opera*
el televidente	*television viewer*
la televisión por satélite	*satellite television*

La computadora

los audífonos	*headphones*
el buscador	*search engine*
el Internet	*Internet*
el MP3	*MP3 player*
la pantalla	*screen*

el ratón	*mouse*
las redes sociales	*social networks*
el reproductor de CDs	*CD player*
el tablero	*keyboard*

El cine

la butaca	*seat*
el éxito de taquilla	*box office hit*
las golosinas	*candy*

las palomitas de maíz	*popcorn*

Verbos

chatear	*to chat online*
censurar	*to censor*
hacer clic (en)	*to click (on)*

limitar	*to limit*
transmitir	*to broadcast*

Palabras adicionales

adolescente	*adolescent*
adulto	*adult*

infantil	*for children, childish*
la revista	*magazine*

Diccionario personal

_____

_____

_____

_____

Learning Strategy

Think in Spanish

When speaking, try to think in Spanish and speak spontaneously rather than translating everything. If you find you need to use a word that you don't know, rather than saying it in English or looking it up in the dictionary, try explaining the concept using other words. With a little practice, this skill will become easier.

In this chapter you will learn how to:
- Discuss health issues with a doctor
- Discuss hypothetical situations
- Express opinions regarding world issues
- Tell what had happened prior to other events in the past

¿Vivimos en un mundo sin fronteras?

© AFP/Getty Images

Exploraciones gramaticales
Conditional
Imperfect subjunctive
Subjunctive with adverbial clauses
Past perfect

En vivo
Guías para la alimentación
Organizaciones intra-gubernamentales

Conexiones culturales
Manteniéndonos saludables
Relaciones internacionales

Lectura
El valor de la salud
Latinoamérica y la inmigración

▶ Exploraciones profesionales
La medicina

Exploraciones **léxicas**

Los servicios de salud son muy importantes en todas las comunidades.

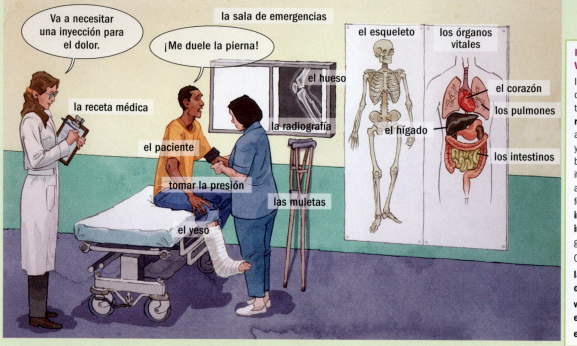

Va a necesitar una inyección para el dolor.

¡Me duele la pierna!

la sala de emergencias

el esqueleto

los órganos vitales

el hueso

la receta médica

la radiografía

el corazón

los pulmones

el paciente

el hígado

tomar la presión

las muletas

los intestinos

el yeso

INVESTIGUEMOS EL VOCABULARIO

In some countries different words are used to refer to a cold: **el resfriado, el catarro,** and **la gripe.** In recent years, it has come to be called **el flu** when it is more severe. There are also specific names for new types of flu: **influenza aviaria** and **influenza H1N1 A** are good examples.

Other variations:

la cirugía/la operación

vomitar/volver del estómago

el asco/la náusea

Los síntomas — Symptoms
- la alergia — allergy
- la cortada — cut
- el desmayo — faint
- la diarrea — diarrhea
- el dolor (de) — pain (in)
- el estornudo — sneeze
- la fractura — fracture
- la náusea — nausea
- la presión baja/alta — low/high blood pressure
- la tos — cough

Algunas enfermedades
- el cáncer — cancer
- la diabetes — diabetes
- la gripe — flu
- la hipertensión — high blood pressure

- el insomnio — insomnia
- la obesidad — obesity
- el resfriado — cold
- el SIDA — AIDS

Los medicamentos y procedimientos
- la aspirina — aspirin
- la cirugía — surgery
- la curita — small adhesive bandage
- las gotas — drops
- el jarabe — syrup (cough)
- la pastilla — pill
- la vacuna — vaccination
- el vendaje — bandage

Verbos
- cortarse — to cut oneself
- desmayarse — to faint

- estar mareado — to be dizzy
- estornudar — to sneeze
- examinar — to examine
- fracturarse — to fracture
- recuperarse — to recuperate, to recover
- respirar — to breathe
- torcerse (ue) — to twist, to sprain
- toser — to cough
- vomitar — to vomit

Palabras adicionales
- los primeros auxilios — first aid
- la salud — health
- la sangre — blood
- el tratamiento — treatment

A practicar

14.1 Escucha y responde En un papel escribe "síntoma" y en otro "tratamiento". Vas a escuchar una serie de palabras del vocabulario. Levanta el papel correspondiente si la palabra que escuches es un síntoma o un tratamiento.

CD2-27

14.2 **La salud** Escoge la opción más lógica para completar cada idea.

1. El (corazón / cerebro / hígado) sirve para pensar y regular el sistema nervioso.

2. Un síntoma de los resfriados es la (cirugía / obesidad / tos).

3. Le recomiendo tomar vitaminas si usted (se enferma / se recupera / se corta) con frecuencia.

4. El doctor (tose / examina / vomita) al paciente.

5. El órgano que sirve para respirar es (el hígado / el pulmón / el corazón).

6. Los paramédicos llevan en una (silla de ruedas / curita / inyección) a un hombre que se desmayó.

7. El paciente se sentó un momento porque estaba muy (mareado / cortada / resfriado).

8. A veces, las mujeres embarazadas sienten (estornudos / vacunas / náusea).

14.3 **Asociaciones** Con un compañero, relacionen los problemas de la primera columna con una palabra de la segunda columna y expliquen la relación. Hay varias posibilidades.

Modelo obesidad   diabetes
   La obesidad es un factor que puede causar diabetes.

1. la inyección	a. el yeso
2. las venas	b. la sangre
3. la presión alta	c. el hueso
4. la náusea	d. el vendaje
5. la cortada	e. la tos
6. la radiografía	f. la vacuna
7. la fractura	g. las pastillas
8. el resfriado	h. vomitar

14.4 **Con el doctor** Trabaja con un compañero e imaginen que son doctores. Túrnense para darles recomendaciones a pacientes que sufran de los síntomas en la lista.

Modelo estornudos, ojos irritados
   Tome una pastilla para las alergias y no salga a su jardín o al parque.

1. náusea, mareos
2. tos, dolor de garganta
3. dolor de estómago, vómito
4. dolor de cabeza, mareos
5. la presión alta
6. falta de energía, insomnio

14.5 **Encuesta** Trabajen en grupos de cuatro o cinco estudiantes para averiguar quiénes han tenido las experiencias de la lista. Acuérdense de hacer las preguntas adicionales y de tomar notas para después reportarle la información a la clase.

1. Pasar una noche en el hospital (¿Por qué?)
2. Tener gripe recientemente (¿Qué tratamiento siguió?)
3. Recibir una inyección (¿Cuándo?)
4. Fracturarse un hueso (¿Cómo?)
5. Administrar los primeros auxilios alguna vez (¿Por qué?)
6. Desmayarse alguna vez (¿Por qué?)

iTunes
Listen to Spanish singers Juan Serrat and Joaquín Sabina's song "Pastillas para no soñar." What do they suggest that one do in order to live 100 years?

¿Conoces la pirámide nutricional? En pocas palabras ¿qué recomienda? ¿La utilizas para guiar tu alimentación? Lee el artículo sobre otras guías de alimentación. ¿Qué otras guías para la alimentación se mencionan? ¿Por qué son necesarias otras guías para la alimentación en los países que se mencionan?

Guías para la alimentación

El modelo de una pirámide nutricional fue creado en los Estados Unidos para ayudar al público a entender lo que significa una dieta balanceada. La imagen de esta pirámide es conocida en muchos lugares del mundo. Sin embargo, varios países latinoamericanos han decidido crear sus propios modelos de alimentación, ya que cada nación cuenta con sus propias tradiciones y cultura. Además, los alimentos fácilmente disponibles no son los mismos debido a cuestiones geográficas y climáticas.

Entre estos modelos, se destacan dos: el modelo cubano y el llamado óvalo argentino de la nutrición. Para crear la guía de alimentación argentina se trabajó durante cuatro años. Su diseño consideró muchas variables, entre las que se cuentan las enfermedades más comunes en el país y la disponibilidad de los alimentos. Además de adaptarse mejor a la idiosincrasia y cultura de los argentinos, según sus creadores, el óvalo es más flexible y fácil de comprender. Una diferencia evidente entre el óvalo y la pirámide alimenticia es que el primero inicia con la imagen del agua, la base de la vida. El gráfico se propone comunicar claramente varios mensajes, entre los que destaca el comer variado.

CONSUMA FRUTAS FRESCAS Y AUMENTARÁ SU VITALIDAD

© fao.org/ess.nutrition/dietera_guidelines/cub

Otro ejemplo de guía para la alimentación lo realizó el gobierno de Cuba. En la guía destacan consejos sencillos como comer verduras todos los días, consumir frutas frescas y preferir la carne de pollo y el pescado. Los consejos están alineados con la realidad de la cultura y sociedad cubanas, y crean conciencia sobre datos importantes, como que mientras más se recalienten las grasas, más daño hacen.

Los objetivos de la guía cubana incluyen aumentar el conocimiento de la población sobre la alimentación y la nutrición, fomentar hábitos saludables y, a largo plazo, mejorar la salud de la población mediante la alimentación.

Source: U.S. Department of Agriculture, Center for Nutrition Policy and Promotion.

Más allá

Diseña un modelo sencillo y realista para ayudar a estudiantes universitarios a tener una mejor alimentación. Puedes usar como modelo la guía argentina. Trata de ser (*Try to be*) realista con la comida que se puede conseguir en donde vives, y con los precios.

Exploraciones **gramaticales**

A analizar

Lee la conversación y observa los verbos en negritas. Luego contesta la pregunta que sigue.

> Alicia: Mamá, estoy enferma con la gripe, y tengo una presentación muy importante el lunes. ¿Qué hago?
>
> Mamá: Yo **me quedaría** en casa y **tomaría** muchos líquidos. **Me mantendría** calientita y **dormiría** todo lo posible.
>
> Alicia: Gracias, Mamá. ¿Qué **haría** sin ti?

The verbs in bold are in the conditional. How are they formed?

A comprobar

Conditional

1. To form the conditional, add the following endings to the infinitive. Notice that all verbs take the same endings.

	hablar	volver	ir
yo	hablaría	volvería	iría
tú	hablarías	volverías	irías
él, ella, usted	hablaría	volvería	iría
nosotros(as)	hablaríamos	volveríamos	iríamos
vosotros(as)	hablaríais	volveríais	iríais
ellos, ellas, ustedes	hablarían	volverían	irían

2. The irregular verbs have the same irregular stems as the future tense. The endings are same as those for regular verbs.

decir	**dir-**	yo diría
hacer	**har-**	tú harías
poder	**podr-**	él podría
poner	**pondr-**	ella pondría
salir	**saldr-**	usted saldría
tener	**tendr-**	nosotros tendríamos
venir	**vendr-**	vosotros vendríais
querer	**querr-**	ellos querrían
saber	**sabr-**	ellas sabrían

3. The conditional is similar to the English construction *would* + verb.

> Yo **tomaría** esa pastilla sin hablar con un médico.
> I **wouldn't take** that pill without talking with a doctor.

> Me dijo que **estaría** en la sala de emergencias.
> He told me he **would be** in the emergency room.

4. The conditional form of **haber** is **habría.** You will remember that there is only one form of the verb regardless of whether it is followed by a singular or plural noun.

> Pensé que **habría** más enfermeras.
> I thought there **would be** more nurses.

5. The conditional is also used for conjecture about past activities.

> ¿Por qué **no tomaría** las pastillas?
> Why **wouldn't he take** the pills? (I **wonder** why he **didn't take** the pills.)

> **Tendría** la gripe.
> He **probably had** the flu.

6. The conditional is often used to demonstrate politeness or to soften a request.

> **Me gustaría** ver las radiografías.
> I **would like** to see the X-rays.

> ¿**Irías** al hospital conmigo?
> **Would you go** to the hospital with me?

A practicar

14.6 **Remedios** Eres padre o madre de un niño de cinco años. ¿Qué harías en los siguientes casos?

1. Tu hijo tiene un resfriado.

   a. Le prepararía comidas con vitamina C.

   b. Lo llevaría inmediatamente a la sala de emergencias.

2. Tu hijo se quema (*burn*) la mano en la estufa.

   a. Le pondría pasta de dientes en la quemadura.

   b. Sumergiría la mano en agua fresca.

3. Tu hijo tiene una cortada muy profunda.

   a. La limpiaría con jabón y un cepillo.

   b. Le aplicaría presión con un vendaje.

4. Tu hijo tiene mucha fiebre.

   a. Le daría agua o jugo.

   b. Le daría un baño caliente.

5. Tu hijo se rompe un brazo mientras juega en el parque.

   a. Le pondría hielo en el brazo.

   b. Movería el brazo para saber si le duele mucho.

6. A tu hijo le duele la garganta.

   a. Le daría antibióticos que tengo en casa.

   b. Le haría un té con limón y miel (*honey*).

INVESTIGUEMOS LA GRAMÁTICA

The verb **doler,** like the verb **gustar,** requires the indirect object pronoun and is conjugated in the third person singular or plural in agreement with the subject. Remember to use the definite article rather than the possessive before parts of the body.

Me duelen los brazos.
My arms hurt.

14.7 **¿Es lógico?** Primero completa la oración con la forma apropiada del condicional. Luego decide si la oración es lógica o no.

1. Tú _____ (poner) un vendaje en una cortada.

2. El doctor _____ (sacar) radiografías del hueso roto.

3. Una persona con diabetes _____ (estornudar) mucho.

4. Nosotros _____ (tomar) una aspirina para curar un dolor de estómago.

5. Las enfermeras _____ (poder) desmayarse al dar una inyección.

6. Yo _____ (venir) a la clase con una fiebre de 100 grados.

14.8 **En busca de...** Pregúntales a diferentes personas si harían las siguientes cosas al ganar la lotería. Pide información adicional para reportársela a la clase después. Recuerda que necesitas buscar a alguien que conteste que **sí.**

Modelo comprar un coche nuevo (¿Por qué?)

   Estudiante 1: *¿Comprarías un coche nuevo?*
   Estudiante 2: *Sí, compraría un coche nuevo.*
   Estudiante 1: *¿Por qué?*
   Estudiante 2: *Porque mi auto se descompone con frecuencia.*

1. trabajar (¿Dónde?)

2. comprarles regalos a tus amigos (¿A quiénes?)

3. darles dinero a los necesitados (¿Para qué causas?)

4. seguir estudiando (¿Por qué?)

5. hacer un viaje (¿Adónde?)

6. salir a restaurantes muy caros (¿Qué comerías?)

7. tener una gran fiesta para todos tus amigos (¿Qué harían?)

8. poner parte del dinero en el banco (¿Cuánto?)

14.9 **¿Qué harías?** Con un compañero, hablen de lo que harían en las siguientes situaciones.

Modelo Tu doctor habla muy poco y no hace muchas preguntas.
Estudiante 1: *Le haría muchas preguntas.*
Estudiante 2: *Yo cambiaría de doctor.*

1. Te sientes mareado.
2. Un amigo te pide que le regales pastillas para el dolor.
3. Tienes insomnio.
4. Un amigo tiene un resfriado.
5. Estás con una amiga cuando de repente se desmaya.
6. Te rompes una pierna y tienes que llevar un yeso.
7. El médico te dice que tienes la presión alta.
8. Es la temporada de gripe.
9. Te duele mucho la cabeza.
10. Eres médico y tienes un paciente hipocondríaco.

14.10 **¿Qué pasaría?** Mira los dibujos y explica lo que pasó. Después, usa el condicional para expresar una conjetura sobre cómo occurrió.

Modelo *Los médicos operaron al paciente. El paciente tendría problemas cardíacos y necesitaría la cirugía para no morir.*

1.

2.

3.

4.

5.

6.

Conexiones culturales
Manteniéndonos saludables

Cultura

Hoy en día muchos problemas de salud son comunes en todas las regiones del mundo; ejemplos de estos problemas son las enfermedades del corazón, la diabetes y la obesidad. Sin embargo, no todas las personas siguen un tratamiento de medicina moderna. Algunas personas no confían en estos tratamientos, o sufren de alergias que no les permiten tomar ciertas medicinas; otras personas no los toman porque no les han dado buenos resultados, o porque tienen más confianza en otros métodos que han ayudado a sus ancestros o conocidos a curarse. En algunas comunidades remotas de muchos países, y aún en las grandes ciudades, hay quienes prefieren seguir las recomendaciones de los curanderos. Generalmente los curanderos son personas mayores que saben curar enfermedades a base de remedios naturales, como el uso de hierbas.

Los remedios naturales siempre han sido populares.

En el caso de México, la medicina tradicional indígena está reconocida en la Constitución Política del país como derecho cultural de los pueblos indígenas, y este reconocimiento incluye el respeto a la cosmovisión indígena, la cual reconoce al universo como una totalidad interconectada, y al cuerpo humano como al conjunto de mente y espíritu. Algunos aspectos que distinguen a la medicina indígena son que toma en cuenta mecanismos que rompen el equilibrio frío-calor del cuerpo, y otras causas de desequilibrio, como desórdenes alimenticios, y alteraciones de la fuerza vital.

Los remedios van más allá del uso de plantas medicinales, e incluyen tratamientos terapéuticos como el uso de ciertos productos animales y minerales, masajes, limpias (*cleansings*) y otros ritos.

En la actualidad existe un movimiento para rescatar el conocimiento prehispánico acerca del uso de plantas para curar a la gente. El movimiento está apoyado por el gobierno y gracias a este apoyo se han abierto centros en donde se enseñan las bases de la medicina indígena.

¿Qué remedios o tratamientos naturales conoces? ¿Alguna vez has conocido a algún curandero? ¿Piensas que su medicina es tan efectiva como la medicina tradicional de los hospitales? ¿Por qué?

> Investiga en Internet tratamientos naturales que son comunes en los países hispanohablantes.

Comunidad

Investiga qué servicios de salud existen en tu comunidad. ¿Ofrecen estos servicios en español? Después, comunícate con uno de los centros de salud para averiguar las respuestas a las siguientes preguntas:

1. ¿Reciben a personas que no hablan inglés? ¿Tienen intérpretes? ¿Qué idiomas habla el personal en el centro de salud?

2. ¿Hay documentos para pacientes que hablen español? Si los hay, pide algunas muestras. ¿De qué hablan estos documentos? ¿Son los mismos que se ofrecen en inglés?

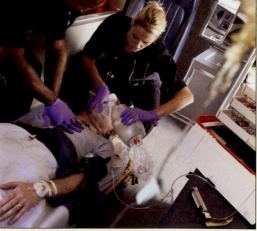

¿Qué servicios de salud existen en tu comunidad?

Comparaciones

No es secreto que la dieta de una persona afecta su salud. Tampoco es secreto que los cambios en nuestra sociedad han cambiado la manera en la que las personas se alimentan. El libro *Hungry Planet: What the World Eats* del fotógrafo Peter Menzel y la escritora Faith D'Aluisio, documenta visualmente la dieta semanal de 30 familias de diferentes países.

Observa las fotografías de las familias de estos dos países. ¿Son semejantes sus dietas? ¿Cuál piensas que es mejor? ¿Cuál se parece más a tu dieta? ¿En cuál de estos países piensas que hay más problemas de salud?

La familia Revises de Carolina del Norte, Estados Unidos

La familia Casales de Cuernavaca, México

👭 Conexiones... a la filosofía

Con un compañero, lean los siguientes refranes para determinar qué significan. ¿Hay refranes similares en inglés? Después digan si están de acuerdo.

> La naturaleza, el tiempo y la paciencia son tres grandes médicos.
> Quien quiera vivir sano, coma poco y cene temprano.
> A quien come muchos manjares (*delicacies*) no le faltarán enfermedades.
> Gástalo en la cocina y no en medicina.
> No hay buena salud, donde no entra la luz.
> Échate a enfermar, verás quién te quiere bien o quién te quiere mal.
> La salud no es conocida hasta que es perdida.
> Entre salud y dinero, salud quiero.
> Más vale prevenir que curar.

Más vale prevenir que curar.

A analizar

Ayer Rebeca se despertó con fiebre. Lee las reacciones de las personas de su familia y contesta las preguntas que siguen.

A su madre le preocupaba que **tuviera** una enfermedad grave.

Su hermana recomendó que **fuera** a ver al médico.

Su abuela le dijo que **se acostara.**

Su padre dudaba que **estuviera** muy enferma.

1. The verbs in bold are in the imperfect subjunctive. What is the stem for each of the verbs?

2. You have studied a variety of uses of the subjunctive. Look at each of the sentences, and explain why the subjunctive is required.

A comprobar

Imperfect subjunctive

1. In the last three chapters, you learned to use the present subjunctive. You will notice in the following examples that the verb in the main clause is in the present tense and that the verb in the dependent clause is in the present subjunctive.

Main clause	Dependent clause
Espero	que Clara **se recupere** pronto.
Es una lástima	que **tenga** un resfriado.

2. When the verb in the main clause is in the past (preterite or imperfect), the verb in the dependent clause must be in the imperfect subjunctive.

Main clause	Dependent clause
El médico le **recomendó**	que **tomara** unas pastillas.
Era necesario	que **usara** las muletas.

3. The imperfect subjunctive is formed using the third person plural (**ellos, ellas, ustedes**) of the preterite. Eliminate the **-on** and add the endings as indicated. You will notice that the endings are the same, regardless of whether the verb ends in **-ar, -er,** or **-ir.** Verbs that are irregular in the preterite are also irregular in the imperfect subjunctive.

	hablar	tener	dormir
yo	habla**ra**	tuvie**ra**	durmie**ra**
tú	habla**ras**	tuvie**ras**	durmie**ras**
él, ella, usted	habla**ra**	tuvie**ra**	durmie**ra**
nosotros(as)	hablá**ramos**	tuvié**ramos**	durmié**ramos**
vosotros(as)	habla**rais**	tuvie**rais**	durmie**rais**
ellos, ellas, ustedes	habla**ran**	tuvie**ran**	durmie**ran**

*Notice that it is necessary to add an accent in the **nosotros** form.

4. The imperfect subjunctive form of **haber** is **hubiera.**

> No me gustó que **hubiera** tantas personas en la sala de espera.
> *I didn't like it that **there were** so many people in the waiting room.*

5. In general, the same rules that apply to the usage of the present subjunctive also apply to the past subjunctive.

To express an opinion using personal expressions:

> **Era importante** que **habláramos** con el médico.
> *It was important that we talk with the doctor.*

To express doubt:

El médico **dudaba** que **fuera** necesario operar.
The doctor doubted it would be necessary to operate.

To express desire:

El paciente no **quería** que le **pusieran** una inyección.
The patient did not want them to give him a shot.

To talk about the unknown using adjective clauses:

Leo **buscaba** un medicamento que no **causara** náusea.
Leo was looking for medication that wouldn't make him nauseous.

To express an emotion:

A Juana **le preocupaba** que su hijo **tuviera** gripe.
Juana was worried that her son had the flu.

6. When using an "if clause" to express what would happen in a hypothetical situation or a situation that is not likely or impossible, it is necessary to use the imperfect subjunctive and the conditional.

si	+	imperfect subjunctive	+	conditional
		dependent clause		**main clause**

Si **tuviera** tiempo, iría con el doctor.
*If **I had** time, I'd go to the doctor.*

A practicar

14.11 Una visita al médico Lee las siguientes oraciones y ponlas en un orden lógico.

1. _____ El doctor le dijo que tenía gripe y sugirió que tomara un antibiótico.

2. _____ Era necesario que pasara por la farmacia camino a la casa.

3. _____ Sandra no creía que tuviera nada serio, pero decidió ver al médico.

4. _____ Le sorprendió que el medicamento costara tanto.

5. _____ Buscó una clínica que estuviera cerca de su casa.

6. _____ Sandra se sentía mal y su esposo le sugirió que fuera al médico.

14.12 Recomendaciones Completa las oraciones con la forma apropiada del imperfecto del subjuntivo del verbo entre paréntesis.

1. Fui al médico ayer porque tenía gripe. Él me recomendó que (tomar) unas pastillas.

2. Mis hermanos quieren perder peso. Yo les sugerí que (comer) menos dulces.

3. Mi esposo y yo queremos dejar de fumar. Un amigo nos recomendó que no (salir) a lugares donde muchas personas fuman.

4. Mis hijos tienen fiebre. Yo les dije que (acostarse).

5. Mi amiga está embarazada. Su esposo le sugirió que (dejar) de trabajar.

6. Mi esposo tiene insomnio. Yo le recomendé que (leer) antes de acostarse.

14.13 ¿Qué pasaría? Pon el verbo entre paréntesis en la forma apropiada del imperfecto del subjuntivo y completa la idea, usando el condicional.

Modelo Si no _____ (haber) tantas personas en la sala de espera... *no sería necesario esperar mucho tiempo.*

1. Si los pacientes no _____ (necesitar) una receta médica para conseguir medicinas...

2. Si nadie _____ (sufrir) de alergias...

3. Si el cuidado médico no _____ (ser) tan caro...

4. Si yo nunca _____ (enfermarse)...

5. Si los científicos _____ (poder) encontrar una cura para el cáncer...

6. Si nosotros _____ (cuidarse) más...

14.14 **Todos opinan** Lean las situaciones y completen las oraciones de una forma lógica para indicar las reacciones y sugerencias de los amigos y familiares. ¡OJO! Tendrán que usar el imperfecto del subjuntivo.

Modelo Virginia tuvo una entrevista de trabajo.
Su esposo le sugirió que... *llevara un traje.*

1. Cecilia estaba muy enferma.
   a. Su médico le aconsejó que...
   b. Su madre temía que...
   c. Sus amigas esperaban que...
2. Donato tuvo un accidente de coche.
   a. El policía le pidió que...
   b. Sus padres preferían que...
   c. Su amigo le recomendó que...
3. Marlene tuvo una cita anoche.
   a. Su padre le dijo que...
   b. Su mejor amiga quería que...
   c. Al muchacho le alegró que...

14.15 **Consejos médicos** Los pacientes del doctor Orozco no llevaban una vida muy saludable. Con un compañero, túrnense para darles una recomendación del doctor a sus pacientes. Usen el imperfecto del subjuntivo.

Modelo Paulina siempre tenía mucho estrés en el trabajo.
Estudiante 1: *El doctor le recomendó que se relajara más.*
Estudiante 2: *También le recomendó que buscara otro trabajo.*

1. José Luis y su esposa fumaban.
2. Magdalena comía muchos dulces.
3. Claudia y su hermano miraban la televisión seis horas al día.
4. Jaime usaba drogas.
5. Esmeralda bebía dos litros de soda todos los días.
6. Bety y Rosaura no hacían ejercicio.
7. Vicente solo dormía cinco horas cada noche.
8. Edwin y Nelson tomaban mucho alcohol.

14.16 **Reacciones** En parejas, túrnense para poner la primera cláusula en el condicional y completar las ideas de forma lógica, usando una "clausula si" y el imperfecto del subjuntivo.

Modelo sorprenderse
Estudiante 1: *Me sorprendería si no tuviera una buena nota en la clase. ¿Y tú?*
Estudiante 2: *Me sorprendería si ganara la lotería.*

1. estar preocupado
2. estar triste
3. molestarse
4. alegrarse
5. estar enojado
6. tener miedo

14.17 **Se sienten mal** Con un compañero, miren las fotos y después túrnense para completar las oraciones correspondientes. ¡OJO! Algunas oraciones requieren el subjuntivo y otras el indicativo.

1.

© Monkey Business Images/Shutterstock

a. Era necesario que...

b. La paciente esperaba que...

c. La enfermera creía que...

2.

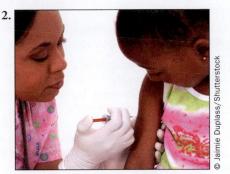

© Jaimie Duplass/Shutterstock

a. La niña tenía miedo que...

b. La enfermera le recomendó que...

c. La niña le pidió que...

3.

© Gina Sanders/Shutterstock

a. Era obvio que...

b. Le frustró que...

c. No conocía a nadie que...

14.18 **La adolescencia** Con un compañero, túrnense para completar las oraciones con sus experiencias personales. Recuerden que necesitarán usar el imperfecto del subjuntivo.

Modelo mis vecinos no querían que...

 Estudiante 1: *Cuando era adolescente, mis vecinos no querían que mis hermanos y yo*
  jugáramos frente a su casa.

 Estudiante 2: *Mis vecinos no querían que molestara a su perro.*

Cuando era adolescente,

1. mis padres no permitían que yo...

2. yo no quería que mis padres...

3. dudaba que...

4. temía que...

5. era importante que...

6. buscaba amigos que...

7. mis amigos preferían que yo...

8. nadie creía que...

Lectura

Antes de leer

1. ¿Qué crees que significa "ofrecer servicios de salud universal"? ¿Qué países hispanos piensas que tienen servicios de salud universal para sus ciudadanos?

2. ¿Crees que estos países gastan (*spend*) más en salud que los países que no ofrecen servicios de salud universal? ¿Por qué?

3. ¿De qué piensas que va a tratar el artículo? ¿Puedes anticipar un par de ideas?

A leer

El valor de la salud

Como dice el refrán, nadie sabe cuánto vale la salud hasta que la pierde. Visto a un nivel económico, el valor de la salud también es muy significativo. El costo de los días que los trabajadores toman por estar enfermos es enorme para cada país, pero las consecuencias son aún más grandes para los trabajadores que no tienen esta **prestación** y no reciben dinero si no van a trabajar. Claramente, mantener una buena salud es de primordial importancia para todos.

benefit

¿En qué países se enferma más la gente?
En un estudio de la comunidad europea se encontró que el número de **días tomados por enfermedad** varía enormemente de país a país. La conclusión más evidente fue que en los países del norte la gente toma muchos más días que en los países del sur de Europa. Por ejemplo, el 24% de los finlandeses y el 21.8% de los holandeses dijeron haber tomado al menos un día por enfermedad durante el último año, en contraste con el 6.7% de los griegos, el 8.5% de los italianos y el 11.8% de los españoles. Los hombres tomaron más días que las mujeres. ¿Será que las mujeres tienen mejor salud que los hombres? Es posible argumentar que en los países en donde es más fácil conseguir una "incapacidad", un día con goce de sueldo sin ir a trabajar, la gente toma más de estos días.

sick days

[nadie sabe cuánto vale la salud hasta que la pierde]

En México si una persona está enferma por más de tres días debe ir a una clínica del Seguro Social y conseguir de su médico un documento llamado "incapacidad". El médico especifica cuántos días se necesitan para recuperarse, y es **indispensable** presentar este papel para recibir el sueldo de los días que se faltó al trabajo. La compañía pagará el 75% del sueldo, y el Seguro Social pagará el 25%. Desafortunadamente, este servicio de salud se le ofrece solamente a una parte de la población. Mientras que en México se está planeando implementar un programa de salud universal en un futuro próximo, este servicio ya existe en varios países latinoamericanos desde hace muchos años. Estos países son Argentina, Chile, Costa Rica, Cuba y Uruguay.

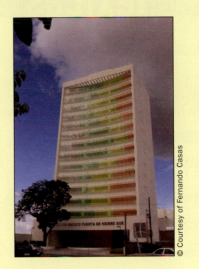

© Courtesy of Fernando Casas

essential

Ofrecer servicios de salud adecuados es uno de los grandes retos que enfrentan casi todos los países del mundo, y probablemente no haya ninguna solución que funcione para todas las naciones.

Comprensión

Lee las siguientes afirmaciones y decide si son ciertas o falsas. Corrige las falsas.

1. Según un estudio, los europeos del norte se enferman mucho más que los europeos del sur.
2. En Europa, los españoles son los que menos días faltan al trabajo por enfermedad.
3. Los hombres toman más días por enfermedad que las mujeres.
4. En México la incapacidad permite al empleado faltar el trabajo por enfermedad y recibir su sueldo.
5. En México, Cuba y Uruguay existe el servicio de salud universal.

Después de leer

Escribe una lista de ideas sobre cómo se puede mejorar la salud de las personas en tu país.

El español es un idioma que une a veintiún países.

Argentina (argentino)

Bolivia (boliviano)

Chile (chileno)

Colombia (colombiano)

Costa Rica (costarricense)

Cuba (cubano)

Ecuador (ecuatoriano)

El Salvador (salvadoreño)

España (español)

Guatemala (guatemalteco)

Guinea Ecuatorial (ecuatoguineano)

Honduras (hondureño)

México (mexicano)

Nicaragua (nicaragüense)

Panamá (panameño)

Paraguay (paraguayo)

Perú (peruano)

Puerto Rico (puertorriqueño)

República Dominicana (dominicano)

Uruguay (uruguayo)

Venezuela (venezolano)

Conceptos políticos

el ciudadano	*citizen*
el desempleo	*unemployment*
los derechos humanos	*human rights*
la emigración	*emigration*
la guerra	*war*
la globalización	*globalization*
la inmigración	*immigration*
el (la) inmigrante	*immigrant*
la ley	*law*
los organismos internacionales	*international organizations*
la paz	*peace*
la pobreza	*poverty*
el refugiado	*refugee*
la riqueza	*wealth*
el tratado de comercio	*trade agreement*

Verbos

emigrar	*emigrate*
inmigrar	*immigrate*
mudarse	*to move (to another place)*
votar	*to vote*

Práctica

14.19 **Escucha y responde** Vas a escuchar una serie de ideas. Si una idea te parece lógica, señala con el pulgar hacia arriba. Si es ilógica, señala con el pulgar hacia abajo.

14.20 **¿Cuál es la palabra correcta?** Para cada país, selecciona el gentilicio (la nacionalidad) correcta.

1. Cuba
   a. cubense   **b.** cubano   **c.** cubeño

2. Puerto Rico
   a. puertorricano   **b.** puertorricense   **c.** puertorriqueño

3. Guatemala
   a. guatemalteco   **b.** guatemaltense   **c.** guateco

4. Panamá
   a. panamano   **b.** panamense   **c.** panameño

5. Chile
   a. chileño   **b.** chileno   **c.** chilense

6. Paraguay
   a. paraguayo   **b.** paragüense   **c.** paraguano

14.21 **Famosos** Observa la siguiente lista de personalidades hispanohablantes. Trabajen en grupos de tres para identificar la nacionalidad de cada persona y decir lo que saben de ellos.

1. Rigoberta Menchú   5. Franklin Díaz-Chang   9. Frida Kahlo
2. José Martí   6. Antonio Gaudí   10. Albert Pujols
3. Óscar Romero   7. Eva Perón   11. Shakira
4. Pablo Neruda   8. Carolina Herrera   12. Rubén Blades

14.22 **Opiniones** Lee las siguientes afirmaciones y decide si estás de acuerdo o no. Después compara tus respuestas con las de un compañero. En cada caso deben explicar por qué están de acuerdo o no, y dar ejemplos concretos.

1. Todos los derechos humanos se respetan.

2. Las leyes deben obedecerse siempre.

3. La globalización causa pobreza.

4. Los organismos internacionales son los principales responsables de cuidar los derechos humanos.

5. Un refugiado es básicamente un inmigrante.

14.23 **Hablemos** Trabaja con un compañero para expresar sus experiencias y opiniones sobre las siguientes preguntas.

1. ¿Qué países conoces? ¿Menciona cinco países que te gustaría visitar y explica por qué?

2. ¿Cuáles crees que sean los tres problemas más importantes de la comunidad internacional?

3. ¿Cuáles son tres ventajas de la inmigración? ¿Cuáles son tres desventajas?

4. ¿Hay inmigrantes/emigrantes en la historia de tu familia? ¿De dónde y adónde fueron? ¿Por qué?

5. ¿Conoces a inmigrantes? ¿De dónde son? ¿En qué trabajan?

6. ¿Cuáles son dos consecuencias positivas de la globalización? ¿Cuáles son dos consecuencias negativas?

Existen muchas organizaciones en el mundo en las que participan varios países. Algunas de estas organizaciones son intra-gubernamentales, y otras son organizaciones privadas de alcance internacional, como la Cruz Roja Internacional, Amnistía Internacional y Médicos sin Fronteras. ¿Puedes listar otras organizaciones internacionales y sus objetivos?

A continuación aparece una breve descripción de varias organizaciones importantes para países de habla hispana. ¿Qué tipos de objetivos diferentes se listan? ¿Cuál es la organización con más miembros? ¿Cuál es la más antigua? ¿Y la más reciente?

Nombre: Organización de las Naciones Unidas
Países participantes: 192 países
Sede: Nueva York
Fundación: 1945
Tipo de organización: Unión supranacional

Nombre: Organización de Estados Iberoamericanos para la Educación, las Ciencias y la Cultura
Países participantes: España, Argentina, Bolivia, Brasil, Chile, Colombia, Costa Rica, Cuba, República Dominicana, Ecuador, El Salvador, Guatemala, Honduras, México, Nicaragua, Panamá, Paraguay, Perú, Portugal, Puerto Rico, Venezuela.
Sede: Madrid
Fundación: 1985
Tipo de organización: Organismo de cooperación

Nombre: Organización de Estados Americanos
Países participantes: 34 países americanos
Sede: Washington D.C.
Fundación: 1948
Tipo de organización: Organismo internacional

Nombre: Tratado de Libre Comercio de América del Norte
Países participantes: Canadá, Estados Unidos, México.
Sede: Ottawa, Washington D.C., México D.F.
Fundación: 1994
Tipo de organización: Bloque comercial

Nombre: Sistema de Integración Centroamericano
Países participantes: Belice, Costa Rica, El Salvador, Guatemala, Honduras, Nicaragua, Panamá
Sede: Ciudad de Guatemala
Fundación: 1993
Tipo de organización: Bloque comercial

Nombre: Comunidad del Caribe
Países participantes: Antigua y Barbuda, Bahamas, Barbados, Belice, Dominica, Granada, Guyana, Haití, Jamaica, Montserrat, San Cristóbal y Nieves, Santa Lucía, San Vicente y las Granadinas, Surinam, Trinidad, Tobago.
Sede: Georgetown
Fundación: 1973
Tipo de organización: Bloque comercial

Nombre: Unión de Naciones Sudamericanas
Países participantes: Argentina, Bolivia, Brasil, Chile, Colombia, Ecuador, Guyana, Paraguay, Perú, Surinam, Uruguay, Venezuela.
Sede: Brasilia, Cochabamba
Fundación: 2008
Tipo de organización: Integración en todos los niveles

Nombre: Mercado Común del Sur
Países participantes: Argentina, Brasil, Paraguay, Uruguay
Sede: Montevideo
Fundación: 1991
Tipo de organización: Bloque comercial

Nombre: Comunidad Andina
Países participantes: Bolivia, Ecuador, Colombia, Perú
Sede: Lima
Fundación: 1969
Tipo de organización: Bloque comercial

Nombre: Alianza Bolivariana para las Américas
Países participantes: San Vicente y las Granadinas, Antigua y Barbuda, Bolivia, Cuba, Dominica, Ecuador, Honduras, Nicaragua, Venezuela.
Sede: Caracas
Fundación: 2004
Tipo de organización: Organismo internacional

Source: Author-generated; logos from international organizations.

Más allá

Aunque existe una organización que agrupa a todas las naciones donde se habla francés, no hay una para las naciones donde se habla español. Imagínate que se debe crear un organismo internacional para todos los países hispanohablantes. ¿Dónde estaría la sede (*headquarters*) y por qué? ¿Cuáles serían los objetivos de la organización? ¿Recomendarías que se excluye a algún país? ¿Por qué?

© Ian MacLellan/Shutterstock

A analizar

Lee el siguiente párrafo y observa las expresiones en negritas y los verbos que las siguen. Luego contesta las preguntas.

> **Cuando** comenzó la guerra el año pasado, la vida de los ciudadanos cambió radicalmente; ahora viven en la pobreza y con mucho miedo. Todos esperan el día **cuando** llegue la paz de nuevo. Desafortunadamente, **después de que** termine la guerra, pasarán muchos años **antes de que** la vida pueda volver a la normalidad.

1. Each of the expressions in bold is related to time. Identify the expressions followed by the subjunctive. Considering what you know about the use of the subjunctive, why do you think the subjunctive was needed after these expressions?
2. Which of the expressions is followed by the indicative? Why do you think this is?

A comprobar

Subjunctive with adverbial clauses

1. The following adverbial conjunctions always require the subjunctive. Because they indicate that the action is contingent upon another action, the outcome is unknown.

a fin de que	*in order that, so that*
antes (de) que	*before*
a menos que	*unless*
con tal (de) que	*as long as; in order that, so that*
en caso de que	*in case*
para que	*in order that, so that*
sin que	*without*

> No es posible entrar en el país **a menos que** uno **tenga** visa.
> *It is not possible to enter the country **unless** one **has** a visa.*

> Fedra se mudó **a fin de que** sus hijos **tuvieran** una mejor vida.
> *Fedra moved **in order that** her children **would have** a better life.*

2. With the exception of **a menos que,** the expressions above are often used with the infinitive if there is no change of subject. The **que** after the preposition is omitted.

> Hay que luchar **para eliminar** la pobreza.
> *It is necessary to fight **in order to eliminate** poverty.*

> **Antes de emigrar,** hay muchos factores a considerar.
> *Before emigrating, there are many factors to consider.*

3. The following adverbial conjunctions of time require the subjunctive when referring to actions that have not yet occurred. When referring to actions that are already taking place or are habitual, they require the indicative.

cuando	*when*	**hasta que***	*until*
después (de) que*	*after*	**tan pronto**	*as soon as*
en cuanto	*as soon as*	**(como)**	

> *****Después (de) que** and **hasta que** are often used with the infinitive if there is no change of subject. Again, the **que** after the preposition is omitted.

Present indicative

> **Cuando hay** violaciones de derechos humanos, Amnistía Internacional responde.
> *When there are human rights violations, Amnesty International responds.*

INVESTIGUEMOS EL VOCABULARIO

The expression **con tal de que** can be a little tricky in its usage. It generally implies that the subject doesn't really want to do something but is willing to because of the end result.

Seguiré trabajando en esta compañía **con tal de que** me aumenten el sueldo.

*I will continue to work for this company **as long as** they give me a raise.*

Rafa se mudó **con tal de que** sus hijos pudieran ver a sus abuelos.

*Rafa moved (although he really didn't want to) **in order that** his children could see their grandparents.*

Siempre viajamos a Europa **tan pronto como terminan** las clases.
*We always travel to Europe **as soon as** classes **end.***

Subjunctive

Cuando tenga el dinero, viajaré a África.
***When I have** the money, I will travel to Africa.*

Podemos trabajar **tan pronto como lleguemos** a una solución.
*We can work **as soon as we come** to a solution.*

4. The following adverbial conjunctions require the indicative when referring to something that is known or is definite. However, when referring to something that is unknown or indefinite, they require the subjunctive.

aunque	*although, even though, even if*
como	*as, how, however*
(a)donde	*where, wherever*

Quiero ir a Asia **aunque es** caro.
*I want to go to Asia **even though it is** expensive.*

Quiero ir a Asia **aunque sea** caro.
*I want to go to Asia **even if it is** expensive.*

Adonde iremos hay pobreza.
***Where we are going,** there is poverty.*

Adonde vayamos hay pobreza.
***Wherever we (may) go,** there is poverty.*

A practicar

14.24 **¿Quién sabe?** Contesta las preguntas y explica tus respuestas.

1. ¿Quién sabe cuánto cuesta estudiar en otro país, Belinda o Walter?
   a. Belinda prefiere estudiar en otro país aunque <u>cuesta</u> mucho dinero.
   b. Walter prefiere estudiar en otro país aunque <u>cueste</u> mucho dinero.
2. ¿Quién sabe dónde hay libertad, Ernesto o Isabel?
   a. Ernesto quiere vivir donde <u>hay</u> libertad.
   b. Isabel quiere vivir donde <u>haya</u> libertad.
3. ¿Quién sabe cuáles son las instrucciones del formulario de inmigración, Eva o Ana?
   a. Eva va a completar el formulario de inmigración como <u>dicen</u> las instrucciones.
   b. Ana va a completar el formulario de inmigración como <u>digan</u> las instrucciones.
4. ¿Quién sabe si hay otras oportunidades en otra ciudad, Bárbara o Sebastián?
   a. Bárbara no quiere mudarse aunque <u>hay</u> oportunidades en otra ciudad.
   b. Sebastián no quiere mudarse aunque <u>haya</u> oportunidades en otra ciudad.

14.25 **Antes y después** Completa las oraciones con la forma apropiada del indicativo o del subjuntivo del verbo entre paréntesis y añade información personal. **¡OJO!** Presta atención a los tiempos verbales.

1. a. En cuanto _____ (encontrar) mi primer trabajo, yo salí para celebrar con mis amigos.
   b. En cuanto _____ (encontrar) un buen trabajo, yo voy a mudarme.
2. a. Cuando _____ (tener) diez años, yo jugaba al fútbol.
   b. Cuando _____ (ser) mayor, yo quiero tener hijos.
3. a. Después de que yo _____ (graduarse) de la escuela secundaria, mi familia me hizo una fiesta.
   b. Después de que yo _____ (graduarse) de la universidad, mi familia estará muy feliz.
4. a. Antes de que yo _____ (hacer) mi primer viaje, era importante trabajar para ganar el dinero necesario.
   b. Antes de que yo _____ (hacer) otro viaje, es importante terminar mis estudios.
5. a. Tan pronto como _____ (terminar) el semestre pasado, yo salí de vacaciones a la playa.
   b. Tan pronto como _____ (terminar) este semestre, yo buscaré un trabajo.

14.26 **La situación mundial** Completa las oraciones, añadiendo una de las siguientes expresiones para conectar las dos frases: **a fin de que, a menos que, antes de que, con tal de que, en caso de que, para que** y **sin que.** Luego conjuga el verbo en la forma apropiada del presente del subjuntivo. Por último, crea un final original, usando las expresiones adverbiales.

1. El nuevo presidente no quiere aprobar la nueva ley...

    a. sus ministros le (dar) consejos. **b.** el Congreso la (aprobar) primero.   **c.** ¿?

2. Cada ciudadano debe votar...

    a. se (escuchar) su voz (*voice*). **b.** su voto (poder) ayudar a mejorar la situación. **c.** ¿?

3. Los soldados irán a la guerra...

    a. (haber) justicia en el país. **b.** los presidentes (llegar) a un acuerdo primero. **c.** ¿?

14.27 **¿Cuándo?** Con un compañero completen las oraciones usando una de las siguientes expresiones adverbiales: **cuando, después de que, en cuanto, hasta que, tan pronto como.** ¡OJO! Presten atención al uso del indicativo y del subjuntivo. Intenten usar algunas de las expresiones conversacionales que aprendieron en el **Capítulo 13.**

    Modelo Esta noche voy a acostarme...

        Estudiante 1: *Esta noche voy a acostarme después de que mis hijos se duerman.*

        Estudiante 2: *¿De veras? Yo voy a acostarme tan pronto como pueda.*

  1. a. Siempre estudio...   **b.** Hoy pienso estudiar...

  2. a. Esta mañana me levanté...   **b.** Mañana me levantaré...

  3. a. Me gusta cenar...   **b.** Esta noche voy a cenar...

  4. a. Compré mi primer coche...   **b.** Voy a comprar un coche nuevo...

  5. a. Conseguí mi primer trabajo...   **b.** Buscaré un nuevo trabajo...

14.28 **Destino España** Rodolfo es argentino y quiere viajar a España. Usando algunas de las expresiones adverbiales (**a fin de que, en caso de que, para que**), explica por qué necesita los artículos de la lista. Luego, con un compañero imagínense que van de vacaciones a España. Mencionen otros cuatro artículos que van a necesitar y expliquen por qué.

    Modelo la dirección de la embajada (*embassy*) argentina

        Lleva la dirección de la embajada argentina en caso de que tengas alguna emergencia.

  1. una visa de turista   **4.** un par de zapatos cómodos

  2. su currículum (*resumé*)   **5.** una maleta grande

  3. un traje   **6.** yerba mate

14.29 **Descripción de fotos** Con un compañero, escojan una de las fotos y expliquen las circunstancias, mencionando quiénes son las personas y qué hacen. Usen algunas de las expresiones adverbiales y decidan si se requiere el indicativo o el subjuntivo.

a fin de que	a menos que	antes de que	para que	sin que
en caso de que	hasta que	aunque	cuando	después de que

© fotorobs/Shutterstock   © absolut/Shutterstock   © kojoku/Shutterstock

Cultura

Si el mundo fuera un pueblo de 100 habitantes y reflejara proporcionalmente nuestro mundo actual, esto sería lo que veríamos:

Si el mundo fuera un pueblo, ¿cómo sería?

60 habitantes serían asiáticos (20 chinos y 17 indios), 14 americanos (6 del norte y 8 del sur), 13 africanos, 12 europeos y una persona de Oceanía.

Habría 52 mujeres y 48 hombres.

89 serían heterosexuales y 11 homosexuales.

50.5 vivirían en el pueblo y 49.5 estarían esparcidos en el campo.

6 personas poseerían 59% de la riqueza total del pueblo (varios de ellos serían de los Estados Unidos).

50 habitantes vivirían con 2 dólares al día y 25 con solo 1 dólar al día.

25 consumirían el 75% de la energía total, los 75 otros consumirían el restante 25%.

17 no tendrían ni servicios médicos, ni vivienda adecuada, ni agua potable.

50 padecerían malnutrición.

20 habitantes controlarían el 86% del PNB (Producto Nacional Bruto) y 74% de las líneas telefónicas.

11 habitantes utilizarían un coche y dispondrían del 87% de todos los vehículos.

9 tendrían acceso a Internet.

1 tendría estudios universitarios.

La gente del pueblo tendría problemas para comunicarse porque unos 16 hablarían mandarín, 8 inglés, unos 7 hablarían español, 6 se comunicarían en ruso... y la mitad (*half*) de los habitantes hablarían otras lenguas.

Sources: http://www.sustainer.org/dhm_archive/index.php?display_article=vn338villageed

¿Te sorprende está información? ¿Por qué?

> Investiga en Internet cómo sería este pueblo en cuanto a edad, religión, ingresos y educación.

Conexiones... a la economía

El nuestro es un mundo en movimiento. Entre 1960 y 2005, el número de migrantes internacionales pasó de 75 millones a 191 millones, es decir, el 3% de la población mundial. Estados Unidos es un país que recibe a muchos inmigrantes, pero no es el único, ni la región que más gente recibe. La Comunidad Europea ha sido el destino de millones y millones de inmigrantes. Dentro de esta comunidad, España es el país que más inmigrantes recibe cada año.

En general, los inmigrantes tienden a trabajar en puestos que no requieren mucha educación. Aun cuando los migrantes tengan una educación, es común que los países que los reciben no validen sus estudios, o que no puedan trabajar en esa área debido a no hablar bien el idioma. Típicamente, altos porcentajes de migrantes trabajan en campos relacionados con la agricultura, la construcción y la manufactura.

¿Puedes identificar tres áreas sociales o económicas que sean afectadas por la inmigración? Explica los efectos con ejemplos concretos en los países que reciben inmigrantes y en los países que los pierden, ya sean efectos positivos o negativos.

El número de migrantes internacionales ha aumentado mucho.

Comparaciones

Se dice que una de las consecuencias más graves de la globalización es la desaparición de culturas. Esta consecuencia afecta en particular los idiomas en nuestro planeta. Los diferentes idiomas que existen son una forma palpable de las culturas que las hablan. Con la desaparición de idiomas, desaparece también gran parte de la diversidad cultural de los seres humanos. Se calcula que en el mundo existen en la actualidad unas seis mil lenguas, pero dentro de menos de cincuenta años el número se habrá reducido a la mitad *(half)*.

Aunque hay quienes dicen que un idioma está en peligro cuando el número de hablantes se reduce a menos de 50 000, algunos estudiosos consideran que un idioma está realmente en peligro cuando se observa que las nuevas generaciones dejan de usarlo. En contraste, un idioma hablado por unos cuantos cientos de personas podría no estar en peligro, si es el único idioma hablado por una comunidad entera, y es necesario para su subsistencia.

Con la expansión de los medios de comunicación se ha acelerado el dominio de unos cuantos idiomas sobre todos los demás. De acuerdo a *Ethnologue,* el 94% de la población habla 389 idiomas (el 6% del total). El restante 6% de la población habla el restante 94% de las lenguas. Los tres idiomas más hablados en el mundo son chino, español e inglés.

Elige un país hispano e investiga cuántos idiomas se hablan en él. Después compara la información con el número de lenguas que se hablan en Estados Unidos ¿Cómo se pueden explicar las diferencias y semejanzas?

Hay también una gran diversidad de idiomas dentro de algunos países.

iTunes

Listen to "Las Cruces de Tijuana," by the Spanish rock group Jarabe de Palo. What two places does he compare? Do you think his view of immigration is positive or negative? Why? What are key words that lead you to such a conclusion?

Comunidad

La inmigración es un fenómeno humano natural. Ha existido desde el principio de la humanidad, cuando grupos de nuestros ancestros se trasladaban de un lugar a otro para buscar mejores condiciones de vida. En el mundo en el que vivimos hay enormes cantidades de seres humanos que dejan sus lugares de origen por diferentes motivos, entre ellos encontrar un mejor trabajo, huir de la guerra, vivir en un clima más benigno, o estudiar. Aunque la mayor parte de la migración ocurre dentro de las fronteras de un mismo país (por ejemplo, la migración del campo a la ciudad), hay un número significativo de personas que se han desplazado a otros países y enfrentan grandes retos. De acuerdo a la Organización Internacional de Migración, hay más de 200 millones de migrantes en el mundo. Europa ocupa el primer lugar en el mundo por el número de inmigrantes que ha recibido, y Norteamérica ocupa el segundo lugar.

Investiga sobre el fenómeno de la inmigración en tu comunidad: ¿Cuántos inmigrantes se calcula que hay? ¿Hay organizaciones para ayudarlos en donde tú vives? ¿Qué organizaciones son? ¿En qué idiomas se ofrece ayuda? ¿Qué servicios ofrecen? ¿De qué países emigraron las personas que ayudan? Escribe una lista de los servicios que piensas que son los más urgentes para un inmigrante recién llegado a una comunidad. Comparte la información con la clase.

¿Qué organizaciones ofrecen servicios para inmigrantes?

Exploraciones gramaticales

A analizar

Lee el párrafo que aparece a continuación y observa los verbos en negritas. Luego contesta las preguntas que siguen.

Antes de solicitar la ciudadanía, Andrés ya **había vivido** en España por diez años y **había aprendido** español. También **se había casado** con una mujer española y **habían tenido** un hijo.

1. You learned the present perfect in **Capítulo 12.** The verbs in bold are in the past perfect. How are these verbs formed?

2. These verbs are used to talk about the past. When do the actions of the verbs in the past perfect take place in relation to the action first mentioned (**solicitar la ciudadanía**)?

A comprobar

Past perfect

1. Similar to the present perfect, the past perfect (also known as the **pluscuamperfecto**) combines the imperfect form of the verb **haber** with the past participle.

yo	**había**	nosotros(as)	**habíamos**
tú	**habías**	vosotros(as)	**habíais**
él, ella, usted	**había**	ellos, ellas, ustedes	**habían**

Habían inmigrado a México.
They had immigrated to Mexico.

¿**Habías viajado** a Europa antes?
Had you traveled to Europe before?

2. The past perfect is used to express a past action that already took place before another past action.

```
1998
  |   aprendió inglés
  |   se mudó a Estados Unidos
  |   estableció la residencia
  |   se hizo ciudadano
  ↓
presente
```

Camilo ya **había aprendido** inglés cuando se mudó a los Estados Unidos.
Camilo had already learned English when he moved to the United States.

Antes de hacerse ciudadano, él **había establecido** la residencia.
Before becoming a citizen, he had established residency.

3. Remember the irregular past participles from **Capítulo 11:**

abrir	**abierto**	romper	**roto**
decir	**dicho**	poner	**puesto**
escribir	**escrito**	ver	**visto**
hacer	**hecho**	volver	**vuelto**
morir	**muerto**	devolver	**devuelto**

4. As with the present perfect, when using direct object, indirect object, or reflexive pronouns, they are placed in front of the conjugated form of **haber.**

No **se** habían mudado antes.
They hadn't moved before.

Ya **lo** habíamos visto.
We had already seen it.

A practicar

14.30 **¿Qué habían hecho?** Muchos latinos famosos han tenido una vida muy interesante. Relaciona el evento en la primera columna con el evento que ocurrió primero en la segunda columna.

1. _____ Julio Iglesias empezó a tocar la guitarra como terapia.

2. _____ Desi Arnaz hizo el papel de músico en el programa de televisión *I Love Lucy*.

3. _____ Carlos Santana empezó a tocar la guitarra a los ocho años.

4. _____ Shakira escribió su primera canción a los ocho años.

5. _____ Benicio del Toro tuvo su primer papel en la película *Big Top Pee-wee*.

6. _____ Óscar de la Renta trabajó para Elizabeth Arden por dos años.

a. Había escrito poesía desde los cuatro años.

b. Había dibujado para unas casas de moda en España.

c. Había tenido un accidente de coche.

d. Pero antes ya había tocado el violín.

e. Había dejado sus estudios de negocios para estudiar actuación.

f. Había tenido un grupo musical exitoso.

14.31 **Entrevista** Con un compañero, túrnense para preguntar si habían hecho las siguientes actividades antes de graduarse de la escuela secundaria. Añade (*Add*) detalles al contestarle a tu compañero.

Modelo viajar a Nueva York
> Estudiante 1: *Antes de graduarte de la escuela secundaria ¿habías viajado a Nueva York?*
> Estudiante 2: *Sí, había viajado a Nueva York. Fui con mi familia un verano. /*
> *No, no había viajado a Nueva York. Nunca he ido allí.*

1. comprar su primer coche
2. hacer un viaje solo
3. enamorarse
4. tener un accidente
5. asistir a una clase de español
6. empezar a trabajar
7. tomar un curso universitario
8. participar en algún equipo deportivo

14.32 **Un poco de historia** Con un compañero, completen las oraciones con dos eventos históricos anteriores a los mencionados, usando el pluscuamperfecto.

Modelo Antes de que Hernán Cortés llegara a México...
> Estudiante 1: *Antes de que Hernán Cortés llegara a México, había estado en Cuba.*
> Estudiante 2: *También había estado en La Hispaniola.*

1. Antes de que comenzara la Revolución cubana en 1956...

2. Antes de que Puerto Rico llegara a ser un Estado Libre Asociado de los Estados Unidos en 1952...

3. Antes de que el Canal de Panamá pasara a ser la responsabilidad de Panamá en 1999...

4. Antes de que Napoleón y sus tropas invadieran España en 1808...

5. Antes de que empezara la Guerra entre México y los Estados Unidos en 1846...

6. Antes de que se formara la organización de las Provincias Unidas de América Central en 1823...

14.33 **Una catástrofe** Con un compañero, observen la ilustración de un accidente que ocurrió en la calle, y mencionen todos los eventos que podrían haber pasado antes del accidente.

Modelo *Antes de que ocurriera el accidente, un hombre había comprado un periódico.*

Antes de que ocurriera el accidente...

14.34 **Un mal día** Norma tuvo un muy mal día ayer. Con un compañero, túrnense para imaginarse lo que podría haber pasado antes para causar los siguientes eventos. Usen el pluscuamperfecto.

Modelo Norma no pudo encontrar su mochila.
Estudiante 1: *Su hermano la había escondido.*
Estudiante 2: *La había dejado en la universidad.*

1. Norma llegó tarde a su clase de inglés.
2. Recibió una mala nota en su composición.
3. No le entregó (*to hand in*) la tarea al profesor de español.
4. No pudo ver lo que el profesor escribía en la pizarra.
5. No comió nada a mediodía.
6. No estuvo preparada para el examen de historia.
7. Tuvo un accidente cuando iba a su casa.
8. No pudo llamar a la policía con su teléfono celular.
9. Cuando por fin llegó a casa, no pudo entrar.
10. Se acostó temprano, pero tuvo dificultades para dormir.

© Jason Stitt/Shutterstock

Redacción

A narrative composition tells a story. You will write an article on an international event that could appear in a newspaper.

Paso 1 Think of something that has happened internationally or invent a fictitious international event for a newspaper article. Write a brief list of the chronological sequence of events.

Paso 2 Jot down a few sentences that someone involved in the event or witnessing it might say.

Paso 3 Write a topic sentence that presents what you are going to be writing about and that will grab your reader's interest.

> **Modelo** *Miles de inmigrantes indocumentados llegaron a la capital para protestar contra la nueva ley.*

Paso 4 Look back at your list of chronological events in **Paso 1.** Write three or four paragraphs that give the details of what happened. Be sure to add a quote or two from people interested in the event or involved in it where appropriate.

Paso 5 Write a concluding paragraph in which you give a final commentary or final statement that tells why the event is relevant or supposes what might be the results of the event.

Paso 6 Edit your article:

  a. Is the information clearly organized in a logical sequence?
  b. Do all of the sentences in each of the paragraphs support their topic sentences?
  c. Did you include ample details?
  d. Do your adjectives and your verbs agree with the subject?
  e. Did you use the past tenses (preterite, imperfect, past perfect) accurately?
  f. Did you use subjunctive where necessary?

Lectura

Antes de leer

Contesta las preguntas.

1. ¿Por qué emigra la gente? Menciona al menos cuatro razones.

2. ¿Conoces a algún inmigrante? ¿De dónde es? ¿Por qué dejó su país?

3. ¿Qué países crees que reciben más inmigrantes en el mundo? ¿Por qué?

4. ¿Sabes qué se necesita para inmigrar legalmente a los Estados Unidos?

A leer

Latinoamérica y la inmigración

Cuando se habla de inmigración, muchos piensan en los trabajadores agrícolas que inmigran a países como los Estados Unidos. Sin embargo, la inmigración ha ocurrido en todas las etapas de la historia y ha sido decisiva en la formación de los países latinoamericanos.

En algunos países como Argentina, Chile y Uruguay, la mayor parte de la población desciende de inmigrantes europeos que llegaron a estas tierras en los siglos XVIII y XIX, buscando mejorar su vida. En el caso de Argentina, la

Una celebración menonita en Cuautémoc, México

promoted

inmigración europea se **promovió** activamente, ya que se percibía como una forma de hacer progresar al país. Entre 1870 y 1914 llegaron al país alrededor de seis millones de extranjeros. Los nuevos inmigrantes se establecieron y mezclaron su idioma y sus costumbres con los ya existentes, creando los diferentes sabores culturales de cada región que conocemos hoy.

Otro país que recibió un número significativo de inmigrantes fue Cuba, adonde llegaron aproximadamente 124 000 chinos entre 1853 y 1874 para trabajar en el campo. Esta inmigración se sumó a la de los españoles que se establecieron en la isla, y a la de los africanos que habían sido llevados en masa contra su voluntad para trabajar como esclavos.

A principios del siglo XX la Guerra Civil Española y la Primera y la Segunda Guerra Mundial trajeron como consecuencia una nueva **ola** de inmigrantes que **huían** de la violencia y de la pobreza que la guerra ocasionó en Europa.

wave
were fleeing

[la inmigración europea se promovió activamente]

A Argentina llegaron numerosos grupos de **judíos.** México y Chile recibieron un gran número de exiliados políticos de España,

Jews

muchos de ellos intelectuales, quienes se establecieron y fundaron escuelas y ayudaron a crear nuevas e importantes corrientes culturales de gran impacto en la literatura, la educación y la cinematografía. Más tarde en la década de los 70, las dictaduras militares de Argentina, Chile, Uruguay y Paraguay empujaron a miles de personas a abandonar su patria y a buscar asilo político en otros países hispanoparlantes, en particular en España y México.

Aunque no es posible hablar en este reducido espacio de todos los grupos que han inmigrado y que siguen inmigrando, a países latinoamericanos, los ejemplos citados hacen evidente el impacto de la inmigración en las sociedades latinoamericanas. La migración es un fenómeno económico y social que continúa transformando la faz de todos los países del planeta.

Comprensión

Decide si las afirmaciones son ciertas o falsas. Corrige las falsas.

1. En los siglos XVIII y XIX Argentina quería parar la inmigración de Europa.
2. Los inmigrantes a Argentina no tuvieron efecto en la cultura del país.
3. Cuba es un país de gran diversidad cultural, debido a los numerosos inmigrantes.
4. La Guerra Civil Española creó una nueva ola de inmigración hacia Latinoamérica.
5. Las personas que emigraron a México huyendo de la Guerra Civil Española eran principalmente trabajadores sin mucha educación.
6. Muchas personas inmigraron a Chile, Argentina, Paraguay y Uruguay para huir de las dictaduras.
7. La inmigración es un fenómeno social que sigue cambiando la cultura de los países hispanoparlantes.

Después de leer

España es uno de los países que recibe proporcionalmente al mayor número de inmigrantes, comparado con otras naciones del mundo. Investiga de dónde llegan estos inmigrantes y lo que hace el gobierno español para ayudarlos y fomentar la asimilación.

Abra la boca.

© Frank Siteman/age fotostock

Vocabulario

Especialistas

el (la) dermatólogo(a)	*dermatologist*
el (la) endocrinólogo(a)	*endocrinologist*
el (la) ginecólogo(a)	*gynecologist*
el (la) internista	*internist*
el (la) obstetra	*obstetrician*
el (la) oncólogo(a)	*oncologist*
el (la) ortopedista	*orthopedist*
el (la) otorrino(a)	*throat, nose and ear specialist*
el (la) psiquiatra	*psychiatrist*
el (la) radiólogo(a)	*radiologist*
el (la) urólogo(a)	*urologist*

Sustantivos

la higiene	*hygiene*
la temperatura	*temperature*
el termómetro	*thermometer*

Verbos

atender	*to take care of*
extraer	*to withdraw*
pesar	*to weight*
revisar	*to check*

Expresiones útiles

¿Es alérgico a algún medicamento?
Are you allergic to any medication?

Necesito tomar su presión arterial.
I need to take your blood pressure.

Respire hondo.
Take a deep breath.

DATOS IMPORTANTES

Educación: Estudios universitarios o terciarios como enfermero registrado.

Salario: Entre $20 000 y $40 000, dependiendo de los años de experiencia y del hospital o clínica, entre 1 y 20 años.

Dónde se trabaja: En hospitales, clínicas privadas, laboratorios, escuelas, clubes deportivos.

Saúl Salerno es enfermero y trabaja en un hospital local. En el video verás a Saúl atendiendo a un paciente.

Antes de ver

Los enfermeros trabajan constantemente para cuidar a los pacientes del hospital. Realizan muchas tareas y luego les dan el informe a los médicos. Los pacientes se sienten bien cuando los enfermeros son amables y cuidadosos. ¿Qué elementos interesantes encuentras en el trabajo de un enfermero? ¿Qué preguntas le harías a un enfermero con respecto a su trabajo? ¿Serías enfermero? ¿Por qué?

Al ver

© Heinle/Cengage Learning

1. ¿Tiene fiebre el paciente?
2. ¿Dónde le duele?
3. ¿Había estado en el hospital antes?
4. ¿Cuánto pesa el paciente?
5. ¿Qué problema tuvo antes el paciente?
6. ¿Está comiendo mucho el paciente?
7. ¿Cómo está la presión arterial del paciente?
8. ¿Qué le da el enfermero para tomar?
9. ¿Para qué necesita una orden del médico?
10. ¿De dónde le va a extraer sangre?

Después de ver

En grupos de dos, representen a un enfermero que está ayudando a un paciente. El enfermero debe hablarle al paciente sobre lo que le duele, cuándo empezó a sentirse mal y después darle recomendaciones.

14.35 **¿Por qué?** El asistente del doctor Navárez hace muchas preguntas sobre los pacientes. Contesta las preguntas, usando el pluscuamperfecto del verbo entre paréntesis.

Modelo *¿Por qué operó a Leonor? (tener un accidente)*
Porque había tenido un accidente.

1. ¿Por qué le puso un yeso en la pierna a Jaime? (romperse)
2. ¿Por qué le sacó radiografías del brazo a Gaby? (caerse)
3. ¿Por qué le puso una curita en la mano a Chuy? (cortarse)
4. ¿Por qué le hicieron una prueba de embarazo a la señora Núñez? (desmayarse)
5. ¿Por qué le puso un vendaje en la muñeca de Sabino? (torcerse)
6. ¿Por qué le examinó los ojos a Ernesto? (comenzar a perder la vista)

14.36 **Hablemos de doctores** Combina la primera columna con la segunda columna para completar las ideas lógicamente. Cuando identifiques la idea más lógica, usa la forma apropiada del verbo en el presente del subjuntivo o del indicativo, según se necesite.

1. Cada mañana hablo con los primeros pacientes en cuanto...
2. Ana toma medicamentos sin que...
3. Visitaré Panamá antes de que...
4. Mis primos visitan una clínica en La Habana para que...
5. Inés va a llamar al hospital a fin de que...
6. Iremos al hospital tan pronto como...

a. la recepcionista le (dar) una cita.
b. los doctores me (operar).
c. un experto les (examinar) los ojos.
d. yo (llegar) al hospital.
e. la ambulancia (llegar) a nuestra casa.
f. su doctor se los (recetar).

14.37 **El pasado y el presente** Completa los siguientes comentarios con la forma apropiada del verbo entre paréntesis. Necesitarás usar el subjuntivo, el indicativo y el infinitivo. **¡OJO!** Algunos están en el presente y otros en el pasado.

1. En el pasado no había tantas personas que (a.) _____ (estudiar) idiomas en los Estados Unidos. Mucha gente no creía que esto (b.) _____ (ser) necesario. Es obvio que el mundo (c.) _____ (ser) más pequeño hoy a causa de la tecnología, y es importante que todos (d.) _____ (aprender) a hablar otro idioma.

2. Antes algunas universidades estadounidenses requerían (*required*) que los estudiantes (a.) _____ (tener) una clase de lenguas para (b.) _____ (poder) graduarse. Pienso que ahora las universidades (c.) _____ (deber) requerir nuevamente que los estudiantes (d.) _____ (tomar) una clase de lenguas antes de (e.) _____ (graduarse).

3. En el pasado era muy difícil que la gente (a.) _____ (viajar) mucho. Hoy es muy común que la gente (b.) _____ (ir) a otro país de vacaciones, de negocios o para seguir sus estudios. Por eso, es buena idea que los estudiantes (c.) _____ (asitir) a algún curso donde el profesor (d.) _____ (enseñar) acerca de otros países para que ellos (e.) _____ (poder) entender mejor otras culturas.

14.38 **¡Imaginemos!** ¿Qué harías si tu vida fuera diferente? Con un compañero, túrnense para explicar qué harían en estas circunstancias.

Modelo Trabajas en el mundo del espectáculo (cine, televisión, etc.).
Estudiante 1: *Si trabajara en el mundo del espectáculo, siempre comería en los mejores restaurantes. ¿Qué harías tú?*
Estudiante 2: *Viviría en California.*

1. No hay electricidad.
2. Eres del sexo opuesto.
3. Eres presidente.
4. Vives en otro país.
5. Hablas español perfectamente.
6. Eres invisible.
7. Te puedes convertir en un animal.
8. Puedes cambiar algo en el mundo.

14.39 **Los idiomas** En grupos de tres o cuatro estudiantes respondan las siguientes preguntas.

1. ¿Por qué decidiste estudiar español?
2. ¿Habías estudiado español antes de entrar en la universidad? ¿Por cuánto tiempo?
3. ¿Era necesario que estudiaras un idioma para graduarte de la escuela secundaria?
4. ¿Piensas seguir con tus estudios de español cuando termine el semestre? ¿Por qué?
5. ¿Te gustaría aprender otro idioma aparte el español? ¿Cuál?
6. ¿Qué pasaría si no se enseñaran otros idiomas en las escuelas y universidades de Estados Unidos?
7. ¿Cuáles son las ventajas y las desventajas de aprender otro idioma?
8. ¿Cómo se puede ayudar a los inmigrantes a aprender el idioma de su nuevo país?

14.40 **Nacionalidades** Trabaja con un compañero. En esta página uno de ustedes va a ver una lista de personas y la ciudad de donde son, y el otro estudiante va a ver una lista diferente en el apéndice A. Túrnense para compartir la información. **¡OJO!** No mencionen el país, solo la capital. Tu compañero deberá dar la nacionalidad de cada persona.

Modelo Estudiante 1: *Alfonso es de la Ciudad de México.*
Estudiante 2: *Es mexicano.*

Nombre	Capital
Mireya	Bogotá, Colombia
Simón	Montevideo, Uruguay
Diego	La Habana, Cuba
Celia	Caracas, Venezuela
Gisela	Lima, Perú
Miguel	Sucre, Bolivia
Lulú	Quito, Ecuador
Zoyla	Tegucigalpa, Honduras

Alfonso es de la Ciudad de México.

Vocabulario 1

CD2-29

En el hospital

el corazón	heart	la radiografía	x-ray
el esqueleto	skeleton	la receta médica	prescription
el hígado	liver	la sala de	emergency room
el hueso	bone	emergencias	
el intestino	intestine	la salud	health
el órgano vital	vital organ	la sangre	blood
el (la) paciente	patient	el tratamiento	treatment
los primeros auxilios	first aid	el yeso	cast
el pulmón	lung		

Los síntomas

la alergia	allergy	el estornudo	sneeze
el asco	nausea	la fractura	fracture
el desmayo	faint	la presión baja/alta	low/high blood pressure
la diarrea	diarrhea	la tos	cough
el dolor	pain		

Algunas enfermedades

el cáncer	cancer	el insomnio	insomnia
el catarro	cold	la obesidad	obesity
la diabetes	diabetes	el resfriado	cold
la gripe	flu	el SIDA	AIDS
la hipertensión	high blood pressure		

Los medicamentos y procedimientos

la aspirina	aspirin	la inyección	injection
la cirugía	surgery	el jarabe	syrup (cough)
la curita	small adhesive bandage	la pastilla	pill
		la vacuna	vaccine
las gotas	drops	el vendaje	bandage

Verbos

cortarse	to cut oneself	recuperarse	to recuperate, to recover
desmayarse	to faint	respirar	to breathe
doler (ue)	to hurt	tomar la presión	to take someone´s blood pressure
estar mareado	to be dizzy		
estornudar	to sneeze	torcerse (ue)	to twist, to sprain
examinar	to examine	toser	to cough
fracturarse	to fracture	vomitar	to vomit

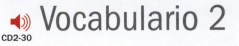

Vocabulario 2

CD2-30

Nacionalidades

argentino	*Argentine*	hondureño	*Honduran*
boliviano	*Bolivian*	mexicano	*Mexican*
chileno	*Chilean*	nicaragüense	*Nicaraguan*
colombiano	*Colombian*	panameño	*Panamanian*
costarricense	*Costa Rican*	paraguayo	*Paraguayan*
cubano	*Cuban*	peruano	*Peruvian*
dominicano	*Dominican*	puertorriqueño	*Puerto Rican*
ecuatoguineano	*Ecuatorial Guinean*	salvadoreño	*Salvadoran*
ecuatoriano	*Ecuadorian*	uruguayo	*Uruguayan*
español	*Spanish*	venezolano	*Venezuelan*
guatemalteco	*Guatemalan*		

Conceptos políticos

el (la) ciudadano(a)	*citizen*	la ley	*law*
los derechos humanos	*human rights*	el organismo internacional	*international organization*
el desempleo	*unemployment*	la paz	*peace*
la emigración	*emigration*	la pobreza	*poverty*
la globalización	*globalization*	el (la) refugiado(a)	*refugee*
la guerra	*war*	la riqueza	*wealth*
la inmigración	*immigration*	el tratado de comercio	*trade agreement*
el (la) inmigrante	*immigrant*		

Verbos

emigrar	*emigrate*	mudarse	*to move (to another location)*
inmigrar	*immigrate*	votar	*to vote*

Adverbios

a fin de que	*in order that, so that*	en cuanto	*as soon as*
a menos que	*unless*	hasta que	*until*
antes (de) que	*before*	para que	*in order that, so that*
aunque	*although, even if*	sin que	*without*
con tal (de) que	*provided that*	tan pronto (como)	*as soon as*
después (de) que	*after*		
en caso de que	*in case*		

Diccionario personal

_____

_____

Gregorio López y Fuentes

Biografía

Gregorio López y Fuentes (1899–1966) nació en la región de la Huasteca, Veracruz, en una familia de comerciantes y campesinos (*farm workers*). Estudió en la Escuela Nacional de Maestros en la Ciudad de México, donde posteriormente trabajó como maestro de literatura y más tarde como periodista. Después de varios intentos para publicar, encontró el éxito al escribir novelas sobre la Revolución Mexicana y la vida de los campesinos. Su primera novela, *El Vagabundo*, apareció en la revista *El Universal Ilustrado* en 1922, y en 1935 recibió el Premio Nacional Mexicano por su novela *La India*.

Antes de leer

1. ¿Alguna vez trabajaste mucho tiempo en algo que luego perdiste? ¿Qué? ¿Cómo reaccionaste?

2. ¿Qué pasa cuando un agricultor pierde toda la cosecha (*harvest*)?

3. En tu opinión o experiencia personal, ¿qué le piden a Dios las personas religiosas? ¿Qué tipo de respuesta crees que esperan estas personas de Dios? Explica.

Investiguemos la literatura: La ironía

Irony is a literary device in which the author creates an incongruity between what appears to be true and what is true. There are different types of irony, some of which include: dramatic irony in which there is a discrepancy between what the characters know and what the audience knows; situational irony in which there is a discrepancy between what is expected to happen and what really happens; and cosmic irony in which the universal forces (God, destiny, or fate) react contrary to what the character expects.

Una carta a Dios

    La casa—única en todo el valle—
estaba subida en uno de esos **cerros**
flat-top hills   **truncados** que, a manera de pirámides
rudimentarias, dejaron algunas tribus
5   al continuar sus peregrinaciones. Desde
plains   allí se veían las **vegas,** el río, rastrojos
maíz   y, lindando con el corral, la **milpa,** ya a
to form ears of corn/   punto de **jilotear.** Entre las **matas** del
plantas   maíz, el frijol con su florecilla morada,
10   promesa inequívoca de una buena
harvest   **cosecha.**

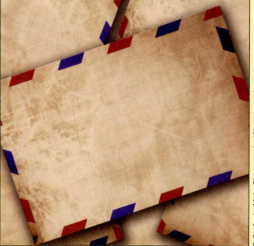

© Stefanie Mohr Photography/Shutterstock

Lo único que estaba haciendo falta a la tierra era una lluvia, cuando lo menos un fuerte aguacero, de esos que forman charcos entre los surcos. Dudar que llovería hubiera sido lo mismo que dejar de creer en la experiencia de quienes, por

to plant — 15 tradición enseñaron a **sembrar** en determinado día del año.

Durante la mañana, Lencho—conocedor del campo, apegado a las viejas costumbres y creyente a puño cerrado—no había hecho más que examinar el cielo por el rumbo del noreste.

—Ahora sí que viene el agua, vieja.

20 Y la vieja, que preparaba la comida, le respondió:

—Dios lo quiera.

weeds — Los muchachos más grandes limpiaban de **hierba** la siembra, mientras
corrían — que los más pequeños **correteaban** cerca de la casa, hasta que la mujer les gritó a todos:

pegar — 25 —Vengan que les voy a **dar en la boca**…

Fue durante la comida cuando, como lo había asegurado Lencho, comenzaron a
drops — caer gruesas **gotas** de lluvia. Por el noreste se veían avanzar grandes montañas de
earthen jar — nubes. El aire olía a **jarro** nuevo.

—Hagan de cuenta, muchachos—exclamaba el hombre mientras sentía la
to get wet/tools — 30 fruición de **mojarse** con el pretexto de recoger algunos **enseres** olvidados sobre una
fence/coin — **cerca** de piedra—, que no son gotas de agua las que están cayendo; son **monedas** nuevas; las gotas grandes son de a diez y las gotas chicas son de a cinco…

Y dejaba pasear sus ojos satisfechos por la milpa a punto de jilotear,
rows — adornada con las **hileras** frondosas del frijol, y entonces toda ella cubierta por
35 la transparente cortina de la lluvia. Pero, de pronto, comenzó a soplar un fuerte
hailstones — viento y con las gotas de agua comenzaron a caer **granizos** tan grandes como
acorns — **bellotas**. Ésos sí parecían monedas de plata nueva. Los muchachos, exponiéndose a la lluvia, corrían a recoger las perlas heladas de mayor tamaño.

—Esto sí que está muy malo—exclamaba mortificado el hombre.—Ojalá que
40 pase pronto…

hit — No pasó pronto. Durante una hora el granizo **apedreó** la casa, la huerta, el
salt marsh — monte, la milpa y todo el valle. El campo estaba blanco que parecía una **salina**.
destruido — Los árboles, deshojados. El maíz **hecho pedazos**. El frijol, sin una flor. Lencho,
tristeza — con el alma llena de **tribulaciones**. Pasada la tormenta, en medio de los surcos,
45 decía a sus hijos:

locusts — —Más hubiera dejado una nube de **langostas** … El granizo no ha dejado nada:
ear of corn — ni una sola mata de maíz dará una **mazorca,** ni una mata de frijol dará una
pod — **vaina** …

La noche fue de lamentaciones:

50 —¡Todo nuestro trabajo, perdido!

—¡Y ni a quién acudir!

—Este año pasaremos hambre…

Pero muy en el fondo espiritual de cuantos convivían bajo aquella casa solitaria en mitad del valle, había una esperanza: la ayuda de Dios.

55 —No te mortifiques tanto, aunque el mal es grande. ¡Recuerda que nadie se muere de hambre!

—Eso dicen: Nadie se muere de hambre...

dawn Y mientras llegaba el **amanecer,** Lencho pensó mucho en lo que había visto en la iglesia del pueblo los domingos: un triángulo y dentro del triángulo un ojo, un

60 ojo que parecía muy grande, un ojo que, según le habían explicado, lo mira todo, hasta lo que está en el fondo de las conciencias.

course Lencho era un hombre **rudo** y él mismo solía decir que el campo embrutece, pero no lo era tanto que no supiera escribir. Ya con la luz del día y aprovechando la circunstancia de que era domingo, después de haberse afirmado en su idea de

watches over 65 que sí hay quien **vele** por todos, se puso a escribir una carta que él mismo llevaría al pueblo para echarla al correo.

Era nada menos que una carta a Dios.

Dios—escribió—si no me ayudas, pasaré hambre con todos los míos, durante este año: necesito cien pesos para volver a sembrar y vivir mientras viene la nueva

70 cosecha, pues el granizo...

escribió/envelope/papel **Rotuló** el **sobre** "A Dios", metió el **pliego** y, aun preocupado, se dirigió al

stamp pueblo. Ya en la oficina de correos, le puso un **timbre** a la carta y echó ésta en el

mailbox **buzón.**

Un empleado, que era cartero y todo en la oficina de correos, llegó riéndose

75 con toda la boca ante su jefe: le mostraba nada menos que la carta dirigida a Dios.

residence Nunca en su existencia de repartidor había conocido ese **domicilio.** El jefe de la

amable oficina—gordo y **bonachón**—también se puso a reír, pero bien pronto **se le plegó**

frowned **el entrecejo** y, mientras daba golpecitos en la mesa con la carta comentaba:

faith —**¡La fe!** ¡Quién tuviera la fe de quien escribió esta carta! ¡Creer como él cree!

80 ¡Esperar con la confianza con que él sabe esperar! ¡Sostener correspondencia con Dios!

Y, para no defraudar aquel tesoro de fe, descubierto a través de una carta que

delivered no podía ser **entregada,** el jefe postal concibió una idea: contestar la carta. Pero

will una vez abierta, se vio que contestarla necesitaba algo más que buena **voluntad,**

he didn´t give up/ 85 **tinta** y papel. **No por ello se dio por vencido:** exigió a su empleado una **dádiva,**

donación/ él puso parte de su sueldo y a varias personas les pidió su **óbolo** "para una obra

contribución piadosa".

Fue imposible para él reunir los cien pesos solicitados por Lencho, y se conformó con enviar al campesino cuando menos lo que había recibido: algo más

90 que la mitad. Puso los billetes en un sobre dirigido a Lencho y con ellos un pliego que no tenía más que una palabra, a manera de firma: Dios.

Al siguiente domingo Lencho llegó a preguntar, más temprano que de costumbre, si había alguna carta para él. Fue el mismo repartidero quien **le hizo**

dio **entrega** de la carta, mientras que el jefe, con la alegría de quien ha hecho una

scratched glass 95 buena acción, espiaba a través de un **vidrio raspado,** desde su despacho.

Lencho no mostró la menor sorpresa al ver los billetes—tanta era su seguridad—pero hizo un gesto de cólera al contar el dinero... ¡Dios no podía haberse equivocado, ni negar lo que Lencho se le había pedido!

Inmediatamente, Lencho se acercó a la ventanilla para pedir papel y tinta.

wrinkling

100 En la mesa destinada al público, se puso a escribir, **arrugando** mucho la frente a causa del esfuerzo que hacía para dar forma legible a sus ideas. Al terminar, fue a

blow of the fist

pedir un timbre, el cual mojó con la lengua y luego aseguró con un **puñetazo**.

En cuanto la carta cayó al buzón, el jefe de correos fue a recogerla. Decía:
"Dios: Del dinero que te pedí, sólo llegaron a mis manos sesenta pesos.

105 Mándame el resto, que me hace falta; pero, no me los mandes por conducto de la

thieves

oficina de correos, porque los empleados son muy **ladrones.**—Lencho".

Lic. Manuel Arredondo, Instituto Nacional del Derecho del Autor, México.

Después de leer

A. Comprensión

1. ¿Cómo se sintió Lencho cuando comenzó a llover? ¿Por qué?
2. ¿Cuál fue el resultado de la tormenta?
3. ¿Cuál era la única esperanza de la familia?
4. ¿Qué decidió hacer Lencho?
5. ¿Cuál fue la reacción inicial del cartero y de su jefe?
6. ¿Por qué estaba sorprendido el jefe?
7. ¿Qué decidió hacer el jefe de correos?
8. ¿Cuál fue el problema del jefe? ¿Qué hizo al final?
9. ¿Por qué el jefe miraba mientras Lencho recogía la carta?
10. ¿Por qué Lencho no se sorprendió cuando vio el dinero?
11. ¿Cuál fue la reacción de Lencho cuando contó el dinero? ¿Qué hizo después?
12. ¿Cual es la ironía del cuento?

B. Conversemos

1. ¿Qué hubieras hecho si tú hubieras abierto la primera carta de Lencho?
2. ¿Cómo piensas que reaccionó el jefe de correos al abrir la segunda carta de Lencho?

Exploraciones del mundo hispano

Argentina ▶

INFORMACIÓN GENERAL

Nombre oficial: República Argentina

Nacionalidad: argentino(a)

Área: 2 780 400 km² (el país de habla hispana más grande del mundo, aproximadamente 2 veces el tamaño de Alaska)

Población: 41 343 201 (2010)

Capital: Buenos Aires (f. 1580) (3 000 000 hab.)

Otras ciudades importantes: Córdoba (1 350 000 hab.), Rosario (1 250 000 hab.), Mar del Plata (600 000 hab.)

Moneda: peso (argentino)

Idiomas: español (oficial), guaraní, inglés, italiano, alemán, francés

DEMOGRAFÍA

Alfabetismo: 97,2%

Religiones: católicos (92%), protestantes (2%), judíos (2%), otros (4%)

ARGENTINOS CÉLEBRES

Eva Perón
primera dama (1919–1952)

Jorge Luis Borges
escritor (1899–1986)

Julio Cortázar
escritor (1914–1984)

Adolfo Pérez Esquivel
Premio Nobel de la Paz (1931–   )

Diego Maradona
futbolista (1960–   )

Charly García
músico (1951–   )

Puerto Madero, en Buenos Aires

INVESTIGA EN INTERNET 🌐

La geografía: las cataratas del Iguazú, la Patagonia, las islas Malvinas, las pampas

La historia: la inmigración, los gauchos, la guerra sucia, la Guerra de las Islas Malvinas, Carlos Gardel, Mercedes Sosa, José de San Martín

Películas: *Valentín, La historia oficial, Quién toca a mi puerta, El secreto*

Música: el tango, la milonga, la zamba, la chacarera, Fito Páez, Soda Stereo, Charly García

Comidas y bebidas: el asado, los alfajores, las empanadas, el mate, los vinos cuyanos

Fiestas: 25 de mayo (Día de la Revolución), 9 de julio (Día de la Independencia)

© Corey Wise/age fotostock

Interior del antiguo mercado de San Telmo

Pablo H Caridad/Shutterstock

Un puente de hielo del glaciar Perito Moreno

CURIOSIDADES

- Argentina es un país de inmigrantes europeos. A partir de la última parte del siglo XIX hubo una fuerte inmigración, especialmente de Italia, España e Inglaterra. Estas culturas se mezclaron y ayudaron a crear la identidad argentina.

- Argentina se caracteriza por la calidad de su carne vacuna por ser uno de los principales exportadores del mundo.

- El instrumento musical característico del tango, la música tradicional argentina, se llama *bandoneón*, y es de origen alemán.

Bolivia ▶

INFORMACIÓN GENERAL

Nombre oficial: Estado Plurinacional de Bolivia

Nacionalidad: boliviano(a)

Área: 1 098 581 km² (2800 km de costas) (aproximadamente 4 veces el área de Wyoming, o la mitad de México)

Población: 9 947 418 (2010)

Capital: Sucre (poder judicial) (350 000 hab.) y La Paz (sede del gobierno) (f. 1548) (900 000 hab.)

Otras ciudades importantes: Santa Cruz de la Sierra (1 800 000 hab.), Cochabamba (1 200 000 hab.), El Alto (900 000 hab.)

Moneda: peso (boliviano)

Idiomas: español (oficial), quechua, aymará

DEMOGRAFÍA

Alfabetismo: 86,7%

Religiones: católicos (95%), protestantes (5%)

BOLIVIANOS CÉLEBRES

María Luisa Pacheco
pintora (1919–1982)

Jaime Escalante
ingeniero y profesor de matemáticas (1930–2010)

Evo Morales
primer indígena elegido presidente de Bolivia (1959–   )

Edmundo Paz Soldán
escritor (1967–   )

La montaña Huayna Potosí desde La Paz

Celso Diniz/Shutterstock

INVESTIGA EN INTERNET 🌐

La geografía: el lago Titikaka, Tihuanaco, el salar de Uyuni

La historia: los incas, los aymará, la hoja de coca, Carnaval de Oruro Festival de la Virgen de Urkupiña, Simón Bolivar

Música: la música andina, las peñas, la lambada, Los Kjarkas

Comidas y bebidas: las llauchas, la papa (más de dos mil variedades), la chicha

Fiestas: 6 de agosto (Día de la Independencia)

Un barco tradicional hecho con totora, una planta que crece en el lago Titikaka

Jenny Leonard/Shutterstock

Peter McFarren/AP Images

El cerro Rico donde se encuentra la mina Pailaviri

CURIOSIDADES

- Bolivia tiene dos capitales. Una de ellas, La Paz, es la más alta del mundo a 3640 metros sobre el nivel del mar.

- El lago Titikaka es el lago navegable más alto del mundo con una altura de más de 3800 metros (12 500 pies) sobre el nivel del mar.

- En Bolivia se consumen las hojas secas del coca para soportar mejor los efectos de la altura extrema.

- Bolivia es uno de los dos países de Sudamérica que no tiene costa marina.

Chile ▶

INFORMACIÓN GENERAL

Nombre oficial: República de Chile

Nacionalidad: chileno(a)

Área: 756 102 km² (un poco más grande que Texas)

Población: 16 746 491 (2010)

Capital: Santiago (f. 1541) (6 400 000 hab.)

Otras ciudades importantes: Valparaíso (350 000 hab.), Viña del Mar (325 000 hab.), Concepción (300 000 hab.)

Moneda: peso (chileno)

Idiomas: español (oficial), mapuche, mapudungun, alemán, inglés

DEMOGRAFÍA

Alfabetismo: 95,7%

Religiones: católicos (70%), evangélicos (15%), testigos de Jehová (1%), otros (14%)

CHILENOS CÉLEBRES

Pablo Neruda
poeta, Premio Nobel de Literatura
(1904–1973)

Gabriela Mistral
poetisa, Premio Nobel de Literatura
(1889–1957)

Isabel Allende
escritora (1942–   )

Michelle Bachelet
primera mujer presidente de Chile (1951–   )

Violeta Parra
poetisa, cantautora (1917–1967)

El cerro Toro en Valparaíso

SF photo/Shutterstock

Galina Barskaya/Shutterstock

Los famosos moáis de la Isla de Pascua

La geografía: Antofagasta, el desierto de Atacama, la isla de Pascua, Tierra del Fuego, el estrecho de Magallanes, los pasos andinos

La historia: los indígenas mapuches, Salvador Allende, Augusto Pinochet, Bernardo O'Higgins

Películas: *Obstinate Memory, La nana*

Música: el Festival de Viña del Mar, Víctor Jara, Quilapayún, La Ley, Inti Illimani

Comidas y bebidas: las empanadas, los pescados y mariscos, el pastel de choclo, los vinos chilenos

Fiestas: 18 de septiembre (Día de la Independencia)

ELISEO FERNANDEZ / Reuters / Landov

Un festival de payasos en Valparaíso

CURIOSIDADES

■ Chile es uno de los países más largos del mundo, pero también es muy angosto. En algunas partes del país se necesitan solo 90 km para atravesar el país. Gracias a su longitud, en el sur de Chile hay glaciares y fiordos, mientras que en el norte está el desierto más seco del mundo: el desierto de Atacama. La cordillera de los Andes también contribuye a la gran variedad de zonas climáticas y geográficas de este país.

■ Es un país muy rico en minerales, en particular el cobre, que se exporta a nivel mundial.

■ En febrero del 2010, Chile sufrió uno de los terremotos (*earthquakes*) más fuertes registrados en el mundo, con una magnitud de 8.8. Chile también es el escenario del terremoto más violento desde que se tiene registro: ocurrió en 1960, y tuvo una magnitud de 9.4.

Colombia ▶

INFORMACIÓN GENERAL

Nombre oficial: República de Colombia

Nacionalidad: colombiano(a)

Área: 1 139 914 km² (aproximadamente 4 veces el área de Arizona)

Población: 44 205 293 (2010)

Capital: Bogotá D.C. (f. 1538) (8 000 000 hab.)

Otras ciudades importantes: Medellín (2 200 000 hab.), Cali (2 100 000 hab.), Barranquilla (1 200 000 hab.)

Moneda: peso (colombiano)

Idiomas: español (oficial), chibcha, guajiro y apróximadamente 90 lenguas indígenas

DEMOGRAFÍA

Alfabetismo: 90,4%

Religiones: católicos (90%), otros (10%)

COLOMBIANOS CÉLEBRES

Gabriel García Márquez
escritor, Premio Nobel de Literatura (1928–)

Fernando Botero
pintor y escultor (1932–)

Shakira
cantante y benefactora (1977–)

Tatiana Calderón Noguera
automovilista (1994–)

© Ildi Papp/Shutterstock.

Colombia es un país con una gran biodiversidad

La geografía: los Andes, el Amazonas, las playas de Santa Marta y Cartagena

La historia: los araucanos, Simón Bolívar, la leyenda de El Dorado, el Museo del Oro, las FARC

Películas: *María llena de gracia*

Música: la cumbia, el vallenato, Shakira, Juanes, Carlos Vives, Aterciopelados

Comidas y bebidas: el ajiaco, las arepas, la picada, el arequipe, las cocadas, el café, el aguardiente

Fiestas: 20 de julio (Día de la Independencia)

La playa Santa Marta

rm/Shutterstock

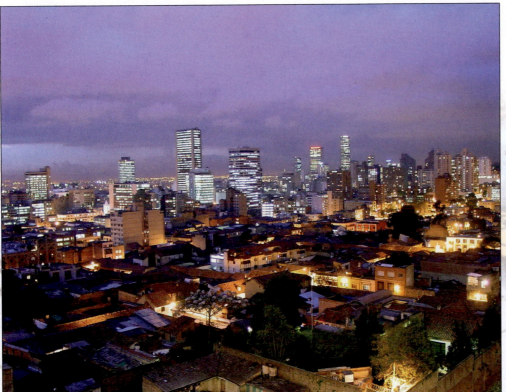

Marinko Tarlac/Shutterstock

Bogotá, capital de Colombia

CURIOSIDADES

- El 95% de la producción mundial de esmeraldas se extrae del subsuelo colombiano. Sin embargo, la mayor riqueza del país es su diversidad, que incluye culturas del Caribe, del Pacífico, del Amazonas y de los Andes.

- Colombia, junto con Costa Rica y Brasil, es uno de los principales productores de café de Latinoamérica.

- Colombia tiene una gran diversidad de especies de flores. Es el primer productor de claveles y el segundo exportador mundial de flores después de Holanda.

Costa Rica ▶

INFORMACIÓN GENERAL

Nombre oficial: República de Costa Rica

Nacionalidad: costarricense

Área: 51 100 km² (aproximadamente 2 veces el área de Vermont)

Población: 4 516 220 (2010)

Capital: San José (f. 1521) (1 500 000 hab.)

Otras ciudades importantes: Alajuela (700 000 hab.), Cartago (450 000 hab.)

Moneda: colón

Idiomas: español (oficial), inglés

DEMOGRAFÍA

Alfabetismo: 94,9%

Religiones: católicos (76,3%), evangélicos y otros protestantes (15,7%), otros (4,8%), ninguna (3,2%)

COSTARRICENCES CÉLEBRES

Oscar Arias
político, Premio Nobel de la Paz, presidente (1949–   )

Carmen Naranjo
escritora (1928–   )

Claudia Poll
atleta olímpica (1972–   )

Una garza en el Parque Nacional Tortuguero

Bruce Raynor/Shutterstock

INVESTIGA EN INTERNET

La geografía: Monteverde, Tortuguero, el Bosque de los Niños, el volcán Poás, los Parques Nacionales, ecoturismo

La historia: las plantaciones de café, Juan Mora Fernández, los ticos

Música: El Café Chorale

Comidas y bebidas: el gallo pinto, el café

Fiestas: 15 de septiembre (Día de la Independencia)

El volcán Poás, uno de los volcanes activos más visitados del mundo

Mujeres cocinando comida típica en la región de Guanacaste

CURIOSIDADES

■ Costa Rica es uno de los pocos países del mundo que no tiene ejército *(army)*. En noviembre de 1949, 18 meses después de la Guerra Civil, abolieron el ejército en la nueva constitución.

■ Se conoce como un país progresista gracias a su apoyo a la democracia, el alto nivel de vida de los costarricenses y la protección de su medio ambiente.

■ Costa Rica posee una fauna y flora sumamente ricas. Un ejemplo de ello es el Parque Nacional Tortuguero.

■ Costa Rica produce y exporta cantidades importantes de café, por lo que este producto es muy importante para su economía. Además, el café costarricense es de calidad reconocida en todo el mundo.

Cuba ▶

INFORMACIÓN GENERAL

Nombre oficial: República de Cuba

Nacionalidad: cubano(a)

Área: 110 860 km² (aproximadamente el área de Tennessee)

Población: 11 477 459 (2010)

Capital: La Habana (f. 1511) (2 200 000 hab.)

Otras ciudades importantes: Santiago (450 000 hab.), Camagüey (300 000 hab.)

Moneda: peso cubano

Idiomas: español (oficial)

DEMOGRAFÍA

Alfabetismo: 99,8%

Religiones: católicos (85%), santería y otras religiones (15%)

CUBANOS CÉLEBRES

José Martí
político, periodista, poeta (1853–1895)

Alejo Carpentier
escritor (1904–1980)

Wifredo Lam
pintor (1902–1982)

Alicia Alonso
bailarina, fundadora del Ballet
Nacional de Cuba (1920–   )

Silvio Rodríguez
poeta, cantautor (1946–   )

Giovanni Rinaldi/iStockphotos

Niños nadando en el malecón de La Habana en Cuba

INVESTIGA EN INTERNET 🌐

La geografía: las cavernas de Bellamar, la Ciénaga de Zapata, la península de Guanahacabibes

La historia: los taínos, los ciboneyes, Fulgencio Batista, Bahía de Cochinos, la Revolución Cubana

Películas: *Vampiros en La Habana, Fresa y chocolate, La última espera*

Música: el son, Buena Vista Social Club, Celia Cruz, Pablo Milanés, Santiago Feliú, Silvio Rodríguez

Comidas y bebidas: la ropa vieja, los moros y cristianos, el ron

Fiestas: 10 de diciembre (Día de la Independencia), 1º de enero (Día de la Revolución)

Peeter Viisimaa/iStockphotos

Los autos viejos son una vista típica en toda la isla.

RoxyFer/Shutterstck

Músicos cubanos tradicionales tocando en las calles de Trinidad

CURIOSIDADES

■ Cuba se distingue por tener uno de los mejores sistemas de educación del mundo, por su sistema de salud y por su apoyo a las artes.

■ La población de la isla es una mezcla de los pobladores nativos (taínos), descendientes de esclavos africanos, y europeos, mezcla que produce una cultura única.

■ A principios de la década de 1980, un movimiento musical conocido como la Nueva Trova Cubana presentó al mundo entero la música testimonial.

Ecuador ▸

INFORMACIÓN GENERAL

Nombre oficial: República del Ecuador

Nacionalidad: ecuatoriano(a)

Área: 283 561 km² (aproximadamente el área de Colorado)

Población: 14 790 608 (2010)

Capital: Quito (f. 1556) (2 500 000 hab.)

Otras ciudades importantes: Guayaquil (2 200 000 hab.), Cuenca (460 000 hab.)

Moneda: dólar

Idiomas: español (oficial), quechua

DEMOGRAFÍA

Alfabetismo: 91%

Religiones: católicos (95%), otros (5%)

ECUATORIANOS CÉLEBRES

Jorge Carrera Andrade
escritor (1903–1978)

Oswaldo Guayasamín
pintor (1919–1999)

Rosalía Arteaga
abogada, política, ex vicepresidenta (1956–   )

Las Peñas es un barrio muy conocido de la ciudad de Guayaquil

Marcos Aspiazu/Shutterstck

INVESTIGA EN INTERNET

La geografía: La selva amazónica, las islas Galápagos, el volcán Cotopaxi

La historia: José de Sucre, la Gran Colombia, los indígenas tagaeri

Música: música andina, la quena, la zampoña

Comida: la papa, el plátano frito, el ceviche

Fiestas: 10 de agosto (Día de la Independencia)

AIZAR RALDES/AFP/Getty Images

Un grupo de campesinos aymará tocando zampoñas durante una feria

XuRa/Shutterstck/iStockphotos

Vista aérea del sector financiero de la ciudad de Quito

CURIOSIDADES

- Este país cuenta con una gran diversidad de zonas geográficas como costas, altas montañas con nieve y selva. Las famosas islas Galápagos le pertenecen y presentan una gran diversidad biológica. A principios del siglo XX, estas islas fueron utilizadas como prisión.

- Ecuador toma su nombre de la línea ecuatorial, que divide el globo en dos hemisferios: norte y sur.

- La música andina es tradicional en Ecuador, con instrumentos indígenas como el charango, el rondador y el bombo.

- Ecuador es famoso por sus tejidos de lana de llama y alpaca, dos animales de la región andina.

El Salvador ▶

INFORMACIÓN GENERAL

Nombre oficial: República de El Salvador

Nacionalidad: salvadoreño(a)

Área: 21 041 km² (un poco más grande que Nueva Jersey)

Población: 6 052 064 (2010)

Capital: San Salvador (f. 1524) (400 000 hab.)

Otras ciudades importantes: San Miguel (250 000 hab.), Santa Ana (250 000 hab.)

Moneda: dólar estadounidense

Idiomas: español (oficial), náhuatl, otras lenguas amerindias

DEMOGRAFÍA

Alfabetismo: 80,2%

Religiones: católicos (57%), protestantes (21%), otros (22%)

SALVADOREÑOS CÉLEBRES

Óscar Arnulfo Romero
arzobispo, defensor de los derechos humanos (1917–1980)

Claribel Alegría
escritora (nació en Nicaragua pero se considera
salvadoreña) (1924–   )

Alfredo Espino
poeta (1900–1928)

Un mural en Concepción de Ataco que muestra a mujeres salvadoreñas lavando ropa

Vespasian/Alamy

INVESTIGA EN INTERNET 🖥️

La geografía: el bosque lluvioso (Parque Nacional Montecristo), el puerto de Acajutla, el volcán Izalco, los planes de Renderos

La historia: Tazumal, Acuerdos de Paz de Chapultepec, José Matías Delgado, FMLN, Ana María

Películas: *Romero, Voces inocentes*

Música: Taltipac, la salsa y la cumbia (fusión)

Comidas y bebidas: las pupusas, los tamales, la semita, el atole

Fiestas: 6 de agosto (Día del Divino Salvador del Mundo); 15 de septiembre (Día de la Independencia)

Andre Nantel/Shutterstock

Una de las numerosas cascadas en el área de Juayua

Michael Obert/age fotostock

El Lago de Coatepeque

CURIOSIDADES

- El Salvador es el país más pequeño de Centroamérica pero el más denso en población.

- Hay más de veinte volcanes y algunos están activos.

- El Salvador está en una zona sísmica, por lo que ocurren terremotos con frecuencia. En el pasado, varios sismos le causaron muchos daños al país.

- Entre 1980 y 1990, El Salvador vivió una guerra civil. Durante esos años, muchos salvadoreños emigraron a los Estados Unidos.

España ▶

INFORMACIÓN GENERAL

Nombre oficial: Reino de España

Nacionalidad: español(a)

Área: 505 370 km² (aproximadamente 2 veces el área de Oregón)

Población: 40 548 753 (2010)

Capital: Madrid (f. siglo X) (3 300 000 hab.)

Otras ciudades importantes: Barcelona (1 600 000 hab.), Valencia (840 000 hab.), Sevilla (710 000 hab.), Toledo (85 000 hab.)

Moneda: euro

Idiomas: castellano (oficial), catalán, vasco, gallego

DEMOGRAFÍA

Alfabetismo: 97,9%

Religiones: católicos (94%), otros (6%)

ESPAÑOLES CÉLEBRES

Miguel de Cervantes Saavedra
escritor (1547–1616)

Federico García Lorca
poeta (1898–1936)

Camilo José Cela
escritor, Premio Nobel de Literatura (1916–2002)

Pedro Almodóvar
director de cine (1949–   )

Antonio Gaudí
arquitecto (1852–1926)

Rafael Nadal
tenista (1986–   )

Vinicius Tupinamba/Shutterstck

La Plaza Mayor es un lugar lleno de historia en el centro de Madrid.

La geografía: las islas Canarias, las islas Baleares

La historia: la conquista de América, la Guerra Civil, el rey Fernando y la reina Isabel, la Guerra de la Independencia Española

Películas: *Ay, Carmela, Mala educación, Hable con ella, Mar adentro, Volver*

Música: las tunas, el flamenco, Paco de Lucía, Mecano, Rosario, Joaquín Sabina

Comidas y bebidas: paella valenciana, tapas, tortilla española, crema catalana, vinos, sangría, horchata

Fiestas: Festival de la Tomatina, San Fermín, procesiones de Semana Santa

GlowImages Cuisine / SuperStock

El puerto de Barcelona al atardecer

Matt Trommer/Shutterstock

El Alcázar en la ciudad de Toledo

CURIOSIDADES

- España se distingue por una gran cantidad de pintores y escritores. En el siglo XX se destacaron los pintores Pablo Picasso, Salvador Dalí y Joan Miró. Entre los clásicos figuran Velázquez, El Greco y Goya.

- El Palacio Real de Madrid presenta una arquitectura hermosa. Contiene pinturas de los artistas mencionados arriba. Originalmente era un fuerte, construido por los musulmanes en el siglo IX. Más tarde, los reyes de Castilla construyeron allí el Alcázar. En 1738, el rey Felipe V ordenó la construcción del palacio. Desde entonces fue la residencia del rey. Actualmente, Juan Carlos I lo usa en las ceremonias de estado, aunque ya no habita en él.

- Aunque el castellano se habla en todo el país, cada región de España mantiene vivo su propio idioma. De todos, el más interesante quizás sea el vasco, que es el único idioma que no deriva del latín y cuyo origen no se conoce.

- En la ciudad de Toledo se fundó la primera escuela de traductores, en el año 1126.

Guatemala ▶

INFORMACIÓN GENERAL

Nombre oficial: República de Guatemala

Nacionalidad: guatemalteco(a)

Área: 108 890 km² (un poco más grande que el área de Ohio)

Población: 13 550 440 (2010)

Capital: Guatemala (f. 1524) (14 000 000 hab.)

Otras ciudades importantes: Mixco (410 000 hab.), Villa Nueva (400 000 hab.)

Moneda: quetzal

Idiomas: español (oficial), lenguas mayas y otras lenguas amerindias

DEMOGRAFÍA

Alfabetismo: 70,6%

Religiones: católicos (94%), protestantes (2%), otros (4%)

GUATEMALTECOS CÉLEBRES

Augusto Monterroso
escritor (1921–2003)

Miguel Ángel Asturias
escritor (1899–1974)

Carlos Mérida
pintor (1891–1984)

Rigoberta Menchú
activista por los derechos humanos,
Premio Nobel de la Paz (1959–   )

Ricardo Arjona
cantautor (1964–   )

Mujer tejiendo en la región del departamento de Sololá

SUETONE Emilio/age fotostock

INVESTIGA EN INTERNET 🖥

La geografía: el lago Atitlán, Antigua

La historia: los mayas, Efraín Ríos Mont, la matanza de indígenas durante la dictadura, quiché, el Popul Vuh

Películas: *El norte*

Música: punta, Ricardo Arjona

Comida: los tamales, la sopa de pepino

Fiestas: 15 de septiembre (Día de la Independencia)

Un detalle arquitectónico en el centro de la Ciudad de Guatemala

Vista del lago Atitlán

CURIOSIDADES

■ Guatemala es famosa por la gran cantidad de ruinas mayas y por las tradiciones indígenas, especialmente los tejidos de vivos colores.

■ Antigua es una famosa ciudad que sirvió como la tercera capital de Guatemala. Es reconocida mundialmente por su bien preservada arquitectura renacentista y barroca.

■ En Guatemala se encuentra Tikal, uno de los más importantes conjuntos arqueológicos mayas.

Guinea Ecuatorial ▶

INFORMACIÓN GENERAL

Nombre oficial: República de Guinea Ecuatorial

Nacionalidad: ecuatoguineano(a)

Área: 28 051 km² (aproximadamente el área de Maryland)

Población: 650 702 (2010)

Capital: Malabo (f. 1827) (157 000 hab.)

Otras ciudades importantes: Bata (175 000 hab.), Ebebiyín (26 000 hab.)

Moneda: franco CFA

Idiomas: español y francés (oficiales), lenguas bantúes (fang, bubi)

DEMOGRAFÍA

Alfabetismo: 87%

Religiones: católicos y otros cristianos (95%), prácticas paganas (5%)

ECUATOGUINEANOS CÉLEBRES

Eric Moussambani
nadador olímpico (1978–)

Leoncio Evita
escritor del primer libro guineano y primera novela africana en español (1929–1996)

Christine Nesbitt/AP Images

Niños jugando frente a una iglesia en Malabo

Mujeres del pueblo de Ur-a
pescando en la playa

La geografía: la isla de Bioko, el río Muni

La historia: los Bantú, los Igbo, los Fang

Música: Las Hijas del Sol

Comidas y bebidas: la sopa banga, el pescado a la plancha, el puercoespín, el antílope, los vinos de palma, la malamba (aguardiente de caña de azúcar)

Fiestas: 12 de octubre (Día de la Independencia)

Un río en un bosque de la isla
de Bioko

CURIOSIDADES

- Se piensa que los primeros habitantes de esta región fueron pigmeos.

- Guinea Ecuatorial obtuvo su independencia de España en 1968.

- Parte de su territorio fue colonizado por los portugueses y por los ingleses.

- Macías Nguema fue dictador de Guinea Ecuatorial hasta 1979.

- El país cuenta con una universidad, la universidad Nacional de Guinea Ecuatorial, situada en la capital.

Honduras ▶

INFORMACIÓN GENERAL

Nombre oficial: República de Honduras

Nacionalidad: hondureño(a)

Área: 112 090 km² (aproximadamente el área de Pennsylvania)

Población: 7 989 415 (2010)

Capital: Tegucigalpa (f. 1762) (1 200 000 hab.)

Otras ciudades importantes: San Pedro Sula (640 000 hab.), El Progreso (90 000 hab.)

Moneda: lempira

Idiomas: español (oficial), dialectos amerindios

DEMOGRAFÍA

Alfabetismo: 80%

Religiones: católicos (97%), protestantes (3%)

HONDUREÑOS CÉLEBRES

Lempira
héroe indígena (1499–1537)

José Antonio Velásquez
pintor (1906–1983)

Ramón Amaya Amador
escritor (1916–1966)

David Suazo
futbolista (1979–   )

Una cabeza maya entre las ruinas de Copán, declarado Patrimonio Universal por la UNESCO

Grigory Kubatyan/Shutterstck

INVESTIGA EN INTERNET 🌐

La geografía: islas de la Bahía, Copán

La historia: los mayas, los garífunas, los Miskito, Ramón Villedas Morales

Personalidades: Saúl Martínez, Carlos Mencía

Comidas y bebidas: el arroz con leche, los tamales, las pupusas, el atol de elote, la chicha, el ponche de leche

Fiestas: 15 de septiembre (Día de la Independencia)

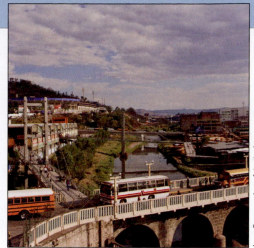

Autobuses cruzando el río Choluteca en Tegucigalpa

Jane Sweeney/ age fotostock

Devon Stephens/iStockphotos

Vista aérea de la isla Roatán en el Caribe hondureño

CURIOSIDADES

- El nombre original del país fue Comayagua, el mismo nombre que su capital. A mediados del siglo XIX adoptó el nombre República de Honduras, y en 1880 la capital se trasladó a Tegucigalpa.

- Honduras basa su economía en la agricultura, especialmente en las plantaciones de banana, cuya comercialización empezó en 1889 con la fundación de Standard Fruit Company.

- En 1998, el huracán Mitch golpeó severamente la economía nacional, destruyendo gran parte de la infraestructura del país y de los cultivos. Se calcula que el país retrocedió 25 años a causa del huracán.

México ▶

INFORMACIÓN GENERAL

Nombre oficial: Estados Unidos Mexicanos

Nacionalidad: mexicano(a)

Área: 1 964 375 km² (aproximadamente 4 1/2 veces el área de California)

Población: 112 468 855 (2010)

Capital: México, D.F. (f. 1521) (9 000 000 hab.)

Otras ciudades importantes: Guadalajara (1 600 000 hab.), Monterrey (2 200 000 hab.), Puebla (5 600 000 hab.)

Moneda: peso

Idiomas: español (oficial), náhuatl, maya, zapoteco, mixteco, otomi, totonaca (se hablan aproximadamente 280 idiomas)

DEMOGRAFÍA

Alfabetismo: 92,2%

Religiones: católicos (90,4%), protestantes (3,8%), otros (5,8%)

MEXICANOS CÉLEBRES

Octavio Paz
escritor, Premio Nobel de Literatura (1914–1998)

Diego Rivera
pintor (1886–1957)

Frida Kahlo
pintora (1907–1954)

Emiliano Zapata
revolucionario (1879–1919)

Armando Manzanero
cantautor (1935–   )

Rafa Márquez
futbolista (1979–   )

Gael García Bernal
actor (1978–   )

La Bolsa de valores en la Ciudad de México

andres balcazar/iStockphoto

INVESTIGA EN INTERNET 🌐

La geografía: el cañón del Cobre, el volcán Popocatépetl, las lagunas de Montebello, Sierra Tarahumara, Acapulco

La historia: mayas, aztecas, toltecas, la conquista, la colonia, Pancho Villa, Porfirio Díaz, Hernán Cortés, Miguel Hidalgo, Los Zapatistas

Películas: *Amores perros, Frida, Y tu mamá también, Babel, El laberinto del fauno, La misma luna*

Música: mariachis, ranchera, Pedro Infante, Vicente Fernández, Luis Miguel, Maná, Jaguares

Comidas y bebidas: los chiles en nogada, el mole poblano, el pozole, los huevos rancheros, el tequila (alimentos originarios de México: chocolate, tomate, vainilla)

Fiestas: 16 de septiembre (Día de la Independencia), 1° y 2 de noviembre (Día de los Muertos)

La ciudad colonial de Taxco, una ciudad minera muy importante

El amanecer en el puerto de Zihuatanejo

CURIOSIDADES

■ La Ciudad de México (D.F.) es la segunda ciudad más poblada del mundo, después de Tokio. La ciudad fue fundada por los aztecas sobre un lago; algunas partes se están hundiendo por la desaparición del lago. Es una de las capitales más altas (a 2500 metros sobre el nivel del mar) y una urbe cosmopolita y llena de historia.

Nicaragua ▶

INFORMACIÓN GENERAL

Nombre oficial: República de Nicaragua

Nacionalidad: nicaragüense

Área: 130 370 km² (aproximadamente el área del estado de Nueva York)

Población: 5 995 928 (2010)

Capital: Managua (f. 1522) (2 000 000 hab.)

Otras ciudades importantes: León (200 000 hab.), Chinandega (180 000 hab.)

Moneda: córdoba

Idiomas: español (oficial), misquito, inglés y lenguas indígenas en la costa atlántica

DEMOGRAFÍA

Alfabetismo: 67,5%

Religiones: católicos (58%), evangélicos (22%), otros (20%)

NICARAGÜENSES CÉLEBRES

Rubén Darío
poeta, padre del Modernismo (1867–1916)

Ernesto Cardenal
sacerdote, poeta (1925–   )

Violeta Chamorro
periodista, ex presidenta (1929–   )

Juergen Richter/age fotostock

Los volcanes Concepción y Madera desde la isla de Ometepe

INVESTIGA EN INTERNET

La geografía: el lago Nicaragua, la isla Ometepe

La historia: Misquitos, Anastasio Somoza, Augusto Sandino, Revolución Sandinista

Películas: *Ernesto Cardenal*

Música: polca, mazurca, Camilo Zapata, Carlos Mejía Godoy

Comidas y bebidas: los tamales, la sopa de pepino, el triste, el tibio, la chicha

Fiestas: 15 de septiembre (Día de la Independencia)

rj Ierich/Shutterstck

La Catedral Santo Domingo en Managua

rj Ierich/Shutterstck

Una de las Islas del Maíz

CURIOSIDADES

■ Nicaragua se conoce como tierra de poetas y volcanes.

■ Es el país más grande de Centroamérica, y también cuenta con el lago más grande de la región, el lago Nicaragua, con más de 370 islas. La isla más grande, Ometepe, tiene dos volcanes.

Panamá ▶

INFORMACIÓN GENERAL

Nombre oficial: República de Panamá

Nacionalidad: panameño(a)

Área: 75 420 km² (aproximadamente la mitad del área de Florida)

Población: 3 410 676 (2010)

Capital: Panamá (f. 1519) (900 000 hab.)

Otras ciudades importantes: San Miguelito (300 000 hab.), David (128 000 hab.)

Moneda: balboa

Idiomas: español (oficial), inglés

DEMOGRAFÍA

Alfabetismo: 91,9%

Religiones: católicos (85%), protestantes (15%)

PANAMEÑOS CÉLEBRES

Rubén Blades
cantautor, actor, abogado, político (1948–)

Omar Torrijos
militar (1929–1981), presidente

Joaquín Beleño
escritor y periodista (1922–1988)

El canal de Panamá

Matt Ragen/Shutterstck

INVESTIGA EN INTERNET 🌐

La geografía: el canal de Panamá

La historia: los Cunas, la construcción del canal de Panamá, la dictadura de Manuel Noriega

Películas: *El plomero, Los puños de una nación*

Música: salsa, Rubén Blades

Comidas y bebidas: el chocao panameño, el sancocho de gallina, las carimaolas, la ropa vieja, los jugos de fruta, el chicheme

Fiestas: 3 de noviembre (Día de la Independencia)

Steven Miric/iStockphoto

La Catedral Metropolitana en la ciudad de Panamá

tonisalado/Shutterstock

Bocas del Toro, Panamá

CURIOSIDADES

■ El canal de Panamá se construyó entre 1904 y 1914. Mide 84 kilómetros de longitud y funciona con un sistema de esclusas que elevan y bajan los barcos (los océanos Atlántico y Pacífico tienen diferentes elevaciones). Cada año cruzan unos 14 000 barcos o botes por el canal, el cual estuvo bajo control de los Estados Unidos hasta el 31 de diciembre de 1999. En promedio, cada embarcación paga 54 000 dólares por cruzar el canal. La tarifa más baja la pagó un aventurero estadounidense, quien pagó 36 centavos por cruzar nadando en 1928.

Paraguay ▶

INFORMACIÓN GENERAL

Nombre oficial: República del Paraguay

Nacionalidad: paraguayo(a)

Área: 406 750 km² (aproximadamente el área de California)

Población: 6 375 830 (2010)

Capital: Asunción (f. 1537) (690 000 hab.)

Otras ciudades importantes: Ciudad del Este (320 000 hab.), San Lorenzo (300 000 hab.)

Moneda: guaraní

Idiomas: español y guaraní (oficiales)

DEMOGRAFÍA

Alfabetismo: 94%

Religiones: católicos (90%), protestantes (6%), otros (4%)

PARAGUAYOS CÉLEBRES

Augusto Roa Bastos
escritor, Premio Cervantes de Literatura (1917–2005)

José Luis Chilavert
futbolista (1965–   )

Olga Bliner
pintora (1921–   )

Berta Rojas
guitarrista (1966–   )

JORGE ROMERO/AFP/Getty Images

La calle Palma en la ciudad de Asunción

La geografía: las cataratas del Iguazú, los ríos Paraguay y Paraná, la presa Itaipú, el Chaco

La historia: guaraníes, misiones jesuitas, la Guerra de la Triple Alianza, Alfredo Stroessner

Películas: *Nosotros*, *Hamacas paraguayas*

Música: polca, baile de la botella, arpa paraguaya

Comidas y bebidas: el chipá paraguayo, el surubí, las empanadas, la sopa paraguaya, el mate, el tereré

Fiestas: 14 de mayo (Día de la Independencia), 24 de junio (Verbena de San Juan)

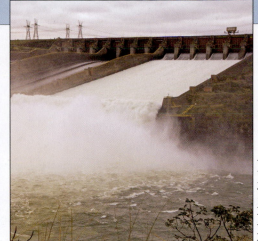

Schulz, I /age fotostock

La presa de Itaipú entre Paraguay y Brasil

Michal Wozniak/iStockphoto

La Catedral de Asunción

CURIOSIDADES

■ Por diversas razones históricas, Paraguay es un país bilingüe. Se calcula que el 90% de sus habitantes hablan español y guaraní, el idioma de sus pobladores antes de la llegada de los españoles. En particular, la llegada de los jesuitas tuvo importancia en la preservación del idioma guaraní y en el mestizaje. Actualmente se producen novelas y programas de radio y televisión en guaraní. Por otra parte, el guaraní ha influenciado notablemente el español de la región.

Perú ▶

INFORMACIÓN GENERAL

Nombre oficial: República del Perú

Nacionalidad: peruano(a)

Área: 1 285 216 km² (aproximadamente 2 veces el área de Texas)

Población: 29 907 003 (2010)

Capital: Lima (f. 1535) (8 000 000 hab.)

Otras ciudades importantes: Callao (2 000 000 hab.), Arequipa (1 300 000 hab.), Trujillo (1 000 000 hab.)

Moneda: nuevo sol

Idiomas: español y quechua (oficiales), aymará y otras lenguas indígenas

DEMOGRAFÍA

Alfabetismo: 92,9%

Religiones: católicos (82%), evangélicos (13%), otros (5%)

PERUANOS CÉLEBRES

Mario Vargas Llosa
escritor, político (1936–   ),
Premio Nobel de Literatura

César Vallejo
poeta (1892–1938)

Javier Pérez de Cuellar
secretario general de las Naciones Unidas
(1920–   )

Tania Libertad
cantante (1952–   )

Galyna Andrushko/Shutterstck

Machu Picchu

La geografía: los Andes, el Amazonas, Machu Picchu, el lago Titikaka, Nazca

La historia: los incas, los aymará, el Inti Raymi, los uros, José de San Martín

Películas: *Todos somos estrellas*

Música: música andina, valses peruanos, jaranas

Comidas y bebidas: la papa (más de 2000 variedades), la yuca, la quinoa, el ceviche, el pisco

Fiestas: 28 de julio (Día de la Independencia)

Karel Navarro/AP Images

La tradición de tirar cartas con deseos al pozo de la iglesia de Santa Rosa de Lima

Catherine Karnow/CORBIS

El puerto de El Callao

CURIOSIDADES

■ En Perú vivieron muchas civilizaciones diferentes que se desarrollaron entre el año 4000 a.C. y la llegada de los españoles en el siglo XVI. La más importante fue la civilización de los incas, que dominaba la región a la llegada de los españoles.

■ Otra civilización importante fueron los nazcas, quienes trazaron figuras de animales en la tierra, pero solo se pueden ver desde el aire. Hay más de 2000 km de líneas. Su origen es un misterio y no se sabe por qué las hicieron.

Puerto Rico ▶

INFORMACIÓN GENERAL

Nombre oficial: Estado Libre Asociado de Puerto Rico (*Commonwealth of Puerto Rico*)

Nacionalidad: puertorriqueño(a)

Área: 13.790 km² (un poco menos que el área de Connecticut)

Población: 3 997 663 (2010)

Capital: San Juan (f. 1521) (450 000 hab.)

Otras ciudades importantes: Ponce (200 000 hab.), Caguas (150 000 hab.)

Moneda: dólar estadounidense

Idiomas: español, inglés (oficiales)

DEMOGRAFÍA

Alfabetismo: 94,1%

Religiones: católicos (85%), protestantes y otros (15%)

PUERTORRIQUEÑOS CÉLEBRES

Francisco Oller y Cestero
pintor (1833–1917)

Esmeralda Santiago
escritora (1948–)

Rosario Ferré
escritora (1938–)

Rita Moreno
actriz (1931–)

Raúl Juliá
actor (1940–1994)

Ricky Martin
cantante, benefactor (1971–)

Una calle en el viejo San Juan

Lori Froeb/Shutterstck

La cascada de La Mina en el Bosque Nacional El Yunque

INVESTIGA EN INTERNET

La geografía: el Yunque, Vieques, El Morro

La historia: los taínos, Juan Ponce de León, la Guerra hispanoamericana

Películas: *Lo que le pasó a Santiago, 12 horas, Talento de barrio*

Música: salsa, bomba y plena, Gilberto Santa Rosa, Olga Tañón, Daddy Yankee, Tito Puente

Personalidades: Roberto Clemente

Comidas y bebidas: el lechón asado, el arroz con gandules, el mofongo, los bacalaítos, la champola de guayaba, el coquito, la horchata de ajonjolí

Fiestas: 4 de julio (Día de la Independencia de EE.UU.), 25 de julio (Día de la Constitución de Puerto Rico)

Una playa en Fajardo

CURIOSIDADES

- A los puertorriqueños también se los conoce como "boricuas", ya que antes de la llegada de los europeos la isla se llamaba Borinquen.

- A diferencia de otros países, los puertorriqueños también son ciudadanos estadounidenses, con la excepción de que no pueden votar en elecciones presidenciales de los Estados Unidos, a menos que sean residentes de un estado.

- El gobierno de Puerto Rico está encabezado por un gobernador.

República Dominicana ▶

INFORMACIÓN GENERAL

Nombre oficial: República Dominicana

Nacionalidad: dominicano(a)

Área: 48 670 km² (aproximadamente 2 veces el área de Vermont)

Población: 9 794 487 (2010)

Capital: Santo Domingo (f. 1492) (2 500 000 hab.)

Otras ciudades importantes: Santiago de los Caballeros (2 000 000 hab.), La Romana (300 000 hab.)

Moneda: peso

Idiomas: español

DEMOGRAFÍA

Alfabetismo: 87%

Religiones: católicos (95%), otros (5%)

DOMINICANOS CÉLEBRES

Juan Pablo Duarte
héroe de la independencia (1808–1876)

Julia Álvarez
escritora (1950–   )

Sammy Sosa
pelotero (1968–   )

Juan Luis Guerra
músico (1957–   )

Wilfrido Vargas
músico (1949–   )

Gary Blakeley/Shutterstck

El Convento de la Orden de los Predicadores en Santo Domingo

La geografía: Puerto Plata, Pico Duarte, Sierra de Samana

La historia: los taínos, los arawak, la dictadura de Trujillo, las hermanas Mirabal

Películas: *Nueba Yol, Cuatro hombres y un ataúd*

Música: merengue, bachata, Juan Luis Guerra, Wilfrido Vargas

Comidas y bebidas: el mangú, el sancocho, el asopao, el refresco rojo, la mamajuana

Fiestas: 27 de febrero (Día de la In dependencia)

Puerto Plata

emin kuliyev/Shutterstock

Yann Arthus-Bertrand/CORBIS

Bailando merengue en la playa
en Las Terrenas

CURIOSIDADES

- La isla que comparten la República Dominicana y Haití, La Española, estuvo bajo control español hasta 1697, cuando la parte oeste pasó a ser territorio francés.

- La República Dominicana tiene algunas de las construcciones más antiguas dejadas por los españoles.

- Se piensa que los restos de Cristóbal Colón están enterrados en Santo Domingo, pero Colón también tiene una tumba en Sevilla, España.

- En Santo Domingo se construyeron la primera catedral, el primer hospital, la primera aduana y la primera universidad del Nuevo Mundo.

- Santo Domingo fue declarada Patrimonio de la Humanidad (*World Heritge*) por la UNESCO.

Uruguay ▶

INFORMACIÓN GENERAL

Nombre oficial: República Oriental del Uruguay

Nacionalidad: uruguayo(a)

Área: 176 215 km² (casi exactamente igual al estado de Washington)

Población: 3 510 386 (2010)

Capital: Montevideo (f. 1726) (1 500 000 hab.)

Otras ciudades importantes: Salto (130 000 hab.), Paysandú (90 500 hab.)

Moneda: peso

Idiomas: español

DEMOGRAFÍA

Alfabetismo: 98%

Religiones: católicos (47%), protestantes (11%), otros (42%)

URUGUAYOS CÉLEBRES

Horacio Quiroga
escritor (1878–1937)

Mario Benedetti
escritor (1920–2009)

Alfredo Zitarrosa
compositor (1936–1989)

Julio Sosa
cantor de tango (1926–1964)

Diego Forlán
futbolista (1979–   )

Delmira Agustini
poetisa (1886–1914)

La conmemoración del cumpleaños de José Artigas en la Plaza Independencia en Montevideo

Eduardo Rivero/Shutterstck

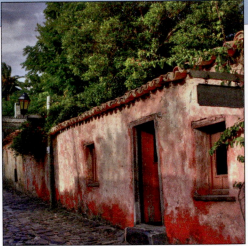

gary yim/Shutterstck

La ciudad Colonia del Sacramento

INVESTIGA EN INTERNET 🌐

La geografía: Punta del Este, Colonia

La historia: el Carnaval de Montevideo, los tablados, José Artigas

Películas: *Whisky, 25 Watts, Una forma de bailar*

Música: tango, milonga, candombe, Jorge Drexler, Rubén Rada

Comidas y bebidas: el asado, el dulce de leche, la faina, el chivito, el mate

Fiestas: 25 de agosto (Día de la Independencia)

gary yim/Shutterstck

El Río de la Plata

CURIOSIDADES

■ La industria ganadera es una de las más importantes del país. La bebida más popular es el mate. Es muy común ver a los uruguayos caminando con el termo bajo el brazo, listo para tomar mate en cualquier lugar.

■ Los descendientes de esclavos africanos que vivieron en esa zona dieron origen a la música típica de Uruguay: el candombe.

■ Uruguay fue el anfitrión y el primer campeón de la Copa Mundial de Fútbol en 1930.

Venezuela ▶

INFORMACIÓN GENERAL

Nombre oficial: República Bolivariana de Venezuela

Nacionalidad: venezolano(a)

Área: 912 050 km² (2800 km de costas) (aproximadamente 6 veces el área de Florida)

Población: 27 223 228 (2010)

Capital: Caracas (f. 1567) (3 300 000 hab.)

Otras ciudades importantes: Maracaibo (2 000 000 hab.), Valencia (900 000 hab.), Maracay (500 000 hab.)

Moneda: bolívar

Idiomas: español (oficial), lenguas indígenas (araucano, caribe, guajiro)

DEMOGRAFÍA

Alfabetismo: 93%

Religiones: católicos (96%), protestantes (2%), otros (2%)

VENEZOLANOS CÉLEBRES

Simón Bolívar
libertador (1783–1830)

Andrés Eloy Blanco
escritor (1897–1955)

Rómulo Gallegos
escritor (1884–1969)

rm/Shutterstock

El Salto del Ángel, la catarata más alta del mundo

Pescadores en la isla Margarita

Alberto Pomares/iStockphoto

Alexander Chaikin/Shutterstock

La plaza Francia, Caracas

CURIOSIDADES

■ La isla Margarita es un lugar turístico muy popular. Cuando los españoles llegaron hace más de 500 años, los indígenas de la isla, los guaiqueríes, pensaron que eran dioses y les dieron regalos y ceremonia de bienvenida. Gracias a esto, los guaiqueríes fueron los únicos indígenas del Caribe que tuvieron el estatus de "vasallos libres".

■ En la época moderna, Venezuela se destaca por sus concursos de belleza y por su producción internacional de telenovelas.

Los Latinos en los Estados Unidos ▶

INFORMACIÓN GENERAL

Nombre oficial: Estados Unidos de América

Nacionalidad: estadounidense

Área: 9 826 675 km² (aproximadamente el área de China o 3 1/2 veces el área de Argentina)

Población: 310 232 863 (2010) (aproximadamente el 15% son latinos)

Capital: Washington, D.C. (f. 1791) (6 000 000 hab.)

Otras ciudades importantes: Nueva York (8 500 000 hab.), Los Ángeles (4 000 000 hab.), Chicago (3 000 000 hab.), Miami (460 000 hab.)

Moneda: dólar estadounidense

Idiomas: inglés, español y otros

DEMOGRAFÍA

Alfabetismo: 97%

Religiones: protestantes (51,3%), católicos (23,9%), mormones (1,7%), judíos (1,7%), budistas (0,7%), musulmanes (0,6%), otros (14%), no religiosos (4%)

LATINOS CÉLEBRES DE ESTADOS UNIDOS

Ellen Ochoa
astronauta (1958–   )

César Chávez
activista por los derechos de
los trabajadores (1927–1993)

Jessica Alba
actriz (1981–   )

Sandra Cisneros
escritora (1954–   )

Edward James Olmos
actor (1947–   )

Jennifer López
actriz, cantante (1969–   )

Marc Anthony
cantante (1969–   )

Christina Aguilera
(cantante) (1980–   )

La Pequeña Habana en Miami, Florida

©Jeff Greenberg/The Image Works

Un mural de Benito Juárez en Chicago, Illinois

El famoso Riverwalk en San Antonio, Texas

CURIOSIDADES

- Los latinos son la primera minoría de Estados Unidos (más de 46 millones). Este grupo incluye personas que provienen de los veintiún países de habla hispana y a los hijos y nietos de estas que nacieron en los Estados Unidos. Muchos hablan español perfectamente y otros no apenas lo hablan. El grupo más grande de latinos es el de mexicanoamericanos, ya que territorios como Texas, Nuevo México, Utah, Nevada, California, Colorado y Oregón eran parte de México.

- Actualmente, casi toda la cultura latinoamericana está presente en los Estados Unidos. Las tradiciones dominicanas son notables en la zona de Nueva Inglaterra; y los países sudamericanos, cuya presencia no era tan notable hace algunos años, cuentan con comunidades destacadas, como es el caso de La Pequeña Buenos Aires, una fuerte comunidad argentina en South Beach, Miami.

Partner Activities

1.37 Diferencias Working with a partner, one of you will look at the picture on this page, and the other will look at the picture on page 35. Take turns describing the pictures using the expression **hay**, numbers, and the classroom vocabulary. Find the eight differences.

> **MODELO** Estudiante 1: *En A hay una computadora.*
> Estudiante 2: *Sí. En B, hay una silla.*
> Estudiante 1: *No, en A no hay una silla.*

B.

2.39 Datos personales Working with a partner, one of you will look at the chart below and the other will look at the chart on page 71. Take turns asking questions in order to fill in the missing information.

> **MODELO** ¿Cuántos años tiene Diego? — Diego tiene veinte años.
> ¿Qué parientes hay en la familia de Diego? — Diego tiene dos hermanos.
> ¿Qué clase tiene Diego? — Diego tiene informática.
> ¿Diego estudia ahora (now)? — No, Diego limpia la casa.

Nombre	Edad	Familia	Clase	Actividad
Diego	20	dos hermanos	informática	limpia la casa
Alonso		una sobrina		esquia
Magdalena				
Cristina	30	cinco primos		nada
Pablo	62			cocina
Gabriel	25		cálculo	
Rufina		un esposo	alemán	

3.38 **Mi agenda** Tú y tu compañero deben encontrar una hora para estudiar español. Uno mira la agenda aquí y el otro mira la agenda en la página 107 . Túrnense para preguntar sobre las horas libres que tienen. (*You and your partner should find a time to study Spanish. One of you look at this agenda and the other look at the agenda on page 107, and take turns asking about the times you have available.*)

MODELO Estudiante 1: *¿Quieres estudiar a las nueve?*
Estudiante 2: *No, nado con Armando a las diez..*

miércoles, 20 de octubre	
8:30	comprar libros
9:15	
10:00	nadar con Armando
11:30	
12:00	
1:15	asistir a clase de geometría
2:45	llamar a Valentina
3:30	leer novela para clase
4:15	
5:00	

4.38 **Cinco diferencias** Trabaja con un compañero. Uno mira el dibujo aquí y el otro mira el dibujo en la página 143. Túrnense para describirlos y buscar cinco diferencias.

5.40 **Información, por favor** Trabaja con un compañero. Uno debe mirar el gráfico en esta página y el otro debe mirar el gráfico en la página 179. Túrnense para preguntarse y completar el gráfico con la información necesaria. Necesitan identificar sus profesiones, sus orígenes, dónde están ahora y cómo están. Atención al uso de **ser** y **estar.**

Nombre	Profesión	Origen	Localización	Emoción
Carlota	pintora			alegre
Éric	arquitecto	Bogotá	el banco	
César			el café	
Paloma		Santiago		nerviosa
Samuel	escritor			ocupado
Camila		Montevideo	el teatro	

6.42 Unos monstruos Trabaja con un compañero. Uno mira el dibujo aquí, y el otro mira el dibujo en la página 215. Túrnense para describir los monstruos. Deben encontrar las cinco diferencias.

 7.39 Comparemos Trabaja con un compañero. Uno va a mirar el dibujo en esta página y el otro va a mirar el dibujo en la página 251. Túrnense para describir los dibujos y encontrar cinco diferencias.

8.40 Crucigrama Trabaja con un compañero. Uno de ustedes va a usar el crucigrama en esta página, y el otro va a usar el crucigrama en la página 287. Ayuda a tu compañero a completar su crucigrama, explicándole las palabras en español. No debes mencionar la palabra que aparece en tu crucigrama.

MODELO #0 horizontal

Se hace de los tomates. Se pone en la hamburguesa.

9.40 Contradicciones Tú y tu compañero son testigos de un accidente, pero hay diferencias entre las dos versiones. Mira uno de los dibujos y tu compañero va a mirar el otro en la página 323. Busquen las cinco diferencias. Después narren lo que ocurrió en el accidente, usando el pretérito y el imperfecto.

10.43 **En la agencia de viajes** Trabaja con un compañero. Uno de ustedes es el cliente, y mira la información en esta página. El otro es el agente de viajes y mira la información en la página 359. El cliente llama al agente de viajes para comprar un boleto. El agente de viajes debe intentar encontrar el mejor boleto para el cliente y conseguir su información (nombre, teléfono, etc.) y su tarjeta de crédito.

el cliente
Necesitas viajar a Santiago, Chile para una reunión el viernes por la mañana.

- Quieres viajar el jueves.
- Prefieres viajar por la tarde.
- No quieres tener escalas.
- Te gusta sentarte al lado de la ventanilla.
- No quieres pagar más de $750.

11.38 **Un pedido** Trabaja con un compañero. Uno de ustedes es vendedor, y el otro es el cliente. El cliente necesita ropa para un viaje a la playa y mira el catálogo en la página 395. El vendedor mira el inventario que aparece a continuación *(below)* y ayuda al cliente con su pedido.

MODELO Estudiante 1: *Buenas tardes.*
Estudiante 2: *Buenas tardes. Necesito una camiseta de algodón azul en talla extra grande.*
Estudiante 1: *Lo siento. No la tenemos en talla extra grande.*
Estudiante 2: *¿Qué colores tienen en talla extra grande?*

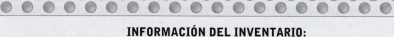

INFORMACIÓN DEL INVENTARIO:

C1050 Camiseta de algodón
Colores: azul (P, M, G), amarillo (P, M, G, XG), negro (agotado *sold out*), beige (M, G, XG)
Precio: 25 € (Rebajado a 20 €)

C4325 Camisa con estampado hawaiano
Colores: azul (agotado), verde (M, G, XG), rojo (P, XG)
Precio: 35 €

B2219 Blusa de lunares
Colores: blanco/negro (P, G, XG); negro/rosado (P, M, XG), rojo/blanco (P, M, G, XG)
Precio: 42 €

P6750 Pantalones cortos a rayas
Colores: blanco/azul (P, M, G), blanco/verde (P, M, G, XG), gris/negro (agotado), café/beige (M, G)
Precio: 55 €

P7382 Pantalones cortos a cuadros
Colores: azul/verde (P, M, G, XG), negro/rojo (P, G, XG), rosado/gris (P, M)
Precio: 48 €

F9124 Falda con estampado de flores
Colores: blanco/rosado (P, G, XG), azul marino/rojo (P, M, XG), anaranjado/amarillo (P, M, G, XG)
Tallas: P, M, G, XG
Precio: 57 €

S5320 Sandalias de cuero
Colores: café (35, 37, 39, 41, 43), negro (36, 38, 40, 42)
Precio: 70 €

12.42 **La granja** Trabaja con un compañero. Uno de ustedes debe observar la ilustración de una granja en esta página, y el otro va a ver el dibujo en la página 431. Túrnense para describir las granjas. Deben encontrar las cinco diferencias.

13.38 **¿Cuál es la pregunta?** Trabaja con un compañero. Uno de ustedes debe ver las preguntas en esta página, y el otro deber verlas en la página 467. El objetivo es hacer la mayor cantidad de puntos. Se consiguen puntos adivinando la pregunta exacta que tiene tu compañero. Para ayudarte, tu compañero te va a dar la respuesta a la pregunta. Tienes tres oportunidades cada vez.

MODELO *¿Qué es extrañar?*
Estudiante 1: *Es cuando no estás con una persona y estás triste. Piensas mucho en la persona.*
Estudiante 2: *¿Qué es extrañar?*

1. 10 puntos: ¿Qué es el noviazgo?

2. 20 puntos: ¿Qué hay en una recepción?

3. 30 puntos: ¿Qué es la unión libre?

4. 40 puntos: ¿Qué hacemos en la vejez?

5. 50 puntos: ¿Quién es la prometida?

14.40 **¿Nacionalidades** Trabaja con un compañero. En esta página uno de ustedes va a ver una lista de personas y la ciudad de dónde son, y el otro estudiante va a ver una lista diferente en la página 503. Túrnense para compartir la información. **¡OJO!** No mencionen el país, sólo la capital. El compañero deberá dar la nacionalidad de cada persona.

MODELO Estudiante 1: *Alfonso es de la Ciudad de México.*
Estudiante 2: *Es mexicano.*

Nombre	Capital
Mónica	Santiago, Chile
Alberto	San Juan, Puerto Rico
José	Malabo, Guinea Ecuatorial
Alma	Buenos Aires, Argentina
Rosario	San José, Costa Rica
Lombardo	San Salvador, El Salvador
Nuria	Managua, Nicaragua
Verónica	Asunción, Paraguay

Acentuación

In Spanish, as in English, all words of two or more syllables have one syllable that is stressed more forcibly than the others. In Spanish, written accents are frequently used to show what syllable in a word is the stressed one.

Words without written accents

Words without written accents are pronounced according to the following rules:

A. Words that end in a vowel (**a, e, i, o, u**) or the consonants **n** or **s** are stressed on the next to last syllable.

| **tar**des | capi**ta**les | **gran**de | es**tu**dia | **no**ches | **co**men |

B. Words that end in a consonant other than **n** or **s** are stressed on the last syllable.

| bus**car** | ac**triz** | espa**ñol** | liber**tad** | ani**mal** | come**dor** |

Words with written accents

C. Words that do not follow the two preceding rules require a written accent to indicate where the stress is placed.

| ca**fé** | sim**pá**tico | fran**cés** | na**ción** | José **Pé**rez |

Words with a strong vowel (a, o, u) next to a weak vowel (e, i)

D. Diphthongs, the combination of a weak vowel (**i, u**) and a strong vowel (**e, o, a**), or two weak vowels, next to each other, form a single syllable. A written accent is required to separate diphthongs into two syllables. Note that the written accent is placed on the weak vowel.

| **se**is | estu**dia** | inter**ior** | **ai**re | **au**to | ciu**dad** |
| re**ír** | **dí**a | **rí**o | ma**íz** | ba**úl** | veinti**ún** |

Monosyllable words

E. Words with only one syllable never have a written accent unless there is a need to differentiate it from another word spelled exactly the same. The following are some of the most common words in this category.

Unaccented	Accented	Unaccented	Accented
como (*like, as*)	cómo (*how*)	que (*that*)	qué (*what*)
de (*of*)	dé (*give*)	si (*if*)	sí (*yes*)
el (*the*)	él (*he*)	te (*you D.O., to you*)	té (*tea*)
mas (*but*)	más (*more*)	tu (*your*)	tú (*you informal*)
mi (*my*)	mí (*me*)		

F. Keep in mind that in Spanish, the written accents are an extremely important part of spelling since they not only change the pronunciation of a word, but may change its meaning and/or its tense.

publico (*I publish*)   **público** (*public*)   **publicó** (*he/she/you published*)

Los verbos regulares

Simple tenses

	Present Indicative	Imperfect	Preterite	Future	Conditional	Present Subjunctive	Past Subjunctive	Commands
hablar (to speak)	hablo	hablaba	hablé	hablaré	hablaría	hable	hablara	
	hablas	hablabas	hablaste	hablarás	hablarías	hables	hablaras	habla (no hables)
	habla	hablaba	habló	hablará	hablaría	hable	hablara	hable
	hablamos	hablábamos	hablamos	hablaremos	hablaríamos	hablemos	habláramos	hablemos
	habláis	hablabais	hablasteis	hablaréis	hablaríais	habléis	hablarais	hablad (no habléis)
	hablan	hablaban	hablaron	hablarán	hablarían	hablen	hablaran	hablen
aprender (to learn)	aprendo	aprendía	aprendí	aprenderé	aprendería	aprenda	aprendiera	
	aprendes	aprendías	aprendiste	aprenderás	aprenderías	aprendas	aprendieras	aprende (no aprendas)
	aprende	aprendía	aprendió	aprenderá	aprendería	aprenda	aprendiera	aprenda
	aprendemos	aprendíamos	aprendimos	aprenderemos	aprenderíamos	aprendamos	aprendiéramos	aprendamos
	aprendéis	aprendíais	aprendisteis	aprenderéis	aprenderíais	aprendáis	aprendierais	aprended (no aprendáis)
	aprenden	aprendían	aprendieron	aprenderán	aprenderían	aprendan	aprendieran	aprendan
vivir (to live)	vivo	vivía	viví	viviré	viviría	viva	viviera	
	vives	vivías	viviste	vivirás	vivirías	vivas	vivieras	vive (no vivas)
	vive	vivía	vivió	vivirá	viviría	viva	viviera	viva
	vivimos	vivíamos	vivimos	viviremos	viviríamos	vivamos	viviéramos	vivamos
	vivís	vivíais	vivisteis	viviréis	viviríais	viváis	vivierais	vivid (no viváis)
	viven	vivían	vivieron	vivirán	vivirían	vivan	vivieran	vivan

Compound tenses

Present progressive	estoy / estás / está / estamos / estáis / están	hablando, aprendiendo, viviendo
Present perfect indicative	he / has / ha / hemos / habéis / han	hablado, aprendido, vivido
Past perfect indicative	había / habías / había / habíamos / habíais / habían	hablado, aprendido, vivido

Los verbos con cambios en la raíz

Infinitive / Present Participle / Past Participle	Present Indicative	Imperfect	Preterite	Future	Conditional	Present Subjunctive	Past Subjunctive	Commands
pensar *to think* e → ie pensando pensado	pienso piensas piensa pensamos pensáis piensan	pensaba pensabas pensaba pensábamos pensabais pensaban	pensé pensaste pensó pensamos pensasteis pensaron	pensaré pensarás pensará pensaremos pensaréis pensarán	pensaría pensarías pensaría pensaríamos pensaríais pensarían	piense pienses piense pensemos penséis piensen	pensara pensaras pensara pensáramos pensarais pensaran	piensa (no pienses) piense pensemos pensad (no penséis) piensen
acostarse *to go to bed* o → ue acostándose acostado	me acuesto te acuestas se acuesta nos acostamos os acostáis se acuestan	me acostaba te acostabas se acostaba nos acostábamos os acostabais se acostaban	me acosté te acostaste se acostó nos acostamos os acostasteis se acostaron	me acostaré te acostarás se acostará nos acostaremos os acostaréis se acostarán	me acostaría te acostarías se acostaría nos acostaríamos os acostaríais se acostarían	me acueste te acuestes se acueste nos acostemos os acostéis se acuesten	me acostara te acostaras se acostara nos acostáramos os acostarais se acostaran	acuéstate (no te acuestes) acuéstese acostémonos acostaos (no os acostéis) acuéstense
sentir *to feel* e → ie, i sintiendo sentido	siento sientes siente sentimos sentís sienten	sentía sentías sentía sentíamos sentíais sentían	sentí sentiste sintió sentimos sentisteis sintieron	sentiré sentirás sentirá sentiremos sentiréis sentirán	sentiría sentirías sentiría sentiríamos sentiríais sentirían	sienta sientas sienta sintamos sintáis sientan	sintiera sintieras sintiera sintiéramos sintierais sintieran	siente (no sientas) sienta sintamos (no sintáis) sentid sientan
pedir *to ask for* e → i, i pidiendo pedido	pido pides pide pedimos pedís piden	pedía pedías pedía pedíamos pedíais pedían	pedí pediste pidió pedimos pedisteis pidieron	pediré pedirás pedirá pediremos pediréis pedirán	pediría pedirías pediría pediríamos pediríais pedirían	pida pidas pida pidamos pidáis pidan	pidiera pidieras pidiera pidiéramos pidierais pidieran	pide (no pidas) pida pidamos pedid (no pidáis) pidan
dormir *to sleep* o → ue, u durmiendo dormido	duermo duermes duerme dormimos dormís duermen	dormía dormías dormía dormíamos dormíais dormían	dormí dormiste durmió dormimos dormisteis durmieron	dormiré dormirás dormirá dormiremos dormiréis dormirán	dormiría dormirías dormiría dormiríamos dormiríais dormirían	duerma duermas duerma durmamos durmáis duerman	durmiera durmieras durmiera durmiéramos durmierais durmieran	duerme (no duermas) duerma durmamos dormid (no durmáis) duerman

Los verbos con cambios de ortografía

Infinitive Present Participle Past Participle	Present Indicative	Imperfect	Preterite	Future	Conditional	Present Subjunctive	Past Subjunctive	Commands
comenzar (e → ie) *to begin* **z → c** before e comenzando comenzado	comienzo comienzas comienza comenzamos comenzáis comienzan	comenzaba comenzabas comenzaba comenzábamos comenzabais comenzaban	**comencé** comenzaste comenzó comenzamos comenzasteis comenzaron	comenzaré comenzarás comenzará comenzaremos comenzaréis comenzarán	comenzaría comenzarías comenzaría comenzaríamos comenzaríais comenzarían	**comience comiences comience comencemos comencéis comiencen**	comenzara comenzaras comenzara comenzáramos comenzarais comenzaran	comienza (no **comiences**) **comience comencemos** comenzad (no **comencéis**) **comiencen**
conocer *to know* **c → zc** before a, o conociendo conocido	**conozco** conoces conoce conocemos conocéis conocen	conocía conocías conocía conocíamos conocíais conocían	conocí conociste conoció conocimos conocisteis conocieron	conoceré conocerás conocerá conoceremos conoceréis conocerán	conocería conocerías conocería conoceríamos conoceríais conocerían	**conozca conozcas conozca conozcamos conozcáis conozcan**	conociera conocieras conociera conociéramos conocierais conocieran	conoce (no **conozcas**) **conozca conozcamos** conoced (no **conozcáis**) **conozcan**
pagar *to pay* **g → gu** before e pagando pagado	pago pagas paga pagamos pagáis pagan	pagaba pagabas pagaba pagábamos pagabais pagaban	**pagué** pagaste pagó pagamos pagasteis pagaron	pagaré pagarás pagará pagaremos pagaréis pagarán	pagaría pagarías pagaría pagaríamos pagaríais pagarían	**pague pagues pague paguemos paguéis paguen**	pagara pagaras pagara pagáramos pagarais pagaran	paga (no **pagues**) **pague paguemos** pagad (no **paguéis**) **paguen**
seguir (e → i, i) *to follow* **gu → g** before a, o siguiendo seguido	**sigo** sigues sigue seguimos seguís siguen	seguía seguías seguía seguíamos seguíais seguían	seguí seguiste siguió seguimos seguisteis siguieron	seguiré seguirás seguirá seguiremos seguiréis seguirán	seguiría seguirías seguiría seguiríamos seguiríais seguirían	**siga sigas siga sigamos sigáis sigan**	siguiera siguieras siguiera siguiéramos siguierais siguieran	sigue (no **sigas**) **siga sigamos** seguid (no **sigáis**) **sigan**
tocar *to play, to touch* **c → qu** before e tocando tocado	toco tocas toca tocamos tocáis tocan	tocaba tocabas tocaba tocábamos tocabais tocaban	**toqué** tocaste tocó tocamos tocasteis tocaron	tocaré tocarás tocará tocaremos tocaréis tocarán	tocaría tocarías tocaría tocaríamos tocaríais tocarían	**toque toques toque toquemos toquéis toquen**	tocara tocaras tocara tocáramos tocarais tocaran	toca (no **toques**) **toque toquemos** tocad (no **toquéis**) **toquen**

Los verbos irregulares

Infinitive Present Participle Past Participle	Present Indicative	Imperfect	Preterite	Future	Conditional	Present Subjunctive	Past Subjunctive	Commands
andar *to walk* andando andado	ando andas anda andamos andáis andan	andaba andabas andaba andábamos andabais andaban	**anduve** **anduviste** **anduvo** **anduvimos** **anduvisteis** **anduvieron**	andaré andarás andará andaremos andaréis andarán	andaría andarías andaría andaríamos andaríais andarían	ande andes ande andemos andéis anden	**anduviera** **anduvieras** **anduviera** **anduviéramos** **anduvierais** **anduvieran**	anda (no andes) ande andemos andad (no andéis) anden
*dar *to give* dando dado	**doy** das da damos dais dan	daba dabas daba dábamos dabais daban	**di** **diste** **dio** **dimos** **disteis** **dieron**	daré darás dará daremos daréis darán	daría darías daría daríamos daríais darían	**dé** des **dé** demos deis den	diera dieras diera diéramos dierais dieran	da (**no des**) **dé** demos dad (**no deis**) den
*decir *to say, tell* **diciendo** **dicho**	**digo** **dices** **dice** decimos decís **dicen**	decía decías decía decíamos decíais decían	**dije** **dijiste** **dijo** **dijimos** **dijisteis** **dijeron**	**diré** **dirás** **dirá** **diremos** **diréis** **dirán**	**diría** **dirías** **diría** **diríamos** **diríais** **dirían**	**diga** **digas** **diga** **digamos** **digáis** **digan**	**dijera** **dijeras** **dijera** **dijéramos** **dijerais** **dijeran**	**di (no digas)** **diga** **digamos** decid (**no digáis**) **digan**
*estar *to be* estando estado	**estoy** **estás** **está** estamos estáis **están**	estaba estabas estaba estábamos estabais estaban	**estuve** **estuviste** **estuvo** **estuvimos** **estuvisteis** **estuvieron**	estaré estarás estará estaremos estaréis estarán	estaría estarías estaría estaríamos estaríais estarían	**esté** **estés** **esté** **estemos** **estéis** **estén**	estuviera estuvieras estuviera estuviéramos estuvierais estuvieran	**está (no estés)** **esté** **estemos** estad (**no estéis**) **estén**
haber *to have* habiendo habido	**he** **has** **ha [hay]** **hemos** **habéis** **han**	había habías había habíamos habíais habían	**hube** **hubiste** **hubo** **hubimos** **hubisteis** **hubieron**	**habré** **habrás** **habrá** **habremos** **habréis** **habrán**	**habría** **habrías** **habría** **habríamos** **habríais** **habrían**	**haya** **hayas** **haya** **hayamos** **hayáis** **hayan**	hubiera hubieras hubiera hubiéramos hubierais hubieran	he (no hayas) haya hayamos habed (no hayáis) hayan
*hacer *to make, to do* haciendo **hecho**	**hago** haces hace hacemos hacéis hacen	hacía hacías hacía hacíamos hacíais hacían	**hice** **hiciste** **hizo** **hicimos** **hicisteis** **hicieron**	**haré** **harás** **hará** **haremos** **haréis** **harán**	**haría** **harías** **haría** **haríamos** **haríais** **harían**	**haga** **hagas** **haga** **hagamos** **hagáis** **hagan**	hiciera hicieras hiciera hiciéramos hicierais hicieran	**haz (no hagas)** **haga** **hagamos** haced (**no hagáis**) **hagan**

*Verbs with irregular *yo* forms in the present indicative

(continued)

Infinitive / Present Participle / Past Participle	Present Indicative	Imperfect	Preterite	Future	Conditional	Present Subjunctive	Past Subjunctive	Commands
ir / *to go* / yendo / ido	voy	iba	fui	iré	iría	vaya	fuera	
	vas	ibas	fuiste	irás	irías	vayas	fueras	ve (no vayas)
	va	iba	fue	irá	iría	vaya	fuera	vaya
	vamos	íbamos	fuimos	iremos	iríamos	vayamos	fuéramos	vamos (no vayamos)
	vais	ibais	fuisteis	iréis	iríais	vayáis	fuerais	id (no vayáis)
	van	iban	fueron	irán	irían	vayan	fueran	vayan
*oír / to hear / oyendo / oído	oigo	oía	oí	oiré	oiría	oiga	oyera	
	oyes	oías	oíste	oirás	oirías	oigas	oyeras	oye (no oigas)
	oye	oía	oyó	oirá	oiría	oiga	oyera	oiga
	oímos	oíamos	oímos	oiremos	oiríamos	oigamos	oyéramos	oigamos
	oís	oíais	oísteis	oiréis	oiríais	oigáis	oyerais	oíd (no oigáis)
	oyen	oían	oyeron	oirán	oirían	oigan	oyeran	oigan
poder (o → ue) / *can, to be able* / pudiendo / podido	puedo	podía	pude	podré	podría	pueda	pudiera	
	puedes	podías	pudiste	podrás	podrías	puedas	pudieras	puede (no puedas)
	puede	podía	pudo	podrá	podría	pueda	pudiera	pueda
	podemos	podíamos	pudimos	podremos	podríamos	podamos	pudiéramos	podamos
	podéis	podíais	pudisteis	podréis	podríais	podáis	pudierais	poded (no podáis)
	pueden	podían	pudieron	podrán	podrían	puedan	pudieran	puedan
*poner / *to place, to put* / poniendo / puesto	pongo	ponía	puse	pondré	pondría	ponga	pusiera	
	pones	ponías	pusiste	pondrás	pondrías	pongas	pusieras	pon (no pongas)
	pone	ponía	puso	pondrá	pondría	ponga	pusiera	ponga
	ponemos	poníamos	pusimos	pondremos	pondríamos	pongamos	pusiéramos	pongamos
	ponéis	poníais	pusisteis	pondréis	pondríais	pongáis	pusierais	poned (no pongáis)
	ponen	ponían	pusieron	pondrán	pondrían	pongan	pusieran	pongan
querer (e → ie) / *to like* / queriendo / querido	quiero	quería	quise	querré	querría	quiera	quisiera	
	quieres	querías	quisiste	querrás	querrías	quieras	quisieras	quiere (no quieras)
	quiere	quería	quiso	querrá	querría	quiera	quisiera	quiera
	queremos	queríamos	quisimos	querremos	querríamos	queramos	quisiéramos	queramos
	queréis	queríais	quisisteis	querréis	querríais	queráis	quisierais	quered (no queráis)
	quieren	querían	quisieron	querrán	querrían	quieran	quisieran	quieran
*saber / *to know* / sabiendo / sabido	sé	sabía	supe	sabré	sabría	sepa	supiera	
	sabes	sabías	supiste	sabrás	sabrías	sepas	supieras	sabe (no sepas)
	sabe	sabía	supo	sabrá	sabría	sepa	supiera	sepa
	sabemos	sabíamos	supimos	sabremos	sabríamos	sepamos	supiéramos	sepamos
	sabéis	sabíais	supisteis	sabréis	sabríais	sepáis	supierais	sabed (no sepáis)
	saben	sabían	supieron	sabrán	sabrían	sepan	supieran	sepan

*Verbs with irregular *yo* forms in the present indicative

(continued)

Infinitive Present Participle Past Participle	Present Indicative	Imperfect	Preterite	Future	Conditional	Present Subjunctive	Past Subjunctive	Commands
*salir to go out saliendo salido	salgo sales sale salimos salís salen	salía salías salía salíamos salíais salían	salí saliste salió salimos salisteis salieron	saldré saldrás saldrá saldremos saldréis saldrán	saldría saldrías saldría saldríamos saldríais saldrían	salga salgas salga salgamos salgáis salgan	saliera salieras saliera saliéramos salierais salieran	sal (no salgas) salga salgamos salid (no salgáis) salgan
ser to be siendo sido	soy eres es somos sois son	era eras era éramos erais eran	fui fuiste fue fuimos fuisteis fueron	seré serás será seremos seréis serán	sería serías sería seríamos seríais serían	sea seas sea seamos seáis sean	fuera fueras fuera fuéramos fuerais fueran	sé (no seas) sea seamos sed (no seáis) sean
*tener (e → ie) to have teniendo tenido	tengo tienes tiene tenemos tenéis tienen	tenía tenías tenía teníamos teníais tenían	tuve tuviste tuvo tuvimos tuvisteis tuvieron	tendré tendrás tendrá tendremos tendréis tendrán	tendría tendrías tendría tendríamos tendríais tendrían	tenga tengas tenga tengamos tengáis tengan	tuviera tuvieras tuviera tuviéramos tuvierais tuvieran	ten (no tengas) tenga tengamos tened (no tengáis) tengan
*traer to bring trayendo traído	traigo traes trae traemos traéis traen	traía traías traía traíamos traíais traían	traje trajiste trajo trajimos trajisteis trajeron	traeré traerás traerá traeremos traeréis traerán	traería traerías traería traeríamos traeríais traerían	traiga traigas traiga traigamos traigáis traigan	trajera trajeras trajera trajéramos trajerais trajeran	trae (no traigas) traiga traigamos traed (no traigáis) traigan
*venir (e → ie, i) to come viniendo venido	vengo vienes viene venimos venís vienen	venía venías venía veníamos veníais venían	vine viniste vino vinimos vinisteis vinieron	vendré vendrás vendrá vendremos vendréis vendrán	vendría vendrías vendría vendríamos vendríais vendrían	venga vengas venga vengamos vengáis vengan	viniera vinieras viniera viniéramos vinierais vinieran	ven (no vengas) venga vengamos venid (no vengáis) vengan
ver to see viendo visto	veo ves ve vemos veis ven	veía veías veía veíamos veíais veían	vi viste vio vimos visteis vieron	veré verás verá veremos veréis verán	vería verías vería veríamos veríais verían	vea veas vea veamos veáis vean	viera vieras viera viéramos vierais vieran	ve (no veas) vea veamos ved (no veáis) vean

*Verbs with irregular yo forms in the present indicative

Supplemental Structures

1. Perfect tenses

In **Capítulo 13** you learned that the perfect tense is formed by combining the present indicative of the verb **haber** with the past participle. Similarly, you learned in **Capítulo 14** that the past perfect is formed by combining the imperfect of the verb **haber** with the past participle. The future perfect and conditional perfect tenses are formed by combining the imperfect, future, and conditional of **haber** with the past participle.

Future perfect		Conditional perfect	
habré		habría	
habrás		habrías	
habrá	+ past	habría	+ past
habremos	participle	habríamos	participle
habréis		habríais	
habrán		habrían	

In general, the use of these perfect tenses parallels their use in English.

Para el año 2015, **habremos terminado** nuestros estudios aquí.

Yo lo **habría hecho** por ti.

By the year 2015, we will have finished our studies here.

I would have done it for you.

The present perfect subjunctive and past perfect subjunctive are likewise formed by combining the present subjunctive and past subjunctive of **haber** with the past participle.

Present perfect subjunctive		Past perfect subjunctive	
haya		hubiera	
hayas		hubieras	
haya	+ past	hubiera	+ past
hayamos	participle	hubiéramos	participle
hayáis		hubierais	
hayan		hubieran	

These tenses are used whenever the independent clause in a sentence requires the subjunctive and the verb in the dependent clause represents an action completed prior to the time indicated by the verb in the independent clause. If the time of the verb in the independent clause is present or future, the present perfect subjunctive is used; if the time is past or conditional, the past perfect subjunctive is used.

Dudo que lo **hayan leído.**

Si **hubieras llamado,** no tendríamos este problema ahora.

I doubt that they have read it.

If you had called, we would not have this problem now.

2. Past progressive tense

In **Capítulo 3** you learned that the present progressive tense is formed with the present indicative of **estar** and a present participle. The past progressive tense is formed with the imperfect of **estar** and a present participle.

The past progressive tense is used to express or describe an action that was in progress at a particular moment in the past.

Past progressive tense	
estaba	
estabas	
estaba	+ present
estábamos	participle
estabais	
estaban	

Estábamos comiendo cuando llamaste.	*We were eating when you called.*
¿Quién **estaba hablando** por teléfono?	*Who was talking on the phone?*

Another past progressive tense can also be formed with the preterite of **estar** and the present participle. However, its use is of much lower frequency in Spanish.

3. Stressed possessive adjectives and pronouns

In **Capítulo 2** you learned to express possession using **de** or the possessive adjectives **mi(s), tu(s), su(s), nuestro(a, os, as), vuestro(a, os, as)**. Possession may also be expressed using the stressed possessive adjectives equivalent to the English *of mine, of yours, of ours, of theirs*.

Stressed possessive adjectives and pronouns					
mío	**mía**	*my, (of) mine*	**nuestro**	**nuestra**	*our, (of) ours*
míos	**mías**		**nuestros**	**nuestras**	
tuyo	**tuya**	*your, (of) yours*	**vuestro**	**vuestra**	*your, (of) yours*
tuyos	**tuyas**		**vuestros**	**vuestras**	
suyo	**suya**	*its, his, (of) his*	**suyo**	**suya**	*their, (of) theirs*
suyos	**suyas**	*hers, (of) hers* / *your, (of) yours*	**suyos**	**suyas**	*your, (of) yours*

A. As adjectives, the stressed possessives must agree in number and gender with the thing possessed.

Una amiga **mía** viene a visitarme hoy.	*A friend of mine is coming to visit me today.*
¿Qué hay en las maletas **suyas**, señor?	*What do you have in those suitcases, of yours?*
El coche **nuestro** nunca funciona.	*Our car never works.*

Note that stressed possessive adjectives *always* follow the noun they modify. Also note that the noun must be preceded by an article.

B. Stressed possessive adjectives can be used as possessive pronouns by eliminating the noun.

¿Dónde está **la suya,** señor?   *Where is yours, sir?*
El nuestro nunca funciona.   *Ours never works.*

Note that both the article and possessive adjective must agree in number and gender with the noun that has been eliminated.

C. A stressed possessive pronoun may be used without the article after the verb **ser.**

Esta maleta no es **mía,** señor.   *This suitcase is not mine, sir.*
¿Es **suya,** señora?   *Is it yours, ma'am?*

4. Present subjunctive of stem-changing verbs

A. Stem-changing **-ar** and **-er** verbs follow the same stem changes in the present subjunctive as in the present indicative. Note that the stems of the **nosotros** and **vosotros** forms do not change.

contar (ue)	
cuente	contemos
cuentes	contéis
cuente	cuenten

perder (ie)	
pierda	perdamos
pierdas	perdáis
pierda	pierdan

B. Stem-changing **-ir** verbs follow the same pattern in the present subjunctive, except for the **nosotros** and **vosotros** forms. These change **e → i** or **o → u.**

morir (ue)	
muera	muramos
mueras	muráis
muera	mueran

preferir (ie)	
prefiera	prefiramos
prefieras	prefiráis
prefiera	prefieran

pedir (i)	
pida	pidamos
pidas	pidáis
pida	pidan

5. Present subjunctive of verbs with spelling changes

As in the preterite, verbs that end in **-car, -gar,** and **-zar** undergo a spelling change in the present subjunctive in order to maintain the consonant sound of the infinitive.

A. -car: c changes to **qu** in front of **e**

buscar: bus**que,** bus**ques,** bus**que**...

B. -zar: z changes to **c** in front of **e**

almorzar: almuer**ce,** almuer**ces,** almuer**ce**...

C. -gar: g changes to **gu** in front of **e**

jugar: jue**gue,** jue**gues,** jue**gue**...

D. -ger: g changes to **j** in front of **a**

proteger: prote**ja,** prote**jas,** prote**ja**...

6. Irregular verbs in the present subjunctive

The following verbs are irregular in the present subjunctive:

dar	dé, des, dé, demos, deis, den
haber	haya, hayas, haya, hayamos, hayáis, hayan
ir	vaya, vayas, vaya, vayamos, vayáis, vayan
saber	sepa, sepas, sepa, sepamos, sepáis, sepan
ser	sea, seas, sea, seamos, seáis, sean

7. Past subjunctive and Conditional *Si* clauses

The past subjunctive of *all* verbs is formed by removing the -**ron** ending from the **ustedes** form of the preterite and adding the past subjunctive verb endings: -**ra**, -**ras**, -**ra**, -**ramos**, -**rais**, -**ran**. Thus, any irregularities in the **ustedes** form of the preterite will be reflected in all forms of the past subjunctive. Note that the **nosotros** form requires a written accent.

comprar	
compra~~ron~~	
compra**ra**	comprá**ramos**
compra**ras**	compra**rais**
compra**ra**	compra**ran**

tener	
tuvie~~ron~~	
tuvie**ra**	tuvié**ramos**
tuvie**ras**	tuvie**rais**
tuvie**ra**	tuvie**ran**

ser	
fueron	
fue**ra**	fué**ramos**
fue**ras**	fue**rais**
fue**ra**	fue**ran**

An alternate form of the past subjunctive uses the verb endings -**se**, -**ses**, -**se**, -**semos**, -**seis**, -**sen**. This form is used primarily in Spain and in literary writing.

A. The past subjunctive has the same uses as the present subjunctive, except that it generally applies to past events or actions.

Insistieron en que **fuéramos.**	*They insisted that we go.*
Era imposible que lo **terminaran** a tiempo.	*It was impossible for them to finish it on time.*

B. In Spanish, as in English, conditional sentences express hypothetical conditions usually with an *if*-clause: *I would go if I had the money.* Since the actions are hypothetical and one does not know if they will actually occur, the past subjunctive is used in the *if*-clause.

Iría a Perú si **tuviera** el dinero.	*I would go to Peru if I had the money.*
Si **fuera** necesario, pediría un préstamo.	*If it were necessary, I would ask for a loan.*

C. Conditional sentences in the present use either the present indicative or the future tense. The present subjunctive is never used in *if*-clauses.

Si me **invitas,** iré contigo.	*If you invite me, I'll go with you.*

Grammar Guide

For more detailed explanations of these grammar points, consult the Index on pages 599–602 to find the places where these concepts are presented.

ACTIVE VOICE (La voz activa) A sentence written in the active voice identifies a subject that performs the action of the verb.

Juan	cantó	la canción.
Juan	*sang*	*the song.*
subject	verb	direct object

In the sentence above Juan is the performer of the verb **cantar**.

(*See also* **Passive Voice.**)

ADJECTIVES (Los adjetivos) are words that modify or describe **nouns** or **pronouns** and agree in **number** and generally in **gender** with the nouns they modify.

Las casas **azules** son **bonitas.**
*The **blue** houses are **pretty.***

Esas mujeres **mexicanas** son mis **nuevas** amigas.
*Those **Mexican** women are my **new** friends.*

- **Demonstrative adjectives (Los adjetivos demostrativos)** point out persons, places, or things relative to the position of the speaker. They always agree in **number** and **gender** with the **noun** they modify. The forms are: **este, esta, estos, estas / ese, esa, esos, esas / aquel, aquella, aquellos, aquellas.** There are also neuter forms that refer to generic ideas or things, and hence have no gender: **esto, eso, aquello.**

Este libro es fácil.	***This** book is easy.*
Esos libros son difíciles.	***Those** books are hard.*
Aquellos libros son pesados.	***Those** books (**over there**) are boring.*

Demonstratives may also function as **pronouns**, replacing the **noun** but still agreeing with it in **number** and **gender:**

Me gustan esas blusas verdes.	*I like those green blouses.*
¿Cuáles, **estas?**	*Which ones, **these?***
No. Me gustan **esas.**	*No. I like **those.***

- **Stressed possessive adjectives (Los adjetivos posesivos acentuados)** are used for emphasis and follow the noun that they modifiy. These adjectives may also function as pronouns and always agree in **number** and in **gender.** The forms are: **mío, tuyo, suyo, nuestro, vuestro, suyo.** Unless they are directly preceded by the verb **ser,** stressed possessives must be preceded by the **definite article.**

Ese perro pequeño es **mío.**	*That little dog is **mine.***
Dame el **tuyo;** el **nuestro** no funciona.	*Give me **yours; ours** doesn't work.*

- **Unstressed possessive adjectives (Los adjetivos posesivos no acentuados)** demonstrate ownership and always precede the **noun** that they modify.

La señora Elman es **mi** profesora.	*Mrs. Elman is **my** professor.*
Debemos llevar **nuestros** libros a clase.	*We should take **our** books to class.*

ADVERBS (Los adverbios) are words that modify **verbs, adjectives,** or other adverbs and, unlike **adjectives,** do not have **gender** or **number.** Here are examples of different classes of adverbs:

Practicamos **diariamente.**	*We practice **daily.*** (adverb of manner)
Ellos van a salir **pronto.**	*They will leave **soon.*** (adverb of time)
Jennifer está **afuera.**	*Jennifer is **outside.*** (adverb of place)
No quiero ir **tampoco.**	*I don't want to go **either.*** (adverb of negation)
Paco habla **demasiado.**	*Paco talks **too much.*** (adverb of quantity)
Esta clase es **extremadamente** difícil.	*This class is **extremely** difficult.* (modifies adjective)
Ella habla muy **poco.**	*She speaks **very** little.* (modifies adverb)

AGREEMENT (La concordancia) refers to the correspondence between parts of speech in terms of **number, gender,** and **person.** Subjects agree with their verbs; articles and adjectives agree with the nouns they modify, etc.

Toda**s** la**s** lengua**s** son interesante**s.**	*All languages are interesting.* (number)
Ella es bonit**a.**	*She is pretty.* (gender)
Nosotros somos de España.	*We are from Spain.* (person)

ARTICLES (Los artículos) precede nouns and indicate whether they are definite or indefinite persons, places, or things.

- **Definite articles (Los artículos definidos)** refer to particular members of a group and are the equivalent of *the* in English. The definite articles are: **el, la, los, las.**

El hombre guapo es mi padre.	***The*** *handsome man is my father.*
Las mujeres de esta clase son inteligentes.	***The*** *women in this class are intelligent.*

- **Indefinite articles (Los artículos indefinidos)** refer to any unspecified member(s) of a group and are the equivalent of *a(n)* and *some.* The indefinite articles are: **un, una, unos, unas.**

Un hombre vino a nuestra casa anoche.	***A*** *man came to our house last night.*
Unas niñas jugaban en el parque.	***Some*** *girls were playing in the park.*

CLAUSES (Las cláusulas) are subject and verb combinations; for a sentence to be complete it must have at least one main clause.

- **Main clauses** (Independent clauses) **(Las cláusulas principales)** communicate a complete idea or thought.

Mi hermana va al hospital.	*My sister goes to the hospital.*

- **Subordinate clauses** (Dependent clauses) **(Las cláusulas subordinadas)** depend upon a main clause for their meaning to be complete.

Mi hermana va al hospital	cuando está enferma.
My sister goes to the hospital	*when she is ill.*
main clause	**subordinate clause**

In the sentence above, *when she is ill* is not a complete idea without the information supplied by the main clause.

COMMANDS (Los mandatos) (*See* **Imperatives.**)

COMPARISONS (Las comparaciones) are statements that describe one person, place, or thing relative to another in terms of quantity, quality, or manner.

- **Comparisons of equality (Las formas comparativas de igualdad)** demonstrate an equal share of a quantity or degree of a particular characteristic. These statements use a form of **tan(to)(ta)(s)** and **como.**

Ella tiene **tanto** dinero **como** Elena.	*She has **as much** money **as** Elena.*
Fernando trabaja **tanto como** Felipe.	*Fernando works **as much as** Felipe.*
Jim baila **tan** bien **como** Anne.	*Jim dances **as well as** Anne.*

- **Comparisons of inequality (Las formas comparativas de desigualdad)** indicate a difference in quantity, quality, or manner between the compared subjects. These statements use **más/menos... que** or comparative **adjectives** such as **mejor/peor, mayor/menor.**

México tiene **más** playas **que** España.	*Mexico has **more** beaches **than** Spain.*
Tú hablas español **mejor que** yo.	*You speak Spanish **better than** I.*

(*See also* **Superlative statements.**)

CONJUGATIONS (Las conjugaciones) represent the inflected form of the verb as it is used with a particular **subject** or **person.**

Yo **bailo** los sábados.	*I dance on Saturdays.* (1st-person singular)
Tú **bailas** los sábados.	*You dance on Saturdays.* (2nd-person singular)
Ella **baila** los sábados.	*She dances on Saturdays.* (3rd-person singular)
Nosotros **bailamos** los sábados.	*We dance on Saturdays.* (1st-person plural)
Vosotros **bailáis** los sábados.	*You dance on Saturdays.* (2nd-person plural)
Ellos **bailan** los sábados.	*They dance on Saturdays.* (3rd-person plural)

CONJUNCTIONS (Las conjunciones) are linking words that join two independent **clauses** together.

Fuimos al centro **y** mis amigos compraron muchas cosas.
*We went downtown **and** my friends bought a lot of things.*

Yo quiero ir a la fiesta, **pero** tengo que estudiar.
*I want to go to the party, **but** I have to study.*

CONTRACTIONS (Las contracciones) in Spanish are limited to preposition/article combinations, such as **de + el = del** and **a + el = al,** or preposition/pronoun combinations such as **con + mí = conmigo** and **con + ti = contigo.**

DIRECT OBJECTS (Los objetos directos) in sentences are the direct recipients of the action of the verb. Direct objects answer the questions *What?* or *Whom?*

¿Qué hizo?	*What did she do?*
Ella hizo **la tarea.**	*She did her **homework.***
Y luego llamó **a su amiga.**	*And then called **her friend.***

(*See also* **Pronoun, Indirect Object, Personal *a*.**)

EXCLAMATORY WORDS (Las palabras exclamativas) communicate surprise or strong emotion. Like interrogative words, exclamatory words also carry accents.

¡**Qué** sorpresa!	***What** a surprise!*
¡**Cómo** canta Miguel!	***How well** Miguel sings!*

(*See also* **Interrogatives.**)

IDIOMATIC EXPRESSIONS (Las frases idiomáticas) are phrases in Spanish that do not have a literal English equivalent.

Hace mucho frío.	*It is very cold.* (Literally, *It makes a lot of cold.*)

IMPERATIVES (Los imperativos) represent the mood used to express requests or commands. It is more direct than the **subjunctive** mood. Imperatives are commonly called commands and fall into two categories: affirmative and negative. Spanish speakers must also choose between using formal commands and informal commands based upon whether one is addressed as **usted** (formal) or **tú** (informal).

Habla conmigo.	**Talk** to me. (informal, affirmative)
No me hables.	**Don't talk** to me. (informal, negative)
Hable con la policía.	**Talk** to the police. (formal, singular, affirmative)
No hable con la policía.	**Don't talk** to the police. (formal, singular, negative)
Hablen con la policía.	**Talk** to the police. (formal, plural, affirmative)
No hablen con la policía	**Don't talk** to the police. (formal, plural, negative)
Hablad con la policía.	**Talk** to the police. (informal, plural, affirmative)
No habléis con la policía.	**Don't talk** to the police. (informal, plural, negative)

(*See also* **Mood.**)

IMPERFECT (El imperfecto) The imperfect tense is used to make statements about the past when the speaker wants to convey the idea of 1) habitual or repeated action, 2) two actions in progress simultaneously, or 3) an event that was in progress when another action interrupted. The imperfect tense is also used to emphasize the ongoing nature of the middle of the event, as opposed to its beginning or end. Age and clock time are always expressed using the imperfect.

Cuando María **era** joven, ella **cantaba** en el coro.
*When María **was** young, she **used to sing** in the choir.*

Aquel día **llovía** mucho y el cielo **estaba** oscuro.
*That day **it was raining** a lot and the sky **was dark**.*

Juan **dormía** cuando sonó el teléfono.
*Juan **was sleeping** when the phone rang.*

(*See also* **Preterite.**)

IMPERSONAL EXPRESSIONS (Las expresiones impersonales) are statements that contain the impersonal subjects of *it* or *one*.

Es necesario estudiar.	***It is necessary** to study.*
Se necesita estudiar.	***One needs** to study.*

(*See also* **Passive Voice.**)

INDEFINITE WORDS (Las palabras indefinidas) are **articles**, **adjectives**, **nouns** or **pronouns** that refer to unspecified members of a group.

Un hombre vino.	*A man came. (indefinite article)*
Alguien vino.	*Someone came. (indefinite noun)*
Algunas personas vinieron.	*Some people came. (indefinite adjective)*
Algunas vinieron.	*Some came. (indefinite pronoun)*

(*See also* **Articles.**)

INDICATIVE (El indicativo) The indicative is a mood, rather than a tense. The indicative is used to express ideas that are considered factual or certain and, therefore, not subject to speculation, doubt, or negation.

Josefina **es** española.	*Josefina **is** Spanish.*
(present indicative)	
Ella **vivió** en Argentina.	*She lived in Argentina.*
(preterite indicative)	

(*See also* **Mood.**)

INDIRECT OBJECTS (Los objetos indirectos) are the indirect recipients of an action in a sentence and answer the questions *To whom?* or *For whom?* In Spanish it is common to include an indirect object **pronoun** along with the indirect object.

Yo **le** di el libro **a Sofía.**	*I gave the book **to Sofía.***
Sofía **les** guardó el libro **a sus padres**.	*Sofía kept the book **for her parents.***

(*See also* **Direct Objects** *and* **Pronouns.**)

INFINITIVES (Los infinitivos) are verb forms that are uninflected or **not conjugated** according to a specific **person.** In English, infinitives are preceded by *to: to talk, to eat, to live*. Infinitives in Spanish end in **-ar (hablar)**, **-er (comer)**, and **-ir (vivir).**

INTERROGATIVES (Las formas interrogativas) are used to pose questions and carry accent marks to distinguish them from other uses. Basic interrogative words include: **quién(es), qué, cómo, cuánto(a)(s), cuándo, por qué, dónde, cuál(es).**

¿**Qué** quieres?	***What** do you want?*
¿**Cuándo** llegó ella?	***When** did she arrive?*
¿De **dónde** eres?	***Where** are you from?*

(*See also* **Exclamatory Words.**)

MOOD (El modo) is like the word *mode*, meaning *manner* or *way*. It indicates the way in which the speaker views an action, or his/her attitude toward the action. Besides the **imperative** mood, which is simply giving commands, two basic moods in Spanish: the **subjunctive** and the **indicative.** Basically, the subjunctive mood communicates an attitude of uncertainty or negation toward the action, while the indicative indicates that the action is certain or factual. Within each of these moods there are many **tenses.** Hence you have the present indicative and the present subjunctive, the present perfect indicative and the present perfect subjunctive, etc.

- **Indicative mood (El indicativo)** is used to talk about actions that are regarded as certain or as facts: things that happen all the time, have happened, or will happen. It is used in contrast to situations where the speaker is voicing an opinion, doubts, or desires. (*See* **Mood** and **Subjunctive**.)

Yo **quiero** ir a la fiesta.	*I want to go to the party.*
¿**Quieres** ir conmigo?	*Do you want to go with me?*

- **Subjunctive mood (El subjuntivo)** indicates a recommendation, a statement of uncertainty or negation, or a hypothetical situation.

Yo recomiendo que tú **vayas** a la fiesta.	*I recommend that **you go** to the party.*
Dudo que **vayas** a la fiesta.	*I doubt that **you'll go** to the party.*
No creo que **vayas** a la fiesta.	*I don't believe that **you'll go** to the party.*
Si **fueras** a la fiesta, te divertirías.	*If **you were to go** to the party, you would have a good time.*

- **Imperative mood (El imperativo)** is used to make a command or request.

¡**Ven** conmigo a la fiesta!	***Come** with me to the party!*

(*See also* **Indicative, Imperative,** *and* **Subjunctive**.)

NEGATION (La negación) takes place when a negative word, such as **no,** is placed before an affirmative sentence. In Spanish, double negatives are common.

Yolanda va a cantar esta noche.	*Yolanda will sing tonight.* (affirmative)
Yolanda **no** va a cantar esta noche.	*Yolanda will **not** sing tonight.* (negative)
Ramón quiere algo.	*Ramón wants something.* (affirmative)
Ramón **no** quiere **nada.**	*Ramón **doesn't** want **anything.*** (negative)

NOUNS (Los sustantivos) are persons, places, things, or ideas. Names of people, countries, and cities are proper nouns and are capitalized.

Alberto	*Albert* (person)
el pueblo	*town* (place)
el diccionario	*dictionary* (thing)

ORTHOGRAPHY (La ortografía) refers to the spelling of a word or anything related to spelling such as accentuation.

PASSIVE VOICE (La voz pasiva), as compared to **active voice (la voz activa),** places emphasis on the action itself rather than the subject (the person or thing that is indirectly responsible for committing the action). The passive **se** is used when there is no apparent subject.

Luis vende los coches.	*Luis sells the cars.* (active voice)
Los coches **son vendidos por** Luis.	*The cars **are sold by** Luis.* (passive voice)
Se venden los coches.	*The cars **are sold.*** (passive voice)

(*See also* **Active Voice**.)

PAST PARTICIPLES (Los participios pasados) are verb forms used in compound tenses such as the **present perfect.** Regular past participles are formed by dropping the **-ar** or **-er/-ir** from the **infinitive** and adding **-ado** or **-ido.** Past participles are the equivalent of verbs ending in *-ed* in English. They may also be used as **adjectives,** in which case they agree in **number** and **gender** with their nouns. Irregular past participles include: **escrito, roto, dicho, hecho, puesto, vuelto, muerto, cubierto.**

Marta ha **subido** la montaña.	*Marta has **climbed** the mountain.*
Hemos **hablado** mucho por teléfono.	*We have **talked** a lot on the phone.*
La novela **publicada** en 1995 es su mejor novela.	*The novel **published** in 1995 is her best novel.*

PERFECT TENSES (Los tiempos perfectos) communicate the idea that an action has taken place before now (present perfect) or before a moment in the past (past perfect). The perfect tenses are compound tenses consisting of the verb **haber** plus the **past participle** of a second verb.

Yo **he comido.**	*I have eaten.* (present perfect indicative)
Antes de la fiesta, yo ya **había comido.**	*Before the party **I had already eaten.*** (past perfect indicative)
Yo espero que **hayas comido.**	*I hope that **you have eaten.*** (present perfect subjunctive)
Yo esperaba que **hubieras comido.**	*I hoped that **you had eaten.*** (past perfect subjunctive)

PERSON (La persona) refers to changes in the subject pronouns that indicate if one is speaking (first person), if one is spoken to (second person), or if one is spoken about (third person).

Yo hablo.	*I speak.* (1st-person singular)
Tú hablas.	*You speak.* (2nd-person singular)
Ud./Él/Ella habla.	*You/He/She speak(s).* (3rd-person singular)
Nosotros(as) hablamos.	*We speak.* (1st-person plural)
Vosotros(as) habláis.	*You speak.* (2nd-person plural)
Uds./Ellos/Ellas hablan.	*They speak.* (3rd-person plural)

PREPOSITIONS (Las preposiciones) are linking words indicating spatial or temporal relations between two words.

Ella nadaba **en** la piscina.	*She was swimming **in** the pool.*
Yo llamé **antes de** las nueve.	*I called **before** nine o'clock.*
El libro es **para** ti.	*The book is **for** you.*
Voy **a** la oficina.	*I'm going **to** the office.*
Jorge es **de** Paraguay.	*Jorge is **from** Paraguay.*

PRESENT PARTICIPLE (El participio del presente) is the Spanish equivalent of the *-ing* verb form in English. Regular participles are created by replacing the infinitive endings (**-ar, -er/-ir**) with **-ando** or **-iendo.** They are often used with the verb **estar** to form the present progressive tense. The present progressive tense places emphasis on the continuing or progressive nature of an action. In Spanish, this form is referred to as a gerund.

Miguel está **cantando** en la ducha.	*Miguel is **singing** in the shower.*
Los niños están **durmiendo** ahora.	*The children are **sleeping** now.*

(*See also* **Gerunds**)

GERUNDS (Los gerundios) in Spanish refer to the present participle. In English gerunds are verbals (based on a verb and expressing an action or a state of being) that function as nouns. In most instances where the gerund is used in English, the infinitive is used in Spanish.

(El) **Ser** cortés no cuesta nada.	***Being** polite is not hard.*
Mi pasatiempo favorito es (el) **viajar.**	*My favorite pasttime is **traveling.***
Después de **desayunar,** salió de la casa.	*After **eating** breakfast, he left the house.*

(*See also* **Present Participle.**)

PRETERITE (El pretérito) The preterite tense, as compared to the **imperfect tense,** is used to talk about past events with specific emphasis on the beginning or the end of the action, or emphasis on the completed nature of the action as a whole.

Anoche yo **empecé** a estudiar a las once y **terminé** a la una.
*Last night I **began** to study at eleven o'clock and **finished** at one o'clock.*

Esta mañana **me desperté** a las siete, **desayuné, me duché** y **vine** al campus para las ocho.
*This morning **I woke up** at seven, **I ate** breakfast, **I showered,** and **I came** to campus by eight.*

PERSONAL A (La *a* personal) The personal **a** refers to the placement of the preposition **a** before the name of a person or a pet when it is the **direct object** of the sentence.

Voy a llamar **a** María.	*I'm going to call María.*
El veterinario curó **al** perro.	*The veterinarian treated the dog.*

PRONOUNS (Los pronombres) are words that substitute for **nouns** in a sentence.

Yo quiero **este.**	*I want **this one.*** (demonstrative—points out a specific person, place, or thing)
¿**Quién** es tu amigo?	***Who** is your friend?* (interrogative—used to ask questions)
Yo voy a llamar**la.**	*I'm going to call **her.*** (direct object—replaces the direct object of the sentence)
Ella va a dar**le** el reloj.	*She is going to give **him** the watch.* (indirect object—replaces the indirect object of the sentence)
Juan **se** baña por la mañana.	*Juan bathes **himself** in the morning.* (reflexive—used with reflexive verbs to show that the agent of the action is also the recipient)

Es la mujer **que** conozco.	*She is the woman **that** I know. (relative—used to introduce a clause that describes a noun)*
Nosotros somos listos.	*We are clever. (subject—replaces the noun that performs the action or state of a verb)*

SUBJECTS (Los sujetos) are the persons, places, or things which perform the action of a verb, or which are connected to a description by a verb. The **conjugated** verb always agrees with its subject.

Carlos siempre baila solo.	***Carlos** always dances alone.*
Colorado y **California** son mis estados preferidos.	***Colorado** and **California** are my favorite states.*
La cafetera produce el café.	*The **coffee pot** makes the coffee.*

(*See also* **Active Voice.**)

SUBJUNCTIVE (El subjuntivo) The subjunctive mood is used to express speculative, doubtful, or hypothetical situations. It also communicates a degree of subjectivity or influence of the main clause over the subordinate clause.

No creo que **tengas** razón.	*I don't think that **you're** right.*
Si yo **fuera** el jefe, es pagaría más a mis empleados.	*If I **were** the boss, I would pay my employees more.*
Quiero que **estudies** más.	*I want **you to study** more.*

(*See also* **Mood, Indicative.**)

SUPERLATIVE STATEMENTS (Las frases superlativas) are formed by adjectives or adverbs to make comparisons among three or more members of a group. To form superlatives, add a definite article (**el, la, los, las**) before the comparative form.

Juan es **el más alto** de los tres.	*Juan is **the tallest** of the three.*
Este coche es **el más rápido** de todos.	*This car is **the fastest** of them all.*

(*See also* **Comparisons.**)

TENSES (Los tiempos) refer to the manner in which time is expressed through the **verb** of a sentence.

Yo estudio.	*I study. (present tense)*
Yo estoy estudiando.	*I am studying. (present progressive)*
Yo he estudiado.	*I have studied. (present perfect)*
Yo había estudiado.	*I had studied. (past perfect)*
Yo estudié.	*I studied. (preterite tense)*
Yo estudiaba.	*I was studying. (imperfect tense)*
Yo estudiaré.	*I will study. (future tense)*

VERBS (Los verbos) are the words in a sentence that communicate an action or state of being.

Helen **es** mi amiga y ella **lee** muchas novelas.	*Helen **is** my friend and she **reads** a lot of novels.*

- **Auxiliary verbs (Los verbos auxiliares)** or helping verbs **haber, ser,** and **estar** are used to form the passive voice, compound tenses, and verbal periphrases.

Estamos estudiando mucho para el examen mañana.	***We are** studying a lot for the exam tomorrow. (verbal periphrases)*
Helen **ha** trabajado mucho en este proyecto.	*Helen **has** worked a lot on this project. (compound tense)*
La ropa fue hecha en Guatemala.	*The clothing **was** made in Guatemala (passive voice)*

- **Reflexive verbs (Los verbos reflexivos)** use reflexive **pronouns** to indicate that the person initiating the action is also the recipient of the action.

Yo **me afeito** por la mañana.	***I shave (myself)** in the morning.*

- **Stem-changing verbs (Los verbos con cambios de raíz)** undergo a change in the main part of the verb when conjugated. To find the stem, drop the **-ar, -er,** or **-ir** from the **infinitive: dorm-, empez-, ped-.** There are three types of stem-changing verbs: **o** to **ue**, **e** to **ie** and **e** to **i.**

dormir: Yo d**ue**rmo en el parque.	*I sleep in the park. (**o** to **ue**)*
empezar: Ella siempre emp**ie**za su trabajo temprano.	*She always starts her work early. (**e** to **ie**)*
pedir: ¿Por qué no p**i**des ayuda?	*Why don't you ask for help? (**e** to **i**)*

Asking questions
Question words

¿Adónde? To where?
¿Cómo? How?
¿Cuál(es)? Which? What?
¿Cuándo? When?
¿Cuánto/¿Cuánta? How much?
¿Cuántos/¿Cuántas? How many?
¿Dónde? Where?
¿Para qué? For what reason?
¿Por qué? Why?
¿Qué? What?
¿Quién(es)? Who? Whom?

Requesting information

¿Cómo es su (tu) profesor/profesora favorito/favorita? What's your favorite professor like?
¿Cómo se (te) llama(s)? What's your name?
¿Cómo se llama? What's his/her name?
¿Cuál es su (tu) facultad? What's your school/college?
¿Cuál es su (tu) número de teléfono? What's your telephone number?
¿De dónde es (eres)? Where are you from?
¿Dónde hay...? Where is/are there ...?
¿Qué estudia(s)? What are you studying?

Asking for descriptions

¿Cómo es...? What is . . . like?
¿Cómo son...? What are . . . like?

Asking for clarification

¿Cómo? What?
Dígame (Dime) una cosa. Tell me something.
Más despacio. More slowly.
   No comprendo./No entiendo. I don't understand.
   ¿Perdón? Pardon me?
   ¿Qué? Otra vez, por favor. What? One more time, please.
   Repita (Repite), por favor. Please repeat.

Asking about and expressing likes and dislikes

¿Te (le) gusta(n)? Do you like it (them)?
No me gusta(n). I don't like it (them).
Sí, me gusta(n). Yes, I like it (them).

Asking for confirmation

... ¿de acuerdo? . . . agreed? (*Used when some type of action is proposed.*)
... ¿no? . . . isn't that so? (*Not used with negative sentences.*)
... ¿no es así? . . . isn't that right?

... ¿vale? . . . okay?
... ¿verdad? ¿cierto? . . . right?
... ¿está bien? . . . OK?

Asking for clarification

Disculpe. No entiendo. Excuse me. I don't understand.
¿Qué significa...? What does . . . mean?
¿Voleibolista? What is a *voleibolista*?

Complaining

Es demasiado caro/cara (costoso/costosa). It's too expensive.
Esto es el colmo. This is the last straw.
No es justo. It isn't fair.
¡No, hombre/mujer! No way!
No puedo esperar más. I can't wait anymore.
No puedo más. I can't take this anymore.
Pero, por favor... But, please . . .

Expressing belief

Es cierto/verdad. That's right./That's true.
Estoy seguro/segura. I'm sure.
Lo creo. I believe it.
No cabe duda de que... There can be no doubt that . . .
No lo dudo. I don't doubt it.
No tengo la menor duda. I haven't the slightest doubt.
Tiene(s) razón. You're right.

Expressing disbelief

Caben dudas. There are doubts.
Dudo si... I doubt/I'm doubtful whether . . .
Es poco probable. It's doubtful/unlikely.
Lo dudo. I doubt it.
No lo creo. I don't believe it.
No tienes razón. You're wrong.
Tengo mis dudas. I have my doubts.

Expressing frequency of actions and length of activities

¿Con qué frecuencia...? How often . . .?
de vez en cuando from time to time
durante la semana during the week
frecuentemente frequently
los fines de semana on the weekends
nunca never
por la mañana/por la tarde/por la noche in the morning/afternoon/evening
siempre always
todas las tardes/todas las noches every afternoon/evening
todos los días every day
Hace un año/dos meses/tres semanas que... for a year/two months/three weeks

Listening for instructions in the classroom

Abran los libros en la página... Open your books to page . . .
Cierren los libros. Close your books.
Complete (Completa) (Completen) la oración. Complete the sentence.
Conteste (Contesta) (Contesten) en español. Answer in Spanish.
Escriba (Escribe) (Escriban) en la pizarra. Write on the board.
Formen grupos de...estudiantes. Form groups of . . . students.
Practiquen en parejas. Practice in pairs.
¿Hay preguntas? Are there any questions?
Lea (Lee) en voz alta. Read aloud.
Por ejemplo... For example . . .
Prepare (Prepara) (Preparen)...para mañana. Prepare . . . for tomorrow.
Repita (Repite), (Repitan) por favor. Please repeat.
Saque (Saca) (Saquen) el libro (el cuaderno, una hoja de papel). Take out the book (the notebook, a piece of paper).

Greeting and conversing
Greetings

Bien, gracias. Fine, thanks.
Buenas noches. Good evening.
Buenas tardes. Good afternoon.
Buenos días. Good morning.
¿Cómo está usted (estás)? How are you?
¿Cómo le (te) va? How is it going?
Hola. Hi.
Mal. Ill./Bad./Badly.
Más o menos. So so.
Nada. Nothing.
No muy bien. Not too well.
¿Qué hay de nuevo? What's new?
¿Qué tal? How are things?
Regular. Okay.
¿Y usted (tú)? And you?

Introducing people

¿Cómo se (te) llama(s)? What is your name?
¿Cómo se llama(n) él/ella/usted(es)/ellos/ellas? What is (are) his/her, your, their name(s)?
¿Cuál es su (tu) nombre? What is your name?
El gusto es mío. The pleasure is mine.
Encantado/Encantada. Delighted.
Igualmente. Likewise.
Me llamo... My name is . . .
Mi nombre es... My name is . . .
Mucho gusto. Pleased to meet you.
Quiero presentarle(te) a... I want to introduce you to . . .
Se llama(n)... His/Her/Their name(s) is/are . . .

Entering into a conversation

Escuche (Escucha). Listen.
(No) Creo que... I (don't) believe that . . .
(No) Estoy de acuerdo porque... I (don't) agree because . . .
Pues, lo que quiero decir es que... Well, what I want to say is . . .
Quiero decir algo sobre... I want to say something about . . .

Saying good-bye

Adió s. Good-bye.
Chao. Good-bye.
Hasta la vista. Until we meet again.
Hasta luego. See you later.
Hasta mañana. Until tomorrow.
Hasta pronto. See you soon.

Chatting

(Bastante) bien. (Pretty) well, fine.
¿Cómo está la familia? How's the family?
¿Cómo le (te) va? How's it going?
¿Cómo van las clases? How are classes going?
Fenomenal. Phenomenal.
Horrible. Horrible.
Mal. Bad(ly).
Nada de nuevo. Nothing new.
¿Qué hay de nuevo? What's new?
¿Qué tal? How's it going?

Using exclamations

¡Caray! Oh! Oh no!
¡Dios mío ! Oh, my goodness!
¡Estupendo! Stupendous!
¡Fabuloso! Fabulous!
¡Qué barbaridad! How unusual! Wow! That's terrible!
¡Qué bien! That's great!
¡Qué desastre! That's a disaster!
¡Qué gente más loca! What crazy people!
¡Qué horrible! That's horrible!
¡Qué increíble! That's amazing!
¡Qué lástima! That's a pity! That's too bad!
¡Qué mal! That's really bad!
¡Qué maravilla! That's marvelous!
¡Qué padre! That's cool!
¡Qué pena! That's a pain! That's too bad!

Extending a conversation using fillers and hesitations

A ver... Let's see . . .
Buena pregunta... That's a good question . . .
Bueno... Well . . . .
Es que... It's that . . .
Pues...no sé. Well . . . I don't know.
Sí, pero... Yes, but . . .
No creo. I don't think so.

Expressing worry

¡Ay, Dios mío! Good grief!
¡Es una pesadilla! It's a nightmare!
¡Eso debe ser horrible! That must be horrible!

¡Pobre! Poor thing!
¡Qué espanto! What a scare!
¡Qué horror! How horrible!
¡Qué lástima! What a pity!
¡Qué mala suerte/pata! What bad luck!
¡Qué terrible! How terrible!
¡Qué triste! How sad!
¡Qué pena! What a shame!

Expressing agreement

Así es. That's so.
Cierto./Claro (que sí)./Seguro. Certainly. Sure(ly).
Cómo no./Por supuesto. Of course.
Correcto. That's right.
Es cierto/verdad. It's true.
Eso es. That's it.
(Estoy) de acuerdo. I agree.
Exacto. Exactly.
Muy bien. Very good. Fine.
Perfecto. Perfect.
Probablemente. Probably.

Expressing disagreement

Al contrario. On the contrary.
En absoluto. Absolutely not. No way.
Es poco probable. It's doubtful/not likely.
Incorrecto. That's not right.
No es así. That's not so.
No es cierto. It's not so.
No es verdad. It's not true.
No es eso. That's not it.
No está bien. It's no good/not right.
No estoy de acuerdo. I don't agree.
Todo lo contrario. Just the opposite./ Quite the contrary.

Expressing sympathy

Es una pena. It's a pity.
Le doy mi pésame. You have my sympathy.
Lo siento mucho. I'm very sorry.
Mis condolencias. My condolences.
¡Qué lástima! What a pity!

Expressing encouragement

¡A mí me lo dice(s)! You're telling me!
¿De veras?/¿De verdad? Really? Is that so?
¿En serio? Seriously? Are you serious?
¡No me diga(s)! You don't say!
¿Qué hizo (hiciste)? What did you do?
¿Qué dijo (dijiste)? What did you say?
¡Ya lo creo! I (can) believe it!

Expressing obligation

Necesitar + _infinitive_ To need to . . .
(No) es necesario + _infinitive_ It's (not) necessary to . . .
(No) hay que + _infinitive_ One must(n't) . . ., One does(n't) have to . . .
(Se) debe + _infinitive_ (One) should (ought to) . . .
Tener que + _infinitive_ To have to . . .

In the hospital
Giving instructions

Aplicar una pomada. Apply cream/ ointment.
Bañarse con agua fría/caliente. Take a bath in cold/hot water.
Lavar la herida. Wash the wound.
Llamar al médico. Call the doctor.
Pedir información. Ask for information.
Poner hielo. Put on ice.
Poner una tirita/una venda. Put on a Band-Aid®/a bandage.
Quedarse en la cama. Stay in bed.
Sacar la lengua. Stick out your tongue.
Tomar la medicina/las pastilles después de cada comida (dos veces al día/antes de acostarse). Take the medicine/ the pills after each meal (two times a day/ before going to bed).

Describing symptoms

Me duele la cabeza/la espalda, etc. I have a headache/backache, etc.
Me tiemblan las manos. My hands are shaking.
Necesito pastillas (contra fiebre, mareos, etc.). I need pills (for fever, dizziness, etc.).
Necesito una receta (unas aspirinas, un antibiótico, unas gotas, un jarabe). I need a prescription (aspirin, antibiotics, drops, cough syrup).

Invitations
Extending invitations

¿Le (Te) gustaría ir a...conmigo? Would you like to go to . . . with me?
¿Me quiere(s) acompañar a...? Do you want to accompany me to . . .?
¿Quiere(s) ir a...? Do you want to go to . . .?
Si tiene(s) tiempo, podemos ir a... If you have time, we could go to . . .

Accepting invitations

Sí, con mucho gusto. Yes, with pleasure.
Sí, me encantaría. Yes, I'd love to.
Sí, me gustaría mucho. Yes, I'd like to very much.

Declining invitations

Lo siento mucho, pero no puedo. I'm very sorry, but I can't.
Me gustaría, pero no puedo porque... I'd like to, but I can't because . . .

Making reservations and asking for information

¿Dónde hay...? Where is/are there . . .?
¿El precio incluye...? Does the price include . . .?
Quisiera reservar una habitación... I would like to reserve a room . . .

Opinons and suggestions

Asking for opinions

¿Cuál prefiere(s)? Which do you prefer?
Le (Te) gusta(n)...? Do you like . . .?
Le (Te) interesa(n)...? Are you interested in . . .?
¿Qué opina(s) de...? What's your opinion about . . .?
¿Qué piensa(s)? What do you think?
¿Qué le (te) parece(n)? How does/ do . . . seem to you?

Giving opinions

Creo que... I believe that . . .
Me gusta(n)... I like . . .
Me interesa(n)... I am interested in . . .
Me parece(n)... It seems . . . to me. (They seem . . . to me.)
Opino que... It's my opinion that . . .
Pienso que... I think that . . .
Prefiero... I prefer . . .

Adding information

A propósito/De paso... By the way . . .
Además... In addition . . .
También... Also . . .

Giving suggestions

Es bueno. It's good.
Es conveniente. It's convenient.
Es importante. It's important.
Es imprescindible. It's indispensable.
Es mejor. It's better.
Es necesario./Es preciso. It's necessary.
Es preferible. It's preferable.

Negating and contradicting

¡Imposible! Impossible!
¡Jamás!/¡Nunca! Never!
Ni hablar. Don't even mention it.
No es así. It's not like that.
No está bien. It's not all right.

Making requests

¿Me da(s)...? Will you give me . . .?
¿Me hace(s) el favor de...? Will you do me the favor of . . .?
¿Me pasa(s)...? Will you pass me . . .?
¿Me puede(s) dar...? Can you give me . . .?

¿Me puede(s) traer...? Can you bring me . . .?
¿Quiere(s) darme...? Do you want to give me . . .?
Sí, cómo no. Yes, of course.

In a restaurant

Ordering a meal in a restaurant

¿Cuánto es la entrada? How much is the cover charge?
¿Está incluida la propina? Is the tip included?
Me falta(n)... I need . . .
¿Me puede traer..., por favor? Can you please bring me . . .?
¿Puedo ver la carta/el menú/la lista de vinos? May I see the menu/the wine list?
¿Qué recomienda usted? What do you recommend?
¿Qué tarjetas de crédito aceptan? What credit cards do you accept?
Quisiera hacer una reserva para... I would like to make a reservation for . . .
¿Se necesitan reservaciones? Are reservations needed?
¿Tiene usted una mesa para...? Do you have a table for . . .
Tráigame la cuenta, por favor. Please bring me the check/bill.

Describing food

Contiene... It contains . . .
Es como... It's like . . .
Es dulce (agrio/agria, etc.)... It's sweet (bitter, etc.) . . .
Huele a... It smells like . . .
Sabe a... It tastes like . . .
Se parece a... It looks like . . .
Su textura es blanda/dura/cremosa, etc. Its texture is soft/hard/creamy, etc.

Shopping

Asking how much something costs and bargaining

¿Cuál es el precio de...? What's the price of . . .?
¿Cuánto cuesta...? How much is . . .?
El precio es... The price is . . .
Cuesta alrededor de...almes. It costs around . . . per month.

¿Cuánto cuestan? How much do they cost?
¿Cuánto cuesta(n)? How much does it (do they) cost?
¿Cuánto vale(n)? How much is it (are they) worth?
De acuerdo. Agreed. All right.
Es demasiado. It's too much.
Es una ganga. It's a bargain.
No más. No more.
No pago más de... I won't pay more than . . .
sólo only
última oferta final offer

Describing how clothing fits

Me queda bien./Me quedan bien. It fits me well./They fit me well.
Te queda mal./Te quedan mal. It fits you badly. They fit you badly.
Le queda bien./Le quedan bien. It fits him/her/you well. They fit him/her/ you well.

Getting someone's attention

con permiso excuse me
discúlpeme excuse me
oiga listen
perdón pardon
perdóneme pardon me

Expressing satisfaction and dissatisfaction

El color es horrible. The color is horrible.
El modelo es aceptable. The style is acceptable.
Es muy barato/barata. It's very inexpensive.
Es muy caro/cara. It's very expensive.
Me gusta el modelo. I like the style.

Thanking

De nada./Por nada./No hay de qué. It's nothing. You're welcome.
¿De verdad le (te) gusta? Do you really like it?
Estoy muy agradecido/agradecida. I'm very grateful.
Gracias. Thanks./Thank you.
Me alegro que le (te) guste. I'm glad you like it.
Mil gracias. Thanks a lot.
Muchas gracias. Thank you very much.
Muy amable de su (tu) parte. You're very kind.

This vocabulary includes all the words and expressions listed as active vocabulary in **Exporaciones.** The number following the definition refers to the chapter in which the word or phrase was first used actively. For example, an entry followed by **13** is first used actively in **Capítulo 13.** Nouns that end in **-o** are maculine and in **-a** are feminine unless unless otherwise indicated.

All words are alphabetized according to the 1994 changes made by the Real Academia: **ch** and **ll** are no longer considered separate letters of the alphabet.

Stem-changing verbs appear with the vowel change in parentheses after the infinitive: **(ie), (ue), (i), (ie, i), (e, i), (ue, u),** or **(i, i).** Most cognates, conjugated verb forms, and proper nouns used as passive vocabulary in the text are not included in this glossary.

The following abbreviations are used:

adj. adjective *n.* noun
adv. adverb *pl.* plural
art. article *pp.* past participle
conj. conjunction *poss.* possessive

dem. **demonstrative** *prep.* **preposition**
dir. obj. **direct object** *pron.* **pronoun**
f. feminine *refl.* reflexive
f. feminine

form. formal *s.* singular
indir. obj. indirect object *subj.* subject
interj. interjection *v.* verb
m. masculine

A

a to, at; **a causa de** on account of; **a cuadros** checkered; plaid (11); **a diferencia de** unlike; in contrast to; **a fin de que** so (that) (14); in order to (14); **a la derecha (de)** to the right (of) (4); **a la izquierda (de)** to the left (of) (4); **a lo largo (de)** along; **a lunares** polka-dotted; **a menos que** unless (14); **a menudo** frequently, often; **a pesar de** in spite of; **a propósito** by the way; **a rayas** striped (11); **a tiempo completo** full-time; **a tiempo** on time (10); **a tiempo parcial** part-time; **a veces** at times; **a ver** let's see; **al contrario** on the contrary; **al contrario de** unlike; **al día** per day; **al fin y al cabo** after all; when all is said and done; **al final** in the end; **al fondo (de)** in (the) back (of); **al horno** baked (7); **al igual que** like; **al lado (de)** alongside (of); beside, next to (4); **al mes** per month; **al principio** at the beginning
abajo *adv.* below; **abajo de** under
abdomen *m.* abdomen
abogado(a) lawyer (5); attorney
abordar to board (10); **pase** *m.* **de abordar** boarding pass
abrazar (c) to hug (13)
abrigo coat (3)
abril *m.* April (3)
abrir to open (3)
abstracto(a) abstract; **arte** *m.* **abstracto** abstract art (11)
abuelo(a) grandfather/grandmother (2)
aburrido(a) bored (5); boring (1)
aburrirse to become bored (9)
acabar to finish (11); **acabar de (+ *inf.*)** to have just (*done something*)
acampar to go camping
acaso perhaps
acción *f.* action
aceite *m.* oil
aceituna olive
aceptar to accept
acera sidewalk (9)
acercarse (qu) to approach
acompañar to accompany
acondicionado(a): aire acondicionado *m.* air-conditioning
acontecimiento event
acostarse (ue) to lie down (6); to go to bed (6)
actividad activity
actor *m.* actor (5)
actriz *f.* actress (5)
actual current
acuerdo agreement; **de acuerdo** agreed, all right; **estar de acuerdo** to agree
adelgazar (c) to lose weight

además besides; furthermore; in addition
adiós good-bye (1)
adjetivo adjective
administración *f.* **de empresas** business and management
adolescencia adolescence (13)
adolescente *m. f.* adolescent (13)
¿adónde? to where? (3)
aduana customs (10); **agente de aduana** customs official
adulto adult (13)
aéreo(a) *adj.* air; **línea aérea** airline
aerolínea airline
aeropuerto (internacional) (international) airport (10)
afeitarse to shave (6)
aficionado(a) fan (6)
afuera *adv.* outside
agasajado(a) guest of honor
agenda date book, agenda
agente *m. f.* agent; **agente de aduana** customs official; **agente de seguridad** security agent (10); **agente de viajes** travel agent (5)
agosto August (3)
agradecido(a) grateful
agregar (gu) to add (8)
agresivo(a) aggressive (1)
agua *f.* (*but* **el agua**) water; **esquiar en el agua** to water ski
aguacate *m.* avocado
águila *f.* (*but* **el águila**) eagle
ahí there
ahora now; **hasta ahora** up to now, so far
aire acondicionado *m.* air-conditioning
ajedrez *m.* chess (8)
ajo garlic
alberca swimming pool
albergue estudiantil *m.* youth hostel
alegrarse to become happy (9)
alegre happy (5)
alemán *m.* German (*language*) (2)
alergia allergy (14)
alfombra carpet (4); rug
álgebra *m.* algebra
algo something (6); **algo que declarar** something to declare
algodón *m.* cotton (11)
alguien someone, somebody (6)
algún/alguno(a) some (6)
aliviar to relieve, alleviate
allá over there (11)
allí there (11)
almacén *m.* department store
almohada pillow
almorzar (ue) (c) to have lunch (4)
almuerzo lunch (7)
aló hello (*telephone response in some countries*)
alojamiento lodging (7)
alojarse to lodge (7), to stay (*in a hotel*) (7)

alpinismo mountain climbing (6); **hacer alpinismo** to climb mountains (6)
alquilar to rent (4)
alto(a) high; tall (1); **presión** *f.* **alta** high blood pressure (14)
amable kind (1)
amarillo(a) yellow (3)
ambiente *m.* atmosphere, environment
ambulancia ambulance (9)
americano: fútbol americano football (6)
amigo(a) friend (2)
amo(a) de casa homemaker (5)
anaranjado(a) orange (3)
ándale there you go
andar to walk (6); **andar en bicicleta** to ride a bike (6)
andén *m.* platform (10)
anfibio amphibian (12)
anfitrión(-ona) host
anillo ring (13)
animado(a) excited; **dibujos animados** cartoons (13)
ánimo encouragement
aniversario (wedding) anniversary (9)
anoche last night (6)
ante todo first of all, first and foremost
anteayer the day before yesterday
anterior before, prior
antes previously; **antes de** (+ *inf.*) before (*doing something*) (6); **antes (de) que** before
antibiótico antibiotic
antipático(a) unfriendly (1)
antropología anthropology
anuncio comercial commercial (13)
añadir to add
año year; **el año pasado** last year; **los quince años** girl's fifteenth birthday celebration (9); **tener... años** to be . . . years old (2)
apagar (gu) to turn off (11)
aparcamiento parking lot
apartamento apartment (4)
apio celery
aplicarse (qu) to apply
apreciar to appreciate (11); to enjoy (11)
aprender (a +*inf.*) to learn (*to do something*) (3)
apretado(a) tight (11)
aprobar (ue) to approve
aquel(la) *adj.* that (over there)
aquél(la) *pron.* that (one) (over there)
aquello *pron.* that (one)
aquellos(as) *adj.* those (over there)
aquéllos(as) *pron.* those (over there)
aquí here (11); **hasta aquí** up to now, so far
árbol *m.* tree (12); **trepar un árbol** to climb a tree (8)
ardilla squirrel (12)
arena sand (12)

arete *m.* earring
argentino(a) Argentine (14)
árido(a) dry, arid
armario closet, armoire (4)
arquitecto(a) architect (5)
arquitectura architecture
arreglar to arrange; **arreglarse** to get ready (6)
arriba up (with)
arroz *m.* rice (7)
arte *m.* art (2); **arte abstracto** abstract art (11); **arte dramático** theater; **artes marciales** *f. pl.* martial arts; **bellas artes** *f. pl.* fine arts
arterial: presión *f.* **arterial** blood pressure
artesanías handicrafts
artículo article; **artículos de limpieza** cleaning materials
artista *m. f.* artist
asado(a) grilled (7)
ascensor *m.* elevator (7)
así like this, thus, in this manner; **así es** that's so; **así que** thus, therefore; **¿no es así?** isn't that so?
asiento seat (10)
asistente *m. f.* **de vuelo** flight attendant (5); **asistir (a)** to attend (3)
aspiradora vacuum cleaner; **pasar la aspiradora** to vacuum (10)
aspirante *m. f.* job candidate
aspirina aspirin (14)
astronomía astronomy
asustado(a) scared (5)
asustarse to become frightened (9)
atención *f.* attention
atender (ie) a to wait on; to attend to; to pay attention to (*other people*)
aterrizar (c) to land (10)
ático small attic apartment
atleta *m. f.* athlete
atlético(a) athletic (1)
atracción *f.* attraction; **parque** *m.* **de atracciones** amusement park
atrasado(a) late; **estar atrasado(a)** to be late
atravesar (ie) to cross (9)
atropellar to run over (9)
atún *m.* tuna
audiencia audience (13)
audífonos headphones (13)
aumento increase
aunque although, though
auto car
autobús *m.* bus; **estación** *f.* **de autobuses** bus station
autorretrato self-portrait (11)
auxilio help; **primeros auxilios** first aid (14)
ave *f.* (*but* **el ave**) poultry; bird (12)
avergonzado(a) embarrassed (5)
avión *m.* plane
ayer yesterday (6)
ayudar to help (2)
ayuntamiento city hall
azafata *f.* flight attendant
azúcar *m.* sugar (7)
azul blue (3)
azulejo tile

B

bádminton *m.* badminton (6)
bahía bay (12)
bailar to dance (2)
bailarín/bailarina dancer
bajar de to get out of (*a vehicle*) (9)
bajo(a) short (1); **presión** *f.* **baja** low blood pressure (14)
balcón *m.* balcony
ballena whale (12)
balneario spa
balón *m.* (volley)ball

baloncesto basketball
banco bank (4)
bandera flag (1)
bañarse to bathe (6); to take a bath; to shower (*Mex.*) (6)
bañera bathtub (4)
baño bath; bathtub; bathroom (4); **traje de baño** bathing suit
bar *m.* bar (4)
barato(a) inexpensive, cheap (11)
barbilla chin
barco ship, boat
barrer to sweep (10)
básquetbol *m.* basketball (6)
basura trash, garbage, litter (10); **bote** *m.* **de basura** trashcan (10); **sacar (qu) la basura** to take the trash out (10)
batido(a) whipped; **crema batida** whipped cream
batir to beat (8)
bautizo baptism (9)
beber to drink (3)
bebida drink (7)
béisbol *m.* baseball (6)
bellas artes *f. pl.* fine arts
beneficios benefits
besar to kiss (13)
biblioteca library (4)
bibliotecario(a) librarian
bicicleta bicycle; **andar en bicicleta** to ride a bike (6)
bien fine (1); well; **llevarse bien** to get along well (13); **pasarlo bien** to have a good time; **¡qué bien te queda esa falda!** that skirt really fits you well! (11); **sentirse (e, i) bien** to feel well
billete *m.* ticket
biología biology (2)
birth nacimiento (13)
bisabuela great grandmother
bisabuelo great grandfather
blanco(a) white (3); **vino blanco** white wine (7)
blando(a) soft
blusa blouse (3)
bluyíns *m., pl.* blue jeans (3)
boca mouth (6)
bocadillo snack (9)
boda wedding (9)
boleto ticket (10)
bolígrafo pen (1)
boliviano(a) Bolivian (14)
bolsa bag; purse (11); handbag
bolso bag; beach bag; purse (11); handbag
bombero(a) firefighter; **estación** *f.* **de bomberos** fire station
bonito(a) pretty (1); **¡qué color tan bonito!** what a pretty color! (11)
borracho(a) drunk (5)
borrador *m.* (chalk) eraser
bosque *m.* forest (12); wood(s)
bota boot (3)
bote *m.* **de basura** trashcan (10)
botella bottle
botones *m. f., sing. pl.* bellhop (7)
brazo arm (6)
brillante bright, shiny
brindar to toast (9)
brindis *m.* toast (*with a drink*) (9)
brócoli *m.* broccoli (8)
bucear con tubo de respiración to snorkel
bucear to scuba dive (6)
buen/bueno(a) good (1); **buen provecho** enjoy your meal; **buenas noches** good night (1); **buenas tardes** good afternoon (1); **buenos días** good morning (1); **hace buen tiempo** it's nice weather (3); **¡que tengas un buen día!** have a nice day (1)
bufanda scarf (3)

burro ironing board
buscador *m.* search engine (13)
buscar (qu) to look for (2)
butaca seat (*theater*) (13)

C

caballero gentleman
caballo horse (2); **montar a caballo** to ride horseback
cabello hair
caber to fit; **no cabe duda** there can be no doubt
cabeza head (6); **me duele la cabeza** I have a headache
cablevisión *f.* cablevision (13)
cabo: al fin y al cabo after all; when all is said and done
cactus *m.* cactus
cada each, every
cadera hip
caer(se) to fall (9)
café *m.* coffee (7); café (4); brown (3); **tomar café** to drink coffee
cafetera coffee maker (4)
cafetería cafeteria
caja cash register (11)
calabacita zucchini
calabaza squash; pumpkin
calcetines *m. pl.* socks (3)
calculadora calculator
cálculo calculus
calefacción *f.* heat
caliente warm, hot
calle *f.* street (4)
calor *m.* warmth; heat; **hace calor** it's hot; **tener (mucho) calor** to be (very) hot (2)
calvo(a) bald (1)
cama bed (4); **cama matrimonial** double bed; **coche** *m.* **cama** sleeping car (10); **hacer la cama** to make the bed (10)
camarero(a) (hotel) maid (7)
camarón *m.* shrimp (7)
cambiar to change
cambio change; **en cambio** on the other hand
camilla stretcher (9)
caminar to walk (2)
camisa shirt (3)
camiseta T-shirt (3)
campo field (6)
cáncer *m.* cancer (14)
cancha court (*sports*) (6)
cangrejo crab
canicas *pl.* marbles (8)
cansado(a) tired (5)
cantante *m. f.* singer (5)
cantar to sing (2)
cara face (6)
característica characteristic
¡caray! oh!; oh no!
cariñoso(a) loving (1)
carne *f.* meat (7); **carne de res** beef; **carne de vacuno** beef
carnicería butcher shop
caro(a) expensive (11); **¡qué caro(a)!** how expensive! (11)
carretera highway
carrito toy car (8)
carta letter (4); menu; *pl.* playing cards (8)
cartel *m.* poster (1)
cartera billfold, wallet
casa house
casarse (con) to get married to (9)
cascada waterfall (*small*) (12)
caso: en caso (de) (que) in case (that) (14)
catarata waterfall (12)
catarro cold (*illness*) (14)
catedral *f.* cathedral
catorce fourteen (1)

catsup *m.* ketchup (8)
causa cause; **a causa de** on account of
causar to cause
caza hunting (12)
cazar (c) to hunt (12)
CD *m.* CD; **reproductor de CDs** CD player (13)
cebolla onion (8)
cebra zebra (12)
ceja eyebrow
celebrar to celebrate (9)
celos *m. pl.* jealousy; **tener celos** to be jealous
celoso(a) jealous (5)
cena dinner (7)
cenar to eat dinner (7)
censurar to censor (13)
centro center; **centro comercial** shopping center
cepillarse to brush (6)
cerca (de) close (to) (4)
cerdo pork (7); pig (12)
cerebro brain (14)
ceremonia ceremony (13); **maestro(a) de ceremonias** master of ceremony
cereza cherry
cero zero (1)
cerrar (ie) to close (3); to shut
cerro hill
certeza certainty
cerveza beer (7)
césped *m.* lawn; **cortar el césped** to mow the lawn (10)
cesta basket
ceviche (cebiche) *m. raw fish marinated in lime juice*
chaleco vest (3)
chalet *m.* villa
champán *m.* champagne (9)
champú *m.* shampoo (6)
chao good-bye (1)
chaqueta jacket (3)
charlar to chat
charlatán(-ana) gossipy
chatear to chat (*online*) (13)
cheque *m.* check; **cheque de viaje** traveler's check; **cheque de viajero** traveler's check
chico(a) child; *adj.* small (11)
chileno(a) Chilean (14)
chimenea fireplace
chismear to gossip
chiste *m.* joke (8)
chocar (qu) (con) to crash (*into something*) (9)
ciclista *m. f.* cyclist (9)
cielo sky (12)
cien/ciento one hundred (1) (7); **cien mil** (one) hundred thousand; **cien millones** (one) hundred million; **ciento uno** one hundred one (1) (7)
ciencias *f. pl.* science; **ciencias de la computación** computer science; **ciencias de la pedagogía** education; **ciencias económicas** economics; **ciencias naturales** natural science (2); **ciencias políticas** political science (2); **ciencias sociales** social science (2)
científico(a) scientist (5)
cierto(a) *adj.* sure, certain, true; *adv.* certainly, surely; **¿cierto?** right?
cinco five (1)
cincuenta fifty (1)
cine *m.* movie theater (4); cinema
cintura waist
cinturón *m.* belt (3); **cinturón de seguridad** safety (seat) belt (10)
circo circus
cirugía surgery (14)
cita date (13)

ciudadano(a) citizen (14)
civil civil
claro(a) *adj.* sure; clear; *adv.* certainly, surely; **claro que no** of course not; **claro que sí** certainly, surely, of course
clase *f.* class; **compañero(a) de clase** classmate (2); **hotel de primera clase** first-class hotel; **primera clase** first class (10); **salón** *m.* **de clase** classroom (1); **segunda clase** second class (10)
clásico(a) classic
clasificación *f.* TV rating (13)
clic: hacer clic (en) to click on (13)
clínica clinic
club *m.* club (4)
coche *m.* car; **coche cama** sleeping car (10)
cocina kitchen (4); **papel de cocina** paper towel
cocinar to cook (2)
cocinero(a) cook
cocodrilo crocodile (12)
coctel *m.* cocktail (7)
codo elbow (6)
cognado cognate
cola line, queue; **hacer cola** to stand in line
coleccionar to collect
colega *m. f.* colleague
colegio school (*secondary*)
colgar (ue) to hang (10)
colina hill (12)
collar *m.* necklace
colmo height; **¡esto es el colmo!** this is the last straw!
colombiano(a) Colombian (14)
color *m.* color; **¡qué color tan bonito!** what a pretty color! (11)
columna vertebral spinal column
comedor *m.* dining room (4)
comenzar (ie) (c) to begin (3); to start
comer to eat (3) (5)
comerciante *m. f.* merchant
comercio: tratado de comercio trade agreement (14)
comestibles *m. pl.* groceries
cometa kite (8)
cómico(a) funny (1); **tira cómica** comic strip (8)
comida meal; food (7); lunch (7)
comercial: anuncio comercial commercial (13); **centro comercial** shopping center
como like, as; **como consecuencia** as a consequence; **como resultado** as a result
¿cómo? how? (3); what?; **¿cómo está usted?** how are you (*form.*) (1); **¿cómo estás?** how are you (*fam.*) (1); **cómo no** of course
cómoda chest of drawers; bureau
compañero(a) companion, significant other, partner; **compañero(a) de clase** classmate (2); **compañero(a) de cuarto** roommate
comparación *f.* comparison
comparado(a) con compared with
comparar to compare
compartir to share
compasión *f.* sympathy
competencia competition
competición *f.* competition
competir (i, i) to compete (3)
completar to complete; to fill out
completo(a) complete; **a tiempo completo** full-time; **pensión** *f.* **completa** full board
complicado(a) complex (11)
componer to repair
comprar to buy (2)
comprender to understand (3)

comprobante *m.* voucher, credit slip
comprometerse (con) to get engaged (to) (13)
compromiso engagement (13)
computación: ciencias de la computación computer science
computadora computer (1)
con with; **con mucho gusto** with pleasure; **con tal (de) que** provided (that) (14)
concierto concert
concluir (y) to conclude
conclusión *f.* conclusión; **en conclusión** in conclusion
concurso contest; game show (13)
condición *f.* condition
condimentos condiments
condolencias condolences
condominio condominium
conducir (zc) to drive (5)
conductor(a) driver (9); TV host (13)
conejo rabbit (12)
conexión *f.* connection (10)
conferencia lecture
confirmar to confirm
confundido(a) (5)
conjunción *f.* conjunction
conjunto outfit
conmigo with me
conocer (zc) to know (5); to be acquainted with (5)
conocimiento knowledge
consecuencia consequence; **como consecuencia** as a consequence
conseguir (i, i) to get, obtain
consejero(a) adviser
conserje *m. f.* concierge
conservador(a) conservative (1) (11)
construir (y) to build, construct
consultar to look up (a webpage, a text, etc.); to consult
consultorio doctor's office
contabilidad *f.* accounting
contable *m. f.* accountant
contador(a) accountant (5)
contaminación pollution (12); contamination (12)
contar (ue) to count (8); to tell a story (8)
contener (*like* **tener**) to contain
contento(a) happy (5)
contestar to answer
continente *m.* continent
contra against
contradecir to contradict
contrario(a) opposite, contrary; **al contrario** on the contrary; **al contrario de** unlike
contraste *m.* contrast
control *m.* control; **control de pasaporte** passport control; **control de seguridad** security check; **control remoto** remote control (13)
conveniente convenient
conversación *f.* conversation
copa wine glass (7)
corazón *m.* heart (14)
corbata tie (3)
cordero lamb
cordillera mountain range
correcto(a) that's right
correo mail; post office (4); **oficina de correos** post office
correr to run (3); **pista de correr** track
cortacésped *m.* lawnmower (10)
cortar to cut (8); **cortarse** to cut (oneself) (6) (14); **cortar el césped** to cut, to mow the lawn (10)
cortina curtain
corto(a) short (1); **pantalones** *m. pl.* **cortos** shorts

cosa thing
costa coast (12)
costar (ue) to cost (4)
costarricense m. f. Costa Rican (14)
costoso(a) expensive
coyuntura join
crédito credit; tarjeta de crédito credit card
(11)
creer to believe (3); to think
crema cream (8); crema batida whipped
cream
cremoso(a) creamy
criminología criminology (2)
cruce m. crosswalk (9)
crucigrama m. crossword puzzle
cruel cruel (1)
cruzar (c) to cross (9)
cuaderno notebook (1)
cuadro square; painting (4); picture (4);
a cuadros checkered; plaid (11)
¿cuál(es)? which? (3)
cuando when
¿cuándo? when? (3)
cuanto: en cuanto as soon as (14)
¿cuánto(a)? how much? (3)
¿cuántos(as)? how many? (3)
cuarenta forty (1)
cuarto quarter (of an hour); room; cuarto
de baño bathroom; cuarto oscuro
darkroom; compañero(a) de cuarto
roommate
cuarto(a) adj. fourth (4)
cuatro four (1)
cuatrocientos(as) four hundred (7)
cubano(a) Cuban (14)
cubanoamericano(a) Cuban-American
cubierto(a) covered
cubiertos m. pl. table setting; cutlery
cubista m. f. cubist (11)
cuchara soupspoon (7)
cucharita teaspoon
cuchillo knife (7)
cuello neck (6)
cuenta bill (restaurant)(7); check
cuento story (8)
cuerda jumping rope (8)
cuero leather
cuerpo body
cuidado care; tener (mucho) cuidado to
be (very) careful (2)
cuidar (de) to take care (of)
culpa fault
cultivar el jardín to garden (flowers)
cumpleañero(a) birthday boy (girl)
cumpleaños m. sing., pl. birthday (3) (9);
fiesta de cumpleaños birthday party
cuñado(a) brother-in-law/sister-in-law (2)
curita small adhesive bandage (14)
curso term (2)
cutis m. complexion
cuyo(a), cuyos(as) whose

D

dama lady; pl. checkers (8)
dañado(a) damaged; estar dañado(a) to be
damaged (9)
dañar to damage
dar to give (5); dar a luz to give birth (13);
darse cuenta de to realize
de of, from; de acuerdo agreed, all right; de
diamantes (of) diamonds; ¿de dónde
eres tú? were are you (fam.) from? (1);
¿de dónde? from where? (3); de flores
floral; flowered; de ida one-way; de ida
y vuelta round-trip; de la mañana a.m.;
de la noche p.m.; de la tarde p.m.; de
lunares polka-dotted (11); de moda
fashionable (11); de nuevo new; again;
de paso by the way; de repente suddenly

(9); ¿de veras? really, is that so?; de verdad
really; del mismo modo similarly
debajo (de) below; under (4)
deber (+ inf.) should/ought to (do something)
(3)
décimo(a) tenth (4)
decir to say (5); to tell (5); querer decir to mean
declarar to declare; algo que declarar something to declare
decoración m. decoration (9)
dedo finger (6); dedo del pie toe (6)
definido(a) definite
deforestación f. deforestation (12)
dejar to leave; dejar una propina to leave a
tip (7)
delante (de) in front (of)
delantero(a) front
delgado(a) thin (1)
delicioso(a) delicious
demasiado(a) too, too much
dentista m. f. dentist
dentrífico toothpaste (6)
dentro (de) inside (of) (4)
dependiente(a) clerk (5)
deportes m. pl. sports; practicar (qu)
deportes to play sports (2)
deportivo(a) related to sports, sporting
depositar to deposit
depresión f. depression
deprimido(a) depressed (5)
derecha right; a la derecha (de) to the right
(of) (4)
derecho law; right; derechos humanos
human rights (14); seguir (i) derecho to
go straight (10)
desacuerdo disagreement
desastre m. disaster
desayunar to eat breakfast (7)
desayuno breakfast (7)
descomponer to break down (a machine) (11)
describir to describe
descripción f. description
descriptivo(a) descriptive
desear to wish (2) (13); to desire (13);
to want
desembarcar (qu) to deplane
desempleado(a) unemployed
desempleo unemployment (14)
desfile m. parade (9)
deshacer la maleta to unpack one's suitcase
deshechos industriales industrial waste (12)
desierto desert (12)
desmayarse to faint (14)
desmayo faint (14)
despacio slowly
despedida farewell; despedida de soltera
bridal shower; despedida de soltero bachelor party
despedir (i, i) to fire; despedirse to say good-
bye
despegar (gu) to take off (10)
despejado(a) clear (weather)
despertador m. alarm clock (6)
despertarse (ie) to wake up (6)
después then, next; después de (que) after
(14); después de (+ inf.) after (doing something) (6)
destino destination
destruir (y) to destroy (5) (12)
desván m. attic
detergente m. para platos dish detergent
detrás (de) in back (of); behind (4)
devolver (ue) to return (something) (4)
día m. day (3); al día per day; día de santo
saint's day; día festivo holiday; ¡que tengas
un buen día! have a nice day (1); todos los
días every day (3)
diabetes f. diabetes (14)
diario(a) daily

diarrea diarrhea (14)
dibujar to draw (8)
dibujos animados cartoons (13)
diccionario dictionary (1)
diciembre m. December (3)
diecinueve nineteen (1)
dieciocho eighteen (1)
dieciséis sixteen (1)
diecisiete seventeen (1)
diente m. tooth (6)
diez ten (1)
diferencia difference; a diferencia de
unlike; in contrast to
diferente different; diferente de unlike
digestión f. digestion
dinero money (4)
Dios m. God; Dios mío oh, my goodness
dirección f. direction; address
directo(a) direct
discoteca nightclub (4)
disculparse to excuse oneself
diseñador(a) designer (5)
diseñar to design (11)
disfrutar to enjoy
disponible available (7)
distraerse to get distracted (9)
diversión f. entertainment; hobby, pastime
divertido(a) funny (5); fun
divertirse (ie, i) to have fun (6)
divorciarse (de) to divorce (13)
doblar to bend; to turn (10)
doble double (7); habitación doble double
room
doce twelve (1)
docena dozen
doctor(a) doctor
documental m. documentary (13)
doler (ue) to hurt (14); me duele la cabeza
I have a headache
dolor m. pain(14); ache; dolor de garganta
sore throat; dolor muscular muscle ache
doméstico(a) domestic, household
domingo m. Sunday (3)
dominicano(a) Dominican (14)
dominó sing. dominos (8)
donde where (3)
¿dónde? where; ¿de dónde? from where?
(3); ¿de dónde eres tú? where are you
(fam.) from? (1)
dormir (ue, u) to sleep (4) (5); dormirse
(ue, u) to fall asleep (6); saco de dormir
sleeping bag (6)
dormitorio bedroom (4)
dos two (1)
doscientos(as) two hundred (7)
dramático(a) dramatic; arte m. dramático
theater
ducha shower (4)
ducharse to shower (6)
duda doubt; no cabe duda there can be no
doubt
dudar to doubt (12)
dudoso(a) doubtful
dulce sweet; salsa de tomate dulce tomato
sauce; ketchup; n. pl. candies (9)
durazno peach (8)
duro(a) tough, hard

E

ecología ecology (12)
economía economics ; economy (2)
económico(a) adj. economical; inexpensive; ciencias económicas economics;
hotel m. económico inexpensive hotel
ecuatoguineano Ecuatorial Guinean (14)
ecuatoriano(a) Ecuadorian (14)
edificio building (4)
efectivo cash (11)
efecto effect

eficiente efficient

egoísta selfish (1)

ejemplo example; **por ejemplo** for example

ejercicio exercise; **ejercicios aeróbicos** aerobics

el *def. art. m.* the; **el cual(es)** which, whom; **el que** that, which, whom, the one

él *sub. pron.* he

electrodoméstico electrical (household) appliance (4)

elefante *m.* elephant (12)

elegante elegant; **¡qué pantalones tan elegantes!** what elegant pants! (11)

elegir (i, i) (j) to elect; to choose

ella she

embarazada pregnant; **estar embarazada** to be pregnant (13)

embargo: sin embargo nevertheless; however

emergencia: sala de emergencias emergency room (14)

emigración *f.* emigration (14)

emigrar to emigrate (14)

emisora de radio radio station

emoción *f.* emotion

empatar to tie (*score*)

empezar (ie) (c) to begin (3); to start; **para empezar** to begin with

empresa firm, business; **administración** *f.* **de empresas** business and management

en in; on; at; **en cambio** on the other hand; **en caso (de) (que)** in case (that) (14); **en conclusión** in conclusion; **en particular** in particular; **en principio** in principle; **en resumen** in summary; **en suma** in conclusion; **en venta** on sale; **en voz alta** aloud

enamorado(a) (de) in love (*with*) (5)

encantado(a) delighted; nice to meet you (1)

encantador(a) enchanting

encantar to love, to be delighted

encerrar (ie) to lock up

encima (de) on top (of) (4)

encontrar (ue) to find (4)

enero January (3)

enfermero(a) nurse (5)

enfermo(a) sick (5)

enfrente (de) in front (of) (4)

engordar to gain weight

enojado(a) angry (5)

enojarse to become angry (9)

ensalada salad (7)

enseñar to teach (2)

entender (ie) to understand (3)

entonces then, next

entrada entrance; cover charge; ticket (6)

entrar to enter

entre among; between (4)

entregar (gu) to hand in, hand over

entremés *m.* appetizer (7)

entrenador(a) coach

entrenar to train, to coach

entreplanta loft

entrevista interview (5)

entusiasta enthusiastic

envolver (ue) to wrap

equipaje *m.* luggage (10); **facturar equipaje** to check luggage (10); **reclamo de equipaje** baggage claim (10); **revisión** *f.* **de equipaje** luggage screening (10)

equipo team (6); equipment (6); **equipo escolar** school supplies

equivocado(a) wrong (5)

equivocarse (qu) to make a mistake

escala layover (10); **hacer escala** to make a stop, layover

escalera stairs (7)

escoba broom (10)

escolar *adj.* school; **equipo escolar** school supplies

escondidas *f.* hide and seek (8)

escribir (un mensaje) to write (a message) (3)

escritor(a) writer (5)

escritorio desk; teacher's desk (1)

escuchar to listen (2)

escuela school (4)

esculpir to sculpt (11)

escultura sculpture (11)

ese(a) *adj.* that

ése(a) *pron.* that (one)

esmog *m.* smog (12)

eso *pron.* that (one); **por eso** therefore

esos(as) *adj.* those

ésos(as) *pron.* those

espalda back (6)

espanto fright

España Spain

español *m.* Spanish (*language*)

español(a) *m.* (*f.*) native of Spain; *adj.* Spanish (14)

especial special

espejo mirror

espera: sala de espera waiting room (10)

esperar to hope (for) (13); to expect; to wait

espinaca spinach

esponja sponge

esposo(a) husband/wife; spouse (2)

esqueleto skeleton (14)

esquí acuático *m.* water-skiing

esquiar to ski (2); **esquiar en el agua** to water ski (6); **esquiar en tabla** to snowboard (6)

esquina corner (9)

estación *f.* station; season; **estación de autobuses** bus station; **estación de bomberos** fire station; **estación de ferrocarril** train station; **estación de policía** police station

estacionar to park (9)

estadio stadium

Estados Unidos United States

estadounidense *m. f.* citizen of the United States

estampado(a) patterned (11)

estante *m.* shelf

estar to be (5); **¿cómo está usted?** how are you (*form.*) (1); **¿cómo estás?** how are you (*fam.*)? (1); **estar embarazada** to be pregnant (13); **estar atrasado(a)** to be late; **estar dañado(a)** to be damaged (9); **estar de acuerdo** to agree; **estar de moda** to be in style; **estar herido(a)** to be injured (9); **estar mareado(a)** to be dizzy (14); **está lloviendo** it's raining; **está nevando** it's snowing; **está nublado** it is cloudy (3); **está despejado** it is clear (3); **fuera de** outside of (4)

estatura height

este(a) *adj.* this

éste(a) *pron.* this (one)

estilográfico(a): pluma estilográfica fountain pen

estirarse to stretch (6)

esto *pron.* this (one); **¡esto es el colmo!** this is the last straw!

estómago stomach (6)

estornudar to sneeze (14)

estornudo sneeze (14)

estos(as) adj. these

éstos(as) *pron.* these

estrecho strait

estreñimiento constipation

estudiante *m. f.* student (1)

estudiantil *adj.* student; **albergue estudiantil** *m.* youth hostel

estudiar to study (2)

estudio efficiency apartment, studio

estufa stove (4)

estupendo(a) stupendous

evidente evident

exacto(a) exactly

examen *m.* exam (2); **examen médico** medical examination

examinar to examine (14)

exclamación *f.* exclamation

excursión: ir de excursión to hike (6)

excusarse to make an excuse

exhibición *f.* exhibition (11)

exhibir to exhibit (11)

éxito success; **éxito de taquilla** box office hit (13); **tener (mucho) éxito** to be (very) successful (2)

experiencia experience

expresar to express

expresión *f.* expression; **expresión oral** speech (2)

extinción: peligro de extinción danger of extinction (12)

extranjero: al extranjero abroad

extranjero(a) foreigner

extrañar to miss (13)

extremidad *f.* extremity

extrovertido(a) extrovert

F

fábrica factory

fabuloso(a) fabulous

fácil easy (1)

facturar equipaje to check luggage (10)

facultad *f.* school, college

falda skirt (3); **¡qué bien te queda esa falda!** that skirt really fits you well! (11)

falso(a) false

falta lack

familia family

famoso(a) famous (1)

farmacéutico(a) pharmacist

farmacia pharmacy (4)

fascinante fascinating

fascinar to fascinate, be fascinated by

fatal fatal

favor *m.* favor; **por favor** please

favorito(a) favorite

febrero February (3)

fecha date (*calendar*) (3)

felicitar to congratulate

feliz happy (5); **ponerse feliz** to become happy

femenino(a) feminine

feminista feminist

fenomenal phenomenal

feo(a) ugly (1)

ferrocarril *m.* railroad **estación** *f.* **de ferrocarril** train station

festejado(a) guest of honor

festejar to entertain, to celebrate

festival *m.* festival

festivo: día *m.* **festivo** holiday

fiambre *m.* luncheon meat, cold cut

fiebre *f.* fever

fiesta party; **fiesta de canastilla** baby shower; **fiesta de cumpleaños** birthday party; **fiesta sorpresa** surprise party

filosofía philosophy (2); **filosofía y letras** liberal arts

fin *m.* end; **fin de semana** weekend (3); **a fin de que** so (that) (14); in order that (14); **al fin y al cabo** after all; when all is said and done; **por fin** finally

final *m.* end; **al final** in the end

finalmente finally

física physics (2)

físico(a) physical

flan *m.* flan (7)

flojo(a) loose

flor *f.* flower (4); **de flores** floral, flowered

fluorescente fluorescent

forma shape; **mantenerse** (*like* **tener**) **en forma** to stay fit, keep in shape
formar to form
foto *f.* photo(graph); **revelar fotos** to develop photos; **sacar (qu) fotos** to take photos
fotógrafo(a) photographer (5)
fractura broken bone; fracture (14)
fracturarse to fracture (14)
francés *m.* French (*language*) (2)
frase *f.* phrase
fregadero kitchen sink (4)
fregar (ie) (gu) to mop; to scrub
freír (í, i) to fry (8)
frente a facing
frente *f.* forehead
fresa strawberry (8)
fresco(a) fresh, cool; **hace fresco** it's cool (*weather*)
frijol *m.* bean
frío(a) cold; **hace frío** it's cold (*weather*); **tener (mucho) frío** to be (very) cold (2)
frito(a) fried (7)
frustrado(a) frustrated (5)
frustrarse to become frustrated (9)
fruta fruit (7)
frutería fruit store
fuego fire; **fuegos artificiales** fireworks (9)
fuente *f.* soup bowl
fuera (de) outside (of) (4)
funeral *m.* funeral
furioso(a) furious
fútbol *m.* soccer (6); **fútbol americano** football
futbolista *m. f.* football (soccer) player

G

gafas *pl.* glasses; **gafas de sol** sunglasses
galería gallery (11)
gallina hen (12)
gallo rooster (12)
gamba shrimp
gana desire, wish; **tener ganas de** (+ *inf.*) to feel like (*doing something*)
ganar to earn (5); to win
ganga bargain
garaje *m.* garage (4)
garganta throat; **dolor** *m.* **de garganta** sore throat; **inflamación** *f.* **de la garganta** strep throat
gastar to spend
gato(a) cat (2)
gemelo(a) twin
general: por lo general generally
generalmente generally
generoso(a) generous (1)
gente *f.* people
geografía geography (2)
geología geology
geometría geometry
gerente *m. f.* manager
gimnasio gym(nasium) (4)
gis *m.* chalk
globalización *f.* globalization (14)
globo balloon (9)
golf *m.* golf (6)
golfo gulf
golosina candy (13)
goma (pencil) eraser
gordo(a) fat (1); plump
gorila gorilla (12)
gorra cap
gorro cap (3)
gota drop (14)
grabado engraving (11); print (11)
grabadora tape recorder
gracias thanks, thank you
gracioso(a) funny; charming
graduación *f.* graduation (9)
gran/grande great; big (1); large (11)

granja farm (12)
gripe *f.* flu (14)
gris gray (3)
grupo group; **grupo de música** musical group (9); band (9)
guante *m.* glove (3)
guapo(a) handsome (1)
guardar to keep; to put away (10)
guatemalteco(a) Guatemalan (14)
guerra war (14)
guineano(a) Guinean
guisante *m.* pea
gustar to like; to please; to be pleasing; **me gusta** I like (3); **le gusta** he/she likes (3); **te gusta** you (*fam. sing.*) like (3)
gusto pleasure; taste; **con mucho gusto** with pleasure; **mucho gusto** nice to meet you (1)

H

habitación *f.* room (4) (7); **habitación doble** double room; **habitación sencilla** single room
hablar to talk (2) (5); to speak; **hablar por teléfono** to talk on the phone (2)
hacer to do (5); to make (5); **hace buen tiempo** the weather is nice (3); **hace calor** it's hot (3); **hace fresco** it's cool (*weather*) (3); **hace frío** it's cold (*weather*) (3); **hace mal tiempo** the weather is bad (3); **hace sol** it's sunny (3); **hace viento** it's windy (3); **hacer alpinismo** to climb mountains (6); **hacer clic (en)** to click on (13) **hacer cola** to stand in line; **hacer escala** to make a stop, layover; **hacer juego** to match (11); **hacer la cama** to make the bed (10); **hacer la maleta** to pack one's suitcase; **hecho(a) a mano** handmade (11); **¿qué tiempo hace?** what's the weather like?; **hacer travesuras** to do mischievous things (8)
hambre *f.* hunger; **tener (mucha) hambre** to be (very) hungry (2)
hamburguesa hamburger (7)
hasta until; **hasta ahora** up to now, so far; **hasta aquí** up to now, so far; **hasta hace poco** until a little while ago; **hasta luego** see you later (1); **hasta mañana** see you tomorrow (1); **hasta pronto** see you soon (1); **hasta que** until
hay there is/are (1); **hay que** (+ *inf.*) one should (+ *verb*); it's necessary to (+ *verb*); **¿qué hay de nuevo?** what's new? (1)
helada frost
helado ice cream (7)
hembra female (12)
hepatitis *f.* hepatitis
herida wound
herido(a): estar herido(a) to be injured (9)
hermanastro(a) stepbrother/stepsister
hermano(a) brother/sister (2); **medio(a) hermano(a)** half brother/half sister (2)
hermoso(a) beautiful
hielo ice; **patinar sobre hielo** to ice skate
hierba grass
hígado liver (14)
hijastro(a) stepson/stepdaughter
hijo(a) son/daughter (2)
hipertensión *f.* hypertension; high blood pressure (14)
historia history (2); **historia médica** medical history
hogar *m.* home
hoja de papel piece of paper
hola hello (1)
holandés(esa) Dutch
hombre *m.* man (1)
hombro shoulder (6)
hondureño(a) Honduran (14)
honesto(a) honest (1)

hora time (*of day*)
hornear to bake (8)
horno oven (4); **al horno** baked (7)
horrible horrible
horror *m.* horror
hospital *m.* hospital (4)
hostal *m.* hostel
hotel *m.* hotel (4); **hotel económico** inexpensive hotel; **hotel de lujo** luxury hotel; **hotel de primera clase** first-class hotel
hoy today (3)
huelga strike
hueso bone (14)
huésped *m. f.* guest (7)
huevo egg (8)
huipil *m.* embroidered blouse
humano(a) human

I

ida: de ida one-way; **de ida y vuelta** round-trip
ideal ideal
idealista idealist (1)
identificación *f.* identification
iglesia church (4)
igual equal; **al igual que** like
igualmente likewise
impaciente impatient (1)
impermeable *m.* raincoat (3)
impersonal impersonal
importancia importance
importante important
imposible impossible
imprescindible indispensable
impresionante impressive
impresora printer
impuesto tax
incluido(a) included
incluir (y) to include
incorrecto(a) not right, incorrect
increíble incredible, amazing
independiente independent
indicar (qu) to indicate
indirecto(a) indirect
infantil childish, for children (13)
inferior lower
infinitivo infinitive
inflamación *f.* **de la garganta** strep throat
información *f.* information
informática computer science (2)
ingeniería engineering (2)
ingeniero(a) engineer
inglés *m.* English (*language*)
ingrediente *m.* ingredient
inicialmente initially
inmigración *f.* immigration (14)
inmigrante *m. f.* immigrant (14)
inmigrar to immigrate (14)
inodoro toilet (4)
insistir (en + *inf.*) to insist (*on*) (13)
insomnio insomnia (14)
instrucciones *f. pl.* instructions
instructor(a) instructor
inteligente intelligent (1)
interesado(a) interested (5)
interesante interesting (1)
interesar to interest, be interested in
internacional international; **aeropuerto internacional** international airport (10); **organismo internacional** international organization (14)
Internet *m.* Internet (13)
interno(a) internal
interrogativo(a) interrogative
intestino intestine (14)
introvertido(a) introvert
invierno winter (3)
invitación *f.* invitation (9)

invitado(a) guest (9)
invitar to invite
inyección f. injection (14); shot; **poner(le) una inyección** to give (him/her) an injection
ir to go (4); **irse** to leave, go away (6); **ir de excursión** to hike (6); **ir de pesca** to go fishing (6)
irracional irrational
irresponsable irresponsible
isla island (12)
izquierda left; **a la izquierda (de)** to the left (of) (4)

J

jabón m. soap (6); **jabón para platos** dish soap (10)
jade m. jade; **objeto de jade** jade object
jaguar m. jaguar (12)
jamás never (6)
jamón m. ham (8)
jarabe m. cough syrup (14)
jardín m. yard; garden (4); **jardín botánico** botanical garden; **cultivar el jardín** to garden (flowers)
jaula cage (12)
jeans m. pl. jeans
jirafa giraffe (12)
joven (pl. **jóvenes**) young (1)
jubilado(a) retired
judía verde green bean
juego game; **juego de mesa** board game (8); **hacer** irreg. **juego** to match (11)
jueves m. Thursday (3)
jugar (ue, u) (gu) to play (4)
jugo juice (7)
juguete m. toy (8)
juicio judgment
julio July (3)
junio June (3)
junto a beside, next to
jurar to swear, give one's word
justo(a) fair
juventud f. youth (13)

K

kilo kilogram (2.2 pounds)
kiosco kiosk, stand

L

la f. the; d.o. you (form. sing.); d.o. her/it/you (form. sing.)
labio lip
laboratorio laboratory
lado side; **al lado (de)** alongside (of); beside, next to (4)
lago lake (12)
lámpara lamp (4)
lana wool (11)
langosta lobster
lápiz m. (pl. **lápices**) pencil(s) (1)
largo(a) long (1); **a lo largo (de)** along
las f. pl. the; d.o. pron. you (form. pl.) them
lástima pity
lavabo bathroom sink (4)
lavadora washing machine (4)
lavandería laundry, laundry room
lavaplatos m. sing., pl. dishwasher (4)
lavar(se) to wash (6); **lavar platos** to do dishes (10); **lavar ropa** to do laundry
le i.o. you (form. sing.); to/for him, her, it; **le presento a...** I'd like to introduce you (form.) to ... (1)
leal loyal
lección f. lesson
leche f. milk (8)
lechería dairy store
lechuga lettuce (8)
leer to read (3) (5)

lejos (de) far (from) (4)
lengua language (2); tongue; **lenguas modernas** modern languages; **sacar (qu) la lengua** to stick out one's tongue
lentes m. pl. glasses (3)
león m. lion
les i.o. pron. to, for you (form. pl.) them
letras: filosofía y letras liberal arts
levantar to lift; **levantarse** to get up (6); **levantar pesas** to lift weights (6)
ley f. law (14)
liberal liberal (1)
libra pound
libre free; **unión** f. **libre** common-law union (13)
librería bookstore (4)
libro book (1)
licuado smoothie made with fruits, juices, and ice
limitar to limit (13)
límite de velocidad speed limit (9)
limón m. lemon; lime
limpiador m. liquid cleaner; **limpiador para el hogar** all-purpose cleaner; **limpiador para ventanas** window cleaner
limpiar to clean (2)
limpieza: artículos de limpieza cleaning materials
lindo(a) pretty; **¡qué lindos zapatos!** what pretty shoes! (11)
línea aérea airline
lino linen (11)
liquidación f. sale
liso(a) solid (color) (11)
lista list
litera bunk (bed)
literatura literature (2)
litro liter
llama llama (12)
llamar to call (2); **llamarse** to be called/named; **me llamo...** my name is . . . (1)
llano plains (12)
llave f. key (7)
llegada arrival (10)
llegar (gu) to arrive (2)
lleno(a) full
llevar to take; to carry; to wear (3)
llevarse bien/mal to (not) get a long (13)
llover (ue) to rain; **está lloviendo** it's raining; **llueve** it is raining, it rains (3)
lluvia rain
lo m. d.o. you (form. sing.); him,/it; **lo cual** which; **lo que** what, which; **lo siento (mucho)** I'm (very) sorry
lobo wolf (12)
loco(a) crazy (5); **volverse loco(a)** to go crazy
locutor(a) announcer (13)
los def. art. m. pl. the; d.o. them/you (form. pl.)
lucha fight, struggle
luchar to fight, struggle
lucir (zc) to wear; to show off, sport (wear)
luego then, next; **hasta luego** see you later (1)
lugar m. place **tener lugar** to take place
lujo luxury (7); **hotel** m. **de lujo** luxury hotel
luna de miel honeymoon (13)
lunar: de lunares polka-dotted (11)
lunes m. Monday (3)
luz f. (pl. **luces**) light; **dar a luz** to give birth (13)

M

macho male (12)
madrastra stepmother
madre f. mother (2)
madrina godmother
maestro(a) teacher; **maestro(a) de ceremonias** master of ceremony
maíz m. corn (8); **palomitas de maíz** popcorn (13)

mal adv. badly; bad (1), not well; **hace mal tiempo** the weather is bad (3); **llevarse mal** to not get along (13); **sentirse (e, i)** to feel badly, ill
mal, malo(a) bad (1)
maleta suitcase (7); **deshacer la maleta** to unpack one's suitcase; **hacer la maleta** to pack one's suitcase
maletero porter
mamá mother (2)
mamífero mammal (12)
manantial m. spring (of water)
mandar to order (13); **mandar** to send (4)
mandato command
manejar to drive
manera way
mango mango
manguera hose (10)
mano f. hand (6); **equipaje** m. **de mano** hand luggage (10); **hecho(a) a mano** handmade (11); **me tiemblan las manos** my hands are shaking
mansión f. mansion
mantel m. tablecloth
mantenerse (like **tener**) **en forma** to stay fit, keep in shape
mantequilla butter (8)
manzana apple (8)
mañana tomorrow (3); morning; **de la mañana** a.m.; **hasta mañana** see you tomorrow (1)
mapa m. map (1)
maquillarse to put on make-up (6)
mar m. sea (12)
maravilla marvel, wonder
marcador m. marker
marcharse to leave, to go away
marcial: artes marciales f. pl. martial arts
mareado dizzy; **estar mareado(a)** to be dizzy (14)
marearse to feel dizzy
mareo dizziness; **tener mareos** to be dizzy
mariscal m. raw shellfish marinated in lime juice
mariscos shellfish
marrón brown
martes m. Tuesday (3)
marzo March (3)
más more; plus (in mathematical functions); **más que** more than
máscara mask (11)
masculino(a) masculine
masticar (qu) to chew
matemáticas pl. mathematics (2)
materia course, subject
materialista materialistic
matrimonial: cama matrimonial double bed
matrimonio: marriage proponer matrimonio to propose marriage (13)
mayo May (3)
mayonesa mayonnaise (8) (8)
mayor older (11); **el/la mayor** the oldest
me d.o., i.o. pron. me
mecánico(a) mechanic (5)
media stocking
mediano(a) medium (11)
medianoche f. midnight (3)
medias pl. panty hose
medicamento medication
medicina medicine
médico(a) adj. medical; **examen** m. **médico** medical examination; **historia médica** medical history; **receta médica** prescription (14)
médico(a) n. doctor (5)
medio(a) half; **medio(a) hermano(a)** half brother/half sister (2); **media pensión** half board (breakfast and one other meal)

mediodía *m.* noon (3)
mejilla cheek
mejillón *m.* mussel
mejor better (11); **el/la mejor** the best
melón *m.* melon (8)
menor younger (11); **el/la menor** the youngest
menos less; **minus** (*in mathematical functions*); **menos que** less than; **a menos que** unless (14)
mentir (ie, i) to lie (3) (5)
menú *m.* menu
menudo: a menudo frequently, often
mercado market
merecer (zc) to deserve
merendar (ie) to eat a snack
merienda snack
mermelada jam
mes *m.* month; **el mes anterior** the month before
mesa table; **poner la mesa** to set the table (10); **recoger (j) la mesa** to pick up the table (10); to clear the table (10)
mesero(a) (*Mex.*) (*restaurant*) waitperson; waiter (5)
meseta plateau
mesita coffee table (4); end table; **mesita de noche** night table
metro subway
mexicano(a) Mexican (14)
mezclar to mix (8)
mezclilla denim (11)
mezquita mosque (4)
mi my
microondas *m.* microwave (4)
miedo fear; **tenerle miedo a** to be afraid of (*person*); **tener (mucho) miedo** to be (very) afraid (2)
miel *f.* honey; **luna de miel** honeymoon (13)
miembro member
mientras while
miércoles *m.* Wednesday (3)
mil one thousand (7); **cien mil** (one) hundred thousand; **dos mil** two thousand (7)
millón *m.* million (7); **cien millones** (one) hundred million
mío(a) mine
mirar (la tele) to watch (TV) (2); to look (at)
misa mass
mismo(a) same; **del mismo modo** similarly
mochila backpack (1)
moda fashion, style; **de moda** fashionable (11); **estar de moda** to be in style; **pasado(a) de moda** out of style
modelo *m. f.* model (5)
moderno(a) modern; **lenguas modernas** modern languages
modesto(a) modest
modista dressmaker
modo way; **del mismo modo** similarly
molestar to bother, be bothered by
momento moment
mono monkey (12)
montaña mountain (12)
montañoso(a) mountainous
montar to climb; get on; **montar a caballo** to ride horseback
morado(a) purple (3)
moreno(a) dark-skinned/dark-haired (1), brunette
morir (ue, u) to die (4) (5)
mostaza mustard (8)
mostrador *m.* counter (10)
mostrar (ue) to show
motel *m.* motel
moto(cicleta) motorcycle
mover (ue) to move (*something*)

MP3 *m.* MP3 (13)
mucho(a) much; many; a lot (2); **lo siento (mucho)** I'm (very) sorry; **mucho gusto** nice to meet you (1)
mudarse to move (14)
muebles *m. pl.* furniture
muerte *f.* death (13)
muerto(a) dead; **naturaleza muerta** still life (11)
mujer *f.* woman (1); **mujer policía** police officer (5)
multa fine (9); ticket (9)
municipalidad *f.* city hall
muñeca wrist
muñeco(a) doll (8)
mural *m.* mural (11)
muscular muscular; **dolor** *m.* **muscular** muscle ache
museo museum (4)
música music (2)
músico(a) musician (5)
muslo thigh (6)
muy very (1)

N

nacer (zc) to be born (13)
nacionalidad *f.* nationality
nada nothing (1)
nadar to swim (2)
nadie no one (6), nobody (6)
naipes *m. pl.* (playing) cards
naranja orange (7) (8)
nariz *f.* nose (6)
natural natural; **recursos naturales** natural resources (12)
naturaleza nature (12); **naturaleza muerta** still life (11)
navegar (gu) a la vela to sail
necesario(a) necessary
necesitar to need (2)
negar (ie) (gu) to deny, to negate
negocios *pl.* business (2)
negro(a) black (3)
nevar (ie) to snow (3); **está nevando** it's snowing; **nieva** it is snowing, it snows (3)
ni... ni neither . . . nor
nicaragüense *m. f.* Nicaraguan (14)
niebla fog
nieto(a) grandson/granddaughter (2)
nieve *f.* snow
nilón *m.* nylon
ningún/ninguno(a) none, not any
niñera baby-sitter (8)
niñez *f.* childhood (13)
no no; **¿no?** isn't that so?; **¿no es así?** isn't that right?; **no obstante** however
noche *f.* night; **de la noche** p.m.; **mesita de noche** night table
nombre *m.* name
noreste *m.* northeast
normal normal
normalmente normally
noroeste *m.* northwest
norte *m.* north
norteamericano(a) North American
nos *d.o.* us; *i.o.* to/for us; *refl. pron.* ourselves; **nos vemos** see you later (1)
nosotros(as) *subj. pron.* we
nota grade (2); **nota adhesiva** sticky note; **sacar (qu) una buena/mala nota** to get a good/bad grade
noticiario news (13)
novecientos(as) nine hundred (7)
novelista *m. f.* novelist
noveno(a) ninth (4)
noventa ninety (1)

noviazgo engagement (13); relationship (13)
noviembre *m.* November (3)
novio(a) groom/bride; fiancé(e); boyfriend/girlfriend (2); *pl.* bride and groom (9)
nube *f.* cloud (12)
nublado(a) cloudy; **está nublado** it is cloudy (3)
nuboso(a) cloudy
nuera daughter-in-law
nuestro(a) *poss.* our
nueve nine (1)
nuevo(a) new; **de nuevo** new; again; **¿Qué hay de nuevo?** What's new? (1)
número number; size (*shoe*) (11)
nunca never (6)

O

o or; **o...o** either . . . or (6)
obesidad *f.* obesity (14)
objeto object; **objeto directo** direct object; **objeto indirecto** indirect object
obligación *f.* obligation
obra work (*of art, literature, theater, etc.*) (11)
obstante: no obstante however
obstinado(a) obstinate, stubborn
obtener to get
obvio(a) obvious
océano ocean
ochenta eighty (1)
ocho eight (1)
ochocientos(as) eight hundred (7)
octavo(a) eighth (4)
octubre *m.* October (3)
ocupado(a) busy (5)
ocurrir to occur
odiar to hate (13)
oferta offer
oficina office (4); **oficina de correos** post office
oficio occupation
oído inner ear
oír to hear (5)
ojalá (que) I hope (that) (13)
ojo eye
ola wave (12)
óleo oil painting (11)
oler (ue) to smell
olfato sense of smell
olla de cerámica ceramic pot
olvidar to forget (11)
once eleven (1)
onomástico saint's day
ópera opera
opinar to give one's opinion
opinión *f.* opinion
optimista *m., f.* optimist (1)
oración *f.* sentence
orden *f.* order (7)
ordenador *m.* computer
ordenar to tidy up (10); to straighten up (10)
ordinal ordinal
oreja (*outer*) ear (6)
organismo internacional international organization (14)
organizar (c) to organize, to tidy up
órgano organ; **órgano vital** vital organ (14)
orgulloso(a) (de) proud (of)
origen *m.* origin
oro gold
oscuro(a) dark; **cuarto oscuro** darkroom
oso bear (12)
otoño autumn (3)

otro(a) other; **otra vez** again; **por otra parte** moreover; on the other hand
oveja sheep (12)

P

pachanga (rowdy) party
paciente patient (1) (14)
padrastro stepfather (2)
padre *m.* father (2); *pl.* parents
padrino godfather
pagado: viaje *m.* **todo pagado** all-inclusive trip (7)
pagar (gu) to pay
página page
paisaje *m.* landscape (11)
pájaro bird
palabra word
palacio palace
paleta pallet (11)
palmera palm tree (12)
palomitas de maíz popcorn (13)
pampa grasslands (12)
pan *m.* bread (7)
panadería bakery
panameño(a) Panamanian (14)
pantalla screen (13)
pantalones *m. pl.* pants (3); **pantalones cortos** shorts (3)
papá *m.* father (2)
papa potato (8)
papaya papaya
papel *m.* paper (1); **hoja de papel** piece of paper; **papel de cocina** paper towel
paperas mumps
para for; in order to; to (*in the direction of*)
para empezar to begin with; **para que** so (that) (14); **¿para qué?** for what reason?
parada stop (10)
parador *m.* **nacional** *government run historical inn, castle, or palace* (*Sp.*)
paraguas *m. sing., pl.* umbrella (3)
paraguayo(a) Paraguayan (14)
paramédico paramedic (9)
parcial partial; **a tiempo parcial** part-time
PARE: pasarse una señal de PARE to run a STOP sign (9)
parecer (zc) to seem
parecerse a to look like; to be similar/like
pared *f.* wall
pareja pair; couple (2) (13); partner (2)
pariente relative (2)
párpado eyelid
parque *m.* park (4); **parque de atracciones** amusement park
parquímetro parking meter (9)
parte *f.* part; **por otra parte** moreover; on the other hand
particular: en particular in particular
partido match; game (*sports*) (6)
pasa raisin
pasado(a) past; last; **el año pasado** last year; **la semana pasada** last week (6); **pasado(a) de moda** out of style
pasaje *m.* ticket (*transportation*)
pasajero(a) passenger (10)
pasaporte *m.* passport (10); **control de pasaporte** passport control
pasar to pass; to happen; **pasar la aspiradora** to vacuum (10); **pasarlo bien** to have a good time; **pasar por seguridad** to go through security (10); **pasarse un semáforo en rojo** to run a red light; **pasarse una señal de PARE** to run a STOP sign (9); **¿qué pasa?** what's going on? (1)
pase: pase *m.* **de abordar** boarding pass (10)
pasear to walk

paseo: dar un paseo to go on a walk (8)
pasillo hallway; aisle (10)
paso: de paso by the way
pastel *m.* pastry; cake (7) (9)
pastelería pastry shop
pastilla pill (14)
pasto grass, pasture (12)
patín *m.* skate
patinar to skate (6) (8); **patinar en hielo** to ice skate (6); **patinar sobre ruedas** to roller-skate, roller-blade
patineta skateboard (8)
patio patio (4); courtyard; yard; flower garden
patrocinador sponsor (13)
pato duck (12)
patrocinar to sponsor (13)
patrulla police car (9)
pavo turkey (7)
paz *f.* peace (14)
pecho chest (6)
pedagogía pedagogy; **ciencias de la pedagogía** education
pedir (i, i) to ask for (3) (5); to request
peinarse to comb/style one's hair (6)
pelar to peel (8)
pelear to fight (8); to argue (8)
película movie (4); film
peligro (de extinción) danger (of extinction) (12)
pelirrojo(a) red-haired (1)
pelo hair (6)
pelota ball (6)
península peninsula (12)
pensar (ie) to think (3); to intend
peor worse (11); **el/la peor** the worst
pepinillo pickle (8)
pepino cucumber (8)
pequeño(a) small (1)
pera pear
perder (ie) to lose (3)
perdón *m.* pardon
perdonarse to excuse oneself; **perdón** pardon me, excuse me
perezoso(a) lazy (1)
perfecto(a) perfect
periodismo journalism (2)
periodista *m. f.* journalist (5)
permiso permission (8)
pero *conj.* but
perro dog (2)
persona person
peruano(a) Peruvian (14)
pesa weight; **levantar pesas** to lift weights (6)
pesadilla nightmare
pésame *m. sing.* condolences
pesar to weigh
pesar: a pesar de in spite of
pesca: ir de pesca to go fishing (6)
pescadería fish store, fish market
pescado fish (*food*) (7)
pescar (qu) to fish
pesimista *adj. m. f.* pessimist (1)
pestaña eyelash
petróleo oil (12)
pez *m.* (*pl.* **peces**) fish (2)
piano piano; **tocar (qu) el piano** to play the piano
picar (qu) to snack
pico mountain peak
pie *m.* foot (6)
piel *f.* skin; leather (11)
pierna leg (6)
pijama *m. sing.* pajamas (3)
piloto *m. f.* pilot (5)
pimienta pepper (7)
pincel *m.* paintbrush (11)
ping-pong *m.* ping-pong (6)

pingüino penguin (12)
pintor(a) painter (5)
pintura paint
piña pineapple (8)
piñata piñata (9)
Pirineos Pyrenees
piscina swimming pool (4)
piso apartment; floor (*of a building*) (4)
pista (de correr) track
pizarra chalkboard (1)
plancha iron (10)
planchar to iron (10)
planta plant (4); floor (*building*)
plata silver
plátano banana (8)
platillo saucer
plato plate; dish; **detergente** *m.* **para platos** dish detergent; **jabón** *m.* **para platos** dish soap (10); **lavar platos** to do dishes (10); **plato principal** main dish (7)
playa beach
plaza city square (4)
pluma (estilográfica) (fountain) pen
pobre poor (1)
pobreza poverty (14)
poco(a) little, few (2); **hasta hace poco** until a little while ago
poder to be able to (4)
policía *f.* police (*force*); **estación** *f.* **de policía** police station
policía *m.* police officer (5); **mujer** *f.* **policía** police officer (5)
poliéster *m.* polyester
político(a) *n.* politician (5); *adj.* political; **ciencias políticas** political science
pollo chicken (7); chick (12)
pomada cream; ointment
poner to put, place; to put on; to put up; **poner la mesa** to set the table (10); **poner(le) una inyección** to give (him/her) an injection; **ponerse** to get (+ *adj.*) to become (+ *adj.*); **ponerse feliz** to become happy; **ponerse la ropa** to put on clothing (6); **ponerse triste** to become sad
por by; through; because of; due to; on account of; times (*in mathematical functions*); **por adelantado** in advance; **por ejemplo** for example; **por eso** therefore; **por favor** please; **por fin** finally; **por lo general** generally; **por otra parte** moreover; on the other hand; **por otro lado** on the other hand; **¿por qué?** why? (3); **por supuesto** of course; **por último** lastly, finally
porque because
portero door attendant
posada inn; *pl.* nine-day celebration before Christmas
posar to pose (11)
posesivo(a) possessive
posible possible
postre *m.* dessert (7)
postura posture
práctica activity; practice
practicar (qu) to practice; **practicar deportes** to play sports (2)
prado meadow
precio price
precioso(a) precious; lovely; beautiful
preciso(a) necessary
preferible preferable
preferir (ie, i) to prefer
pregunta question
preguntar to ask (2)
preguntón(-ona) inquisitive
prenda garment (11); article of clothing
preocupación *f.* worry

preocupado(a) worried (5)
preocuparse to worry
preparar to prepare
preposición *f.* preposition
presentar to introduce; **le presento a...** I'd like to introduce you (*form.*) to . . . (1); **te presento a...** I'd like to introduce you (*fam.*) to . . . (1)
preservar to preserve (12)
presidente *m. f.* president
presión *f.* **arterial** blood pressure; **presión alta/baja** high/low blood pressure (14); **tomar la presión** to take someone's blood pressure (14)
pretérito preterite
previamente previously
primavera spring (3)
primer, primero(a) first (4); **hotel** *m.* **de primera clase** first-class hotel; **primera clase** first class (10); **Primera Comunión** *f.* First Communion; **primeros auxilios** first aid (14)
primo(a) cousin (2)
principal main; **plato principal** main dish (7)
principio beginning; principle; **al principio** at the beginning; **en principio** in principle
prisa hurry, haste; **tener (mucha) prisa** to be in a (big) hurry (2)
privado(a) private
probable probable; likely
probablemente probably
probador *m.* dressing room (11); fitting room
probar(se) (ue) to try (on) (11); to test
problema *m.* problem
problemático(a) problematic
profesión *f.* profession
profesor(a) professor (1)
profundo(a) deep
programación *f.* programming (13)
programador(a) programmer
prohibir to prohibit
prometer to promise
prometido(a) fiancé(e) (13)
pronombre *m.* pronoun
pronto soon; **hasta pronto** see you soon (1); **tan pronto como** as soon as (14)
propina tip; **dejar una propina** to leave a tip (7)
proponer (matrimonio) to propose (marriage) (13)
propósito: a propósito by the way
propuesta proposal
proteger (j) to protect (12)
protesta protest
provecho: buen provecho enjoy your meal
prueba test
psicología psychology (2)
psicólogo(a) psychologist (5)
público(a) public; **funcionario(a) público(a)** public official
puerta door (1); **puerta de salida** gate (10)
puerto port, harbor
puertorriqueño(a) Puerto Rican (14)
puesto de trabajo position, job
pulgar *m.* thumb
pulmón *m.* lung (14)
pulpo octopus
pulsera bracelet
pulso pulse
punto point
puntual punctual
pupitre *m.* student desk (1)

Q

que that, which; than; **¡que tengas un buen día!** have a nice day (1)
¡qué! what!; **¡qué bien te queda esa falda!** that skirt really fits you well! (11); **¡qué**

caro(a)! how expensive! (11); **¡qué color tan bonito!** what a pretty color! (11); **¡qué lindos zapatos!** what pretty shoes! (11); **¡qué pantalones tan elegantes!** what elegant pants! (11)
¿qué? what? (3); **¿qué hay de nuevo?** what's new? (1); **¿qué pasa?** what's going on? (1); **¿qué tal?** how's it going? (1); **¿qué tiempo hace?** what's the weather like?
quedar to remain (11); to fit (11); **quedarse** to stay; **¡qué bien te queda esa falda!** that skirt really fits you well! (11)
quedarle to fit
quehacer *m.* chore (10)
quejarse to complain
quemadura de sol sunburn
querer to want (3); to love (13); **querer decir** to mean; **quisiera** I would like
queso cheese (8)
quien(es) who, whom
¿quién(es)? who? (3)
química chemistry (2)
quince fifteen (1); **los quince años** girl's fifteenth birthday celebration (9)
quinceañera girl celebrating her fifteenth birthday (9)
quinientos(as) five hundred (7)
quinto(a) fifth (4)
quitarse to take off (*clothing*)
quizá(s) perhaps

R

racional rational
radio: emisora de radio radio station
radiografía x-ray (14)
raíz *f.* (*pl.* **raíces**) root
rana frog (12)
rápido fast
raqueta racket (6)
ráquetbol *m.* racquetball
raro(a) strange
ratón *m.* mouse (2) (13)
raya stripe; **a rayas** striped (11)
rayos X X-rays; **sacar (qu) rayos X** to take X-rays
razón *f.* reason; **no tener razón** to be wrong; **tener razón** to be right (2)
realista realist (1) (11)
rebajado(a) on sale (11)
rebelde rebel (1)
recado message
recepción *f.* reception (13)
recepcionista *m. f.* desk clerk; receptionist (7)
receta médica prescription
rechazar (c) to decline, reject
recibir to receive (3)
recibo receipt
reciclaje *m.* recycling (12)
recién casado(a) newlywed (13)
recinto campus
reclamo de equipaje baggage claim (10)
recoger (j) la mesa to clear the table (10); to pick up the table (10)
recomendación *f.* recomendación
recomendar (ie) to recommend
recordar (ue) to remember (4)
recreación *f.* recreation; **sala de recreación** rec room
recreo recess (8); **sala de recreo** rec room
recuperarse to recover (14)
recursos naturales natural resources (12)
red *f.* net
redacción *f.* writing (2)
redes *f. pl.* **sociales** social networks (13)
refresco soda (7)
refrigerador *m.* refrigerator (4)
refugiado(a) refugee (14)

regalo gift (9)
regar (ie) (gu) to water (10)
regatear to bargain
regla ruler
regresar (a casa) to return (home) (2)
regular so-so (1); okay
reír (í, i) to laugh (3)
relación *f.* relationship
relacionado(a) related
relámpago lightning
relativo(a) relative
religioso(a) religious
rellenar to fill out
reloj *m.* clock (1); watch
remediar to remedy
remedio remedy
remoto: control *m.* **remoto** remote control (13)
renunciar to resign
reparar to repair
repente: de repente suddenly (9)
repetición *f.* repetition
repetir (i, i) to repeat (3) (5)
representante *m. f.* representative
reproductor: reproductor de CDs CD player (13); **reproductor de DVDs** DVD player (13)
reptil *m.* reptile (12)
res: carne de res beef
resaca hangover
reserva reservation
reservación *f.* reservation
resfriado cold (*illness*) (14)
resguardo voucher; credit slip
residencia dormitory
resistir to resist
resolución *f.* resolution
resolver (ue) to solve
respiración *f.* breathing; **bucear con tubo de respiración** to snorkel
respirar to breathe (14)
responder to respond
responsabilizar (c) to make (someone) responsible
responsable responsible
respuesta reply, answer
restaurante *m.* restaurant (4)
resultado result; **como resultado** as a result
resultar (de/en) to result (in)
resumen *m.* summary; **en resumen** in summary
retrasado(a) delayed (10)
retrato portrait (11)
revelar fotos to develop photographs
revisar to inspect
revisión *f.* **de equipaje** luggage screening (10)
revisor *m.* controller
revista magazine (13)
rezar (c) to pray (4)
rico(a) rich (1); delicious
riñón *m.* kidney
río river (12)
riqueza wealth (14)
rocoso(a) rocky
rodilla knee (6)
rojo(a) red (3); **pasarse un semáforo en rojo** to run a red light (9)
romántico(a) romantic
romper(se) to break (9) (11); **romper con** to break up with (relationship) (13)
ropa clothes; clothing; **lavar ropa** to do laundry (10)
ropero closet
rosado(a) pink (3); **vino rosado** rosé wine
rotulador *m.* marker
rubio(a) blond(e) (1)
rueda wheel; **patinar sobre ruedas** to roller-skate, roller-blade
rutina routine

sábado *m.* Saturday (3)
saber to know (*facts, how to do something*) (5)
sabroso(a) delicious
sacar (qu) to take (out); **sacar fotos** to take photographs; **sacar la basura** to take the trash out (10); **sacar la lengua** to stick out one's tongue; **sacar una buena/mala nota** to get a good/bad grade; **sacar rayos X** to take X-rays
saco suit coat; sport coat; **saco de dormir** sleeping bag
sacudidor *m.* duster (10)
sacudir to dust (10)
sal *f.* salt (7)
sala living room (4); **sala de emergencias** emergency room (14); **sala de espera** waiting room (10); **sala de recreación** rec room; **sala de recreo** rec room
salado(a) salty
salchicha sausage
salida departure (10); **puerta de salida** gate (10)
salir to leave, to go out
salmón *m.* salmon
salón *m.* living room; sitting room; hall; **salón de clase** classroom (1)
salsa de tomate (dulce) tomato sauce; ketchup
saltar to jump (8)
salud *f.* health (5) (14)
saludar to greet
saludo greeting
salvadoreño(a) Salvadorian (14)
salvaje wild
sandalia sandal (3)
sandia watermelon
sándwich *m.* sandwich (7)
sangre *f.* blood
sano(a) healthy
santo saint; saint's day (9); **día** *m.* **de santo** saint's day
sarampión *m.* measles
sastre *m.* tailor
satisfacción *f.* satisfaction
satisfecho(a) full (*stomach*); satisfied
sauna *m.* sauna (7)
secadora dryer (4)
secar(se) (qu) to dry (oneself) (6); to dry (10)
secretario(a) secretary (5)
secreto secret
sed *f.* thirst; **tener (mucha) sed** to be (very) thirsty (2)
seda silk (11)
seguir (i, i) to follow (5); **seguir (i) derecho** to go straight (10)
segundo(a) second (4); **segunda clase** second class (10)
seguridad *f.* security; **agente de seguridad** security agent (10); **cinturón** *m.* **de seguridad** safety (seat) belt (10); **control de seguridad** security check; **pasar por seguridad** to go through security (10)
seguro(a) *adj.* sure (5); *adv.* certainly; surely
seis six (1)
seiscientos(as) six hundred (7)
selva jungle (12); **selva tropical** tropical rain forest
semáforo stoplight; **pasarse un semáforo en rojo** to run a red light (9)
semana week (3); **fin de semana** weekend (3); **semana pasada** last week (6)
sencillo(a) single (*room*) (7); simple (11); **habitación** *f.* **sencilla** single room
sensacional sensational
sensible sensitive
sentarse (ie) to sit (down)

sentido sense
sentimental sentimental
sentir (ie, i) to feel; **lo siento (mucho)** I'm (very) sorry; **sentirse bien** to feel well; **sentirse mal** to feel badly, ill
señal *f.* sign; **pasarse una señal de PARE** to run a STOP sign (9)
separarse (de) to separate (from) (13)
septiembre *m.* September (3)
séptimo(a) seventh (4)
ser *m. humano* human being
ser to be (1); **¿de dónde eres tú?** where are you (*fam.*) from? (1); **yo soy de...** I'm from . . . (1)
serenata serenade (9)
serio(a) serious (1)
serpiente *f.* snake (12)
servicios utilities
servilleta napkin (7)
servir (i, i) to serve (3) (5)
sesenta sixty (1)
setecientos(as) seven hundred (7)
setenta seventy (1)
sexto(a) sixth (4)
si if, whether
sí yes
sicología psychology
sicólogo(a) psychologist
SIDA *m. sing.* AIDS (14)
siempre always (6)
sierra mountain range
siete seven (1)
silla chair (1)
sillón *m.* armchair (4)
sin without; **sin embargo** nevertheless; however; **sin que** without (14)
sino but (rather), instead; **sino (que)** *conj.* but
sobre on; on top of; over; about
sobremesa after-dinner conversation
sobrino(a) nephew/niece (2)
social social; **redes** *f. pl.* **sociales** social networks (13)
sociología sociology
sofá *m.* couch (4)
sol *m.* sun; **gafas de sol** sunglasses; **hace sol** it's sunny; **quemadura de sol** sunburn
solicitar to apply
solicitud *f.* application (5); want ad (5)
solidaridad *f.* solidarity
sólo only
soltero(a) single person; unmarried person (13); **despedida de soltera** bridal shower; **despedida de soltero** bachelor party
solución *f.* solution
solucionar to solve
sombrero hat (3)
sombrilla beach umbrella
sonreír (í, i) to smile (3)
soñar (ue) to dream (*about*) (4)
sopa soup (7)
sorprenderse to be surprised (9)
sorprendido(a) surprised (5)
sorpresa surprise; **fiesta sorpresa** surprise party
sostener to support
sótano basement
su *poss.* your (*form. sing., pl.*); his; her; its; their
subir a to get into (*a vehicle*) (9)
suegro(a) father-in-law/mother-in-law (2)
sueldo salary (5)
suelo floor
sueño dream; sleep; **tener (mucho) sueño** to be (very) sleepy (4)
suerte *f.* luck; **tener (mucha) suerte** to be (very) lucky (2)
suéter *m.* sweater (3)
sugerencia suggestion
sugerir (ie, i) to suggest (13)

suma sum; summary; **en suma** in conclusion
súper super (*used as prefix*)
superar to overcome
superior superior; upper
supermercado supermarket (4)
supersticioso(a) superstitious
supuesto: por supuesto of course
sur *m.* south
sureste *m.* southeast
suroeste *m.* southwest
surrealista *m. f.* surrealist
suspender to fail

tabla: esquiar en tabla to snowboard (6)
tablero keyboard (13)
tacto touch
tal vez perhaps
tal: ¿qué tal? how's it going? (1); **con tal (de) que** provided that (14)
taller *m.* workshop; garage
también also (6); in addition
tampoco neither (6), either (6)
tan so; **tan... como** as . . . as; **tan pronto como** as soon as (14); **¡qué color tan bonito!** what a pretty color! (11); **¡qué pantalones tan elegantes!** what elegant pants! (11)
tanto(a) *adj.* so much; *pl.* so many; **tanto(s)/ tanta(s)... como** as many . . . as
tapete *m.* throw rug
taquilla ticket window (10); box office; **éxito de taquilla** box office hit (13)
tarde *adv.* late (6)
tarde *f.* afternoon; **de la tarde** P.M.
tarea homework
tarjeta de crédito credit card (11)
tarta pie
taza cup
tazón *m.* soup bowl
te *d.o.* you (*fam. sing.*); *i.o.* to/for you (*fam. sing.*); *refl.* yourself; **te presento a...** I'd like to introduce you (*fam.*) to . . . (1)
té *m.* tea, afternoon tea
teatro theater (2) (4)
techo ceiling
técnico(a) technician
tejer to knit (8)
tela fabric
teléfono telephone; **teléfono celular** cell phone (8)
telenovela soap opera (13)
televidente *m. f.* television viewer (13)
televisión *f.* television (*medium*); **televisión por satélite** satellite television (13)
televisor *m.* television set (1)
temblar (ie) to shake; **me tiemblan las manos** my hands are shaking
temer to fear
temperatura temperature
templo temple (4)
temprano early
tenedor *m.* fork (7)
tener to have; **tener que** (+ *inf.*) to have to (+ *verb*); **no tener razón** to be wrong; **¡que tengas un buen día!** have a nice day (1); **tener (mucha) hambre** to be (very) hungry (2); **tener (mucha) prisa** to be in a (big) hurry (2); **tener (mucha) sed** to be (very) thirsty (2); **tener (mucha) suerte** to be (very) lucky (2); **tener (mucho) calor** to be (very) hot (2); **tener (mucho) cuidado** to be (very) careful (2); **tener (mucho) éxito** to be (very) successful (2); **tener (mucho) frío** to be (very) cold (2); **tener (mucho) miedo** to be afraid of (2); **tener (mucho) sueño** to be (very)

sleepy (2); **tener celos** to be jealous; **tener ganas de** (+ *inf.*) to feel like (*doing something*); **tener lugar** to take place; **tener mareos** to be dizzy; **tener razón** to be right (2); **tener... años** to be . . . years old (2); **tenerle miedo a** to be afraid of (*person*)

tenis *m.* tennis (6); tennis shoes (3)
tercer, tercero(a) third (4)
terminal *m.* terminal
terminar to finish
ternera veal
terraza terrace
terrible terrible
testigo *m. f.* witness
textura texture
tiburón *m.* shark (12)
tiempo time; weather; **a tiempo** on time (10); **a tiempo completo** full-time; **a tiempo parcial** part-time; **hace buen tiempo** the weather is nice (3); **hace mal tiempo** the weather is bad (3); **¿Qué tiempo hace?** What's the weather like?
tienda shop; store (4); **tienda de campaña** camping tent (6)
tierno(a) tender
Tierra Earth (*planet*)
tierra land, earth
tigre *m.* tiger (12)
tinta ink (11)
tinto: vino tinto red wine (7)
tintorería dry cleaners
tío(a) uncle/aunt (2)
tira cómica comic strip (8)
tiza chalk
toalla towel (6); **toalla de papel** paper towel
tobillo ankle (6)
tocador *m.* dressing table
tocar (qu) to touch; **tocar (el piano)** to play (*the piano*) (8); to touch
tocino bacon
todo(a) all, every; **todos los días** every day (3)
tomar to take; **tomar (café)** to drink (coffee) (2); **tomar la presión** to take someone's blood pressure (14)
tomate *m.* tomato (7); **salsa de tomate (dulce)** tomato sauce; ketchup
tonto(a) dumb (1)
topografía topography
torcerse (ue) (z) to twist (14)
tormenta storm
toro bull (12)
toronja grapefruit
torre *f.* tower
tortuga turtle (12)
tos *f.* cough (14)
toser to cough (14)
totopos *pl.* tortilla chips (7)
trabajador(a) *adj.* hard-working (1)
trabajador(a) social social worker (5)
trabajar to work
trabajo work; job; **solicitud** *f.* **de trabajo** job application
tradicional traditional (11)
traductor(a) translator
traer to bring (5)
traidor(a) traitorous
traje *m.* suit (3); **traje de baño** swimming suit (3)
tranquilo(a) tranquil; calm
transicional transitional
transmitir to broadcast (13)
transporte *m.* transportation (7)
trapeador *m.* mop (10)
trapear to mop (10)
trapo dust cloth; rag (10); cleaning cloth (10)

tratado de comercio trade treaty (14)
tratamiento treatment (14)
travesura mischief (8); **hacer travesuras** to do mischievous things (8)
trece thirteen (1)
treinta thirty (1)
tren *m.* train
trepar (un árbol) to climb (a tree) (8)
tres three (1)
trescientos(as) three hundred (7)
triple triple (7)
triste sad (5); **ponerse triste** to become sad
tronco trunk
tropezar (ie) (c) to trip (9)
tropical tropical; **selva tropical** tropical rain forest
trucha trout
trueno thunder
tú *subj. pron.* you (*fam. sing.*); **¿de dónde eres tú?** where are you (*fam.*) from? (1); **¿y tú?** and you (*fam.*) (1)
tu(s) *poss.* your (*fam. sing.*)
tubo: bucear con tubo de respiración to snorkel
tuna cactus fruit
turista *m. f.* tourist (7)

U

ubicación *f.* location
último(a) final; last; **por último** lastly; finally
un/uno(a) a, an, one (1)
único(a) unique; only
unión *f.* **libre** common-law union (13)
universidad *f.* university
unos(as) some
urgente urgent
uruguayo(a) Uruguayan (14)
usado(a) used
usar to use
usted *subj. pron.* you (*form. sing.*); **¿cómo está usted?** how are you (*form.*)? (1); **¿y usted?** and you (*form.*)? (1)
usualmente usually
uva grape (8)

V

vaca cow (12)
vacaciones *f. pl.* vacation
vacuna vaccine (14)
vacunar to vaccinate
vacuno: carne de vacuno beef
vagón *m.* car, wagon (10)
valer to be worth; to cost; **¿vale?** okay?
valiente valiant, courageous
valle *m.* valley (12)
valor *m.* value
vanguardista *m. f.* revolutionary (11); avant-garde (11)
varicela chicken pox
varios several (2)
vaso glass
veinte twenty (1)
veinticinco twenty-five (1)
veinticuatro twenty-four (1)
veintidós twenty-two (1)
veintinueve twenty-nine (1)
veintiocho twenty-eight (1)
veintiséis twenty-six (1)
veintisiete twenty-seven (1)
veintitrés twenty-three (1)
veintiuno twenty-one(1)
vejez *f.* old-age (13)
vela candle (9)
velocidad: límite *m.* **de velocidad** speed limit (9)
vena vein

venado deer (12)
venda bandage
vendaje *m.* bandage (14)
vendedor(a) salesperson (5)
vender to sell (3)
venezolano(a) Venezuelan (14)
venir to come (5)
venta sale; **en venta** on sale
ventana window (1); **limpiador para ventanas** window cleaner
ventanilla window (10)
ver to see (5); **verse** to see oneself (6); **a ver** let's see; **nos vemos** see you later (1)
verano summer (3)
verbo verb
verdad *f.* truth; **¿verdad?** right?; **de verdad** really
verde green (3)
verduras *f. pl.* vegetables
vestido dress (3)
vestirse (i, i) to get dressed (6)
veterinaria veterinary medicine
veterinario(a) veterinarian (5)
vez *f.* time; **a veces** at times; **de vez en cuando** from time to time; **dos veces** two times, twice
viajar to travel (2)
viaje *m.* trip; **agente de viajes** travel agent (5); **cheque** *m.* **de viaje** traveler's check; **viaje todo pagado** all-inclusive trip
viajero(a) traveler; **cheque** *m.* **de viajero** traveler's check
videojuego videogame (8)
viejo(a) old (1)
viento wind; **hace viento** it's windy
viernes *m.* Friday (3)
VIH *m.* HIV
vinagre *m.* vinegar
vino wine; **vino blanco** white wine (7); **vino rosado** rosé wine; **vino tinto** red wine (7)
violeta violet
visa visa (10)
visitar to visit
vista view; sight
viudo(a) widower/widow (13)
vivienda housing
vivir to live (3) (5); **viva...** long live . . .
volar (ue) to fly (8)
volcán *m.* volcano (12)
voleibol *m.* volleyball (6)
voleibolista *m. f.* volleyball player
volver (ue) to return; to come back (4); **volverse loco(a)** to go crazy
vomitar to vomit (14)
vosotros(as) *subj. pron.* you (*fam. pl.*) (*Sp.*)
votar to vote (14)
voz *f.* voice; **en voz alta** aloud
vuelo flight (10); **asistente** *m. f.* **de vuelo** flight attendant
vuestro(a) *poss.* your (*fam. sing.*) (*Sp.*)

Y

y and; **¿y tú?** and you (*fam.*)? (1); **¿y usted?** and you (*form.*)? (1)
yerno son-in-law
yeso cast (14)
yo I; **yo soy de...** I'm from . . . (1)

Z

zanahoria carrot (8)
zapatilla slipper
zapato shoe (3); **¡qué lindos zapatos!** what pretty shoes! (11)
zona area
zoológico zoo (4)
zorro fox (12)

A

a, an un/uno(a)
a lot mucho(a) (2)
a.m. de la mañana
abdomen abdomen *m.*
able, to be poder (4)
about sobre
abstract art arte *m.* abstracto (11)
accept, to aceptar
accompany, to acompañar
account of, on a causa de
accountant contador(a) (5); contable *m. f.*
accounting contabilidad *f.*
ache dolor *m.*; **muscle ache** dolor muscular
acquainted with, to be conocer (zc) (5)
action acción *f.*
activity actividad *f.*, práctica
actor actor *m.* (5)
actress actriz *f.* (5)
ad, want solicitud *f.* (5)
add, to agregar (gu) (8); añadir
addition, in además; también
adjective adjetivo
adolescence adolescencia (13)
adolescent adolescente *m. f.* (13)
adopted adoptivo(a)
adult adulto (13)
adviser consejero(a) (5)
aerobics ejercicios aeróbicos
afraid, to be (very) tener (mucho) miedo; tener miedo de (*of a thing*) (2)
after (*doing something*) después de (+ *inf.*) (6); después (de) (que) (14)
after-dinner conversation sobremesa
afternoon tarde *f.*; **good afternoon** buenas tardes (1); **in the afternoon** por la tarde
again otra vez
against contra
agent agente *m. f.*; **security agent** agente *m., f.* de seguridad (10); **travel agent** agente *m., f.* de viajes (5)
aggressive agresivo(a) (1)
agree, to estar de acuerdo
agreed de acuerdo
agreement acuerdo; **trade agreement** tratado de comercio (14)
aid: first aid primeros auxilios (14)
AIDS SIDA *m.* (14)
air-conditioning aire acondicionado
airline aerolínea; línea aérea
airport aeropuerto (10); **international airport** aeropuerto international (10)
aisle pasillo (10)
alarm clock despertador *m.* (6)
algebra álgebra *m.* (2)
all todo(a)
all todo(a)(s); **after all** al fin y al cabo; **all right** de acuerdo; **when all is said and done** al fin y al cabo
all-inclusive trip viaje todo pagado (7)
allergy alergia (14)
alleviate, to aliviar
along a lo largo (de)
alongside (of) al lado (de)
aloud en voz alta
also también (6)
although aunque
always siempre (6)
amazing increíble
ambulance ambulancia (9)
among entre
amphibian anfibio (12)
amusement park parque *m.* de atracciones
and y; **and you?** ¿y tú? (*fam. sing.*) (1); ¿y usted? (*form. sing.*) (1)
angry enojado(a) (5); **to become angry** enojarse

ankle tobillo (6)
anniversary aniversario (*wedding*) (9)
announcer locutor(a) (13)
answer respuesta; **to answer** contestar
anthropology antropología
antibiotic antibiótico
any ninguno/ninguno(a) (6)
apartment apartamento (4); piso; **efficiency apartment** estudio
appetizer entremés *m.* (7)
apple manzana
appliance, electrical electrodoméstico (4)
application solicitud *f.* (5)
apply, to solicitar; aplicarse (qu)
appreciate, to apreciar (11)
approach, to acercarse (qu)
approve, to aprobar (ue)
April abril *m.* (3)
architect arquitecto(a) (5)
architecture arquitectura
area zona
Argentine argentino(a) (14)
argue, to pelear (8)
arm brazo (6)
armchair sillón *m.* (4)
armoire armario (4)
arrange, to arreglar
arrival llegada (10)
arrive llegar (gu) (2)
art arte *m.* (2); **abstract art** arte *m.* abstracto (11); **fine arts** bellas artes *f. pl.*; **liberal arts** filosofía y letras; **martial arts** artes *f. pl.* marciales
article artículo
artist artista *m. f.*
as como; **as... as** tan . . . como; **as many... as** tanto(s)/tanta(s) . . . como; **as soon as** tan pronto como (14); en cuanto (14)
ask, to preguntar (2); **to ask (for)** pedir (i, i) (3) (5)
aspirin aspirina (14)
astronomy astronomía
at a; en (4); **at the beginning** al principio
athlete atleta *m. f.*; deportista *m. f.* (5)
athletic atlético(a) (1)
attend, to (*function*) asistir a (3); **to attend to** atender (ie) a
attention atención *f.*
attic ático; desván *m.*
attorney abogado(a)
audience audiencia (13)
August agosto (3)
aunt tía (2)
autumn otoño (3)
available disponible (7)
avant-garde vanguardista *m. f.* (11)
avocado aguacate *m.*
away: to put away guardar (10)

B

baby-sitter niñera (8)
bachelor party despedida de soltero
back espalda (6); **in the back (of)** al fondo (de)
backpack mochila (1)
bacon tocino
bad mal (1); malo(a) (1)
badly mal; **to feel badly** sentirse (ie, i) mal
badminton bádminton *m.* (6)
bag bolsa; bolso; **bags** (*luggage*) equipaje *m.* (10)
baggage claim reclamo de equipaje (10)
bake, to hornear (8)
baked al horno (7)
bakery panadería
balcony balcón *m.*
bald calvo(a) (1)

ball balón *m.*; pelota (6)
balloon globo (9)
banana plátano (8)
band grupo de música (9)
bandage venda; vendaje *m.* (14); **small adhesive bandage** curita (14)
bank banco (4)
baptism bautizo (9)
bar bar *m.* (4)
bargain ganga; **to bargain** regatear
baseball béisbol *m.* (6)
basement sótano
basket cesta
basketball básquetbol *m.* (6); baloncesto
bath baño; **to take a bath** bañarse
bathe, to bañarse (6)
bathroom baño (4); **bathroom sink** lavabo (4)
bathtub bañera (4)
bay bahía (12)
beach playa; **beach umbrella** sombrilla
bean frijol *m.*; **green bean** judía verde
bear oso (12)
beat, to batir (8)
beautiful precioso(a); hermoso(a)
because porque; **because of** por
become: to become angry enojarse (9); **to become bored** aburrirse (9); **to become frustrated** frustrarse (9); **to become happy** alegrarse (9); **to become frightened** asustarse (9)
bed cama (4); **bunk bed** litera (10); **double bed** cama matrimonial; **to go to bed** acostarse (ue) (6); **to make the bed** hacer la cama (10)
bedroom dormitorio (4)
beef carne *f.* de res; carne *f.* de vacuno
beer cerveza (7)
before anterior; antes (de) (que) (14); **before** (*doing something*) antes de que (+ *inf.*) (6)
begin, to comenzar (ie) (c) (3); empezar (ie) (c) (3); **to begin with** para empezar
beginning principio
behind detrás (de) (4)
believe, to creer (3)
bellhop botones *m. f., sing. pl.* (7)
below debajo (de)
belt cinturón *m.* (3); **safety (seat) belt** cinturón *m.* de seguridad (10)
bend, to doblar
benefits beneficios
beside al lado (de) (4); junto a
besides además
best, the el/la mejor (11)
better mejor (11)
between entre (4)
bicycle bicicleta
big gran, grande (1)
bill cuenta (4)
billfold cartera
biology biología (2)
bird pájaro (2); ave *f.* (*but* el ave) (12)
birth nacimiento (13); **to give birth** dar a luz (13)
birthday cumpleaños *m. sing., pl.* (3) (9); **birthday boy(girl)** cumpleañero(a)
black negro(a) (3)
blackboard pizarra
blond(e) rubio(a) (1)
blood sangre *f.* (14); **blood pressure** presión *f.* arterial; **high blood pressure** hipertensión *f.* (14); presión *f.* alta (14); **to take someone's blood pressure** tomar la presión (14)
blouse blusa (3)
blue azul (3)
blue jeans bluyíns *m., pl.* (3)

board game juego de mesa (8)
board, to abordar (10)
board: ironing board burro (10)
boarding pass pase *m.* de abordar (10)
boat barco
body cuerpo
Bolivian boliviano(a) (14)
bone hueso (14); **broken bone** fractura (14)
book libro (1)
bookstore librería (4)
boot bota (3)
bored aburrido(a) (5); **to become bored** aburrirse (9)
boring aburrido(a) (1)
born, to be nacer (zc) (13)
bother, to molestar; **to be bothered by** molestar
bottle botella
bottom fondo
box office taquilla; **box office hit** éxito de taquilla (13)
boyfriend novio (2)
bracelet pulsera
brain cerebro (14)
bread pan *m.* (7)
break, to romper (9) (11); fracturarse (*bone*); **to break down** (*machine*) descomponer (11); **to break up with** (*relationship*) romper con (13)
breakfast desayuno (7); **to eat breakfast** desayunar (7)
breathe, to respirar (14)
breathing respiración *f.*
bridal shower despedida de soltera
bride novia (9)
bridge puente (9)
bright brillante
bring, to traer (5)
broadcast, to transmitir (13)
broccoli brócoli *m.* (8)
broken bone fractura
broom escoba (10)
brother hermano
brother-in-law cuñado (2)
brown marrón; café (3)
brush, to cepillarse (6)
build, to construir (y)
building edificio (4)
bull toro (12)
bunk (bed) litera (10)
bureau cómoda
bus autobús *m.*; **bus station** estación *f.* de autobuses
business empresa; negocios (*subject*) (2); **business and management** administración *f.* de empresas
busy ocupado(a) (5)
but *conj.* pero;
butcher shop carnicería
butter mantequilla (8)
buy, to comprar (2)
by por; **by the way** a propósito; de paso

C

cablevision cablevisión *f.* (13)
cactus cactus *m.* (12); **cactus fruit** tuna
cafeteria cafetería
cage jaula (12)
cake pastel *m.* (7) (9)
calculator calculadora
calculus cálculo (2)
call, to llamar (2)
calm tranquilo(a)
camping, to go acampar (6); **camping tent** tienda de campaña (6)
campus recinto
cancer cáncer *m.* (14)
candidate, job aspirante *m. f.*
candies dulces *m. pl.* (9) golosinas (13)
candle vela (9)
cap gorro (3)

car auto; vagón *m.* (10); **toy car** carrito (8); **sleeping car** coche *m.* cama (10)
card tarjeta; **credit card** tarjeta de crédito (11)
cards (*playing*) cartas (8); naipes *m. pl.*
care cuidado
careful, to be (very) tener (mucho) cuidado
carpet alfombra (4)
carrot zanahoria (8)
carry, to llevar
cartoons dibujos animados (13)
cascade cascada (12)
case (that), in en caso (de) (que) (14)
cash efectivo (11); **cash register** caja (11)
cast yeso (14)
cat gato(a) (2)
cathedral catedral *f.*
cause causa; **to cause** causar
CD player reproductor *m.* de CDs (13)
ceiling techo
celebrate, to festejar; celebrar (9)
celery apio
cell phone teléfono celular (8)
censor, to censurar (13)
center centro
ceremony ceremonia (13)
certain cierto(a)
certainly cierto; claro (que sí); seguro
certainty certeza
chair silla (1)
chalk gis *m.*; tiza
chalkboard pizarra (1)
champagne champán *m.* (9)
change cambio; **to change** cambiar
characteristic característica
charming gracioso(a)
chat, to charlar (8); chatear (*online*) (13)
cheap barato(a) (11)
check cuenta (*restaurant*) (7); cheque *m.* (*bank*); **traveler's check** cheque de viaje/viajero
check, to consultar (*webpage, text, etc.*); **check luggage, to** facturar el equipaje (10)
checkered a cuadros (11)
checkers damas (8)
cheek mejilla
cheese queso (8)
chemistry química (2)
cherry cereza
chess ajedrez *m.* (8)
chest pecho (6)
chew, to masticar (qu)
chick pollo (12)
chicken pollo (7)
chicken pox varicela
child niño(a) (1)
childhood niñez *f.* (13)
childish infantil (13)
children, for infantil (13)
Chilean chileno(a) (14)
chin barbilla
chips, tortilla totopos (7)
choose, to elegir (i, i) (j)
chore quehacer *m.* (10)
Christmas Navidad *f.*; **nine-day celebration before Christmas** posadas (9)
church iglesia (4)
cinema cine *m.*
circus circo
citizen ciudadano(a) (14)
city ciudad; **city hall** ayuntamiento; **city square** plaza (4)
civil civil
claim: baggage claim reclamo de equipaje (10)
class clase *f.*; **first class** primera clase (10); **second class** segunda clase (10)
classic clásico(a)
classmate compañero(a) de clase (2)
classroom salón *m.* de clases (1)
clean, to limpiar (2)
cleaner (*liquid*) limpiador *m.*

cleaning: cleaning cloth trapo (10); **cleaning materials** artículos de limpieza
clear claro(a); despejado(a) (*weather*); **it is clear** está despejado (3); **to clear the table** recoger (j) la mesa (10)
clerk dependiente(a) (5); **desk clerk** recepcionista *m. f.*
click (on), to hacer clic (en) (13)
climb, to montar; **to climb a tree** trepar un árbol (8); **to climb mountains** hacer alpinismo (6)
climbing, mountain alpinismo (6)
clinic clínica
clock reloj *m.* (1); **alarm clock** despertador (6)
close (to) cerca (de) (4)
close, to cerrar (ie) (3)
closet ropero; armario (4)
cloth: cleaning cloth trapo (10)
clothes/clothing ropa; prenda; **to put on clothing** ponerse la ropa (6); **to take off clothing** quitarse la ropa (6)
cloud nube *f.* (12)
cloudy nublado(a); nuboso(a); **it is cloudy** está nublado (3)
club club *m.* (4)
coach entrenador(a)
coach, to entrenar
coast costa (12)
coat abrigo (3); **suit coat** saco; **sport coat** saco
cocktail coctel *m.* (7)
coffee café *m.* (7); **coffee maker** cafetera (4); **coffee table** mesita (4); **to drink coffee** tomar café
cold *adj.* frío(a); **it's cold** (*weather*) hace frío; **to be(very) cold** tener (mucho) frío; *n.* catarro (14); resfriado (14)
colleague colega *m. f.*
collect, to coleccionar
college (*university division*) facultad *f.*
Colombian colombiano(a) (14)
color color *m.*; **what a pretty color!** ¡qué color tan bonito! (11)
comb one's hair, to peinarse (6)
come, to venir (5); **come back, to** volver (ue) (4)
comic strip tira cómica (8)
command mandato
commercial anuncio comercial (13)
common-law union unión *f.* libre (13)
companion compañero(a)
compare, to comparar; **compared with** comparado(a) con
comparison comparación *f.*
compete, to competir (i, i) (3)
competition competencia; competición *f.*
complain, to quejarse
complete completo(a); **to complete** completar
complex complicado(a) (11)
complexion cutis *m.*
computer computadora (1); ordenador; **computer science** informática (2); ciencias de la computación
concert concierto
concierge conserje *m. f.*
conclude, to concluir (y)
conclusion conclusión *f.*; **in conclusion** en conclusión; en suma
condiments condimentos
condition condición *f.*
condolences condolencias
condominium condominio
confirm, to confirmar
congratulate, to felicitar
conjunction conjunción *f.*
connection conexión *f.* (10)
consequence, as a como consecuencia
conservative conservador(a) (1) (11)
constipation estreñimiento
construct, to construir (y)
contain, to contener (ie)
contamination contaminación *f.* (12)
contest concurso

continent continente *m.*
contradict, to contradecir
contrary contrario(a); **on the contrary** al contrario
contrast contraste *m.*; **in contrast to** a diferencia de
control control *m.*; **remote control** control *m.* remoto (13)
controller revisor *m.* (10)
convenient conveniente
conversation conversación *f.*
cook cocinero(a); **to cook** cocinar (2)
cool fresco(a); **it's cool** (*weather*) hace fresco
corn maíz *m.* (8)
corner esquina (9)
cortacésped *m.* lawnmower (10)
cost, to costar (ue) (4)
Costa Rican costarricense *m. f.* (14)
cotton algodón *m.* (11)
couch sofá *m.* (4)
cough tos *f.* (14); **cough syrup** jarabe *m.* (14); **to cough** toser (14)
count, to contar (ue) (8)
counter mostrador *m.* (10)
couple pareja (2) (13)
courageous valiente
course materia
court (*sports*) cancha (6)
courtyard patio
cousin primo(a) (2)
cover charge entrada
covered cubierto(a)
cow vaca (12)
crab cangrejo
crash (into something), to chocar (qu) (con) (9)
crazy loco(a) (5)
cream crema (8); pomada (*ointment*)
creamy cremoso(a)
credit crédito; **credit card** tarjeta de crédito (11); **credit slip** comprobante *m.*; resguardo
criminology criminología (2)
crocodile cocodrilo (12)
cross, to atravesar (ie) (9); cruzar (c) (9)
crosswalk cruce *m.* (9)
crossword puzzle crucigrama *m.*
cruel cruel (1)
Cuban cubano(a) (14); **Cuban-American** cubanoamericano(a)
cubist cubista *m. f.*
cucumber pepino (8)
cup taza (7)
current actual
curtain cortina (4)
customs aduana (10); **customs official** agente *m. f.* de aduana
cut, to cortar (8); **to cut oneself** cortar(se) (6) (14); **to cut the lawn** cortar el césped (10)
cutlery cubiertos *m. pl.*
cyclist ciclista *m., f.* (9)

D

daily diario(a)
dairy store lechería
damage, to dañar (9)
damaged: to be damaged estar dañado(a) (9)
dance, to bailar (2)
dancer bailarín/bailarina (5)
danger (of extinction) peligro (de extinción) (12)
dark oscuro(a)
dark-haired moreno(a) (1)
dark-skinned moreno(a) (1)
darkroom cuarto oscuro
date book agenda
date fecha (*calendar*) (3); cita (13)
daughter hija
daughter-in-law nuera
day día *m.* (3); **day before yesterday** anteayer; **every day** todos los días (3); **per day** al día
death muerte *f.* (13)

December diciembre *m.* (3)
declare, to declarar
decline, to rechazar (c)
decoration decoración *f.* (9)
deep profundo(a)
deer venado (12)
definite definido(a)
deforestation deforestación *f.* (12)
delayed retrasado(a) (10)
delicious delicioso(a), rico(a), sabroso(a)
delighted encantado(a); **to be delighted** encantar
denim mezclilla (11)
dentist dentista *m. f.*
deny, to negar (ie) (gu)
department store almacén *m.*
departure salida (10)
deplane, to desembarcar (qu)
deposit, to depositar (4)
depressed deprimido(a) (5)
depression depresión *f.*
describe, to describir
description descripción *f.*
descriptive descriptivo(a)
desert desierto (12)
deserve, to merecer (zc)
design, to diseñar (11)
designer diseñador(a) (5)
desire, to desear (13)
desk pupitre *m.* (*student*) (1); escritorio (*teacher's*) (1); **desk clerk** recepcionista *m. f.*; **ticket window** taquilla (10); ventanilla
dessert postre *m.* (7)
destination destino
destroy, to destruir (y) (5) (12)
develop photographs, to revelar fotos
diabetes diabetes *f.* (14)
diarrhea diarrea (14)
dictionary diccionario (1)
die, to morir (ue, u) (4) (5)
difference diferencia
different diferente
difficult difícil (1)
digestion digestión *f.*
dining room comedor *m.* (4)
dinner cena (7); **to eat dinner** cenar (7)
direct directo(a); **direct object** objeto directo
direction dirección *f.*
disagreement desacuerdo
disaster desastre *m.*
dish plato; **dish detergent** detergente *m.* para platos; **dish soap** jabón *m.* para platos (10); **main dish** plato principal (7); **to do dishes** lavar platos (10)
dishwasher lavaplatos *m.* (4)
distracted, to get distraerse (9)
dive: to scuba dive bucear (6)
divorce, to divorciarse (de) (13)
dizziness mareo
dizzy mareado(a); **to be dizzy** estar mareado(a) (14); **dizzy, to be** tener mareos, marearse
do, to hacer (5); **to do dishes** lavar platos (10); **to do laundry** lavar ropa (10); **to do mischievous things** hacer travesuras (8)
doctor doctor(a), médico(a) (5); **doctor's office** consultorio
documentary documental *m.* (13)
dog perro (2)
doll muñeco(a) (8)
domestic doméstico
Dominican dominicano(a) (14)
dominos dominó *sing.* (8)
door puerta (1); **door attendant** portero
dormitory residencia
double doble (7); **double room** (*hotel*) habitación *f.* doble
doubt duda; **there is no doubt** no cabe duda; **to doubt** dudar (12)
doubtful dudoso(a)

down (below) abajo
dozen docena
draw, to dibujar (8)
dream sueño; **to dream** soñar (ue) (4)
dress vestido (3)
dressed, to get vestirse (i, i) (6)
dresser tocador
dressing room probador *m.* (11)
dressing table tocador
dressmaker modista
drink bebida (7); **to drink** tomar (2); beber (3)
drive, to conducir (zc) (5), manejar
driver conductor(a) (9)
drop gota (14)
drunk borracho(a) (5)
dry árido(a); **to dry (oneself)** secar(se) (qu) (6) (10)
dry cleaners tintorería
dryer secadora (4)
duck pato (12)
due to por
dumb tonto(a) (1)
dust cloth trapo; **to dust** sacudir (10)
duster sacudidor *m.* (10)
Dutch holandés(esa)
DVD player reproductor *m.* de DVDs (13)

E

each cada
eagle águila *f.* (*but* el águila) (12)
ear oído (*inner*); oreja (*outer*) (6)
early temprano (6)
earn, to ganar (5)
earring arete *m.*; **dangling earring** pendiente *m.*
earth tierra; **Earth** Tierra (*planet*)
easy fácil (1)
eat, to comer (3) (5)
ecology ecología (12)
economics ciencias económicas; economía
economy economía (2)
Ecuadorian ecuatoriano(a) (14)
education ciencias de la pedagogía; **physical education** educación física (2)
effect efecto
efficiency apartment estudio
efficient eficiente
egg huevo (8)
eight ocho (1)
eighteen dieciocho (1)
eighth octavo(a) (4)
eighty ochenta (1)
either... or o . . . o (6); tampoco (6)
elbow codo (6)
elect, to elegir (i, i) (j)
elegant elegante; **what elegant pants!** ¡qué pantalones tan elegantes! (11)
elephant elefante *m.* (12)
elevator ascensor *m.* (7)
eleven once (1)
embarrassed avergonzado(a) (5)
emergency emergencia; **emergency room** sala de emergencias; **emergency service** servicio de emergencias (9)
emigrate, to emigrar (14)
emigration emigración *f.* (14)
emotion emoción *f.*
enchanting encantador(a)
encouragement ánimo
end, in the al final
engaged (to), to get comprometerse (con) (13)
engagement compromiso (13); noviazgo (13)
engine: search engine buscador *m.* (13)
engineer ingeniero(a) (5)
engineering ingeniería (2)
English (*language*) inglés *m.* (2)
engraving grabado (11)
enjoy, to apreciar (11); disfrutar; **enjoy your meal** buen provecho
enter, to entrar (en)
entertain, to festejar
entertainment diversión *f.*

enthusiastic entusiasta
entrance entrada
entrée plato principal (7)
environment ambiente *m.*
equal igual
Equatorial Guinean ecuatoguineano (14)
equipment (6)
eraser borrador *m.* (*chalk*); goma (*pencil*)
evening noche *f.*; **in the evening** por la noche
event acontecimiento
every todo(a); cada; **every day** todos los días (3)
evident evidente
exactly exacto(a)
exam examen (2)
examination (*medical*) examen médico *m.*
examine, to examinar (14)
example ejemplo; **for example** por ejemplo
excited animado(a)
exclamation exclamación *f.*
excuse excusa; **to excuse oneself** disculparse; **to make an excuse** excusarse
exercise ejercicio
exhibit, to exhibir (11)
exhibition exhibición *f.* (11)
expect, to esperar
expensive caro(a) (11); costoso(a); **how expensive!** ¡qué caro(a)! (11)
experience experiencia
express, to expresar
expression expresión *f.*
extinction: danger of extinction peligro de extinción (12)
extrovert(ed) extrovertido(a)
eye ojo (6)
eyebrow ceja
eyelash pestaña
eyelid párpado

F

fabric tela (11)
fabulous fabuloso(a)
face cara (6)
facing frente a
factory fábrica
fail, to (*class*) suspender
faint desmayo (14); **faint, to** desmayarse (14)
fair justo(a)
fall, to caer(se) (9); **to fall asleep** dormirse (ue, u) (6); **to fall in love with** enamorarse (de) (13)
false falso(a)
family familia (2)
famous famoso(a) (1)
fan aficionado(a) (6)
far (from) lejos (de) (4)
farm granja (12)
fascinate, to fascinar (8)
fascinated by, to be fascinar
fascinating fascinante
fashion moda, modo
fashionable de moda (11)
fast rápido
fat gordo(a) (1)
fatal fatal
father padre *m.*, papá *m.* (2)
father-in-law suegro (2)
fault culpa
favor favor *m.*
favorite favorito(a)
fear miedo; **to fear** temer
February febrero (3)
feel, to sentirse (ie, i) (9); **to feel like (doing something)** tener ganas de (+ inf.)
female hembra (12)
feminine femenino(a)
feminist feminista
festival festival *m.*
fever fiebre *f.*
few, (a) poco(a) (2)
fiancé(e) novio(a); prometido(a) (13)

field cancha (*sports*); campo (*sports*) (6)
fifteen quince (1); **girl's fifteenth birthday celebration** los quince años (9)
fifteen-year-old (female) quinceañera
fifteenth: girl celebrating her fifteenth birthday quinceañera (9)
fifth quinto(a) (4)
fifty cincuenta (1)
fight lucha; **to fight** luchar; pelear (8)
fill out, to completar, rellenar
film película (4)
final último(a)
finally por último, finalmente, por fin
find, to encontrar (ue) (4)
fine *adv.* bien (1); *n.* multa (9)
fine arts bellas artes *f. pl.*
finger dedo (6)
finish, to acabar (11); terminar
fire station estación *f.* de bomberos
fire, to despedir (i, i)
firefighter bombero(a)
fireplace chimenea
fireworks fuegos artificiales (9)
firm empresa
first primer/primero(a) (4); **first aid** primeros auxilios (14); **first and foremost** ante todo; **first class** primera clase (10); **first-class hotel** hotel *m.* de lujo; hotel *m.* de primera; **first of all** ante todo
fish pescado (*food*) (7); pez (*pl.* peces) (2); **fish store/market** pescadería; *raw fish marinated in lime* ceviche *m.*
fishing, to go ir de pesca (6)
fit, to quedar (11); caber; **that skirt really fits you well!** ¡qué bien te queda esa falda! (11)
fitting room probador *m.*
five cinco (1)
five hundred quinientos(as) (7)
flag bandera (1)
flan flan *m.* (7)
flight vuelo (10); **flight attendant** asistente *m. f.* de vuelo (5); azafata *f.*
flip-flop zapatilla
floor suelo; piso (*of a building*) (4); planta (*of a store or business*)
floral de flores
flower flor *f.* (4)
flowered de flores
flu gripe *f.* (14)
fluorescent fluorescente
fly, to volar (ue) (8)
fog niebla
follow, to seguir (i, i) (5)
food comida
foot pie *m.* (6)
football fútbol *m.* americano (6); **football player** futbolista *m. f.*
for para; **for example** por ejemplo
forehead frente *f.*
foreigner extranjero(a)
forest bosque *m.* (12); **tropical rain forest** bosque tropical
forget, to olvidar (11)
fork tenedor *m.*
form, to formar
forty cuarenta (1)
four cuatro (1)
four hundred cuatrocientos(as) (7)
fourteen catorce (1)
fourth cuarto(a) (4)
fox zorro (12)
fracture fractura (14); **to fracture** fracturarse (14)
French (*language*) francés *m.* (2)
frequency repetición *f.*; frecuencia
frequently a menudo
fresh fresco(a)
Friday viernes *m.* (3)
fried frito(a)
friend amigo(a) (2)
friendly amable
fright espanto

frightened: to become frightened asustarse (9)
frog rana (12)
from de; **where are you** (*fam.*) **from?** ¿de dónde eres tú? (1); **I am from...** yo soy de . . . (1)
front delantero(a); **in front (of)** enfrente (de) (4)
fruit fruta
fruit store frutería
frustrated frustrado(a) (5); **to become frustrated** frustrarse (9)
full lleno(a); satisfecho(a) (*after eating*)
full-time a tiempo completo
fun, to have divertirse (ie, i) (6)
fun *adj.* divertido(a)
funeral funeral *m.*
funny cómico(a) (1); divertido(a) (5); gracioso(a)
furious furioso(a)
furniture muebles *m. pl.* (4)
furthermore además

G

gain weight, to engordar
gallery galería (11)
game juego; partido (*sports match*) (6); **board game** juego de mesa (8); **game show** concurso (13)
garage garaje *m.* (4); taller *m.* (*shop*)
garbage basura (10)
garden, jardín *m.* (4); **to garden** (*flowers*) cultivar el jardín
garlic ajo
garment prenda (11)
gate puerta (de salida) (10)
generally generalmente, por lo general
generous generoso(a) (1)
gentleman caballero
geography geografía (2)
geology geología
geometry geometría (2)
German (*language*) alemán *m.* (2)
get, to conseguir (i, i) (g); obtener; **to get a good/bad grade** sacar (qu) una buena/mala nota; **to (not) get along** llevarse bien/mal (13); **to get distracted** distraerse (9); **to get dressed** vestirse (ie, i) (6); **to get into** montar; subir a (*a vehicle*) (9); **to get married (to)** casarse (con) (9); **to get out of** (*vehicle*) bajar de (9); **to get ready** arreglarse (6); **to get up** levantarse (6)
gift regalo (9)
giraffe jirafa (12)
girlfriend novia (2)
give, to dar (5); **to give birth** dar a luz (13)
glad, to be alegrarse
glass vaso; **wine glass** copa (7)
glasses gafas *f. pl.*; lentes *m. pl.* (3)
globalization globalización *f.* (14)
glove guante *m.* (3)
go, to ir (4); **to go away; to go out** salir (5); **to go straight** seguir (i) derecho (10)
God dios *m.*
godfather padrino
godmother madrina
gold oro
golf golf *m.* (6)
good buen/bueno(a) (1); **good afternoon** buenas tardes (1); **good morning** buenos días (1); **good night** buenas noches (1)
good-bye adiós (1); chao (1)
gorilla gorila (12)
gossip, to chismear
gossipy charlatán(-ana)
grade nota (2)
graduation graduación *f.* (9)
granddaughter nieta (2)
grandfather abuelo (2); **great-grandfather** bisabuelo
grandmother abuela (2); **great-grandmother** bisabuela
grandson nieto (2)

grape uva (8)
grapefruit toronja
grass hierba; pasto (12)
grasslands pampa (12)
grateful agradecido(a)
great gran/grande
green verde (3); **green bean** judía verde
greet, to saludar
greeting saludo
grey gris (3)
grilled asado(a) (7)
groceries comestibles
groom novio (9)
group grupo; **musical group** grupo de música (9)
Guatemalan guatemalteco(a) (14)
guest invitado(a) (9); huésped *m. f.* (7); **guest of honor** agasajado(a); festejado(a)
Guinean guineano(a)
gulf golfo
gym(nasium) gimnasio (4)

H

hair cabello; pelo (6); **to comb/style one's hair** peinarse (6)
half medio(a); **half board** (*breakfast and one other meal*) media pensión *f.*; **half brother** medio hermano (2); **half sister** media hermana (2)
hall (*banquet, event*) salón *m.*
hallway pasillo
ham jamón *m.* (8)
hamburger hamburguesa (7)
hand mano *f.* (6); **hand luggage** equipaje *m.* de mano (10); **my hands are shaking** me tiemblan las manos; **on the other hand** por otra parte, en cambio, por otro lado
handbag bolso/bolsa
handicrafts artesanías
handmade hecho(a) a mano (11)
handsome guapo(a) (1)
hang, to colgar (ue) (10)
hangover resaca
happen, to pasar
happy feliz (5); alegre (5); contento(a) (5); **to become happy** ponerse feliz; alegrarse (9)
harbor puerto
hard duro(a); difícil (*difficult*)
hard-working trabajador(a) (1)
haste prisa
hat sombrero (3)
hate, to odiar (13)
have, to tener (ie); **to have fun** divertirse (ie, i) (6); **to have to** (*do something*) deber (+ *inf.*); tener que (+ *inf.*)
he él
head cabeza (6)
headache dolor *m.* de cabeza; **I have a headache** me duele la cabeza
headphones audífonos (13)
health salud *f.* (5) (14)
healthy sano(a)
hear, to oír (5)
hearing (*sense*) oído
heart corazón *m.* (14)
heat calor *m.*; calefacción *f.* (*system*)
height estatura
hello hola (1); aló (*telephone*)
help, to ayudar (2)
hen gallina (12)
hepatitis hepatitis *f.*
her *poss.* su(s); *d.o.* la; **to/for her** *i.o.* le
here aquí (11)
hi hola (1)
hide and seek escondidas *pl.* (8)
high alto(a) (1); **high blood pressure** hipertensión *f.* (14); presión *f.* alta (14)
highway carretera
hike, to ir de excursión (6)
hill cerro; colina (12)

him lo *d.o.*; **to/for him** le *i.o.*
hip cadera
his *poss.* su(s); *d.o.* le; **to/for him** *i.o.* le
history historia (2)
hit: box office hit éxito de taquilla (13)
HIV VIH *m.*
hobby diversión *f.*
holiday día *m.* festivo
home hogar *m.*; **to return home** regresar a casa
homemaker amo(a) de casa (5)
homework tarea (2)
Honduran hondureño(a) (14)
honest honesto(a) (1)
honeymoon luna de miel (13)
hope (for), to esperar (13); **I hope** ojalá (13)
horrible horrible
horror horror *m.*
horse caballo (2)
horseback, to ride montar a caballo (6)
hose manguera (10)
hospital hospital *m.* (4)
host anfitrión(-ona); **TV host** conductor(a) (13)
hostel hostal *m.*; **youth hostel** albergue *m.* estudiantil
hot caliente; **it's hot** (*weather*) hace calor; **to be (very) hot** tener mucho calor
hotel hotel *m.* (4); **first-class hotel** hotel de lujo, hotel de primera clase; **inexpensive hotel** hotel económico
house casa
household *adj.* doméstico
housing vivienda
how expensive! ¡qué caro(a)! (11)
how? ¿cómo? (3); **how are you** (*form. sing.*)? ¿cómo está usted? (1); **how are you** (*fam. sing.*)? ¿cómo estás? (1); **how many?** ¿cuántos(as)? (3); **how much?** ¿cuánto(a)? (3); **how's it going?** ¿qué tal? (1)
however sin embargo, no obstante
hug, to abrazar (c) (13)
human humano(a); **human being** ser *m.* humano
hundred million, one cien millones
hundred thousand, one cien mil
hundred, one cien/ciento (1) (7); **one hundred one** ciento uno (1) (7)
hunger hambre *f.*
hungry, to be (very) tener (mucha) hambre
hunt, to cazar (c) (12)
hunting caza (12)
hurry prisa; **to be in a (big) hurry** tener (mucha) prisa
hurt, to doler (ue) (14)
husband esposo (2)
hypertension hipertensión *f.*

I

I yo; **I am from...** yo soy de . . . (1); **I hope** ojalá (13)
ice cream helado (7)
ice hielo; **to ice skate** patinar en hielo (6)
ideal ideal
idealist idealista (1)
identification identificación *f.*
if si
ill enfermo(a); mal; **to feel ill** sentirse (ie, i) mal
immigrant inmigrante *m. f.* (14)
immigrate, to inmigrar (14)
immigration inmigración *f.* (14)
impatient impaciente (1)
importance importancia
important importante
impossible imposible
impressive impresionante
in en (4); **in back (of)** detrás (de); **in front (of)** delante (de)
include, to incluir (y)
included incluido(a)
incorrect incorrecto(a)
increase aumento
incredible increíble
independent independiente

indirect indirecto(a); **indirect object** objeto indirecto
indispensable imprescindible
industrial waste deshechos industriales (12)
inexpensive barato(a) (11)
infinitive infinitivo
information información *f.*
ingredient ingrediente *m.*
initially inicialmente
injection inyección *f.* (14)
injured: to be injured estar herido
ink tinta (11)
inn posada; parador *m.* nacional (*government-run historical inn*) (*Sp.*)
inquisitive preguntón(-ona)
inside (of) dentro (de) (4)
insist (on), to insistir (en + *inf.*) (13)
insomnia insomnio (14)
inspect, to revisar
instructions instrucciones *f. pl.*
instructor instructor(a)
intelligent inteligente (1)
intend, to pensar (ie) (3)
interest, to interesar (8)
interested interesado (a) (5); **to be interested in** interesar
interesting interesante (1)
internacional international; **international airport** aeropuerto internacional (10); **international organization** organismo internacional (14)
internal interno(a)
Internet Internet *m.* (13)
interrogative interrogativo(a)
interview entrevista (5)
intestine intestino (14)
introduce, to presentar; **I'd like to introduce you to...** le presento a . . . (*form. sing.*) (1); te presento a . . . (*fam. sing.*) (1)
introvert(ed) introvertido(a)
invitation invitación *f.* (9)
invite, to invitar
iron plancha (10); **to iron** planchar (10)
ironing board burro (10)
irrational irracional
irresponsible irresponsable
is that so? ¿de veras?
island isla (12)
isn't: isn't that right? ¿no es así?; **isn't that so?** ¿no?
it *d.o.* lo, la; **to/for it** *i.o.* le; **it is raining** llueve (3); **it is snowing** nieva (3)
its *poss.* su(s)

J

jacket chaqueta (3)
jaguar jaguar *m.* (12)
jam mermelada (8)
January enero (3)
jealous celoso(a) (5); **to be jealous** tener celos
jealousy celos *m. pl.*
jeans jeans *m. pl.*
job candidate aspirante *m. f.*
job puesto de trabajo
joint coyuntura
joke chiste *m.* (8)
journalism periodismo (2)
journalist periodista *m. f.* (5)
judgment juicio
jugo juice (7)
July julio (3)
jump, to saltar (8)
June junio (3)
jungle selva (12)
just (*done something*), **to have** acabar de (+ *inf.*)

K

keep, to guardar; **to keep in shape** mantenerse en forma
ketchup catsup *m.* (8); salsa de tomate (dulce)

key llave *f.* (7)
keyboard tablero (13)
kidney riñón *m.*
kilogram kilo
kind amable (1)
kiosk kiosco
kiss, to besar (13)
kitchen cocina (4); **kitchen sink** fregadero (4)
kite cometa (8)
knee rodilla (6)
knife cuchillo (7)
knit, to tejer (8)
know, to saber (*facts, how to do something*) (5); conocer (zc) (*a person*) (5)
knowledge conocimiento

L

laboratory laboratorio
lack falta; **to lack** faltar
lady dama
lake lago (12)
lamb cordero
lamp lámpara (4)
land tierra; **to land** aterrizar (c) (10)
landscape paisaje *m.* (11)
language lengua (2); **modern languages** lenguas modernas
large gran/grande (11)
last último(a) (*final*); pasado(a) (*past*); **last night** anoche (6); **last year** el año pasado
lastly por último
late *adv.* tarde (6); *adj.* atrasado (a); **to be late** estar atrasado(a)
later luego; **see you later** hasta luego (1); nos vemos (1)
laugh, to reír (í, i) (3)
laundromat lavandería
laundry/laundry room lavandería; **to do laundry** lavar ropa (10)
law derecho; ley *f.* (14)
lawn césped *m.*; **to cut, mow the lawn** cortar el césped (10)
lawyer abogado(a) (5)
layover escala (10)
lazy perezoso(a) (1)
learn (*to do something*)**, to** aprender a (+ *inf.*) (3)
leather cuero; piel *f.* (11)
leave, to dejar; salir (5); irse (6), marcharse; **to leave a tip** dejar una propina (7)
lecture conferencia
left (of), to the a la izquierda (de) (4)
leg pierna (6)
lemon limón *m.*
less menos; **less than** menos que; menos de (+ *number*)
lesson lección *f.*
letter carta (4)
lettuce lechuga (8)
liberal liberal (1); **liberal arts** filosofía y letras
librarian bibliotecario(a)
library biblioteca (4)
lie, to mentir (ie, i) (3) (5); **to lie down** acostarse (ue) (6)
lift, to levantar; **to lift weights** levantar pesas (6)
light: to run a red light pasarse un semáforo en rojo (9)
lightning relámpago
like como; al igual que; **like this** así
like, to gustar; **I like** me gusta (3); **I would like** quisiera; **he/she likes** le gusta (3); **you like** te gusta (3)
likely probable
likewise igualmente
lime limón *m.*
limit limitar (13)
limit: speed limit límite *m.* de velocidad (9)
line (*queue*) cola; **to stand in line** hacer cola
linen lino (11)
lion león *m.* (12)
lip labio

liquid cleaner limpiador *m.*
list lista
listen, to escuchar (2)
liter litro
literature literatura (2)
litter basura (10)
little (bit), a un poco (1)
live, to vivir (3) (5); **long life** viva
liver hígado (14)
living: living area zona de estar; **living room** sala (4)
llama llama (12)
lobster langosta
lock up, to encerrar (ie)
lodge, to alojarse (7)
lodging alojamiento (7)
long largo(a) (1)
look: to look (at) mirar (2); **to look for** buscar (qu) (2); **to look like** parecerse (zc) a; **to look up** consultar
loose flojo(a)
lose, to perder (ie); (3) **to lose weight** adelgazar (c)
lot: a lot mucho(a) (2)
love, to querer (13); encantar; **in love (with)** enamorado (de) (5); **to fall in love with** enamorarse de (13)
lovely precioso(a)
loving cariñoso(a) (1)
low blood pressure presión *f.* baja (14)
lower inferior
loyal leal
luck suerte *f.*
lucky, to be (very) tener (mucha) suerte (2)
luggage equipaje *m.* (10); **hand luggage** equipaje *m.* de mano (10); **facturar equipaje** to check luggage (10); **luggage screening** revisión *f.* de equipaje (10)
lunch almuerzo (7); comida (7); **to have lunch** almorzar (ue) (c) (4)
lung pulmón *m.* (14)
luxury lujo (7)

M

magazine revista (13)
maid camarero(a) (*hotel*) (7)
mail correo
main dish plato principal (7)
make-up, to put on maquillarse (6)
make, to hacer (5); **to make the bed** hacer la cama (10)
male macho (12)
mammal mamífero (12)
man hombre *m.* (1)
manager gerente *m. f.*
mango mango
manner, in this así
mansion mansión *f.*
many muchos(as)
map mapa *m.* (1)
marbles canicas (8)
March marzo (3)
marker marcador *m.*; rotulador *m.*
market mercado (4)
marriage matrimonio; **to propose marriage** proponer matrimonio (13)
married: to get married (to) casarse (con) (9)
martial arts artes *f. pl.* marciales
masculine masculino(a)
mask máscara (11)
mass Misa
master of ceremonies maestro(a) de ceremonias
match (*sports*) partido; **to match** hacer *irreg.* juego (11)
materialistic materialista
mathematics matemáticas (2)
May mayo (3)
mayonnaise mayonesa (8)
me *d.o.* me; **to/for me** *i.o.* me

meadow prado
meal comida; **enjoy your meal** buen provecho
mean, to querer decir
measles sarampión *m.*; **German measles** rubéola
meat carne *f.* (7); **luncheon meat** fiambre *m.*
mechanic mecánico(a) (5)
medical médico(a)
medication medicamento (14)
medicine medicina; **veterinary medicine** veterinaria (2)
medium mediano(a) (11)
meet, to conocer (zc) a; **nice to meet you** encantado(a) (1); mucho gusto (1)
melon melón *m.* (8)
member miembro
menu carta, menú *m.*
merchant comerciante *m. f.*
message recado, mensaje *m.*; **escribir un mensaje** to write a message (3)
Mexican mexicano(a) (14)
microwave microondas *m.* (4)
midnight medianoche *f.* (3)
milk leche *f.* (8)
million millón *m.* (7); **one hundred million** cien millones
mine mío(a)
minus (*in mathematical functions*) menos
mirror espejo (4)
mischief travesura (8)
mischievous things, to do hacer travesuras (8)
miss, to extrañar (13)
mistake, to make a equivocarse (qu)
mix, to mezclar (8)
model modelo *m. f.* (5)
modern moderno(a)
modest modesto(a)
moment momento
Monday lunes *m.* (3)
money dinero (4)
monkey mono (12)
month mes *m.*; **per month** al mes; **the month before** el mes anterior
mop trapeador *m.* (10); **to mop** fregar (ie) (gu); trapear (10)
more más; **more than** más que; más de (+ *number*)
moreover por otra parte
morning mañana; **in the morning** por la mañana; **good morning** buenos días (1)
mosque mezquita (4)
motel motel *m.*
mother madre *f.* (2); mamá (2)
mother-in-law suegra (2)
motorcycle motocicleta
mountain montaña (12); **mountain climbing** alpinismo (6); **mountain pass** puerto; **mountain peak** pico; **mountain range** cordillera, sierra; **to climb mountains** hacer alpinismo (6)
mountainous montañoso(a)
mouse ratón *m.* (2) (13)
mouth boca (6)
move, to (*something*) mover (ue); (*houses*) mudarse (14)
movie película (4); **movie theater** cine *m.* (4)
mow the lawn, to cortar el césped (10)
MP3 MP3 *m.* (13)
much mucho(a)
mumps paperas
mural mural *m.* (11)
muscle ache dolor *m.* muscular
muscular muscular
museum museo (4)
music música (2)
musical group grupo de música (9)
musician músico(a) (5)
mussel mejillón *m.*
must (*do something*) deber (+ *inf.*)

mustard mostaza (8)
my *poss.* mi(s)

N

name nombre *m.*; **my name is...** me llamo … (1)
named, to be llamarse
napkin servilleta
nationality nacionalidad *f.*
natural natural; **natural resources** recursos naturales (12); **natural science** ciencias naturales (2)
nature naturaleza (12)
near cerca de (4)
necessary necesario(a); preciso(a); **it's necessary to** (+ *verb*) hay que (+ *inf.*)
neck cuello (6)
necklace collar *m.*
need, to necesitar (2); faltar
negate, to negar (ie) (gu)
neither tampoco (6); **neither... nor** ni … ni (6)
nephew sobrino (2)
nervous nervioso(a)
net red *f.* (6)
networks, social redes *f. pl.* sociales (13)
never jamás (6), nunca (6)
nevertheless sin embargo
new nuevo(a); **what's new?** ¿qué hay de nuevo? (1)
newlywed recién casado(a) (13)
news (*program*) noticiario (13)
next después, entonces, luego; **next to** al lado de (4)
next to junto a
Nicaraguan nicaragüense *m. f.* (14)
nice: nice to meet you encantado(a) (1); mucho gusto (1); **have a nice day!** ¡que tengas buen día! (1)
niece sobrina (2)
night noche *f.*; **good night** buenas noches (1); **last night** anoche (6)
night table mesita de noche
nightclub discoteca (4)
nightmare pesadilla
nine hundred novecientos(as)
nine nueve (1)
nineteen diecinueve (1)
ninety noventa (1)
ninth noveno(a) (4)
no no; **no one** nadie (6)
nobody nadie (6)
none ningún/ninguno(a) (6)
noon mediodía *m.* (3)
nor: neither... nor ni … ni (6)
normal normal; **normally** normalmente
North American norteamericano(a)
north norte *m.*
northeast noreste *m.*
northwest noroeste *m.*
nose nariz *f.* (6)
not: not well mal; **not right** incorrecto(a)
notebook cuaderno (1)
nothing nada (1)
novelist novelista *m. f.*
November noviembre *m.* (3)
now ahora
number número
nurse enfermero(a) (5)
nylon nilón *m.*

O

obesity obesidad *f.* (14)
object objeto; **direct object** objeto directo; **indirect object** objeto indirecto
obligation obligación *f.*
obstinate obstinado(a)
obtain, to conseguir (i, i) (g)
obvious obvio(a)
occupation oficio
occur, to ocurrir
ocean océano

October octubre *m.* (3)
octopus pulpo
of de; **of course** claro que sí; cómo no; por supuesto; **of course not** claro que no
offer oferta
office oficina (4); **box office** taquilla; **box office hit** éxito de taquilla (13); **doctor's office** consultorio; **post office** correo (4); oficina de correos
officer, police policía *m.* (5); mujer *f.* policía (5)
official, customs agente *m. f.* de aduana
often a menudo
oh: oh (no)! ¡caray!; **oh, my goodness** Dios mío
oil aceite *m.*; petróleo (12); **oil painting** óleo (11)
ointment pomada
okay regular; **okay?** ¿vale? ¿está bien?
old viejo(a) (1)
old-age vejez *f.*
older mayor (11)
oldest, the el/la mayor (11)
olive aceituna
on en (4); sobre; **on top (of)** encima (de) (4)
one uno (1); **one thousand** mil (7); **the one(s)** el(la) / los(las) que (1)
one-way (*ticket*) de ida
onion cebolla (8)
only sólo; único(a)
open house banquete *m.*; convite *m.*
open, to abrir (3)
opera ópera; **soap opera** telenovela (13)
opinion opinión *f.*; **to give one's opinion** opinar
opposite contrario(a)
optimist optimista (1)
or o; **either... or** o … o (6)
orange anaranjado(a) (*color*) (3); naranja (*fruit*) (7) (8)
order orden *f.* (7); **to order** mandar (13); **in order that** a fin de que (14)
ordinal ordinal
organ órgano; **vital organ** órgano vital (14)
organization: international organization organismo internacional (14)
organize, to organizar (c)
origin origen *m.*
other otro(a)
ought to deber
our *poss.* nuestro(a)
out: to get out of (*a plane, train, etc.*) bajar de; **to take the trash out** sacar (qu) la basura (10)
outfit conjunto
outside afuera; **outside of** fuera de (4)
oven horno (4)
over sobre; **over there** allá (11)
overcome, to superar

P

p.m. de la tarde; de la noche
pack one's suitcase, to hacer la maleta
page página
pain dolor *m.* (14)
paintbrush pincel *m.* (11)
painter pintor(a) (5)
painting cuadro (4); **oil painting** óleo (11)
pair pareja; par
pajamas pijama *m. f.* (3)
pal amiguito(a)
palace palacio
pallet paleta (11)
palm tree palmera (12)
Panamanian panameño(a) (14)
pants pantalones *m. pl.* (3); **what elegant pants!** ¡qué pantalones tan elegantes! (11)
panty hose medias *pl.* (3)
papaya papaya
paper papel *m.* (1); **paper towel** papel de cocina, toalla de papel; **piece of paper** hoja de papel
parade desfile *m.* (9)
Paraguayan paraguayo(a) (14)
paramedic paramédico (9)

pardon perdón *m.*
parents padres *m. pl.* (2)
park parque *m.* (4); **amusement park** parque de atracciones; **to park** estacionar (9)
parking lot aparcamiento
parking meter parquímetro (9)
part parte *f.*
part-time a tiempo parcial
partial parcial
particular, in en particular
partner compañero(a); pareja (2)
party fiesta; pachanga (*rowdy*); **bachelor party** despedida de soltero; **birthday party** fiesta de cumpleaños; **surprise party** fiesta sorpresa
pass, to pasar
pass: boarding pass pase *m.* de abordar; **mountain pass** puerto
passenger pasajero(a) (10)
passport pasaporte *m.* (10); **passport control** control *m.* de pasaporte
past pasado(a)
pastime diversión *f.*
pastry pastel *m.*; **pastry shop** pastelería
pasture pasto (12)
patient paciente (1) (14)
patio patio (4)
patterned estampado(a) (11)
pay, to pagar (gu); **to pay attention to** prestar atención
pea guisante *m.*
peace paz *f.* (14)
peach durazno (8)
peak, mountain pico
pear pera
pedestrian peatón, peatona (9)
peel, to pelar (8)
pen pluma; bolígrafo (1); **fountain pen** pluma estilográfica
pencil lápiz *m.* (*pl.* lápices) (1)
penguin pingüino (12)
peninsula península (12)
people gente *f.*
pepper pimienta (7)
per: per day al día; **per month** al mes
perfect perfecto(a)
perhaps acaso, quizá(s), tal vez
permission permiso (8)
person persona; **unmarried person** soltero(a) (13)
Peruvian peruano(a) (14)
pessimist pesimista (1)
pharmacist farmacéutico(a)
pharmacy farmacia (4)
phenomenal fenomenal
philosophy filosofía (2)
photo(graph) foto *f.*; **to develop photographs** revelar fotos; **to take photographs** sacar (qu) fotos
photographer fotógrafo(a) (5)
phrase frase *f.*
physical education educación física (2)
physics física (2)
piano piano; **to play the piano** tocar (qu) el piano (8)
pick up the table, to recoger (j) la mesa (10)
pickle pepinillo (8)
picture cuadro (4)
pie tarta
pig cerdo (12)
pill pastilla (14)
pillow almohada
pilot piloto *m. f.* (5)
piñata piñata (9)
pineapple piña (8)
ping-pong ping-pong *m.* (6)
pink rosado(a) (3)
pity lástima
place lugar *m.*; **to place** poner; **to take place** tener lugar

plaid a cuadros (11)
plains llano (12)
plane avión *m.*
plant planta (4)
plate plato (7)
plateau meseta
platform andén *m.* (10)
play, to jugar (ue) (gu) (4); **to play sports** practicar (qu) deportes (2); **to play (the piano)** tocar (qu) (el piano)
player: CD player reproductor *m.* de CDs (13); **DVD player** reproductor *m.* de DVDs (13); **football player** futbolista *m. f.*; **volleyball player** voleibolista *m. f.*
please por favor; **to please** gustar
pleasure gusto
police policía *f.* (*force*); **police car** patrulla (9); **police officer** policía *m.* (5); mujer *f.* policía (5)
political science ciencias políticas (2)
politician político(a) (5)
polka dots, with de lunares (11)
pollution contaminación *f.* (12)
pool, swimming piscina (4)
poor pobre (1)
popcorn palomitas de maíz (13)
pork cerdo (7)
portrait retrato (11)
pose, to posar (11)
post poste *m.* (9)
poster cartel *m.* (1)
potato papa (8)
poverty pobreza (14)
practice, to practicar (qu) (2)
pray, to rezar (c) (4)
pregnant, to be estar embarazada (13)
prepare, to preparar
prescription receta médica (14)
preserve, to preservar (12)
preterite pretérito
pretty bonito(a) (1); lindo; **what a pretty color!** ¡qué color tan bonito! (11); **what pretty shoes!** ¡qué lindos zapatos! (11)
previously previamente
principle principio; **in principle** en principio
print grabado (11)
prior anterior
probably probablemente
profession profesión *f.*
professor profesor(a) (1)
programmer programador(a)
programming programación *f.* (13)
prohibit, to prohibir
promise, to prometer
pronoun pronombre *m.*
propose (marriage), to proponer (matrimonio) (13)
protect proteger (j) (12)
provided that con tal (de) que (14)
psychologist psicólogo(a) (5)
psychology psicología (2)
Puerto Rican puertorriqueño(a) (14)
pulse pulso
pumpkin calabaza
purple morado (3)
purse bolsa (11)
put, to poner (5); **to put away** guardar (10); **to put on clothing** ponerse (6); **to put on make-up** maquillarse (6)
puzzle, crossword crucigrama *m.*

Q

question pregunta

R

rabbit conejo (12)
racket raqueta (6)
rag trapo (10)
rain lluvia; **to rain** llover (ue) (3); **it is raining** llueve (3)

raincoat impermeable *m.* (3)
raining: it is raining llueve (3)
rather sino, sino (que); bastante
rational racional
read, to leer (3) (5)
ready listo(a); **to get ready** arreglarse (6)
realist realista (1) (11)
realize, to darse cuenta de
really? de veras
rebel rebelde (1)
rec room sala de recreo
receipt recibo
receive, to recibir (3)
reception recepción *f.* (13)
receptionist recepcionista *m. f.* (7)
recess recreo (8)
recommend, to recomendar (ie)
recommendation recomendación *f.*
recover, to recuperarse (14)
recreation recreación
recycling reciclaje *m.* (12)
red rojo(a) (3); **to run a red light** pasarse un semáforo en rojo (9); **red wine** vino tinto (7)
red-haired pelirrojo(a) (1)
refrigerator refrigerador *m.* (4)
refugee refugiado(a) (14)
register, cash caja (11)
related relacionado(a)
relationship relación; noviazgo (13)
relative pariente (2)
religioso(a) religious
remain, to quedar (11)
remedy remedio; **to remedy** remediar
remember, to recordar (ue) (4)
rent, to alquilar (4)
repair, to reparar
repeat, to repetir (3) (5)
repetition repetición *f.*
representative representante
reptile reptil *m.* (12)
reservation reserva; reservación
resign, to renunciar
resist, to resistir
resource recurso; **natural resources** recursos naturales (12)
responsible responsable; **to make (someone) responsible** responsabilizar (c)
restaurant restaurante *m.* (4)
result resultado; **as a result** como resultado; **to result in** resultar (de/en)
return, to regresar (*place*) (2); devolver (ue) (*something*) (4); **to return home** regresar a casa (2)
revolutionary vanguardista *m. f.* (11)
rice arroz *m.* (7)
rich rico(a) (1)
ride, to (*animal*) montar a (6); **to ride a bike** andar en bicicleta (6); **to ride horseback** montar a caballo
right derecha; derecho; **a la derecha (de)** to the right (of) (4); **human rights** derechos humanos (14) **to be right** tener razón (2)
ring anillo (13)
river río (12)
rollerblade, to patinar sobre ruedas
rollerskate, to patinar sobre ruedas
room habitación *f.* (4) (7); **waiting room** sala de espera (10)
rooster gallo (12)
root raíz *f.* (*pl.* raíces)
rope (*jumping*) cuerda (8)
round-trip de ida y vuelta
routine rutina
rug alfombra (4)
run, to correr; **to run over** atropellar (9); **to run a red light** pasarse un semáforo en rojo (9); **to run a STOP sign** pasarse una señal de PARE (9)

S

sad triste (5)
safety belt cinturón *m.* de seguridad (10)
saint's day santo (9); onomástico
salt sal (7)
salad ensalada (7)
salary sueldo (5)
sale liquidación *f.*; **on sale** rebajado(a) (11); en venta
salesperson vendedor(a) (5)
salmon salmón *m.*
salty salado(a)
Salvadoran salvadoreño(a) (14)
sand arena (12)
sandal sandalia (3)
sandwich sándwich *m.* (7)
Saturday sábado (3)
sauna sauna *m.* (7)
sausage salchicha
say, to decir (5)
scared asustado(a) (5)
scarf bufanda (3)
school escuela (4); colegio (*secondary*); **school supplies** equipo escolar
science ciencia; **computer science** informática (2); **natural science** ciencias naturales (2); **political science** ciencias políticas (2); **social science** ciencias sociales (2)
scientist científico(a) (5)
screen pantalla (13)
screening: luggage screening revisión *f.* de equipaje (10)
scrub, to fregar (ie) (gu)
scuba dive, to bucear (6)
sculpt, to esculpir (11)
sculpture escultura (11)
sea mar *m.* (12)
search engine buscador *m.* (13)
season estación *f.* (3)
seat asiento (10); butaca (*theater*) (13); **seat belt** cinturón *m.* de seguridad (10)
second segundo(a) (4); **segunda clase** second class (10)
secret secreto
secretary secretario(a) (5)
security seguridad *f.* ; **security agent** agente *m., f.* de seguridad (10); **to go through security** pasar por seguridad (10)
see, to ver (5); **let's see** vamos a ver; **see you later** hasta luego (1); **nos vemos** (1); **see you soon** hasta pronto (1); **see you tomorrow** hasta mañana (1); **to see oneself** verse (6);
seek: hide and seek escondidas *pl.* (8)
seem, to parecer(zc)
self-portrait autorretrato (11)
selfish egoísta (1)
sell, to vender (3)
send, to mandar (4)
sentence oración
separate (from), to separarse (de) (13)
September septiembre *m.* (3)
serenade serenata (9)
serious serio(a) (1)
serve, to servir (3) (5)
server mesero(a), camarero(a)
servicio de emergencias emergency service (9)
set, to poner (5); **to set the table** poner la mesa (10)
seven hundred setecientos(as) (7)
seven siete (1)
seventeen diecisiete
seventh séptimo(a) (4)
seventy setenta (1)
several varios(as) (2)
shampoo champú *m.* (6)
shape, to keep in mantenerse en forma
shark tiburón *m.* (12)
shave, to afeitarse (6)
sheep oveja (12)
shiny brillante

ship barco
shirt camisa (3)
shoe zapato (3); **what pretty shoes!** ¡qué lindos zapatos! (11)
shopping center centro comercial
short corto(a) (*length*) (1); bajo(a) (*height*) (1)
shorts pantalones *m. pl.* cortos (3)
should deber (3)
shoulder hombro
show: game show concurso (13); **to show** mostrar (ue)
shower ducha (4); **baby shower** fiesta de canastilla; **bridal shower** despedida de soltera; **to shower** bañarse (*Mex.*) (6); ducharse (6)
shrimp camarón *m.* (7); gamba
shy tímido (1)
sick enfermo(a) (5)
sidewalk acera (9)
sign señal *f.* (9); **to run a STOP sign** pasarse una señal de PARE (9)
silk seda (11)
similarly del mismo modo
simple sencillo(a) (11)
sing, to cantar (2)
singer cantante *m., f.* (5)
single sencillo (*room*) (7)
sister-in-law cuñada (2)
six hundred seiscientos(as) (7)
six seis (1)
sixteen dieciséis (1)
sixth sexto(a) (4)
sixty sesenta (1)
size talla (*clothing*) (11); número (*shoe*) (11)
skate patín *m.* (6); **to skate** patinar (6) (8)
skateboard patineta (8)
skeleton esqueleto (14)
ski, to esquiar (2); **to water ski** esquiar en el agua (6)
skin piel *f.*
skirt falda (3); **that skirt really fits you well!** ¡qué bien te queda esa falda! (11)
sky cielo (12)
sleep, to dormir (ue, u) (4) (5)
sleeping: sleeping bag saco de dormir (6); **sleeping car** coche *m.* cama (10)
sleepy: to be (very) sleepy tener (mucho) sueño (2)
slip: credit slip comprobante *m.*
slipper zapatilla
small pequeño(a) (1); chico(a) (11)
smell (*sense*) olfato
smile, to sonreír (í, i) (3)
smog esmog *m.* (12)
snack bocadillo (9); **to eat a snack** merendar (ie)
snake serpiente *f.* (12)
sneeze estornudo; **to sneeze** estornudar (14)
snorkel, to bucear con tubo de respiración
snow nieve *f.*; **to snow** nevar (ie) (3); **it is snowing** nieva (3)
snowboard, to esquiar en tabla (6)
snowing: it's snowing nieva (3)
so that a fin de que (14); para que (14)
so, so regular (1)
soap jabón *m.* (6); **dish soap** jabón *m.* para platos (10); **soap opera** telenovela (13)
soccer fútbol *m.* (6)
sociable sociable (1)
social social; **social networks** redes *f. pl.* sociales (13); **social sciences** ciencias sociales (2); **social worker** trabajador(a) social (5)
sociology sociología
socks calcetines *m. pl.* (3)
soda refresco (7)
soft blando(a)
solid (*color*) liso(a) (11)
solidarity solidaridad *f.*
solve, to resolver (ue); solucionar
some algún/alguno(a) (6)
somebody alguien (6)
someone alguien (6)

something algo (6)
son-in-law yerno
soon pronto; **as soon as** en cuanto (14); tan pronto como (14); **see you soon** hasta pronto (1)
sorry: I'm sorry lo siento
soup sopa (7)
soupspoon cuchara (7)
south sur *m.*
southeast sureste *m.*
southwest suroeste *m.*
spa balneario
Spanish (*language*) español *m.; adj.* español(a) (14)
speech (*class*) expresión *f.* oral (2)
speed limit límite *m.* de velocidad (9)
spinach espinaca
spinal column columna vertebral
spite: in spite of a pesar de
sponsor patrocinador *m.* (13); **to sponsor** patrocinar
spouse esposo(a) (2)
spring primavera (3)
square cuadro; **city square** plaza (4)
squash calabaza
squirrel ardilla (12)
stairs escalera (7)
stand in line, to hacer cola
station estación *f.*
stay, to (*hotel room*) alojarse (7)
stepbrother hermanastro (2)
stepfather padrastro (2)
stepmother madrastra (2)
stepsister hermanastra (2)
still life naturaleza muerta (11)
stomach estómago (6)
stop parada (10); **to make a stop** hacer escala; **to run a STOP sign** pasarse una señal de PARE (9)
store tienda (4)
story cuento (8); **to tell a story** contar (ue) (8)
stove estufa (4)
straight, to go seguir (i) derecho (10)
straighten up, to ordenar (10)
strawberry fresa (8)
street calle *f.* (4)
strep throat inflamación *f.* de garganta
stretch, to estirarse (6)
stretcher camilla (9)
strip, comic tira cómica (8)
stripe raya
striped a rayas (11)
struggle, to luchar
student estudiante *m., f.* (1); *adj.* estudiantil
study, to estudiar (2)
style one's hair, to peinarse (6)
subject materia
subway metro
successful: to be (very) successful tener (mucho) éxito (2)
suddenly de repente (9)
sugar azúcar *m.* (7)
suggest, to sugerir (ie, i) (13)
suggestion sugerencia
suit traje *m.* (3); **suit coat** saco; **swimming suit** traje *m.* de baño (3)
suitcase maleta (7); **to pack one's suitcase** hacer la maleta; **to unpack one's suitcase** deshacer la maleta
summary resumen *m.*; **in summary** en resumen
summer verano (3)
sunburn quemadura de sol
Sunday domingo (3)
sunglasses gafas de sol
supermarket supermercado (4)
support, to sostener
sure seguro(a) (5)
surgery cirugía (14)

surprised sorprendido(a) (5); **to be surprised** sorprenderse (9)
surrealist surrealista *m. f.* (11)
swear, to jurar
sweater suéter *m.* (3)
sweep, to barrer (10)
swim, to nadar (2)
swimming pool piscina (4)
swimming suit traje *m.* de baño (3)
sympathy compasión *f.*
syrup, cough jarabe (14)

T

T-shirt camiseta (3)
table mesa; **coffee table** mesita (4); **table setting** cubiertos; **to clear the table** recoger (j) la mesa (10); **to pick up the table** recoger (j) la mesa (10); **to set the table** poner la mesa (10)
tailor sastre *m.*
take, to tomar (2); **take off, to** despegar (gu) (*airplane*) (10); **to take off clothing** quitarse la ropa (6); **to take place** tener lugar; **to take someone's blood pressure** tomar la presión (14); **to take the trash out** sacar (qu) la basura (10)
talk, to hablar (2) (5); **to talk on the telephone** hablar por teléfono (2)
tall alto(a)
tea té *m.*
teach, to enseñar (2)
team equipo (6)
technician técnico(a)
telephone teléfono; **to talk on the telephone** hablar por teléfono (2)
television (*medium*) televisión *f.*; **satellite television** televisión *f.* por satélite (13); **television viewer** televidente *m. f.* (13); **to watch television** mirar la tele (2)
television set televisor *m.* (1)
tell, to decir (5); **to tell a story** contar (ue) (8)
temperature temperatura
temple templo (4)
ten diez (1)
tenth décimo
tennis tenis *m.* (6); **tennis shoes** tenis *m. pl.* (3)
tent, camping tienda de campaña (6)
tenth décimo (4)
term curso (2)
terrible terrible
that ese(a) (11); aquel(la) (*over there*) (11)
theater teatro (2) (4); **movie theater** cine *m.* (4); arte *m.* dramático
there allí (11); **over there** allá (11)
there is/are hay (1)
therefore así que; por eso
thigh muslo (6)
thin delgado (1)
think, to pensar (ie) (3)
third tercero(a) (4)
thirsty: to be (very) thirsty tener (mucha) sed (2)
thirteen trece (1)
thirty-one treinta y uno (1)
this este(a) (11)
thousand, one mil (7); **two thousand** dos mil (7)
three hundred trescientos(as) (7)
three tres (1)
thunder trueno
Thursday jueves *m.* (3)
thus así; así que
ticket boleto (10); pasaje; ; entrada (*to event*) (6); multa (*fine*) (9)
tidy up, to ordenar (10)
tie corbata (3)

tiger tigre *m.* (12)

tight apretado(a) (11)

time (*of day*) hora; at times a veces; on time a tiempo (10); to have a good time pasarlo bien

tip, to leave a dejar una propina (7)

tired cansado(a) (5)

toast *n.* (*with a drink*) brindis *m.* (9); to toast brindar (9)

today hoy (3)

toe dedo del pie (6)

toilet inodoro (4)

tomato tomate *m.* (7)

tomorrow mañana (3); see you tomorrow hasta mañana (1)

tongue lengua; to stick out one's tongue sacar la lengua

tooth diente *m.* (6)

toothpaste dentrífico (6)

tortilla chips totopos (7)

touch, to tocar (qu)

tough duro(a)

tourist turista *m. f.* (7)

towel toalla (6)

tower torre *f.*

toy juguete *m.* (8)

trade agreement tratado de comercio (14)

traditional tradicional (11)

train, to entrenar

tranquil tranquilo(a)

translator traductor(a)

transportation transporte *m.* (7)

trash basura (10); to take the trash out sacar (qu) la basura (10)

trashcan bote *m.* de basura (10)

travel agent agente de viajes (5)

travel, to viajar (2)

traveler's check cheque *m.* de viaje; cheque *m.* de viajero

treatment tratamiento (14)

tree árbol *m.* (12); to climb a tree trepar un árbol (8)

treinta thirty (1)

trip viaje *m.*; all-inclusive trip viaje todo pagado (7); to trip tropezar (ie) (c) (9)

triple triple (7)

tropical tropical; tropical rain forest selva tropical

trout trucha

try, to (*to do something*) tratar (de + *inf.*); to try on probarse (ue) (11)

Tuesday martes *m.* (3)

tuna atún *m.*

turkey pavo (7)

turn, to doblar (10); to turn off apagar (gu) (11); to turn years old cumplir años (9)

turtle tortuga (12)

TV televisión *f.*; TV host conductor(a) (13); TV rating clasificación *f.* (13)

twelve doce (1)

twenty veinte

twenty-eight veintiocho (1)

twenty-five veinticinco (1)

twenty-four veinticuatro (1)

twenty-nine veintinueve (1)

twenty-one veintiuno (1)

twenty-seven veintisiete (1)

twenty-six veintiséis (1)

twenty-three veintitrés (1)

twenty-two veintidós (1)

twist, to torcerse (ue) (z) (14)

two dos (1); two hundred doscientos(as) (7); two thousand dos mil

U

ugly feo(a) (1)

umbrella paraguas *m. sing., pl.* (3); beach umbrella sombrilla

uncle tío (2)

under abajo de; debajo de (4)

understand, to comprender (3); entender (ie) (3)

unemployed desempleado(a)

unemployment desempleo (14)

unfriendly antipático(a) (1)

union: common-law union unión *f.* libre (13)

unique único(a)

university universidad *f.*

unless a menos que (14)

unmarried person soltero(a) (13)

unpack one's suitcase, to deshacer la maleta

up to now hasta aquí

Uruguayan uruguayo(a) (14)

use, to usar

usually usualmente

utilities servicios

V

vacation vacaciones *f. pl.*

vaccinate vacunar

vaccine vacuna (14)

vacuum cleaner aspiradora (10)

vacuum, to pasar la aspiradora (10)

valiant valiente

valley valle *m.* (12)

value valor *m.*

vegetable verdura

Venezuelan venezolano(a) (14)

very muy (1)

vest chaleco (3)

veterinarian veterinario(a) (5)

veterinary medicine veterinaria (2)

videogame videojuego (8)

viewer: television viewer televidente *m. f.* (13)

visa visa (10)

volcano volcán *m.* (12)

volleyball voleibol (6); balón *m.* (*ball*)

vomit, to vomitar (14)

vote, to votar (14)

voucher comprobante *m.*

W

wagon vagón *m.* (10)

wait, to esperar; to wait on atender (ie) a

waiter/waitress mesero(a) (5)

waiting room sala de espera (10)

waitperson camarero(a)

wake up, to despertarse (ie) (6)

walk, to andar (6); caminar (2); to go on a walk dar un paseo (8)

want ad solicitud *f.* (5)

want, to querer (3)

war guerra (14)

warmth calor *m.*

wash, to lavar(se) (6)

washing machine lavadora (4)

waste, industrial deshechos industriales (12)

watch reloj *m.*; to watch mirar (2); to watch television mirar la tele (2)

water agua (*f., but* el agua); to water regar (ie) (gu) (10); to water ski esquiar en el agua (6)

water-skiing esquí *m.* acuático

watermelon sandia

waterfall cascada (12); catarata (12)

wave ola (2)

way manera; by the way a propósito

wealth riqueza (14)

wear, to llevar (3)

weather tiempo; hace buen tiempo the weather is nice (3); hace mal tiempo the weather is bad (3)

wedding boda (9)

Wednesday miércoles *m.* (3)

week semana (3); last week la semana pasada (6)

weekend fin *m.* de semana (3)

weight: to gain weight engordar; to lose weight adelgazar (c)

weights pesas; to lift weights levantar pesas (6)

whale ballena (12)

what? ¿qué? (3); what's going on? ¿qué pasa? (1); what's new? ¿qué hay de nuevo? (1)

what...!: what a pretty color! ¡qué color tan bonito! (11); what elegant pants! ¡qué pantalones tan elegantes! (11); what pretty shoes! ¡qué lindos zapatos! (11)

wheel rueda

when? ¿cuándo? (3)

where? ¿dónde? (3); from where? ¿de dónde? (3)

whether si

which lo cual; lo que

which? ¿cuál(es)? (3)

whipped batido(a); whipped cream crema batida

white blanco(a) (3); white wine vino blanco

who? ¿quién(es)? (3)

whose cuyo(a)

why? ¿por qué? (3)

widow viudo (13)

widower viuda (13)

wind viento

window ventana (1); ventanilla (10); ticket window taquilla (10)

windy: it is windy hace viento (3)

wine vino; red wine vino tinto (7); wine glass copa (7); white wine vino blanco

winter invierno (3)

wish, to desear (2) (13)

without sin; sin que (14)

witness testigo *m., f.* (9)

wolf lobo (12)

woman mujer *f.* (1)

wonder maravilla

wool lana (11)

word palabra

work (*of art, literature, theater, etc.*) obra (11); to work trabajar (2)

worker, social trabajador(a) social (5)

workshop taller *m.*

worried preocupado(a) (5)

worry, to preocuparse

worse peor (11)

wound herida

wrap, to envolver (ue)

wrist muñeca

write, to escribir (3); to write a message escribir un mensaje (3)

writer escritor(a) (5)

writing redacción *f.* (2)

wrong equivocado(a) (5)

X

x-ray radiografía (14)

Y

yard patio

year año; to be... years old tener . . . años (2)

yellow amarillo(a) (3)

yes sí

yesterday ayer (6); day before yesterday anteayer

you tú (*fam. sing.*); usted (*form. sing.*); ustedes (*pl.*); vosotros(as) (*pl. fam.*)

young joven (*pl.* jóvenes) (1)

younger menor (11)

youth juventud *f.*; youth hostel albergue *m.* estudiantil

Z

zebra cebra (12)

zero cero (1)

zoo zoológico (4)

Vocabulario 1

🔊 CD1–7

Saludos

bien	*fine*
buenas noches	*good night*
buenas tardes	*good afternoon*
buenos días	*good morning*
¿Cómo estás?	*How are you? (informal)*
¿Cómo está usted?	*How are you? (formal)*
hola	*hello*
mal	*bad*
nada	*nothing*
¿Qué hay de nuevo?	*What's new?*
¿Qué pasa?	*What's going on?*
¿Qué tal?	*How's it going?*
regular	*okay*
¿y tú?	*and you? (informal)*
¿y usted?	*and you? (formal)*

Presentaciones

Encantado(a).	*Nice to meet you.*
Me llamo...	*My name is . . .*
Mucho gusto.	*Nice to meet you.*
Le presento a...	*I'd like to introduce you to . . . (formal)*
Te presento a...	*I'd like to introduce you to . . . (informal)*

Despedidas

adiós	*good-bye*
chao	*bye*
Hasta luego.	*See you later.*
Hasta mañana.	*See you tomorrow.*
Hasta pronto.	*See you soon.*
Nos vemos.	*See you later.*
¡Qué tengas un buen día!	*Have a nice day!*

El salón de clases

bandera	*flag*
bolígrafo	*pen*
cartel (m.)	*poster*
computadora	*computer*
cuaderno	*notebook*
diccionario	*dictionary*
escritorio	*teacher's desk*
estudiante (m.f.)	*student*
lápiz (m.)	*pencil*
libro	*book*
mapa (m.)	*map*
la mesa	*table*
mochila	*backpack*
papel (m.)	*paper*
pizarra	*chalkboard*
profesor(a)	*professor*
puerta	*door*
pupitre (m.)	*student desk*
reloj (m.)	*clock*
salón de clases	*classroom*
silla	*chair*
televisor (m.)	*television set*
ventana	*window*

Palabras adicionales

hay	*there is/there are*
¿De dónde eres tú?	*Where are you from?*
Yo soy de...	*I am from . . .*

Gramática

Gender and number of nouns

1. A noun is a person, place, or thing. In order to make a noun plural, add an **-s** to words ending in a vowel. Add **-es** to words ending in a consonant, unless that consonant is **-z** in which case the **-z** changes to **-c** before adding **-es**. (lápiz → lápices)

2. Some nouns lose an accent mark or gain an accent mark when they become plural. (examen → exámenes) You will learn more about accents in **Capítulo 2**.

3. Nouns have gender (masculine / feminine) whether or not they refer to people. In general, if they are not referring to people, nouns that end in **-o** are masculine, and nouns that end in **-a** are feminine. Exceptions include **el** día (m.), **el** mapa (m.), **el** problema (m.), **la** mano (f.), **la** foto (f.), and **la** moto (f.).

Definite and indefinite articles

1. Definite articles mean *the*, and are used to refer to specific nouns or nouns already mentioned. They agree in gender and number with the noun they modify.

	masculino	femenino
singular	el	la
plural	los	las

2. Indefinite articles mean *a / an* or *some*, and are used to refer to non-specific nouns. They also agree in gender and number with the noun they modify.

	masculino	femenino
singular	un	una
plural	unos	unas

Hay

1. **Hay** means *there is* when followed by a singular noun and *there are* when followed by a plural noun.

> Hay un libro en el pupitre.
> *There is a book on the desk.*

> Hay veinte estudiantes en la clase.
> *There are twenty students in the class.*

Los números

uno	*one*		veintiuno	*twenty-one*
dos	*two*		veintidós	*twenty-two*
tres	*three*		veintitrés	*twenty-three*
cuatro	*four*		veinticuatro	*twenty-four*
cinco	*five*		veinticinco	*twenty-five*
seis	*six*		veintiséis	*twenty-six*
siete	*seven*		veintisiete	*twenty-seven*
ocho	*eight*		veintiocho	*twenty-eight*
nueve	*nine*		veintinueve	*twenty-nine*
diez	*ten*		treinta	*thirty*
once	*eleven*		treinta y uno	*thirty-one*
doce	*twelve*		cuarenta	*forty*
trece	*thirteen*		cincuenta	*fifty*
catorce	*fourteen*		sesenta	*sixty*
quince	*fifteen*		setenta	*seventy*
dieciséis	*sixteen*		ochenta	*eighty*
diecisiete	*seventeen*		noventa	*ninety*
dieciocho	*eighteen*		cien	*one hundred*
diecinueve	*nineteen*		ciento uno	*one hundred one*
veinte	*twenty*			

Vocabulario 2

🔊 CD1–8

Describir la personalidad

aburrido(a)	boring
agresivo(a)	aggressive
amable	nice
antipático(a)	mean
atlético(a)	athletic
bueno(a)	good
cariñoso(a)	loving
cómico(a)	funny
conservador(a)	conservative
cruel	cruel
egoísta	selfish
famoso(a)	famous
generoso(a)	generous
honesto(a)	honest
idealista	idealist
impaciente	impatient
inteligente	intelligent
interesante	interesting
liberal	liberal
malo(a)	bad
optimista	optimist
paciente	patient
perezoso(a)	lazy
pesimista	pessimist
pobre	poor
realista	realist
rebelde	rebel
rico(a)	rich
serio(a)	serious
simpático(a)	nice
sociable	sociable
tímido(a)	timid, shy
tonto(a)	dumb
trabajador(a)	hard-working

Describir el aspecto físico

alto(a)	tall
bajo(a)	short
bonito(a)	pretty
calvo(a)	bald
delgado(a)	thin
feo(a)	ugly
gordo(a)	fat
grande	big
guapo(a)	handsome
joven	young
moreno(a)	dark-skinned/dark-haired
pelirrojo(a)	red-haired
pequeño(a)	small
rubio(a)	blond(e)
viejo(a)	old

Palabras adicionales

corto(a)	short (length)
difícil	difficult
fácil	easy
el hombre	man
largo(a)	long
la mujer	woman
muy	very
el (la) niño(a)	child
un poco	a little
ser	to be

Gramática

Subject pronouns

1. The subject pronouns in Spanish are **yo, tú, él, ella, usted, nosotros/nosotras, vosotros/vosotras, ellos, ellas,** and **ustedes.**

2. **Tú** and **usted (Ud.)** both mean *you.* **Tú** is informal, **usted** is formal.

3. The subject pronouns **nosotros, vosotros,** and **ellos** must be made feminine when referring to a group of only females (**nosotras , vosotras, ellas**). If there is a mixed-gender group, the subject pronouns remain in the masculine form.

4. **Vosotros** and **ustedes** both mean *you* (plural). **Vosotros** is used in Spain with a familiar group of people. **Ustedes** is always used to address a group formally, and in Latin America, it is also used to address a familiar group.

Ser

1. The verb **ser** means *to be,* and its forms are as follows:

yo	soy	nosotros / nosotras	somos
tú	eres	vosotros / vosotras	sois
usted	es	ustedes	son
él / ella	es	ellos / ellas	son

2. **Ser** is used when describing someone's traits (tall, intelligent, etc.) and to say where someone is from.

Adjective agreement

1. Adjectives describe a person, place, or thing. In Spanish, adjectives must agree in gender and number with the nouns that they modify.

2. If a singular masculine adjective ends in **-o,** the ending must be changed to **-a** when modifying a feminine noun (**alto → alta**).

3. If a singular masculine adjective ends in **-a** or **-e,** it does not need to be changed when modifying a feminine noun (**idealista, paciente**).

4. If a singular masculine adjective ends in a consonant, it does not need to be made feminine, unless the ending is **-or,** in which case you would add an **-a** (**trabajador → trabajadora**).

5. Once you have made the adjective agree in gender, you must make it also agree in number. To modify plural nouns, you add **-s** to adjectives that end in vowels or **-es** to adjectives that end in consonants.

Vocabulario 1

🔊 CD1–12

Las materias académicas

alemán (m.)	German
álgebra (m.)	Algebra
arte (m.)	Art
biología	Biology
cálculo	Calculus
ciencias naturales	Natural Science
ciencias políticas	Political Science
ciencias sociales	Social Science
criminología	Criminology
economía	Economy
educación física (f.)	Physical Education
expresión oral (f.)	Speech
filosofía	Philosophy
física (f.)	Physics
francés (m.)	French
geografía	Geography
geometría	Geometry
historia	History
informática	Computer Science
ingeniería	Engineering
inglés (m.)	English
literatura	Literature
matemáticas	Mathematics
música	Music
negocios	Business
periodismo	Journalism
psicología	Psychology
química	Chemistry
redacción (f.)	Writing
teatro	Theater
veterinaria	Veterinary Medicine

Expresiones con *tener*

tener... años	to be . . . years old
tener (mucho) calor	to be (very) hot
tener (mucho) cuidado	to be (very) careful
tener (mucho) éxito	to be (very) successful
tener (mucho) frío	to be (very) cold
tener (mucha) hambre	to be (very) hungry
tener (mucho) miedo	to be (very) afraid
tener (mucha) prisa	to be in a (big) hurry
tener razón	to be right
tener (mucha) sed	to be (very) thirsty
tener (mucho) sueño	to be (very) sleepy
tener (mucha) suerte	to be (very) lucky

Palabras adicionales

compañero(a) de clase	classmate
curso	term
examen (m.)	exam
lenguas	languages
mucho	a lot
nota	grade
poco	a little, few
tarea	homework
varios	several

Gramática

The verb *tener*

1. The verb **tener** means *to have*, and its forms are as follows:

yo	**tengo**	nosotros(as)	**tenemos**
tú	**tienes**	vosotros(as)	**tenéis**
él / ella / usted	**tiene**	ellos / ellas / ustedes	**tienen**

2. The verb **tener** can also mean *to be* when used in certain expressions. See **expresiones con *tener*** on the left-hand column of this page.

Mi mejor amiga **tiene** diecinueve años.
*My best friend **is** nineteen years old.*

Yo siempre **tengo** hambre antes del almuerzo.
*I **am** always hungry before lunch.*

Adjective placement

1. In Spanish, adjectives are generally placed after the noun they describe.

La química no es una clase **fácil.**
*Chemistry is not an **easy** class.*

2. Adjectives such as **mucho, poco,** and **varios** that indicate quantity or amount are placed in front of the object.

Tengo **varias** clases los jueves, pero no tengo clase los viernes.
I have several classes on Thursdays, but I don't have class on Fridays.

3. When using more than one adjective to describe a noun, use commas between adjectives and **y** (*and*) before the last adjective.

Mis clases son largas, difíciles **y** aburridas.
My classes are long, difficult, and boring.

Vocabulario 2

🔊 CD1–13

La familia

abuelo(a)	grandfather/grandmother
amigo(a)	friend
cuñado(a)	brother-in-law/sister-in-law
esposo(a)	spouse
hermanastro(a)	stepbrother/stepsister
hermano(a)	brother/sister
hijo(a)	son/daughter
madrastra	stepmother
madre (mamá)	mother
medio(a) hermano(a)	half brother/half sister
nieto(a)	grandson/granddaughter
novio(a)	boyfriend/girlfriend
padrastro	stepfather
padre (papá)	father
pareja	couple; partner
pariente (m.)	relative
primo(a)	cousin
sobrino(a)	nephew/niece
suegro(a)	father-in-law/mother-in-law
tío(a)	uncle/aunt

Las mascotas

caballo	horse
gato(a)	cat
pájaro	bird
perro(a)	dog
pez (m.)	fish
ratón (m.)	mouse

Los verbos

ayudar	to help
bailar	to dance
buscar	to look for
caminar	to walk
cantar	to sing
cocinar	to cook
comprar	to buy
desear	to wish
enseñar	to teach
escuchar	to listen
esquiar	to ski
estudiar	to study
hablar (por teléfono)	to talk (on the phone)
limpiar	to clean
llamar	to call
llegar	to arrive
mirar (la tele)	to look, to watch (TV)
nadar	to swim
necesitar	to need
perder	to lose
practicar (deportes)	to practice (to play sports)
preguntar	to ask
regresar (a casa)	to return (home)
tomar (café)	to take, to drink (coffee)
trabajar	to work
viajar	to travel

Gramática

Regular -ar verbs

1. The verbs presented on the left are in the *infinitive* form. This form identifies the action, and is translated as *to (do something)* in English. (**Bailar** means <u>to</u> dance.)

2. Verbs in the infinitive form need to be conjugated when you are identifying the person who is doing the action. Regular **-ar** verbs are all conjugated in the same way. To form a present tense verb, the **-ar** is dropped from the infinitive and an ending is added that reflects the subject (the person doing the action).

nadar

yo	-o	nad**o**	nosotros(as)	-amos	nad**amos**
tú	-as	nad**as**	vosotros(as)	-áis	nad**áis**
él / ella / usted	-a	nad**a**	ellos / ellas / ustedes	-an	nad**an**

3. When using two verbs together that are dependent upon each other, the second verb remains in the infinitive.

Los estudiantes **necesitan estudiar.**
The students need to study.

However, both verbs are conjugated if they are not dependent on each other.

Mi primo **trabaja, practica** deportes y estudia en la universidad.
My cousin works, plays sports, and studies at the university.

4. Place the word **no** before the conjugated verb to make a statement negative.

5. To form a yes/no question, you simply use intonation to raise your voice and place the subject after the conjugated verb. There is no need for a helping word in Spanish.

¿**Cocinas tú** bien?
Do you cook well?

Possessive adjectives

1. The possessive adjectives in Spanish are as follows:

mi(s)	my	nuestro(a)(s)	our
tu(s)	your	vuestro(a)(s)	your (plural, informal)
su(s)	his, her, its, your (formal)	su(s)	their, your (plural, informal or formal)

2. Possessive adjectives, like other adjectives, must agree in gender and number with the nouns that they modify. **Nuestro** and **vuestro** are the only possessive adjectives that need to change for gender.

Nuestra familia es muy grande. *Our family is very big.*
Mis primos son jóvenes. *My cousins are young.*

3. In Spanish, the 's does not exist. Instead, if you want to be more specific about who possesses or owns something, it is necessary to use **de.**

Elena es la hija **de** Juan.
Elena is Juan's daughter.

4. When **de** is followed by **el** in Spanish, you form the contraction **del.**

Anita es una amiga **del** profesor.
Anita is the professor's friend.

Vocabulario 1

🔊 CD1–16

Los días de la semana

lunes (m.)	Monday
martes (m.)	Tuesday
miércoles (m.)	Wednesday
jueves (m.)	Thursday
viernes (m.)	Friday
sábado (m.)	Saturday
domingo (m.)	Sunday

Los meses

enero	January
febrero	February
marzo	March
abril	April
mayo	May
junio	June
julio	July
agosto	August
septiembre	September
octubre	October
noviembre	November
diciembre	December

Los verbos

abrir	to open
aprender (a + infinitive)	to learn (to do something)
asistir (a)	to attend
beber	to drink
comer	to eat
comprender	to understand
correr	to run
creer	to believe
deber	should, ought to
escribir (un mensaje)	to write (a message)
leer	to read
recibir	to receive
vender	to sell
vivir	to live

Palabras adicionales

cumpleaños (m.)	birthday
día (m.)	day
fecha	date
fin de semana (m.)	weekend
hoy	today
mañana	tomorrow
medianoche (f.)	midnight
mediodía (m.)	noon
semana	week
todos los días	every day

Expresiones importantes

me gusta	I like
te gusta	you like
le gusta	he/she likes

Gramática

Me gusta / te gusta / le gusta

1. The Spanish equivalent of *I like* is **me gusta**, which literally means *it pleases me*. The expressions **me gusta** *(I like)*, **te gusta** *(you like)*, and **le gusta** *(he/she likes)* are followed by singular nouns.

> **¿Te gusta** la clase?
> *Do you like the class? (Does the class please you?)*

> No **me gusta** la pizza.
> *I don't like pizza. (Pizza doesn't please me.)*

2. The expressions **me gustan, te gustan,** and **le gustan** are followed by plural nouns.

> No **me gustan** los exámenes.
> *I don't like exams.*

> **Nos gustan** las lenguas.
> *We like languages.*

3. When followed by a verb or a series of verbs, the singular form **gusta** is used.

> A Julio **le gusta** practicar deportes y leer.
> *Julio likes to play sports and read.*

4. When using **gustar** with a noun, you must use the definite article as well.

> No me gusta **el** invierno.
> *I don't like winter.*

5. To clarify who he or she is, it is necessary to use an **a** in front of the name.

> **A Marta** le gusta correr.
> *Marta likes to run.*

6. To express different degrees, use the terms **mucho** *(a lot)*, **poco** *(a little)*, and **para nada** *(not at all)*.

> No me gusta trabajar **para nada.**
> *I don't like working at all.*

Regular -*er* and -*ir* verbs

1. When conjugating regular **-er** and **-ir** verbs, you follow the same steps as you would to conjugate an **-ar** verb.

2. The endings for regular **-er** verbs are as follows:

comer

yo	-o	como	nosotros(as)	-emos	comemos
tú	-es	comes	vosotros(as)	-éis	coméis
él / ella / usted	-e	come	ellos / ellas / ustedes	-en	comen

3. The endings for regular **-ir** verbs are as follows:

vivir

yo	-o	vivo	nosotros(as)	-imos	vivimos
tú	-es	vives	vosotros(as)	-ís	vivís
él / ella / usted	-e	vive	ellos / ellas / ustedes	-en	viven

Vocabulario 2

🔊 CD1–17

La ropa y los accesorios

abrigo	coat
blusa	blouse
bluyíns (m.)	blue jeans
botas	boots
bufanda	scarf
calcetines (m.)	socks
camisa	shirt
camiseta	T-shirt
chaleco	vest
chaqueta	jacket
cinturón (m.)	belt
corbata	tie
falda	skirt
gorro	cap
guantes (m.)	gloves
impermeable (m.)	raincoat
lentes (m.)	glasses
medias	panty hose
pantalones (m.)	pants
pantalones cortos	shorts
paraguas (m.)	umbrella
pijama	pajamas
sandalias	sandals
sombrero	hat
suéter (m.)	sweater
tenis (m.)	tennis shoes
traje (m.)	suit
traje de baño (m.)	swimming suit
vestido	dress
zapatos	shoes

El tiempo

Está despejado.	It is clear.
Está nublado.	It is cloudy.
Hace buen tiempo.	The weather is nice.
Hace calor.	It's hot.
Hace fresco.	It is cool.
Hace frío.	It's cold.
Hace mal tiempo.	The weather is bad.
Hace sol.	It's sunny.
Hace viento.	It is windy.
Llueve.	It rains./It is raining.
Nieva.	It snows./It is snowing.

Las estaciones

invierno	winter
otoño	fall
primavera	spring
verano	summer

Los verbos

cerrar (ie)	to close
comenzar (ie)	to begin
competir (i)	to compete
empezar (ie)	to begin
entender (ie)	to understand
llevar	to wear
mentir (ie)	to lie
nevar (ie)	to snow
pedir (i)	to ask for
pensar (ie)	to think
preferir (ie)	to prefer
reír (i)	to laugh
repetir (i)	to repeat
querer (ie)	to want
servir (i)	to serve
sonreír (i)	to smile

Los colores

amarillo	yellow
anaranjado	orange
azul	blue
blanco	white
café	brown
gris	grey
morado	purple
negro	black
rojo	red
rosado	pink
verde	green

Gramática

Interrogatives

1. In most questions:
   - the subject is placed after the verb.
   - the question word is often the first word of the question.
   - it is not necessary to have a helping word such as *do* or *does*.
   - it is necessary to have an inverted question mark at the beginning of the questions and another question mark at the end.

2. Prepositions (**a, con, de, en, por, para,** etc.) cannot be placed at the end of the question. They must be in front of the question word.

   ¿**Con** quién estudias?
   With whom do you study?

3. **Quién** and **cuál** must agree in number with the noun that follows, and **cuánto** must agree in both gender and number with the noun it precedes.

4. **Qué** and **cuál** could both be translated as *what* or *which*. **Qué** is used to ask for a definition or an explanation when it is used in front of a verb. When it is used in front of a noun, it implies choice. **Cuál** often implies choice. It can be used in front of a verb or the preposition **de,** but is generally not used in front of a noun.

   ¿**Qué** libro lees?
   What book are you reading?

   ¿**Cuáles** de los libros te gustan más?
   Which of the books do you like the most?

Stem-changing verbs e → *ie* and e → *i*

1. Most of the verbs that appear in the **verbos** section of vocabulary, to the left, are stem-changing verbs. That means that their stems change in all forms, except **nosotros** and **vosotros** forms. For all forms the endings are the same as regular **-ar, -er,** and **-ir** verbs.

2. **Querer** is an **e → ie** stem-changing verb:

quiero	queremos
quieres	queréis
quiere	quieren

3. The **e → ie** stem-changing verbs **comenzar** and **empezar** are followed by the preposition **a** when used with an infinitive.

   Empieza a llover.
   It's starting to rain.

4. **Pedir** is an **e → i** stem-changing verb. Note that **pedir** means to ask *for* something or to order, where as **preguntar** means to ask a question. Here are the forms of **pedir:**

pido	pedimos
pides	pedís
pide	piden

5. The verbs **reír** and **sonreír** require accents on the **í** in the conjugated forms.

   Los niños **sonríen** en la foto.
   The children smile in the photo.

Palabras interrogativas

¿Adónde?	To where?
¿Cómo?	How?
¿Cuál(es)?	Which?
¿Cuándo?	When?
¿Cuánto(a)?	How much?
¿Cuántos(as)?	How many?
¿De dónde?	From where?
¿Dónde?	Where?
¿Por qué?	Why?
¿Qué?	What?
¿Quién(es)?	Who?

Vocabulario 1

🔊 CD1-21

Los lugares

banco	bank
bar (m.)	bar
biblioteca	library
café (m.)	cafe
calle (f.)	street
cine (m.)	movie theater
club (m.)	club
correo	post office
discoteca	nightclub
edificio	building
escuela	school
farmacia	pharmacy
gimnasio	gym
hospital (m.)	hospital
hotel (m.)	hotel
iglesia	church
librería	bookstore
mercado	market
mezquita	mosque
museo	museum
oficina	office
parque (m.)	park
piscina	swimming pool
plaza	city square
restaurante (m.)	restaurant
sinagoga	synagogue
supermercado	supermarket
teatro	theater
templo	temple
tienda	store
zoológico	zoo

Los verbos

depositar	to deposit
ir	to go
mandar	to send
rezar	to pray

Palabras adicionales

carta	letter
dinero	money
película	movie

Las preposiciones

a la derecha de	to the right of
a la izquierda de	to the left of
al lado de	beside, next to
cerca de	near
debajo de	under
dentro de	inside
detrás de	behind
en	in, on, at
encima de	on top of
enfrente de	in front of
entre	between
fuera de	outside
lejos de	far from

Gramática

Estar with prepositions

1. Estar means *to be* when talking about position or location. Its forms are as follows:

estoy	estamos
estás	estáis
está	están

2. You will always use **estar** when using any of the **prepositions** listed on the left of this page.

El café **está entre** la farmacia y la biblioteca.
The coffee shop is (located) between the pharmacy and the library.

The verb *ir* and *ir* + *a* + infinitive

1. The verb **ir** means *to go*:

voy	vamos
vas	vais
va	van

2. To tell where someone is going, it is necessary to use the preposition **a** *(to)*. When asking where someone is going, the preposition **a** is added to the word **dónde (adónde).** When **a** is followed by the definite article **el,** you must use the contraction **al.**

¿**Adónde** van?
(To) where are they going?

Mis amigos van **al** museo.
My friends are going to the museum.

3. Note that most of the prepositional phrases listed in this chapter include the word **de.** Remember to form the contraction **del** when **de** is followed by the definite article **el.**

Vivo lejos **del** supermercado.
I live far from the supermarket.

3. Similar to English, the verb **ir** can be used to talk about the future. To tell what someone is going to do use the structure **ir** + **a** + *infinitive*.

El viernes, **vamos a bailar.**
On Friday, we're going to dance.

Miguel **va a estudiar** este fin de semana.
Miguel is going to study this weekend.

Vocabulario 2

🔊 CD1–22

Habitaciones de la casa

baño	bathroom
cocina	kitchen
comedor (m.)	dining room
dormitorio	bedroom
garaje (m.)	garage
jardín (m.)	garden
patio	patio
sala	living room

Muebles, utensilios y aparatos electrodomésticos

alfombra	carpet
armario	closet, armoire
bañera	bathtub
cafetera	coffee maker
cama	bed
cortinas	curtains
cuadro	painting, picture
ducha	shower
espejo	mirror
estufa	stove
flor (f.)	flower
fregadero	kitchen sink
horno	oven
horno de microondas	microwave oven
inodoro	toilet
lámpara	lamp
lavabo	bathroom sink
lavadora	washer
lavaplatos (m.)	dishwasher
mesita	coffee table
planta	plant
refrigerador (m.)	refrigerator
secadora	dryer
sillón (m.)	armchair
sofá (m.)	couch

Los verbos

almorzar (ue)	to have lunch
alquilar	to rent
costar (ue)	to cost
devolver (ue)	to return (something)
dormir (ue)	to sleep
encontrar (ue)	to find
jugar (ue)	to play
llover (ue)	to rain
morir (ue)	to die
poder (ue)	to be able to
recordar (ue)	to remember
soñar (ue) (con)	to dream (about)
volver (ue)	to come back

Palabras adicionales

apartamento	apartment
habitación (f.)	room
mueble (m.)	furniture
piso	floor
planta baja	ground floor

Gramática

Stem-changing verbs (o → ue)

1. Most of the verbs that appear in the **verbos** section of vocabulary, to the left, are stem-changing verbs. That means that their stems change in all forms, except **nosotros** and **vosotros** forms. For all forms the endings are the same as regular **-ar, -er,** and **-ir** verbs.

2. Poder is an **o → ue** stem-changing verb:

puedo	podemos
puedes	podéis
puede	pueden

3. The verb **jugar** follows the same pattern, but its stem changes from **u → ue**:

juego	jugamos
juegas	jugáis
juega	juegan

Adjective placement

1. As you remember from **Capítulo 2,** other than adjectives of quantity, adjectives are generally placed behind the noun they modify. However, there are some other exceptions. **Bueno** and **malo** are often used in front of the noun they modify, and they drop the **o** when used in front of a masculine singular noun.

La señora es una **buena** profesora.
The woman is a good teacher.

Es un **mal** día.
It is a bad day.

2. Ordinal numbers are used to sequence. They also go before the noun that they modify. As with adjectives, these words must agree in gender and number with the noun. Like **bueno** and **malo,** the ordinal numbers **primero** and **tercero** drop the **-o** before a masculine noun. The ordinal numbers are as follows:

Los números ordinales

1º primero	6º sexto
2º segundo	7º séptimo
3º tercero	8º octavo
4º cuarto	9º noveno
5º quinto	10º décimo

Ana es la **séptima hija** de su familia.
Ana is the seventh daughter in her family.

Carlos es el **tercer estudiante** en su clase.
Carlos is the third student in his class.

3. Grande can be used in front of a noun; however, its meaning normally changes from *big* to *great.* **Grande** becomes **gran** when used in front of singular nouns.

En la casa **grande** vive una **gran** familia.
In the big house lives a great family.

Vocabulario 1

🔊 CD1-26

Los estados de ánimo y otras expresiones con el verbo *estar*

aburrido(a)	*bored*
alegre	*happy*
asustado(a)	*scared*
avergonzado(a)	*embarrassed*
borracho(a)	*drunk*
cansado(a)	*tired*
celoso(a)	*jealous*
confundido(a)	*confused*
contento(a)	*happy*
deprimido(a)	*depressed*
divertido(a)	*to be entertained; to be in a good mood*
enamorado(a)	*in love*
enfermo(a)	*sick*
enojado(a)	*angry*
equivocado(a)	*wrong*
feliz	*happy*
frustrado(a)	*frustrated*
interesado(a)	*interested*
loco(a)	*crazy*
nervioso(a)	*nervous*
ocupado(a)	*busy*
preocupado(a)	*worried*
sano(a)	*healthy*
seguro(a)	*sure*
sorprendido(a)	*surprised*
triste	*sad*

Palabras adicionales

salud (f)	*health*

Los verbos

comer	*to eat*
destruir	*to destroy*
dormir	*to sleep*
estar	*to be*
hablar	*to speak*
leer	*to read*
mentir	*to lie*
morir	*to die*
pedir	*to ask for*
repetir	*to repeat*
servir	*to serve*
traer	*to bring*
vivir	*to live*

Gramática

Estar with adjectives and present progressive

1. Remember that **estar** is an irregular verb:

estar

estoy	estamos
estás	estáis
está	están

2. Apart from indicating location, the verb **estar** is also used to express an emotional, mental, or physical condition.

> Mis padres **están** felices.
> *My parents **are** happy.*

3. The verb **estar** is also used with present participles to form the present progressive. The present progressive is used to describe actions in progress. To form the present participle, add **-ando** (**-ar** verbs) or **–iendo** (**-er** and **-ir** verbs) to the stem of the verb.

> El profesor **está hablando** con Tito ahora.
> *The professor **is talking** to Tito now.*

4. The present participle of the verb **ir** is **yendo**. However, it is much more common to use the present tense of the verb when the action is in progress.

5. When the stem of an **-er** or an **-ir** verb ends in a vowel, **-yendo** is used instead of **-iendo**.

6. Stem changing **-ir** verbs have an irregular present participle. An **e** in the stem becomes an **i**, and an **o** in the stem becomes a **u**.

> mentir – m**i**ntiendo   dormir – d**u**rmiendo

7. In the present progressive, the verb **estar** must agree with the subject; however, you will notice that the present participle does NOT agree in gender (masculine/feminine) or number (singular/plural) with the subject.

> Mis hijos están estudiando inglés.
> *My children are studying English.*

Ser and *estar*

1. The verb **ser** is used in the following ways:
   a. to describe characteristics of people, places, or things

   > La profesora **es** inteligente.
   > *The professor **is** intelligent.*

   b. to identify a relationship, occupation, or nationality

   > Mi novia **es** peruana.
   > *My girlfriend **is** Peruvian.*

   c. to express origin

   > Yo **soy** de Bolivia.
   > *I **am** from Bolivia.*

   d. to express possession

   > El libro **es** de Álvaro.
   > *The book **belongs** to Álvaro.*

   e. to tell time and give dates

   > **Son** las dos.
   > *It **is** two o'clock.*

2. The verb **estar** is used in the following ways:
   a. to indicate location

   > Ella **está** en la casa.   She **is** in the house.

   b. to express an emotional, mental, or physical condition

   > Mi madre **está** enferma hoy.
   > *My mother **is** sick today.*

   c. in the present progressive

   > **Estoy** estudiando.   *I **am** studying.*

3. It is important to realize that the use of **ser** and **estar** with some adjectives can change the meaning of the adjectives. The use of ser indicates a characteristic or a trait, while the use of **estar** indicates a condition. Some common adjectives that change meaning are: **aburrido(a), alegre, feliz, bueno(a), malo(a), guapo(a), listo(a),** and **rico(a).**

   > Carlos **es** aburrido.
   > *Carlos is boring. (personality)*

   > Graciela **está** aburrida.
   > *Graciela is bored. (present condition)*

Vocabulario 2

🔊 CD1-27

Las profesiones

abogado(a)	lawyer
actor (m.)	actor
actriz (f.)	actress
agente de viajes	travel agent
ama de casa (m.)	housewife
arquitecto(a)	architect
asistente de vuelo (m.f.)	flight attendant
bailarín (balarina)	dancer
cantante (m.f.)	singer
científico(a)	scientist
cocinero(a)	cook
consejero(a)	adviser
contador(a)	accountant
dependiente (m.f.)	clerk
deportista (m.f.)	athlete
diseñador(a)	designer
enfermero(a)	nurse
escritor(a)	writer
fotógrafo(a)	photographer
ingeniero(a)	engineer
jefe(a)	boss
maestro(a)	elementary/high school teacher
mecánico(a)	mechanic
médico(a)	doctor
mesero(a)	waiter
modelo	model
músico(a)	musician
periodista	journalist
piloto (m.f.)	pilot
pintor(a)	painter
policía (m.) mujer policía (f.)	police officer
político(a)	politician
psicólogo(a)	psychologist
secretario(a)	secretary
trabajador(a) social	social worker
vendedor(a)	salesperson
veterinario(a)	veterinary

Palabras adicionales

entrevista (f.)	interview
solicitud (f.)	application, want ad
sueldo (m.)	salary

Los verbos

conducir	to drive
conocer	to know, to be acquainted with
dar	to give
decir	to say, to tell
ganar	to earn, to make money
hacer	to do, to make
oír	to hear
poner	to put, to set
saber	to know (facts, how to do something)
salir	to go out, to leave
seguir	to follow
traer	to bring
venir	to come
ver	to see

Gramática

Verbs with changes in the first person

1. The following verbs have irregular first person forms:

poner → pongo   conducir → conduzco
salir → salgo   dar → doy
traer → traigo   ver → veo

2. The following verbs are not only irregular in the first person form, but also have other changes:

decir

digo	decimos
dices	decís
dice	dicen

venir

vengo	venimos
vienes	venís
viene	vienen

seguir

sigo	seguimos
sigues	seguís
sigue	siguen

oír

oigo	oímos
oyes	oís
oye	oyen

Saber and conocer

1. *Saber* and *conocer* are irregular in the first person form.

saber

sé	sabemos
sabes	sabéis
sabe	saben

conocer

conozco	conocemos
conoces	conocéis
conoce	conocen

2. While the verbs **saber** and **conocer** both mean *to know*, they are used in different contexts. **Saber** is used to express knowledge of facts or information as well as skills. **Conocer** is used to express acquaintance or familiarity with a person, place or thing.

Ana **conoce** Chile. (*famililiarity*)
Ana **sabe** dónde está Chile. (*fact*)

3. When using **saber** to mean *to know how to do something*, it is followed by the infinitive.

El profesor **sabe** enseñar.
*The professor **knows how to** teach.*

4. Remember to use the *personal **a*** with **conocer** when referring to a person or a pet.

Conozco al piloto. *I **know** the pilot.*

Vocabulario 1

🔊 CD1-29

Los verbos reflexivos

acostarse (ue)	to lie down, to go to bed
afeitarse	to shave
arreglarse	to get ready
bañarse	to bathe, to shower (Mex.)
cepillarse	to brush
cortarse	to cut
despertarse (ie)	to wake up
divertirse (ie)	to have fun
dormirse (ue)	to fall asleep
ducharse	to shower
estirarse	to stretch
irse	to leave, to go away
lavarse	to wash
levantarse	to get up
maquillarse	to put on make-up
peinarse	to comb or style one's hair
ponerse (la ropa)	to put on (clothing)
quitarse (la ropa)	to take off (clothing)
secarse	to dry oneself
sentarse (ie)	to sit down
verse	to see oneself
vestirse (i)	to get dressed

Las partes del cuerpo

boca	mouth
brazo	arm
cabeza	head
cara	face
codo	elbow
cuello	neck
dedo	finger
dedo (del pie)	toe
diente (m.)	tooth
espalda	back
estómago	stomach
hombro	shoulder
mano (f.)	hand
muslo	thigh
nariz (f.)	nose
ojo	eye
oreja	ear
pecho	chest
pelo	hair
pie (m.)	foot
pierna	leg
rodilla	knee
tobillo	ankle

Palabras adicionales

antes de + infinitive	before (doing something)
champú (m.)	shampoo
dentrífico	toothpaste
despertador (m.)	alarm clock
después de + infinitive	after (doing something)
jabón (m.)	soap
tarde	late
temprano	early
toalla	towel

Expresiones indefinidas y negativas

algo	something
alguien	someone, somebody
algún (alguno), alguna	some
jamás	never
nada	nothing
nadie	no one, nobody
ni... ni	neither . . . nor
ningún (ninguno), ninguna	none, any
nunca	never
o... o	either . . . or
siempre	always
también	also
tampoco	neither, either

Gramática

Reflexive verbs

1. Reflexive verbs are verbs whose subject also receives the action performed. Simply put, they describe what one does to oneself. In Spanish, these verbs are characterized by the reflexive pronoun **se** that follows the infinitive form of the verb. Many of the verbs used to talk about daily routine are reflexive verbs.

2. Reflexive verbs are conjugated like regular verbs, except that the reflexive pronoun **se** must also be changed to reflect the subject.

levantarse

me levanto	nos levantamos
te levantas	os levantáis
se levanta	se levantan

3. The reflexive pronoun can always go in front of the conjugated verb. If you are using two verbs, it will precede the first verb.

   Nos lavamos las manos antes de comer.
   We wash our hands before eating.

   Paula **se está estirando.**
   Paula is stretching.

4. When using a reflexive verb with the infinitive, you can attach the pronoun to the infinitive.

Indefinite and negative words

1. Indefinite and negative words are listed on the left-hand side of this page.

2. In Spanish, it is correct to use a double negative. When using a negative expression after a verb, be sure to put **no** before the verb.

   Jaime **no** estudia **nunca**.

   No tengo **ningún** dinero.

3. **Nadie, jamás, nunca,** and **tampoco** can all be placed before the verb. **Nada** can go before the verb only if it is used as the subject.

   Andrés no quiere ir, y yo **tampoco** quiero ir.
   Andrés doesn't want to go, and I don't want to go either.

When using a reflexive verb with the present participle, you can attach the pronoun to the present participle, but you must then add an accent to maintain the original stress. The pronoun will still always agree with the subject.

   ¿**Vas a ducharte** antes de salir?

   Gilberto **está poniéndose** la ropa en su habitación.

5. Verbs may be reflexive or nonreflexive depending on who receives the action.

   Roberto **se lava.**

   Roberto **lava** a su perro.

6. Use the definite article rather than the possessive adjective after a reflexive verb.

   Mariana **se cepilla** los dientes.

7. Using a reflexive pronoun may change the meaning of a verb.

   Vivián **se va** porque está enojada con su novio.
   Vivian left because she was angry at her boyfriend.

   Mi prima **va** a la iglesia a las diez.
   My cousin goes to church at ten.

   Nada es mejor que la familia.
   Nothing is better than family.

4. The words **ningún** and **algún** are used before singular masculine nouns. The words **ninguno** and **alguno** must agree in gender and number with the nouns that they modify.

   ¿Tienes **algunos amigos** que puedan venir con nosotros?

   Los estudiantes no tienen **ninguna tarea** durante las vacaciones.

Vocabulario 2

🔊 CD1-31

Los deportes

alpinismo	mountain climbing
bádminton (m.)	badminton
básquetbol (m.)	basketball
béisbol (m.)	baseball
fútbol (m.)	soccer
fútbol americano	American football
golf (m.)	golf
ping-pong (m.)	ping-pong, table tennis
tenis (m.)	tennis
voleibol (m.)	volleyball

El equipo

campo	field
cancha	court
equipo	equipment, team
patín (m.)	skate
pelota	ball
raqueta	racquet
red (f.)	net
saco de dormir	sleeping bag
tienda de campaña	camping tent

Los verbos

acampar	to go camping
andar (en bicicleta)	to walk, (to ride a bike)
bucear	to scuba dive
esquiar en el agua	to water-ski
esquiar en tabla	to snowboard
hacer alpinismo	to climb mountains
ir de excursión	to hike
ir de pesca	to go fishing
levantar pesas	to lift weights
montar a	to ride (an animal)
patinar	to skate
patinar en hielo	to ice skate
pescar	to fish

Palabras adicionales

aficionado(a)	fan (of a sport)
entrada	ticket
partido	game
anoche	last night
ayer	yesterday
la semana pasada	last week

Gramática

The preterite

1. The preterite is used to discuss actions completed in the past. To form the preterite of regular **-ar** verbs, add these endings to the stem of the verb.

ballar			
yo	bail**é**	nosotros(as)	bail**amos**
tú	bail**aste**	vosotros(as)	bail**asteis**
él / ella / usted	bail**ó**	ellos / ellas / ustedes	bail**aron**

José **viajó** a México.   *José traveled (did travel) to Mexico.*

2. The preterite endings for regular **-er** and **-ir** verbs are identical. They are as follows:

beber / vivir			
yo	beb**í** / viv**í**	nosotros(as)	beb**imos** / viv**imos**
tú	beb**iste** / viv**iste**	vosotros(as)	beb**isteis** / viv**isteis**
él / ella / usted	beb**ió** / viv**ió**	ellos / ellas / ustedes	beb**ieron** / viv**ieron**

¿**Escribiste** tú una carta?   *Did you write a letter?*

3. -Ar and -er verbs that have stem changes in the present tense do not change in the preterite tense. You will learn about stem-changing -ir verbs below.

4. Verbs ending in -**car**, -**gar**, and -**zar** have spelling changes in the **yo** form in the preterite. Notice that the spelling changes preserve the original sound of the infinitive for -**car** and -**gar** verbs.

car → qué   **Busqué** el libro. *I looked for the book.*

gar → gué   **Llegué** tarde a la fiesta. *I arrived late to the party.*

zar → cé   **Empecé** a estudiar español el año pasado. *I started studying Spanish last year.*

5. The third person singular and plural of **oír** and **leer** also have spelling changes when conjugated in the preterite tense. These verbs carry accents in all forms of the preterite except for the third person plural.

oír → oyó, oyeron   leer → leyó, leyeron

Stem-changing verbs in the preterite

1. -**Ir** verbs that have stem changes in the present tense also have stem changes in the preterite. The third person singular and plural change **e → i** and **o → u**.

pedir		**dormir**	
pedí	pedimos	dormí	dormimos
pediste	pedisteis	dormiste	dormisteis
p**i**dió	p**i**dieron	d**u**rmió	d**u**rmieron

Mi hermano **pidió** pollo, pero yo **pedí** la sopa.
My brother ordered chicken, but I ordered soup.

2. Other common stem-changing verbs:

conseguir (i)	morir (u)	repetir (i)	servir (i)
divertirse (i)	preferir (i)	seguir (i)	vestirse (i)

Vocabulario 1

🔊 CD1-34

El hotel

alojamiento	lodging
ascensor (m.)	elevator
botones (m./f.)	bellhop
camarero (a)	maid
escaleras	stairs
habitación (f.)	room
huésped (m./f.)	guest
llave (f.)	key
maleta	suitcase
recepción (f.)	reception
recepcionista (m./f.)	receptionist
sauna (m.)	sauna
transporte (m.)	transportation
turista (m./f.)	tourist

Verbos

alojarse	to lodge, to stay (in a hotel)
bajar	to go down
quedarse	to lodge, to stay
subir	to go up

Palabras adicionales

clase turista (f.)	economy class
disponible	available
doble	double
lujo	luxury
sencillo	single
triple	triple
viaje pagado (m.)	all-inclusive trip

Los números

cien	100
ciento uno	101
doscientos	200
trescientos	300
cuatrocientos	400
quinientos	500
seiscientos	600
setecientos	700
ochocientos	800
novecientos	900
mil	1000
dos mil	2000
un millón	1 000 000

Gramática

Irregular verbs in the preterite

1. There are a number of verbs that are irregular in the preterite. **Ser** and **ir** have the same forms in the preterite.

ser/ir

fui	fuimos
fuiste	fuisteis
fue	fueron

2. The verbs **dar** and **ver** have similar conjugations in the preterite.

dar

di	dimos
diste	disteis
dio	dieron

ver

vi	vimos
viste	visteis
vio	vieron

3. Other irregular verbs can be divided into three groups. Notice that there are no accents on these verbs and that they all take the same endings (with the exception of the 3rd person plural of the verbs with **j** in the stem).

Verbs with *u* in the stem: tener

tuve	tuvimos
tuviste	tuvisteis
tuvo	tuvieron

Verbs with *i* in the stem: venir

vine	vinimos
viniste	vinisteis
vino	vinieron

Verbs with *j* in the stem: traer

traje	trajimos
trajiste	trajisteis
trajo	trajeron

Other irregular verbs with similar patterns

andar	anduv-	hacer	hic-
estar	estuv-	querer	quis-
poder	pud-	conducir	conduj-
poner	pus-	decir	dij-
saber	sup-	producir	produj-
tener	tuv-	traducir	traduj-

4. The preterite tense of **hay** is **hubo**.

   Hubo mucha información para estudiar.

Por and *para* and prepositional pronouns

1. Por and **para** can both be translated as *for* in English, but they have different uses in Spanish. **Por** is used to indicate:

a. cause, reason, or motive (*because of, on behalf of*)

   Nos tuvimos que poner los abrigos **por** el frío.

b. duration, period of time (*during, for*)

   El presidente habló **por** una hora y media.

c. exchange (*for*)

   Mi padre pagó diez mil dólares **por** el coche.

d. general movement through space (*through, around, along, by*)

   Pasamos **por** el parque porque es más bonito.

e. expressions:

por ejemplo	for example
por eso	that's why
por favor	please
por fin	finally
por supuesto	of course

2. Para is used to indicate:

a. goal or purpose (*in order to, used for*)

   Fueron al cine **para** ver una película.
   They went to the movie theater to see a film.

b. recipient (*for*)

   La abuela preparó la comida **para** sus nietos.
   The grandmother prepared the food for her grandchildren.

c. destination (*to*)

   Vamos **para** la playa este verano.
   We're going to the beach this summer.

d. deadline (*for, due*)

   Tenemos que leer el texto **para** el lunes.
   We have to read the text for Monday.

e. contrast to what is expected.

   Para un turista, Marcos sabe mucho de la ciudad.
   For a tourist, Marcos knows a lot about the city.

f. expressions:

para colmo	to top it all off
para nada	not at all
para siempre	forever
para variar	for a change

3. After a preposition, use the same pronoun that you use as a subject pronoun, except for **yo** and **tú**. **Yo** becomes **mí** after a preposition, and **tú** becomes **ti**.

   La habitación grande es **para ellos**.
   The large room is for them.

4. Instead of **mí** or **ti** with **con**, **conmigo** and **contigo** are used.

   ¿Puedo venir **contigo**?
   Can I come with you?

   ¡Claro que sí! Puedes venir **conmigo**.
   Of course! You can come with me.

Vocabulario 1

🔊 CD1-34

El hotel

alojamiento	lodging
ascensor (m.)	elevator
botones (m./f.)	bellhop
camarero (a)	maid
escaleras	stairs
habitación (f.)	room
huésped (m./f.)	guest
llave (f.)	key
maleta	suitcase
recepción (f.)	reception
recepcionista (m./f.)	receptionist
sauna (m.)	sauna
transporte (m.)	transportation
turista (m./f.)	tourist

Verbos

alojarse	to lodge, to stay (in a hotel)
bajar	to go down
quedarse	to lodge, to stay
subir	to go up

Palabras adicionales

clase turista (f.)	economy class
disponible	available
doble	double
lujo	luxury
sencillo	single
triple	triple
viaje todo pagado (m.)	all-inclusive trip

Los números

cien	100
ciento uno	101
doscientos	200
trescientos	300
cuatrocientos	400
quinientos	500
seiscientos	600
setecientos	700
ochocientos	800
novecientos	900
mil	1000
dos mil	2000
un millón	1 000 000

Gramática

Irregular verbs in the preterite

1. There are a number of verbs that are irregular in the preterite. **Ser** and **ir** have the same forms in the preterite.

ser/ir

fui	fuimos
fuiste	fuisteis
fue	fueron

2. The verbs **dar** and **ver** have similar conjugations in the preterite.

dar

di	dimos
diste	disteis
dio	dieron

ver

vi	vimos
viste	visteis
vio	vieron

3. Other irregular verbs can be divided into three groups. Notice that there are no accents on these verbs and that they all take the same endings (with the exception of the 3rd person plural of the verbs with **j** in the stem).

Verbs with *u* in the stem: tener

tuve	tuvimos
tuviste	tuvisteis
tuvo	tuvieron

Verbs with *i* in the stem: venir

vine	vinimos
viniste	vinisteis
vino	vinieron

Verbs with *j* in the stem: traer

traje	trajimos
trajiste	trajisteis
trajo	trajeron

Other irregular verbs with similar patterns

andar	anduv-	hacer	hic-
estar	estuv-	querer	quis-
poder	pud-	conducir	conduj-
poner	pus-	decir	dij-
saber	sup-	producir	produj-
tener	tuv-	traducir	traduj-

4. The preterite tense of **hay** is **hubo**.

Hubo mucha información para estudiar.

Por and *para* and prepositional pronouns

1. **Por** and **para** can both be translated as *for* in English, but they have different uses in Spanish. **Por** is used to indicate:

   a. cause, reason, or motive *(because of, on behalf of)*

   Nos tuvimos que poner los abrigos **por** el frío.

   b. duration, period of time *(during, for)*

   El presidente habló **por** una hora y media.

   c. exchange *(for)*

   Mi padre pagó diez mil dólares **por** el coche.

   d. general movement through space *(through, around, along, by)*

   Pasamos **por** el parque porque es más bonito.

   e. expressions:

por ejemplo	for example
por eso	that's why
por favor	please
por fin	finally
por supuesto	of course

2. **Para** is used to indicate:

   a. goal or purpose *(in order to, used for)*

   Fueron al cine **para** ver una película.
   They went to the movie theater to see a film.

   b. recipient *(for)*

   La abuela preparó la comida **para** sus nietos.
   The grandmother prepared the food for her grandchildren.

   c. destination *(to)*

   Vamos **para** la playa este verano.
   We're going to the beach this summer.

   d. deadline *(for, due)*

   Tenemos que leer el texto **para** el lunes.
   We have to read the text for Monday.

   e. contrast to what is expected.

   Para un turista, Marcos sabe mucho de la ciudad.
   For a tourist, Marcos knows a lot about the city.

   f. expressions:

para colmo	to top it all off
para nada	not at all
para siempre	forever
para variar	for a change

3. After a preposition, use the same pronoun that you use as a subject pronoun, except for **yo** and **tú**. **Yo** becomes **mí** after a preposition, and **tú** becomes **ti**.

   La habitación grande es **para ellos**.
   The large room is for them.

4. Instead of **mí** or **ti** with **con**, **conmigo** and **contigo** are used.

   ¿Puedo venir **contigo**?
   Can I come with you?

   ¡Claro que sí! Puedes venir **conmigo**.
   Of course! You can come with me.

Vocabulario 1

🔊 CD2–4

Frutas

durazno	peach
fresa	strawberry
melón (m.)	melon
naranja	orange
piña	pineapple
plátano	banana
sandía	watermelon
uvas	grapes

Verduras

brócoli (m.)	broccoli
cebolla	onion
lechuga	lettuce
maíz (m.)	corn
papa	potato
pepino	cucumber
zanahoria	carrot

Lácteos y otros alimentos

cátsup (m.)	ketchup
cereal (m.)	cereal
crema	cream
huevo	egg
jamón (m.)	ham
leche (f.)	milk
mantequilla	butter
mayonesa	mayonnaise
mermelada	jam
mostaza	mustard
pepinillo	pickle
queso	cheese

Verbos

agregar	to add
batir	to beat
cortar	to cut
freír	to fry
hornear	to bake
mezclar	to mix
pelar	to peel

Palabras adicionales

rebanada	slice

Gramática

Indirect object pronouns

1. An indirect object pronoun indicates **to whom** or **for whom** an action takes place.

> Marcos siempre **les** dice la verdad a sus padres.
> *Marcos always tells the truth **to his parents.***

2. In Spanish, the indirect object pronoun must always be used when mentioning the indirect object, even though it may seem redundant. This is true even if you clarify or emphasize the indirect object pronoun using the preposition **a**.

> Lola **les** sirvió la cena **a su familia.**
> *Lola served dinner **to her family.***

> Mis amigos **me** dieron el dinero **a mí.**
> *My friends gave the money **to me.***

3. The indirect object pronouns are:

yo **me**	nosotros(as) **nos**
tú **te**	vosotros(as) **os**
él / ella / usted **le**	ellos / ellas / ustedes **les**

4. An indirect object pronoun can be placed before a conjugated verb or attached to the end of an infinitive or present participle.

> **Te** voy a cortar algunas fresas para comer.
> *I'm going to cut up some strawberries **for you** to eat.*

Constructions with *se*

1. The pronoun **se** is used when the subject is not known or not relevant. When **se** is used, the verb is conjugated in the third person form, either singular or plural, depending on the number of the noun.

> **Se habla** español en la clase.
> *Spanish is spoken in class.*

> En esta cocina, solo **se usan** frutas y verduras frescas.
> *In this kitchen, only fresh fruits and vegetables are used.*

2. When followed by an infinitive, the verb is often conjugated in the singular form.

> Mi mamá está preparándo**nos** unas enchiladas.
> *My mom is preparing some enchiladas **for us.***

5. The following verbs are frequently used with indirect object pronouns:

contar (ue)	pedir
dar	prestar
decir	preguntar
devolver (ue)	servir
mostrar (ue)	

6. The verb **gustar** is always conjugated with an indirect object pronoun. The following verbs work just like **gustar:**

> **caer (bien/mal)** *to like/dislike a person*
> **encantar** *to really like, to enjoy immensely*
> **fascinar** *to fascinate*
> **importar** *to be important*
> **interesar** *to interest*
> **molestar** *to bother*

> No **les** gusta cocinar.
> *They don't like to cook. (Cooking is not pleasing **to them.**)*

> A Julián **le** fascina trabajar en su jardín.
> *Julián really likes working in his garden. (Working in his garden is fascinating **to Julián.**)*

> **Se debe** cortar las zanahorias antes de ponerlas en la sopa.
> *The carrots should be cut before putting them in the soup.*

3. If the verb is not used with a noun, it is conjugated in the third person singular form. The pronoun **se** translates to *one, you* or *they* in English.

> **Se dice** que es importante no comer mucho azúcar.
> *They say it's important to not eat a lot of sugar.*

> Por lo general, **se almuerza** con la familia en España.
> *In general, they eat lunch with family in Spain.*

Vocabulario 1

🔊 CD2–4

Frutas

durazno	*peach*
fresa	*strawberry*
melón (m.)	*melon*
naranja	*orange*
piña	*pineapple*
plátano	*banana*
sandía	*watermelon*
uvas	*grapes*

Verduras

brócoli (m.)	*broccoli*
cebolla	*onion*
lechuga	*lettuce*
maíz (m.)	*corn*
papa	*potato*
pepino	*cucumber*
zanahoria	*carrot*

Lácteos y otros alimentos

cátsup (m.)	*ketchup*
cereal (m.)	*cereal*
crema	*cream*
huevo	*egg*
jamón (m.)	*ham*
leche (f.)	*milk*
mantequilla	*butter*
mayonesa	*mayonnaise*
mermelada	*jam*
mostaza	*mustard*
pepinillo	*pickle*
queso	*cheese*

Verbos

agregar	*to add*
batir	*to beat*
cortar	*to cut*
freír	*to fry*
hornear	*to bake*
mezclar	*to mix*
mostrar (ue)	*to show*
pelar	*to peel*
prestar	*to lend*

Palabras adicionales

rebanada	*slice*

Gramática

Indirect object pronouns

1. An indirect object pronoun indicates **to whom** or **for whom** an action takes place.

> Marcos siempre **les** dice la verdad a sus padres.
> *Marcos always tells the truth **to his parents.***

2. In Spanish, the indirect object pronoun must always be used when mentioning the indirect object, even though it may seem redundant. This is true even if you clarify or emphasize the indirect object pronoun using the preposition **a.**

> Lola **les** sirvió la cena **a su familia.**
> *Lola served dinner **to her family.***

> Mis amigos **me** dieron el dinero **a mí.**
> *My friends gave the money **to me.***

3. The indirect object pronouns are:

yo **me**	nosotros(as) **nos**
tú **te**	vosotros(as) **os**
él / ella / usted **le**	ellos / ellas / ustedes **les**

4. An indirect object pronoun can be placed before a conjugated verb or attached to the end of an infinitive or present participle.

> **Te** voy a cortar algunas fresas para comer.
> *I'm going to cut up some strawberries **for you** to eat.*

Constructions with *se*

1. The pronoun **se** is used when the subject is not known or not relevant. When **se** is used, the verb is conjugated in the third person form, either singular or plural, depending on the number of the noun.

> **Se habla** español en la clase.
> *Spanish is spoken in class.*

> En esta cocina, solo **se usan** frutas y verduras frescas.
> *In this kitchen, only fresh fruits and vegetables are used.*

2. When followed by an infinitive, the verb is often conjugated in the singular form.

Mi mamá está preparándo**nos** unas enchiladas.
*My mom is preparing some enchiladas **for us.***

5. The following verbs are frequently used with indirect object pronouns:

contar (ue)	pedir
dar	prestar
decir	preguntar
devolver (ue)	servir
mostrar (ue)	

6. The verb **gustar** is always conjugated with an indirect object pronoun. The following verbs work just like **gustar:**

caer (bien/mal) *to like/dislike a person*
encantar *to really like, to enjoy immensely*
fascinar *to fascinate*
importar *to be important*
interesar *to interest*
molestar *to bother*

> No **les** gusta cocinar.
> *They don't like to cook. (Cooking is not pleasing **to them.**)*

> A Julián **le** fascina trabajar en su jardín.
> *Julián really likes working in his garden. (Working in his garden is fascinating **to Julián.**)*

> **Se debe** cortar las zanahorias antes de ponerlas en la sopa.
> *The carrots should be cut before putting them in the soup.*

3. If the verb is not used with a noun, it is conjugated in the third person singular form. The pronoun **se** translates to *one, you* or *they* in English.

> **Se dice** que es importante no comer mucho azúcar.
> *They say it's important to not eat a lot of sugar.*

> Por lo general, **se almuerza** con la familia en España.
> *In general, they eat lunch with family in Spain.*

Vocabulario 1

🔊 CD7–8

En la fiesta

bocadillos	snacks
brindis (m.)	toast
champán (m.)	champagne
decoraciones (f.)	decorations
desfile (m.)	parade
dulces (m.)	candies
fuegos artificiales	fireworks
globos	balloons
grupo de música	music group/band
invitación (f.)	invitation
invitado	guest
novios	bride and groom
pastel (m.)	cake
piñata	piñata
quinceañera	girl celebrating her fifteenth birthday
regalo	gift
serenata	serenade
vela	candle

Las celebraciones

aniversario	anniversary
bautizo	baptism
boda	wedding
cumpleaños (m.)	birthday
graduación (f.)	graduation
posadas	nine-day celebration before Christmas
quince años	a girl's fifteenth birthday celebration
santo	saint's day

Verbos

brindar	to toast
casarse (con)	to get married (to)
celebrar	to celebrate
cumplir años	to be/to turn __ years old
romper	to break

Gramática

A comparison of the preterite and the imperfect

1. The **imperfect** is used in the following situations:

a. to describe past actions in progress

> Miguel **trabajaba** el viernes por la noche, y no pudo venir a la fiesta.
> *Miguel was working Friday night, and couldn't come to the party.*

b. to describe habitual actions in the past

> Al regresar de la escuela, siempre **comíamos** un bocadillo.
> *When we got home from school, we always used to eat a snack.*

c. to describe conditions, people, and places in the past

> Cuando **era** joven, mi abuela **era** muy bonita.
> *When she was young, my grandmother was very pretty.*

d. to give the background information or details when telling a story

> **Hacía** mal tiempo y **llovía** el día que tuve mi accidente.
> *The weather was bad and it was raining the day I had my accident.*

2. The **preterite** is used in the following situations:

a. to describe completed actions in the past

> Mi familia y yo **fuimos** a México el año pasado.
> *My family and I went to Mexico last year.*

b. to narrate the main events of a story

> Primero, José **entró** en el salón, **tomó** una cerveza y **empezó** a hablar con María.
> *First, José came into the room, had a beer, and started talking to María.*

Uses of the preterite and the imperfect

When relaying a past event, the actions can usually be expressed in one of three ways:

1. Two simultaneous actions: When talking about two actions that are going on at the same time in the past, use the imperfect, as both actions are *in progress.*

> Mientras Juan **preparaba** los bocadillos, Pilar **ponía** las decoraciones.
> *While Juan was preparing the snacks, Pilar was putting up decorations.*

2. A series of completed actions: When listing a series of events that occurred, use the preterite.

> Primero, **mandamos** invitaciones. Después, **compramos** globos y velas. Por fin, **hicimos** el pastel.
> *First, we sent invitations. Then, we bought balloons and candles. Finally, we made the cake.*

3. One action in progress when another begins: In the past when an action is in progress and a second action begins or is completed, both the preterite and the imperfect are used. The imperfect is used for the action in progress and the preterite is used for the new action that began or interrupted the first action.

> Mis amigos **estaban** en la cocina cuando yo **llegué.**
> *My friends were in the kitchen when I arrived.*

Vocabulario 2

CD2–9

En la calle

acera	sidewalk
ambulancia	ambulance
camilla	stretcher
carretera	highway
ciclista	cyclist
conductor(a)	driver
cruce (m.)	crosswalk
esquina	corner
límite (m.) de velocidad	speed limit
multa	fine/ticket
paramédico(a)	paramedic
parquímetro	parking meter
patrulla	police car
peatón (peatona) (peatones)	pedestrian
poste (m.)	post
puente (m.)	bridge
semáforo	traffic light
señal (f.)	sign
servicio de emergencias	emergency service
testigo(a)	witness

Los verbos

aburrirse	to become bored
alegrarse	to become happy
asustarse	to become frightened
atravesar (ie)	to cross
atropellar	to run over
bajar de	to get out of (a vehicle)
caer (se)	to fall
chocar (con)	to crash (against something)
cruzar	to cross
dañar	to damage
distraerse	to get distracted
enojarse	to become angry
estacionar	to park
frustrarse	to become frustrated
pasarse un semáforo en rojo	to run a red light
pasarse una señal de PARE	to run a STOP sign
sentirse	to feel
sorprenderse	to be surprised
subir a	to get into (a vehicle)
tropezar (ie)	to trip

Expresiones adicionales

de repente	suddenly
estar dañado(a)	to be damaged
estar herido(a)	to be injured

Gramática

Preterite and imperfect with emotions and mental states

1. When describing emotions or mental states in the past, use the same guidelines as with past actions. To express that someone was feeling a certain way over time, use the imperfect. To express that someone felt a certain way during a specific period, use the preterite.

Nora **estaba contenta** porque ganó mucho dinero.
Nora was happy because she won a lot of money.

El Señor López **se enojó** cuando vio la ventana rota.
Mr. López got angry when he saw the broken window.

2. The following verbs are generally used in the preterite, as they describe a specific change in emotion or feeling:

aburrirse	asustarse	frustrarse
alegrarse	enojarse	sorprenderse

3. The verb **sentirse** (e → ie) is used to express how one feels.

Me sentí deprimida después de la película porque era muy triste.
I felt depressed after the movie because it was very sad.

¿Te sentías cansado anoche?
Were you feeling tired last night?

4. Use **ponerse** in the preterite followed by an adjective to express a change in emotion.

Cecilia **se puso** nerviosa porque no podía encontrar su tarea.
Cecilia became nervous because she couldn't find her homework.

5. A verb's meaning may change depending on whether it is used in the preterite or the imperfect.

	Imperfect	Preterite
conocer	to know, to be acquainted with	to meet
saber	to know (about)	to find out
haber	there was/were (descriptive)	there was/there were (occurred)
poder	was able to (circumstances)	succeeded in
no poder	was not able to (circumstances)	failed to
querer	wanted	tried to
no querer	didn't want	refused to

Preterite and imperfect: An overview

1. To summarize, the **preterite** is used to express:

a. a past action or a series of actions that are completed as of the moment of reference.

Anoche, **fui** al cine y **vi** una buena película.
Last night, I went to the movies and saw a good movie.

b. an action that is beginning or ending

Empezó a llover a las cuatro de la tarde.
It began to rain at four in the afternoon.

c. a change of condition or emotion

Esteban **se frustró** con el examen, y no lo terminó.
Esteban got frustrated with the exam and didn't finish it.

2. The **imperfect** is used to express:

a. an action in progress with no emphasis on the beginning or end of the action

Los estudiantes **estaban** trabajando duro.
The students were working hard.

b. a habitual action

Siempre **salía** con mis amigos, pero ahora solo salimos un día la semana.
I always used to go out with my friends, but now we only go out one day a week.

c. a description of a physical or mental condition

Javier **se sentía** alegre al ver a su novia.
Javier felt happy to see his girlfriend.

d. other descriptions such as, time, date, and age

Mi madre **tenía** diez años en 1970.
My mom was ten years old in 1970.

Vocabulario 1

🔊 CD2-12

De viaje

a tiempo	on time
aduana	customs
aeropuerto internacional	international airport
agente de seguridad	security agent
asiento	seat
boleto	ticket
cinturón de seguridad (m.)	safety belt
conexión (f.)	connection
equipaje (m.)	luggage
equipaje de mano	hand luggage
escala	layover
llegada	arrival
mostrador (m.)	counter
pasajero(a)	passenger
pasaporte (m.)	passport
pase de abordar (m.)	boarding pass
pasillo	aisle
primera clase	first class
puerta (de salida)	gate
reclamo de equipaje	baggage claim
retrasado	delayed
revisión de equipaje (f.)	luggage screening
sala de espera	waiting room
salida	departure
segunda clase	second class
ventanilla	window
visa	visa
vuelo	flight

En la estación de tren

andén (m.)	platform
coche-cama (m.)	sleeping-car
litera	bunk
parada	stop
revisor(a)	controller
taquilla	ticket window
vagón (m.)	car, wagon

Los verbos

abordar	to board
aterrizar	to land
despegar	to take off
doblar	to turn
facturar equipaje	to check luggage
pasar por seguridad	to go through security
seguir derecho	to go straight

Gramática

Relative pronouns

1. The relative pronouns **que** and **quien** are used to combine two sentences with a common noun or pronoun into one sentence. When used as relative pronouns, **que** and **quien** do not carry accents.

> El vuelo estaba retrasado. El vuelo despegó a las nueve, no a las ocho.

> El vuelo **que** estaba retrasado despegó a las nueve, no a las ocho.

2. **Que** is the most commonly used relative pronoun. It can be used to refer to people or things.

> El tren tiene un coche-cama **que** es muy pequeño.

Formal and *nosotros* commands

Commands, or **mandatos** in Spanish, are used to tell someone to do something. You do not use the subject when giving a command.

1. Formal commands are used with people you would address with **usted** or **ustedes**. To form these commands, drop the **-o** from the present tense first person (**yo** form) and add the opposite ending (**-e(n)** for **-ar** verbs, and **-a(n)** for **-er** and **-ir** verbs).

	trabajar	tener	dormir
usted	trabaj**e**	teng**a**	duerm**a**
ustedes	trabaj**en**	teng**an**	duerm**an**

> **Aborden** el avión a tiempo.
> *Board the plane on time.*

2. Negative formal commands are formed by placing **no** before the verb.

> **No traigan** demasiado equipaje.
> *Don't bring too much luggage.*

3. Infinitives that end in **-car**, **-gar**, and **-ger** have spelling changes in order to maintain the same sound as the infinitive. Infinitives that end in **-zar** also have a spelling change.

> tocar → to**que**(n) escoger → esco**ja**(n)
> llegar → lle**gue**(n) almorzar → almuer**ce**(n)

> **Escojan** los asientos de ventanilla, si es posible.
> *Choose window seats if it's possible.*

3. **Quien(es)** refers only to people and is used after a preposition (**a, con, de, para, por, en**).

> El agente de seguridad es la persona **con quien** debes hablar.

4. **Quien(es)** may replace **que** when the dependent clause is set off by commas.

> Andrés y Julián, **quienes** viajaron en primera clase, no se sentaron con nosotros.

4. These verbs have irregular command forms:

dar	**dé (den)**
estar	**esté(n)**
ir	**vaya(n)**
saber	**sepa(n)**
ser	**sea(n)**

> **Sea** paciente con los empleados.
> *Be patient with the employees.*

5. To make suggestions with *Let's*, use commands in the **nosotros** form. **Nosotros** commands are very similar to formal commands. Add **-emos** for **-ar** verbs, and **-amos** for **-er** and **-ir** verbs.

> **Almorcemos** antes de irnos.
> *Let's eat lunch before leaving.*

6. Note the irregular verbs in number 4. They follow a similar pattern for **nosotros** commands, but they use the **nosotros** endings.

> **Seamos** tranquilos. No vamos a llegar tarde.
> *Let's be calm. We're not going to arrive late.*

7. **Ir** has two different forms. While it is possible to use **vayamos**, the present tense **vamos** is often used with affirmative commands and **vayamos** with negative commands.

8. **-Ar** and **-er** verbs with stem changes do <u>not</u> change in **nosotros** command. However, **-ir** verbs do stem change.

> **Juguemos** cartas mientras esperamos.
> *Let's play cards while we wait.*

> **Pidamos** algo para tomar.
> *Let's order something to drink.*

Vocabulario 2

🔊 CD2-13

Lo necesario para limpiar

basura	*trash, garbage, litter*
bote de basura (m.)	*trashcan*
burro	*ironing board*
cortacésped (f.)	*lawnmower*
escoba	*broom*
jabón para platos (m.)	*dish soap*
manguera	*hose*
plancha	*iron*
quehacer (m.)	*chore*
sacudidor (m.)	*duster*
sucio	*dirty*
trapeador (m.)	*mop*
trapo	*cleaning cloth, rag*

Verbos

barrer	*to sweep*
colgar (ue)	*to hang*
cortar (el césped)	*to cut, to mow (the lawn)*
guardar	*to keep*
hacer la cama	*to make the bed*
lavar platos	*to do the washing up*
lavar ropa	*to do laundry*
ordenar	*to tidy up, to straighten up*
pasar la aspiradora	*to vacuum clean*
planchar	*to iron*
poner la mesa	*to set the table*
recoger (la mesa)	*to pick up (to clear the table)*
regar (ie)	*to water*
sacar la basura	*to take the trash out*
sacudir	*to dust*
secar	*to dry*
tender (ie) la cama	*to make the bed*
trapear	*to mop*

Gramática

Informal commands

1. Informal commands are used with anyone you have an informal relationship with, such as family members or friends. To form the affirmative informal (**tú**) commands, use the third person singular (**él/ella**) of the present tense.

> **Tiende** la cama.   *Make the bed. (Note that stem-changing verbs keep their changes in the informal command forms.)*

2. The following verbs have irregular forms for the affirmative informal commands:

decir **di**	salir **sal**	ir **ve**	tener **ten**
hacer **haz**	ser **sé**	poner **pon**	venir **ven**

3. When forming negative informal commands, use the formal **usted** commands and add an **–s**.

Verb	*Usted* command	Negative *tú* command
comer	coma	**no comas**
tener	tenga	**no tengas**
ir	vaya	**no vayas**

> No **pongas** la mesa ahora porque la cena no está lista.
> *Don't set the table now because dinner isn't ready.*

4. In Spain, the **ustedes** commands are formal. To give commands to two or more friends or family members, they use **vosotros** commands. **Vosotros** affirmative commands are formed by dropping the **–r** from the infinitive and replacing it with **–d**. Negative commands are formed by using the base of the **usted** commands and adding the **vosotros** ending (**-éis, -áis**).

Verb	Affirmative *vosotros* command	Negative *vosotros* command
hablar	**hablad**	**no habléis**
ir	**id**	**no vayáis**
poner	**poned**	**no pongáis**

> **Ordenad** la casa antes de salir.   *Tidy up the house before you (all) leave.*

Commands with pronouns

1. When using affirmative commands, the pronouns are attached to the end of the verb.

> **Pedro:** No voy a hacer la cama.   *I'm not going to make the bed.*
>
> **Su madre:** Pedro, ¡**hazla** ahora!   *Pedro, make it now!*
>
> **Pedro:** Tampoco quiero lavar los platos.   *I don't want to wash the dishes, either.*
>
> **Su madre:** ¡**Lávalos!**   *Wash them!*

2. When using negative commands, the pronouns are placed directly before the verb.

> La mesa no está limpia. No **la pongas.**
> *The table isn't clean. Don't set it.*

Vocabulario 1

🔊 CD2-17

En la tienda

a cuadros	*plaid*
a rayas	*striped*
algodón (m.)	*cotton*
bolsa	*purse*
caja	*cash register*
de lunares	*with polka dots*
de moda	*fashionable*
efectivo	*cash*
estampado	*patterned*
lana	*wool*
lino	*linen*
mezclilla	*denim*
número	*size (shoe)*
piel (f.)	*leather*
prenda	*garment*
probador (m.)	*dressing room*
seda	*silk*
talla	*size (clothing)*
tarjeta de crédito	*credit card*

Palabras adicionales

apretado	*tight*
barato	*cheap, inexpensive*
caro	*expensive*
chico	*small*
grande	*large*
hacer juego	*to match*
hecho a mano	*handmade*
liso	*solid*
mediano	*medium*
probarse (ue)	*to try on*
quedar	*to fit*
rebajado	*on sale*

Expresiones útiles

¡Qué bien te queda esa falda!	*That skirt really fits you well!*
¡Qué caros!	*How expensive!*
¡Qué color tan bonito!	*What a pretty color!*
¡Qué lindos zapatos!	*What pretty shoes!*
¡Qué pantalones tan elegantes!	*What elegant pants!*
allá	*over there*
allí	*there*
aquel	*that (over there)*
aquí	*here*
ese	*that*
este	*this*
mayor	*older (age)*
mejor	*better*
menor	*younger*
peor	*worse*

Gramática

Demonstrative adjectives and pronouns

1. Demonstrative adjectives are used to point out specific people, objects, or places.

> **este, esta, estos, estas** *this, these (close to the speaker)*
> **ese, esa, esos, esas** *that, those (further away from the speaker)*
> **aquel, aquella, aquellos, aquellas** *that, those over there (quite far from the speaker)*

2. Demonstrative adjectives agree in gender and number with the item they describe.
3. A demonstrative adjective is placed in front of the noun it modifies.

> Me encanta **esta** falda, pero no me gustan **esos** pantalones.
> *I love this skirt, but I don't like those pants.*

Aquella tienda tiene zapatos bonitos.
That store (over there) has pretty shoes.

4. Demonstrative pronouns replace the noun and have the same forms as demonstrative adjectives.

> -¿Te gustan estos zapatos?
> *Do you like these shoes?*
>
> -No, prefiero **esos**, que son hechos a mano.
> *No, I prefer those, which are handmade.*

5. The demonstrative forms of **esto** and **eso** are neuter and are used to refer to something abstract such as an idea or a situation. They are also used to refer to items not yet identified.

> La ropa debe ser de buena calidad.
> **Eso** es importante.
> *The clothing should be good quality.*
> *That is important.*

Comparisons

1. Comparisons of equality:
   a. to compare equal qualities use
      tan + adjective/adverb + **como**

   > La camisa es **tan barata como** la falda.
   > *The shirt is as cheap as the skirt.*

   b. to compare equal quantities, use
      tanto(s) / tanta(s) + noun + como

   > Katia tiene **tanta ropa como** su hermana.
   > *Katia has as many clothes as her sister.*

   c. to compare equality in actions, use
      verb + **tanto como**

   > Mis amigos van de compras **tanto como** trabajan.
   > *My friends go shopping as much as they work.*

2. Comparisons of inequality:
   a. to express that one thing is greater than another, use
      más + adjective/adverb/noun + **que**

   > Los pantalones negros me quedan **más apretados que** los azules.
   > *The black pants are tighter on me than the blue ones.*

   b. to express that one thing is less than another, use **menos** + adjective/ adverb/ noun + **que**

   > Este suéter de lana es **menos cómodo que** el suéter de algodón.
   > *This wool sweater is less comfortable than the cotton sweater.*

   c. to compare unequal actions, use
      verb + **más que / menos que**

   > Pilar gasta **más que** gana.
   > *Pilar spends more than she earns.*

3. The following adjectives and adverbs do not use **más** or **menos** in their constructions:

> **bueno/bien** → **mejor** *better*
> **joven** → **menor** *younger*
> **malo/mal** → **peor** *worse*
> **viejo** (age of a person) → **mayor** *older*

> Cecilia tiene amigos que son **menores que** ella.

4. Superlatives are used when someone or something is referred to as *the most, the least, the best,* etc. This is expressed through the following construction:

   article **(el, la, los, las)** + noun (optional) + **más / menos** + adjective

   > Héctor es **el más guapo** del grupo.
   > *Héctor is the most handsome in the group.*

   > La prenda que tienes es **la menos cara** de la tienda.
   > *The garment that you have is the least expensive of the store.*

   As with the other comparisons, when using **bueno/bien, malo/mal, joven,** and **viejo** (age), you must use the irregular constructions **mejor, peor, menor,** and **mayor.**

   > Esta tienda tiene **las mejores** rebajas.

5. The preposition **de** is often used with superlatives to express *in* or *of.*

Vocabulario 2

🔊 CD2-18

El arte

arte abstracto (m.)	abstract art
autorretrato	self-portrait
escultura	sculpture
exhibición (f.)	exhibit
galería	gallery
grabado	engraving; print
máscara	mask
mural (m.)	mural
naturaleza muerta	still life
obra	work (of art, literature, theater, etc.)
óleo	oil painting
paisaje (m.)	landscape
paleta	pallet
pincel (m.)	paintbrush
retrato	portrait
tinta	ink

Verbos

acabar	to finish, to run out
apagar	to go off, to go out
apreciar	to apreciate; to enjoy
descomponer	to break down (a machine)
diseñar	to design
esculpir	to sculpt
exhibir	to exhibit
olvidar	to forget
posar	to pose
quedar	to leave (behind)
romper	to break

Adjetivos

complicado	complex
conservador	conservative
cubista	cubist
impresionista	impressionist
realista	realistic
sencillo	simple
surrealista	surrealist
tradicional	traditional
vanguardista	revolutionary; avant-garde

Gramática

Estar with the past participle

1. The past participle is formed by changing the verb as follows:

-ar verb → add -ado   diseñado, apagado
-er & -ir verb → add –ido   vendido, esculpido

The following verbs are the irregular past participles:

abrir	**abierto**	morir	**muerto**
decir	**dicho**	romper	**roto**
despertar	**despierto**	poner	**puesto**
devolver	**devuelto**	ver	**visto**
escribir	**escrito**	volver	**vuelto**
hacer	**hecho**		

2. The past participle can be used as an adjective to show condition. You have already learned some of them, such as **aburrido, cansado,** and **muerto.** Like other adjectives, they must agree in gender and number with the nouns they describe.

El museo está **abierto** todos los días, menos lunes.
The museum is open every day except Monday.

Carlos tiene unos cuadros **pintados** por Picasso.
Carlos has paintings painted by Picasso.

3. They are often used with the verb **estar,** however they can also be placed after the noun they describe.

Las obras **esculpidas** por Señor Ramos **están conocidas** por todos.
The works sculpted by Mr. Ramos are familiar to everyone.

Se to indicate accidental occurrences

1. In **Capítulo 8,** you learned to use the pronoun **se** in order to indicate that the subject is either unknown or unimportant. Use the following construction with **se** to indicate unintentional or accidental occurrences:

se + indirect object pronoun + verb

Se me perdieron los libros.
I lost the books. / The books were lost by me (unintentionally).

Notice that the verb agrees with the subject (**los libros**). The indirect object pronoun (**me**) identifies who is affected by this action.

2. The following are common verbs used with this construction:

acabar	olvidar
apagar	perder
caer	quedar
descomponer	romper

A Rodrigo **se le acabó** la pintura antes de terminar el mural.
Rodrigo ran out of paint before finishing the mural.

Jugábamos en la casa y **se nos rompió** la escultura de mamá.
We were playing in the house, and we broke Mom's sculpture.

Vocabulario 1

🔊 CD2-21

El medio ambiente

árbol(m.)	tree
arena	sand
cactus (m.)	cactus
cascada	cascade, waterfall (small)
catarata	waterfall
cielo	sky
contaminación(f.)	contamination
deforestación (f.)	deforestation
desechos industriales	industrial waste
ecología	ecology
esmog (m.)	smog
naturaleza	nature
nube(f.)	cloud
ola	wave
palmera	palm tree
pasto	grass
petróleo	oil
reciclaje (m.)	recycling
recursos naturales	natural resources
volcán (m.)	volcano

Lugares

bahía	bay
bosque(m.)	forest
colina	hill
costa	coast
desierto	desert
isla	island
lago	lake
llano	plain
mar (m.)	sea
montaña	mountain
pampa	grasslands
península	peninsula
río	river
selva	jungle
valle (m.)	valley

Verbos

destruir	to destroy
preservar	to preserve
proteger	to protect

Gramática

Future tense

1. Things that are going to happen in the near future can be expressed in the present tense or using the construction **ir + a+** an infinitive.

   Salgo para las montañas.
   I'm leaving for the mountains today.

   Vamos a visitar la selva.
   We are going to visit the jungle.

2. Another way to express what will happen is to use the future tense; however, it tends to be a little more formal and is generally used to refer to a more distant future. To form the future tense, add the following endings to the infinitive. In the future tense, **-ar, -er,** and **-ir** verbs take the same endings.

proteger

Subject	Ending	Verb form
yo	-é	protegeré
tú	-ás	protegerás
él / ella / usted	-á	protegerá
nosotros(as)	-emos	protegeremos
vosotros(as)	-éis	protegeréis
ellos / ellas / Uds.	-án	protegerán

Present Perfect

1. The present perfect is used to express actions that we have and have not done. It combines the present tense of the verb **haber** with the past participle.

haber

he	hemos
has	habéis
ha	han

2. Remember, to form past participles, you add **-ado** to the stem of an **-ar** verb, and **-ido** to the stem of an **-er** or **-ir** verb. The past participles **creído, leído, oído,** and **traído** all carry accents. Note the remaining irregular forms listed here:

abierto	hecho	roto
dicho	muerto	visto
devuelto	puesto	vuelto
escrito		

Ellos **protegerán** el medio ambiente.
They will protect the environment better.

The following are irregular stems for the future tense:

decir	dir-	querer	querr-
haber	habr-	saber	sabr-
hacer	har-	salir	saldr-
poder	podr-	tener	tendr-
poner	pondr-	venir	vendr-

   ¿Podrá venir con nosotros?
   Will he be able to come with us?

3. The future tense is also used to express probability or to speculate about present conditions.

   A Julio le gusta el fútbol. **Tendrá** boletos para el partido este sábado.
   Julio likes soccer. He might have tickets for the game this Saturday.

3. When using the participle with **haber,** it is part of the verb, and it does not agree with the subject.

   Raquel no **ha leído** el texto.
   Raquel hasn't read the text.

4. When using direct object, indirect object, or reflexive pronouns, they are placed in front of the conjugated form of **haber.**

   Ya **los** hemos devuelto.
   We have already returned them.

5. In Spanish, the present perfect is generally used as it is in English to talk about something that has happened or something that someone has done. It is usually either unimportant when it happened or it has some relation to the present.

6. The following expressions are often used with the present perfect: **alguna vez, no...todavía, nunca, recientemente,** and **ya.**

Vocabulario 2

🔊 CD2-22

Los animales

águila	eagle
ardilla	squirrel
ballena	whale
cebra	zebra
cerdo	pig
cocodrilo	crocodile
conejo	rabbit
elefante (m.)	elephant
gallina	hen
gallo	rooster
gorila (m.)	gorrilla
jaguar (m.)	jaguar
jirafa	giraffe
león (m.)	lion
llama	llama
lobo	wolf
mono	monkey
oso	bear
oveja	sheep
pato	duck
pavo	turkey
pingüino	penguin
pollo	chick
rana	frog
serpiente (f.)	snake
tiburón (m.)	shark
tigre (m.)	tiger
toro	bull
tortuga	turtle
vaca	cow
venado	deer
zorro	fox

Clasificaciones

anfibios	amphibians
aves (f.)	birds
mamíferos	mammals
reptiles (m.)	reptiles

Palabras adicionales

caza	hunting
cazar	to hunt
granja	farm
hembra	female
jaula	cage
macho	male
peligro (de extinción)	danger (of extinction)

Gramática

Subjunctive with impersonal expressions

Until now, all the verb tenses you have studied have been in the indicative. The indicative is an objective mood that is used to state facts and to talk about things that you are certain have occurred or will occur.

Las águilas están en peligro.   *Eagles are endangered.*

In contrast, the subjunctive is a subjective mood that is used to convey uncertainty, anticipated or hypothetical events, or the subject's wishes, fears, doubts, and emotional reactions.

Es terrible que las águilas desaparezcan.
It is terrible (that) the eagles may disappear.

1. You will notice that the subjunctive verb forms are very similar to formal commands. To form the present subjunctive, drop the **-o** from the first person (**yo**) present tense form and add the opposite ending. Add the **-er** endings for **-ar** verbs, and the **-ar** endings for **-er** and **-ir** verbs.

> **hablar:** hable, hables, hable, hablemos, habléis, hablen
> **comer:** coma, comas, coma, comamos, comáis, coman
> **escribir:** escriba, escribas, escriba, escribamos, escribáis, escriban

Es bueno que las tortugas **naden** en el mar, y no en un acuario.
It's good that the turtles swim in the sea, and not in an aquarium.

2. Verbs that are irregular in the first person present indicative have the same stem in the present subjunctive.

Es importante que **tengamos** paciencia.   *It's important that we have patience.*

3. Stem-changing **-ar** and **-er** verbs follow the same pattern as in the present indicative, changing in all forms except the **nosotros** and **vosotros** forms.

Es necesario que tú **pienses** en el medio ambiente.   *It's necessary that you think of the environment.*

4. Stem-changing **-ir** verbs follow the same pattern as in the present indicative, however there is an additional change in the **nosotros** and **vosotros** forms. The additional stem change is similar to that in the third person preterite. (e → i and o → u)

Es terrible que no **durmáis** mejor.   *It's terrible that you don't sleep better.*

5. You will recall that the formal commands of verbs whose infinitives end in **-car, -gar,** and **-zar** have spelling changes. These same spelling changes occur in the subjunctive as well. There is also a spelling change for verbs ending in **-ger**; change the **g** to **j** and add the subjunctive ending.

Es recomendable que **lleguemos** a tiempo.   *It's recommended that we arrive on time.*

6. The subjunctive of the following verbs is irregular: **dar (dé), estar (esté), haber (haya), ir (vaya), saber (sepa),** and **ser (sea).** You will notice that once again the subjunctive form is similar to the formal command forms.

Es ridículo que Jorge no **sepa** más de los animales que viven en esta parte del país.
It's ridiculous that Jorge doesn't know more about the animals that live in this part of the country.

7. Impersonal expressions do not have a specific subject and can include a large number of adjectives: **es bueno, es difícil, es importante, es triste,** etc. They can be negative or affirmative.

8. Note that the **que** is required as a conjunction between the main clause and the dependent (subjunctive) clause, even though it may be omitted in English.

Es una lástima que no **podamos** hacer más.   *It's a shame (that) we can't do more.*

Subjunctive with expressions of doubt

1. When expressing doubt or uncertainty about an action or a condition, you must use the subjunctive. The following are some common expressions of doubt that require the use of the subjunctive:

Dudar que, No creer que, No pensar que, No suponer que, No estar seguro(a) que, No ser cierto/verdad/obvio/evidente que

No es cierto que vayamos a ayudar las águilas con este programa de preservación.
It's not certain that we are going to help the eagles with this preservation program.

No creo que haya ovejas en esta granja.   *I don't think that there are sheep on this farm.*

2. When using the following expressions to affirm a belief or express certainty, you must use the indicative.

Creer que, Pensar que, Suponer que, Estar seguro(a) de que, Ser cierto/verdad/obvio/evidente que

Inés está segura de que hay elefantes en este zoológico.

Vocabulario 1

🔊 CD2-25

Relaciones personales

anillo	ring
ceremonia	ceremony
cita	date
compromiso	engagement
luna de miel	honeymoon
muerte (f.)	death
nacimiento	birth
noviazgo	engagement, relationship
pareja	couple
prometido (a)	fiancé(e)
recepción (f.)	wedding reception
recién casado (a)	newlywed
soltero (a)	unmarried person
unión libre (f.)	common-law union
viudo (a)	widower (widow)

Verbos

abrazar	to hug
besar	to kiss
comprometerse (con)	to get engaged (to)
dar a luz	to give birth
desear	to desire, to wish
divorciarse (de)	to divorce
enamorarse (de)	to fall in love (with)
esperar	to hope
estar embarazada	to be pregnant
extrañar	to miss
insistir (en)	to insist (on)
llevarse (bien/mal)	to (not) get along
mandar	to order
nacer	to be born
odiar	to hate
proponer (matrimonio)	to propose (marriage)
querer	to love
romper	to break (a relation)
separarse (de)	to separate (from)
sugerir	to suggest

Palabras adicionales

adolescencia	adolescence
juventud (f.)	youth
madurez (f.)	maturity
niñez (f.)	childhood
vejez (f.)	old-age

Gramática

Reciprocal verbs

1. In **Capítulo 6** you learned to use reflexive pronouns when the subject of the sentence does something to himself or herself.

> Ellos **se miran** en el espejo.
> *They **look at themselves** in the mirror.*

2. In English the expressions *each other* and *one another* express reciprocal actions. In order to express a reciprocal action in Spanish, use the plural reflexives.

> Ellos **se miran** con amor.
> *They **look at each other** with love.*

3. Only the plural forms (**nos, os,** and **se**) are used to express reciprocal actions as the action must involve more than one person.

> Paco y Carlota **se vieron** en la fiesta.
> *Paco and Carlota **saw each other** at the party.*
> Mi primo y yo **nos abrazamos.**
> *My cousin and **I hugged each other.***

Subjunctive with expressions of desire

1. When expressing the desire to do something, you use a verb of desire or influence such as **querer** or **preferir** followed by an infinitive.

> **Prefiero tener** un noviazgo corto.
> *I **prefer to have** a short engagement.*

2. When expressing the desire for someone else to do something, you use a verb of influence plus **que** followed by the subjunctive.

> **Prefiero que tengamos** un noviazgo corto.
> *I **prefer that we have** a short engagement.*

3. You will notice in the sample sentence above that when there are two different subjects and the verb in the main clause is in the indicative, the verb in the second clause is in the subjunctive.

4. There are other verbs besides **querer** and **preferir** that express desire or influence. These verbs also require the use of the subjunctive when there are different subjects in the two clauses.

4. It is usually evident by context whether the verb is reflexive or reciprocal. However, if there is need for clarification, **el uno al otro** can be used. The expression must agree with the subject(s); however, if there are mixed sexes, the masculine form is used for both.

> En mi familia, nos cuidamos **los unos a los otros.**
> *In my family, we all care for **each other.***

5. When used in the infinitive form after another verb, the pronoun can be attached to the verb or placed in front of the conjugated verb.

> Vamos a ver**nos** todos los días.
> *We are going to see each other every day.*
> Mariana y Jorge no **se** quieren hablar.
> *Mariana and Jorge don't want to talk to each other.*

desear	mandar	preferir
esperar	necesitar	recomendar
insistir (en)	pedir	sugerir

> Rogelio **recomienda que vayamos** a la recepción juntos.
> *Rogelio **recommends that we go** to the reception together.*

5. **Ojalá** is another way to express hope. This expression does not have a subject and therefore does not change forms. It always requires the use of the subjunctive in the dependent clause; however, the use of **que** is optional.

> **Ojalá (que)** los recién casados se diviertan en su luna de miel.
> *I hope (that) the newlyweds have fun on their honeymoon.*

Vocabulario 2

🔊 CD2-26

La televisión

anuncio comercial	commercial
audiencia	audience
cablevisión (f.)	cablevision
canal (m.)	TV channel
clasificación (f.)	TV rating (for adults, for the whole family, etc.)
concurso	game show
conductor (m.)	TV host
control remoto (m.)	remote control
documental (m.)	documentary
dibujos animados	cartoons
locutor(a)	announcer
noticiario	news
programación (f.)	programming
reproductor de DVDs (m.)	DVD player
telenovela	soap opera
televidente	television viewer
televisión por satélite (f.)	satellite television

La computadora

audífonos	headphones
buscador (m.)	search engine
Internet (m.)	Internet
MP3 (m.)	MP3 player
pantalla	screen
ratón (m.)	mouse
redes sociales (f.)	social networks
reproductor de CDs (m.)	CD player
tablero	keyboard

El cine

butaca	seat
éxito de taquilla	box office hit
golosina	snack
palomitas de maíz	popcorn

Verbos

chatear	to chat online
censurar	to censor
hacer clic (en)	to click (on)
limitar	to limit
patrocinar	sponsor
transmitir	to broadcast

Palabras adicionales

adolescente	adolescent
adulto	adult
infantil	for children, childish
revista	magazine

Gramática

The subjunctive with expressions of emotion

1. When expressing an emotion or feeling about something, it is necessary to use the subjunctive if there are two different subjects. Again, the verb in the main clause is in the indicative, and the verb in the second clause is in the subjunctive.

Tengo miedo de que <u>haya</u> demasiada información falsa en la televisión.
Main Clause   Dependent Clause

2. Some verbs that express emotion are:

estar contento de	**sentir**
estar triste de	**temer/tener miedo de**

3. Other verbs that express emotion are:

alegrar	**gustar**	**sorprender**
enojar	**molestar**	
encantar	**preocupar**	

You will recall that the verbs **gustar, encantar,** and **molestar** require the use of the indirect object. The other verbs in this list also require the use of the indirect object.

Al productor **le preocupa que nadie vaya** a patrocinar su programa.
The producer is worried that nobody is going to sponsor his program.

4. If there is only one subject, the **que** is not necessary and the infinitive is used with the expression of emotion rather than the subjunctive.

Me molesta leer una revista con artículos tan infantiles.
It bothers me to read a magazine with such childish articles.

The subjunctive with adjective clauses

1. When using an adjective clause to describe something that the speaker knows exists the indicative is used.

Quiero comprar las golosinas <u>que **son** de chocolate.</u>
I want to buy the sweets that are chocolate.

2. However, when using an adjective clause to describe something that the speaker does not know exists or believes does not exist the subjunctive is used.

Necesitamos una actriz <u>que **sea** talentosa.</u>   *We need an actress who is talented.*

3. Some common verbs used with adjective clauses that can require either the subjunctive or the indicative are: **buscar, necesitar,** and **querer.**

Busco un televisor que **tenga** una pantalla grande.
Busco el televisor que **tiene** una pantalla grande.

In the first sentence the person does not have a specific television in mind and does not necessarily know if one exists, while in the second sentence he/she is looking for a specific television.

4. When asking about the existence of something, it is also necessary to use the subjunctive, as you do not know whether or not it exists.

En tu familia, ¿hay alguien que no **tenga** una computadora?

5. When using a negative statement in the main clause, it also necessary to use the subjunctive.

No hay nadie que no **tenga** una computadora.

Vocabulario 1

CD2-29

En el hospital

corazón (m.)	heart
esqueleto	skeleton
hígado	liver
hueso	bone
intestino	intestine
órgano vital	vital organ
paciente	patient
primeros auxilios	first aid
pulmón (m.)	lung
radiografía	x-ray
receta médica	prescription
sala de emergencias	emergency room
salud (f.)	health
tratamiento	treatment
yeso	cast

Los síntomas

alergia	allergy
asco	nausea
desmayo	faint
diarrea	diarrhea
dolor (m.)	pain
estornudo	sneeze
fractura	fracture
presión baja/	low/high blood
alta (f.)	pressure
tos (f.)	cough

Algunas enfermedades

cáncer (m.)	cancer
catarro	cold
diabetes (f.)	diabetes
gripe (f.)	flu
hipertensión (f.)	high blood pressure
insomnio	insomnia
obesidad (f.)	obesity
resfriado	cold
SIDA (m.)	AIDS

Los medicamentos y procedimientos

aspirina	aspirin
cirugía	surgery
curita	small adhesive bandage
gotas	drops
inyección (f.)	injection
pastilla	pill
vacuna	vaccine
vendaje (m.)	bandage

Verbos

cortarse	to cut oneself
desmayarse	to faint
doler (ue)	to hurt
estar mareado	to be dizzy
estornudar	to sneeze
examinar	to examine
fracturarse	to fracture
recuperarse	to recuperate, recover
respirar	to breathe
tomar la presión	to take someone´s blood pressure
torcerse (ue)	to twist, to sprain
toser	to cough
vomitar	to vomit

Gramática

Conditional

1. To form the conditional, add the following endings to the infinitive. Notice that all verbs take the same endings.

hablar	volver	ir
hablar**ía**	volver**ía**	ir**ía**
hablar**ías**	volver**ías**	ir**ías**
hablar**ía**	volver**ía**	ir**ía**
hablar**íamos**	volver**íamos**	ir**íamos**
hablar**íais**	volver**íais**	ir**íais**
hablar**ían**	volver**ían**	ir**ían**

2. The irregular stems for the conditional are the same as the irregular stems for the future tense. The endings are the same as the regular forms of the conditional.

> ¿Qué **harías** con un millón de dólares?
> *What would you do with a million dollars?*

> Yo **querría** viajar.
> *I would want to travel.*

3. The conditional is similar to the English construction *would* + verb.

> Patricia no **iría** a la sala de emergencias.
> *Patricia **wouldn't go** to the emergency.*

Imperfect Subjunctive

1. In the last three chapters, you learned to use the present subjunctive. When the verb in the main clause is in the past (preterite or imperfect), the verb in the dependent clause must be in the imperfect subjunctive.

> **Era** necesario que le **pusieran** un yeso a Tomás.

2. The imperfect subjunctive is formed using the third person plural (**ellos, ellas, ustedes**) of the preterite. Eliminate the **-on** and add the endings as indicated. Endings are the same, regardless of whether the verb ends in **-ar, -er,** or **-ir**. Verbs that are irregular in the preterite are also irregular in the imperfect subjunctive.

hablar	tener	dormir
hablar**a**	tuvier**a**	durmier**a**
hablar**as**	tuvier**as**	durmier**as**
hablar**a**	tuvier**a**	durmier**a**
hablár**amos**	tuviér**amos**	durmiér**amos**
hablar**ais**	tuvier**ais**	durmier**ais**
hablar**an**	tuvier**an**	durmier**an**

*Notice that it is necessary to add an accent in the **nosotros** form.

4. The conditional form of **haber** is **habría.** You will remember that there is only one form of the verb regardless of whether it is followed by a singular or plural noun.

> Creí que **habría** más vacunas necesarias antes de viajar.
> *I thought **there would be** more necessary vaccinations before traveling.*

5. The conditional is also used for conjecture about past activities.

> ¿Por qué **no le pondrían** un vendaje a Cristina?
> *Why **wouldn't they put** a bandage on Cristina?*
> *(I **wonder** why **they didn't put** a bandage on Cristina.)*

6. The conditional is often used to demonstrate politeness or to soften a request.

> ¿**Me daría** usted una aspirina?
> *Would you please give me an aspirin?*

3. The imperfect subjunctive form of **haber** is **hubiera.**

4. In general, the same rules that apply to the usage of the present subjunctive also apply to the past subjunctive.

· To express an opinion using personal expressions

· To express doubt

· To express desire

· To express an emotion

· To talk about the unknown using adjective clauses

5. When using an "if clause" to express what would happen in a hypothetical situation or a situation that is not likely or impossible, it is necessary to use the imperfect subjunctive and the conditional.

si + imperfect subjunctive + conditional

> **Si yo recuperara** pronto, **iría** al concierto con ustedes.
> *If I recovered soon, I would go to the concert with you.*

Vocabulario 2

🔊 CD2-30

Nacionalidades

argentino	*Argentine*
boliviano	*Bolivian*
chileno	*Chilean*
colombiano	*Colombian*
costarricense	*Costa Rican*
cubano	*Cuban*
dominicano	*Dominican*
ecuatoguineano	*Ecuatorial Guinean*
ecuatoriano	*Ecuadorian*
español	*Spanish*
guatemalteco	*Guatemalan*
hondureño	*Honduran*
mexicano	*Mexican*
nicaragüense	*Nicaraguan*
panameño	*Panamanian*
paraguayo	*Paraguayan*
peruano	*Peruvian*
puertorriqueño	*Puerto Rican*
salvadoreño	*Salvadoran*
uruguayo	*Uruguayan*
venezolano	*Venezuelan*

Conceptos políticos

ciudadano(a)	*citizen*
derechos humanos	*human rights*
desempleo	*unemployment*
emigración (f.)	*emigration*
globalización (f.)	*globalization*
guerra	*war*
inmigración (f.)	*immigration*
inmigrante	*immigrant*
ley (f.)	*law*
organismo internacional	*international organization*
paz (f.)	*peace*
pobreza	*poverty*
refugiado(a)	*refugee*
riqueza	*wealth*
tratado de comercio	*trade treaty*

Verbos

emigrar	*emigrate*
inmigrar	*immigrate*
mudarse	*to move (to another location)*
votar	*to vote*

Adverbios

a fin de que	*in order that, so that*
a menos que	*unless*
antes (de) que	*before*
con tal (de) que	*provided that*
después (de) que	*after*
en caso de que	*in case*
en cuanto	*as soon as*
hasta que	*until*
para que	*in order that, so that*
sin que	*without*
tan pronto (como)	*as soon as*

Gramática

Subjunctive in adverbial clauses

1. The following adverbial conjunctions always require the subjunctive. Because they indicate that the action is contingent upon another action, the outcome is unknown: **a fin de que, antes (de) que, a menos que, con tal (de) que, en caso de que, para que, sin que**

> Aníbal cambió de trabajo **para que** su esposa pudiera estar con su familia.
> *Aníbal changed jobs so that his wife could be with his family.*

2. With the exception of **a menos que,** the expressions above are often used with the infinitive if there is no change of subject. The **que** after the preposition is omitted.

> Los políticos tuvieron que trabajar mucho **para cambiar** esa ley.
> *The politicians had to work hard in order to change that law.*

3. The following adverbial conjunctions of time require the subjunctive when referring to actions that have not yet occurred. When referring to actions that are already taking place or are habitual, they require the indicative: **cuando, después (de) que*, en cuanto, hasta que*, tan pronto, (como)**

   *Después (de) que and **hasta que** are often used with the infinitive if there is no change of subject. Again, the **que** after the preposition is omitted.

   Present indicative

> **Tan pronto como recibo** mi cheque, mando dinero a mi familia.
> *As soon as I receive my check, I send money to my family.*

   Subjunctive

> **Cuando tengamos** los recursos necesarios, nos mudaremos a los Estados Unidos.
> ***When we have*** *the necessary resources, we will move to the United States.*

4. The following adverbial conjunctions require the indicative when referring to something that is known or is definite. However, when referring to something that is unknown or indefinite, they require the subjunctive: **aunque, como, (a)donde**

> Mi familia va de viaje **aunque hay** una guerra muy cerca de su destino.
> *My family is taking a trip even though there is a war near to their destination.*

> Mi familia va de viaje **aunque haya** una guerra muy cerca de su destino.
> *My family is taking a trip even if there may be a war near to their destination.*

Past perfect tense

1. Similar to the present perfect, the past perfect (also known as the **pluscuamperfecto**, combines the imperfect form of the verb **haber** with the past participle: **había, habías, había, habíamos, habíais, habían.**

> **Habían obtenido** su visa antes de salir.   ***They had obtained*** *their visa before leaving.*

2. The past perfect is used to express a past action that already took place before another past action.

> Camilo ya había aprendido inglés cuando llegó a los Estados Unidos.
> *Camilo had already learned English when he arrived in the United States.*

3. Remember the irregular past participles from **Capítulo 11: abierto, devuelto, dicho, escrito, hecho, muerto, roto, puesto, visto, vuelto**

4. As with the present perfect, when using direct object, indirect object, or reflexive pronouns, they are placed in front of the conjugated form of **haber.**

Capítulo 1 Hola, ¿Qué tal?

In this chapter I have learned how to:

❑ Greet and say good-bye to people in formal and informal situations
❑ Describe my classroom, my friends, and other people
❑ Use numbers up to 100 and exchange telephone numbers
❑ Spell names

I need to review: _____

_____

_____

Capítulo 2 ¿Cómo es tu vida?

In this chapter I have learned how to:

❑ Talk about my classes
❑ Describe my family and tell ages
❑ Talk about what people do routinely
❑ Express ownership

I need to review: _____

_____

_____

Capítulo 3 ¿Qué tiempo hace hoy?

In this chapter I have learned how to:

❑ Communicate dates, time, and seasons
❑ Talk about the weather
❑ Discuss clothing
❑ Discuss likes and dislikes
❑ Use question words to ask for specific information

I need to review: _____

_____

_____

Capítulo 4 ¿Dónde vives?

In this chapter I have learned how to:

❑ Describe my town or city
❑ Describe my house
❑ Tell what my friends and I are going to do in the near future
❑ Request information about the cost of things

I need to review: _____

_____

_____

Capítulo 5 ¿Estás feliz en el trabajo?

In this chapter I have learned how to:

❑ Describe my feelings, emotions, and physical states
❑ Talk about ongoing actions
❑ Discuss abilities needed for certain jobs and professions

I need to review: _____

_____

_____

_____

Capítulo 6 ¿Cómo pasas el día?

In this chapter I have learned how to:

❑ Talk about my daily routine
❑ Discuss my hobbies and pastimes
❑ Talk about sports
❑ Discuss events that occurred in the past

I need to review: _____

_____

_____

_____

Capítulo 7 ¿Cómo pasaste las vacaciones?

In this chapter I have learned how to:

❑ Request a room in a hotel and any of their services
❑ Use numbers above 100
❑ Order food in a restaurant

I need to review: _____

_____

_____

_____

Capítulo 8 ¿Qué te gustaba de niño?

In this chapter I have learned how to:

❏ Give instructions
❏ Talk about my hobbies and pastimes
❏ Talk about what I used to do in the past

I need to review: _____

_____

_____

Capítulo 9 ¿Qué pasó?

In this chapter I have learned how to:

❏ Describe past events in detail
❏ Talk about holidays and celebrations
❏ Give the details of an accident

I need to review: _____

_____

_____

Capítulo 10 ¿Estás preparado?

In this chapter I have learned how to:

❏ Discuss daily chores
❏ Give and receive directions
❏ Make travel arrangements
❏ Suggest activities
❏ Make informal and formal requests

I need to review: _____

_____

_____

Capítulo 11 ¿Es la moda arte?

In this chapter I have learned how to:

❏ Express preferences and make comparisons
❏ Describe the state of objects and people

I need to review: _____

_____

_____

Capítulo 12 ¿Qué será del planeta?

In this chapter I have learned how to:

- ❏ Talk about the future
- ❏ Talk about what I have done
- ❏ Discuss the environment
- ❏ Express my opinions and knowledge about the animal world and the environment
- ❏ Express doubt and certainty

I need to review: _____

_____

_____

_____

Capítulo 13 ¿Es tu vida una telenovela?

In this chapter I have learned how to:

- ❏ Talk about relationships
- ❏ Express desires and give recommendations
- ❏ Talk about popular culture
- ❏ Discuss emotional reactions to events

I need to review: _____

_____

_____

_____

Capítulo 14 ¿Vivimos en un mundo sin fronteras?

In this chapter I have learned how to:

- ❏ Discuss health issues with a doctor
- ❏ Discuss hypothetical situations
- ❏ Express opinions regarding world issues
- ❏ Tell what had happened prior to other events in the past

I need to review: _____

_____

_____

_____